The American Irish

The American Irish

A Political and Social Portrait

by

WILLIAM V. SHANNON

Second Edition

Foreword by
Senator Edward M. Kennedy

The University of Massachusetts Press
Amherst

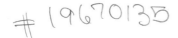

Copyright © 1963, 1966 by William V. Shannon
"Foreword to the Second Edition" © 1989 by
Edward M. Kennedy
All rights reserved
Printed in the United States of America
LC 89-33218
ISBN 0−87023−689−x

Library of Congress Cataloging-in-Publication Data

Shannon, William Vincent.
    The American Irish : a political and social
    portrait / by William V. Shannon. — 2nd ed. /
    foreword by Edward M. Kennedy.
        p.   cm.
    Reprint. Originally published: New York :
    Macmillan, 1963.
    Bibliography: p.
    Includes index.
    ISBN 0−87023−689−x (alk. paper)
    1. Irish Americans—History.   I. Title.
E184.I6S5   1989
973′.049162—dc20   89−33218
                                               CIP

British Library Cataloguing in Publication data are
available.

Acknowledgments of permission to reprint material
can be found on page 486

This book is published with the support and cooperation of the University of Massachusetts at Boston.

This book is dedicated to my mother

NORA McNAMARA SHANNON

and to the memory of my father

PATRICK JOSEPH SHANNON

two who made the great journey

from Ireland to America

Contents

Foreword to the Second Edition

Senator Edward M. Kennedy

I N THE REVISED EDITION of his classic work, *The American Irish*, our friend William Shannon wrote these words about my brother Jack— "He was loved more than he knew." And that simple, eloquent tribute is just as true of Bill Shannon, for he too was loved more than he knew.

In remembering Bill, we also honor the extraordinarily loving Shannon family that was the core and foundation of his life—his wife, Elizabeth (Liz), who was also his life-long partner in all he did and achieved, and his three children, Liam, Christopher, and David.

Of the many friends I inherited from Jack, Bill Shannon was one of the best—and certainly the brightest.

He had a long and enduring affection for President Kennedy. One spring day, while Bill was serving in Ireland as ambassador, he made a point of traveling down to Wexford from Dublin, so that he could pay tribute to Jack on May 29, my brother's birthday.

Bill probably never fully knew what that perceptive gesture meant to me and to our family. For he was one of the first to understand how much we wished to remember Jack by marking the date of his birth, not the date of his death.

Later, Bill sent me a photograph of himself from that day, standing beside a memorial to President Kennedy that consisted of a stone fountain with some of Jack's most famous words inscribed in Gaelic—"Ask not what your country can do for you—ask what you can do for your country." I asked Bill how he knew what the inscription said. He replied that Gaelic was still Greek to him but that he had managed to learn just enough to be sure of the words.

In Bill's remarks that day in Wexford, he recounted a story about Jack that I recalled when Liz telephoned my Senate office with the sad news of Bill's death.

The original edition of *The American Irish* was published in January 1964.

---

*Adapted from the text of a tribute to William V. Shannon, delivered at St. Aidan's Church, Brookline, Massachusetts, September 30, 1988.

But advance copies had been sent out a few weeks earlier to newspapers and magazines. Publishers knew that President Kennedy liked to read, and many of them had begun sending him copies of their new books.

Two or three times a day, Jack used to step out of the Oval Office to look over the letters and packages piled on the desk in the adjoining room. One day in November 1963, he noticed that several new volumes had come in, and *The American Irish* happened to be on top. Jack leafed through it and said, "This looks interesting. I'll read it when I get back from Texas."

For a quarter century, that was a poignant memory for Bill, and it is doubly poignant for me now, because when his illness came, Bill had just begun working closely with me in his spare time to gather recollections of my brothers and my family. I had come to know him especially well in these sessions. He was like a member of the family, and we loved him all the more.

I admired Bill for many things—most of all for the warm and caring and thoughtful friend he always was, but also for his intellect and judgment and the wide range of his interests. He loved to talk and fret about the Red Sox. Sad as Bill's death has been for us, it may just be that with the playoffs and the World Series coming up, God, in His wisdom, decided He needed an expert on the Sox—to teach all the heavenly hosts about the fine points of the game.

In 1967 Bill had published another book, *The Heir Apparent*, a well-received campaign biography of Robert Kennedy—so I respected Bill's political advice as well. One day in the spring of 1979, he stopped by my Senate office to brief me on developments in Dublin and Northern Ireland. When the briefing was over and conversation turned to other things, he remarked, "Ted, the presidential polls look great; 1980 is your year for the White House." So I took Bill's advice—but this time the "heir apparent" was apparent only to Bill and me.

I recalled that conversation again last spring—when I opened the *Boston Globe* one morning, turned to the weekly William V. Shannon column, and saw Bill's endorsement of Senator Albert Gore.

Irish to the core, Bill was proud of his roots in County Clare. He loved the Irish in all their ramifications and contradictions—the legends and stereotypes, the scholars and brawlers, the priests and politicians, the art and history, and especially the wit. Recently we were regaling each other with the tale of the renegade Irishman jailed for thirty days for stealing a ham. It seems that after three weeks, his wife couldn't stand it any longer, so she went before the judge to plead for her husband's release.

"Is he good to you?" asked the judge.

"Well no, sir, he isn't."

"Does he treat the children well?"

"No, sir, he's mean to them."

"Does he stay at home when he's not in jail?"

"No, sir, he runs around a lot."

"Why on earth do you want him back again?"

"Well, to tell the truth, Judge—we're about to run out of ham."

Because of Bill we have a richer understanding not only of Irish wit but also of the many other dimensions of Ireland's hold on the United States. He wrote eloquently of these dimensions in *The American Irish*—about the saints and sinners who came to this country over the past century and more and who did so much to make this land of their dreams a reality. They built our New England mills and cities, dug the canals, and laid the railroad tracks that took America to the West. Even today, it is said, under every railroad tie, an Irishman is buried. And Bill Shannon told their story well, with the characteristic brilliance and sensitivity that have always been his trademark.

Writing that classic tale was a labor of love for Bill. But it was often frustrating too. I understand that at one point, Bill was ready to pack the project in. But Liz came to the rescue, saying: "Look, it's like a pile of wet laundry down in the cellar. You just have to pick it all up and iron it."

Later, in the 1970s, Ireland became not only history and heritage, but headlines and heartaches too. "The troubles" had come again to that other land Bill loved. He was quick to comprehend the truth that all the news from Ireland was not fit to print. And so he traded in the editorial board of New York for the embassy desk of Dublin.

At first, there was grumbling about Bill's nomination. The Foreign Service professionals, the big campaign contributors, and the thoroughbred horse-breeders all thought they owned the embassy. There was stiff competition for the post, and few observers gave much chance to the intellectual editorial writer from Brookline, Massachusetts. But Bill got a little help from his friends. As a White House liaison man remarked in the spring of 1977, President Carter had no intention of stepping in between Bill Shannon and Tip O'Neill and Ted Kennedy.

And so to his portfolio as reporter, columnist, and author, Bill Shannon added the role of distinguished diplomat. I often thought he liked the last best, because he liked the action most.

It is said that editorial writers are people who come down from the hills after the battle is over and shoot the wounded.

Now, I do not think Bill Shannon was that way, or his colleague Marty Nolan of the *Boston Globe* either.

But I do know that when Bill Shannon stopped writing editorials in New York for the *Times* and started writing cables in Dublin, the State Department in Washington became swiftly and miraculously transformed with a much more even-handed posture on the Irish issue.

It is a tribute to the irresistible logic of Bill's diplomacy that when President Reagan took over from President Carter, he took over Bill Shannon's

Irish policy too—and did not change a thing. We are closer to peace in Northern Ireland today because of Bill Shannon, and closer to unity for all of Ireland too.

Finally, let me mention one other quality of Bill's that captivated Jack and Bobby and me, and so many others who knew him. He was a gentle, loving friend, with a powerful, infectious sparkle in his eyes. It made all his soft-spoken words and precise pronunciations echo with insight and delight.

I have often thought that they wrote "When Irish Eyes Are Smiling" for people like Bill Shannon. And the words are an especially appropriate farewell:

> When Irish eyes are smiling,
> It's like a morn in spring.
> In the lilt of Irish laughter,
> You can hear the angels sing.
> When Irish hearts are smiling,
> They'll steal your heart away.

You stole our hearts away, Bill. We loved you, and we miss you.

Preface

WHEN A BOSTON NEWSPAPER referred to him as an Irishman, Joseph P. Kennedy expostulated: "I was born here. My children were born here. What the hell do I have to do to be called an American?"[1]

There are many kinds of Americans, from Comanche Indians to Kansas wheat farmers, from Alabama Negroes to Boston Saltonstalls—and Kennedys. To describe one group of Americans in terms of their ancestry and background is not to say that they are any less American for what they did and are. Rather, it is an effort to show what kind of Americans they are and why their history took the form that it did. The Irish are now among the oldest and best integrated groups in our society. The election of John F. Kennedy to the Presidency demonstrates how much they are taken for granted by other Americans. Paradoxically enough, this happy circumstance has made the uniqueness of the Irish past and the Irish character more, not less, significant. What was formerly private and of parochial concern has become public and of general interest. The life of the Irish in East Boston a century ago, for example, seems much more relevant since the grandson of an East Boston politician entered the White House.

This is true despite the fact that President Kennedy was not Irish in most of the obvious ways. As one biographer has observed, "he doesn't speak with a brogue; he never dances a jig or sings 'Danny Boy.' "[2] But as I demonstrate in my concluding chapter, he was in accord with Irish political experience and with the Irish past in other, more fundamental ways.

A book which discusses racial characteristics requires a preliminary word about the whole idea of race. Anthropologists and biologists have amply demonstrated that race is not a reliable scientific concept. Moreover, human beings do not inherit the acquired characteristics of their parents. But every people has a history and a culture. The members of each generation learn from their parents of the triumphs and griefs of their ancestors; they share in common experiences, repeat established rituals, adopt some of the models and aspirations of their parents, and their outlook on the present and the future is shaped by many influences from the past. This book puts forward an interpretation of the Irish based upon their history and culture, not upon their race in any biological sense.

The Catholic religion has been a major component in the history and culture of the American Irish. With minor exceptions, this book discusses only the Catholic Irish. It is true that there have been American Irish who were belligerently proud of their Irishness but who were not Catholics. It is also true that there have been times when Irish and Catholic diverged, particularly in the 1880's and 1890's when the Catholic hierarchy in Ireland opposed the Land League agitation and later condemned Charles Stewart Parnell, the nationalist leader, for his liaison with a married woman. It was then that some ardent patriots repeated the bitter epigram, "The better the Catholic, the worse the Irishman." But in America, broadly speaking, the opposite has been true. Most Irish have been strongly bound up with their Catholic religion even when, as is true with the individuals I discuss in my chapters on the theater and literature, they rejected it and sought to escape it. The Irish put their stamp on the Catholic Church in America, and the Church in turn has put its stamp on them. Catholicism was important in defining the Irish community, keeping it cohesive, and making the Irish distinctive.

Because I am interested only in those who thought of themselves as Irish and who are related to the Irish community in some meaningful way, I have not tried in the name of racial imperialism to track down and annex to this story every person of remote Irish ancestry. Doubtless, there have been over the past two centuries many Irish who have merged into the general society and ceased to be Irish in any significant sense. As Thomas Beer remarked, "They melted easily into the westward movements of the [1830's] and '40's, shedding their habits from prairie to prairie so that families named O'Donnell, Connor and Delehanty are now discovered drowsing in Protestant pews of Texas and Kansas."[3]

I am content to let them drowse in peace.

Similarly, I think we can lay at rest the old quarrel over those much-disputed people, the Scotch-Irish. In an earlier generation, filiopietistic historians of the American Irish sought to prove that the term "Scotch-Irish" had no factual content. It was, they contended, a deliberate invention of bigoted historians who, in writing about the colonial period and the Revolutionary War, ascribed the accomplishments of the Irish to the virtues of the Scots.[4] These investigators turned up interesting material, and some of their arguments have merit. But the main story of the Irish in America begins with the famine generation who began to come to this country after 1830, and no historian, bigoted or otherwise, has affixed the term "Scotch-Irish" to these immigrants. Unless one drops this argument and lets the Protestant immigrants from eighteenth century Ireland be denominated as a separate group, the Scotch-Irish, one is forced into the awkward position of identifying a person such as Woodrow Wilson as "Irish," which he certainly was not in any sense in which he or his Irish Catholic contemporaries used the term.

On March 18, 1962, the United Press International distributed a dispatch from Philadelphia headlined, "Toast to President Starts Donnybrook," which read: "The friendly Sons of St. Patrick were anything but at their annual dinner Saturday night when Sen. Joseph S. Clark (D-Pa), proposed a toast to President John F. Kennedy, the 'only Irishman ever elected President of the United States.'

"About a dozen lumpy noses resulted during a disagreement at three tables over how many other presidents had Irish ancestry. After the brawl was over a spokesman said six others had claimed roots in the auld sod."[5]

In this as in other matters of public controversy, I think Senator Clark is right.

My principle in organizing this book has been to emphasize those activities in which the presence of the Irish has made a significant difference as against what might have occurred if no Irish had come to this country. These fields are politics, religion, the theater, literature, and such specialized activities as prizefighting and law enforcement. I should like to have devoted more space to the role of Irish in other fields, including my own profession of journalism; in medicine, and in the trade-union movement, but on balance I think I have accurately identified the major themes. Naturally, some readers will quarrel with my judgment, but that is nothing new in a work about the Irish. Two hundred years ago, Samuel Johnson was remarking to Boswell, "The Irish are a fair people; they never speak well of one another." I happen to think disagreement is also a good thing. As a columnist who has to make up his mind several times a week on a broad range of public issues, some of them in bitter dispute, I have always taken comfort from the old Irish proverb, "Contention is better than loneliness."

And so let it be with this book.

Acknowledgments

I N WRITING THIS WORK, I am first of all indebted to my wife, Elizabeth, whose presence in my life inspired and sustained me in the completion of a long task. I also owe much to my mother, Nora Mc-Namara Shannon, whose fondness for reading and keen interest in public affairs have been shaping influences in my life.

Moses Rischin, once my classmate in the Harvard Graduate School and my longtime friend, has done much through his conversations, postcards, and letters over the years to keep alive my interest in the history of the American Irish. His own work, *The Promised City: New York's Jews, 1870–1914* (Harvard University Press, 1962), is a brilliant contribution to a companion field of immigrant history. He and his wife Ruth read the first two-thirds of my manuscript, and I am indebted to them both for saving me from errors of fact and suggesting many improvements in style.

I owe much of my understanding of immigrant history to Professor Oscar Handlin of Harvard. Professors Frederick Merk and Arthur Schlesinger, Jr., from their different perspectives, enriched my understanding of politics.

I would not have been able to complete this book were it not for the year I spent as a fellow at the Center for the Study of Democratic Institutions in Santa Barbara, California. I profited greatly from the spirited discussions and the opportunities for uninterrupted reflection which the Center afforded me. I express my thanks to Robert Maynard Hutchins, whose imaginative and humane leadership has made the Center a uniquely valuable enterprise in our nation's intellectual life. John Cogley, the director of the American Character project at the Center, helped me to understand better the complex relationship between politics and ethics, and was unfailing in his kindness and encouragement. William Gorman, another of my Center colleagues, read my chapter on McCarthyism, and subjected it to his characteristically exacting and perceptive analysis.

My brother John J. Shannon read the entire manuscript and made valuable corrections and criticisms.

Harriet "Tommy" Bush has for intervals over the past decade served as my secretary and research assistant. I am deeply grateful for her accuracy, skill, and enthusiastic devotion to this project. I was most fortunate during my year in Santa Barbara to have Virginia Medeiros as my secretary. No author could hope to have a better one.

I am grateful to James A. Wechsler, my editor at the *New York Post*, for arranging my leave of absence in 1961–1962; to W. H. Ferry for the loan of books from his personal library; to Florence Mischel for her astute criticism of several chapters and her gift of a tape-recording; to Judah Rubinstein for the gift of an out-of-print volume and for his thoughtful criticism of a draft of my first chapter; to Ethel O'Banion, the librarian at the Center for the Study of Democratic Institutions, for her energetic assistance; to the librarians of the Library of Congress, the Washington and Santa Barbara public libraries, and the library of the University of California at Santa Barbara for their many courtesies; to Helene V. Sheriff for her generous help in typing the final draft; to Elizabeth Donahue for her helpful comments on my section on Philip Barry; and to Donald and Paula Jeffries for their warm hospitality to an itinerant writer. In conclusion, I want to add that I accept, of course, full responsibility for any errors that may have persisted despite the vigilance of friends.

WASHINGTON, D.C.
March 27, 1963

CHAPTER ONE

The Irish Inheritance

THE TIME WAS AUGUST, 1847.

Into the river Liffey the steamship *Duchess of Kent*, homeward bound from Italy, moved toward Dublin. Aboard the vessel lay the body of Daniel O'Connell, the first great political leader of modern Ireland. He was called "the Liberator" because of his success in helping to obtain the passage of the Catholic Emancipation Act of 1829. He had been the first Irish Catholic member of the House of Commons and the first Catholic Lord Mayor of modern Dublin. His intellectual brilliance, indefatigable energy, and courage as a lawyer practicing before hostile British judges had long made him a living legend in Irish courtrooms. Turning to politics, he took "all Ireland for his client," and broke his health in her service. He set out for Rome to recover his strength, but in Genoa death had met him on the way.

Another vessel, the *Birmingham*, outward bound for America and thronged with emigrants, passed the funeral ship. Word of it passed among the passengers. From their midst rose the "keen," that crooning, wailing, shouting threnody with which the Irish mourn their dead. They had much to mourn, for the great chief was dead and in death he returned to an Ireland that was dying.[1]

Famine was dark upon the land. From O'Connell's native hills of Kerry and the limestone Cliffs of Moher fronting the Atlantic in the west, along the valleys of the Shannon and the Lee, across the fertile fields of Leinster and Kilkenny to the edge of Dublin, hunger stalked the stricken Irish people. For the third year, blight had touched the potato crop. The smell of the potato rotting in the fields rose and mingled with the odors of death in the cottages, by the roadsides, and along the hedgerows. Already half a million persons had starved to death. Hundreds of thousands of others were fleeing to England, to Canada, and, like these passengers of the *Birmingham*, to America. Many more were to follow.

A few months before, in February, 1847, O'Connell, already mortally ill, had made his last appearance in the House of Commons.

"Ireland is in your hands," he cried out in a voice only a feeble echo of its old strength. "She is in your power. . . . If you do not save her she can't save herself. And I solemnly call on you to recollect that I predict with the sincerest conviction that one-quarter of her population will perish unless you come to her relief."

The House cheered him, but the House did not act.

1

The famine of 1845–1847 was the nadir of Irish history, which in the preceding two thousand years had known few sunlit peaks. Although racial qualities are not inherited, every people has a history, and an awareness of that history goes far toward shaping their outlook on life. A brief backward glance at Irish history clarifies much about the Irish and the national character traits that they brought to America.

The modern Irish, a Celtic people from northwest Europe of the same family as the Welsh, Cornish, and Bretons, are believed to have settled the island around 350 B.C. The Romans knew Ireland as Hibernia, but the country, unlike Britain and Gaul, never experienced the stabilizing effects of government. When the Roman world was in its twilight, the Irish were converted to Christianity primarily under the leadership of St. Patrick, who came to Ireland in A.D. 432.* During the following five centuries, the Irish developed a flourishing group of monasteries that conserved the Greek and Latin learning of the ancient world and sent scores of scholars and missionaries to Europe. "Whoever on the continent in the days of Charles the Bald (in the ninth century) knew Greek was an Irishman, or at least his knowledge was transmitted to him through an Irishman, or the report which endows him with this glory is false," one modern paleographer has observed.[2]

The Irish made these accomplishments in religion and learning without developing comparably high political or economic forms of organization. Ireland remained a country of shepherds, farmers, and fishermen. No town or city life developed.

The first foreign invaders were the Danes who began raids in the coastal areas around 800. The Danes founded the first Irish towns along the seacoast—Dublin, Wexford, and Wicklow in the east along the Irish Sea separating Ireland and England, Cork in the south, and Limerick at the mouth of the Shannon River in the west—but the Danes, a sea-

---

* Christianity had beginnings in the country somewhat earlier than this. St. Jerome, writing on the Continent in 416, took note of an Irishman who disputed with him on a doctrinal point: "an ignorant calumniator . . . full of Irish porridge."

faring people, never penetrated the inner reaches of the country. At Clontarf, in 1014, the Irish won a decisive victory, and turned back the Danish thrust to power. It was Ireland's last successful stand against foreign invaders.

A century and a half later, the Normans, who had conquered England in 1066, began to extend their power to Ireland. Henry II crossed the Irish sea in 1169 and conquered the eastern portions of the country. This began the "seven hundred years of enslavement" referred to in song and story that did not end until the formation of the Irish Free State in 1922. England and Ireland, islands "divided by nature but united by force," became interlocked in history.

The Irish, unlike the English, had not developed a coherent feudal system. In Ireland the landowner did not surrender his lands to the most powerful lord and receive them back again as a vassal after a pledge of knightly obedience. Lands belonged to the family. Gaelic custom permitted their division among several sons rather than the observance of the strict Continental and English practice of primogeniture. The great chiefs, who styled themselves "king," were elected by their followers and allies, a practice which led to countless intrigues and local wars. (Almost every present-day Irishman can with some color of truth say he is descended from a king, since there were so many of them.) There was no central government. Under this loose social system, the Irish were ill-prepared to unite for military action against Henry II and his successors. Since they did not take feudal oaths too seriously among themselves, they felt, once defeated in battle, even less bound by oaths of fealty they were forced to swear to a remote monarch who lived across the sea.

The Norman lords who followed in Henry II's wake made themselves masters of certain areas in the south and east, built stone castles, founded towns and constructed roads, but they did not effectively conquer the country. Nor did the local Irish chieftains merge with them as had their counterparts in England in the centuries after 1066. The more important Irish leaders came to terms, surrendered portions of their lands to the Normans, and continued to control the remainder. The Norman castles often were isolated military outposts surrounded by purely Irish enclaves. The Irish from time to time engaged in sporadic forays, burning Norman towns and raiding Norman strongholds. These expeditions did not break the invaders' power, but they were testaments of the rebellious Irish spirit. Through great portions of central and western Ireland the Norman influence did not penetrate at all, and the Irish language and Irish customs held undisputed sway.

English monarchs during succeeding centuries repeatedly journeyed to Ireland to restore a semblance of order. Richard II made two such journeys. On the occasion of the second visit in 1395 he received the personal homage of the leading Irish noblemen and granted them formal title to their lands. In return they agreed to surrender the lands they had been seizing from the Normans. As a practical matter, however, the English sovereigns were too preoccupied during the Middle Ages with wars in France and the dynastic "War of the Roses" at home to pay much attention to Ireland.

By the early sixteenth century, the Norman conquest had clearly failed. The Irish had absorbed the Norman stock. The original Norman names had taken on an Irish cast—the De Burgos became Burkes and the Geraldines became Fitzgeralds—and the Norman families knew the Gaelic language as well as they knew English. Effective English control existed only in the "Pale" extending twenty to thirty miles outside Dublin. One of Henry VIII's agents wrote him in 1536: "Your Highness must understand that the English blood of the English conquest is in manner worn out of this land, and at all seasons, in manner, without any restoration, is diminished and enfeebled; and contrariwise the Irish blood, ever more and more, without such decay, encreaseth."

Henry VIII became preoccupied with Ireland since he was endeavoring to extend his break with the Catholic Church and was encountering unexpected difficulties. The Irish, "these barbarians," were resisting the new religious dispensations as they resisted everything that came from London. The struggle of the English Crown to subdue and control the Irish became the worst form of human strife: a religious war.

The English government decided only the infusion of new blood could make Ireland properly obedient. It began the long process of "colonizing" Ireland, depriving Catholic Irish noblemen of their property, driving the Irish off the land, and settling "plantations" of English settlers. It was as if Ireland were Maryland or Virginia, unpopulated virgin country except for hostile Indians whose rights and long-standing tenure need not be taken seriously. The Irish nobility fought back and sought allies. In 1570, Pope Pius V issued a Papal Bull depriving Queen Elizabeth of her claim to rule either Ireland or England. From that time, the Irish cause and the Catholic faith were indissolubly linked.[3]

Elizabeth's armies defeated numerous insurrections, but she died before England achieved the decisive victory by crushing the revolt led by Hugh O'Neill, the Catholic Earl of Tyrone. The year of the latter's defeat—1603—marked the downfall of the Irish aristocracy. The Irish had lost their last good opportunity to reverse the tide of English conquest.

O'Neill's stronghold was Ulster in northern Ireland. The English government "planted" his domain with thousands of Lowland Scots, most of them Presbyterians. Within two generations Scottish settlers owned 3,000,000 of the 3,500,000 acres in the northern counties. The political and religious division between Ulster and the rest of Ireland that still vexes the country had been established.

The seventeenth century, from 1603 onward, was for Ireland a slow and prolonged descent into agonizing defeat and utter subjection, marked by recurring outbursts of rebellion followed inexorably by further liquidation of the old Irish Catholic aristocracy and renewed "plantings" of English and Scotch settlers. In 1641 the Irish allied their cause to that of the Stuart kings and the English lords of Royalist sympathies in the "Pale." Civil war raged intermittently for the next eight years. Cromwell, following his conclusive triumph in England and the execution of Charles I in 1649, led an invasion of Ireland that took on the character of a religious crusade and a war of extermination. Capturing an important Irish force at Drogheda, he ordered a total massacre. Soldiers, civilians, priests, 2,800 persons in all, were executed.

"This hath been a marvellous great mercy. . . . I do not believe, neither do I hear, that any officer escaped with his life, save only one lieutenant who, I hear, going to the enemy said that he was the only man that escaped of all the garrison. The enemy were filled upon this with much terror. And truly I believe this bitterness will save much effusion of blood, through the goodness of God," Cromwell wrote.

But the struggle continued until 1652 when all Ireland had been crushed. By then, 616,000 persons, one-third of the population, had died in the wars, plague, and famine of the preceding ten years. There then followed a ravishment of unprecedented severity. Cromwell parceled out two-thirds of the land in Ireland to his soldiers and adherents. Several thousand Irish were sent in chains to the West Indies and sold as slaves on the plantations. Others roamed the country as vagabonds. The great majority remained to work the land for their conquerors.

In 1688 the Irish rallied to the support of the deposed James II. The Protestant armies of William and Mary broke this last revolt in the Battle of the Boyne in 1690 and brought it to a close in the successful siege of Limerick the following year.

The Irish in the sixteenth and seventeenth centuries did not fight for national independence in the modern sense. They fought for the right to hold their lands, for their religion, for the glory of the Catholic Stuart kings, for the righting of some ancient grievance or local quarrel, or as a stubborn protest against the misery of their common lot and the progressive darkening of their common future.

The year 1691 ended it all. The strength of resistance was spent at last. The flame of rebellion that flickered so long guttered out. The remnants of the Irish nobility and the best of the fighting men fled abroad to the courts of England's enemies and enlisted in the armies of the Continent, as had Irish exiles since the beginning of the century. They were the "Wild Geese" of Irish history. In later years, their names cropped up again and again in the far corners of the world—at Fontenoy in the armies of Louis XV, at Jena in the army of the Prussian king, and at Paris in 1871 where Marshal Patrice de Mac-Mahon became the first president of the Third Republic. In South America a later exile of humbler status, Bernardo O'Higgins, became the liberator of Chile.

Behind them in Ireland, the Irish aristocrats left a people invertebrate. Their manor houses were burned, abandoned, or occupied by strangers. Their people toiled in squalor for English landlords and merchants who possessed three-fourths of the land and two-thirds of the trade. For three centuries, the Irish farmers had been sinking into the status of a landless peasantry. They by now had no legal right or even fixed tenure to the soil. They held their cottages and their pinched acre or quarter-acre only if they paid annual rent to the landlord, often an absentee in London or Bath who never showed his face in the neighborhood from one end of his life to the other.

To this economic subjugation, the English added after 1691 the Draconian penalties of a new Penal Code. Under these laws the Irish were beggars in their own land, deprived of civil rights, mercilessly exploited, and subject to hanging or deportation for trivial offenses. No Irish Catholic could vote, serve on a jury, enter the army or navy, teach school, carry a gun, or own a horse of the value of more than five guineas. No Irish Catholic could enter a university, become a lawyer, or work for the government. Every Irish Catholic had to pay tithes for the support of the established Anglican Church. No Catholic Church could have a spire. No Irish Catholic could marry a Protestant or buy land from a Protestant. No Irish Catholic tradesman could have more than two apprentices. Those few Irish who clung to sizable pieces of land did so at the price of swearing allegiance to the Anglican Church. When an Irish Catholic died, his estate was divided among his sons unless the eldest became a Protestant, in which event all of it went to him. Priests were subject to arrest and deportation. The Irish language was forbidden, and schools became almost unknown.

This Penal Code was not, of course, enforced everywhere in the country with equal severity or success, but it survived for the next 125 years. Its effects were deep, severe, and lasting. The Ireland of the Penal Code formed the modern Irish character. The majority of Irish settlers in America carried this background with them.

2

The Irish mind and temper on the eve of immigration were the product of many conflicting forces. The first of these was the land itself. The basic Irish immigrant type was the transplanted countryman.

People who dwell on the land, live by the crops they plant and harvest, turn the soil over in their hands, dig the turf which warms their hearth, watch the common mystery of birth among the animals of their barnyards, and work long days in the fields under sun, sky, and rain come to know deep in their bones and spirit an appreciation of the natural world. They learn its unchangeable rhythms and innate order, its cruelty and beneficence and its power. This knowledge is the common possession of country people the world over. It is a knowledge that breeds patience, fatalism, a sense of awe. In Ireland, this knowledge was deepened by the surrounding sea.

No part of the island is much more than seventy miles from that ocean. It has a maritime climate, never really hot, and with little snow in winter. Rain and scudding gray clouds and cool winds predominate for nine months of the year. Even in the warm days of August the afternoon sea wind has an edge to it. During long winter nights the waves pound the shore, and great storms from the Atlantic bend the trees, send wind whistling around the cottage, and lace the traveler's cheek with rain and chill. The ocean, vast, wide, deep, terrible in its destructive power and brooding lonely emptiness, deepens the feeling of isolation on the farms. It is no wonder then that the Irish, for all the hard practicality that necessity required of them, have forever been hospitable to mysticism and romantic excess and dreams—often dark dreams.

In pre-Christian times the Irish somewhat in the manner of the ancient Greeks, also an island and maritime people, developed a rudimentary cosmology peopled by pagan gods and holy spirits. Yeats recaptured these dim imaginings in his poem "The Unappeasable Host":

"The Danaan children laugh, in cradles of wrought gold,
And clap their hands together, and half-close their eyes,
For they will ride the North when the ger-eagle flies,

With heavy whitening wings, and a heart fallen cold:
I kiss my wailing child and press it to my breast,
And hear the narrow graves calling my child and me.
Desolate winds that cry over the wandering sea;
Desolate winds that hover in the flaming West;
Desolate winds that beat the doors of Heaven, and beat
The doors of Hell and blow there many a whimpering ghost;
O heart the winds have shaken, the unappeasable host
Is comelier than candles at Mother Mary's feet."[4]

During the Middle Ages the first great Irish Christian figures were wild ascetics dwelling alone or missionaries driven by their own zeal to wander across the Continent. The Church with its own richer mythos slowly disciplined this zeal and incorporated these feelings, but not entirely. The receptivity to belief in fairies, fancies, and unseen natural powers has lingered for centuries in the Irish mind, coloring the present.

Every Irishman was prepared to shake hands with Doom, since that gentleman had been so frequent a visitor in the past. He had no difficulty believing Christianity's doctrines of evil and original sin. These were the most congenial truths of his religion, for they were pertinent in organizing his own experience. Man's frailty and man's death were not alien facts. They were realities he had to take into account in his daily life. They conditioned his thinking about all his most intimate concerns. It could not be otherwise in a captive, overcrowded society living on the economic ragged edge on an island where the forces of nature met few human barriers. This was not a strong, vital urban world with its own resources and organization to defeat nature and affirm human strength. This was life on the land, hard and lonely. Melancholy in these circumstances was a common cast of mind, death familiar and even looked forward to, and opportunities for social gathering the more dearly prized. Irish social customs accommodated and reflected these needs. The Irish wake, that national institution, expressed death's integral role. The "kitchen racket," that dance in which neighbors young and old foregathered in the main room of the cottage, became a permanent feature of country life. Paradoxically enough in the midst of poverty, hospitality and openhandedness were enshrined as virtues. Only in this way could they beat back the loneliness of the land and deny the darkness of the common lot. Hard games ("hurling," a wild, tough version of field hockey), hard drinking ("poteen," a villainously powerful drink brewed illegally in home stills), and "faction fighting" gave vent to cramped passions. Learning was prized, since it was so hard to come by in a country where schools were few. The oral arts of poetry, oratory, and storytelling were valued highly because many could not read and write.

Out of this tradition emerges one of the archetypes of Irish character —the man with the gift for words. The Irish have produced writers, poets, dramatists, and teachers out of all proportion to their numbers. The Irish have been preoccupied with explaining themselves to themselves, to one another and to the rest of the world. The national genius, driven back upon itself, rediscovered its unique identity by drawing upon the wellsprings of fantasy and emotion.

The Irish in these years developed inwardness and stubbornness. Within the outlook formed by the rhythms of life on the land and the nearness of the sea, the narrower tradition of national defeat bred these enduring qualities in the Irish character. The repetitive nature of Irish political griefs, the collapse of the Gaelic nobility, and the many lost rebellions reared a tradition of hopeless gallantry and military failure. "They always went forth to battle and they always fell," the poet wrote. The long losing struggle to lead their own life free from English interference rubbed into every Irish mind a primitive tragic sense. From childhood, each generation learned of these old defeats and heard retold these tales of lost battles and fallen heroes. The grinding realities of economic exploitation by a foreign landlord class reiterated to each generation the painful meaning of that tradition. History seemed to have laid a heavy hand on this island and this people. ("History," Stephen Dedalus said in *Ulysses*, "is a nightmare from which I am trying to awake.") Too often they had seen "the moment of my greatness flicker"—and die. There grew among the Irish a sense of themselves as a fated race. A man at the bottom who knows he is at the bottom must conserve and endure, or crack up. The Irish did not break. They mustered their aggressiveness, rolled and twisted their anger into a knot, and tried to hold on to what was theirs: their rights in the land, their family identity, their memories, their pattern of speech, their way of looking at the world. Rebellion had failed, social movement was blocked, individual talent brought no reward, social wrongs no relief, and appeals for understanding no quarter. Then let the outsiders, the government, and the world be damned, and let each man look to his own and his family's interest. The Irish became an ever more conservative people. They became dedicated to holding together the family unit, and independent and "touchy" where their rights were concerned.

3

The Irish did not dwell alone in the eighteenth century, that dark, closed world of frustration and defeat. Living side by side with the English who owned the land and ruled the government, they were not free simply to turn inward upon themselves. They must of necessity cope with these interlopers, and in their response to this conflict their character was further shaped. They produced another Irish national type, the lawyer turned politician.

Daniel O'Connell, their greatest man in the early nineteenth century, once wrote in his diary: "A man, I believe, meets with many difficulties in playing even his own character." These difficulties also confront a people. Their character is their fortune, but their character cannot be wholly of their own making. What they think of themselves and what others think of them are inevitably to some extent different. Yet the two conceptions constantly interact on each other in complex fashion. They are matters of great importance, for the one defines their integrity and the other may define their fate. When, as in Ireland, the outsiders are of a different religious faith and an alien way of life and occupy the land, control the government, and usurp the sources of economic power, the pressures and counterpressures in this subtle interplay become intense. The formation of national character, which is ordinarily an unconscious affair, a silent guerrilla war between memory and desire, rises spectacularly to the conscious level. The result is the emergence of a national character sharply etched, at once versatile and cohesive, and yet, since synthesis is not easy or even possible, deeply flawed by divisions within.

The lines of battle between English and Irish, fluxing and refluxing, merging and parting but knowing no truce, were most sharply drawn in the administration of justice. The Irish, with their strong familial loyalties and ancient Gaelic tribal tradition, were accustomed to appealing to some chieftain or local strong man to defend their rights. The common-law system with its juries and its weighing of truth on the basis of individual testimony under oath was alien to them. It seemed scandalous to have to testify against a relative or a neighbor. Oaths of fealty and ties of blood were one thing, but oaths to tell the truth when it was against one's own interest or the interest of a friend were quite another. The claim of abstract justice that it served the common good in the long run held little appeal. In the long run everyone will be dead, and of what use is the common good if it is not also a personal good? The Irish did not want justice; they wanted equity. Justice not tempered by charity, mercy, and a feeling of common humanity was, in their view, no justice at all.

("We are a generous people but we must also be just," the Englishman remarked. "I fear those big words," Stephen said, "which make us so unhappy.")

The Irishman had sound practical reasons for distrusting the complex of English law. The local justices of the peace were the English landlords or their agents. These officers were a good deal less than disinterested, and their rulings often arbitrary and mercurial. The Irish took their private quarrels to them only if one party or the other had some reason to hope for favoritism. Otherwise, they preferred to settle their disputes among themselves. One observer noted, " 'I'll have the law on you' is the saying of an Englishman who expects justice. 'I'll have you before his honor' is the threat of an Irishman who hopes for partiality."

The Irish had equal grounds to distrust the workings of the higher levels of English jurisprudence. The Irish courts were the neglected dumping ground and patronage hutch of the English judicial system. Many of the judges had bought their way onto the bench. They were often ignorant or brutal men. During one term of a judicial circuit in rural Ireland, the judge heard one hundred criminal cases, found ninety-eight defendants guilty of capital offenses, and ninety-seven of them were hanged. The most infamous of these "hanging judges" was Lord Norbury. He once sentenced a man to death for stealing a watch. On pronouncing sentence, he remarked lightheartedly, "Ha-ha! You made a grab at time, egad, but you caught eternity!"

On another occasion while holding court in Dublin, he ordered the prisoner to be flogged for as long as it took him to walk from College Green to the docks. "Thank you, my lord, you have done your worst," the wretched victim remarked bitterly, at which point Norbury added, "—and back again!"[5]

The Irish coped with the toils of this insensate law machine by developing the art of soft deception ("blarney") and the disingenuous oath which is not really an oath at all. These were acts of the imagination designed to oblige the hearer with the fiction of compliance while preserving fidelity to one's own conception of justice. They were dangerous, self-destructive arts, perhaps, but a people with no tangible resources to meet adversity must rely on inscrutable silence or the resources of wit and speech. The Irish, it seemed, were not good at cultivating silence. They preferred what Sean O'Faolain has termed "that so typically Kerry-ish form of silence, an affluence of volubility."[6]

The word "blarney" dates from the sixteenth century when Queen

Elizabeth endeavored to get Cormac Carthy, the Lord of Blarney, to renounce his ancestral claim to his land and acknowledge that he held tenure only by virtue of a grant from the Crown. Carthy, while pretending to agree to this request, put off its fulfillment repeatedly "with fair words and soft speech" until Elizabeth expostulated, "This is all Blarney. What he says he never means." From this incident sprang the tradition that to kiss the stone at Blarney Castle would automatically confer the gift of eloquence.

William Carleton in his *Traits and Stories of the Irish Peasantry* has described how the concoction of oaths became a fine art: "When relating a narrative, or some other circumstance of his own invention, if contradicted, he will corroborate it, in order to sustain his credit or produce the proper impression, by an abrupt oath upon the first object he can seize. 'Arrah, nonsense! By this pipe in my hand, it's as thrue as'—and then, before he completes the illustration, he goes on with a fine specimen of equivocation—'By the stool I'm sittin' an, it is; an' what more would you have from me, barrin' I take my book oath of it?' Thus does he, under the mask of an insinuation, induce you to believe that he has actually sworn it, whereas the oath is always left undefined and incomplete."[7]

This is not to suggest that every Irishman became a great talker or a supple casuist, but rather that the Irish developed a lasting admiration for those among them who were. Once the Irish had begun to respond to their difficulties in this fashion, the English and the rest of the world came to expect this eloquence and verbal inventiveness of them, and they came to expect it of themselves. A character ideal had been set up, and succeeding generations lived up to it. Ambitious Irish youths dreamed of winning fame as orators and admiration as good talkers just as Prussian youths turned naturally to the army as a career and sought to emulate the great Prussian generals.

A critical date in this development was 1792. Parliament that year passed a Catholic Relief Act, one of several laws enacted in the latter part of the eighteenth century to ameliorate the Penal Code. The act permitted Irish Catholics to study law and join the bar, though not to serve on the bench. Daniel O'Connell, then a youth of seventeen, chose this profession and over the next half-century became the greatest figure among the first two generations of Irish Catholic lawyers.

O'Connell, being Irish himself and having grown up among country people, could comprehend the workings of the minds of his countrymen in the courtroom and penetrate their casual deceptions with greater ease than any English or Anglo-Irish lawyer. Witnesses came to fear him greatly. His cross-examination, if not a model of proper procedure, was often a brilliant tour de force alive with human interest. On one occasion when a witness denied he had been drunk at the time of the crime, O'Connell pressed him to tell how much he had drunk.

"I only drank my share of the cup," he replied.

"And your share was all but the pewter," O'Connell shot back. The witness smiled in agreement.

Defending a man charged with stealing a dead cow, O'Connell got him off by arguing that the charge was for larceny of a cow when it should have been for larceny of beef.

One old lady in the witness chair summed up the common opinion when she burst out, "Ah! You knows all about the roguery of it, but you don't know at all about the honesty of it!"

O'Connell and his Irish Catholic contemporaries of the bar had to summon up bluff and courage to make their way successfully in the courts dominated by hostile English judges and packed juries. Early in O'Connell's career, a judge rebuked him for interfering in a case in which he held no brief.

"It was not in this way I behaved," said his lordship, "when I was at the bar."

"No," retorted O'Connell, "but when you were at the bar I never took you for a model, and now that you are on the bench I am not going to submit to your dictation."

In another case, the judge first forbade him to introduce certain evidence and the next day reversed himself.

O'Connell observed sharply: "Had your lordship known as much law yesterday as you do today, you would have saved me a vast amount of time and trouble and my client a considerable amount of injury. Crier! Call up the witnesses!"

These tactics did not always go unchallenged. Sir Robert Peel, later to be O'Connell's most obdurate political antagonist, wrote in 1813, "I hope the Chief Justice will not allow the court to be again insulted and made the vehicle for treason but that he will interrupt O'Connell's harangue by committing him to Newgate for contempt."

Working in this violent cockpit, O'Connell and his contemporaries established in the minds of the people the ideal of the Irish lawyer: quick-witted, aggressive, shrewd, equally adept at staging a gigantic bluff, fencing endlessly over technicalities and meanings of words, or making sentimental or impassioned pleas to the jury.

O'Connell did not devote his virtuoso talents solely to private ends. Through a succession of sensational libel and conspiracy trials, he argued Ireland's larger grievances. It is common in English-speaking countries that almost as many great political issues are fought out in courtrooms as are decided at elections or in legislatures. The courts are forums where causes are argued and principles established that transcend the merits of the case at hand. This was especially true in Ireland, which had no parliament or representative bodies of any kind. The Irish were not slow to seize the opportunity the courts afforded them; cases that began innocently enough over such a question as who stole Mrs. Kelly's cow were often transformed into dramatic indictments of English misrule and exploitation. The admission of the Irish Catholics to the bar in 1792 thus marked a merging of the legal and the political. The characteristics of the lawyer and the politician mingled to form a single stereotype. To say the best Irish lawyers were political lawyers became a redundancy. The courts were thought of not as mere places where crimes were judged and property disputes settled but as battlegrounds where political and national causes were fought. (O'Connell's twin titles symbolize this duality; to the Irish public he was known interchangeably as "the Counselor" and "the Liberator.") To the Irish peasant's customary distrust of the courts as places where telling the truth would do any good was thus added the concept of the lawyer not as an officer of the court but as a skilled political advocate. Courts, the machinery of the law and, by easy extension, the whole government are, in this view, not instruments for securing justice and the common good but mechanisms for winning battles for oneself, one's family, or one's political point of view. What is at stake is not abstract moral and legal conceptions, but power. This way of looking at these institutions does not strengthen ideas of corporate virtue and individual responsibility. Power is neutral and has no morals, but the pursuit of it can be corrupting.

It is easy to understand how this power concept of law and government developed. England helped show the way. When O'Connell was arrested in 1843 for "incitement to sedition," the government packed the Dublin jury by using an antiquated register that listed only twenty-three Catholic citizens instead of three hundred, and managed to draw from it twelve jurors, none of whom was Catholic. O'Connell's biographer observed that "by every known and hitherto unknown device, the Crown lawyers justified the disrepute with which English law has always been smirched in popular Irish opinion. . . .

"When one considers such methods," he adds, "one humorously wonders whether O'Connell did not learn most of his wiles from the same source and whether the true parentage of Tammany Hall might not be traced to British law in Ireland."[8]

4

The Irish emigrants to America came with a live political tradition. They had learned some understanding of the uses of politics and of the discipline and cohesion successful organization requires. They had passed a threshold of political consciousness that later immigrants from southern Italy, Poland, and the Balkans had not reached.

The first modern Irish political organizations were the Catholic Associations formed to work for Catholic Emancipation (that is, the full repeal of the Penal Code and the right of Irish Catholics to serve in the British Parliament). These Associations were illegal under the sedition laws even if the objective was only the innocuous one of drawing up a petition to the government. Daniel O'Connell, for a time, helped them avoid the law by sponsoring a resolution that the members of the association "were not representative of the Catholic body nor any portion thereof; nor shall they assume or pretend to be representatives of the Catholic body or any portion thereof." It was a simple if ingenious solution which no one was expected to believe but which met the letter of the law. In parliamentary language, it was the equivalent of the peasant's oath that was not an oath.

O'Connell founded the first popular newspaper to argue in behalf of Irish interests, but to write against the government or agitate against the union with England was also illegal. Candor under these circumstances was a dangerous luxury. In his speeches and writings, he became a master of "the double entendre, the mental reservation, the limiting clause, the disingenuous qualification and proviso."

In this tortuous fashion, the Irish of O'Connell's generation labored for a quarter of a century before achieving their first great victory in the Catholic Emancipation Act of 1828. Their struggle aroused the beginnings of a modern political consciousness among the Irish. They learned to work together and sacrifice for a common cause. The Catholic Associations were financed in the style of a modern mass movement by weekly voluntary offerings from the rank and file. Cynics doubted this method would work, since it seemed unlikely the poor, who had scarcely enough to eat, would be able or willing to contribute. Yet the weekly contributions over a twenty-year period from the early 1820's averaged twenty thousand pounds a year and ran sometimes as high as fifty thousand. Thackeray, the novelist, saw this weekly political "rent" being collected at the church doors while on a visit to Dublin.

"Every door was barred, of course, with plate holders," he wrote, "and heaps of pence at the humbler entrances and bank-notes at the front gates told the willingness of the people to reward their champion. The carboy who drove me had paid his little tribute of fourpence at the morning Mass. The waiter who brought me my breakfast had added his humble shilling."

This political movement also made use of the arts of propaganda. The publisher James Duffy issued thousands of small books sold at a few pence apiece on Irish history, literature, art, and music. Reading rooms were organized in hundreds of parishes throughout the country. Each member of the Catholic Association was issued a small card decorated with the shamrock and other traditional insignia.

The Irish before 1848 had adopted the English language as their own. There were no native schools that could perpetuate the Gaelic language in written form. The Irish picked up what learning they could at the Hedge Schools. Held in a cottage or beside the hedgerows, conducted by an itinerant, ill-paid teacher, the schools were rough affairs affording some knowledge of reading, writing, and arithmetic and sometimes of the classics. The schoolmaster often punished pupils who clung to Gaelic, and he did so with the cooperation of the parents. Gaelic was of no use to the farmer dealing with his English landlord: "It would not sell the cow." The politicians encouraged this trend, for their political vision in that era was directed not toward an independent Irish nation but toward an Ireland that could take an equal place with England within the kingdom. A partial survey showed that by 1841, four-fifths of the people knew both Gaelic and English and only one-fifth knew only Gaelic. The surrender of their language was one of the major necessary accommodations the Irish made in their life side by side with their English conquerors. Later-day nationalists mourned the loss, but for the future emigrants it was an unforeseen asset. The Irish were the only immigrants in the United States, other than the English themselves, who spoke the language of their new country.

5

The oppressiveness of economic exploitation by the English landlord class further shaped the Irish character and outlook. The landlords sweated their Irish tenants tirelessly. This evoked cruel physical violence and created a long-lasting Irish tolerance of violent methods. Since English law did not recognize hereditary occupancy on the land as establishing any fixed rights to work it, and since the Irish farmers had no long-term contracts, the landlords could raise the rent at will. This process of "rack-renting" was aptly named, for the more the tenant improved his land or his livestock, the more likely he was to be hit with a rent increase. He was figuratively on a rack, and the landlord was able to exact mean tribute from his tenants in the form of "duty gifts." A character in Maria Edgeworth's novel *Castle Rackrent*, written in 1834, said: "Duty fowls and duty turkeys and duty geese came as fast as we could eat 'em, for my lady kept a sharp look-out, and knew to a tub of butter everything the tenant had, all round. They knew her way, and what with fear of driving for rent, and Sir Murtagh's lawsuits, they were kept in such good order they never thought of coming near Castle Rackrent without a present of something or other—eggs, honey, butter, meal, fish, game, grouse, and herrings, fresh and salt, all went for something. As for their young pigs, we had them, and the best bacon and hams they could make up, with all the young chickens in spring."

This kind of exploitation at close quarters bred smoldering hatred. Moreover, the landlords strove to consolidate the patchy acre and quarter-acre holdings into larger units for more economic farming and to drive the excess tenants off the land. This tendency became pronounced as Irish agriculture was drawn into the vortex of the English market where the demand for meat made the raising of beef cattle profitable. Government agents intensified the bitterness by attempts to collect tithes for the Anglican Church. When they met resistance they knocked down cottages, seized cattle and household goods, and ejected offenders.

The Irish fought these practices with sporadic terror. The Whiteboys in Munster, the Hearts of Steel boys in Antrim, the Terry Alts in Clare, the Molly Maguires, the Black Feet, and other secret organizations flourished. These groups had no political programs or large aims. They took action on specific local grievances. If a landlord converted tilled fields into grazing lands, the Whiteboys maimed his cattle or burned his outbuildings. If a landlord expelled a tenant for failure to meet the rent, few dared to take the farm in his stead for fear of retaliation from the neighbors. If a landlord beat down wages, the landless farm laborers and their brothers and friends among the tenants beat up the landlord's agent or burned his crops.

Murders were common and night raids against offenders of the countryside code were familiar occurrences. Since rural courts were a despised adjunct of the hated landlord system, law enforcement and routine local government sporadically broke down altogether in parts of Ireland. In one year, there were 9,000 "political crimes" and 200 homicides. In 1835 the British government estimated there were 35,000 serious crimes committed the previous year in Ireland, ranging from burglaries and assaults to murders and attempts at murder.

The Irish on the eve of emigration lived in an atmosphere of violence. The old rural society long drained by exploitation at the top was shattering under the pounding blows of new economic demands. The coming catastrophe of the great famine was foreshadowed by brief famines in 1822, 1831, 1835, and 1837 and by a cholera epidemic in 1830. Tension reverberated throughout this sick society. Men got used to lawless ways and rough, direct methods. The Irishman picked up a blunt stick or a shortened pitchfork and "had at" the head of his enemy with unnaturally reckless abandon. Here in the endemic violence of rural Ireland was the breeding ground of the tough "bhoys" who in another decade would tear up paving stones or brandish sticks in election-day riots in New York and Philadelphia. Here also was born another Irish type: the fanatic. Men grown used to violence would become the nationalist zealot and the political gunman in his trench coat. In their most familiar American guise they became the rebel union leaders in the coalfields of Pennsylvania, the copper mines of Butte, and the sandlots of San Francisco. This was a minority tradition compared to that of the hardworking, conservative farmer and the eloquent lawyer-politician, but it existed and was a long time in dying. An old lady summed it up:

"Ten o'clock in the morning and not a blow sthruck yet!"

At the opposite extreme to desperate violence was the response of outward conformity to English standards. This was not a problem for the mass of Irish whose interests did not extend much beyond the horizons of their farms and their villages. For them, there were no incentives to conform. But for the elements in society from which social and political leadership is recruited, the wealthier tradesmen in the towns, the big farmers, the professional men, the bright young men hungering for an intellectual life, and the prospective soldiers and civil servants, conformity was an acute problem. Acceptance of the Protestant faith and of English values was the objective of the Penal Code. It was the easy, open route to honors, careers, and material advancement. Making this choice, however, involved the hardest wrench from the past. It meant the greatest sacrifice of one's image of oneself. It was the ultimate gesture of defeat.

Many went part way to gain an immediate objective. O'Connell's own father was married in a Protestant church. The poet Tom Moore registered as a Protestant to gain admission to Trinity College. Others went further. The Mullins family, the leading merchants of Dublin, accepted a peerage and changed their names to de Moleyns. British government and society stood always ready to purchase compliance with an honor or a sinecure. O'Connell himself was invited in 1831 to become Attorney General.

There was a constant strain not to sell out for social acceptance, a job, a dinner invitation, a peerage. Those who did suffered the special agonies of the parvenu and the social climber. Those who did not cursed their fate. They saw the success in life they worked for and deserved denied them. Their very Irishness seemed a badge of inferiority. They developed a protective cynicism about honors and high position and the worldly ways of achieving them, but in the very act of denial these objectives took on an exaggerated importance. A man who deliberately rejects a prize or an opportunity naturally tends in retrospect to overvalue its significance, for in this way he dramatizes his own decision and builds a prop for his self-esteem. Whether they yielded or not, therefore, the minority of Irish for whom the problem existed developed an anxiety about status, a sensitivity about who sits above and below the salt.

These attitudes interacted with the great-man tradition in politics established by O'Connell and the domineering of the English landholding gentry. The people, inured to the lordly arrogance of the landholding gentry, had a personal and aristocratic rather than democratic concept of politics. Only an extraordinary personality of the dimensions of O'Connell could have rallied and directed them. Decades of Penal Code servitude stamped down and almost snuffed out their natural pride. "They keep us like slaves and then they despise us," a young Irishman told an American visitor in 1845. Their pride under these circumstances was displaced from themselves to their political leaders. In their advancement, the people saw their own hopes mirrored, and aspirations they would not dare hold for themselves fulfilled. To keep this kind of exaggerated confidence, the leaders had to act out the popular conceptions and fantasies. They needed tangible signs of success and authority, whether it be the bric-a-brac of titles, gold chains and robes of office, or the silk hat and frock coat of a gentleman, or material displays of affluence and generosity. Only in these ways could they manifest their acceptance in the highest places and their power to confer patronage and assistance. And so the whole process doubled back upon itself and intensified the importance of place and prestige.

6

The Church was the final formative influence on the Irish character. At every time and at every place the Church formed the life of the people and interlocked the divergent elements of the national character. Here it strengthened and there it counterbalanced, but everywhere its influence was pervasive.

The Church's mere survival affirmed the continuity with the past. Its corporate existence, directed and sustained from Rome, made it the one national institution to persist unchanged through the terrors, miseries, and disintegration of defeat. It was the one Irish institution the people could regard as peculiarly their own and in which they could invest their strength. Its philosophy sketched an intellectual background for the primitive emotions prompted by the forces of nature. Its dogmas made sense out of the legacy of national defeat. Its Sacraments and rituals gave meaning to suffering. Its parish priests (if not always the higher clergy) sustained the fumbling efforts to awaken political consciousness and to organize counterweights to the landlords and the government.

Every priest was ex officio a member of O'Connell's political organization, the Catholic Association.

They were the mainstay of the peaceful revolution of 1826–1828 when O'Connell contested parliamentary seats (long regarded as the private property of the larger landlords) first with sympathetic Protestant candidates and then with Catholic candidates, even though the latter could not take office if elected. The landlords punished their rebellious tenants by evicting them from their land. The climax came when O'Connell personally stood for a seat in County Clare. Since there was no secret ballot, every tenant had to make the anguished choice: vote for O'Connell and be evicted or vote for the landlord candidate and be disgraced in the eyes of his neighbors. The parish priests showed the way.

Sean O'Faolain has described the scene in a passage of his biography of O'Connell based on an eyewitness account by Richard Lalor Sheil:

"Across the cropped fields the old priest waited for his flock. With a voice like subterranean thunder (says Sheil) he silenced the moving balls of tatters that called themselves men and women, 'the looped and windowed raggedness' of the emergent Ireland. Then he drew to the simple altar, as rough-hewn as the chapel itself, recited Mass, and spoke to them. He spoke in Irish, now gently as the wind, now wildly, now with a cold impassioned sarcasm for some renegade wretch who had abandoned faith and country, now raising shouts of laughter from his congregation, but all the time growing more and more inflamed until the sweat shone on his skull and his eye burned. At last, rising to his height, he laid one hand on the altar, lifted the other to the roof-tree, and in a voice of prophetic admonition bade them, by their land and their God, to vote for O'Connell. The shouts that answered told Sheil that three hundred freemen had been born."[9]

Stirred by these appeals, the country people waited all day in the rain in the town of Ennis to welcome O'Connell to County Clare and triumphantly elect him.

These experiences bound together the Irish and their priests for generations to come. The Church in Ireland was a fighting church. Unlike the Church in France, Spain, and Italy, it was poor and landless. It had no vested privileges and no stake in the old order. The British government repeatedly in the early nineteenth century offered to "establish" the Church with annual grants of money to each priest and bishop if Catholics would permit the government a veto over ecclesiastical appointments. The Church consistently rejected the offer. O'Connell fought the "veto proposal" tirelessly for twenty years because he saw in it an ominous threat to his political projects. Unless he could marry the Church to the nationalist movement, he knew he had little hope of success.

"Without the pristhood we cannot succeed," he wrote. "They are not only the natural protectors of the people. They are the only persons who can make the people thoroughly sensible of their political degradation."

What the Church gives it can also take away, as the Young Irelanders discovered in 1848 and as Parnell learned after the scandal of his liaison with Mrs. O'Shea outraged the clergy and tore the nationalist movement apart. Irish politicians early learned the wisdom of the saying, "Never butt your head against a stone wall—particularly a church wall."

One Church figure whose work in an area outside politics was significant was the Capuchin friar Father Theobald Mathew. Taking up the advocacy of temperance in the 1830's, he scored a great success. He was not a spellbinder. His strength was in his simplicity, directness, and quiet force. He did not, it should be noted, preach temperance in the true sense. He urged complete abstinence. The members of the Father Mathew Societies "took the pledge" to shun all intoxicating liquor. This movement ran counter to the spirit of the orthodox theological position of the Church which holds drinking and gambling are not inherently sinful so long as they are practiced in moderation. The personal commitment that Father Mathew inspired did not last, but for a time his achievement was astonishing. In the decade before the great famine the production of whiskey in Ireland fell by a half, and he converted thousands to his cause. His appeal obviously struck a deep chord in the Irish nature. It has persisted in the century after his death as a strong minority strain. For those Irishmen whose hard drinking has made this national trait proverbial in America, there has been an also large, but little-noticed, number of men who were teetotalers and of women whose detestation of the liquor habit among their menfolk was strong and abiding.

Father Mathew's flashing success affords a glimpse of the Church's larger role in the development of Irish puritanism in matters of morals, sexual behavior, censorship, and drinking. Irish puritanism has been much misunderstood. It has been ascribed simply to the influence of the priests and particularly those trained at the Maynooth Seminary in the decades after 1795 when it was largely staffed by exiled French clerics who had fled the revolution in France. These émigré professors brought from France a strong Jansenist tradition. The principal Jansenist teaching is that man is naturally and utterly depraved. He is dependent for salvation not on his own character and striving for good, but on the mysterious flow of God's grace. Grace when it touches the human heart is irresistible, but it cannot be summoned by human will. Jansenism is morally defeatist. It expresses a distrust of natural human instincts and desires, including the sexual. It exalts the virtue of purity and encourages minute examination of one's own conscience. (The story is told of a Maynooth professor who attempted to prevent some Jesuits from hearing confessions because they were too lenient in assigning penance.) This grim doctrine is closely akin to Calvinism with its theory of the elect. In the eyes of Rome, Jansenism is a heresy because it understates the importance of free will and robs the struggle for salvation of its moral sophistication and complexity.

Jansenism was undoubtedly pervasive in Irish Church thinking in the late eighteenth and early nineteenth centuries, but there is no clear evidence that any abrupt shift in Irish moral attitudes took place as a consequence. The Irish moral outlook remained consistent with the past. It was puritanical in certain important respects, but this was due not to Jansenism but rather to the Irish being the kind of people who would find that doctrine congenial.

The Irish, long before the late eighteenth century, had developed the habit of introspection and refined a system of inner checks and balances. They lived, after all, in a predominantly rural, secluded society in which property was not secure; the administration of justice was erratic and unfair; outlets for a freer, more varied life by means of education and trade did not exist or were almost entirely choked off; and where advancement often meant outward conformity to an alien religion and the consequent sacrifice of individuality. In these circumstances, it was natural for them to center their values within the bourne of the family and to guard that retreat jealously against exterior influences and interior tendencies to defilement and impurity. They could not marry casually or improvidently nor could they surrender lightly to wayward passions. If a son's marriage did not bring with it a wife's dowry, then the daughters of the family would not have a dowry to be properly married off in their turn. If the son or daughter married into a landless family, it would degrade their own family's status in the eyes of the community. The delicate balance of mutual interests on which depended the entire family system rested fundamentally on individual self-restraint. The authority of the father had to be respected and obedience paid to it. The role of the mother had to be exalted; and a mother's values, such as devotion to the husband's interests, a willingness to sacrifice on behalf of the children, and absolute chastity outside the marriage relationship, must be accepted and esteemed. These were absolute values, and on them everything depended. There were no competing social institutions to spin a wider web of allegiances or to construct differing hierarchies of value. There was no place for individualism. A man had identity only as a member of a a functioning family. What endangered it endangered him; what lowered its status lowered his. Each member of the family had constantly to examine his own conscience to judge carefully whether his or her behavior met the expected standard. If he fell below that standard, he endangered the foundations of his family's and his own self-respect.

The teachings of the Church reinforced these values. Insofar as those teachings were rigorously Jansenist, they made more arduous and exhausting the reconciliation between personal desires and family duty. But only a people whose vital concerns were contracted and concentrated in such a narrow sphere would have accepted and enthusiastically upheld an external moral discipline of this kind in the first place.

It would be tempting to define the Irish priest as a fifth distinct prototype of the national character in addition to the conservative farmer, the lawyer-politician, the poet, and the two-fisted violent rebel, but in fact the priests as a group did not compose a unified stereotype. They reflected the various configurations of personality and the conflicting styles of the society around them. There were as many different kinds of priests as there were Irishmen: brilliant intellectuals and orators, worldly types skillful at organization and maneuver, hardheaded parochialists devoted to the needs of their parishes and not looking beyond their horizons, and rebellious zealots. Every Irish mother hoped that one of her sons would become a priest. The Church reciprocated by finding a place for every personality and every variety of talent. It was a microcosm of the larger society.

Behind the shifting faces of the national character, flowing within every manifestation of the national spirit was a pervasive, inescapable mirth. The Irish, whatever outsiders thought, never took themselves so seriously as they seemed to do. None knew better than themselves how their tragic view of life could easily crumble into self-pity. No one could mock Irish pretensions, laugh off Irish sorrows, or unmask Irish self-interest parading as patriotism quicker or better than an Irishman.

It is a strange gift, this national capacity for satire and self-burlesque. Sometimes it was a destructive one. Unable to be king, the Irishman frequently settled for court jester, and poked fun at king, commoner, and himself. Too often, it has signified a fatal lack of self-confidence that leads to settling for something less than the highest success. Supreme egotism and utter seriousness are necessary for the greatest accomplishment, and these the Irish find hard to sustain; at some point, the instinct to see life in a comic light becomes irresistible, and ambition falls before it. Perhaps the comic sense is the other half of the instinct for fantasy. If nothing is ever quite real, nothing is ever quite serious.

This national instinct is also a saving grace. It allows the Irish to keep a sense of proportion about their troubles. They more easily escape the sullen pessimism and righteous solemnity that frequently mark defeated peoples and persecuted minorities. A certain gaiety stands always available to turn the tables on life. If looking at the world upside down is not always the best or clearest way of seeing the universe, it is at least a view that keeps man at the center and material things at the periphery.[10]

7

For those who left, Ireland was a bundle of memories.

It was cutting peat on a rainy morning, gathering in the hay on long, warm August days, going to the spa for the fair. It was the picture of grandma churning butter by the door or making bread by the open hearth. It was the memory of Father coming home drawn and exhausted from a long day in the fields. ("I'm as tired as if I'd been drawing stones.") It was going to school on cold winter mornings, mind and feet racing with the knowledge that old Mrs. Boland would warm your hands very well with a stinging application of her cane. It was overhearing the old men around the fire, talking of British foreclosures and chewing over political gossip months old. Later on, it was coming home from country dances over dark roads and remembering uneasily the familiar stories of ghosts and fairies. The political gossip and the fairy stories alike were almost indistinguishable in their awesomeness and unreality.

There were many Irelands, of course, but this is the one the country people knew, and most of those who came to America were country people. For them the brilliant world of Anglo-Irish Dublin, of O'Connell and later of Parnell, of Tom Moore and later of Yeats and Lady Gregory, scarcely existed. The Ireland of the "Celtic twilight," the country which in the early Middle Ages sent saints and scholars wandering to the farthest reaches of Christendom, the country in which monks and minstrels made Gaelic a living language, this, too, was a lost land. For most country people who emigrated to America, the Gaelic language lived on only in tag words and old sayings. Only people in tiny scattered enclaves and an occasional schoolmaster could speak whole sentences in the ancient language. The country people regarded the Gaelic-speaking few, such as the fishermen of the Isles of Aran among whom Synge went to live, as unusual and, indeed, almost freakish persons. Still another Ireland is the land of the faith, the most devoutly and uniformly Catholic country in the modern world. But the ordinary country people, living in the circumscribed routines of farm and village for whom a ten-mile trip was a long journey, never realized there was anything unique about their religious affiliation or their devotion. Going to Church and partaking of the Sacraments were as natural and expected a part of life as milking the cow or gathering the hay. Only later, in America, would this become distinctive, a fact to reflect upon and boast about, a source of national chauvinism.

The life of the Irish people was simple and stripped down. And it was much the same background whether the immigrant came in 1840 or 1920. The surface of life changed greatly in those years, but the traditional rhythms of village life by which the country people lived were slow to change. The farm, the old people, the Church, the fair, the raising of potatoes, hay, and cattle, the cutting of turf, the talk of going to America and of those who had gone, the talk of fairies and magic, the inadequate school, the hardness of life, these things did not change during the ninety years in which the Irish came to America.

Irish life in America begins from a sharp and tragic rejection. To "come out" to the new country meant thrusting behind the old, usually forever, unless in a few instances success brought enough money to visit the old country once more. Even then, however, many who could financially afford the return visit to Ireland never made the trip. It would be a journey back in more than one sense, a journey back into the house of their father, into the womb of old memories and long-forgotten sadnesses. To return would be to reconsider the crucial decision that it was no use to reconsider. The pleasures of nostalgia would not be worth the pain.

Why did they leave and what did they seek?

The answer is that most did not leave willingly. They were hurled out, driven by forces larger and more complex than they could fully understand or cope with. They made the decision to go, of course; the responsibility was theirs and they could not deny it (least of all to themselves in the later and the harder years), but the range of choice was narrow. To the question What did they seek? the answer is the same for them as for all men. They sought a door that would open and give them access to hope.

Irish country life was not unrelievedly drab and hard; the races, the visits to the pub, the outdoor sports, the country dances and other entertainments did much to soften the rigors of existence. But they could not suffice in the sick, tormented society of nineteenth and early twentieth century Ireland. The young, spared to life by the mysterious drop in infant mortality, pressed upon their elders. Young men in their twenties saw ahead bleak years of waiting for a farm of their own, and were plagued by frustration and fears of unfulfillment. The girls, seeing marriage and motherhood delayed by impersonal economic considerations and the dreary calculations of the matchmaker, feared that their best years would slip by, empty and barren. Since parents wanted to keep the family and land system on an even keel, they usually married off their daughters strictly in order of age. Irish folklore is full of sad stories of the pretty young girls who could not marry until their plain-faced older sister was wed. Many an Irish girl decided she would rather join relatives in an overcrowded tenement in Chicago or wash dishes for three dollars a week in "cold roast Boston" than live out her life in an unequal race with those old gypsy men, time and fate. ("I had to go," the mother said to her son; "there was nothing for me in the old country.") Older men and women, squeezed or displaced altogether by the exactions of the landlord or by land consolidations, decided in middle life it was not, after all, too late for them to take the great gamble. And, at times of famine, whole families from infants to grandparents in desperation made the journey.

So it was that in their various ways they decided to leave. Their deep feelings about the familiar village and the gently sloping fields were overborne by the fact of failure and the fear of further defeat. Ireland was beautiful and damned. There was no life for them there. They had to go.

CHAPTER TWO

The Struggle for the City

1

THE HISTORY OF THE IRISH in America is founded on a paradox. The Irish were a rural people in Ireland and became a city people in the United States. The cities of Ireland were founded by Danes, Normans, and English; none was founded by the Irish themselves. The cities were the strongholds of conquerors and centers for the spread of foreign influence. In every revolt from the twelfth century on, the Irish attacked and burned the towns. (As late as the eighteenth century, the city gate of Galway bore the inscription, "O Lord, deliver us from the fury of the O'Flaherties.") When the Irish began to congregate in the cities of Ireland, they were second-class citizens because the Penal Code nominally excluded them. Several of the larger cities were, in fact, encircled by shantytowns where the "Irishies" lived.

In the United States the Irish reversed this pattern. Here they concentrated in the cities and shunned the farms. The first reason was economic. Having arrived in the seacoast cities virtually penniless, they had no funds to travel inland. Moreover, farming on the frontier was radically different from tilling the small plots of intensively cultivated ground in the old country. The open prairie could be a lonely and forbidding place. One Irish farmer who had pioneered successfully in Missouri wrote home in 1821 a poignant letter that showed how profoundly different life on the frontier was from that of Ireland:

"I could then go to a fair, or a wake, or a dance. . . . I could spend the winter's nights in a neighbor's house cracking jokes by the turf fire. If I had there but a sore head I could have a neighbor within every hundred yards of me that would run to see me. But here everyone can get so much land . . . that they calls them neighbors that live two or three miles off."[1]

Beneath these circumstances, there lay a still more profound motivation. The Irish rejected the land for the land had rejected them. By 1848, those who came had survived not one but a dozen crop failures in less than thirty years. Unlike some immigrants from Europe, they had no memories of past prosperity to sustain them in time of crisis. Conditions had been worsening for decades. The immigrants turned away from the fields of Ireland with a sense of relief. They had dropped an ancient, heavy burden; few desired to shoulder it again in their new country.

America in the nineteenth century moved into the urban age. In 1830 only 10 percent of Americans lived in cities. New York was the only city of more than 200,000. In 1900, 40 percent of Americans lived in cities. There were 38 cities with more than 200,000 population and a half-dozen great metropolitan centers. The city was the theater in which the drama of the Irish and other immigrants was played. Beginning in 1820, when statistics were first gathered on foreigners arriving at ports of entry, 19,000,000 immigrants entered the United States in less than a hundred years; 4,500,000, or nearly one-quarter of the total, were Irish. About 700,000 came in the period from 1820 to 1840, an average of about 35,000 a year. These figures jumped spectacularly during the famines of the late forties and the immediate postfamine years. More than 1,700,000 persons left Ireland for the United States in the twenty years before the Civil War, with the all-time peak being reached in 1851 when 216,000 came.

By 1850, 26 percent of the population of New York City (133,000 out of 513,000) were persons born in Ireland. If their children and other second- and third-generation Irish are included, New York was already more than one-third Irish. Boston in 1845 had an Irish-born population of only one in fifty. Ten years later, the ratio was one in five. Philadelphia and Baltimore also showed sharp increases.

The Irish moved out of the Atlantic seaboard principally as laborers working on riverboats and railroad lines. Throughout the nineteenth century every successive railroad town—Albany, Buffalo, Cleveland, Chicago, Peoria, Omaha—became a center of Irish strength. Numbers of Irish also made the long voyage to California after 1849 to work in the goldfields. San Francisco from its earliest boom days had a sizable Irish contingent, and from there they fanned inland to the mining cities of Butte, Denver, and Virginia City.

They were in great part the physical builders of the cities. Their labor met the urgent need of overgrown colonial towns for better streets and sewers, larger water systems, and new housing. The Irish swung the picks, lifted the shovels, and brought down the hammers that transformed the towns into cities. They suffered terrible hardships, for they did the roughest, most dangerous work. After reading of an immigrant's death by drowning in 1836, another Irishman reflected:

"How often do we see such paragraphs in the paper as an Irishman drowned—an Irishman crushed by a beam—an Irishman suffocated in a pit—an Irishman blown to atoms by a steam engine—ten, twenty Irishmen buried alive by the sinking of a bank—and other like casualties and perils to which honest Pat is constantly exposed in the hard toils for his daily bread."[2]

Emerson wrote to Thoreau of his astonishment on discovering Irish laborers in Massachusetts who regularly worked a fifteen-hour day for fifty cents. Theodore Parker observed in Boston in 1846 that he rarely saw a "gray-haired Irishman," inferring that they all died young.[3] One newspaper commented: "America demands for her development an inexhaustible fund of physical energy, and Ireland supplies the most part of it. There are several sorts of power working at the fabric of this Republic —waterpower, steam-power, and Irish-power. The last works hardest of all."

But if the work was hard and the wages were low, at least there was work, and opportunity beckoned. The American cities were in their infancy when the Irish came. Their rise and the rise of the Irish in American life went hand in hand. In Ireland, the Irish had inherited history and suffered it. In America, they became makers of history.

2

The members of the famine generation were not the first Irish immigrants to America. Irish Catholics had been arriving in this country in small numbers throughout the seventeenth and eighteenth centuries. Some who had money or the advantages of an education became merchants, doctors, schoolmasters, and booksellers. Many others came as indentured servants who worked out the cost of their passage after their arrival. But the number was never very great. The first Federal Census in 1790 listed only 44,000 persons of Irish birth; in addition, there were perhaps another 150,000 of Irish ancestry out of a total population of 3,000,000. In that same year, the first Catholic bishop estimated there were only 35,000 Catholics in the country. The Irish Catholics did not come to the colonies in sizable numbers because many of the restrictions of the Penal Code that afflicted Catholics in Ireland were also in effect here. The intensely Protestant atmosphere in the colonies was hostile to Catholics. When the Maryland legislature in 1704 levied a head tax on indentured servants from Ireland, the act expressly stated in its preamble that the purpose of the tax was "to prevent the importing of too great a number of Irish Papists."

The most important Irish Catholic family in the colonial period were the Carrolls, the first of whom came to Maryland in 1688 under the patronage of the Catholic King James II and, despite the latter's overthrow, stayed to become a large landowner. The Carrolls had been part of the Irish aristocracy in the old country. "We derive our descent from princes," Charles Carroll's son wrote later, "and until the Revolution [of 1688], notwithstanding our sufferings under Elizabeth and Cromwell, we were in affluent circumstances and respected." The first Carroll gave several of his Maryland properties the same names as estates his father had once owned in Ireland.[4]

Charles Carroll of Carrollton, who was born in 1737 and lived to be ninety-five, attained the triple distinction of being the only Catholic, the wealthiest, and the longest-lived of the signers of the Declaration of Independence. Daniel Carroll, his cousin, was a delegate to the Constitutional Convention. (A second Irish Catholic participant in the Convention was Thomas FitzSimons, a wealthy Pennsylvania businessman.) Another cousin was John Carroll, the first Catholic bishop of the United States.

Irish Catholics, though few in number, were among the leaders on the military side of the Revolutionary War. The most significant was John Barry who had left Country Wexford as a boy of fourteen and at the outbreak of the war was a merchant captain in Philadelphia. He was the first naval commander commissioned by the Continental Congress and his war exploits ranked with those of John Paul Jones. Years later, when there was danger of war with France in 1798, Barry was recalled to service and given the task of organizing a fleet. He stayed in service until his death in 1803. Because of his skill in training younger officers, he is regarded as "the father of the American Navy."

Scores of descendants of the "Wild Geese," the Irish soldiers and aristocrats who had fled to the Continent after 1691, wrote to Benjamin Franklin, the American agent in Paris, volunteering their services during the Revolution. Among those who wrote him were Comte O'Donnell, colonel of a Polish regiment in Lemberg; Baron O'Cahill, commandant of French troops at Strasbourg; and a Captain O'Heguerty, stationed in Nancy. Franklin's private papers contained nearly one hundred letters from Irishmen scattered through Europe. It is not certain how many of these correspondents made their way to the United States, but one of the army contingents sent by France in 1778 was drawn from the famous Irish Brigade which for generations had served in the armies of the Bourbon kings.[5] Moreover, there were many Irish of humbler origins serving in Washington's army. He took graceful note of their contributions when he occupied Boston after the British evacuated their troops. Since it was March 17, 1776, he had his order of the day countersigned by General John Sullivan and made the password "Saint Patrick." This incident gave a later generation of Boston Irish the pretext to make the date a legal holiday; technically, the city celebrates "Evacuation Day," not St. Patrick's birthday. But it is also important to note that General Sullivan, who figured in this historic event, would have been astonished to be identified as a hero by chauvinistic Boston Irish Catholics. Although he was the grandson of a Catholic officer who went into exile in France with Patrick Sarsfield and the other "Wild Geese" in 1691, his family upon emigrating to New England had long since converted to Protestantism. General Sullivan, according to his biographer, was "violently antagonistic toward Roman Catholicism."[6]

In the half-century between the end of the Revolution and the beginning of large-scale immigration around 1830, individual Irish Catholics attained a leadership in high society that would not be duplicated again for a century. Mrs. Richard Caton, the daughter of Charles Carroll, was the first *grande dame* of American society, occupying the role of social arbiter which Mrs. Astor held in a later day. In the early 1800's, she made White Sulphur Springs the first fashionable resort. Her three daughters were the first of many American heiresses to marry into the British nobility. Known in London as the "American Graces," they became respectively the Duchess of Leeds, the Marchioness of Wellesley, and the Baroness Stafford.

In New York, Dominick Lynch set the social pace. His father had emigrated to the United States shortly after the Revolutionary War, bringing with him a sizable fortune. Dominick was educated in Ireland and France and then entered the wine-importing business. He introduced "Château Margaux" and other fine French wines in this country. He was a gourmet, dressed elegantly, and was an accomplished singer. His social gifts made his handsome town house at 1 Greenwich Street and his estate in Westchester County gathering places for fashionable society. Lynch introduced grand opera in the United States. He went to Europe, recruited a company, and helped coach it in the premiere American performance of *The Barber of Seville* at the Park Theater in November, 1825.

His private musicales were locally famous. The British actress Fanny Kemble recorded irritably that during a party given by the Philip Hones at which Lynch sang, her hosts inquired "whether I had heard of his singing or their musical soirees and seeming all but surprised that I had no revelation of either across the Atlantic."

Lynch died while on a visit to Paris in 1837. At the next meeting of the New-York Historical Society, a speaker eulogized him as "the acknowledged head of the fashionable and festive board, a gentleman of the *ton*." Ward McAllister, the guiding spirit of the Four Hundred a half-century later, ascribed his own social ambitions to a desire to emulate

Lynch whom he had heard spoken of by his father. "He was the greatest swell and beau that New York had ever known," McAllister recalled.[7]

The Irish as a group, however, had made no measurable impact on American life before 1830. The political eminence of the Carrolls, the social successes of Mrs. Caton and Dominick Lynch, the heroism of Captain John Barry, and the accomplishments of various professional men such as Dr. William MacNeven, an exile from the rebellion of 1798 who became a prominent physician in New York, did not comprise a serviceable tradition. The immigrants of the famine era had little in common with these remote personages. The latter were too few to form a welcoming community and could afford no direct leadership. Their individual successes were the material out of which later generations would form a tradition, but precursors who have to be rediscovered have no value to the first generation. The Irish who came after 1830 had to create their own community, evolve their own tradition, and produce their own leaders.

Two excerpts from the many diaries of the period illustrate the sharp break between the individual success stories of the earlier Irish and the difficulties experienced by the impoverished hundreds of thousands who came in the famine generation.

In 1830 Philip Hone paid a visit to Charles Carroll at Carrolton. The old statesman still wore large gold buckles on his shoes and broad lace ruffles at his wrists and shirtfront. He was an extreme conservative who clung to the original Federalist views of Washington and Hamilton; to him, the liberal views of Jefferson and Madison were still unforgiven heresies, and the radical notions of Jacksonian democracy an anathema.

"I paid this morning," Hone wrote, "a visit which I have long been wishing for to the venerable Charles Carroll, the only surviving signer of the Declaration of Independence. He will be ninety-four years of age next September. His faculties are very little impaired, except his sight, which within the last few months has failed a little, and deprived him of the pleasure of reading at all times, which he has heretofore enjoyed. He is gay, cheerful, polite, and talkative. He described to me his manner of living: He takes a cold bath every morning in the summer, plunging headlong into it; rides on horseback from eight to twelve miles; drinks water at dinner; has never drunk spiritous liquors at any period of his life, but drinks a glass or two of madeira wine every day, and sometimes champagne and claret; takes as much exercise as possible; goes to bed at nine o'clock, and rises before day."

But Hone, who was also a close personal friend of Dominick Lynch, while paying tribute to Carroll was also deploring in his diary "a gang of low Irishmen." At one public celebration, he rejoiced everything was "so decidedly American; no foreign influence; no grating brogue."[8]

George Templeton Strong, another conservative diarist of the period, wrote: "Yesterday morning I was spectator of a strange, weird, painful scene. Certain houses of John Watts DePeyster are to be erected on the northwest corner of this street and Fourth Avenue, and deep excavations therefore are in progress. Seeing a crowd on the corner, I stopped and made my way to a front place. The earth had caved in a few minutes before and crushed the breath out of a pair of ill-starred Celtic laborers. They had just been dragged, or dug, out and lay white and stark on the ground where they had been working, ten or twelve feet below the level of the street. Around them were a few men who had got them out, I suppose, and fifteen or twenty Irish women, wives, kinfolk, or friends who had got down there in some inexplicable way.

"The men were listless and inert enough, but not so the women. I suppose they were 'keening'; all together were raising a wild, unearthly cry, half shriek and half song, wailing as a score of daylight Banshees, clapping their hands and gesticulating passionately. Now and then one of them would throw herself down on one of the corpses, or wipe some trace of defilement from the face of the dead man with her apron, slowly and carefully, then resume her lament. It was an uncanny sound to hear, quite new to me. . . .

"Our Celtic fellow citizens are almost as remote from us in temperament and constitution as the Chinese," Strong concluded.[9]

No human sympathy closed the breach between patrician and peasant. Americans might venerate Carroll, the aged grandee, or admire Lynch, the man of wit and fashion, but they did not connect them meaningfully with the bewildered newcomer just off the boat or the dead laborer on the city street.

3

The generation of Irish who fled from the famines of the 1830's and 1840's developed a new way of life in the American cities. It was a way of life quite different from what the older inhabitants of the cities had been accustomed to and also different from what the Irish themselves had known in the old country. In short, neither the cities nor the Irish were ever the same again.

Let us look first at the impact of the cities on the Irish. In the shanty-towns and tenements, the Irish lived by an unstable, unformulated compromise between the neighborly code of the old country village and the individualistic code of the open American society. To succeed in America in American terms, an Irish countryman learned that he would have to alter his values and turn his personality inside out. He began to learn this lesson as soon as he started the journey to America. He saw that it was the pushy, aggressive, fast-talking fellow who got along best in the seaport, on the boat, and with the immigration officials. The man who was selfish and individualistic, who refused to share his food or water or money or bedding with the sick and the old, survived more easily and reached America in the best shape. But these were not the standards of the village and the farm. These were the morals and manners of tinkers and fishmongers, of the wayward sons and the irresponsible. The good peasant in the old country was the man who shared of what little he had with his neighbor in time of need. The good peasant helped relatives and neighbors bring in their hay before the rains came. The good peasant knew his appointed place in the community and kept it. He respected his fellows who did likewise.

America, he learned, was not the land of the good peasant. It was the first of many sad disillusionments to observe that in this new homeland the ruthless fellow, the mean, tightfisted man who grabbed what he could and shared nothing made out best. Much of the sense of status was lost. The ex-peasant could not keep his place because he could not find it. He had to go out and fight to find whatever place he could.[10]

This was too demanding and profound a reorientation for most members of the first generation to make. As a counterpressure to the individualistic values of their environment, they instinctively re-created, within the larger city, neighborhood communities where they could practice and sustain their own values. Whenever possible, they followed old routes of settlement to neighborhoods where other Irish who had come a few years earlier were already established. Each family tried to live near friends and relatives from the same village. Those already arrived held Saturday-night "kitchen rackets" to welcome the "greenhorns." These parties were the equivalents of the "American wakes," which the neighbors who had stayed at home gave for the immigrants before their departure from Ireland. The men helped newcomers find work on the same construction project or on the same horsecar line on which they themselves were employed. For decades these new communities formed a world within a world. Mayor Gaynor once asked Al Smith what he thought of vice conditions in midtown Manhattan. "I don't know, Mr. Mayor," Smith replied. "I don't get above Fourteenth Street once in a year."

The home, the church, and the saloon were the centers of life in the community. Home might be a shanty or two rooms in a tenement, but the family made it do. The home was a hive of activity. The children were born at home, played and grew up there; meals were eaten together around the table in the kitchen; the mother did the washing and cooking, the neighbors visited, and the father drank his pint of beer and took his ease after a day's labor all within these cramped and crowded quarters. There was no privacy or room of one's own. No emotions and no secrets could be kept hidden from the rest of the family within those walls. It was a triumph if they could even be kept secret from the neighbors. It was a warm, gregarious, communal style of life that bred strong family and neighborhood loyalties and permitted the avowal of strong passions.

The Catholic Church played a significant role in the affections of the Irish, for the church buildings in the American cities were not inheritances accepted from the past. If there was to be a church and later a parish school, the parishioners had to pay for their construction by contributing small sums each week for many years. Until the money was raised, they could worship only in a store or a rented hall. The church when it finally rose in the neighborhood was often an ugly enough structure, with its dull red brick, squat lines, square tower, and heavy Romanesque decoration. These fortresses of faith, however, were grand indeed compared to the small country churches of Ireland. Best of all, they had been built by the efforts of the people themselves. The Church in America, like that in Ireland, was the Church of the poor. There were few wealthy patrons and no government assistance. No brick would have been laid, no pews installed, and no altar erected if the parishioners had not paid their own pennies to see these things accomplished. The priests had to be close to the people in spirit and sympathy to make such enormous undertakings successful. They also had to possess or acquire certain traits of character. They needed to be good administrators and careful money managers. They needed the administrator's characteristic gifts of energy, perseverance, enthusiasm, and practical vision. The Irish Catholic clergy stamped the Church in America with these habits of mind. Native converts and foreign travelers accustomed to the urbane tone and richly realized intellectual life of the Church in Europe regarded American Catholics as materialistic, parochial, and culturally impoverished. There was a measure of truth in these indictments, but they overlooked the context in which the American clergy and laity operated. The insistent need for physical expansion drained them of energy and focused attention narrowly on parish concerns.

From the crowded homes, the children escaped to the streets. The children, the second generation in America, could not make the same adjustment as their fathers and mothers had. To them the village in the old country was a lost world, a hand-me-down memory. They felt the pressure of the public schools where a different, competing picture of life was held before their eyes. The message of the schools came through

to them notwithstanding that it was muffled and phrased in alien terms.
The textbooks spoke only of persons with Anglo-Saxon names like Jones
and Robinson. The illustrations and references were exclusively rural or
small town in character. (How much does a story about sheep and goats
mean to a child who has never seen either? What does he think of a story-
book world where everyone lives in white cottages surrounded by trees
and grass when he lives in a cold-water, walk-up tenement house?) Yet
the children apprehended that they were to enter a world of individual
striving where competition set the tone, and commercial success was the
criterion. They arrived at a reconciliation of these conflicts in the boyhood gangs of the streets. The gang put together in an amalgam of its
own the precepts of loyalty, obedience, and neighborly cooperation emphasized in the home with the ideals of aggressiveness, daring, and self-
help acquired in the school. The gang exacted loyalty from its members.
It had a leader to whom obedience was owed. It engaged in raids and
street fights with rival gangs to achieve a common purpose, if only the
purpose of showing who was running that block. Yet within the gang,
one's status depended on individual acts of daring and bravado. One's
place in the hierarchy and even one's nickname depended very much on
oneself. The boyhood gang was a durable institution. Young adults
formed successor groups, and these organizations helped shape their lives.

The nature of business life within the Irish community reflected community values and the old village ideals of mutual help. The early Irish
businessmen, like most immigrant entrepreneurs, did not have the capital
resources or the personal connections to make a frontal entry into the
main areas of business such as manufacturing, mining, and banking.
Rather, they operated in its interstices. They were the blacksmiths,
saloonkeepers, grocery-store owners, small contractors, and makers and
sellers of soap, leather, meat, and other provisions. Success in these businesses and in the professions of law and medicine often depended as much
on neighborhood goodwill as on financial resources or personal skill. Only
if a man and his family before him were well regarded by his fellows
would the latter patronize him as a doctor or go to his shop or saloon.
There were two unwritten rules the rising tradesmen and professional
men usually obeyed. One was to live in the neighborhood. It would be
the end of the nineteenth century before any important number of them
could safely move away to better neighborhoods. By then, clearly differ-
entiated middle classes had emerged in the Irish community, and a sizable
segment of them moved away from original bases. Even then, the better-
off families did not detach themselves from the old neighborhood in an
isolated or haphazard fashion; they shifted to better sections of the city
as part of a general movement of Irish out of old neighborhoods that
were being abandoned to newer immigrant groups. The other require-

ment was a willingness to help the worst off in time of need. If a laborer died without insurance, one of his fellow workers was likely to go from house to house in the neighborhood collecting donations, no matter how small, to make up a purse for the widow and her children. These appeals were frequent. No one who hoped to prosper or be well regarded in the community turned them down.

Everything in the end came back to a question of family. A man was judged not only on his own merits but also on the merits of his entire family. Within the family, meanwhile, a process was at work that tightened family bonds and radically departed from the normal American pattern of family life. The fathers in most families were engaged in manual labor that was hard and usually dangerous. These men died young. They wore themselves out dragging, lifting, hauling, digging, standing, or shoveling for ten, twelve, or fourteen hours a day with rarely a break and never a paid holiday. Industrial accidents for which there was no compensation crippled or cut them down. They fell easy victims to tuberculosis and pneumonia, or they exhausted themselves and, like Alfred E. Smith's father, died of nothing more identifiable than a nameless weariness.

The death of the father in his late thirties or early forties was common. These premature deaths of so many heads of families left their mark. The family held together; the youngest children were kept in school; the oldest helped all they could. After the first bitter, impoverished years, the survivors resumed on the same economic level of pinched but not desperate existence as before. The calamity of the father's loss, however, had invisible psychological costs. It pulled the family inward. It curbed and frustrated individual ambitions to an extent that was abnormal in the larger American society which was increasingly committed to individualism, the emancipation of women, and the relaxation of parental control. It was a reversion in an urban setting to a family-centered life that most Americans migrating from farm to city were moving away from.

The younger members of a family deprived of its chief male support began at the age of five or six to peddle papers, pick coke, run errands, and rummage through junkyards for useful and salable items. Upon the older children, just entering adolescence, were thrust the heavy burdens of maturity. At twelve or thirteen, boys took on full-time jobs wrestling freight or carrying a hod. From the oldest to the youngest, the members of the family were inculcated with the conviction that the family must maintain a united front if it were to survive. Sticking together was the only basis of hope for the future of all. Amusements that cost money were evil, not in themselves, but because they wasted the common substance. Here lurked a source, as important as their religious beliefs, for an unexpectedly puritan approach to life on the part of the American Irish.

The mother, as the children's only link to the happier days of the past and the symbol of the family's will to survive, occupied the central role. Her sufferings and sacrifices were crucial in keeping the home together in the critical years after the father's death. Those sacrifices earned from her children obedience and respect for her opinions on every important subject. The "widow woman" thereby became a classic figure in the Irish community. The Irish widow exercised an emotional hegemony rarely equaled in other American families. Few novels on the American Irish have been written that do not include a widow as one of the major characters.

The Irish youths did not escape family ties by running away from the farm to the city, for they were already in the city. As long as they lived within the Irish community, they were bound to their families. They might physically move from the family home, but they did not so easily move from the family and the neighborhood ties that their history had created.

4

The style of life among the Irish contrasted markedly with the Yankee spirit of native Protestant Americans. The Irish were as different as could be imagined in mood and tempo from those natives of Anglo-Saxon Puritan stock whom Whittier described:

> "Church-goers, fearful of the unseen Powers
> But grumbling over pulpit tax and pew-rent,
> Saving, as shrewd economists, their souls
> And winter pork with the least possible outlay
> Of salt and sanctity."

The Yankee, too, was present in the growing cities. Indeed, in their original form the cities had been his creation, and he resented the coming of these Irish intruders. The Yankee peddler, famed in song and story, was the archetype of the early nineteenth century city man. His values were those of the prudent merchant and banker, the rising tradesman, the thrifty, hardworking craftsman. The city's original ethos was a flinty blend of the gospel according to Calvin and the gospel according to Franklin's "Poor Richard." "Early to bed and early to rise makes a man healthy, wealthy and wise" was the native community's guiding maxim if not always its invariable practice. Individual effort, thrift, caution, sobriety, and a canny, tight-lipped self-reliance were its prevailing values.

The newer Irish challenged the code of the community at almost every point. Impoverished on their arrival, ignorant of skilled trades, bereft of any apprenticeship training, they had nothing to offer but their hands and their willingness to work. As day laborers, they competed for the tough and menial jobs and were at the mercy of every shift in the job market. Their presence on the scene in large and growing numbers threatened the old occupational structure of master, journeyman, and apprentice. The native working classes feared and hated them.

The native middle classes worried about the Irish from another vantage point, seeing in them the nucleus of a permanently depressed laboring class. The natives did not foresee the extent to which industry would expand and how important a resource the Irish laborers would be in this industrial expansion. What they did see was that the Irish, crowding into the cities, posed problems in housing, police, and schools; they meant higher tax rates and heavier burdens in the support of poorhouses and private charitable institutions. Moreover, the Irish did not seem to practice thrift, self-denial, and other virtues desirable in the "worthy, laboring poor." They seemed drunken, dissolute, permanently sunk in poverty. Here appearances were partly deceiving. The Irish of the first generation, that is, those who were born in Ireland and made the great journey to America, did not usually conform to native Protestant values and practices. And this was true whether it was the first generation that came in 1845, in 1880, or in 1910. It was rare for an Irishman of the first generation to have a rags-to-riches success story; to rise economically in the customary American fashion demanded more in terms of relentless perseverance, financial acumen, familiarity with new ways, and plain good luck than the Irish were able to summon from themselves or their environment. This was a task for the second and third and succeeding generations. But within the bounds of what was humanly possible, the Irish laborers and housemaids of the first generation were not so thriftless as the native stereotype of them suggested. Remittances to Ireland from individuals in this country were at the rate of $1,000,000 annually in the 1840's and rose to ten times that figure over the next twenty years. Thousands of individuals earning only fifty cents a day or, in the case of domestic servants, a dollar a week were methodically saving pennies and quarters to send to dependents in the old country. The Emigrant Industrial Savings Bank of New York, chartered by the Irish Emigrant Society in 1851, opened with 2,300 depositors whose average savings were $238.56. In the next thirty years, this bank alone sent $30,000,000 in remittances to Ireland.[11]

The two-fisted aggressiveness of the Irish, however, seemed to confirm the contrary image. The Irishman first entered the popular folklore and the comic stage in the guise of "the bhoy"—the swaggering, rough-talking, free-swinging tough. Irish gangs battled fiercely on election days. In the famous Astor Place Riot in New York, they mobbed the performance of William Macready, an English actor, when he tried to present a production of *Macbeth* competing with one by Edwin Forrest, the theatrical favorite of the Irish. When the police attempted to quell the riot, one Irishman tore open his shirt, bared his chest, and shouted, "Fire into this! Take the life of a free-born American for a bloody English actor! Do it! Ay, you darsen't!"

When Protestants marched on the anniversary of the Battle of Boyne, the Irish broke up their parades. When the Prince of Wales visited New York in 1860, an Irish regiment embarrassed the city fathers by refusing to parade in his honor.

"It is a fact," declared Samuel F. B. Morse, the inventor of the telegraph and a foremost nativist of the period, "that an unaccountable disposition to riotous conduct has manifested itself within a few years when exciting topics are publicly discussed, wholly at variance with the former peaceful, deliberative character of our people."

The Irish did not enter city politics. They erupted. Their politicians pressed to the fore; their priests raised new issues of religious discrimination in the public schools. The activities of both disturbed the smug, clublike atmosphere in which the large towns had formerly been governed. Their "grating brogue" was heard everywhere.

If Irish manners were objectionable to the Yankee community, their morals seemed deplorable. There were two thousand saloons in lower New York City alone by 1840. Not all of them were Irish-run or Irish-patronized, but there was no doubt that the status of the liquor seller was different in the Yankee and Irish communities. In the former, he tended increasingly to be a pariah; in the latter, he was a respected figure. The Irish had their own temperance leader in Father Theobald Mathew who came from Ireland in the 1840's to preach the cause of total abstinence, but he was an isolated figure compared to the solid phalanx of Protestant clergymen who inveighed Sunday in and Sunday out against the evils of "Demon Rum." How could the ministers dry up the land when every day some new Irishman was selling or buying "a drop of the creature?"

The Irish could also produce and esteem a figure like John "Old Smoke" Morrissey. John, born in Tipperary and brought as a child to the river town of Troy, New York, was a great "broth of a bhoy." In 1853, at twenty-two, he won the American heavyweight championship from Yankee Sullivan in a bare-knuckles bout lasting thirty-seven rounds. (Yankee Sullivan retired to California where Vigilantes put him in jail and an unknown assailant strangled him to death.) "Old Smoke" Morrissey earned his name when he tipped over a stove in a barroom in the course of a friendly difference of opinion, fell on his back on the burning coals, but rose, coattails smoking, and knocked out his adversary. Unlike Sullivan, he died quietly in his bed twenty-five years later. In the interim, he served in Congress, amassed a fortune of two million dollars, and founded the first fashionable gambling salon in America at Saratoga Springs.

Prizefighting was illegal and so was gambling. The Irish dominated both, and the natives were scandalized.

The mood of the era before the Civil War was dynamic and expansive; it spoke naturally in a raucous tone. As one observer remarked, "The cities of America were not clean, spotless havens of virtue before the immigrants came and they would not be if all the immigrants suddenly disappeared." Nevertheless, the older elements of the community understandably associated the quickened tempo, the heightened tension, and the unexpected stresses of the growing cities with the most conspicuous newcomers—the Irish.

5

The natives responded in convulsive bursts of violence and prolonged withdrawals. A native mob burned a convent in Charlestown, Massachusetts in 1834; another mob sacked a Catholic Church in Philadelphia in 1844; respectable ministers and civic leaders endorsed the comic opera "disclosures" of Maria Monk in the late 1830's; and reputable politicians flirted with organized bigotry on and off for thirty years, culminating in the brief Know-Nothing upheaval of 1854–1858. Meanwhile, Yankee employers everywhere in the seaboard cities published advertisements, "No Irish Need Apply." It is not easy to distinguish to what extent the nativist crusade of these three decades was directed against Catholicism as such or against the Irish, but it appears that the prevailing motive was an antipathy to the Irish as an alien group. They threatened the patterns of job and trade competition, the old values, the homogeneity of the once-small cities. Religious sentiment was probably an available, respectable pretext rather than the motive for action. The old community, particularly its lower-middle class and working class, feeling threatened, found the religious differences an easy rationale, sanctioned by the anti-Catholic tradition of the colonial era. The Irish workingman in the next block and not the Pope in Rome was the real enemy.[12]

The raid on the Charlestown convent represented the first *démarche* of the Boston workingmen against the Irish. It was also a gesture of defiance against a darkening future. Boston in 1830 was economically a sick city; only half of the persons born there in 1790 still dwelt in the city by 1820. Only emigration from the farming hinterland prevented the city from suffering an absolute shrinkage in population. The old trade with the Far East, the glittering superstructure of the city's former maritime supremacy, had declined. New York, even before the opening of the Erie Canal in 1825, had pulled ahead in prosperity. The growth of factory towns along nearby rivers where electric current was cheap provided Boston entrepreneurs with new wealth, but afforded native craftsmen a glimpse of a dark future in which the factory system would be triumphant.[13] Hemmed in by these pressures, the workingmen searched for a scapegoat.

The imposing red-brick convent conducted by the Ursuline Nuns on the crest of Mount Benedict Hill in Charlestown across the Charles River from Boston was a convenient symbol. Ironically, the pupils in this convent, established in 1818, were drawn largely not from Catholic but from wealthy liberal Protestant homes. The hold of orthodox Congregationalism was breaking down under the impact of liberal Unitarian and Transcendentalist ideas about religion. A number of parents who desired a more cosmopolitan kind of education for their daughters than could be obtained in the female seminaries run by the Congregational Church entered them in the Ursuline Convent. All the hatreds born of the struggle then going on between liberal and fundamentalist religion in Massachusetts thus became centered on the Charlestown convent. "To the lower classes, with whom Congregationalism was a sacred creed, Catholics and Unitarians seemed to be combining against their religion."

On Sunday evening, August 11, 1834, after weeks of rising tension, a mob gathered before the convent. The Mother Superior pleaded with the crowd to go away. When her entreaties failed, she tried intimidation.

"The Bishop has twenty thousand Irishmen at his command in Boston," she cried.

Her threat was not only injudicious but also inaccurate (it is doubtful if there were that many Irish adults in Boston in that year). By prearranged signal, mob leaders ignited barrels of tar in a neighboring field. Fire bells began ringing. Hundreds of persons streamed up the hill to join the crowd and watch the fun. As midnight approached, a gang of forty or fifty men forced their way into the convent. The Mother Superior, the dozen nuns, and some sixty frightened pupils fled by the rear entrance. The gang set fire to the building and a neighboring farmhouse owned by the order. The crowd stood and cheered as the two buildings went down in flames.

Eight men were ultimately accused of arson in connection with the burning of the convent, but their trial was an orgy of anti-Catholic prejudice. All but one was swiftly acquitted, and the latter was pardoned soon after when leading Boston Catholics, in a gesture of conciliation, signed a petition asking clemency. The nuns resumed teaching a year later in another Boston suburb, but few pupils cared to risk studying with them. In 1838 the Ursulines abandoned their work in Boston and withdrew to Canada.[14]

The burning of the convent brought the smoldering fires of anti-Catholic, anti-Irish feeling to the surface of national life. Equally incendiary in its own way was the publication in 1836 of Maria Monk's *Awful Disclosures.* In this inspired work of fiction, the author told of her education in a Catholic convent in Montreal, her conversion to Catholicism, her decision to become a nun, and her subsequent shocking discoveries. The Mother Superior of the Convent instructed her, she reported, to "obey the priests in all things," and this, she discovered, meant "to live in the practice of criminal intercourse with them." The children born of these liaisons were, she reported, baptized and immediately strangled. Nuns who refused to cooperate were murdered. Hers was a colorful picture of convent life complete with mass graves in the basement, a secret passageway to the priest's quarters, and midnight orgies. Maria explained that having become pregnant after relations with a priest, she hed fled to New York to save the life of her unborn child.

Awful Disclosures, which apparently was ghosted by a professional writer, had a tremendous vogue. Maria was taken up by a sponsoring committee of Protestant clergymen and enjoyed a brief personal success. But then her mother in Montreal disclosed that Maria had never been a resident in the convent described in the book, that she had instead been in a Catholic asylum for delinquent girls, and had run away with the help of a former boyfriend, the probable father of her child. Maria's associates in the writing of the book cheated her out of most of the profits. When she gave birth to a second fatherless child, she did not bother to name him after a priest. One Protestant journal insisted her second pregnancy was arranged by crafty Jesuits to discredit her revelations, but the explanation did not catch on. Her respectable defenders deserted her, and she disappeared into obscurity. Years later she was arrested for picking the pockets of a man in a house of prostitution, and she died in prison. But the book outlived its nominal author. It went through twenty printings, sold 300,000 copies, and down to the Civil War served as the "Uncle Tom's Cabin" of the Know-Nothing movement.*

The most serious outburst of violence came in Philadelphia, the City

---

* The book was again in circulation on a small scale in the presidential campaign of 1960.

of Brotherly Love. In 1842 Bishop Francis Kenrick persuaded the school board to permit Catholic children to read the Douai rather than the King James version of the Bible in the public schools. Catholic children were also excused from the religious instruction that was then a customary part of the curriculum. Nativists attacked this decision as interference by a "foreign prelate" in American education. Mass meetings were held in Independence Square to denounce the change. In May, 1844, a Protestant group invaded the Philadelphia suburb of Kensington, an industrial section where the Irish predominated, to hold a protest meeting. This gesture of defiance produced street fighting in which the Irish drove off their antagonists. The nativists then called a mass meeting for the following Monday, May 6th, in the same neighborhood and appealed to their supporters to turn out in force. The second meeting resulted in a far more serious melee in which one man was killed. This pitched battle touched off three days of general rioting. Protestant mobs roamed the streets of Kensington, setting blocks of houses in flames, and burning two Catholic churches.

An uneasy quiet reigned for several weeks. Then, on July 4th, the holiday was converted into a testimonial to those nativist dead who had fallen in the May rioting. Seventy thousand persons paraded behind the carriages of the widows and children of these men in downtown Philadelphia. The next day street fighting broke out again. This time the focus of attack was St. Philip de Neri Church in Southwark, another suburb, where the pastor had stored guns in the basement of the church as a precautionary measure. When the rumor of the existence of this cache spread, hostile crowds gathered. Separate searches by the sheriff and by a committee of twenty drawn from members of the crowd turned up eighty-seven guns and a quantity of ammunition. When the crowd still did not disperse, the governor sent militia to protect the church. By nightfall of the second day, "a company of troops had turned the square on which the church was located into an armed fortress with barricades erected and cannon commanding the principal avenues of approach." The rioters obtained a cannon of their own and fired into the soldiers massed before the church doors. The troops returned the attack, and the sound of cannon and musket fire rang across the square for several hours.

Meanwhile, gangs roamed the streets looking for Irishmen. Priests and nuns went into hiding. Thousands of Catholics fled the city. Before these days of open civil war had passed, thirteen persons had been killed and more than fifty were wounded, most of them nativists who had engaged the militia in combat.[15]

The burning of churches and the open war in the streets in Philadelphia caused a strong backlash of public disapproval of the nativists. The middle and upper classes drew back in fear from a movement that seemed to be reenacting the horrors of the French Revolution. The diary entries of a wealthy New Yorker, George Templeton Strong, record the change in opinion in respectable circles during that tumultuous spring and early summer. On April 10th he rejoiced in the victory of the nativists in the New York municipal elections:

"Hurrah for the Natives!" he wrote. "Such a blow hasn't fallen on the Hibernian race since the days of Earl Strongbow."

On May 8th, when news reached New York of the first outbreak of rioting, he wrote: "Great row in Philadelphia. . . . This'll be a great thing for the Natives, strengthen their hands amazingly if judiciously used."

Two months later when the fighting broke forth again, he took a darker view. "Civil war raging [in Philadelphia]," he wrote on July 8th. "Mob pelting the military, not with paving stones, but with grapeshot and scrap-iron out of ten-pounders; the state of things in that city is growing worse and worse every day.

"I shan't be caught voting for a 'Native' ticket again in a hurry," he concluded.[16]

The nativist movement rose and fell in successive waves of passion. In reaction to the episodes in Philadelphia, the movement ebbed for nearly a decade. It did not, however, go out of existence. By the 1840's a broad network of nativist societies, religious propaganda organizations, magazines and newspapers was in existence. Books attacking Catholics had become staples in the publishing industry. One writer observed as early as 1835 that the abuse of Catholics "is a regular trade and the compilation of anti-Catholic books . . . has become a part of the regular industry of the country, as much as the making of nutmegs or the construction of clocks."

The last great surge of nativism came in 1854 with the emergence of the American, or Know-Nothing, Party. (The party drew its name from the fact that members of the Order of the Star-Spangled Banner, a secret nativist organization, when asked about their activities said, "I know nothing.") In the elections of 1854–1855, the Know-Nothings scored unexpectedly sweeping victories. The party and its allies carried Maryland, Delaware, Kentucky, and most of New England and showed strength in other parts of the country. About seventy-five congressmen were elected, pledged to do battle against the Pope and his American adherents. The size of the victory was deceptive. In retrospect, it is clear that the Know-Nothing Party was a halfway house for voters seeking a new political home. The ravaging struggle over slavery was tearing apart the dying Whig Party and transforming the Democratic Party. The new Republican Party, pledged to halt the extension of slavery, had just been born. In this period of rapid political flux, the Know-Nothings represented an effort to divert attention away from the slavery issue to the "safer" issues of anti-Catholicism and anti-immigration about which the native community could more easily agree.

Massachusetts was the stronghold of the Know-Nothings. There they captured the governorship, all state offices, and huge majorities in both houses of the legislature. The election represented a real coming to power of the embittered lower classes of the native community. Of the 378 members of the lower house of the legislature, only thirty-four had ever served in office before. The great majority were "mechanics, laborers, clerks, school teachers, and ministers who understood nothing of the governmental processes and were ill-equipped to learn." The disorganized, disorderly legislative session passed little important legislation. A committee appointed to investigate convents became the butt of jokes in the newspapers. On a visit to Lowell, members of the committee charged to the state their liquor bills and also expenses incurred in their off-duty relations with a lady "answering to the name of Mrs. Patterson." The scandal became so great the legislature canceled the rest of the investigation and expelled the chairman of the committee from the legislature. Before adjourning, the members voted themselves a pay increase. At the next election, only one-sixth of the members were reelected.[17]

The fiasco in Massachusetts and the ineffectiveness of Know-Nothing legislators in other states contributed to the party's rapid decline. By 1860 it had dwindled to an inconsequential faction. Life in the cities, however, retained its violent tone. In the years just before the Civil War, a nativist mob of fifteen hundred persons rioted in the Irish districts of Lawrence, Massachusetts, burning homes and churches; in Baltimore eight men were killed in election-day battles between Know-Nothings and Democrats, and in New York, Philadelphia, and other cities violence flared sporadically.

Throughout these strife-torn decades of the 1840's and 1850's, however, each week during the spring and summer months vessels arrived in Atlantic Coast seaports carrying more Irish to America. While the battle raged intermittently in the streets between the Irish and the natives, the reinforcements poured forth from steerage. The Irish were slowly winning the battle for the city against the Protestant lower classes by sheer force of numbers.

CHAPTER THREE

Politics and Civil War

1

FROM THEIR EARLIEST YEARS in America, the Irish have been identified in American politics with the Jeffersonian tradition and, as it emerged, with the Democratic Party. This strong identification came about by grace of the shortsighted hostility of the Federalist Party. When England took the lead in organizing a coalition against revolutionary France in the 1790's, American conservative opinion took the English side. This meant that the Federalists were also against Ireland, which hoped to win its independence, as the Americans had, with French aid. The Jeffersonians, who were favorable to revolutionary France, were by logical extension also sympathetic to Ireland. The Protestant colonists had brought to America the ancient English stereotype of the Irish as a wild, barbarous, superstitious, rude people. The Federalists under the stress of events in the 1790's gave this stereotype a specific political content. They pictured the Irish as the natural allies of the French revolutionaries, as naturally turbulent and disorderly, as "the most God-provoking democrats this side of Hell." After the Irish revolt of 1798 failed, many rebel leaders fled to the United States. The Federalists received them with suspicion, while Jefferson and the Clintons, his allies in New York, welcomed them.

The Naturalization, Alien, and Sedition Acts, which the Federalist-controlled Congress passed and President John Adams signed in 1798, were directed against not only French but also Irish emigrants and what was deemed their radical tendencies. The Naturalization Act extended the waiting period before an immigrant could be naturalized from five years to fourteen years. The Alien Act, which was never used, gave the President the power to deport foreigners by executive decree. The Sedition Act had among its provisions a section making it a misdemeanor to write or say anything "with the intent to defame" Congress and the President or likely to bring them "into contempt or disrepute." Twenty-five persons were prosecuted under this section

47

before the law was repealed during the Jefferson administration. Not surprisingly, the first person prosecuted was Matthew Lyon, an Irish editor and politician in Vermont, who was an outspoken admirer of Jefferson and of the French Revolution.

The Federalists grossly misread the character of the Irish immigrant. The successful Irish already established here, such as the Carrolls of Maryland and Thomas FitzSimons of Pennsylvania, were themselves Federalists. The rebels of 1798, whether they were Protestants, such as the lawyer Thomas Emmet, or Catholics, such as Dr. William James MacNeven, were thoroughly respectable professional men of middle-class backgrounds. The masses of poorer Irish who came later may have been turbulent in their manners, but in their fundamental outlook they were conservative. Nevertheless, though the stereotype was out of line with the facts, it lingered for nearly a half-century and had a profound influence on the political behavior of the Irish. The hostility of the Federalists and of their Whig successors, particularly in New England and parts of New York where they were strong, drove the Irish into the arms of the Jeffersonians.

2

On the night of April 24, 1817, there was a gathering in Dooley's Long Room in New York City. The subject under discussion was the discrimination practiced against the Irish by the Tammany Society, the city's dominant political organization. The men in the room, mostly laborers and small tradesmen, raised their voices in anger as they expounded their long-standing grievances. It was time, they concluded, that Tammany was compelled to nominate some Irish leader such as Thomas Emmet for Congress.

Two hundred strong, the men stamped out of Dooley's and headed for Tammany Hall. They broke in upon the caucus of party leaders that was then underway and demanded Emmet's nomination. When their request was not politely received, the Irish began to overturn the tables and break the furniture, the better to use pieces of it to inculcate learning on Tammany minds. The Tammany men fought back. Windows were smashed, eyes blackened, and noses broken. The Tammany men obtained reinforcements from neighboring taverns and finally drove the Irish away.

Emmet was not nominated, but it was undoubtedly a highly educational evening.

The Society of St. Tammany had been founded in 1789, a few weeks after the Federal Constitution went into effect. Named in honor of a famous seventeenth century chief of the Delaware Indians, it was intended as primarily a fraternal and charitable order. Its twelve leaders were called sachems (chiefs) headed by a Grand Sachem. The Fourth of July and Tammany Day, May 12th, were occasions for parades with hundreds of Tammany braves marching single file through the streets with painted faces and carrying bows, arrows, and tomahawks. In this innocent merriment was born what was to become the best organized, longest-lived, most famous city political organization in American history, and the single most important vehicle of Irish power in politics.

Made up of native Protestant workingmen and others of the "lower order," Tammany had at first a bias against the pretensions and political privileges of the ruling merchant classes. Its members distrusted the Society of the Cincinnati and the aristocratic politics of Alexander Hamilton and the Federalist Party. Yet Tammany might have remained a genial and obscure fraternal order were it not for the activities of that ambitious politician Aaron Burr. In alliance with Thomas Jefferson against Hamilton, he saw in Tammany an effective means of arousing and channeling popular support. Several of his friends were original Tammany members, and one of them was soon Grand Sachem. Within a decade of its founding, Tammany had become the center of Burr's faction in the city. In the election of 1800, it was instrumental in electing him to the Vice-Presidency. When Burr killed Hamilton in a duel in 1804, the Tammany sachems were with him and one was his second. Tammany, however, no matter how much its members might rejoice in private, was careful to hold a public procession of mourning for Hamilton. Tammany was already bigger than any one man. It survived Burr's disgrace and downfall.

Throughout its early years, the organization remained strictly nativist in outlook. A sentence in its original constitution provided, "No person shall be eligible to the office of Sachem, unless a native of this country." Tammany steadfastly refused to nominate any Irish Catholics for public office. In 1809 it named Patrick McKay for the state assembly, but for several years he remained an isolated exception. Tammany's anti-Irish position was part of a general antiforeign outlook. In 1819 the sachems issued a general denunciation of foreigners, and urged the public to buy only articles made by Americans in America.[1]

The democratic pressures of the age of Jackson broke the barriers to Irish entry into politics. In 1821 the New York State constitutional convention abolished the property qualifications for voting, and granted equal suffrage to every citizen. The Irish, many of them too poor to qualify under the old restrictions, were now able to speak in more authoritative accents. The leaders of Tammany were good listeners. They opened their doors to the Irish. The heavy immigration from Ireland in the 1840's and 1850's pushed those doors open wider. Thirty years after that stormy night that began in Dooley's Long Room, the Irish were well on their way to taking over the organization that had once excluded them.

The Irish identified with the Democratic Party because the opposition Whigs embodied the earlier Federalist tradition of suspicion and hostility to foreigners. The mercantile and professional classes in control of the Whig Party resented the newcomers who endangered their control of the city. They were less able than the Democrats to cross the barriers of class and make the necessary gestures to win the political support of these propertyless impoverished workingmen. As the party of gentlemen, they could not mask the contempt and derision they felt and which Hone and Strong accurately reflected in their diaries. The Jacksonian liberals in the Democratic Party waging a broad fight against the bankers and merchants at the state and national level welcomed the Irish as allies and made them feel at home. The Whigs remained a closed corporation. As a result it eventually became a politically insolvent one.

When it was already too late, the Whigs in the 1840's revised their attitude and tried to make a broader democratic appeal. Governor William Seward and Thurlow Weed, his political manager, adopted the Catholic position on state aid to parochial schools. Horace Greeley, the foremost Whig editor, championed Irish independence in the *Tribune* and made spirited appeals to Irish voters to rally to the Whig Party. William Robinson, an Irish feature writer on the *Tribune*, wrote numerous political articles slanted toward Irish readers and made speaking tours before Irish groups. The party in 1852 hired Patrick O'Dea to edit a campaign weekly entitled the *Irishman*. By this time, however, the Democrats had already consolidated their hold on the loyalties of the great majority of Irish voters. Irishmen were finding their way to the top in the Democratic organization. One of them had been elected district attorney in Manhattan in 1850. Two years later, eighteen American Irish were elected on the Democratic ticket to various offices in the state.[2]

The *Irish American*, the leading newspaper in the Irish community, took note of the Democratic nominations of Irish candidates. "We say to the Whigs, 'Go thou and do likewise, and you may get a slice of the Irish vote!' How many adopted citizens will you nominate, gentlemen: How many? Will you even give Wm. E. Robinson—your hardest workman and your ablest coadjutor—a chance? We need not ask any such question; we know you will not. With these facts, and the contrasts before us, how can you expect the Irish vote?"[3]

In 1852 General Winfield Scott, the last Whig candidate for President, made last-gasp appeals to the Irish voters. He had the special problem of living down indiscreet overtures to nativist prejudices which he had made a dozen years before in an earlier unsuccessful bid for the presidential nomination.

Speaking at Columbus, Ohio, during the 1852 campaign, Scott told an audience: "I think I hear again that rich brogue that betokens a son of old Ireland. I love to hear it! I heard it on the Niagara in '14, and again in the Valley of Mexico. It will always remind me of the gallant men of Erin who in such great numbers have followed me to victory."[4]

The *Irish American* commented sardonically on these effusions: "The sweet, soft, mellifluous, musical Irish brogue has caught the fancy of General Scott. He likes it, he hugs it, he presses it to his heart. . . . Now, at any other time, such a vindication of our countrymen would be most grateful. But larking or sparking with 'that soft Irish brogue' at this moment, immediately before the Presidential Election, has not the grace of modesty or sincerity about it.

"Gineral, Gineral, you are a big deludherer!"[5]

The failure of the Whigs to make headway with the Irish was essentially a failure of sympathy and communication. The Irish could not easily identify themselves with the bankers and merchants who were the hard core of the Whig Party. Greeley compromised his enthusiasm for Irish causes by his endorsement of prohibition laws and his attacks on liquor sellers and saloons. Seward was the only Whig to capitalize politically on his efforts on behalf of the Irish community, and he was not able to transfer his personal popularity to his party. Fundamentally, the Whigs treated the Irish as a client group to whom special appeals were made. Such overtures are always implicitly patronizing. The Irish heard the words but they also caught the overtones and resented them.

The situation within the Democratic Party was more fluid during these thirty years before the Civil War. Martin Van Buren and his liberal "Locofoco" followers were in the majority, but a more conservative faction known as the "Hunkers" (they "hunkered" after patronage) was often in control of Tammany in the city. There were Irish in both factions, but easily the outstanding Irish figure was Michael Walsh, who belonged to neither. Born in Ireland in 1815 and brought to America by his parents as a child, Walsh was apprenticed at an early age to a lithographer, but his real genius was for journalism and politics. He had a wayward temperament and was fond of whiskey and carousing, but he had authentic talent and a basic honesty.

Mike Walsh's career was inseparably linked to the mood of the time. America was entering the democratic age. The abolition of property qualifications for voting meant the laboring class could participate fully in elections. Politics shifted to a popular, mass basis. Open conventions replaced the old caucus system for selecting candidates. The politician who could make a direct bid to the sentiments of the voters superseded the parliamentary orator and the aristocratic wirepuller. For the first time, public opinion in the modern sense became important. New techniques evolved to organize mass sentiments and rally voters to political causes. Street fighting, election-day riots, political parades, and monster mass meetings became common. The process was rough and crude, but it broke fresh ground for democracy.

The Irish arrived in the United States with some knowledge of these techniques. O'Connell's campaigns in Ireland had accustomed them to democratic methods in politics. The Catholic Association had developed a mass membership, had staged monster meetings and popular demonstrations, and had made use of the arts of propaganda in swaying public opinion. The terrorism in rural Ireland and the activities of the Whiteboys and the Terry Alts had accustomed the immigrants to violence and gang warfare to gain their ends.

Mike Walsh was indigenous to this new democratic atmosphere. He had a flair for writing and a mastery of catch-as-catch-can stump speaking. "Slangy, raucous, and sarcastic, with brassy face and cool, undaunted manner, he would drawl out rambling speeches which convulsed his audiences with their wit and ridicule."[6] He organized a gang of young Irish "bhoys" known as the Spartan Band which supported him at mass meetings and helped him muscle his way to the platform at hostile gatherings. Gangs were not new in city politics. As far back as the Jeffersonian period, Tammany and its rivals had made use of them as repeaters on election day, but Walsh was the first political leader to organize such a group on a year-round basis and make it one of the bases of his power.

Walsh articulated the grievances of the impoverished Irish laborers. "The great and fruitful source of crime and misery on earth," he declared, "is the inequality of society—the abject dependence of honest willing industry upon idle and dishonest capitalists."

"Demagogues tell you that you are freemen," he said on another occasion. "They lie; you are slaves. . . . No man, devoid of all other means of support but that which his own labor affords him, can be a freeman, under the present state of society."

"What have we gained by the numberless political victories we have achieved?" he cried. "Nothing but a change of masters!"

He called upon the workingmen to arise and throw out the self-serving hacks who ran Tammany. "I knew that we, the Subterranean

Democracy, possess the power, if we will but exercise it," he declared.

To support his cause, he founded in 1843, and ran for several years thereafter, a weekly called *The Subterranean*. Its motto was, "Independent in Everything—Neutral in Nothing." It was a racy, scrappy sheet which blended radical politics with lively gossip and twice landed its editor in jail for libel.

The more orthodox leaders of Tammany had little enthusiasm for Walsh, but his popular following was great. At Tammany meetings the crowd often shouted insistently for Walsh until the presiding officer had to let him speak. At one such meeting he graphically described the mechanics of the Tammany system.

The "formal ceremony" of electing ward delegates to nominating conventions was "a most ridiculous and insulting farce," he declared. "A meeting of the democratic electors of the ward is called—a number of fellows who either hold or expect office go round amongst the lowest rum holes in the ward—treat the 'setters,' in addition to which, they give the ringleaders a few dollars apiece, to insure the presence of their gangs. Every contractor brings a number of poor men whose spirits have been broken and whose frames have been withered and bowed down by that worst form of slavery—*the slavery of poverty*, and out of whose sorrowing sighs, sweat and blood, this same bloated brute has distilled a fortune, and they are compelled when at the meeting, by the wretchedness and degradation of their condition to respond with counterfeit sincerity, to each mandate of their labor's plunderer; . . . those, with the city watchmen, lamplighters, police officers and a number of selected or favored thieves . . . assemble half an hour before the time specified in the call—arrange the meeting, cry out 'aye,' when the names are called—give three cheers before the 'noes' can be taken, after which the 'contractor' who acts as chairman pronounces everything 'carried unanimously'—then a motion to adjourn is passed, all hands go down and drink, and thus are made nearly all our honorable nominating committees."

At this point the meeting was interrupted by exultant cries of "Go it Mike," "Go it my hero," "Give it to 'em!" and countershouts of "Turn him out, throw him out of the window, pull him off the stand!"

Walsh offered a challenge.

"Come up; come up here, you craven cowardly scoundrels, you that are hallooing I mean, and pull me off yourselves. Is not this a pretty scene, there now are a parcel of watchmen, lamplighters, hirelings, menials, police officers and their companions—the very stool pigeons and thieves I have just been describing!

"You have men to contend with here! Not poor, destitute and forlorn wretches."

Tammany finally gave in to Walsh in 1846 and nominated him for the Assembly. The organization candidate originally slated was Samuel J. Tilden, a sleek, cold, ambitious young man with pale blue eyes and a cautious air. After hearing Mike's Spartan Boys give a series of "three groans for Tilden," he decided it was the better part of valor to step aside. Thirty years later he was to be the party candidate for President.

Walsh was elected. Four years later, he won a seat in Congress, where he served until his death in 1859.[7]

Walsh was an authentic voice of the Irish masses, but he also demonstrated their political limitations in this initial period. He helped give politics a social content, but his erratic personal behavior and his lack of any sustaining social philosophy cut him off from effective cooperation with the Jacksonian wing of the national party which comprised his natural liberal allies. His major contribution was to batter down the barriers within Tammany to Irish participation, but he and his Irish followers in the "eruption of the shirtless and unwashed democracy," as he termed it, were not yet sufficiently integrated in the community to go beyond participation in any significant direction.

3

The slavery issue was another influence that isolated the Irish within the Democratic Party in New York. While most of the population in the North moved toward an antislavery position, the Irish veered in the other direction. While Martin Van Buren and the Jacksonian liberals became "Free-Soilers" and fought slavery expansion, the sympathies of the Irish gravitated toward Calhoun and the planter aristocracy.

The shifting of Irish political attitudes in the late 1840's and 1850's was a complex process. One influence was the natural enthusiasm for American territorial expansion. The imperial vision of annexing Texas, conquering Mexico, and pushing the flag to the Pacific frontier was a romantic notion that had an intrinsic appeal for the Irish, as it did for many other Americans. Mike Walsh claimed to be the first man to advocate the acquisition of Texas. John O'Sullivan, the founder and editor of the *Democratic Review*, the principal Jacksonian monthly, from 1837 to 1846, coined the catchword of the expansionist movement—"manifest destiny." Territorial expansion in Texas and the West signified an important gain for the slave system. The Irish were indifferent to that consequence.

Irish opinion was almost unanimously opposed to abolition. Although Daniel O'Connell wrote his friends in America urging them to oppose slavery, and although the Pope issued a papal bull against the slave trade, these outside influences were not decisive. As the newest and least secure members of society, the American Irish were the most rigid and least generous in extending their sympathy to a submerged minority like the Negroes whose circumstances they scarcely comprehended. There was also an element of economic rivalry, since Irish workingmen feared the upward thrust of the Negro would further depress their own circumstances in the job market. This fear was not, however, the controlling motive. The number of free Negroes in northern cities was simply not great enough to pose that threat in clear terms. The basic cause of Irish hostility to abolition was an obsessive preoccupation with their own problems. They felt it was quixotic and insincere of the northern middle classes to trouble themselves about the alleged misery of the slave in far-off Alabama or Texas when there were so much poverty and suffering among white men right at home in the city of New York that ought to be remedied first.

Mike Walsh displayed the inwardness of Irish concern in the House of Representatives in 1854: "The only difference between the negro slave of the South and the white wage slave of the North is that the one has a master without asking for him, and the other has to beg for the privilege of becoming a slave. . . . The one is the slave of an individual; the other is the slave of an inexorable class.

"It is all very well for gentlemen to get up here and clamor about the wrongs and outrages of the southern slaves but, sir, even in New York, during the last year, there have been over thirteen hundred people deprived of their liberty without any show or color of offense, but because they were poor, and too honest to commit a crime."[8]

The enthusiasm for expansion and the hostility to abolition did not, however, lead the Irish to favor secession. They had a strong allegiance to the Union and the American form of government which contrasted so favorably in their eyes with British rule in Ireland. They wanted to change Ireland over to the image of America, not to change America. The same impulse that sustained their revolutionary zeal for Irish nationalism made them conservative in terms of American institutions.

The *Irish American* consistently attacked northern abolitionists and southern secessionists impartially. "The truth is," the paper declared in 1858, "the 'barbarian foreigners,' as they are pleased to denominate us, are too national, too conservative of the constitution and institutions of this republic to suit these factious demagogues, whose fingers are continually itching to tear the one to shreds and overturn the others in the mire of oligarchism."[9] Here the carry-over from Irish political experience was clear. The Irish were nationalists in America as they had been in Ireland. They opposed the Abolitionists partly because they identified them as a group willing to destroy national unity for the sake of an abstract moral cause.

The shifting political attachments of the Irish to factions in the Democratic Party in the period from 1840 to 1860 represented not reasoned commitments but temporary stops for shelter. In 1844-1848 Calhoun enjoyed an evanescent popularity in the Irish community. Mike Walsh developed a passionate admiration for him. In the early 1850's, support shifted to Franklin Pierce and the conservative "Doughface" Democrats. Pierce gave the Irish their first national political recognition by his appointment of John O'Sullivan as Minister to Portugal. By the end of the decade, Stephen A. Douglas had emerged as the Irish hero. His personal magnetism was attractive. His compromise "squatter sovereignty" position on slavery expansion emphasized what the Irish regarded as the right themes: democratic sovereignty and majority rule. His disdain for the moral fervor of abolitionism and his argument that maintenance of the Union was the highest good were reassuring. In his 1860 campaign tour, Irish admirers mobbed Douglas in every northern city. It was essentially Douglas's credo that a popular Irish poem expressed when the Irish marched to war in 1861:

> "To the tenets of Douglas we tenderly cling,
> Warm hearts to the cause of our country we bring;
> To the flag we are pledged—all its foes we abhor—
> And we ain't for the 'nigger' but are for the war."[10]

When the Confederate forces attacked Fort Sumter, the Irish rallied with enthusiasm to Lincoln's call for volunteers. It has been estimated that 51,000 of the troops who served in the Union Army from New York State were born in Ireland.[11] Colonel Michael Corcoran, who had been relieved as commander of the 69th Regiment in the state militia the year before for his refusal to participate in the parade in honor of the Prince of Wales, was reinstated. The authorities limited his regiment to 1,000 men, although over 5,000 Irishmen volunteered to serve under him. "His problem was one of selection rather than recruiting." The "Fighting 69th" fought with conspicuous gallantry in the disastrous First Battle of Bull Run. Corcoran was taken prisoner, and the losses in the ranks were heavy. In the fall of 1861, the 69th was re-recruited together with two other regiments to form an "Irish Brigade" under the command of General Thomas Meagher, a hero of the Irish Revolution in 1848.

Under the conscription law of 1863, however, the Irish bore a disproportionate burden. Their resentment produced the draft riots in New York in July of that year. The bulk of Irish were laboring men who could not afford the three hundred dollars required to hire a substitute. The first drawing of names, on Saturday, July 11th, produced a list of twelve hundred, the majority of whom were Irish. This announcement came with special impact after two years of fighting in which the Irish regiments had suffered heavy losses. There was widespread anger following Lincoln's Emancipation Proclamation the preceding autumn, for it seemed that a war begun to save the Union had turned into a war to free the Negro. The tension between the Irish and the Negroes had also been growing for three months, since Negro "scabs" were used in April, 1863, to break a bitter dock strike led by Irish longshoremen. On the Monday morning following the publication of the first draft list, Irish workingmen stayed away from their jobs and began to gather in sullen crowds before the draft centers and on vacant lots on the East Side near Central Park. When the police, who themselves included great numbers of Irish, attempted under the leadership of Superintendent John Kennedy to disperse the crowds, they turned and fought. Kennedy was badly beaten. Once the rioting began, it continued for four days. The mobs went from place to place, attacking the Armory on Lexington Avenue and various private houses. The main objects of attack were Negroes. The Colored Orphan Asylum was burned; hapless individual Negroes who were seen on the streets were beaten, and several of them hanged. It was a classic example of the poor in their misery venting their fury on other poor who were even worse off.

A later study of the draft figures showed that Irish complaints of discrimination were justified. Through unintentional blundering by government officials, the draft fell heavier on some wards than on others. One district, for example, with a population of 131,000 had a draft quota of 5,881, while a neighboring and slightly larger district had a quota of only 2,697. To ease public tempers, officials temporarily suspended the draft in the city. When it was resumed six weeks later, a more equitable apportionment had been worked out.

Archbishop John Hughes, the revered leader of the Irish community, used his influence to damp down the dissension. Addressing a great crowd from the balcony of his residence on the fourth day of the uprising, the archbishop said:

"Men of New York: They call you rioters, but I cannot see a riotous face among you. . . . I thank God that I came to this country, where no oppression exists. (Applause) If you are Irishmen—for your enemies say the rioters are Irishmen—I am also an Irishman, but not a rioter.

(Silence) If you are Catholics, as they have reported—then I am a Catholic too. (Cheers) I know that, under the misguidance of real or imaginary evils, people will sometimes get uneasy, and every man has his troubles, for I have my troubles, too; but I think with the poet that it is better to bear out slight inconveniences than to rush to evils that we have not yet witnessed. . . . When these so-called riots are over, and the blame is justly laid on Irish Catholics, I wish you to tell me in what country I could claim to be born? (Voices, 'Ireland') Yes, but what shall I say if these stories be true? Ireland, that has been the mother of heroes and poets, but never the mother of cowards. I thank you for your kindness, and I hope nothing will occur until you return home, and if, by chance, as you go thither, you should meet a police officer or a military man, why, just look at him."[12]

When the passions of the draft riots had died down, *Harper's* editorialized two weeks later:

"It must be remembered in palliation of the disgrace which, as Archbishop Hughes says, the riots of last week have heaped upon the Irish name, that in many wards of the city, the Irish were during the late riot staunch friends of law and order; that Irishmen helped to rescue the colored orphans in the asylum from the hands of the rioters; that a large proportion of the police, who behaved throughout the riot with the most exemplary gallantry, are Irishmen; that the Roman Catholic priesthood to a man used their influence on the side of the law; and that perhaps the most scathing rebuke administered to the riot was written by an Irishman—James T. Brady.

"It is important that this riot should teach us something more useful than a revival of Know-Nothing prejudices."[13]

It is one of the ironies of American Irish history that the draft riots in New York occurred only one week after the Irish in the Union Army had played a heroic role in the decisive battle of the War. At Gettysburg on July 3–4, the "Fighting 69th" and other Irish regiments had suffered heavy losses. The 69th had fought throughout the Peninsular Campaign, at the Second Battle of Bull Run, Antietam, Fredericksburg, and Chancellorsville. At Antietam on October, 1862, nine months before the draft riots, it had lost 196 out of 317 men in the front lines. These troops "held a position so exposed that five flagbearers were killed in five minutes, fifteen in the course of a day." After filling its ranks with new recruits, the regiment lost 128 men out of 238 leading the Union charge at Fredericksburg. The Irish Rifles, the regiment sponsored by Tammany Hall, lost nearly a quarter of its men killed in combat.

Throughout the North, the Irish had volunteered for the army. No fewer than thirty-eight Union regiments had the word "Irish" in their names.

The Civil War, it has been noted, made the United States a nation in the full sense. José Ortega, writing of the making of a nation, has observed:

"Groups which form a state come together and stay together for definite reasons. . . . They do not live together in order merely *to be* together. They live together in order *to do* something together."[14]

The Irish and the rest of the American community had come together to achieve a common purpose in 1861–1865. After that war was over, native-Irish antagonism never again flared in the open violence that had been almost habitual to the generation of 1830–1860. On the fields of Antietam and Fredericksburg and Gettysburg, old hatreds had been submerged and a larger unity forged. There were now common memories and common sacrifices that linked Americans across the rifts of differing cultural backgrounds and national ancestry. The war established a new level of national consciousness. The Irish, who had been excluded from power and participation by the English ruling class in Ireland, were welcomed as partners in the common cause of saving the Union. When the war ended, the expanding open society in America enabled them to share in achieving the common good.

CHAPTER FOUR

The Irish Style in Politics

1

IN THE DECADES after the Civil War, the Irish developed their characteristic style in American politics. The Irishman as politician is the member of the Irish community most familiar to other Americans. The Irish brought to American politics two advantages other immigrants did not have: a knowledge of the English language and an acquaintance with the dominant Anglo-American culture. In addition to a common language and a shared culture, they had gifts of organization and eloquence, a sense of cohesion, and the beginnings of a political tradition in the nationalist agitation in Ireland. Their antagonism toward England offended leaders of opinion along the eastern seaboard, but it did not upset most Americans since, in the nineteenth century, twisting the lion's tail was the national sport.

The Irish made their big move into American politics at a time when both the theory and the practice of politics were at a peculiarly low ebb. The nation's earliest political tradition originated in the seventeenth and eighteenth centuries among the planters of Virginia and the Puritan aristocrats and merchants of New England. This tradition held that politics is a serious affair worthy of the attention of the best class of men. The governing of mankind, in this view, is an enterprise too important for the natural leaders of society, the men of property and education, to leave to intermediaries and underlings. Washington, Jefferson, Madison, Jay, and the Adamses who organized the American Revolution, wrote the Constitution, and founded the national government shared this viewpoint. They were never guilty of the fatuous maxim "It's just politics."

The merchants and industrial entrepreneurs who came to the fore in the early nineteenth century produced a different theory of politics. What has become known as the Whig view of government contended that "that government is best which governs least." The primary task of politics was to make government a tidy, efficient housekeeper. The business community developed the comfortable and useful mythology that social conflict was unreal, that the interests of employers and workers, of farmers and city consumers, of businessmen and customers were actually identical. Since this was true, the two-party system was more a convenience than a necessity. If there were no social conflicts, then party warfare was devoid of meaning. Party affiliations could be regarded as matters of sentiment, as eccentric vestiges of the past rather than reflections of vital interests. By 1870 this view had become dominant in writings and discussions of politics among educated easterners. The "independent voter" who rejected both parties and chose the better man regardless of label was extolled as the best voter. In these years the business community not only attracted the best talents but also imposed upon politics its standards of efficiency and economical operation as ends in themselves rather than as means in attaining the larger public welfare. "Politics" became a naughty word associated with corrupt schemers and raids on the treasury. During the late Victorian age, the genteel tradition was as supreme in American politics as it was in literature.

This outlook was not without its critics. Edward Everett Hale, writing in 1889, argued that extreme laissez faire went counter to much of the nation's experience, pointing to the public ownership of schools and libraries, roads and canals, lighthouses and docks, and the post office. Hale noted that in the earlier years of our history when canals, railroads, and turnpikes had been built by private companies, these corporations had been chartered as public agents in much the same way as the English chartered companies had acted on behalf of the Crown in the development of India and the American colonies. The "friends of strong government," he concluded, "are acting on the lines of our best traditions."[1]

But Hale and other reformers were in the minority as the extreme individualist, antigovernment views of Herbert Spencer became the vogue. The chief exponent of the majority viewpoint was E. L. Godkin, long-time editor of the New York *Evening Post* and of the *Nation* magazine. Although monopolies, slums, child labor, periodic mass unemployment, and other evils ravaged society, Godkin and other writers on politics devoted most of their attention to the introduction of the civil service system and to thinking of ways to lure educated men into politics. Godkin wrote in "The Duty of Educated Men in a Democracy": "We should probably, in a college-graduate government, witness the disappearance from legislation of nearly all acts and resolutions which are passed for what is called 'politics'; that is, for the purpose of pleasing certain bodies of voters, without any reference to their value as contributions to the work of government."[2]

It is not astonishing that with this narrow, uncomprehending theory of politics in the ascendancy, the masses of immigrants crowding into the growing cities had to develop their own political institutions and their own political ethic. The immigrant laborer desperate for a job to feed his family, the immigrant family quarreling with the landlord, the widowed mother deprived of her income, the injured workman, the sweatshop employee, and the truant boy in trouble with the police needed someone or some agency more compassionate and helpful than routine "good government," no matter how purified by civil service reform or economically run by college graduates. Moreover, the immigrants perceived that when government at different levels did exercise positive power, it was usually on behalf of businessmen by granting land subsidies to railroad companies or using police to break strikes. Middle-class "mugwump" politics was unsound in theory, and when it was violated in practice it was always in behalf of a single interest in society.[3]

The Irish, the most numerous and advanced section of the immigrant community, took over the political party (usually the Democratic Party) at the local level and converted it into virtually a parallel system of government. The network of party clubhouses and the hierarchy of party committees with a citywide leader or "boss" at the apex constituted a "shadow government," a supplementary structure of power that performed some functions more vital than those of the nominal, legal government. The main objective of the party, of course, was to capture control of the city government, but even when the party was out of office, it could continue to function. It had revenue from the "tax" it levied upon saloons, houses of prostitution, gamblers, and contractors. Out of these funds, the party machine could provide the food and coal it gave to those who were destitute. It could finance the young lawyers who interceded in court for the delinquent, wrote letters home to the old country for the illiterate, and intervened at city hall for those bewildered by the regulations and intricacies of the government. It could pay for the torchlight parades, the children's picnics, and the one-day excursion trips up the river or to the beach which brought recreation and a touch of color to the lives of working-class families.

When the machine was in office, it could provide that most precious of all commodities: a job. Public construction work was one of the major sources of jobs and income. When reform administrations were in power, they cut back on construction to save money and reduce the tax rate. When the machine was in power, it expanded construction, building courthouses and schoolhouses, paving more streets, digging more subways, and erecting new bridges. The politicians at the top liked building programs because they could collect bribes from those who received the contract, make "a killing" on the sale of the land on the basis of their advance knowledge, profit by writing the insurance on the project, and sometimes organize a sand-and-gravel company and get cut into the actual construction as a subcontractor. This was "honest graft," sometimes known as "white graft" to distinguish it from the "dirty graft" collected via the police department from the underworld. The contractors liked this expansive attitude toward public works projects because it increased their business, and so did the carpenters, plumbers, plasterers, and other skilled craftsmen. But, most of all, the newest and least skilled of the immigrants were enthusiastic because these projects enabled them to find work as laborers. Since, at the outset of their life in America, they were fitted only to do pick-and-shovel work, they were peculiarly dependent upon the machine and its free-and-easy spending of public money. No number of exposés by citizens' committees and good government groups of graft, payroll padding, and excessive spending on public projects shook their loyalty to the machine. If there were no "corrupt machine," they reasoned, there might not be any building projects, and if there were no projects to work on, how would they earn enough to live? Padded payrolls were better than no payrolls. Since the city usually needed the building or public improvement, it was not easy for critics to demonstrate to working-class voters what harm had been done.

2

The political machines the Irish built in most of the major cities of the North and Midwest developed out of the block and the neighborhood. Family friendships and neighborhood loyalties were the basis of power. The boyhood gangs with their emphasis on loyalty and cohesiveness provided the morale and the habits of mind that were easily transmuted, in adult years, into the rationale of the machine. The citywide leaders, the ward and precinct captains, and the rank-and-file members of the party machines developed a set of political ethics and an attitude toward politics and power that were strikingly different from those of the native middle-class code. The Irish viewed municipal politics not as a conflict over how to obtain the best government at the lowest cost but as a struggle for power among competing groups.

The earliest leaders organized the Irish voters as a battering ram to break the power of a hostile majority. They put an end to elementary forms of discrimination such as the exclusive use of the King James Bible in the schools and the assignment of Protestant chaplains to Catholic inmates of hospitals, jails, and charitable institutions. Next, they fought for the appointment of Irish as schoolteachers and as policemen and firemen. Finally, they sought to take all political power into their own hands.

In the course of this struggle for power, the Irish community evolved an attitude of tolerant acceptance of political corruption. This was neither cynicism nor hypocrisy; rather it was close to a straightforward acceptance of graft as necessary and inevitable. Graft was part of the operating compromise between the formal rules of the political system and the facts of life as it was actually lived. Corruption was often viewed as a primitive mechanism for redistributing the wealth because, as people said, "at least it keeps the money in circulation." The Irish and their allies among other immigrants had the attitude typical of those who comprise a client group and not a ruling class. For a long period, they were people who had stature without status, power without responsibility. Only gradually did the social discipline grow to match the power, and only when that happened did the majority detach themselves from the values of the political machine.

For individual Irish, politics was an attractive career. Since newly naturalized voters were usually more willing to give their votes to another "son of the old country" than to a native-born candidate, politics was the only major profession in which it was an asset rather than a drawback to be an immigrant. Politics, like baseball, prizefighting, and the Church, was a career open to talents, a path of social mobility for the ambitious sons of impoverished families.

This Irish concept of politics as another profession—practical, profitable, and pursued every day in the year—diverged sharply from the ordinary civic code that draped politics in the mantle of "public service." According to the genteel tradition, the holding of office was an ephemeral activity; it might be thought of as an accident comparable to a call for jury service that might befall any citizen. For those who regarded the main business of America as business, service in a political office represented a sacrifice. In the Irish community, there was no talk of duty or sacrifice. Nor did those who gave their time to politics regard the holding of public office as an interlude or an accident. Politics was their career. Like every other profession, it was expected to reward its practitioners with money, prestige and, if possible, security. It was generally expected that a politician would make money out of his office, collaterally if not directly, and that if he lost he would be "taken care of" in a sinecure.*

Since Irish politicians were of working-class origin, they entered public

* Shortly after World War II, the author was walking in Boston with a well-known local politician. The politician exchanged greetings with a passerby, an aged, poorly dressed woman. "When her husband was in the City Council with me," he remarked, "he was called 'Honest John.' But I never took it seriously. I figured he had an angle somewhere. But then he died and it was true. He didn't leave her a cent. Now what do you think of a dumbbell like that who wouldn't take a buck when he could get one and now his wife has to go out and work?"

office trailing long strings of needy relatives. Because the public payroll was the politician's only resource, he was expected to use it to succor his family and dependents. The result was the nepotism so frequently and so futilely condemned by civic reformers. This nepotism was usually controlled by some sense of official responsibility. A halfwit or a drunkard would not be placed in a responsible job, but some other provision might be made for him. Indeed, some other provision had to be made for him. (What of his wife and children? If no one else would hire him, what politician would take the responsibility of sending "your own flesh-and-blood" to the relief rolls or the gutter?)

Nepotism had old-country roots. For generations, each immigrant who "went out to the States" had a fixed responsibility to send back money to pay for the subsequent passage of one of his brothers or sisters. In many families the oldest son came first, paid the fare of the next oldest who paid for the next, and so on. This recruitment practice was known as "sending for a greenhorn." The immigrant was also morally obligated to find jobs here for his relatives and for as many of his neighbors from the old country as he could. In this way, the kitchens of many a mansion and the police, fire, and streetcar departments of many a city were regularly staffed.

Conrad Arensberg, when he wrote his study *The Irish Countryman* in the 1930's, provided a graphic example of this process: "One little settlement called Cross, on the Loop Head peninsula which juts from Clare into the Atlantic at the Shannon's mouth, is said locally to be supported by the Shanghai police force. The first man to go is now Chief of Police in the International Settlement there, and many places in the Force have gone to men of Cross."[4]

It is a short step from neighborliness to nepotism. However much such nepotism might be deplored, it could not be otherwise when men were bred from childhood to an urgent and overriding feeling of family duty and parochial loyalty.

Politics as a career not only required a minimum of education, preparation, and money; it also had the advantage over competing occupations that for the few who had the requisite talents it produced its rewards relatively quickly. In this respect, politics had the same appeal as professional athletics. It is significant how many politicians achieved power at an early age. James Curley was a congressman at thirty-six and mayor of Boston at thirty-nine; Joseph Tumulty of Jersey City became President Wilson's chief aide at thirty-three; Alfred E. Smith and James J. Walker were floor leaders in the New York legislature while still in their thirties. Charm, boldness, energy, a quick mind and a fluent tongue brought young politicos to the top; unlike careers in business and the professions, politics required neither long years of saving and scrimping nor any exact training.

The swiftness of success was probably important in shaping the psychology of many of these political leaders. Because of family necessity, a youth would become a part-time wage earner—a newsboy or bootblack or messenger—and thereby be forced into a premature maturity. He found himself drawn out of his own neighborhood, which up until then had seemed exciting and satisfying, and into the larger world. Back on his home block, a dime had been a fortune, pot roast was a Sunday treat, and beer was his father's luxury after a ten- or twelve-hour shift. But in the brighter, faster-moving world in which he now entered, the youth encountered men who wore silk shirts, ate steak for lunch, and seemed to possess large sums of money. The ambitious adolescent went through several kinds of experience simultaneously. He became aware that, in material terms, there were ways of life better than that of his own family; he felt the first pangs of the adult desires for freedom, sex, and money; he felt the sharp twinges of class envy and personal hope. For many youths this accelerated coming of age in a materialistic society must have had permanently distorting effects. They could see that ordinary occupations—tending a machine or pounding a beat, pressing pants or making them, selling spools of thread or pecks of potatoes—were not going to bring quick success. For those with the right blend of imagination, audacity, and style, politics was the obvious answer.

A politician with this psychological background was obviously more vulnerable to the temptations to dishonesty in office than one who enjoyed a more secure and orderly transition through adolescence into adulthood. During the psychological crisis which shaped his personal sense of identity, certain material objects and a certain style of life obtained an excessive hold on his imagination. The keener his imagination and the better his mind, then the greater the potentiality for a certain kind of tragedy. The routine wardheeler may graft on a petty scale because the ethical code of his community condones it, but the abler and more ambitious politico grafts not only because it is permissible but also because he is subject to all the pressures and insecurities of the parvenu. Having entered politics to raise himself from the ranks of laborers and hodcarriers, he travels a long way vertically in a larger society which recognizes material success as its chief criterion. To move in the social circles and live in the manner which he desired took more money than the politician could possibly acquire honestly. This was true even though he remained within the orbit of the rich and successful of his own kind. The races at Saratoga, the summer house at the seashore, daughter's grand piano—all these and other tangibles of success cost money. One does not have to join the Four

Hundred to live beyond one's means. An Alfred E. Smith or Joseph Tumulty would have a code of rigid personal honesty or develop a set of social ideals to protect himself against the grafter's temptation, but the more typical politician could not avoid giving the wrong answer to the uneasy question: If it was not to travel with these people and live this way, then why did he ring doorbells, run for alderman, or go into politics in the first place?

Those who entered politics as a means of rapid personal advancement were acting from a motive that neither the theory of the founders of the nation nor the theory of the late nineteenth century middle classes had taken into account or could accommodate. Moreover, Irish machine politics was carried on in an intellectual void. It was the intuitive response to practical necessities and unrelated to any comprehensive theory of politics and society. Until the emergence of Finley Peter Dunne's "Mr. Dooley" in the late 1890's and the realistic investigations of politics by Lincoln Steffens and other muckraking magazine writers early in this century, the code by which the Irish politicians and their mass of supporters lived and governed remained unarticulated and undefended. As a result, the larger society outside the Irish community looked upon the party bosses as grotesque; politics seemed a morality play in which, despite frequent scandals and exposures, vice always triumphed; and the gloomier observers despaired of democracy. But for the Irish, politics was a functioning system of power and not an exercise in moral judgment. While E. L. Godkin and Henry Adams despaired of the American experiment, the Irish took over City Hall.

CHAPTER FIVE

Tammany

IN 1865 a three-cornered contest for mayor took place in New York City. The Republican candidate was named Marshall Roberts; a Citizens' Reform group nominated John Hecker, while the group of Irish politicians running Tammany Hall shrewdly chose as the Democratic candidate John Hoffman, a descendant of one of the old Dutch families. The election quickly developed into a struggle of the older, native elements in the city to hold off the bid for power of the Irish and their old family allies. An Irish-American newspaper printed this appeal to its readers entitled "The Wearin' of the Green":

> "Oh! Hans and Patrick, have yez heard the news that's goin'
>   roun',
> Of secret combinations made, by which they'll put us down?
> How Gunther and Fernandy Wood, John Hecker and his clan,
> Have joined the Black Republicans to wrong the Irish man! . . .
>
> "If Roberts should be mayor, sure, our liberties would cease;
> The foreign-born would never vote—we'd have a black police;
> A more distressful country there never would be seen;
> They'd be hanging us for taxes and the Wearin' of the Green!"[1]

Hoffman won the election, and the Tweed Ring was on its way.

1

William Marcy Tweed was of Scotch-Irish ancestry, and professed no religion, but he had grown up as a two-fisted member of an Irish gang and of the predominantly Irish "Company Six" of the volunteer firemen. His closest political associates were Peter Sweeny and Richard "Slippery Dick" Connolly.

Tweed, at this time, was forty-two. He was a great hulk of a man, standing just under six feet and weighing nearly three hundred pounds; he had a strong, prominent nose and looked out upon the world with bold, unhesitating eyes; a moustache and a short, square beard of reddish-brown hair covered the lower half of his florid face. There was little of the proverbial jolly fat man in his makeup, but he had a rough kindliness and an engaging candor. Half educated though he was, he seemed born to command, and for the next half-dozen years he dominated wiser rivals and craftier subordinates.

Tweed served as state senator, held minor office in the city administration, and was Grand Sachem of Tammany. Connolly became city comptroller, the "bag man" for the ring's graft. Sweeny, a cautious, laconic lawyer, took the less conspicuous post of city chamberlain. He was the "fixer," reconciling conflicting interests and setting up the deals. Mayor Hoffman, after a year in office, was promoted to governor, and his place as mayor and "front man" taken by Oakey Hall.

Hall's style was like that of Jimmy Walker, New York's playboy mayor of the 1920's. He had a polished manner, was an irrepressible maker of puns, a scribbler of bad plays, and a dapper dresser. While addressing a public meeting on the problem of Chinese immigration, Hall said, "If this was a question one would feel disposed to joke about, we could very well say tonight—on this hot night of June, that the coolie question was a very good one to talk about."

A newspaper turned his punning against him: "New York City is now governed by Oakey Hall, Tammany Hall, and Alcohol."

On St. Patrick's Day, 1870, Hall showed his enthusiasm for his Irish supporters. Not only did he wear the traditional shamrock; he reviewed the parade wearing a green tie, green coat, and green kid gloves.[2] He was a very popular man.

The Board of Aldermen was safely controlled by Tweed men. This organ of government had already earned the name of "The Forty Thieves." When a petition was sent to the state legislature urging that public franchises not be given away except after a public auction, one alderman remarked, "Does anybody suppose that this body of statesmen would give anything away without being paid for it?"[3]

Tweed also packed the courts. The phrase grew up, "It is better to know the judge than to know the law." Judges were especially useful to the organization in speeding up the naturalization process. The number of aliens naturalized rose from 7,428 in 1865 to 15,476 in 1867 and to a climax of 41,112 the following year. The Naturalization Committee of Tammany Hall organized this procedure on an efficient basis. It opened headquarters, many of them in saloons, in almost every ward. The alien came in and received a red ticket reading "Please naturalize the bearer."

He signed his name to the necessary papers or it was signed for him, and the signature of a witness was provided. In court, the prospective witnesses "were brought before the judge in batches of 150 and gathered in groups around five or six Bibles. The men in the center of the group would hold up the Bible and the others would touch or stretch out their hands toward it. The clerk then called out the names, at the same time handing the judge face down an application to be initialed on the back by the magistrate without even an examination."[4]

Horace Greeley's *Tribune* commented on the work of the busiest of these judges: "It is rumored that Judge McCunn has issued an order naturallizing all the lower counties of Ireland, beginning at Tipperary and running down to Cork. Judge Barnard will arrange for the northern counties at the next sitting of the chambers."[5]

Tweed and his associates were narrow-minded politicians adept at putting together a machine but they were without any political purpose or program. They lacked the vision to build bridges connecting the island of Manhattan to its neighboring boroughs. The city's wharves deteriorated. Public buildings were left dirty and uncared for. No adequate service was provided to care for the growing metropolis's health, sanitation, water, and sewer needs. The *New York Times* commented irritably that the streets were so dirty Hercules himself would not undertake to clean them without a ten-year Tammany contract. Another observer said the municipal health and sanitation facilities were the worst of any city in Christendom with the possible exception of Naples. The Tweed group simply did not know what to do with the machinery of government once it was theirs except to steal openly whatever was not nailed down. In their six years of power, they looted the city treasury of at least thirty million dollars. Since New York was rich and expanding economically, it could afford to lose the money, but what it could not afford was the kind of incompetent, irresponsible, and short-sighted government Tweed gave it. Inevitably the pressure of the city's needs would have forced out the Tweed cabal. The only question was whether his political enemies would trip him up in his grafting operations before that happened, and break him for his venial rather than his mortal sins. His enemies won. In July, 1871, the *Times* began printing secret facts and figures on the administration's collusive dealings with contractors which it had obtained from a disgruntled employee in the comptroller's office. As each day brought a fresh sensation, Mayor Hall urbanely observed in the newspaper he owned: "These warm, yet occasionally breezy days . . . are an indication that we are likely to have what befell Adam—an early Fall."

"Slippery Dick" Connolly lost his nerve and betrayed his fellow thieves. The ring lost the off-year elections of 1871, and late in the year

Tweed was indicted on 120 counts ranging from grand larceny to conspiracy. Connolly and Sweeny fled to Europe, escaping with several million dollars of their quickly gained fortunes. Hall stood trial but was acquitted. Tweed alone paid the price. He went to prison after lengthy legal maneuvers failed, and died there several years later. Upon entering jail, which as a member of the County Board of Supervisors he had helped to build, he was asked by the clerk his religion. "None" replied the fallen boss. Occupation? Tweed replied, "Statesman."

Several Irish-Americans played prominent roles in smashing the Tweed Ring. Charles O'Conor, the son of an Irish exile who had fled to America with Thomas Addis Emmet after the failure of the revolution of 1798, was the chief prosecutor in the Tweed trials. Then in his mid-sixties, O'Conor had enjoyed a brilliant career as a corporation lawyer and a member of the most conservative, pro-southern wing of the Democratic Party prior to 1861. Matthew O'Rourke, another attorney, also was energetic in untangling the complex web of fraud.[6]

Unfortunately, however, the journal that seized the leadership of the anti-Tweed crusade from the *Times*, which had broken the original story, was *Harper's Weekly*. The Irish hated both the magazine and Thomas Nast, its famous cartoonist, because of their notorious antagonism toward the Irish, the Catholic Church, and the Democratic Party. For example, when the Democrats nominated Francis Kernan, a reputable upstate politician, for governor in 1872, *Harper's* wrote: "Francis Kernan, the Democratic-Liberal candidate for Governor of New York, is of Irish extraction, a zealous Roman Catholic, and a man of extreme views on the subject of his religious creed. During the war he was a Copperhead of Copperheads, and opposed every measure for the suppression of the rebellion. When Republicans are ready to give up the common schools, and surrender everything gained for universal freedom during the last twelve years, they may be ready to vote a Copperhead and a bigot into the gubernatorial chair."[7] Two days before the election, *Harper's* published a Nast cartoon showing Kernan kneeling before the Pope. In the background was a priest holding pamphlets labeled "Down with the public schools." Kernan was pictured as saying to the Pope, "I will do your bidding as you are infallible."

The enthusiasm of *Harper's* for reform was selective. It was a down-the-line supporter of Roscoe Conkling's Republican machine, and when Grant made notorious appointments to the Customs House, it defended them. Reform, as it so often did, came wearing the cloak of extreme partisanship.

The Irish, thrown on the defensive by Tweed's malefactions, found comfort in regarding the whole scandal as a case of the pot calling the kettle black. They preferred to remember the Tweed who had given $50,000 to charity and distributed free coal in winter and free beer in summer. Several hundred workingmen showed up at his house the day of his funeral and filed past the coffin.

Noting this sentiment, the *Nation* observed a week later: "Let us remember that he fell without loss of reputation among the bulk of his supporters. The bulk of the poorer voters of this city today revere his memory, and look on him as the victim of rich men's malice; as, in short, a friend of the needy who applied the public funds, with as little waste as was possible under the circumstances, to the purposes to which they ought to be applied—and that is to the making of work for the working man. The odium heaped on him in the pulpits last Sunday does not exist in the lower stratum of New York society."[8]

To those who lived in the tenement neighborhoods, Big Bill Tweed passed into history shrouded in the frayed glamour of Robin Hood.

2

The years following the collapse of Tweed were years of transition. The new leader of Tammany Hall was a respectable politician, John Kelly, a former congressman and the brother-in-law of Cardinal Mc-Closkey. Kelly, who cherished the sobriquet of "Honest John," had been safely busy inspecting the antiquities of the Holy Land during the turbulent investigations of 1871. It was said of Kelly that he found Tammany a disorganized horde and left it a disciplined army. He purged Tammany of the remnants of the Tweed group, systematized the collection of an annual percentage of the salaries of officeholders, required candidates to finance their campaigns out of a common campaign fund, and began the development of a modern political machine.

Tammany served several functions. For the very poor, it served as a rudimentary social-service organization. For the Irish it was a pressure group that helped them get municipal jobs, building contracts, and various kinds of recognition. From these vantage points, Tammany could be considered a liberal organization since it assisted the most impoverished and was a vehicle for a new group in society. But Tammany also functioned as a conservative institution. During the fifteen years that he led Tammany from the downfall of Tweed in 1871 until his own death in 1886, Kelly aligned the organization squarely with the business community on economic issues. He drew leading businessmen and their attorneys into Tammany, making some of them sachems. Among these millionaires were William Whitney, William R. Grace, Franklin Edson, Augustus Schell, Abram Hewitt, and August Belmont. These figures were not just window dressing; they represented those elements in the business community who decided not to waste their time on the local Republican Party, a feeble appendage of the GOP organization upstate, nor on futile anti-Tammany reform movements, and chose instead to come to terms with the majority Democratic Party.

The 1870's and 1880's were a period of severe social unrest. The depression of 1873 lasted five years, and a less serious recession occurred in the early 1880's. There were mass unemployment, bitter strikes, and a growing mood of radicalism. The Greenback and Anti-Monopoly parties were formed. In San Francisco, Denis Kearney led mobs which threatened to burn the homes of the rich on Nob Hill. In Chicago, working-class distress erupted in sporadic violence culminating in the Haymarket bombings of 1886. In New York the new, agressive, self-confident men of business who associated themselves with Tammany during these years were alert to the dangers. If they did not give active political leadership, might not Tammany Hall be captured by another and an abler Mike Walsh, a popular leader with a radical program? As it was, Tammany under Kelly's leadership gave no support to the nascent trade unions and afforded radicalism no quarter. Moreover, Kelly cooperated in the election of a series of prominent businessmen to the office of mayor. The first of these was William Havemeyer, a sugar processor and one of the city's wealthiest men, who succeeded Oakey Hall.

In 1880 William R. Grace, the shipping magnate, was elected. Grace was the city's first Irish Catholic mayor. Born in Queenstown, Ireland, in 1832, he had run away to sea as a youth, settled in Peru, and made a fortune dealing in supplies for ocean-going vessels. Arriving in New York after the Civil War, he organized his own shipping line but continued an active interest in Peruvian affairs. After Peru's defeat in a war with Chile, he helped refinance the country's national debt and, as his fee, obtained control over immensely valuable silver mines, guano deposits, and other properties.

Grace was an able and efficient mayor. He reformed administrative procedures, forced several street-railway companies to pay back taxes, and achieved a general reduction in the tax rate. After one term, he was succeeded by Franklin Edson, the president of the Produce Exchange and also a member of the ruling business group. In 1884 Grace returned to serve a second two years in City Hall.

Kelly got on badly most of the time with all of these mayors, although they were generally Democrats and members of Tammany. He was caught in the middle between the businessmen and the lesser politicians who were denied what they regarded as their full share of patronage. The Irish masses, sorely pinched by hard times and deprived of even the bread and circuses of the old days under Tweed, were restive. The businessmen were strong backers of Governors Tilden and Cleveland whom the rank and file of voters in the city disliked on account of their stiff-necked, colorless ways. When one disgruntled party orator described Tilden as "a galvanized mummy," an audience at Tammany Hall roared with applause. Dissension reached such a point that the conservatives formed a rival organization known as the County Democracy to uphold their side in the intraparty struggle.

The conflict became critical in 1886. Kelly, who died in the spring of that year, turned the leadership in his last months over to Richard Croker, his trusted assistant. Croker confronted the challenge of Henry George.

George, the author of the "single-tax" plan, made thousands of converts during the hard times of 1885–1886 among German and Irish voters traditionally in Tammany's fold. Organizing the Workingmen's Party, he entered the race for mayor. His popularity with the Irish was enhanced by the tremendous reception he had received the preceding year in Ireland where many regarded the single tax as the solution to Ireland's land problem. The socialist character of his other proposals gave him an appeal also to the Russian Jews who were growing in numbers on the lower East Side.

Patrick Ford, the gifted editor of the *Irish World*, swung his paper to George's support. Ford had been agitating for a decade in behalf of various panaceas such as Greenbackism to cure unemployment and poverty. He had a wide readership among low-income Irish. Father Edward McGlynn, a native New Yorker of Irish parentage and the pastor of a large Catholic church, championed George's program. The issues of social justice were clearly drawn in a political campaign for the first time since the Jacksonian revolution forty years earlier.

Croker decided to meet this threat, not by nominating a liberal or popular candidate of his own, but by leading from strength. Dragging a reluctant Tammany behind him, he negotiated an *ad hoc* alliance with the conservative County Democracy to support the candidacy of Abram Hewitt, a retired millionaire businessman and politician. Croker calculated that the combination of business money and machine vote-getting techniques would overpower George's mass support.

George, a slight, bald man with a fringe of red hair and a sandy beard, made impassioned speeches which won him the title of "the little red rooster."

He had no money and no organized support, but Samuel Gompers, Daniel De Leon, and other labor leaders stumped in his behalf, and throughout the city Henry George clubs sprang up.

Hewitt deplored George's preoccupation with economic issues. "A new issue has been suddenly sprung upon this community," he declared in apparent surprise in his letter accepting the nomination. "An attempt is being made to organize one class of our citizens against all other classes, and to place the government of the city in the hands of men willing to represent the special interests of this class to the exclusion of the just rights of the other classes." He gloomily warned the voters of "the horrors of the French Revolution" which inevitably follow from this kind of politics. George replied tartly that he was not initiating the class war, but rather was leading a revolt of the masses against the classes.

Hewitt explained to the workers that "between capital and labor there never is and never can be any antagonism. They are natural and inseparable allies." The locked-out brewery workers and street-railway strikers who worked twelve- and sixteen-hour days might not otherwise have perceived this fact. George meanwhile was telling a gathering of brass workers that "hereafter in politics the millionaires will be on one side and the workingmen on the other."[9]

On the Saturday night before election, George's followers staged a parade. Through a cold, drenching rain, with no brass bands and few torches, more than 30,000 men and women marched past George on the reviewing stand in Union Square, cheering as they marched. It was a demonstration dwarfing any parade Tammany had ever organized.

On election day, Croker won his gamble. Hewitt polled 90,552 votes to 68,110 for George and 60,435 for Theodore Roosevelt, the Republican candidate. It would have been easy for Tammany to steal the election. George had few election watchers and no friendly police or judges. It is likely that a combination of fraud plus the votes of frightened Republicans who switched from Roosevelt to Hewitt made the difference. In any event, the city was saved from the radicals, and Tammany had done the saving.

Hewitt was in some respects a capable reform mayor, but he had little comprehension of, or sympathy with, the majority of his fellow citizens whom he was trying to govern. He denounced the Knights of Labor and championed the open shop. Identifying the immigrants with the source of the city's problems, he attacked the people instead of the problems. He urged that immigration be restricted, a literacy test imposed, and the time for naturalization extended from five to fourteen years. This was Know-Nothing nativism in a new guise. Defending these "reforms," he declared: "I think the feeling is very general in this country that the time has come when this country of ours, which has cost so much in sacrifices of every kind, should be the country of Americans. It does not belong to the rest of the world. It belongs to our own people."

In his second year in office, he became the first mayor in forty years to refuse to review the St. Patrick's Day parade or to fly the Irish flag at City Hall on that day. When the aldermen passed a bill giving themselves the right by majority vote to order the flag to be flown, he vetoed it. In his message he pointed out that only 16 percent of the city's population was Irish-born but that this group made up 27 percent of the Board of Aldermen, 28 percent of the police force and, he added, 36 percent of the inmates of the jails and charitable institutions. "The Irish furnish more than double the number of inmates which would naturally belong to their percentage of population, while the Germans and the native-born are below the percentage due to their proportion of the total population. . . . The facts above stated, when properly considered, should impose a modest restraint in claiming new privileges."[10]

The Irish community naturally raged with anger and resentment, while the *Nation, Harper's Weekly,* and other conservative publications lauded the mayor for his "courage." Hewitt's prejudices marked him as unfit to serve as mayor of the city which more than any other symbolized the American Dream of hope and opportunity for men from all lands. Moreover, the Irish were then at the peak of their numerical power. The census of 1890 revealed that out of 1,489,000 persons in the city, 190,000 were Irish-born. Another 409,000 were the children of Irish immigrants. When to this total is added the considerable number of third- and fourth-generation Irish, it is likely that the Irish made up a majority of the city. Although Irish immigration continued fairly heavy for the next thirty years, the Irish majority disappeared as Jews, Italians, and other peoples began to come in large numbers.

The Tammany leaders informed Hewitt in 1888 that any possibility of his being reelected was out of the question, but he insisted upon running. Not unexpectedly, he finished a poor third, trailing the Republican candidate, while Hugh Grant, the Democratic candidate, rolled up a record-smashing vote.

3

When Richard Croker emerged on the New York scene as the boss of Tammany in the spring of 1886, he was forty-two years old, the same age Tweed had been when he had come to power twenty-one years earlier. His contemporaries accepted Croker as an Irishman, although he was descended from a well-to-do English family which had settled in Ireland in the late seventeenth century. He was a Protestant by birth, but as a young man entering politics, Croker joined the Catholic Church and remained a regular if not devout communicant for the rest of his life. In a city whose politics were increasingly dominated by Irish Catholics, he was an example of assimilation in reverse.

Croker, at the age of three, was brought to America from County Cork in 1846 by his father, Eyre Coote Croker, a veterinarian by trade. The Irish depression and famine together with the burdens of his own large brood of children had dropped the elder Croker far down the social scale from that status which his ancestors had enjoyed. The family lived for a time in Irish shantytown on land now part of Central Park. Later, the father obtained a relatively well-paid position as veterinarian in the stables of a horsecar line. He moved his family to twenty-eighth Street on the middle East Side just above the Gashouse district. Young Richard Croker grew up in modest and constricted circumstances, but not in the desperate poverty of the slums which lay just to the south of his neighborhood. He attended a one-room school on the site of Madison Square Garden "where, instead of a blackboard, the teacher traced letters with a pointed stick in a box of white sand."[11] His education did not go beyond the grade-school level, and he was always to remain an ignorant and grossly undereducated man. Once after listening to Bourke Cochran and other sophisticates discuss the intricacies of free coinage of silver, Croker wound up the discussion with the comment: "What's wrong with silver money? I'm in favor of all kinds of money—the more, the better." But Croker had native shrewdness and high ambitions.

Like Tweed, he was bred in the violence of street-fighting and the roistering competitions of the volunteer fire companies. A square-set man with a powerful physique and big hammer-like fists, he had cold green eyes and a stubborn jaw that accurately indicated a hard, ruthless mind. He worked as a machinist in the carshops of the New York Central Railroad and became leader of the Fourth Avenue Tunnel Gang. Jimmy O'Brien, a Tammany ward boss, made use of him as a thug and captain of a gang of repeaters on election day. These services earned him a seat on the Board of Aldermen in 1868, when he was barely twenty-five. After the Tweed debacle, O'Brien sought to organize an independent faction to supplant Tammany. He was opposed by "Honest John" Kelly. Croker made a critical decision. He went over to Kelly, the bigger boss. It is the mark of the successful politician that he perceives—in time—what is destined to become the winning side.

In 1874 O'Brien ran for Congress against Hewitt. On election day he met Croker outside a polling place and upbraided him for deserting an old friend and supporting a "rich man." In the midst of it, someone shot one of O'Brien's adherents. As the man lay dying, he named Croker as his murderer.

Croker went to jail and several months later stood trial. Since the evidence was conflicting, the jury divided, 6-6, and Croker went free. During the several months he spent in jail, he made his temper "bridle-wise." As William Allen White later observed, "There is a fine perspective of the world to be had from behind prison bars that gives a man—and Croker got it well—a bird's eye view of the vanities of this life. Jail makes men silent."[12]

Kelly and Hewitt stood behind him in this crisis, providing him with lawyers and money. "Gratitude is the finest word I know," said Croker. "I would much prefer a man to steal from me than to display ingratitude. All there is in life is loyalty to one's family and friends."[13] Croker carried his concept of loyalty to the full length. His two cellmates in the Tombs were John Scannell, who had killed his brother's murderer, and Edward Stokes, who had shot Jim Fisk for the love of Josie Mansfield. Scannell was declared temporarily insane and put in a mental institution for a year. Later, Croker made him one of his hangers-on at Tammany Hall. When Stokes, after serving seven years in state prison, opened the Hoffman House, Croker made the eating place a financial success by giving it his patronage and that of his Tammany subordinates.

Croker, who had formerly been alderman and coroner, was penniless and disgraced after the trial. Kelly kept him alive with minor jobs as a glorified errand boy. Nine years later, he made a comeback by winning his old seat on the Board of Aldermen. Mayor Edson was then prevailed upon to appoint him one of the fire commissioners. Three years later he replaced the dying Kelly as supreme leader. His first triumph was the election of Hewitt over George, and his first defeat was trying to control his new mayor. But with Grant's election in 1888, he was on his way.

Croker's power in the city lasted for only ten out of the next thirteen years, but "he seen his opportunities and he took 'em." He rapidly accumulated a fortune of more than eight million dollars. He became partner in an auctioneering firm which enjoyed a near monopoly of real-estate sales conducted under court order. This gave him an income of $25,000 a year. He was also partner in the bonding company which bonded city employees. Important financiers often gave him blocks of stock free or at a nominal price to ensure his political goodwill. From his inside knowledge of the city's plans, he was able to make investments in real estate and the stock of gas and street-railway companies that were sure to rise in value. Tammany collected protection money from gamblers, saloonkeepers who violated the law, and houses of prostitution. Some of this money reached Croker, but he was primarily interested in the safer and thoroughly legal forms of honest graft: he had learned the lesson of Tweed's experience. When Frank Moss, the chief counsel for the Mazet Investigating Committee in 1899, asked him: "Then you are working for your own pocket, are you not?" Croker shot back: "All the time—the same as you!"

With his new wealth, Croker began to live up to the popular image of success which he shared. He bought an $80,000 house just off Fifth Avenue. He sported a huge diamond stickpin, wore tailor-made clothes, and had his own Pullman car. Indulging his passion for horse racing, he invested $250,000 in a stud farm.[14]

Croker standardized machine politics in its classic form. He crushed the County Democracy and ousted the conservative businessmen from leadership of the Democratic Party. With the exception of Republican Mayor Strong who served for three years in the mid-nineties, Hewitt was the last businessman ever to be elected mayor of New York. Croker relegated the business leaders to the role of bribe dispensers; business paid Tammany well for what it wanted but surrendered any part in the active management of politics. Croker conciliated labor in the only way a political boss in those days comprehended. He exhibited a benevolent neutrality toward the craft unions in the construction trades, and he tried to find jobs for workingmen in the city's public works projects and in private industry. There were plenty of jobs available in the nineties as the city provided sewer and water service to outlying districts, the street railways converted from horsecars to cable cars, and the gas companies expanded their facilities. Economic distress did not disappear, and the panic of 1893 brought a fresh round of unemployment, but the policies of Tammany Hall kept social unrest damped down. The city's essential services, though often wastefully run, were provided at a higher level of efficiency and effectiveness than had prevailed under Tweed.

The attack on the seemingly invulnerable Tammany system in the nineties came from a new quarter and on a new front. Croker ran a wide-open town: liquor, prostitutes, and gambling were available to all comers and operated under police protection. The Protestant clergy led by Dr. Charles Parkhurst, pastor of the Madison Square Presbyterian Church, began an anti-vice crusade.

Parkhurst prepared himself for his crusade by hiring Charles Gardner, a private detective, to take him in disguise on a tour of the most notorious dives and brothels. Gardner later wrote an account of this trip entitled, *The Doctor and the Devil: Or Midnight Adventures of Doctor Parkhurst.*

In one saloon, Parkhurst had to drink a glass of cheap whiskey to avoid arousing suspicion. "He acted," Gardner wrote, "as if he had swallowed a whole political parade—torchlights and all."

The high spot of their tour came during their visit to a brothel operated by a lady named Hattie Adams. The house presented for their visitors a unique "dance of nature" consisting of five naked girls dancing the can-can to a lively piano accompaniment. Then came a game of leapfrog in which Gardner was the frog and the girls jumped over him.

"The Doctor sat in a corner with an unmoved face through it all," Gardner wrote, "watching us and slowly sipping a glass of beer. Hattie Adams was quite anxious to find out who Dr. Parkhurst was. I told her he was 'from the West' and was 'a gay boy.' Then Hattie tried to pull Dr. Parkhurst's whiskers, but the Doctor straightened up with such an air of dignity that she did not attempt any further familiarities."[15]

New Yorkers naturally found the minister's factual sermons and Gardner's pamphlet highly titillating reading. For a time, Dr. Parkhurst achieved results. A reform administration was elected in 1894 and held office for three years. Easily its most useful accomplishment was Colonel George Waring's reorganization of the Street Department. Waring put the street cleaners in white uniforms so that any citizen could quickly spot them if they were loafing on the job, and for a few years New York's streets were actually kept clean. In the field of vice control, however, the reform administration proved a fiasco. Theodore Roosevelt as one of the three police commissioners tried to enforce a state law permitting only hotels to sell liquor on Sundays. This seemed to the majority of citizens to be class legislation. Only the well-to-do could afford to patronize hotels, but Sunday was the only day of leisure for the Irish and German workingmen who wanted to spend an afternoon drinking beer at the corner saloon. To evade the law, most saloon-keepers rented a few rooms above the barroom and classed themselves as hotels. Since the rooms were rented with no questions asked, the net effect was to transform the saloons into centers of prostitution.

The work of Mayor Strong's reform administration was unpopular and ineffectual, as that kind of reform always was, since it tried to repress the manifestations of social conditions without remedying the roots of the problem—the slum housing, low wages, unemployment, and economic exploitation. Not for another forty years, until Fiorello La Guardia became mayor, did the city produce a leader interested in economic as well as political reform. Significantly, La Guardia was the only reform mayor ever reelected.

The majority of voters naturally disliked an administration that meddled in their public pleasures and left untouched their private burdens. They distrusted the self-righteous business and financial men who sponsored this kind of reform. To most people, it seemed as if the business community liked "reform" because it could go ahead and do for nothing what it at least had to pay Tammany for the privilege of doing. The inimitable Mr. Dooley summed up the attitude of the Irish community succinctly:

"This here wave iv rayform, Jawn," Mr. Dooley explained to his friend Mr. McKenna, "mind ye, that's sweepin' over th' counthry, mind ye, now, Jawn, is raisin' th' divvle, I see be the pa-apers. I've seen waves iv rayform before now, Jawn. Whin th' people iv this counthry gets wurruked up, there's no stoppin' thim. They'll not dhraw breath until ivery man that tuk a dollar iv a bribe is sint down th' r-road. Thim that takes two dollars goes on th' comity iv the wave iv rayform. . . ."[16]

During these three years Croker spent most of his time abroad. He visited the watering places of Germany to restore his health, although the nature of his ailment, other than his political indisposition, was not clear, and raced horses in England. On his English estate, he enjoyed feeding the pigs, to each of whom he gave the name of a New York politician.

In 1897 he returned to resume control. The state legislature had lengthened Mayor Strong's term from two to three years as part of the plan by which Brooklyn, Queens, and Staten Island were added to Manhattan and the Bronx to form Greater New York. It was hoped that Republican strength in the three new boroughs would tip the city permanently into Republican control. This amalgamation was a statesmanlike decision which other metropolitan communities might well have emulated, but it failed in its political purpose.

The Tammany candidate for district attorney coined the slogan "To Hell with Reform!" On the vaudeville stage, singers were giving forth with the song, "I Want What I Want When I Want It!" On election day the Tammany candidate for mayor swept to victory. Celebrating thousands packed the streets, the bars stayed open all night, and New Yorkers enjoyed perhaps the most riotous election night in history. As a character in Alfred Henry Lewis's novel *The Boss* explained it, the reformers had made the cardinal mistake: "They got between the people and its beer!"[17]

Three Republican-sponsored state investigations raked Tammany's administrations during the nineties, but at the end of the decade Croker's power seemed unshaken. Then in April, 1900, the Mazet Committee, on the eve of its going out of existence, uncovered the great "Ice Trust" scandal. Charles Morse, a financial speculator of doubtful reputation, had merged several independent ice concerns to form the American Ice Company. To protect his monopoly, the city officials gave the new firm the exclusive privilege of unloading ice on the municipal docks. Before this arrangement went through, Morse distributed large blocks of stock in the company to leading politicians, including Mayor Robert Van Wyck, Croker, Hugh McLaughlin, the Brooklyn boss, the four dock commissioners, and many others.

The committee's disclosures blocked the granting of exclusive privileges to American Ice and broke the Ice Trust soon after it was launched. This was the kind of scandal that hit home to the voters. It was self-evident that the trust would have reaped huge profits by raising its prices as high as the traffic would bear. Ice was a necessity of life, and every family would have paid a tithe to the firm in which the leading politicians were secret partners.

The following year, Seth Low led a reform coalition to victory using the ice scandal as one of his major issues.

Low's triumph was the signal for Croker's retirement. He gave up the leadership and withdrew voluntarily to Ireland. His stables were successful, and in 1907 his horse *Orby* won the Derby. On April 29, 1922, he died in bed on his Irish estate at the age of seventy-nine, leaving a fortune of five million dollars to the young lady who was his third wife.

4

After a brief interregnum, Charles F. Murphy succeeded to the leadership of Tammany Hall. Murphy, a native of the Gashouse district on the East Side, had been a noted baseball player. He owned several saloons, entered politics, and in 1895 became the leader of his district. He was one of the dock commissioners involved in the Ice Trust scandal. While holding that office, he organized a trucking and contracting company that developed a lucrative business. By the time he became undisputed leader in 1903, he was already a millionaire. Tweed and Croker, though usually silent men, were not averse occasionally to expressing in rough, colloquial speech their views on government and society. Murphy's taciturnity made those gentlemen seem positively garrulous. He is best remembered for his two euphemistic epigrams: When asked the name of his candidate, he always said, "The convention will decide" (which meant "I haven't made up my mind yet"). When asked why his ticket lost, he replied, "We didn't get enough votes" (which usually meant "I was double-crossed but they'll regret it").

Murphy was as thoroughly conservative in his outlook as Croker had been, but he was more flexible and less arrogant. He was indifferent or opposed to labor laws, women's suffrage, tenement-house legislation, and other progressive measures. But if he did not swim with the current neither did he try to dam it up. The result was that during the twenty years of his leadership, Tammany drifted a long way from the old moorings and never realized it had moved at all.

For much of those two decades, Murphy was preoccupied in a duel for supremacy with William Randolph Hearst. The wealthy young publisher seemed about to become for several years early in this century the leader of that fusion between good government and economic reform which had beckoned invitingly on the horizon for so long but had always proved impossible of achievement.

In 1902 Hearst accepted the Tammany nomination to a seat in Congress. He rarely attended the sessions of the House but he showed up long enough to introduce a comprehensive body of liberal bills, including an eight-hour day for employees in firms working on government contracts, direct election of senators, tougher antitrust legislation, and government ownership of telegraph and cable lines. In 1904 he received two hundred votes in a bid for the Democratic nomination for President, with Clarence Darrow among those making seconding speeches.

Later that year, Hearst, Samuel Seabury, and other young Democratic liberals founded the Municipal Ownership League. Running for mayor on the League's ticket in 1905, Hearst was elected, but Tammany counted him out by throwing boxes of ballots into the East River. Mayor George B. McClellan was officially declared the winner by 3,600 votes.

Hearst aroused great popular enthusiasm by his demand for municipal ownership and operation of the gas, ice, and street-railway companies. The *Journal*, his paper, had a big Irish readership. As Henry George had done before him, Hearst was focusing the resentments and class hatreds of the poor on a political objective. He was drawing large numbers of voters from Tammany among the three largest immigrant groups—the Irish, the Germans, and the Russian Jews.

In 1906 Murphy felt it expedient to reach an accommodation. He came to terms with Hearst and steamrollered his nomination for governor through the Democratic state convention. This deal with Murphy, whom he had been attacking savagely for a half-dozen years as a grafter and a friend of the trusts, undermined Hearst's prestige. As one wit observed of the ambitious and unscrupulous young publisher:

> "So I lashed him and I thrashed him in my hot
> reforming zeal,
> Then I clasped him to my bosom in a most
> artistic deal."

When Charles Evans Hughes defeated him by nearly 60,000 votes, Hearst was in the worst of political positions—that of the man who has sacrificed principle for office and then failed to get the office.[18]

Hearst drifted away from his liaison with Murphy. In 1909 he ran as an independent for mayor in a losing race with William Jay Gaynor, the organization candidate. Gaynor, who had once been friendly with Hearst, now denounced him as a man "whose face almost makes me puke."

Gaynor was perhaps the most extraordinary surprise package Tammany ever selected for itself in the grab bag of candidates. He was an outspoken Brooklyn judge, about sixty years old, when Murphy felt obliged for tactical reasons to nominate a fairly respectable candidate. It was a calculated risk for more reasons than one. Gaynor, born the son of an upstate Irish immigrant farmer, always denied his Irish ancestry because he had a low opinion of the American Irish. He even changed his middle name of James to the more stylish Jay. He studied for five years in a Christian Brothers school to become a member of that Catholic order. Then he changed his mind, withdrew from the order, and subsequently married, divorced, and remarried. He drifted away from the Catholic Church and became nominally a High Church Episcopalian. These would seem to be rather formidable obstacles for a candidate in New York City, but except for one priest who spoke out against him, the clergy kept quiet during the campaign. It has been suggested that the Church probably felt that any candidate endorsed by Murphy and Tammany could not be fundamentally unsound as far as the interests of Catholicism were concerned. Or it may simply have been that the rank-and-file Irish Catholic voters were less troubled by such matters as divorce and religious apostasy than was commonly thought.

Gaynor displayed in City Hall a generous disdain for professional politicians, reforming clergymen, inquiring reporters, suffragettes, and many other disturbers of the peace. The National Publicity Bureau asked him for a statement in reply to the question "What would you say to the readers of 3,000 newspapers?" Gaynor replied, "I would say to them to be very careful about believing all they see in the newspapers."

When a reporter followed him to his weekend farm on Long Island and presented his press card for an interview, the mayor handed it back to him: "Never heard of you. I suggest you get the hell off my front porch."

He was heard to refer to the politicians in the state legislature in Albany as "gabby, cagey little fellows who make you shiver when they come near you." Of Dr. Parkhurst, who was still crusading against vice, Gaynor said he was full of "rancor and uncharity," a man "who thinks he is pious when he is only bilious." When Rabbi Stephen S. Wise criticized him, Gaynor unhesitatingly termed him "a rhetorician with a proverbially crooked mouth."

He delighted in telling audiences opinions he knew they disagreed with, and, somewhat like Adlai Stevenson forty years later, he got away with it because persons found such independence attractive. Gaynor, addressing the pro-suffragette State Federation of Women's Clubs, told them, "We generally aspire to the thing we are least fitted for." Speaking to the Advertising Men's League, he quoted Shakespeare: " 'Oh, what a goodly outside falsehood hath.' I think very likely that that is the motto that you people repeat in your own minds very often, especially when you are composing advertising."

To the American Bankers Association, he managed to criticize two professions almost simultaneously. To the bankers he said, "Your reputation was bad even before the time of the elder Cato." Then he turned in an aside to the newspaper reporters taking notes, "Cato, Cato, I said. Did you ever hear of him before?"

"Much of the Mayor's cantankerousness," his biographer has observed, "came from the fact that he had the fatal flaw of the Irishman, a reckless tongue inflamed by an unbridled temper."[19] Gaynor also had a keen sense of humor and of the ridiculous. The day after he was elected, he observed, "Now that the election is over nobody has any immediate reason for lying." He very soon ignored Murphy and the organization in making appointments. "What can we do for Mr. Murphy?" one worried friend inquired. Gaynor pondered a moment and then said, "Suppose we give him a few kind words."

Gaynor was a colorful and honest mayor but, understandably enough, he acquired a disproportionate share of personal enemies. Tammany denied him renomination in 1913, and he died while running for reelection as an independent.

The final resolution of the struggle of Hearst and Murphy and the positive shaping of the Democratic Party in that period awaited the emergence of younger leaders whose experience was more in the main stream of the Irish community. The most important of these leaders was Alfred E. Smith.

CHAPTER SIX

The Gold Coast Irish

THE FIFTY YEARS from the end of the Civil War to the first decade of the twentieth century were the great period of America's industrial expansion. This was the era of the industrial and financial barons, Rockefeller, Morgan, Carnegie, Frick, and Vanderbilt. Socially, it was the Gilded Age when the new millionaries and their wives flaunted their wealth and invaded high society. The Irish were not notably creative or distinctive in business. The Industrial Revolution passed by Ireland, and the Irish did not bring to this country any business tradition. A few such as Thomas Fortune Ryan and Nicholas Brady made great fortunes in public utilities; William R. Grace built his unique empire in shipping and South American mining, and Patrick Cudahy was a major figure in the meatpacking industry. But most affluent Irish climbed slowly to prosperity through the construction industry, food wholesaling, real estate, and transportation. In these fields, the Irish were pupils of the native businessmen, learning their techniques, adopting their habits, accepting their values. For this reason, there never has been a stereotype of an Irish businessman. Evolving slowly over a long period, he did not differ significantly from other businessmen. His progress was, as financial writers were fond of describing Ryan, "noiseless."

Yet if the Irish were not among the movers and shakers of America's industrial expansion, a small group of them and their wives did participate spectacularly in the Gilded Age. These were the Irish who went to the Far West. At a time when hundreds of thousands of Irish were packed in the slums of Boston's North End and New York's East Side and were looked down upon as laborers and kitchen help, other Irish of identical background were amassing millions from the Comstock Lode and the Montana copper mines, running the governments of Nevada and California, and setting the social tone of San Francisco's Nob Hill. The Irish who went to California proved the adage, "The longest way round is the shortest way home."

1

The Irish were among the first settlers in the San Francisco Bay area. In 1828, when California was still part of Mexico, an Irishman (with a Spanish overlay) named Don Timoteo Murphy acquired a land grant near San Rafael, raised cattle, and maintained a kennel of Irish greyhounds and beagles. Soon afterward, John Read, another Irish immigrant, moved into the area, took a Spanish wife, and began farming.[1]

When the great influx began after the gold strike of 1848, the Irish were active and prominent. No important fortunes were made by Irishmen in the goldfields, but in the development of San Francisco they were in the forefront. Peter Donahue, recently arrived from Ireland, foresaw the need for a gas lighting system. He organized a company, imported pipe from the East and coal from Wales, and constructed San Francisco's streetlights. When the lights were turned on for the first time, the city staged a civic celebration. Donahue also established the city's first iron foundry, owned a steamboat line, and organized the San Jose Railroad. He built a mansion in downtown San Francisco and provided his wife with the perfect Cinderella gift: a coach made entirely of glass. At his death he left an estate of $4,000,000.[2]

Mrs. Donahue's brother and sister also had spectacular successes. Her sister Eleanor married Edward Martin, the founder of San Francisco's Hibernia Bank. As her husband grew in wealth, Eleanor Martin launched her social career, and for forty years, down to the 1890's, she reigned as the city's most influential hostess. Her brother was John G. Downey, governor of California during the Civil War. Arriving in California from County Roscommon in 1849 with only $10 in his pocket, he settled in the straggling town of Los Angeles. Knowing a little about pharmacy, he opened the first drugstore. He prospered, entered politics, and thirteen years after he arrived he was the governor of the state.[3]

Another successful Irish businessman was James Phelan who emigrated from Ireland as a youth, worked as a grocery clerk in New York, shipped to San Francisco on the first news of the gold strike, opened a saloon, branched into real estate, and ultimately founded his own bank. By 1870 Phelan was one of the city's ten richest men.

From time to time, the wealthy San Francisco Irish made forays into New York society. One of their number was among the first of the newly rich in the post–Civil War period to marry a titled European. In December, 1883, Mary Ellen Donahue, the daughter of Peter and Anna Downey Donahue, married Baron Henry von Schroeder in a large New

York wedding. Von Schroeder was a former Prussian army officer decorated by von Moltke with the Iron Cross for his services in the Franco-Prussian War. It was an unusual match as titled marriages went: it lasted.

Social satirists could not resist poking fun at the wealthy Irish whose mansions lined Nob Hill. A writer in the *Argonaut*, a local weekly, wrote in the 1870's: "We have a millionaire among us! . . . His name is MacDooligan. . . . The present partner of the joys and sorrows of MacDooligan was once the beautiful Bridget MacShinnegan. . . . The MacShinnegan coat of arms is a spalpeen rampant on a field of gold. . . . The family is going to Paris while father remains to superintend the erection of a palatial mansion on Nob Hill. . . . Louis Quatorze? Renaissance? Their manner is now *distingué*, their society *recherché*, their manner *débonnaire*, their actions breathe a *savoir faire*."[4]

To be satirized in the press is the ultimate fate of the rich in America. The San Francisco Irish had arrived.

2

David Broderick did not find his prospects encouraging in New York in 1848. Born in Kilkenny twenty-eight years before, he had been brought by his father to the United States as a child. His father was an accomplished stonecutter who worked on the renovation of the Capitol in Washington and other large projects. Broderick, disliking his father's trade, tried other routes to success; he worked in a saloon, ran with a fire company, and dabbled in politics. He was ambitious and talented, but he did not succeed. On the first news of the gold rush, he moved to California. There he quickly read law, was elected to the state senate, and became a leading figure in the Democratic Party.

Hubert Howe Bancroft, writing his reminiscences sixty years later, recalled Broderick: "Elected to the State senate, he became speaker and presided with wisdom and decorum. Strong in body and mind, instinctively honest and direct in all his moods, he naturally was assertive and impatient under restraint, which made him enemies as well as friends."

Elected to the United States Senate, Broderick became an outspoken opponent of the extension of slavery and of the Buchanan administration's fumbling policies in "Bleeding Kansas." When he sought reelection in 1859, the administration and the sizable bloc of pro-southern voters in California tried to purge him.

During the campaign, one of the pro-southern "fire-eaters" challenged him to a duel. Broderick "had fought duels before in a big boyish way, not wishing to kill or to be killed. Terry [his opponent] played with blood, not with boys. Nor had the time arrived when a California politician could decline a duel and retain his influence." Broderick fired his pistol into the ground. Terry shot him an inch below the heart.

Broderick, dying, said, "They killed me because I was opposed to the extension of slavery and a corrupt administration."[5]

3

Tom Maguire arrived in San Francisco in the first wave of Forty-Niners. In New York he had driven a hack and tended bar in a saloon near City Hall. In San Francisco he resumed the latter trade on a more impressive scale, opening the Parker House, the city's most lavishly appointed saloon and gambling house. Maguire, however, had larger ambitions, and he loved the stage. In the fall of 1850, he transformed the top floor of the Parker House into the Jenny Lind Theater and imported the first actors from the East to appear in California.

When fire the next year destroyed the theater, Maguire constructed a new and larger Jenny Lind Theater, seating two thousand patrons. This was by far the biggest theater on the West Coast—too big, it developed, for Maguire to operate successfully. Running into financial difficulties, he imperturbably sold the building to the city; it became the San Francisco City Hall. He subsequently erected the smaller San Francisco Theater, established a resident stock company, engaged the younger Junius Brutus Booth from New York to be stage manager, and had a long and successful career as the nation's foremost theatrical impressario outside New York. Edwin Booth, later to become the greatest tragedian of his generation, was for a time a member of Maguire's resident company. Not limiting himself in those early years to Shakespearean roles, he scored his first notable success as the hero of a melodrama about volunteer firemen. Booth's climactic lines were: "Mother, let me go! The fire bells! . . . What is my death if I save the city? . . . A San Francisco fire boy is the noblest work of God!" Naturally, this line never failed to bring down the house.

All the great actors in the decades from 1850 to 1880 made tours of California, often finding larger audiences and higher salaries than they did back in New York. When Edwin Forrest opened at the Opera House in *Richelieu* on May 14, 1886, Maguire found the demand for tickets so overwhelming, he auctioned them off at prices as high as $500.

Tall, jovial, white-haired, and with a sweeping white moustache, Maguire was a popular figure in San Francisco and in the theatrical profession throughout the nation. On New Year's Day, 1870, the city presented him with a $1,000 silver service decorated with medallions representing Adah Menken, Edwin Forrest, Charles Kean, and other stars he had brought to San Francisco.

Maguire also managed lecture tours. He once wired Artemus Ward, "What will you take for twenty nights in California?"

Ward wired back, "Brandy and water."[6]

4

In 1859 gold was discovered in the Sierras, and miners from California arrived in western Nevada. A small mining camp quickly sprang up. Six months later, two Irish miners, while working their claims, were mystified by "heavy black stuff," mixed with the gold. The "black stuff," they learned, was silver; the ore was fabulously rich in both gold and silver. Peter O'Riley and Patrick McLaughlin had discovered the Comstock Lode.

By the spring of 1860, the rush to the new discovery was on and Virginia City had been born. The Comstock Lode took its name from Henry "Old Pancake" Comstock, a veteran prospector who was one of the first arrivals on the scene and busily claimed everything in sight.

Virginia City boomed throughout the Civil War. Native Yankees and Irish moving in from California were the biggest contingents, but Welsh, Cornish, Chinese, and wanderers from half of the globe were present in the thriving town. One of the first to arrive was Old John Kelly. "Kelly the Fiddler" had "scraped the catgut" for the first dance in San Francisco in 1849. He could not read music, but for a round of drinks or a silver nugget he could not only play but make improvisations on the tunes the miners loved best.

Another familiar figure was "Metaliferous" Murphy, a self-styled ore expert. When a sample of ore was presented to him, he would invariably cock his head and say, in his rich brogue, "This specimen is highly metaliferous." Unfortunately, he would usually add that the metals in this "metaliferous" sample were antimony, iron pyrite, or some other nonprecious substance. Murphy also became famous for a statement that reached the ultimate in optimistic prophecy. Of a Virginia City mine, he declared, "With all Niagara for water power and all hell for a dump, that mine would niver be worked out in tin thousand years!"[7]

Irish also showed up from the East to handle their traditional assignment: governing other Americans. Of one such political figure, Mark Twain wrote in *Roughing It:* "I took quarters in the 'ranch' of a worthy French lady by the name of Bridget O'Flannigan, a campfollower of his Excellency the Governor. She had known him in his prosperity as commander-in-chief of the Metropolitan Police of New York, and she would not desert him in his adversity as Governor of Nevada."

Among the earliest settlers in Nevada were Mormons from Utah with whom the miners did not get on well. Twain reported what seemed to be an exception:

"The hired girl of one of the American families was Irish and a Catholic; yet it was noted with surprise that she was the only person outside of the Mormon rite who could get favors from the Mormons. She asked kindnesses of them often and always got them. It was a mystery, to everybody. But one day as she was passing out at the door, a large bowieknife dropped from under her apron, and when her mistress asked for an explanation, she observed that she was going out to 'borry a washtub from the Mormons!' "[8]

Fortunes were quickly made and lost in Virginia City. In that free-and-easy, democratic society where every mineowner was called "Colonel" and every man of book-learning "Judge," a man could readily gauge his relative standing. In his old age, Patrick Quinn, an impoverished prospector who had once struck it rich as a mineowner and later slowly lost his fortune, recalled his rise and fall by listing the names by which he had been called during his career.[9] They were:

> Quinn
> Pat Quinn
> C. Patrick Quinn
> Col. Cornelius Patrick Quinn
> Col. C. P. Quinn
> Patrick Quinn
> Pat Quinn
> Old Quinn

The discoverers of the Comstock Lode were among those who experienced this roller-coaster ride. Peter O'Riley sold his holdings, potentially worth millions, for $50,000, built the city's first stone hotel, speculated in mining stocks, and lost everything. He died in an insane asylum. McLaughlin sold out for an equally small sum, squandered his money, and wound up a mining-camp cook.

Despite the optimistic predictions of "Metaliferous" Murphy and others, Virginia City's mining fortunes began to ebb after the Civil War.

Then in 1873, the biggest strike of all was made. John Mackay and James Fair discovered a rich gold-and-silver mine which was quickly christened the "Bonanza." The ore in this single mining operation proved to be worth $190,000,000.

John Mackay had been born in poverty in Dublin in 1831. At fifteen, he emigrated to New York and worked as a shipyard apprentice. He moved to California two years later, worked in a saloon, and then became a prospector. He began in Virginia City as a manual laborer, but he became a skilled miner and rose to superintendent. In 1869 he entered a partnership with James Graham Fair, a Scotch-Irish emigrant from Ireland. They put together several small mining properties and worked for three years to discover a rich vein that rumor said existed in the locality. To gain further capital, they brought in as partners James M. Walker, a wealthy Virginian, and James Flood and William O'Brien, two Irishmen from New York who were proprietors of a well-known saloon on the San Francisco waterfront. Consolidated Virginia, their new firm, extended its operations. In March, 1873, the partners found the "Bonanza" they had been seeking. They became millionaires overnight. Walker decided he was rich enough, sold his one-fifth to Mackay, and returned to Virginia. Mackay thereby became the most important member of the partnership, and soon the city's leading citizen. Three times he turned down nominations for the United States Senate. For a generation in Nevada, his name was synonymous with high quality and good luck in the expression "It's a John Mackay."[10]

Affable "Billy" O'Brien died less than five years after he and his partners hit the Bonanza. The three remaining members followed diverse careers in later years. Fair took a seat in the Senate where he impressed colleagues more by his awesome display of wealth than by his interest in legislation. His wife and daughters spearheaded the invasion of western millionaries who crashed eastern society in the 1880's and 1890's. His daughter Tessie married Herman Oelrichs, and his daughter Birdie married William K. Vanderbilt, and both were for many years society leaders in Newport and on Park Avenue. Fair died in 1894.

James Flood lived until his death in 1888 in San Francisco. He built the last of the great mansions on Nob Hill. His new home had a good view of the waterfront where less than ten years before he and Billy O'Brien had run the Auction Lunch Room, Jim serving the drinks and Billy mixing the fish chowder.

Mackay, who was the firm's managing partner in Virginia City for some fifteen years after the discovery of the "Bonanza," eventually moved to New York where he invested his mining profits in telegraph lines and a transatlantic cable company. His wife attempted to conquer the New York social world, but she did not find it easy. She had been born in Canada, a barber's daughter, and had been stranded in Virginia City by the death of her first husband. The miners took a collection to send her and her infant daughter home to Canada. Mackay, approached to contribute, asked to meet the lady, and soon solved her problems by marrying her. An exaggerated tale of these early difficulties preceded her to New York where dowagers gossiped about her as "the former washer-woman." Mrs. Mackay moved to Paris where she hired Mrs. Robert Hooper, a diplomat's wife, as social adviser. After a season in Paris, she moved to London, leased a house near Buckingham Palace, and within a few months was receiving the Prince of Wales, the future King Edward VII, at her parties. She climaxed this triumphant invasion of Europe by marrying her daughter (Mackay's stepdaughter) to the Prince of Colonna, a member of a Roman aristocratic family.

Mackay's son, Clarence Hungerford Mackay, was for many years a leading social figure in New York City and on Long Island. He fully achieved the social acceptance that had been denied his mother, but he is best remembered as the father-in-law of a one-time singing waiter named Irving Berlin.

5

Margaret Tobin had started her career as a housemaid. In 1912 when she went aboard the *Titanic* for its maiden voyage to the United States, she could look back on an extraordinary past. She was the wife of John J. "Leadville Johnny" Brown who, starting from poverty, had become one of Colorado's richest mineowners. Denver society had re-fused to accept her back in the 1890's. She was, said the women whose families had made their money a generation or two ahead of the Browns, "vulgar" and "*nouveau riche*." She had left Denver behind her, traveled in Europe, learned to converse in five languages, entertained and been entertained by Continental society, and was now returning on one of her periodic trips to Denver where she was, if not accepted, accorded grudg-ing respect. It took a score of trunks and other pieces of baggage to carry her wardrobe; she wore a $60,000 chinchilla coat.

Five nights later, the *Titanic* struck an iceberg and went down. Margaret Brown escaped aboard Lifeboat Number 6. Legend said she kept the other passengers rowing by brandishing a Colt .45, but the legend was exaggerated. She dominated her companions only by the force of her will. She rowed until her hands bled; she told jokes; she sang snatches of grand opera; she beat back fear by a resolute show of confidence.

When reporters in New York later asked her for details of her performance, "Lady Margaret," as her shipmates had christened her, replied, "You can't wear the *Social Register* for waterwings."

She subsequently dismissed the affair as "typical Brown luck."

"I'm unsinkable," she remarked.

And so she passed into history as "the Unsinkable Mrs. Brown."[11]

CHAPTER SEVEN
Idols of the Crowd

I

MOSTLY LABORERS and small tradesmen, the American Irish in the last decades of the nineteenth cenury had a hard lot. They worked, suffered, prayed, got drunk, sent money home to Ireland, and reared large families. They were turbulent, combative, and proud. This was largely a raw, new people who had not yet had time to produce artists and writers to articulate their experiences and transmute them into literature. But the Irish of these years afford a glimpse of the lives they led by the heroes they cheered, and the strikingly individual characters they produced. What follows is an account of two of these heroes, one from the streets of Boston and the other from the frontiers of Texas.

1

John Lawrence Sullivan found prizefighting a mean, ill-assorted pastime, half rough-and-tumble wrestling, half eye-gouging, hip-and-knee street fighting, and he left it a modern sport. He began as an Irish youth in a Boston tenement house and he ended as an American legend.

He was not an unusually big man; at nineteen, he stood five feet ten and one-half inches tall and weighed one hundred and ninety pounds. His power was in his broad shoulders, long arms, and large, strong hands; those hands which, a battered opponent once said, "have the kick of a mule in them." Mike, his father, a little gamecock of a man standing only five feet three inches and weighing but a hundred and thirty pounds, was the son of the champion shillelagh fighter of Ireland in the days before the famine and in his turn became, despite his size, the champion hod-carrier in the Boston construction business. Mike took no nonsense from anyone, least of all his son.

"You think you're strong, don't you?" he would say. "Well, Dad, I'm champion of the world," John would reply. "Ah, champion of the world," Mike would snort, "Why, there's men in old Ireland that could break you in two with one slap of their hand."

John's mother, who towered over her husband, was a woman of peaceable ambitions. She wanted her boy to become a priest. After public schooling, he went to study with the Jesuits at Boston College, but the life of learning and prayer was not for him. He quit to become a plumber's apprentice, a job he lost when he argued with the boss and broke his jaw.

One night in 1877, he attended a boxing exhibition at the Dudley Street Opera House. Tom Scannel, a well-known local fighter, swaggered to the front of the platform and announced he would take on anyone in the house and finish him off in three rounds or less. Sullivan, seated in the first row, was on his feet in an instant. Off came his collar, tie, and coat; he rolled up his sleeves and mounted the stage. Scannel, "wearing green tights and a confident smile," sparred for a moment and then landed a hard left. Sullivan, without preliminaries, rushed at his man, swinging furiously. It was all over in a minute or two. A crashing right to the jaw sent Scannel flying off the stage into the orchestra pit, senseless.

The brawny nineteen-year-old strode to the edge of the platform, looked down in contempt at Scannel, glared at the audience, and in a throaty, bass voice called out: "My name's John L. Sullivan, and I can lick any sonofabitch alive! If any of 'em here doubts it, come on!"

Nobody did.

"My name's John L. Sullivan and I can lick . . ." It was a boast that was to echo in the next fifteen years through a thousand barrooms and from stage platforms and prize rings from Boston to Australia to the British Isles and back again, and to continue long after Sullivan had been bested by a younger man, as long as men gathered to recall the exploits of the "Boston Strong Boy." It was a proud boast, a defiance hurled in the teeth of the world, a credo of one man's confidence in himself, but it was more than a personal manifesto, it was the credo of the fighting Irish. They had been driven from a beggared homeland. They started in America with nothing but their memories and their own two hands but, by God, they would succeed. They would put their fist in the face of life and knock it down.

"I believe in having a little fight in most everything except funerals," John L. liked to say. "Anything that ain't got some fight in it is like a funeral, and I don't like funerals. Whether it's war, sport, business, or marbles, you've got to do more or less fighting or you're simply talking in your sleep. And if you're satisfied to talk in your sleep all your life, you might as well call in the undertaker now and save time."

But what of the other fellow? John L. had a word for him, too. "The bigger they are, the harder they fall," he was fond of saying.

Sullivan made rapid progress after that challenging night in the Opera House. He easily whipped Dan Dwyer, the recognized champion of Massachusetts. He defeated Joe Goss, a once great English champion and one of the several claimants to the world title. He knocked out several lesser boxers.

He came under the management of William Muldoon, who had a genius for publicity and was an early exponent of ballyhoo methods that Tex Rickard and Mike Jacobs would make familiar a half-century later. He arranged a nationwide tour for his young protégé. In each city he announced Sullivan would take on all comers. The man who could last four rounds in the ring with him was guaranteed fifty dollars. This was an entirely new touch in prizefight promotion. In a year's tour, Muldoon made Sullivan's name known to every sports fan in the country.

In one match, his opponent was a local blacksmith who was seven feet tall and weighed over three hundred pounds. Sullivan's favorite punch, a right cross to the jaw, was not easy to land on an opponent towering more than a foot over him. Sullivan solved the problem by hammering the blacksmith's huge stomach until he involuntarily doubled up, thus bringing his jaw into range. He repeated this several times until the dazed, weakened giant was reduced to lumbering toward him blindly. Sullivan, as he later said, then just stuck his fists straight out "and the fellow ran into them and knocked himself out." Sullivan called his opponent's awestricken son from the audience and said, "Here, bub, take this fifty dollars and run with it to your Ma. Your Daddy tried hard to earn it."

Sullivan's barnstorming was designed to lure Paddy Ryan, the "Troy Terror" and reigning champion, into a title match. The bout finally came off in Mississippi on February 7, 1882. By then, Sullivan's unbroken string of triumphs and Muldoon's publicity had raised national excitement to a high pitch. Metropolitan newspapers carried columns of news and rumor about the coming contest. The Reverend Henry Ward Beecher signed for a series of articles giving his views of boxing. One newspaper sent not only a sportswriter but also a drama critic to cover the "spectacle." Oscar Wilde, then on his famous American lecture tour, wrote up the fight for a British magazine.

The contest was conducted under the so-called London Prize Ring rules then in effect. The ring was pitched on open ground, fighters fought bareknuckled, a round lasted until there was a knockdown, and the fight went on until one or the other fighter quit. Gouging and wrestling were permitted. Fighters often wore hobnails in their shoes (the better to kick the opponent) and kept huge wads of snuff in their mouths (to be squirted in the other man's eye in a clinch).

Despite these obstacles, Sullivan's fists were clearly in control. The "epic fight" ended in the relatively short time of nine rounds. Sullivan was the new world's champion.

Ryan had no excuses. "When Sullivan struck me," he said, "I thought that a telegraph pole had been shoved against me endways."

Sullivan preferred the Marquis of Queensberry Rules recently introduced in England. They provided that each round should last three minutes, five-ounce boxing gloves must be worn, the fight should take place on a board-floor ring, and the interval between each round be extended from thirty seconds to a minute. Wrestling, gouging, kicking with nailed shoes, and other diversions were forbidden. After gaining the championship, Sullivan once again made tours offering to meet any comer for four rounds, but the battles were fought according to the new rules. These tours popularized the Marquis of Queensberry style of fighting and established boxing in its modern form.

Sullivan's distaste for the old method of prizefighting had been born in a contest with Tug Wilson, an English fighter, who had journeyed to the United States solely to meet him. Wilson lasted the full four rounds but only by alternately hugging Sullivan and crawling around on the floor. A newspaper solemnly described this weird match as a display of "the splendid hitting powers of one of the contestants, and the patience and Christian fortitude of the other."

He fought the last bareknuckle defense of the heavyweight title on July 7, 1889, against Jake Kilrain. The battle, lasting two hours and sixteen minutes, went for seventy-five rounds until Kilrain dropped in exhaustion.

Like the Ryan-Sullivan championship match seven years earlier, the fight aroused as much excitement as a presidential election. (There was probably more personal enthusiasm for the two contenders than there had been for Cleveland and Harrison a year earlier.) It seemed a battle of titans. A little boy in Springfield, Illinois, remembered the excitement years later. Setting it down in a poem, "John L. Sullivan, the Strong Boy of Boston," Vachel Lindsay wrote:

> "When I was nine years old, in 1889 . . .
> I heard a battle trumpet sound.
> Nigh New Orleans
> Upon an emerald plain
> John L. Sullivan
> The strong boy
> of Boston
> Fought seventy-five rounds with Jake Kilrain."

Sullivan was the nation's hero. Crowds followed him in the street. Small boys dogged his heels beseeching him to let them "feel his muscles." Sometimes he frightened them off by playing the part of an ogre. One youngster asked him what he ate. Sullivan growled, "Blood! Nothing but blood!" But this was only good-natured play-acting. He was a warm-hearted, jovial figure, generous with money to those with a hard-luck story, and ready to extend his famous right hand in greeting to every comer. This latter aspect of his good fellowship made its way into a popular vaudeville sketch and became part of the nation's folklore. It went this way:

"Are you from Boston?"

"Yes."

"Know any big folks there?"

"Yes."

"Know John L.?"

"Yes."

"Ever shake hands with him?"

"Yes."

"Let me shake the hand that shook the hand of John L. Sullivan!"

In Boston he was an idol. When in town, he ranked with the Bunker Hill Monument as an attraction for visitors. The city in 1887 decided to pay him formal tribute. A great crowd packed the Boston Theater. The mayor and city officials were there in flag-draped boxes and in rows upon the stage. When Sullivan entered, he received an ovation lasting a quarter of an hour. After the tumult died down, a member of the City Council presented him with a huge diamond-and-gold belt. It was four feet long and a foot wide ("the largest piece of flat gold ever seen in this country"), a great center medallion spelled his name in diamonds, and four panels on either side depicted the emblems of America and Ireland and showed John L. in various poses. It was a work of art costing ten thousand dollars.

Sullivan was the embodiment of Irish self-esteem. He left no one in doubt he was Irish, and if there was anyone better than an Irishman it was an Irishman named Sullivan.

"They'd ought to be a Sullivan reunion in Boston," he used to say. "I tried to fix one up once in Mechanics Building, but it only holds ten thousand, and so, of course, it wasn't near big enough. It's a shame that it couldn't be done, for Boston's the greatest Sullivan town in the whole world.

"There's enough Sullivans to make an army big enough to capture Canada from the British and make it Irish, like it ought to be. There's enough of us to man the navy and send all John Bull's ships where they belong.

"Why, if you was to cut the name of Sullivan out of the Boston Directory, it 'ud look like the Bible would if it didn't say nothing about God."

Sullivan toured the country in a stage show, interspersing his theatrical chores with prizefights. Whatever the occasion, whether he had slain an opponent or a play, he would make a little speech on the virtues of boxing, the glory of America, or the wonders of the Irish. He always closed these homilies with, "I thank you one and all very kindly, yours truly, John L. Sullivan."

Sullivan made a triumphant tour of the British Isles in 1887. Mobs thronged the streets in London and Liverpool. The Prince of Wales, later Edward VII, requested a meeting. They greeted one another in genial fashion. The visiting American was said to have responded thus to the Prince's greeting, "I'm proud to meet you. If you ever come to Boston be sure to look me up; I'll see that you're treated right."

Sullivan asked whether the Prince "put up his dukes much nowadays."

"No, I don't spar at all now, but my second son, George, the middy, is a regular slugger," his host replied.

They had a lively two hours together. Sullivan said later, "Anyone can see he's a gentleman." Then he added with typical Irish generosity, "He's the kind of man you'd like to introduce to your family."

Dublin was an even greater success. Two brass bands met him at the dock playing, "See, the Conquering Hero Comes." He left after a week, weighed down with gifts, including a tweed suit, four jugs of whiskey, and seventeen blackthorn sticks.

Time and success were beginning to leave their marks. By 1892 he had been champion for ten years. He had earned half a million dollars, and spent most of it on women and whiskey. "I've always pelted money at the birdies," he mourned. Too many times, he strode into a saloon surrounded by admiring hangers-on and ordered "a round for everyone in the house." He weighed two hundred and fifty pounds and was sadly out of condition.

2

On September 7, 1892, John L. Sullivan lost his title, and John Greenleaf Whittier died. It was a black day for the new and the old Boston. A dapper, soft-spoken, young former bank clerk from San Francisco named James Corbett had brought the mighty John L. low in twenty-one rounds in New Orleans. It seemed impossible. The gamblers had made Sullivan the favorite of five to one. Boston backed him to the last man and the last dollar. The "champion of champions" had shown no concern over his stripling opponent. He prepared for the fight by getting drunk the night before. On the way to the fight that evening, he rolled along in his open carriage lustily singing Irish ballads. He was in fine voice. When he entered the ring, the crowd let out a tremendous roar of applause. Yet it had happened. Corbett outfeinted, outboxed, outmaneuvered, and outran him until, finally wearing him down, he sent a volley of blows to the head, breaking Sullivan's nose, and knocking him to the canvas, face down. There was no cheering at Corbett's triumph. The audience sat in stupefied silence as the referee tolled the fallen champion's fate.

Corbett at twenty-six was eight years younger than Sullivan. In his school days, he had, like other Irish youths, worshiped Sullivan from afar. Eleven years earlier, when Sullivan reached San Francisco on the first nationwide tour Muldoon arranged, Corbett had been in the audience and had seen the "Boston Strong Boy," in his prime, score a knockout.

Corbett reigned as champion for five years, but he was slow to win popular acceptance. Although he, too, was an Irishman, no part of the public disliked him more than the Irish. The sportswriters might call him "Gentleman Jim," but to the Irish he was "that western dude" who had had the effrontery to defeat John L. Sullivan. To them, Corbett's victory, though fairly earned, was almost a betrayal of the race.

Sullivan took his defeat in good grace. He never fought again. He had scored over two hundred ring victories. He knew he had outrun his strength. He toured the country in *Honest Hearts and Willing Hands*. Another vehicle was *Uncle Tom's Cabin*, in which he played Simon Legree (John called the show, "Me and the Bloodhounds,"). Still later he conquered his weakness for liquor and enjoyed a second career as an esteemed, if unorthodox, temperance lecturer. In his old age, he weighed three hundred pounds and retired to the life of a gentleman farmer outside Boston. ("Me look like President Taft? You mean Taft looks like me!") When they buried him on February 6, 1918, thousands lined the streets of Boston, and ten strong men were required to carry the casket.[1]

For years after the debacle in New Orleans, the Irish mourned his downfall. There never was, there never could be, another champion like "the great John L." Whenever men's talk turned to boxing, they remembered him . . . the brawny man in green tights with curly black hair on his chest, his way of opening every fight with a terrifying scowl at his foe and a derisive slap of his left hand on his thigh, and then the smashing blows of his right fist, that sledgehammer right with the kick of a mule in it. He had been the champion of the Irish, the champion of America, the champion of the world. He was a real hero, a two-fisted, hard-drinking fighting man. He was the stuff that dreams are made of. As the cans of beer were passed around, and the evening's conversation persisted, it was as if at any moment the swinging doors might part, the great body thrust through the crowd, hat off and coat open, and the bass voice boom out as of old—

"My name is John L. Sullivan and I can lick any . . ."

II

The Irish in America were not strangers on any frontier, in any activity that involved physical danger, in any calling that required for its practice the presence of bravery. It was natural, therefore, that they should find their way to Texas and take a leading part in shaping the Texas legend.

Of all the Texas Irish, a hallowed name is Leander McNelly, greatest of the Texas Ranger captains. McNelly did not have the look of a hero. Of medium height, slim, almost frail, with a dark brown moustache and chin whiskers giving a touch of authority to his narrow, boyish face, he had gentle blue eyes and a soft voice. In a rough frontier town he could easily be ignored as a clerk or perhaps the new schoolteacher. But he was a natural leader of men, and his relaxed, quiet demeanor concealed extraordinary personal force and firmness of will. He was a lawman, and in the troubled years in Texas, after the Civil War, no name was more feared among murderers and cattle thieves along the Rio Grande than his.

Walter Prescott Webb, writing in 1935, more than fifty years after McNelly's death, reported that along the Mexican border men compared all subsequent Ranger captains with McNelly, "whose name still lives on the river."[2]

1

Lee McNelly was born in Brooke County, Virginia (now West Virginia,) in 1844, the youngest son of immigrants from County Down, Ireland. His parents died when he was a boy, and he grew up in poverty. When he was fifteen, he migrated with his older brother's family to Texas. Not quite seventeen when the Civil War began, he enlisted in the Confederate Army where he saw four years of service, was several times decorated for gallantry under fire, and at war's end had reached the rank of captain. He remained a warrior the rest of his days, merely changing uniforms and substituting outlaws for Yankees.

He first joined the Texas State Police, which was much disliked because it had been organized under Republican "carpetbagger" auspices. McNelly was a devoted Southerner who named his only son Rebel, but he was above all else a law-and-order man. He actively hunted down those who used violence against the freed Negroes. In one such case, he was seriously wounded. A Negro named Sam Jenkins, a few days after testifying to a grand jury that a group of white men had flogged him, was found murdered. McNelly conducted an investigation and arrested four suspects. During a preliminary hearing which lasted three days, public opinion was vehemently in their favor and against the State Police. The judge dismissed charges against one suspect and ordered the other three held for trial at the next term of court. As McNelly and one of his men were taking the prisoners from the court-room, armed sympathizers began shooting, McNelly and the other officer were wounded, and the prisoners made their escape. They were not recaptured until martial law was proclaimed in the county.

When the State Police were abolished and the Texas Rangers re-constituted in 1874, McNelly was appointed a captain. His first assignment was in De Witt County where law enforcement had broken down and where rival factions settled disputes by private warfare. The leader of one gang was "Old Joe" Tumlinson. "I saw him," wrote McNelly in one of his reports, "at the head of seventy-five well-armed men who have no interest but in obeying his orders; he is a man who has always righted his wrongs and he tells me that the only way for this country to have peace is to kill off the Taylor party. He has never been made to feel that the civil law could and should be the supreme arbiter between man and man, and I am satisfied that when the sheriff calls on me to serve papers on Tumlinson that he will resist or at least refuse to go into court without his arms and men as he has done here-tofore."

McNelly brought a measure of peace to the county. He successfully protected prisoners from lynching parties organized by rival gangs. Under the protection of his officers, sessions of court went forward more peacefully. He organized a network of informers to keep track of criminals and potential troublemakers. One of his techniques was to make whirlwind raids on saloons and country stores. "I find," he said, "that it does a great deal of good to disperse congregations that usually meet at grogshops to have difficulties and concoct devilment; most of them, being under indictment in some part of the State, are in constant expectation of the approach of an officer and when they hear of my men coming, they scatter."

McNelly was able to keep Old Joe Tumlinson's activities within bounds, but, to his lasting regret, he was not able to bring him to book. In one of his last reports from De Witt County, he wrote with characteristic dry humor: "Old Joe has just joined the church and I think must be meditating the death of some preacher or some kindred amusement. I have been more on the alert than ever."[3]

2

In the spring of 1875, Lee McNelly took up the task that was to make him famous. In the decade after the Civil War, cattle stealing flourished in southwest Texas. Rustlers, operating from bases in Mexico, developed a wholesale business raiding the large, isolated ranches between the Rio Grande and Nueces rivers and shipping the stolen cattle across the border. By 1875, as many as 200,000 head of cattle were being stolen annually, and there were only one-fourth to one-third the number of cattle in southwest Texas that had been there ten years earlier. The Mexican government made no serious effort to suppress this illegal traffic. Mexicans who participated in the rustling liked to boast, "The gringos are raising cows for me."[4]

When ranchers organized their own posses, and counterattacked, the situation only became worse. Innocent Mexicans were shot on sight; armed bands made the lonely prairie roads unsafe; criminals joined in the looting and violence under cover of the existing disorder, and the thieving did not stop.

On April 18, 1875, the sheriff of Nueces County sent a telegram to the state authorities in Austin:

IS CAPT MCNELLY COMING. WE ARE IN TROUBLE. FIVE RANCHES BURNED BY DISGUISED MEN NEAR LA PARRA LAST WEEK. ANSWER.

McNelly came. In less than a year, and with fewer than fifty Rangers under his command, he put an end to the big raids, greatly reduced the cattle stealing, and restored peace to the border country. He accomplished this result by an unusual combination of prudent judgment and rare personal daring.

There were three highlights in his year-long campaign. First, he took one look at the groups of armed men allegedly organized for self-protection, and ordered their immediate disbanding. These self-appointed posses "could scarcely be distinguished either by appearance or performance from groups whose sole object was to plunder and raid." In a report to his commanding officer in Austin ten days after he arrived at the border, McNelly wrote: "The acts committed by Americans are horrible to relate; many ranches have been plundered and burned, and the people murdered or driven away; one of these parties confessed to me in Corpus Christi as having killed eleven men on their last raid. I immediately issued an order . . . disbanding the minute companies and all armed bands acting without the authority of the state; my order was obeyed, or agreed to be, without hesitation."[5]

Second, McNelly resolved to capture a group of the cattle bandits and make a striking example of them. Throughout May, he hunted them, gradually developing a network of spies to keep him informed of their plans. "I think you will hear from us soon," he wrote his chief.

A leading chieftain of the cattle bandits on the Mexican side was General Juan Cortinas. Early in June, McNelly learned that Cortinas had a steamer waiting off Brownsville, at the mouth of the Rio Grande, to take several hundred head of cattle to Cuba where they were to be sold to the Spanish Army garrisons on duty there. Cortinas had a party of men on the Texas side of the river trying to round up additional cattle to complete this shipment. McNelly determined to intercept them.

What follows is McNelly's official account of his achievement in the succeeding week:

"I have the honor to report that on Saturday the fifth [of June, 1875] I received information of a party of Mexicans, fifteen in number, who had crossed the river at eight miles below Brownsville for the purpose of stealing cattle. . . . I sent a spy on their trail with instructions to follow them until they returned, at the same time keeping my men concealed and secretly guarding all the passes of the Arroyo Colorado for twenty miles in my front.

"On Friday evening . . . the 11th, we caught a Mexican . . . he told the same story . . . as far as number, name, and intention of the raiders and said he was the advance guard and that they had about 300 head of cattle, and would cross the Arroyo that night, and try to drive to the river next day.

"I stationed my men in a motte and remained there until two o'clock, when one of my scouts came in and reported that the thieves had passed four miles east of our post early in the night. I at once started to strike their trail, or get in their front by taking a near cut to Laguna Madre. About seven o'clock next morning, I came in sight of them about eight miles distant. They discovered my command about the same time and commenced running the cattle. They drove about three miles, and finding we were gaining on them, they drove the herd on a little island, in a salt marsh, and took their stand on the opposite side, and *waited* our approach for a *half hour* before we reached the marsh."

The bandits obviously expected to slaughter their pursuers in a battle in which they would fight from a protected position and the Rangers would be firing as they moved across the salt marsh. But at that distance, it proved impossible for them to hit McNelly's men, who were moving targets and did not return their fire. McNelly continues:

"On arriving I found them drawn up in line on the south side of a marsh about six hundred yards wide, filled with mud and water, eighteen or twenty inches deep, and behind a bank four or five feet high. I formed my men as skirmishers and rode into the marsh, not allowing my men to unsling their carbines, or draw their pistols. As soon as we struck the water, the raiders commenced firing on us with Spencers and Winchester carbines. We advanced at a walk (a more rapid gait being impossible) and not firing a shot or speaking a word and keeping our line well dressed.

"On our nearing the position they held, perhaps within seventy-five or one hundred yards, they wheeled their horses round, and galloped off at a slow gait. When we got out on hard ground we pressed forward and soon brought ourselves within shooting distance, fifty or sixty yards. The Mexicans then started at a full run, and I found that our horses could not overtake them. So I ordered three of my best mounted men to pass to their right flank and press them so as to force a stand.

"And as I had anticipated, the Mexicans turned to drive my men off, but they held their ground, and I got up with four or five men, when the raiders broke. After that it was a succession of single hand fights for six miles before we got the last one. Not one escaped out of the twelve that were driving the cattle. They were all killed.

"I have never seen men fight with such desperation. Many of them, after being shot from their horses and severely wounded three or four times, would rise on their elbows and fire at my men as they passed. I lost one man . . . we captured twelve horses, guns, pistols, saddles, and two hundred and sixty-five head of beef cattle belonging in the neighborhood of King's Ranch, Santa Gertrudis."[6]

The dead men turned out to be among Cortina's favorite *bravos*. McNelly ordered their bodies brought to the public square of Brownsville and left there on public exhibition until their relatives claimed them. This gesture created a sensation. For the first time, an entire party of rustlers had paid with their lives. For the first time, also, a substantial number of cattle had been recaptured from rustlers and restored to their owners. Confidence among ranchers rose spectacularly.

By means of an effective intelligence system and hard riding, McNelly and the Rangers were able several times to interrupt raids, forcing the bandits to abandon stolen cattle rather than risk capture and death. McNelly was tirelessly alert. Receiving word that a major raid was expected on August 6th, "I left camp after dark and traveled by trails all night the fourth and fifth, laying in the brush during the days; reached a point of timber on the morning of the sixth and remained there until the night of the seventh when I learned from one of the spies that they [the thieves] had not come over."[7]

The big raid did not come. The summer passed uneventfully.

3

The high point in McNelly's campaign against the rustlers was an adventure so unusual that it will live as long as Texans celebrate their exploits. On the night of November 18, 1875, leading thirty Rangers, he invaded Mexico and attacked Las Cuevas, the heavily fortified headquarters of the cattle thieves.

Las Cuevas, a large ranch three miles inland, was owned by General Juan Flores, a figure in Mexican feudal politics and also a major cattle runner and protector of thieves and smugglers along that part of the Rio Grande. Earlier that month, McNelly had learned that Las Cuevas was to be the rendezous for 18,000 head of Texas cattle which Mexican dealers in stolen livestock had contracted to deliver to purchasers in Monterrey. This was the biggest coup the cattle rustlers had planned in many months. McNelly was convinced that the only way to break this profitable trade was to strike across the river at the seat of the trouble in Mexico itself. Acting entirely on his own initiative, he had been cultivating Army officers and the commander of the Navy gunboat patrolling the Rio Grande in an effort to persuade them to join him in a foray into Mexican territory. These officers were naturally reluctant to invade a country with which the United States was at peace, but they finally agreed that if the Rangers were in hot pursuit of rustlers, the U.S. Cavalry would follow the Rangers as far as they were prepared to go, even into Mexico. As events developed, however, it was the Army, not the Rangers, who first made contact with the rustlers. On November 17th an Army company chased a raiding party, killing two of its members, but arriving at the river only after most of the rustlers and their stolen herd had crossed. The Army set up temporary camp by the river and awaited further orders. At noon the next day, McNelly arrived. He quietly announced that as soon as his Rangers arrived, he would lead them into Mexico on a strike against Las Cuevas. The Rangers, who had been scouting in the brush country fifty-five miles away, meanwhile set out for the Army camp, covering the distance in less than five hours.

In his old age, Bill Callicott, one of McNelly's Rangers, set down what happened that night:

Captain McNelly . . . came to me and said, 'Bill, you go to that near ranch and get two or three muttons and dress them for supper and I will step up and see the U.S. captain again about getting 100 of his men. You boys cook and eat all the mutton you want, and broil a chunk for dinner tomorrow; you won't need any breakfast—it will make us too late getting over. Have everything ready by twelve tonight; we will start crossing by one. I have made arrangements with a Mexican to cross us in a dugout of a canoe that will hold four men. It has a leak in it but one of you can keep the water dipped out so it won't sink. We will swim our horses one at a time. Loosen your flank girths, as a horse can't swim well with the flank girth tight, and take your guns in your hands so that if the horse drowns you won't lose your guns. Take your morral with your cartridges in it and your dinner. Do as I tell you and be ready to start by twelve. I will soon let you know what I can do with the U.S. Captain, and if I can get 100 of his men we are all O.K.'

"When the Captain came back about twelve he said the U.S. captain couldn't let us have any men. He told us to get ready, that we were going over if we never came back. When we were in ranks, the Captain stepped out in front of us and said, 'Boys, you have followed me as far as I can ask you to unless you are willing to go farther. Some of us may get back, or maybe all of us will get back, but if any of you do not want to go over with me, step aside. I don't want you to go unless you are willing to volunteer. You understand there is to be no surrender—we ask no quarter nor give any. If you don't want to go, step aside.'

"We all said, 'Captain, we will go.'

" 'All right,' he said, 'that's the way to talk. We will learn them a Texas lesson that they have forgotten since the Mexican war. Get ready. I will take Casuse, Tom Sullivan and myself first. We will take Casuse's horse. Then I want Lieutenant Robison, John Armstrong, Sergeant George Hall and Sergeant George Orell to bring their horses, and the rest of you come as fast as you can.'

"When these five horses were over, Captain came back and said not to take any more horses because they bogged down and had to be pulled out with ropes. He told us to bring nothing but our guns, pistols, and the morral with our cartridges and grub. The Captain said he wanted us all over by half past three, that it was two or three miles to the ranch and it would take hard walking to make it on time. So we went three at a time in the leaky Mexican boat, and it took one man to dip out the water to keep it from sinking.

"At last we got over and found ourselves all together again in Mexico. It was the 19th of November, 1875, and 4 A.M.

"The Captain said, 'Boys, the pilot tells me that Las Cuevas Ranch is picketed in with high posts set in the ground with bars for a gate. We will march single file as the cowtrail is not wide enough for you to go in two's. The mounted men will go first, and when we get to the ranch the bars will be let down and I want the five men on horses to dash through the ranch yelling and shooting to attract attention and the rest of us will close in behind and do the best we can. Kill all you see except old men, women and children. These are my orders and I want them obeyed to the letter.' Captain always planned his battles before he went in, and he expected everybody to do as he said. Then the Captain and the guide led the way up the cowtrail through underbrush and trees so thick that you could not see a rabbit ten feet away.

"We reached the ranch just at daylight. Just before we got to the bars, Captain waited for us, and as we came up he said 'Halt.' We all stopped. He walked up and down the line of only thirty of us three miles in Mexico afoot and looked each man in the face. 'Boys, I like your looks all right—you are the palest set of men I ever looked at. That is a sign that you are going to do good fighting. In the Confederate army I noticed that just before battle all men get pale.'

"Then the Captain had the pilot let down the bars, and when we got there, he said 'Stand to one side boys. Casuse [a former Mexican] has not had a chance to breathe Mexican air or give a yell in Mexico for over twenty years. We'll let Casuse wake them up.' It was then between daylight and sunup. 'Go through,' said the Captain.

"Old Casuse pushed his hat to the back of his head, drew his pistol, rammed both spurs to his old paint horse, gave a Comanche yell, and away the five went shooting and yelling. The rest of us closed in behind them, and if the angels of heaven had come down on that ranch the Mexicans would not have been more surprised. We were the first Rangers they had seen since the Mexican War."[8]

The Rangers killed four men who were surprised while chopping wood for breakfast fires. But the guide had made a mistake. This was a smaller, outlying ranch house; the main headquarters they were seeking was a half-mile up the trail.

"Well," said McNelly, "you have given my surprise away. Take me to Las Cuevas as fast as you can."

But they arrived at the main ranch just in time to see 250 Mexican soldiers dash into the ranch on horseback. Between the Rangers and the Mexicans was open ground with a tree here and there. McNelly ordered his men to form a line and open fire, but it was soon apparent that an assault was hopeless. After exchanging shots for about ten minutes, he ordered his men to fall back and retreat to the river. As Bill Callicott later wrote, "The Mexicans would think we had taken a scare, stampeded, and were swimming the river back to Texas and that they could kill us while we were swimming." But McNelly was determined to have his surprise one way or another. Instead of sending his men scrambling back to Texas, he concealed them along the Mexican side of the riverbank. A few moments later, when twenty-five Mexican horsemen came galloping to the river, the Rangers opened fire. The leader fell dead from his horse; the rest broke ranks and fled back to a heavy thicket.

When the Rangers advanced to where the dead man lay sprawled, they discovered they had killed the *grand seigneur* of all the Rio Grande bandits, the owner of Las Cuevas, General Flores. McNelly stooped down, picked up Flores's gold-and-silver-plated pistol and placed it in his own belt.

In the midst of this exchange, he had not forgotten his grand design, which was to draw the Army into combat with the Mexican marauders. As soon as the firing began, he had cried out, as if in serious distress, "Randlett, for God's sake, come over and help us." Captain Randlett of the Cavalry, responding to this plea, crossed the river with forty of his men.

The Mexicans having retreated to the thicket, McNelly immediately began urging Randlett to counterattack and make a fresh sortie toward Las Cuevas, but with no success. Randlett would do no more than await orders from his commanding officer. By this time, it was late morning. For the next several hours, the mixed force of Army men and Rangers exchanged shots with the enemy. The Mexicans charged the riverbank repeatedly, but each time the Americans drove them back. As night came on, Randlett's commanding officer arrived at the camp on the American side and ordered the Army to withdraw. The Mexicans, meanwhile, sent an emissary with a white flag and a note asking for a truce. Since the note did not flatly promise to return the stolen cattle, McNelly refused to withdraw. But with disdain, he granted the Mexicans a truce and promised he would give them an hour's notice before he attacked. The American cavalry left; McNelly and the thirty Texas Rangers stayed on the Mexican side with ten times that many Mexican soldiers and cattle bandits in front and the Rio Grande behind. The Rangers passed the night digging a trench.

The next morning, two messages arrived at this curious battlefront. One from the military commander in the area to the Army officer in charge of the cavalry company read:

ADVISE CAPT MCNELLY TO RETURN AT ONCE TO THIS SIDE OF THE RIVER. INFORM HIM THAT YOU ARE DIRECTED NOT TO SUPPORT HIM IN ANY WAY WHILE HE REMAINS ON THE MEXICAN TERRITORY. IF MCNELLY IS ATTACKED BY MEXICAN FORCES ON MEXICAN SOIL DO NOT RENDER HIM ANY ASSISTANCE. KEEP YOUR FORCES IN THE POSITION YOU NOW HOLD AND AWAIT FURTHER ORDERS. LET ME KNOW WHETHER MCNELLY ACTS UPON YOUR ADVICE AND RETURNS.

The second message came from the American consul in Matamoros, Mexico, to his agent in the area:

I UNDERSTAND MCNELLY IS SURROUNDED AND TREATING FOR TERMS OF SURRENDER. IF SO GO TO HIM IMMEDIATELY AND ADVISE HIM TO SURRENDER TO THE MEXICAN FEDERAL AUTHORITIES AND THEN YOU GO WITH HIM TO THIS CITY TO SEE THAT NOTHING HAPPENS ON THE WAY.

McNelly refused to be rescued. He held his ground throughout the day. At four o'clock in the afternoon, he sent word to the Mexicans that he would attack. Whether they were bewildered by the presence of the Army company on the other side of the river or overawed by this mild yet implacable Texas Ranger, no one ever knew. All that is known is that after a few minutes of conference among themselves, the leaders of the Mexican force said they would surrender all the cattle and thieves they could find at ten the next morning.

McNelly and his Rangers sailed back to the American side of the river in their leaky scow and in triumph.

The following day, Mexican officials resorted to the familiar tactic of delay. Their chief sent word: "Because of excessive work on hand, I do not send you the cattle today, but early tomorrow morning you will have them on the other side of the river." McNelly replied at once, and as one historian has put it, "his letter shows him a master of diplomacy and psychology." He reviewed the terms of the agreement, and added: "As the Commanding Officer of the United States forces is here awaiting your action in this matter, I would be glad if you would inform me of the earliest hour at which you can deliver these cattle and any of the thieves you may have apprehended."

The commanding officer was not there and would not have done anything if he were, but the bluff worked. The cattle were returned that afternoon. Of the thousands of stolen cattle that had made the one-way trip across the Rio Grande into Mexico, they were the first ever to be returned. These cattle, like the bodies of the dead cattle thieves in the public square in Brownsville, were visible proof that the Rangers could make rustling unprofitable. The story of McNelly's two-day invasion of Mexico became a legend along the river.

4

At the time of his exploit, Lee McNelly was thirty-one. The hardships, the long rides, the hours on duty without food weakened his slender body, and brought about tuberculosis. He continued his work for another year, capturing several raiding parties and hundreds of stolen cattle. Within that time, cattle stealing, although it continued on a small scale for another five years, declined sharply. The Rangers had made concerted, large-scale cattle thieving too risky. By the end of 1876, McNelly shifted his attention from repelling the incursions of Mexican bandits to the curbing of native American criminals.

In one of his last dispatches to his commanding officer in Austin, he referred to a series of killings in a certain county: "I privately sent the Meanses word that the governor had sent me down here to stop all such things, and that the next man they killed in that quarrel, or in that manner, I would come down direct and . . . shoot them in less than two hours after reaching that neighborhood; that that kind of thing had gone as far as human patience could bear, and that it had to stop, and I don't know but I had better do it."[9]

This passage had the characteristic McNelly mixture of casual colloquialism and quiet menace, but this *hombre de verdad*, as the Mexicans called him, was not to ride against criminals again. Becoming too ill for further duty, he was dropped from the Rangers, and another captain appointed in his place. He received no pension or medical care. An outcry in the press and from the public broke forth at this shabby treatment, but the state adjutant general refused to rectify it. A year later, on September 4, 1877, McNelly died at his home in Burton, Texas.

As Walter Prescott Webb has written, the true Texas Ranger was not a swaggering figure in cowboy boots, a big hat, and a six-shooter moving across the prairie under a cloud of pistol smoke. "No Texas Ranger ever fanned a hammer when he was serious, or made a hip shot if he had time to catch a sight. The real Ranger has been a very quiet, deliberate, gentle person who could gaze calmly into the eye of a murderer, divine his thoughts, and anticipate his action, a man who could ride straight up to death."[10]

Lee McNelly was the model of this real-life Ranger. In Webb's words, "His successors did excellent work, but they never equaled McNelly." He was, moreover, the protagonist of an Irish tradition in America. This was the tradition of the Irish in the law-and-order professions in this country. In towns and cities all over the nation, Irish policemen, lawyers, and judges are and have been familiar figures.* Much of the lawfulness and stability that have been achieved in our turbulent cities and on our once-violent frontiers are due to their efforts and devotion. If Lee McNelly had grown up in a crowded city, he would have been one of the proverbial Irish cops: honest, kindly, good-humored, gentle enough to lead a child through heavy traffic and tough enough to shoot it out with a criminal. Most of them have lived and died unknown. But on the lonely prairies and under the big sky of Texas, men cast a longer shadow and individual deeds linger in the common memory. So it was that Lee McNelly, the quiet one, the exemplar of all Irish law-and-order men, gained a deserved fame and became a legend in which all the forgotten sheriffs and patrolmen of his race can share.

* In 1963, the head of the largest municipal police force in the United States is New York City Police Commissioner Michael J. Murphy who, like most of his predecessors for the past seventy-five years, is of Irish ancestry. The top assistant to J. Edgar Hoover in the Federal Bureau of Investigation is Assistant Director William C. Sullivan, a native of Bolton, Massachusetts.

CHAPTER EIGHT

Cardinal Gibbons

1

B Y 1880 there were more than 6,000,000 Catholics in the United States where forty years earlier there had been only one-tenth that many. For two generations Catholics under the leadership of a predominantly Irish hierarchy had expended their energies on the urgent task of organizing new parishes, building churches and schools, and training priests. The issue of the Catholic community's relationship to the larger American society and the many subsidiary questions deriving from that issue had been left in abeyance. Before the Civil War, Orestes Brownson, the first native Protestant intellectual to be converted to Catholicism, had pondered the implications for the Church if it passed into the hands of the Irish immigrants. Thomas D'Arcy McGee and other Irish "Forty-Eighters" had in the same period tried unsuccessfully to bring the Catholic Irish immigrants into the mainstream of liberal, nationalistic, middle-class politics. But their concerns had been premature. The Irish, surging ahead within the Church by force of numbers, were content with the leadership of conservative clerics, such as Archbishop John Hughes of New York, an able but narrow man. By the 1880's these questions could no longer be ignored. Catholics began to be preoccupied with wider, more subtle, and more complex issues of social policy and intellectual orientation.

What role would the clergy encourage the lay members to play in secular affairs? How would the Church relate itself to the American system of government and to other religious groups in a pluralist society? How would the Church conduct itself in the hurly-burly of democratic politics and opinion making? What social policy would the Church frame to take account of the facts of industrial life and the strivings of the nascent labor movement? There were at least two answers possible to each of these questions, and two parties gradually took form within the Catholic community.

The bulwark of the conservative viewpoint was the hierarchy in New York under the leadership of John Cardinal McCloskey, Archbishop

Michael Corrigan, his successor; and Bishop Bernard McQuaid of Rochester, their longtime collaborator. The leaders of the progressive viewpoint were James Cardinal Gibbons of Baltimore and Archbishop John Ireland of St. Paul, Minnesota. It is a subject for historical speculation as to why the hierarchy in New York down to the present time has usually, although not always, taken an extremely conservative position. It has been due primarily to the accidents of personality, but a second and important cause is that New York was where the Irish first captured political power and held it for a long time. There they first built up a substantial group of upper-middle-class property owners. The fact that Irish Catholics were almost a majority and had power and property subtly conditioned the outlook of the Irish clergy running the Catholic Church in New York.

Gibbons, by contrast, spent four years as Bishop of North Carolina, which was mission territory, and five years as Bishop of Richmond, Virginia, where Catholics were a small minority. Baltimore, his archdiocesan see from 1877 onward, had a large and thriving Catholic community, but Catholics were not in the majority and, among them, the Irish had to contend closely in numbers with the Germans. Similarly, Minnesota, when Ireland became bishop in 1875, was only one generation away from the raw frontier; the city of St. Paul remained an Irish Catholic enclave surrounded by a sea of Protestant Scandinavians, Germans, and Yankees. Neither Maryland nor Minnesota afforded the Irish or their bishops any opportunity to experience the overweening pride of the majority; on the contrary, the circumstances of life in both dioceses emphasized the diversity and pluralism of American life.

The progressive-conservative split began to appear within the Catholic community in the 1880's. Over the next twenty years, the conflict was so acute that it frequently broke into print on the front pages of the nation's daily newspapers. At bottom, it was a question of confidence— the clergy's confidence in the good sense of the laity, and the whole Catholic community's confidence in itself and in Catholic values. Catholics were being drawn into the vortex of general American life, quitting their shantytowns and their Hell's Kitchens, entering politics, labor unions, social-reform movements, fraternal groups, business, education, and the professions. Gibbons and Ireland welcomed this outward movement. They regarded these diffuse gestures as heartening signs of an emergent maturity among the laity. They strove to frame for the Church social policies and definitions of temporal practices flexible and broad enough to accommodate the quickening tempo and to encompass changing interests. They recognized that the education, social routines, and forms of political intercourse could not be for American Catholics the usages of the Old World, sanctified by time. The progressives contemplated this fact without fear. They believed American Catholicism could not secure its faith nor fulfill its opportunities by proscription and withdrawal; it could save its soul only by risking it; it could validate its principles only by practicing them in the American scene.

Their conservative adversaries in the hierarchy had no such optimism as a center of reference. Corrigan and McQuaid wanted to keep lay Catholics within the confines of the Catholic community, and were suspicious of any mixing with non-Catholics in secular organizations. Their distrust extended even to social and fraternal groups such as the Ancient Order of Hibernians. When Catholics joined fraternal societies in search of harmless camaraderie and inexpensive insurance, Corrigan and McQuaid warned gloomily of occasions for sin. They wanted to hold all other religious groups at arm's length, sometimes refusing even minor courtesies. When they saw Catholics participate with non-Catholics in civic meetings, they feared that each handshake betokened a conspiracy and that each statement of common interest represented a scandalous concession to unbelievers. Gibbons, for example, was subject to private criticism because he endorsed President Cleveland's proclamation of Thanksgiving Day which the conservatives characterized as "the damnably Puritanical substitute for Christmas."[1] The conservatives deplored the participation of Gibbons and Ireland in the planning of the Chicago World's Fair and, particularly, its "Parliament of Religions." Similarly, when Gibbons delivered the closing prayer and pronounced benediction at the celebration of the one hundredth anniversary of the Constitution in Philadelphia in September, 1887, he took care to protect himself by writing a full account of his participation to Rome and obtaining the Pope's prior permission.[2]

On all social questions involving strikes by exploited workers or the proposed regulation of industry, Corrigan and McQuaid expounded a stark conservative defense of the rights of private property. When Catholics entered clandestine labor organizations or raised their voices in radical protest movements, these clerics heard the echo of tumbrels rolling over cobblestones. By contrast, Gibbons in his book *Our Christian Heritage* (1889) strongly supported the right of workers to organize unions, condemned child labor, and attacked monopolies. He periodically deplored the rise of colossal fortunes, and once remarked that "one sanctimonious miserly millionaire" did more harm to Christianity than a dozen cases of burglary or drunkenness. He intervened on behalf of striking Baltimore clothing workers who worked fifteen to eighteen hours a day under sweatshop conditions. Corrigan, on the other hand, not only never spoke on behalf of striking workers but also embroiled himself in a spectacular quarrel with the Reverend Edward McGlynn, a radical priest who crusaded for Henry George's single tax plan. McGlynn was a brilliant orator and the idol of many working-class Catholics. Corrigan first suspended and then excommunicated Father McGlynn, but ultimately the archbishop had to back down. In 1892, after a study had been made of McGlynn's views in the light of Pope Leo XIII's Encyclical *Rerum Novarum*, a special Papal legate decided that the priest was not out of line with Catholic social teaching and ordered him reinstated. By this time, McGlynn had been transferred to a small-town parish, his career in the Church ruined but his intellectual rights vindicated.[3]

On the theoretical issue of the ideal relationship between Church and State, the conservatives adhered rigidly to traditional formulas that took no account of the American situation. Worst of all, they treated the democratic process with a certain disdain, acting as if blunt clerical pronouncements were the best way to dispose of public issues, as if to conciliate were to stoop, and as if no one's sensibilities except their own need be considered seriously. On each initiative and innovation that arose, Corrigan's first thought and sometimes his only one was to issue a flat statement of disapproval. The Reverend John Tracy Ellis, Gibbons's biographer, has described succinctly the opposite approach of Gibbons: "The whole mentality of James Gibbons reacted against harsh and unnecessary condemnations of any kind at any time. . . . He fought some of his most notable battles in an effort to ward off condemnations by the Holy See and American ecclesiastical authorities of both men and movements. . . . It was Gibbons' way to win men if at all possible through persuasion and kindliness, not to alienate them through hasty and unsympathetic use of ecclesiastical authority. This reasonable approach was in entire consonance with the man's nature. Gibbons was comfortable in the atmosphere of conciliation, but he felt estranged when the discussion of differences lost that spirit and assumed the air of uncompromising dogmatism."[4]

Unfortunately, "uncompromising dogmatism" was too often the instinctive approach of his opponents. They were pleased only when the laity was complacent and they exalted docility into a major virtue. Implacable in their suspicions, remorseless in their hostility, Corrigan, McQuaid, and their fellow conservatives struggled to ensnare and pinion the live corpus of the faithful in their own petty vision, a vision of a claustral parish world: tidy, thickly curtained, breathing of dust, every antimacassar firmly in place.

Gibbons and Ireland struggled tirelessly against this conservative vision. These two men, so diverse in temper, so contradictory in tactics, were as one in their perception of the problems that engaged the Catholic community and in the strategies to work through those problems. In the 1880's and 1890's, they suffered some partial defeats, but during that twenty-year period they triumphed over the conservatives on the major issues and succeeded in giving Catholicism in America a progressive cast. Their victory by its very nature could not be conclusive or definitive as a clear-cut conservative victory might have been; their battle had to be waged over again in succeeding generations—but only from the points where they left off and making use of the possibilities they opened.

2

In the autumn of 1887 when James Cardinal Gibbons journeyed to Oregon to confer an archbishop's pallium on an old friend recently named a metropolitan archbishop, great crowds turned out to greet him in Chicago, Milwaukee, and lesser cities. It was only six months since he had returned from Rome, the recipient of a cardinal's red hat. He was the first prince of the Catholic Church whom most Americans, Catholic and non-Catholic alike, had ever seen.* The demonstrations reached a climax in St. Paul where Archbishop John Ireland arranged a civic reception for his closest friend and ally in the hierarchy.

Back in Baltimore, local Catholics exulted in these testimonials of respect for their bishop. The editor of the Baltimore *Catholic Mirror* wrote on October 1st, "Reports from points en route indicate that the beloved head of the Church in America has been everywhere received with the strongest tokens of affectionate respect and esteem by all classes of citizens without regard to creed."

There were some who viewed Gibbons's triumphal procession sourly. In Rochester, New York, Bishop McQuaid read the *Catholic Mirror* editorial and grumbled in a letter to his friend Archbishop Corrigan of New York: "This everlasting talk about *head* of the *American church* annoys me. The good little man can't see that he is making himself ridiculous. He will go so far that somebody will have to call him to order."[5]

Archbishop Corrigan agreed with this judgment from Rochester; he had numerous grievances against the "good little man" from Baltimore. Even more, he distrusted the advice that John Ireland in St. Paul sent to Rome by way of Baltimore.

Gibbons enjoyed the applause, was aware of the hostility, and accepted both with imperturbable equanimity. Calmness was his forte. It was perhaps the expression of a first principle of self-preservation he had learned early in life. Below medium height, exceptionally thin,

* Gibbons was the second American cardinal. The first was John McCloskey, Archbishop of New York, who was elevated to Cardinal in 1875 and died in 1885.

he had been a frail and delicate youth. When a young priest, his health broke down and he was required to take a long rest to ward off what was feared to be an incipient case of tuberculosis. Throughout his life he suffered from a "nervous stomach." He ate sparingly and kept to a careful daily regimen. Letters from contemporaries contained frequent admonitions to watch his health and expressions of fear that he would not survive the many burdens of his work. But he outlived all of them and preached funeral sermons over friends who had worried for him. Shortly before his death in 1921 in his eighty-seventh year he was asked his prescription for a long life. He made the famous reply, "Acquire an incurable ailment in your youth."

Gibbons was a paradox in more than his health: he was one of those great figures of history who seem to be men of no talent and yet who triumph over others of brilliance and many talents. With little passion or outward show of conviction, he bested others of ardent determination and combativeness. Gibbons had been an able but not exceptional student in seminary. His mind was unoriginal; during his long leadership of the American episcopacy he sponsored no major projects on his own initiative. He was a mediocre orator and a colorless writer. Notwithstanding all that, he was an extraordinary man and the greatest figure the Church has produced in America.

Gibbons's greatness was as a diplomat. The true diplomat is one of the rarest and most useful servants of human society. The gift for diplomacy is nowhere more needed than in a high-ranking churchman who must move in the spiritual and material spheres simultaneously, and of all churchmen perhaps none needs it more than a Catholic prelate in America who must lead a Church made up of many racial groups, differing social backgrounds, and clashing political opinions within a larger society in which Catholics are a minority. This was particularly true in Gibbons's era. The Church had many pulpit orators and energetic administrators, but it had need for a man to conciliate, to mediate, to offer a discreet lead toward the future. This need Gibbons met. He had the diplomatist's crucial gifts: a sensitivity to the feelings of others, a perception of social currents, a lively feeling for history, a broad tolerance, infinite patience, flexibility in maneuver, and a gentleness and quiet self-confidence that restrained himself and blunted the vanity and vindictiveness of others. He had the fruitful insights of a true moderate: everything is not really simple and clear cut, humans at best "see through a glass darkly," violence means waste and suffering, and in the long slow reach of history what is urgent but insoluble today may be less urgent but more soluble tomorrow. His favorite phrase was "masterly inactivity." This was his shorthand prescription, not for inertia, but for restraint and delicacy of touch.

When former President Taft wrote him in 1915 concerning the League to Enforce Peace, an organization whose non-Utopian program foreshadowed the later League of Nations, Gibbons responded favorably, observing that "the plan is a sane one for it does not make the mistake of disregarding the fact that human nature in the future will be very much the same as today and yesterday." When school boards in several states during the hysteria of World War I banned the study of German, he publicly deplored their action. "We should no more dismiss that language from our curriculum because of the danger of Prussianism," he argued, "than we should do away with the pagan classics, Latin and Greek, because of the fear of our children becoming contaminated with paganism."[6]

His sense for a human situation never failed him. He loved the pageantry of the Church and saw to it that great ecclesiastical occasions in the United States went off with dignity and splendor, but on evenings at home in his rectory in Baltimore he was always in to neighborhood children who came to call. ("He reigned in Baltimore like a king, but he met every man like a comrade," a contemporary remarked.)

An obnoxious woman once accosted him at a social gathering to ask how far he thought the Pope's infallibility extended. With a glimmer of a smile, he said: "Madam, that is not an easy question. All I can say is that a few months ago in Rome His Holiness called me 'Jibbons.'"

Gibbons, like many priests, was an inveterate walker. He never kept a horse and carriage, and in later years rejected the offers of admirers to give him an automobile. But he did like to dine out ("I dine out because Christ dined out,") and to smoke cigars. When visiting in Ireland in his family's ancestral parish, he lived with the local pastor who had an aversion to tobacco. Gibbons discreetly smoked in his room. When a visitor inquired of the pastor if the cardinal was in, the priest replied, "Yes, don't you smell him?" He loved baseball and horse racing, occasionally using a friend as his intermediary to place a small bet at the track. He liked to play cards but disdained bridge because he disliked the boredom of being dummy. He preferred euchre, "and the zest with which he would win a hand of euchre was emphasized by the cardinal rapping his ring in glee on the top of the table as he clinched the game with a trump."[7]

This warmhearted, urbane, shrewd, and principled man was at the peak of his powers and influence in the last two decades of the nineteenth century. Born in Baltimore in 1834, he had been taken back to Ireland as a child of three, lost his father at thirteen when the latter died of fever during the great famine, and returned to the United States to settle in New Orleans with his mother and younger sisters and brothers when he was nineteen. Two years later, in 1855, he entered the seminary to study for the priesthood. He was influenced in his decision about a vocation by reading articles in Orestes Brownson's *Review* and attending a retreat preached by three Redemptorist Fathers who soon afterward joined with Isaac Hecker to found the Paulist congregation. Gibbons thus entered his vocation under the most liberal Catholic auspices of his time. After his ordination, his intelligence and amiability attracted the attention of the Archbishop of Baltimore who made him his secretary. In 1868, at thirty-four, Gibbons became the youngest Catholic prelate in the world, and went to North Carolina as "the boy bishop." After four years there and five years in the Richmond Diocese, he returned to Baltimore to succeed to the archbishopric. A decade later, he was cardinal.

His figure was slight but his face was dominating. The broad forehead, cavernous eyes, large straight nose, and wide mouth were strongly molded. The pale, almost fleshless skin accented the bone structure and gave him, despite his relative youth, a look of ascetic dignity and aged wisdom.

John Ireland, Gibbons's devoted colleague and adviser for more than forty years, posed a striking contrast of temperament and approach.

Tall, burly, vigorous, Ireland was blunt and combative. He once told an audience in Paris, "You will not ever be without voices which will preach to you prudence. As for me, I prefer to preach to you action."[8] He was a powerful orator, his harsh voice ringing out to the farthest reaches of the largest hall and his long arms flailing the air in emphatic gestures. Where Gibbons did not give even his intimates a hint of how he voted, Ireland thought nothing of stumping for the Republican ticket. He attended many Republican state conventions in Minnesota; politicians buzzed about him in the lobbies and filed in and out of his suite much as if he were a party boss. When he heard that Gibbons had been invited to deliver a prayer at the opening of the Democratic National Convention, he wrote him: "Be on your guard while invoking blessings upon the Democratic convention. Pray hard for the country, not so much for the party."

He was a man of tireless energy, the instigator of a hundred different religious and civic projects, and ready to pronounce a public judgment on any of them. He had been well educated in France, and he was more cultured than most of his contemporaries in the American hierarchy. He could converse fluently in French, read the classical authors in the original, and was the patron of a deluxe edition of Horace, but there remained something coarse-grained in his nature.

He was invariably direct in his methods. The evil of liquor was one of his passionate concerns. Most of the clergy, he believed, took too wishy-washy a stand on this issue. Casting aside what he termed "the counsels of fireside philosophers and chancel orators," he made house-to-house tours of the Irish slums in St. Paul and sent whiskey bottles flying out the doorways. He coaxed and badgered backsliders to sign the pledge foreswearing the use of alcohol. He canvassed saloons, collected money for his work from proprietors, "and then, to their dismay, comfortably seating himself before the bar, he would exhort them to give up the trade of making widows and orphans."[9]

His rise in the Church had been almost as rapid as Gibbons's. Born in County Kilkenny in 1838, he moved with his family to the United States during the Irish famine. The family gradually migrated westward from Boston, settling in St. Paul in 1852 where his father took up his trade as a carpenter. A year later, the Reverend Joseph Cretin, a French missionary who had become the first bishop of St. Paul, selected young Ireland and another youth to study in France. Ireland was then fourteen. After more than eight years abroad, he returned as a priest to the St. Paul Diocese. Fourteen years later, at thirty-seven, he became bishop.

During the Civil War, Ireland was a chaplain with the Union Army. He went through numerous bloody battles and comforted many dying men in the front lines under heavy fire. The war was a profound experience for a man of his passionate nature. It made him a convinced Unionist, American patriot, and partisan Republican. More than that, it helped make him a warrior all his life in every cause in which he enlisted. In all their battles against old fogeyism, Ireland was the militant and the provocative antagonist, while Gibbons was the quiet pleader and the peacemaker.

3

On November 10, 1884, the Third Plenary Council of the Catholic Church in America opened in Baltimore. The first gathering of the leaders of the Church in twenty years, it marked the first appearance of Gibbons and Ireland in significant roles.

The Pope had contemplated sending an Italian bishop to preside over the Council as apostolic delegate, but Gibbons and other American bishops had persuaded him this would create an unfortunate impression in the United States. Pope Leo XIII therefore appointed Gibbons as temporary apostolic delegate for the purpose of running the Council. This recognition and the fact that Baltimore, his see, was the traditional site of Plenary Council meetings enhanced his prestige in the hierarchy.

Gibbons invited Ireland to deliver one of the major addresses at the Council. He chose as his theme "The Catholic Church and Civil Society." The speech was an affirmation in terms Orestes Brownson might have used of the interdependence and harmony between the Church and the American Republic.

"There is no conflict between the Catholic Church and America," Ireland declared. "I could not utter one syllable that would belie, however remotely, either the Church or the Republic, and when I assert, as I now solemnly do, that the principles of the Church are in thorough harmony with the interests of the Republic, I know in the depths of my soul that I speak the truth."

He depicted the Church through the ages as the guardian of and the warrior for personal and political liberty, opposing the excesses of feudalism and the ambitions of tyrannical monarchs, condemning slavery, and upholding the moral worth of the individual. "Strange fortune of the Catholic Church. She battled for centuries in giant warfare, and saved Europe to liberty and today she is accused of befriending despotism and crushing out free institutions."

Ireland concluded with an apostrophe to America and the glory of its freedom: "Republic of America, receive from me the tribute of my love and of my loyalty. With my whole soul I do thee homage. I pray from my heart that thy glory be never dimmed. *Esto perpetua.* Thou bearest in thy hands the hopes of the human race, thy mission from God is to show nations that men are capable of highest civil and political liberty. Be thou ever free and prosperous. Through thee may liberty triumph over the earth from the rising to the setting sun. *Esto perpetua.* Believe me, no hearts love thee more ardently than Catholic hearts, no tongues speak more honestly thy praises than Catholic tongues, and no hands will be lifted up stronger and more willing to defend, in war and in peace, thy laws and thy institutions than Catholic hands. *Esto perpetua.*"[10]

It may be difficult to understand eighty years later why Ireland's speech should have signaled the opening of a new era. The sentiments he expressed, except for their florid form, would be considered banal in the mid-twentieth century. They were, however, a commitment and an expression of confidence which many conservatives in the Church did not share. The American system was novel in Catholic experience. The Church had been accustomed elsewhere to dealing with governments that were either Catholic in sympathy and made Catholicism the established religion or were hostile and established rival faiths. Either arrangement was premised on an intimate connection between Church and State. The American Constitution, however, established the State as neutral among all competing systems of belief and nonbelief. The welfare of men's souls, instead of being the State's first concern, was not its concern at all. The Constitution put religion firmly in the category of private belief, not public concern. Ireland contended with obvious logic that this neutrality was a positive good. Catholics were distinctly in the minority. They could under this arrangement freely practice their faith and freely seek to convert others.

But he carried the argument beyond expediency. The Constitution represented the ideal of the "highest civil and political liberty." The Church, which always seeks to safeguard its own liberty, could best do so, Ireland argued, in an atmosphere of political freedom. In terms of traditional Catholic teaching on Church and State relations, this was revolutionary doctrine.

Conservatives in the Catholic community did not accept Ireland's sanguine view. The Constitution's neutrality might seem to imply that all religions were about the same, that religion was solely a matter of private judgment, that tolerance was the highest public good. This neutrality was an expression of the political thinking of Protestant dissenters and of agnostics; Corrigan, McQuaid, and the other conservatives shied away from it instinctively. They had no desire to criticize the Constitution, and they had no practical alternative to offer in terms of the American situation. Their only response was to cling to the practices and policies sanctified by centuries of usage in Europe and to wait for the day when they could be put into effect in the United States.

Ireland's position was that those European practices and policies would not work in the United States. Indeed, they had already failed in Europe, as Bismarck's *Kulturkampf* and mounting anticlerical campaigns in France testified. The Church was not committed to any political order or system of government; it had flourished under absolute monarchies, constitutional monarchies, and republics. The neutrality established by the American Constitution did not necessarily imply that all religions were of equal merit, and therefore that the Catholic Church was not the one true Church; rather the Constitution made clear that this was the kind of judgment the State was not competent to make.

Ireland's views accorded with Lord Acton's dictum: "In politics as in science the Church need not seek her own ends. She will obtain them if she encourages the pursuit of the ends of science, which are truth, and of the State, which are liberty."[11]

American Catholics were well into the twentieth century before this viewpoint became widely accepted.

The Third Plenary Council approved a resolution to establish a national Catholic University. This project originated principally with Bishop John Lancaster Spalding, the brilliant and progressive bishop of Peoria, Illinois, and was strongly backed during the critical beginning period by Archbishop Ireland. Gibbons, lukewarm at first, agreed to serve as chancellor, a post he held for thirty-five years. The original aim of Spalding and the other founders of the university was to establish a center for the postgraduate training of the clergy and ultimately an intellectual center for the entire Catholic community, what might be termed a "Catholic Harvard." The conservatives scoffed at the enterprise. Bishop McQuaid would never allow any collections for the university to be taken in the churches of his diocese. Archbishop Corrigan, although a member of the original committee which reported the project favorably, never gave it his full support. The jealousies of some religious teaching orders, particularly the Jesuits, undercut it. When the university was still in its formative stage, John J. Keane, the former Bishop of Richmond, who had agreed to serve as the first rector, proposed that Rome be requested to withhold its approval for any other university in the United States for twenty-five years.

"This request puzzled Gibbons," according to his biographer. "Knowing nothing of the fact that the previous winter in New York Archbishop Corrigan had told Keane he felt a university in New York under the Jesuits should be established, Gibbons pressed Keane in the meeting to give his reasons for this demand of the Holy See. But since Archbishop Corrigan was present and remained silent, Keane naturally did not feel free to speak. He later explained in private to the Archbishop of Baltimore what lay behind his request, at which, said Keane, 'he was not a little astonished.' "

The Jesuits under Corrigan's patronage were eager to strengthen Fordham University, which naturally drew students and support away from Catholic University. Corrigan also gave his support to intrigues in the Roman curia which led in 1896 to Rome's abrupt dismissal of Keane as rector of the university. The conservatives exulted. McQuaid wrote Corrigan: "What collapses on every side! Gibbons, Ireland and Keane!!! They were cock of the walk for a while and dictated to the country and thought to run our dioceses for us. They may change their policy and repent. They can never repair the harm done in the past."[12]

Despite these and other setbacks, Gibbons and the progressives among the clergy kept the university going and eventually put it on a firm basis, although their dream was never fully realized.[13]

4

The United States in the 1880's experienced its first major wave of labor unrest. The Catholic Church was struggling during these years to formulate a position on the many secret societies, veterans' groups, and fraternal organizations coming into existence. It was only after some difficulty and considerable negotiating that Gibbons and his progressive colleagues persuaded the conservatives to distinguish these harmless organizations from the traditionally anti-Catholic Masonic Order brought over from Europe. The Grand Army of the Republic, the Ancient Order of Hibernians, and similar fraternal organizations escaped clerical condemnation.

The Knights of Labor, the first nationwide union movement, presented a more serious problem. The Knights were, in fact, no threat to the faith and morals of their Catholic members. The Grand Master Workman during the organization's peak years was Terence Vincent Powderly, an Irish Catholic, a local politician in Pennsylvania, and a man of immense goodwill, limited talents, and earnest respectability. He was eventually to pass out of the labor movement into a comfortable niche as President McKinley's immigration commissioner. The Knights, weakly organized and overextended, could not match the massed economic power of the employers. Only in the eyes of Corrigan, McQuaid, and other conservatives did Powderly loom a threatening figure and the Knights seem a source of moral danger.

The first Master Workman of the Knights at its founding in 1869 had been Uriah Stephens, an active Mason who had borrowed freely from the rituals of Masonry in developing the style of the new organization. The Knights of Labor was at first a secret organization to protect its membership rolls from employer spies. The secrecy and the neo-Masonic rituals were the initial targets of criticism by the Catholic conservatives, but beyond these issues their hostility seemed to arise from a basic disapproval of any kind of labor union.

Powderly showed himself cheerfully willing to meet clerical criticisms. In 1881 he persuaded the general assembly of the Knights to make the organization public and substitute a word of honor for the secret oath. Subsequently, he arranged a revision of the ritual. Criticism from conservative elements of the clergy did not abate. The Knights, it was pointed out, still prohibited any member from disclosing the name of a fellow member without the latter's permission, and kept their deliberations private. Powderly countered that Catholic members were not barred from revealing any secrets of the Knights in the privacy of the confessional. Yet, as one pastor wrote Gibbons, was not this "a catch in order to gain the good will of the clergy?"

Powderly sadly observed, "Between the men who love God and the men who don't believe in God I have had a hard time of it."

In Canada, conservative Archbishop Taschereau of Quebec forced the issue in 1883 by appealing for a judgment from Rome. A year later, a decree condemning the union in Canada was granted. Taschereau advised his clergy the union "ought to be considered among those prohibited by the Holy See."

At the Third Plenary Council over which Gibbons presided a few weeks later in Baltimore, the issue arose of applying in the United States the decree announced in Canada. Gibbons argued that the judgment of Rome was based on purely local circumstances and should not be considered binding on this country. He succeeded in getting the problem assigned to a committee on secret societies of which he was chairman.

For the next two years, he temporized in the hope the pressure for condemning the Knights would die down. "With regard to the Knights of Labor it is not easy to determine what action if any should be taken," he wrote Archbishop Elder in Cincinnati two years later. "A masterly inactivity and a vigilant eye on their proceedings is perhaps the best thing to be done in the present junction. . . . But we should be careful not to be too hard on them, otherwise they would suspect us of siding with the moneyed corporations and employers."

This "masterly inactivity" chafed the conservatives. They pressed for an early decision bringing the American policy into line with that of Taschereau in Canada. When Archbishop Corrigan was asked his opinion by the Archbishop of Montreal, he wrote back that the Knights of Labor were *"undoubtedly forbidden"* in both countries.

Gibbons used Bishop Keane of Richmond as his liaison man with Powderly. When the annual convention of the union was held in Richmond in October, 1886, Powderly and other officers attended High Mass and later conferred with Keane. Gibbons meanwhile heard that an adverse decision in Rome might be imminent. On his invitation, nine of the twelve archbishops gathered in his residence on October 28th. Earlier that day he conferred with Powderly. Now he made a strenuous effort to persuade his fellow prelates to reach agreement. He emphasized that there were half a million Catholics in the Knights of Labor and that it would be a grave matter to run the risk of alienating them from the Church. The rough minutes of that meeting record Gibbons: "Labor has rights as well as capital. We should not condemn labor and let capital go free— would regard condemnation of K. of L. as disastrous to the Church. We

should send documents to Rome and if objectionable features are elimi-
nated K. of L. should be tolerated, should not be condemned."

His plea failed. The majority agreed with him, but since the vote was
not unanimous the scene of decision shifted to Rome. Ireland and Keane
left for Rome on other business after this conference. Gibbons rejoiced
that they would be present to influence the final decision. The tide of
opinion at the Vatican, however, was running strongly against his
views. While the issues hung in doubt, Gibbons was informed that he
had been raised to a cardinal. Late in January, he sailed to Italy to receive
the red hat. Ironically enough, he was accompanied by Taschereau, who
had also been elevated to cardinal. Taschereau told reporters, "I shall do
what I can to have it [the Knights of Labor] denounced." Gibbons discreetly declined to comment.

In Rome, Gibbons interviewed the leading members of the Papal
curia, soliciting their support against any condemnation of the Knights.
In a "heated interview" with one of these officials, he warned that he
would hold him personally responsible for the loss of souls in the United
States if the Knights were proscribed. With the aid of Ireland and Keane,
he drafted a cogent summary of the issues at stake. This statement noted
that the Knights were free of any oath, extreme secrecy, or blind obedience, emphasized that it was "natural and just" that workers should
organize, and described the Knights as the workers' "only means of
defense" against "hard and obstinate monopolies." With respect to the
charge that Catholics might lose their faith by relations with Protestants
in such a secular organization, he observed that it would be truer to say
that Protestants were admitted to share in an organization the majority
of whose officers and members were Catholics. To the question whether
Catholic workers in the United States could be organized into exclusively
Catholic unions under the patronage of the clergy, Gibbons replied, "I
answer frankly that I do not believe this either possible or necessary in
our country." In conclusion, he dwelt on the risk of alienating the Church
from the working class. The workers might not obey a command so
hostile to their own interests. "It is necessary to recognize that, in our age
and in our country, obedience cannot be blind," Gibbons observed. The
Church would have to align itself with the masses if it was to accomplish
its spiritual ends.

"To lose the heart of the people would be a misfortune for which the
friendship of the few rich and powerful would be no compensation," he
concluded.

Gibbons and his friends, Ireland and Keane, worked at a high emotional pitch during these feverish winter months of lobbying, letter-
writing and negotiating. They prevailed upon Cardinal Manning of

England to endorse Gibbons's statement to the Vatican. They corresponded for support from friendly quarters in France and Germany. Gibbons wrote at this time to Richard Gilmour, Bishop of Cleveland: "I feel strongly on this subject. We must prove that we are the friends of the working classes; if we condemn or use them harshly we lose them, and they will look upon us with as much hatred and suspicion as they do in the Church of France. They commit excesses now and then. Let us correct them, but they have also real grievances. Let us help them to redress them. I would regard the condemnation of the Knights of Labor, as a signal calamity to the Catholic Church of America."

By the time Gibbons ended his three-month sojourn in Rome late in April, he knew Pope Leo XIII had decided in his favor. The Vatican in its deliberate pace did not issue its decision until several months later. Word of the impending decision, however, reached the public. Conservatives in and out of the Church were dismayed. E. L. Godkin in the *Nation* suggested Gibbons must have been "partaking freely of the labor beverage," and caustically suggested that politics had suffered a loss when he entered the Church. The *New York Times* deplored Gibbons's "weak judgment," and grumbled "the church will make a terrible blunder if it permits him to persuade it into taking the side of an organization which is trying to substitute brute force and intimidation for law, reason, equity, and the precepts of the Christian religion." Catholic liberals exulted. The New York *Catholic Herald* declared, "God reigns, Cardinal Gibbons lives and Labor thrives." (Archbishop Corrigan drove the paper out of business shortly thereafter.)

For Corrigan, news of his defeat came at a bitter moment. He was then embroiled with a local of the Knights of Labor which had organized the workers at Calvary Cemetery and was threatening to strike unless he raised their low wages. The workers at the cemetery took a collection to charter a steamer to escort Gibbons into New York Harbor, and they also planned to parade in his honor. Gibbons, informed of these moves, agreed they should be headed off to avoid "wrong interpretations." When he arrived in New York, he tactfully made his first stop a courtesy call on the archbishop.

The conservatives had no alternative except to reap what satisfaction they could from the Knights' later decline and disintegration. In the fall of 1887, the union lost several strikes and its membership began to fall off. McQuaid wrote to Corrigan: "How does His Eminence [Gibbons] feel now about his pets, the Knights of Labor?

"They are evidently breaking to pieces and are getting many more kicks than kisses. . . . For the countenance his Eminence gave them, he will have to suffer. He exceeded his instruction and must bear his burden."[14]

Far from feeling any burden, Gibbons experienced no surprise as the Knights' power waned. He had suspected from the first that they had neither the leadership nor the cohesion to meet labor's needs in the long run. He had been concerned not with saving the precarious life of any single organization, but with establishing a fundamental principle. The great scandal of the Church in France and Italy during the nineteenth century was that it lost contact with the urban masses. He was determined such a failure should not occur in the United States. In this he succeeded. He kept the door open to the future.[15]

CHAPTER NINE

The Changing Image

1

B Y 1900 the Irish were beginning to emerge from the immigrant community which the first and second generations had created. Through politics, they had achieved a portion of power and a tangible stake in society; within the Catholic Church they had developed a progressive and intellectually responsible leadership; on the far frontiers of Texas and in the boxing rings of Boston, they had begun to develop mythic heroes who would enter the general American folklore; and in a "gilded age" that admired money and conspicuous success, they had produced in the goldfields of California and Nevada several spectacular millionaires. The majority of Irish were still members of the working class and, in hard times, they were not much above the subsistence level. Only a fortunate few had achieved financial and social success, while those who had risen into the middle class, although a sizable group, were still a minority in the Irish community. The flow of new immigrants did not cease; every year thousands came from Ireland and were themselves as much "first generation" as those who had come in 1840. Although their way was made somewhat easier because there was now a welcoming community of relatives and friends, they re-experienced many of the old hardships, and reinforced in Irish neighborhoods the values brought over from the old country. Nevertheless, the Irish as a group had acquired a stake in society and begun to move forward. The poorest and the newest had reason to hope that their sons would achieve what they had not. This stake in society and this feeling of hope were essential for the successful adjustment of any impoverished, deprived group starting out in the competition of American life, as the Irish did, with no assets except themselves. The stake and the hope made up for much that had been painful and disappointing in the lives of the first two generations.

The changing material circumstances and the broadening horizon brought about an image of the Irish different from what it had been thirty years earlier. This was true in both senses: the picture the Irish had of themselves was changing and the way that other Americans looked upon them was altered. The Irish could no longer be patronized in the humorous, affectionate terms of the "comic Irishman" or any other variety of the "stage Irishman." The growing group of respectable merchants, of police and fire officials, of securely established, if meagerly paid, Irish schoolmarms and other civil servants could not possibly be viewed any longer as indolent, feckless, good-humored, and irresponsible folk. They had too much power for that; they might be resented but they now had to be taken seriously.

The Irish, despite their growing power, were aware of the social distance that separated them from the American inner group. This was still very much a Protestant country, and the occupants of the top places in government, business, and intellectual life were usually drawn from the descendants of the pre-Revolutionary War English settlers. There were many Irish mayors and aldermen but rarely one in an important office in Washington;[1] there were many thriving Irish contractors but seldom a John Mackay or a Thomas Fortune Ryan. On the other hand, there was a comparable social distance between the Irish and the newer immigrants from southern and eastern Europe—the Italians, Greeks, Poles, Lithuanians, and Russian Jews who had no knowledge of English, no acquaintance with the dominant Anglo-Saxon culture, and were as lacking in useful skills and helpful friends in an alien land as the Irish had been in 1840. The Irish were therefore the group closest to being "in" while still being "out." They were a sizable community whose presence had to be acknowledged and accommodated, but in some important ways they were not fully accepted.

In this ambiguous, indeterminate state, the Irish reached toward a definition of themselves within the American context. They were, in effect, asking themselves the questions: Who am I? What kind of American am I? This process of querying and affirming is an old enterprise for Americans. As early as 1782, John Crèvecoeur in his *Letters from an American Farmer* asked: Who is this new man, the American? At the turn of the twentieth century, this question had begun to take shape for the American Irish.

On the surface, the answer they had evolved during the previous three decades was a paradox. They defined themselves not only as Americans but as Americans of a superpatriotic kind, and as proof, they offered the fact of their Irishness and their devotion to old Ireland. The term "hyphenated American" had not yet been invented, but outsiders recognized the seeming paradox, and deplored it because they did not understand the logic of these two loyalties. The reality was that the Irish nationalist movement was one of the ways in which the Irish in this country learned what it was like to be American. The leaders of the Irish nationalist movement in this country were the more advanced and sophisticated element of the immigrant community; they were the editors, the school-teachers, the more idealistic political types. The ideals they had for Ireland were the up-to-date, liberal ideals of mid-nineteenth century nationalists everywhere in Western Europe and the United States. They wanted Ireland to be free because they wanted it to govern itself democratically. They wanted the Irish to enjoy the fruits of education and to advance by practicing the individualistic virtues of self-reliance, thrift, pride, and hard work. Closely inspected, these proved to be many of the same values that Protestant Americans admired. The Irish nationalists wanted, in other words, to make Ireland over and to make it over largely in the image of America. They wanted the old country to have its own George Washington, its own constitution, its own republican institutions, its own universal education, its own independent farmers in place of a rack-rented peasantry. This transference of values was an understandable, natural way for millions of uprooted people to assimilate themselves to a new country—that is, by transposing the strange values of their new country back into the familiar setting of the old country. The American Irish could relate themselves to these values more easily in an Irish than in an American context, and in so relating they might not free Ireland but they would do much to educate themselves as Americans. However, the nationalist movement in Ireland was, in fact, critically dependent upon the support of the American Irish. Patrick Ford, the editor of the *Irish World*, wrote in 1874:

"This country is Ireland's base of operations. Here in this Republic—whose flag first flashed on the breeze in defiance of England—whose first national hosts rained an iron hail of destruction upon England's power—here in this land to whose shores English oppression exiled our race—we are free to express the sentiments and to declare the hopes of Ireland. It is your duty, revolutionary chieftains, to realize these hopes! If you are but true to this duty—if you are but true to nature—there are those among you who, perhaps, will yet live to uplift Ireland's banner above the ruins of London, and proclaim with trumpet-tongued voice, whose echoes shall reverberate to the ends of the earth—'The rod of the oppressor is broken! Babylon the great is fallen.' "[2]

Ford, born in Galway, Ireland in 1835 and brought to the United States as a child, founded the *Irish World* in New York in 1870 and edited it until his death in 1913. When Michael Davitt, the leader in the fight for Irish land reform, decided to put his agitation on a systematic basis, he first visited the United States and exchanged ideas with Ford and other leaders of the American Irish. Subsequently, Charles Stewart Parnell, the leader of the Irish party in Parliament, made a similar tour of the United States to raise funds and strengthen the ties between the American and Irish supporters of the nationalist movement. Parnell traveled ten thousand miles through the United States, attracted large crowds, and climaxed his tour on February 2, 1880, in Washington with an address to the House of Representatives. An American Land League was organized, and the American Irish provided most of the funds for the Land League agitation that convulsed Ireland in the 1880's. Ford alone was able in less than two years in 1880–1881 to organize twenty-five hundred branches of the Land League Fund in this country and to raise $345,072.[3]

Americans outside the Irish community caught glimpses of this activity. They were periodically aroused by the frictions that Irish nationalist activities created in America's foreign relations: There were the Fenian raids on Canada in 1866; there were the claims for diplomatic protection by naturalized American citizens of Irish extraction who were arrested by British police for nationalist activities in Ireland; and there was the Irish political pressure in 1888 which forced President Cleveland to expel Sir Lionel Sackville-West, the British minister, after he had written a foolish letter which implied that British interests were safe with Cleveland in office. But what outsiders did not see was the self-educating effect that this nationalist activity had upon the American Irish community. It provided experience in building voluntary organizations, in working for large, impersonal goals, and in writing and reading lively polemical articles. It is not likely that questions such as the tariff and the free coinage of silver which were abstruse or unreal to the immigrant voters could have provided this training in democratic habits. Moreover, we can now see in retrospect that the cause of Irish freedom served two additional, unconscious purposes for the American Irish. It provided an intellectual explanation for the low estate in which they found themselves. The Irish, so the argument ran, would be every bit as strong in the world as anyone else if it were not for hundreds of years of English exploitation and misrule. Any Irish weaknesses could be explained away as the bad effects of English tyranny. This rationalization in terms of nineteenth century nationalism was appealing to other Americans because we were then, more than now, a self-consciously and belligerently patriotic people who traced our success as a people back to the gaining of our independence in 1776. If the Irish had been equally successful in throwing off the yoke of George III, might not they have had an equally glorious history? Whether or not great numbers of other Americans found this explanation persuasive, it was convincing to the American Irish and helped them to think of themselves in the same terms as the majority of

Americans did. In this sense, the loyalty of the American Irish to the cause of Irish nationalism can be understood as a variant of their loyalty to the United States and not an alternative to it.[4]

Second, the cause of Irish freedom provided a binding tie which held the American Irish together, particularly the successive waves of "first-generation" immigrants. Emigration from the old country meant a radical loss of community. The emigrant might be enterprising and individualistic, but he still missed the emotional support and the sense of solidarity that the village and its customary way of life had provided. Once in this country, the newcomers could not ever completely re-establish that lost sense of community; the mobile and diverse character of American urban life did not make it possible. But through their fraternal societies, lodges, and newspapers, they could create a partial substitute: the Irish nationalist movement was that substitute. (The Catholic Church was, of course, another institution that nourished this broken sense of community and kept traditions alive.) The nationalist movement gave the members of the American Irish community a common bond and a common focus. Who was there with soul so dead he would not say a prayer, shed a tear, and give a dollar for the cause of old Ireland?

At the same time, the nationalist leaders, as noted above, stressed American heroes and American (that is, Protestant Yankee) values. Washington, Jefferson, and Jackson were held up as the kind of leaders Ireland needed. John Boyle O'Reilly, the counterpart of Patrick Ford in Boston where he edited *The Pilot*, frequently told his audiences, "We can do Ireland more good by our Americanism than by our Irishism."[5] The latter term—"Irishism"—was not explicitly defined, but the implications of Americanism were clear. This indoctrination extended even to the virtue of temperance. Ford abhorred alcohol and never accepted liquor advertising in the *Irish World*. Many American Irish youths were brought up to "take the pledge" to abstain from intoxicants and to remember that Father Mathew had linked personal temperance with his nation's cause: "Ireland sober is Ireland free." Thus it was that what appeared to outsiders as divisive was actually assimilationist; what seemed to keep the Irish closed off in a subgroup was actually a roundabout way of entering the larger society.

2

While their devotion to Ireland's independence helped maintain their group spirit, the Irish defined another aspect of their identity. They emerged in the role of mediator between the network of newer immigrant communities and the larger American society that was native, Protestant, Angle-Saxon, and middle class in its values. At the turn of the century, the Italians, Poles, Greeks, and other latter-day immigrants could scarcely frame an answer to the question of a distinctively American identity. They looked to the Irish to provide the answers pragmatically, since the Irish were often the only Americans they knew well. Was not an Irishman the straw boss on the job, the cop on the beat, the ward-heeler at the corner clubhouse? The newer immigrants figured—Who should know better how to do things in the American way than an Irishman? The older Protestant America had some contacts with the new immigrants from southern and eastern Europe through teachers in the public schools and through settlement-house workers and social workers, but to a large extent Protestant America abandoned to the Irish the task of politicking, policing, and dealing with the newcomers. Of necessity, the Irishman finding himself the man on the scene became a kind of go-between. This is not to suggest that his services as political broker and social middleman were always disinterested nor that the groups on either side of the Irish in the social spectrum necessarily received their services with gratitude or enthusiasm. Rather, one can only state that the Irish functioned in this way, that by doing so they helped to make a democratic society of many diverse peoples succeed, and that in the process they worked out for themselves a unique role in American life.

Among Catholic immigrants, the Church was a decisive institution. Here the Irish and the Germans vied in the last thirty years of the nineteenth century for the places of leadership. The Irish had only a small edge over the Germans in the number of communicants but they had a wide margin in episcopal offices. In 1886, for example, of the 69 bishops, 35 were Irish-born or of Irish ancestry as against 15 for the Germans (including Austrian and Swiss). The French had 11; the English, 5; and the Dutch, Scotch, and Spanish, 1 each.[6] The Irish influence persisted and inevitably won out because the Irish, speaking English, monopolized the right to define the Church in American terms. The newer immigrants —the Poles, Italians, Lithuanians, and others—could not look to the Germans whose ideals were the preservation of the German language and of a coherent sense of German culture and tradition in this country. These ideals were, by definition, exclusive. The Irish, no matter how parochial they might be, talked in English and bespoke an inclusive "American" ideal. It is easy to satirize the extent to which the Irish clergy monopolized the places of power and to deplore their somewhat less than cosmopolitan intellectual outlook, but, in fact, the Catholic Church in America could not have avoided becoming an "Irish Church." No other group was so well situated in terms of numbers, experience, and familiarity with the American scene to provide leadership. A Church trying to sink deep roots in the American soil could not look elsewhere than to the most aggressively "American" element in its membership.

In politics, the Irish were instrumental in drawing the newer immigrants into politics and creating broad-based political alliances. Their political arts were not always proof against inherent social antagonisms; they were notoriously unsuccessful, for example, in coming to terms with the French Canadians in the New England mill towns. The French Canadians regularly favored the Republicans largely because the Irish were Democrats (until the coming of the depression and the New Deal revolutionized politics in the 1930's.) But, in most cities, the Irish overcame economic rivalries and dislike of the "alien" newcomers to make effective contact with the major urban immigrant groups—the Italians, Poles, and Russian Jews. Irish politicians registered them to vote, helped them organize political clubs, gave their leaders some recognition (never as much recognition, of course, as those leaders felt they deserved), and performed for them the usual services a political machine provided for its constituents.

The career of "Big Tim" Sullivan affords a brief demonstration of the Irish politician at work among the newer groups, in this instance, mostly Russian Jews and Italians. The New York mayoralty election of 1886 alerted the Irish bosses of Tammany to the Potential significance of the Jewish vote.* The election returns followed a pattern in which Abram Hewitt, the Tammany victor, carried or was a close second to Henry George, the independent Labor Party candidate, in the Irish and German wards; Hewitt was second to Theodore Roosevelt, the Republican candidate, in the middle-class wards. The only district in which Hewitt trailed both George and Roosevelt was in the Jewish neighborhood in the Lower East Side. Tammany had clearly failed to establish itself with these new voters. George appealed to all working-class voters regardless of nationality, but the returns in this Jewish neighborhood posed a special, double threat to the Democrats. These newcomers might go not only left toward socialism but also right, in favor of the Republicans and middle-class reform movements. Richard Croker and his Irish colleagues could safely calculate that the George phenomenon was a passing storm, but if the dissenting spirit of the Jews found permanent expression in the Republican Party at the municipal level, the Democrats' hegemony would be seriously endangered.

---

* Individual Jews had, of course, been active in Tammany for many years. In 1834 Mordecai Noah, editor of the *National Advocate*, the Tammany Newspaper, was nominated for sheriff. When someone objected that a Jew ought not to be permitted in a job where he would be hanging Christians, Noah countered, "Pretty Christians to require hanging at all." He was elected.

Croker and his associates moved instinctively to counter this threat. In 1890 they assigned "Big Tim" Sullivan to organize the Bowery, a district of dance halls, saloons, and cheap lodging houses, which also included a stretch of tenement houses rapidly being vacated by Irish and filling up with Jewish immigrant families. Sullivan, at twenty-seven, was young enough and flexible enough to cope with this challenge. He had been born in the slums, left school at the age of eight to make his way in the world as a newsboy, and quickly drifted into pursuits not mentioned in Horatio Alger. He became a leader of the "Whyo Gang" in the tough Five Points District. At the age of twenty-three he was elected to the state assembly as member of a splinter anti-Tammany faction. In Albany, Croker's agents convinced him his future lay with the regular organization.[7]

When he took over the Bowery district four years later, he set out to adapt Tammany methods to fit the new residents. He took his contituents on all-day outings, distributed free ice, free coal, and other largesse. He demonstrated to Jewish storekeepers and pushcart peddlers the advantages of having "a friend at court" when they ran into trouble with the law. He and his assistants busied themselves attending every Jewish social function from a bar mitzvah to a funeral. As George Washington Plunkitt, the Tammany sage, remarked about one of these precinct captains: "He eats corned beef and kosher meat with equal nonchalance, and it's all the same to him whether he takes off his hat in the church or pulls it down over his ears in the synagogue."[8]

Tammany welcomed into the fold many young Jewish politicians who found it unprofitable to stay in a Republican Party that rarely won a local election. "Silver Dollar" Smith, a Republican precinct captain on the East Side for Roosevelt in the 1886 campaign, shifted six years later to the Democratic Party. (Smith, whose real name was probably Charles Solomon, acquired his nickname when he had one thousand silver dollars cemented in the floor of his saloon with a fifty-dollar goldpiece in the center.) By 1895, Smith, Max Hochstim, another saloonkeeper, and Martin Engel controlled the Lower East Side and had converted the Eighth Assembly District into a solid Democratic stronghold.

Tammany also recognized the new immigrant Jewish community's claim to recognition by according it a member in Congress. The American-born Henry Goldfogle was elected to the House of Representatives in 1900.

Big Tim Sullivan himself served a term in Congress but did not like it much; his only pleasant memory of Washington was winning the pinochle championship of Congress. Albany was more to his taste, and until his death in 1913 he served nearly twenty years in the State Senate.

He regularly supported women's suffrage, although most Tammany leaders were opposed to it. Sullivan acted out of gratitude to the memory of a schoolteacher who had bought him a pair of shoes when he was a slum child. He also supported most of the liberal social legislation sponsored by reformers. Frances Perkins recalls that it was Sullivan who saved the bill giving working women a fifty-four hour week, for which she was the principal lobbyist at Albany. He had departed for New York the night the bill came to a vote, believing its passage was assured, but at the last moment she had to call him back.

"When Tim Sullivan came puffing up the hill after being pulled off the Albany boat, he said to me, 'It's all right, me gal, we are wid ya. De bosses thought they was going to kill your bill, but they forgot about Tim Sullivan. I'm a poor man meself. Me father and me mother were poor and struggling. I see me sister go out to work when she was only fourteen and I know we ought to help these gals by giving 'em a law which will prevent 'em from being broken down while they're still young.'

"This was a simple emotional response with no sophisticated political consideration involved. Certainly Tim Sullivan never realized the extent to which this type of measure twenty years later would bring nation-wide support to Franklin Roosevelt.

"Tim Sullivan got the bill passed. True, it was an amended bill, but it made possible shorter hours for hundreds of thousands of women in the factories and mills of New York State."[9]

Sullivan put through two other bills of a more conventional nature. One made Columbus Day a legal holiday, which naturally pleased his Italian constituents. The other was the Sullivan Law which made the carrying of firearms without a license a penal offense. It has been pointed out that the latter bill was not designed to curb lawbreaking since guns could easily be obtained in New Jersey, but rather to keep Sullivan's sometimes unruly gang subordinates under control. Whenever a gangster threatened to get out of hand, he could be arrested by the Tammany-controlled police for carrying a gun or else one could be "planted" on him. A term in state's prison would make him more amenable to reason. The Sullivan Law was thus a useful disciplinary measure in controlling underworld warfare. To escape police frame-ups, one of the leading mobsters of the period wore suits with all the pockets sewed up. When he needed a gun, he had an assistant carry it.

By the turn of the century, Sullivan controlled an empire of vice as well as all the Tammany districts in the southern end of Manhattan below Fourteenth Street. As the underworld put it, "Everything goes south of de' line." The ethnic coalition that Sullivan put together, and its curious amalgam of party regularity, social-welfare liberalism, and organized vice, typified the Irish political machines that began to emerge in the 1890's and flourished in the first forty years of the twentieth century: "Hinky Dink" Kenna and "Bathhouse John" Coughlin and, later, Pat Nash and Ed Kelly in Chicago; Tom Pendergast in Kansas City, Frank Hague in Jersey City, Bernard McFeely in Hoboken, and the O'Connells in Albany. In some of these cities, organized vice played a much less important part than it did in Big Tim Sullivan's operations in Manhattan, and certain kinds of vice, such as prostitution, were suppressed altogether, but in general in the larger cities the pattern obtained.

The labor movement, in addition to the Church and the political machine, was a third important area in which the Irish defined for themselves a mediating role in national life. Aside from President Samuel Gompers, who was of Dutch Jewish extraction, the American Federation of Labor was largely the creation of the Irish. They were dominant in the crafts from which the AFL drew its strength and produced most of the leadership at the second and third levels below Gompers. The largest union in the AFL at the turn of the century was the Brotherhood of Carpenters, whose long-time secretary-treasurer was Peter J. McGuire. The son of Irish immigrants and reared on New York's East Side, "P.J." was "father of Labor Day." He first proposed the idea in 1882, and a dozen years later, Congress made it a national holiday. McGuire, one of the founders of the Federation, served initially as its secretary and later as first vice-president. The Irish were also powerful in most of the related building trades, such as the plumbers,* plasterers, and bricklayers and in the teamsters' and longshoremen's unions. Gompers, in the 1890's and the opening years of this century, fought a running battle with the socialists for control of the AFL. He won because a majority of the members of the Federation in that period were Catholics (and most of them Irish).[10] The Irish opposed socialism because the Catholic Church opposed it; and, perhaps even more important, the Irish workers were expectant capitalists. The rather circumscribed social policies of the AFL accurately reflected the middle-class ideals and aspirations of the Irish community. Until the great depression beginning in 1929 drastically altered both the economic facts and the psychology of the American working class, the pattern of unionization roughly followed that of Irish dominance. That is, in the trades in which the Irish were entrenched and numerically important, there were unions; where they were not an im-

---

* George Meany, an Irish Catholic and an officer of the Plumbers' Union, became President of the AFL in 1952, while the following year Martin Durkin, also a plumber and an Irish Catholic, became Eisenhower's first Secretary of Labor.

portant factor, unionization was weak. The Irish stood, so to speak, on the frontier along a series of "breaking points" between unionization and nonunionization. Because they were the oldest and therefore the most experienced immigrant group, and also the best adjusted and most fluent, they tended to concentrate in the better-paid and more secure trades, such as plumbing and carpentry; these were trades that because of their strategic location in industry and their comparatively small number of members could be most easily unionized. At the same time, in occupations such as those of the teamsters and the longshoremen, which were not intrinsically easier to unionize than other lines of work, the Irish were successful in forming unions because they could draw upon their experience and mastery of the language and, most important, their cohesiveness as a community. The workers had ties to one another not only on the job but also in the neighborhood and, in some cases, dating back to the old country.

There were many reasons why the steel industry and large-scale manufacturing firms were difficult to unionize, but one important reason was that no single nationality group obtained a dominant position in the work force such as the Irish did in teamstering, on the docks, and in the building trades. The only exception in manufacturing was the garment industry where Eastern European Jews concentrated and in which strong unions developed. Otherwise, the work force was made up of workers of various national origins. This heterogeneity was partly an inevitable circumstance but it was also partly a design. Employers tried to keep down the proportion of Irish in the steel mills and coal mines; this same discrimination was exercised against other comparatively advanced immigrants, such as the English and the Welsh. As early as 1875, a steel mill superintendent wrote:

"We must be careful of what class of men we collect. . . . My experience has shown that Germans and Irish, Swedes and what I denominate 'Buckwheats'—young American country boys, judiciously mixed, make the most effective and tractable force you can find."[11]

What was true in 1875 was an even more impressive fact by the turn of the century when Terence Powderly in the Knights of Labor, McGuire in the Carpenters, and many other Irish trade unionists had made the association between "Irish" and "unionism" vivid in many employers' minds. The Irish skill in creating ethnic alliances served them well in party politics, but it could not overcome the barriers to communication and cooperation effectively raised by the managers of mass industry.

3

To the larger society, the Irish presented a single face, but the surface unity of the Irish community masked a growing diversity and stratification. It seems impossible to document the origin of the term "lace curtain," but oral tradition indicates it had come into common usage by the 1890's to denominate those more well-to-do Irish whose rise in the world enabled them to afford, among other prestige symbols, lace curtains on the windows.* The radio comic Fred Allen once offered a capsule definition of "lace curtain": "They have fruit in the house when no one's sick." Like similar terms, "lace-curtain Irish," while denoting a certain level of financial achievement, has connotations that go well beyond mere prosperity. It connotes a self-conscious, anxious attempt to create and maintain a certain level and mode of gentility. The Irish of the middle class were trying to live down the opprobrium deriving from the brawling, hard drinking, and raffish manners of the "shanty Irish" of an earlier generation. The shanty Irish might in some instances have been the individual's own grandmother who did, indeed, smoke a clay pipe and keep a pig or a goat in what, forty years later, became Central Park. Or shanty Irish might be those fellow Irish who at the turn of the century still lived in slums and were poor, hard-drinking, and contentious. Whether the legend of raffishness and rowdiness was personal or just communal, contemporary or far in the past, well founded or largely a mixture of rumor and exaggeration, its effect on that first generation of lace-curtain Irish in the late nineteenth century was chilling and repressive. It produced a mania for the respectable and pious, the sober and genteel. Daughter's piano and music lessons were probably as much a symbol as the lace curtains, and junior's stiffly starched white shirt was not far behind. The complex of lace-curtain values was epitomized in the cliché that hushed many a family quarrel: "Ssh! What will the neighbors think?"

Thomas Beer in his wise and entertaining essay on the Irish of this period relates the anecdote about John McCall, a wealthy Irish insurance company president: "A magnificent female at a dinner in Washington said to my father across McCall: 'He's not at all Irish, is he?' McCall asked her sweetly: 'Did you expect me to bring a pig and a shillelagh with me?' She assured him: 'Oh, dear no! I don't suppose you even keep a pig, do you?' "[12]

One can easily imagine that an Irish matron would experience far

---

* Since lace curtains quickly became familiar items even in working-class homes by World War I, the term "cut glass Irish" was invented to denote the wealthier Irish, but it never caught on to the extent the earlier phrase had. Carved crystal (i.e., "cut glass") is a traditional product of Ireland.

more anguish over remarks of this kind than did the tough and experienced McCall. Unthinking remarks as well as calcuated slurs lay potentially in wait at every children's dancing party, high school prom, mothers' tea, and summer resort as the more successful Irish moved into new neighborhoods and penetrated the social mazes of the middle class. Social rules and conventions in America are set by women, and the standards women enforced in late Victorian America as to what was "nice" behavior and who was a proper partner at a dance could be cruel and rigorous. And to these standards the Irish mothers and maiden aunts often added exacting requirements of their own because resentment and competitiveness impelled them not only to want to be accepted and well thought of but also superior and invulnerable. This defensive quality and this covert aggressiveness might be particularly strongly felt if, as often happened, the family's money had been made in some faintly dubious manner in politics, liquor selling, or contracting. Other Irish did not look down upon these occupations, but the lace-curtain Irish were aware that many of their Protestant neighbors did.

One effect of the rise of the lace-curtain Irish was the decline of the stage Irishman and his variant, the comic Irishman. In 1890 Edward Harrigan, who had written, produced and acted in scores of musical plays about the American Irish, presented his last great success, *Reilly and the Four Hundred*. The show was about the social-climbing, newly rich Irish, and the hit of the show was the song "Maggie Murphy's Home":

"There's an organ in the parlor, to give the house a tone
And you're welcome every evening at Maggie Murphy's home."

This represented a marked shift from the theme of earlier shows in which Harrigan and his partner, Tony Hart, had offered songs such as "Why Paddy's Always Poor," "The Pitcher of Beer," "Remember, Boy, You're Irish," and "Give an Honest Irish Boy a Chance."[13] By the turn of the century, the Irish were no longer represented on the stage as dressed in rags and living in shanties or slums, and the distinctive plays about the American Irish began to disappear. Harrigan and Hart had no successors. The Ancient Order of Hibernians, the most powerful Irish fraternal group, helped along what would, in any event, have been an inevitable trend by organizing a campaign early in the new century against the stereotype of the stage Irishman. The more advanced, self-conscious elements of the Irish community had never liked these popular stereotypes, and they now had enough support from the growing Irish middle class to make their distaste effective.

Another image of the Irish also underwent a subtle change in content

during these years. Previously, the phrase "fighting Irish" had been a
term of disdain. It stemmed from the medieval English conception of
the Irish as wild and barbaric and from the reputation for turbulence
which the Irish earned in the "faction fights" of the eighteenth century.
The older settlers in the growing towns and cities of America after 1830
had often blamed the "fighting Irish," rather than the fighting nativist
toughs or the general social conditions, for increased crime and violence.
The Irish, by their enthusiasm for the Civil War and the Spanish-
American War, gave this term a positive meaning. A half-century of
propaganda on behalf of Irish nationalism in this country also gave Irish
aggressiveness constructive and heroic qualities. Joseph I. C. Clark, for
example, wrote a poem, "The Fighting Race," which glorified the
patriotism of the American Irish. The attractiveness of the great John L.
Sullivan helped give Irish aggressiveness a more popular and genial cast.
Members of the American Irish community had also entered the newspaper profession in increasing numbers after the Civil War; these Irish
newspapermen managed over the years, often probably without consciously intending to do so, to strip the term of its rowdy overtones and
give it favorable, even glamorous, connotations. If history is written by
the victors, popular stereotypes are created by the press. If Thomas Beer
is correct, the press had already effectively invented the new positive
stereotype by 1898: "A group of young journalists went hunting the
first trooper to reach the blockhouse on San Juan Hill, assuring each
other, said Acton Davies, that he would be a red-haired Irishman and
warmly disappointed when he proved an ordinary American of German
ancestry. . . . Nineteen years later, another group of journalists went
hunting a red-haired Irishman who fired the first shot of the American
Expeditionary Force in France. Some clever military commander will
eventually sense an occasion and provide the necessary type."* Without
the cooperation of the military, the phrase "fighting Irish," which had
originated as a hostile label, became a proud boast, and the image of
the two-fisted, freckle-faced, redheaded Irishman who is twice as brave
as anyone else has passed irretrievably into American folklore.

The general image of the Irish, however, was still in transition, as the
comic strips in the new mass journals demonstrated. The Hearst papers,
for example, which from their earliest days attracted a large Irish readership, featured divergent comic strips—"Happy Hooligan," which looked
back toward the raffish shanty Irish, and "Maggie and Jiggs," which

* Beer, *Mauve Decade,* p. 117. Beer, who wrote in 1926, would doubtless have
been aesthetically pleased that the first great hero of World War II was Captain
Colin Kelly and that it was General Anthony McAuliffe who said "Nuts!" to the
German demand for the surrender of Bastogne in 1945.

broadly satirized the social climbing of an Irish matron and her rich husband. Maggie is always trying to make her way to the opera with the Van Snoots while Jiggs aches to take off his shoes and enjoy corned beef and cabbage with the boys at Dinty's.

The Irish, in short, stood at the opening of the twentieth century with a foot in each world. The desire to join the "ins" conflicted with the desire to lead the "outs." The wish to climb socially ran counter to the impulse to champion the rebellious, restless poor. The options for individual Irishmen were numerous: conventional success or frustrated insurgency, individual assimilation or the chauvinism of the Irish community, bleached-out respectability or labor radicalism, adherence to the political machine or acceptance of good government ("goo goo") values, the American-style idealism of Gibbons and Ireland or the clerical reaction of Corrigan and McQuaid. They had come a long way in seventy years. They knew they still had a long way to go.

4

At this point, there stepped forth from the Irish community one of the greatest satirists America has produced—Finley Peter Dunne and his alter ego, "Mr. Dooley."

Dunne, born in Chicago in 1867, created Martin Dooley, "a bachelor, a saloon-keeper, and a Roscommon Irishman," as the central character in a newspaper sketch on October 7, 1893. Despite occasional interruptions, he kept Dooley alive for more than twenty years. The pattern of these sketches was a lengthy monologue by Dooley usually set off and infrequently interrupted by leading comments from a slow-witted patron, Hennessy.

Dooley gently satirized almost every aspect of life in the Irish community. He spoke of the policeman who "dhrinks this beat." He was harder on O'Brien ("O'Broyn"), the grafting alderman. Describing that gentleman's official duties, Dooley explained:

"No work or worry. Nawthin' but sit down with y'er hat cocked over ye'er eye an' ye'er feet on a mahogany table an' let th' roly-boly [easy money] dhrop into ye'er mit. Th' most wurruk an aldherman has to do is to presint himself with a gold star wanst a year so he won't forget he's an aldherman. . . . 'Tis good f'r annythin' fr'm a ball to a christenin' an' by gar Billy O'Broyn wurruked it on th' church. He went to mass over by Father Kelly's wan Sundah mornin' to square himsilf, an' whin Dinnis Nugent passed th' plate to him he showed th' star.

" 'Are ye an aldherman?' says Nugent. 'I am that,' says O'Broyn.

'Thin,' he says, stickin' th' plate under his nose, 'thin,' he says, 'lave half f'r th' parish,' he says."[14]

Dooley could be equally telling about the Irish freedom movement which was long on militant speeches at rallies and picnics but short on militant action. He once observed, "Be hivins, if Ireland could be freed be a picnic, it'd not on'y be free to-day, but an impire, begorra."[15]

He captured the exact quality of the Irish attitude toward the Germans, their rivals in the long-time duel for hegemony within the immigrant world.

"I'm not prejudiced again thim, mind ye" [Mr. Dooley explained to Hennessy one day about Germans]. "They make good beer an' good citizens an' mod-rate polismen, an' they are fond iv their families an' cheese. But wanst a German, always Dutch. Ye cudden't make Americans iv thim if ye called thim all Perkins an' brought thim up in Worcester. A German niver ra-aly leaves Germany. He takes it with him wheriver he goes. Whin an Irishman is four miles out at sea he is as much an American as Presarved Fish. But a German is niver an American excipt whin he goes back to Germany to see his rilitives. He keeps his own language, he plays pinochle, he despises th' dhrink iv th' counthry, his food is sthrange an he on'ly votes f'r Germans f'r office, or if he can't get a German, f'r somewan who's again' th' Irish. I bet ye, if ye was to suddenly ask Schwarzmeister where he is, he'd say: 'At Hockheimer in Schwabia.' He don't ra-aly know he iver come to this counthry. I've heerd him talkin' to himsilf. He always counts in German."[16]

Dooley had a cutting edge to his attacks on financial predators such as Charles T. Yerkes, the corrupt and ruthless owner of Chicago's street railway system. Disapproving of the ceremonies commemorating the Chicago fire of 1871, Dooley observed: "We've had manny other misfortunes an' they're not cillybrated. Why don't we have a band out an' illuminated sthreet cars f'r to commimerate th' day that Yerkuss came to Chicago? An' there's cholera. What's th' matter with cholera?"[17]

Nothing in the realm of politics more troubled the conscience of the Irish community than the obvious gap between its own standard of political morals and that of the larger society. The Irish believed that the political machines they created had the cardinal virtue of recognizing the human needs that the minimalist government of the civic reformers did not: the machines were rudimentary models of the later welfare state. The Irish had no convincing rationale they could offer outsiders on behalf of boodling aldermen and other grafters, yet they also sensed that theirs was not the only form of corruption in American life. Compared to many kinds of corruption aggressively practiced by the business community, it seemed much the mildest evil. Since reform movements always drew their strength from businessmen and lawyers allied with business, such movements were suspect in Irish eyes. In other words, did anyone come to the task of reform with clean hands?

Dunne's essays reflected precisely this interior conflict over ethical standards in politics. Like an increasing minority of Irish, Dunne had detached himself from the values of the machine: he could see clearly that political corruption at any level and in any terms was wrong. He did not try to whitewash the boodling aldermen. But at the same time he still shared so much of the ethos of the Irish community that he could readily articulate its viewpoint. He summed up the difference between personal and family graft as practiced by the crooked Irish politician and the systematic, corporate graft practiced by the businessmen in the famous advice of Mr. Dooley: "Jawn, niver steal a dure mat. If ye do ye'll be invistigated, hanged, an' maybe rayformed. Steal a bank, me boy, steal a bank."

He underscored the contrast in a lightly sardonic profile of John Powers, the head of the machine faction in the Chicago City Council, written in 1898:

"They raise no saints in that part iv th' nineteenth ward, an' they was nawthin' Jawnny Powers seen afther he got into th' council that'd make him think th' worse iv Alick Swan iv Law avnoo. He didn't meet so manny men that'd steal a ham an' thin shoot a polisman over it. But he met a lot that'd steal th' whole West Side iv Chicago an' thin fix a grand jury to get away with it. It must've been a shock to Jawnny Powers, thim first two years in th' council. Think iv this quite, innocent little grocery-man that knew no thieves but thim that lurked along alleys with their hats pulled over their eyes, bein' inthrojooced to bigger thieves that stole in th' light iv day, that paraded their stovepipe hats and goold watches an' chains in Mitchigan avnoo. . . .

"Whin Jawnny Powers wint into th' council I don't suppose he had anny idee what a great man he'd make iv himsilf. He thought iv most all the wurruld except th' nineteenth as honest. He believed that th' lads that presided over th' municipyal purity meetin's was on th' square an' he hated th' ladin' mimbers iv churches an' th' boys that gives money to home missions an' thrainin' schools because he thought they were in-humanly honest. It didn't take long f'r to make him see diff'rent. Inside iv his first term he begun to undherstand that they was rale, flesh-an'-blood, bribe-givin' men. . . . An' whin wanst he got their measure he knew how to threat [treat] thim. He's quick to larn, Jawnny Powers is. None quicker. But I wudden't iv had his expeeryence f'r twict his money. I'd rather set back here an' believe that whin a man dhresses dacint he's respectible an' whin he has money he won't steal."

That same year, Dunne did, in fact, support a reform movement to unseat Powers and his allies. In an editorial, he advised the reformers what it would require to defeat Powers. The passing of more than sixty years has not outdated the wisdom of Dunne's advice to political reformers: "If he is defeated it must be by the use of the weapons similar to his own. The candidate who beats him must be:

"A friend of the poor.

"One whom the people can trust to make reform a perceptible benefit.

"One who won't make reform an affliction and a restraint on personal liberty.

"A candidate who can conform to these specifications may beat Powers. For any one who can't, to try to beat him will be a waste of effort."[18]

Shortly afterward, Dunne's comments on the Spanish-American War made him famous. He moved from Chicago to New York, and he moved also from the strictly Irish and local topics with which he had begun to the national and international issues on which he established his enduring reputation.

Humor resists analysis, but Dunne's insights and satire had a social context. He was an Irishman at a time when the American Irish community was reaching a new level of self-consciousness and self-confidence; the same community could not have produced a satirist of his depth and sophistication thirty years earlier. He was a political commentator at a time when his fellow Irish had amassed considerable experience in running municipal politics but were still on the fringes of national politics; Mr. Dooley's comments reflect both the experience of power at one level and the sharp insights of the ambitious but largely powerless outsiders at the higher level. Although not a practicing Catholic during much of his adult life, Dunne was Catholic in his background and in his sympathies at a time when American Catholicism was beginning to move forward but was still widely regarded as an "alien" religion and under attack by the American Protective Association and similar organizations. This experience, too, sharpened the sensibility of an outsider. Dunne had a keener ear for self-righteousness than he might have had as a member of the majority. He began his account of a pious speech by President McKinley: "Th' proceedin's was opened with a prayer that Providence might remain undher th' protection iv th' administhration."[19] As an Irishman, he naturally viewed the growing Anglophilism of the Establishment in the eastern part of the country as a subject for ridicule. Since Ireland had experienced imperialism and suffered under it, Dunne (and other American Irish) had a different perspective on the wave of imperialist emotion that swept the country during and after the Spanish-American War. He paraphrased the two best-known imperialist slogans as: "Hands acrost th' sea an' into somewan's pocket," and "Take up th' white man's burden an' hand it to th' coons."

Familiar since childhood with the self-seeking, the savage thrust, and the sentimental rhetoric of Chicago ward politics, he was not taken in by the duplicities of national and international politics. He brought to the doings of President and Congress, of czar and kaiser the skepticism learned in observing the maneuvers and pretensions of Charles Yerkes and the Chicago city council. Regarding the annexation of the Philippines, he observed that our message to the Filipinos was: " 'We can't give ye anny votes because we haven't more thin enough to go around now, but we'll treat ye th' way a father shud treat his childher if we have to break ivry bone in ye'er bodies. So come to our arms,' says we."

This skepticism and knowing realism never fell over the edge into hard cynicism not only because of a certain sweetness in Dunne's own character but also because the American Irish community whose experience formed his outlook was basically optimistic about individual success. Dunne was not a radical social reformer and he was a liberal only in a limited sense. His family's experience was typical of those Irish who were slowly but steadily pushing their way up in the world. His father was a self-made man, a thrifty *bourgeois*, hard-working, somewhat dour, who began as a carpenter and became a prosperous lumber dealer. Dunne's mother was a cultivated woman who loved music and inculcated in her children a taste for Thackeray, Scott, and other nineteenth century English authors. Dunne's oldest sister was an elementary-school teacher. The satirical opinions of Mr. Dooley reflected and affirmed the middle-class American values of individual effort and economic and cultural aspiration that were implicit in this family background. But, at the same time, Dunne's acquaintance with Ireland's history and things Irish as well as his experience of Catholic religious teaching imbued his Dooley essays with a sense of history as a cycle of suffering and defeat, a strong feeling for the impermanence of material achievement, and a conviction about the vanity of human wishes. As his biographer has observed, Dunne's writings "often expressed a profound fatalism which was saved from becoming defeatist cynicism only by an intensely emotional sympathy for the under-dog, and a love of humanitarian values."[20]

Dunne, although he attained wealth and success, could never become a conservative because he had an instinctive irreverence toward the afflictions of the comfortable; even in his well-to-do old age, he took delight in espousing Franklin D. Roosevelt's social reforms to his wealthy golfing partners. Yet he was not a conventional liberal because, at bottom, he believed that the only way to achieve real reform was to change men's hearts and not men's social institutions. He lacked the liberal's basic faith in politics as an instrument of human reform.

The opinions of Mr. Dooley were the wisdom of an American Irishman, bred in the Chicago middle class and trained in the newspaperman's craft, who was perpetually fascinated by the men and the ways of politics, a profession in whose larger claims he had no belief.

CHAPTER TEN

The Education of Al Smith

ALFRED E. SMITH of New York and James M. Curley of Boston were the great political leaders of the Irish community in their generation. These two contemporaries had much in common. Sons of impoverished working-class families, they knew what financial hardship and manual labor were. They quit school early and accomplished remarkable feats of self-education. They knocked around in politics in the blood-and-guts nineties and turn-of-the-century days, long before women had the vote and when politics was a lusty man's trade carried on in saloons and at torch-lit street corner rallies. They first achieved prominence in 1913 when Smith was elected Speaker of the Assembly in New York, and Curley was elected mayor of Boston.

A study of their respective careers during the following twenty years until the depression and the New Deal transformed the national scene reveals much about the role of the Irish in politics in this period. To understand Curley requires a prior look at the unique and sometimes baffling Boston Irish.

1

On May 24, 1883, Queen Victoria celebrated a birthday and New York opened a bridge to Brooklyn. The Irish, being a peaceful people, did not riot at the coincidence. They allowed the bridge to open unharmed.

The mile-long structure with its slim, clean lines was the first great masterpiece of functional architecture. It was a harbinger of the coming age of urban industrialism and a symbol of the modern city.

Young Alfred Smith, nine years old, was among the many thousands of eager spectators on that first great day. The anchorage towers at the Manhattan end of the bridge had been completed in 1873, the year he was born. His home at No. 174 South Street lay almost within their shadow.

"The bridge and I grew up together," he recalled later. "I spent a lot of time superintending the job. I have never lost the memory of the admiration and envy I felt for the men swarming up, stringing the cables, putting in the roadways, as the bridge took shape."[1]

One of his earliest memories was of a walk with his father one winter's day across the wooden planks of the bridge before it was finished. His father was eager to enjoy the privilege of saying that he was the first to cross the bridge before its completion. On the first Saturday after its opening, the entire Smith family made the journey across the bridge, each paying the pedestrian's toll—one cent.

Al knew the cost of it was more than dollars. Since pneumatic tools and compressed air were unknown, the bridge was built by hand. "I often heard my mother say—she having knowledge of what was going on, because we lived directly under that tower—that if the people of New York City had had any idea of the number of human lives sacrificed in the sinking of the caissons for the towers of the Brooklyn Bridge, in all probability they would have halted its progress," he wrote years later in his autobiography.[2]

From a practical viewpoint, the bridge brought the island of Manhattan closer to its neighbor city of Brooklyn. In a larger sense it spelled out, in concrete and steel, the American dream. (How many hopeful immigrants bought the Brooklyn Bridge only to discover that what they sought was not to be bought for so cheap a price?) A bridge has many meanings. It is a bringing together and a leading away. It offers adventure because it leads away and harmony because it brings together. The adventure of achievement in America and the promise of integration with America comprised the dream of every immigrant and gave a mythic quality to the greatest bridge in the heart of America's greatest city, a city of immigrants. The toll was much higher than one cent.

The New York in which Al Smith was born was already a cosmopolitan city. It would soon be able to boast that it had more Irish than Dublin, more Italians than Rome, more Jews than Warsaw, and more Negroes than any other city in the world. The Fourth Ward and St. James Parish on the Lower East Side in which Smith grew up in the 1870's and 1880's were solidly Irish. It was a neighborhood of the old-fashioned kind, closely knit, interlaced by a thousand common interests, affections, and rivalries.

Smith's father was a teamster who worked long hours each day driving two horses through the streets. He was a strong, thickly set man with powerful hands, dark eyes, and a sweeping handlebar mustache.

One of the son's few memories of his father was the picture of him returning in the evening from his day's labor "grimy with the dust of the streets, wet with streaky sweat, peeling off garment after garment, plunging his neck, hands, and arms into cold water to cool off."

The origins of Alfred Emanuel Smith the elder are obscure. In later years the story circulated that he was not Irish at all, but a German who had changed his name from Schmidt. Some took this story seriously; Al thought it was very funny.

The father was not much of a businessman. He earned barely enough to provide food for his family and shelter them in their simple, but clean and adequate four-room flat. Though not personally involved, he loved politics, and enjoyed standing at the back of the crowd, listening to the political orators. He was a lively conversationalist with a good memory for anecdotes, which made him popular at gatherings in the corner barbershop. He was a volunteer fireman and active in what was then the community sport of going to fires. He was known and liked throughout the ward for his neighborly qualities. One of his favorite sayings was "A man who cannot do a friend a favor is not a man." Easygoing, good-natured, he enjoyed taking his son for walks and teaching him to swim.[3] But his long workday made these occasions infrequent.

When Al was eleven, his father became too exhausted to continue working at his old job; the horses and equipment were sold to pay doctors' bills and feed the family. As his health declined, the elder Smith took a job as a watchman. After two years, he died.

Before her marriage, Mrs. Smith had learned the trade of making hoopskirts. These were now out of fashion, but she quickly turned to the work of making umbrellas, toiling at piecework at home. Later she ran a small grocery store until Al was old enough to support her.

Catherine Mulvihill Smith was a small, erect, bright-eyed woman. She was serious and reserved by nature, intelligent, and a strict disciplinarian. A faithful churchgoer, devoted to her family, she neither enjoyed nor sought outside amusements. Fifteen years younger than her husband, she survived him by thirty-eight years, dying in 1924.

She watched closely over Al and his younger sister. She instilled in them a few simple precepts: tell the truth, be honest, work hard. Her favorite saying was, "Show a child the difference between right and wrong, and it will choose the right." When Al was an altar boy serving the six o'clock Mass, she got up at five-fifteen to prepare his breakfast. Until his marriage, she always prepared his breakfast, packed his lunch, washed and mended his clothes. She put high value on neatness and cleanliness. Her son was always one of the best scrubbed and neatly dressed boys in the neighborhood. Al came to regard his mother with reverence. After his marriage, she moved to Brooklyn to live with her daughter, but every Sunday for the remaining twenty-four years of her life he spent the day with her. In 1916, when he was inaugurated as sheriff, she expressed one of her rare public opinions.

"Alfred," she said, "has been a good boy."

As a boy, Al was popular and a natural leader, but he did not follow any of the usual routes to prominence and success as a youngster. He was not a good student. He was not an athlete and did not care for most games. He was not attracted to fighting and rarely mixed in the gang fights of the streets. He managed to hold his own in the gang without fighting or becoming a part of the "pecking order," that rough boyhood hierarchy based on gradations of physical strength. He carried this outlook into adult life. He always detested boxing, and when he was governor it took all of Jimmy Walker's charm and persuasive skill to get him to sign Walker's bill legalizing boxing in New York. He cared nothing for basketball or football, and when he had to attend a baseball game to throw out the first ball he sat through the nine innings as bored as Cal Coolidge. He liked the individualistic sports of bicycling and fishing and particularly ocean bathing where he battled only the waves. In later life he took up golf, but played only nine holes and let it go at that; it was the opportunity for sociability and good conversation it afforded that he enjoyed.

In school, he was an indifferent scholar, obedient and regular in his attendance but uninterested in school work and undistinguished in achievement.

"I never read books," he admitted when he was governor. "I never have read them. In all my life I have never read for amusement or to pass away the time. Life furnishes me with all the thrills."[4]

The governor's mansion in Albany when Smith lived there contained a gramophone and a motion-picture projector but almost no books.

Most politicians are oral-minded; Smith was this type in pure form: he liked to learn by listening. In the political clubhouse as a young man, in the Assembly and in investigating committees, on the board of aldermen, and in the governor's office, he listened and learned. When he was inaugurated in 1925 for his third term as governor, he remarked in his address: "I have a deep and abiding affection for the assembly chamber. It has been my high school and my college."[5]

Smith was an inveterate reader of newspapers. As a public official, he pored over countless bills, reports, and public documents of all kinds, but this reading grew out of the practical problem at hand. His disinterest in reading for its own sake reveals itself in his speeches. In them, there are no quotations and few literary flourishes. His talks were simple and direct, enlivened by his own native wit. From his boyhood in poverty and his adolescent working years, Smith was engaged in a contest with life at close quarters. His only earned degrees were an "FFM" from the

Fulton Fish Market and a master of political science from the night school of ward politics. His mind turned instinctively to practical wisdom, to the specific problem, to facts. It was not by chance that he made famous the phrase, "Let's look at the record."

Smith's great passion as a youth was for amateur theatricals. It was the vent for his strong, quick mind and his active imagination. His only triumphs in school were victories in speech contests and a medal for elocution. It took no encouragement to get him to recite "Cohen on the Telephone" or "The Face on the Barroom Floor."

Much of his theatrical activity centered in the lyceum society of St. James Parish Church. Asked years later whether he was an active church member as a boy, he replied, "Of course. What else was there to do?" In the church hall seating eight hundred persons, he played in innumerable comedies, farces, and melodramas of the period, including the roles of Corry Kinchella in *The Shaughraun*, Bradwell Slote in *The Mighty Dollar*, and Jim Dalton in *The Ticket o'Leave Man*.[6]

Smith was a natural actor. He learned his lines quickly and remembered them. He was a shrewd observer of human foibles and a superb mimic. He had an actor's sense of timing and gift for improvisation. Utterly unselfconscious, he could dance a jig or rattle off a song and sweep the heroine and the audience before him.

This flair for the theatrical was inherent in Smith's Irish temperament, and the Irish have contributed much to American minstrelsy.

"Now the theatrical, as opposed to the dramatic, is full of experiment, finding its way to audiences by their quick responses and rejections," Constance Rourke has observed in *American Humor*. "On the stage the shimmer and glow, the minor appurtenances, the jokes and dances and songs, the stretching and changes of plots, are arranged and altered almost literally by the audience or in their close company; its measure is human, not literary."[7]

Smith liked to think he might have been a prominent actor or a famous song-and-dance man in the George M. Cohan manner, and he might well have been if his own serious mind and the relatively greater security of politics had not drawn him away. He carried into politics many of the habits of mind and mannerisms of the theater. Even his major speeches were extemporaneous. Working from a tight outline jotted down on the backs of envelopes, he could ad lib a speech of an hour and a half or two hours in length. His loud, harsh voice carried in the largest hall; when he was speaker of the Assembly it was said of him that he did not need a gavel "because he has a gavel in his throat." His vigorous gestures, and his trick of stooping down to emphasize a point created suspense. He knew the value of humor and of a tag line in aiding the vivid, simplified presentation of an issue.

In 1924 Theodore Roosevelt, Jr., running against Smith for governor, addressed a group of college athletes and made the error of congratulating them for winning over a team other than the one they had played. Seeing the embarrassment on their faces, he turned to one of his aides and asked, "Now, who told me that?"

Smith read of this incident. In a speech of his own, he tore apart young Roosevelt's position on several issues, charging misstatements and inaccuracies, and winding up each portion of his talk with the question, "Now, who told Teddy that?"

On another occasion, he lined up several vacant chairs on the platform and for two hours conducted a multicornered conversation among the Republican strategists, taking each part himself. It was an enormously successful tour de force subsequently imitated by lesser politicians; only an old-time actor sure of his skills could have carried it off.

Smith was a self-confident and self-assured youngster with a touch of cockiness and swagger. Some neighborhood girls were once planning a picnic. Al came by and joined in the conversation.

"We haven't asked you to go," one of them remarked tartly.

"Oh, you'll ask me," he replied. "You won't be able to get along without the talent."[8]

He projected his dramatic picture of himself into his dress. He graduated from the neat clothing homemade by his mother to the stylishness of a local "Dapper Dan." He went in for fancy vests, colorful neckties, and tight trousers. When he was elected to the Assembly at the age of thirty, one of his campaign backers sent him to Albany with a dress suit and a cutaway from Brooks Brothers. Al was pleased. If he was going to be an assemblyman, he wanted to look the part. He often dressed all in brown—brown shoes, brown suit, brown tie, and the brown derby he was to make famous. Later, in the 1920's, as he emerged as a national figure and a potential President, he discarded these snappy clothes for the somber grays and blacks of a statesman. The brown derby was brought out only at campaign time. If this attention to dress was a shade too insistent, it must be remembered that he did not have generations of money and family standing behind him to confer automatic status. Being thoroughly extroverted, he responded to himself and his changing world in an uninhibited way.

2

After his father died, Smith earned a few dollars as a newspaper boy. Later he helped his mother in the store. Then at age fifteen he quit school to work full time. He did not mind leaving the parochial grammar school at the time, but in later years he may have felt the handicaps of having only a grade-school education. He once said if you doubt the value of an education, ask the man who never had one. As governor he signed the largest school appropriation in history up to that time.

His first jobs were as a truck chaser and then as a shipping clerk. In 1892 he went to work in the Fulton Fish Market as a clerk at twelve dollars a week and all the fish he could eat. He worked a twelve-hour shift from 4:00 A.M. to 4:00 P.M. and on Friday from 3:00 A.M. His name was to be forever connected with the Fulton Market, though he actually worked there only a year. He then went to work as a common laborer handling steam pipes at a steam pump plant in Brooklyn. Meanwhile he had been a loyal and active member of the local Democratic club, canvassing before elections and doing errands for the ward leader in the evening. In 1895 he received his reward: an appointment as a subpoena server in the office of the Commissioner of Jurors. The job paid sixteen dollars a week, he wore a white collar, and had more free time for himself than he had had since leaving school. He was twenty-two years old.

He stayed in the Jury Commissioner's office for the next eight years. It was during this time that he met and married Katie Dunn. She was the daughter of a lace-curtain Irish family living in the Bronx. Her parents frowned on Smith at first because they were prosperous and slightly higher on the social scale than he was. They also had a distrust of anyone active in theatricals, which they associated with inebriates and loose living. Smith persevered, however, and he and Katie were married in 1900. Over the next few years, Katie bore him three sons and two daughters. She grew into a plump, motherly person who was devoted to her husband and her family. She kept out of the limelight and took no part behind the scenes in political affairs.

In 1903 the Democratic organization sent Smith to the state Assembly. It was an honor, it paid fifteen hundred dollars a year, and it meant wearing a stiff collar and a cutaway on important occasions, but otherwise it was a most unsatisfactory office. The state Assembly was a cross between an inferior elocution school and a sheep run. Important matters were all decided in committees that were thoroughly Republican-controlled. The leadership on both sides of the aisle rounded up the members when needed and they voted as they were told. Bills were complicated and phrased in obscure legal language. Smith, accustomed to being an active and articulate figure in his neighborhood and in the local Tammany clubhouse, found himself ignored. He received no important committee assignments and no one asked him his opinion about anything. Albany was a long way from his family and friends on the East Side, and fifteen hundred a year did not go far with a new child coming along almost every year. Playing poker and the other nightly diversions of his colleagues bored him. He roomed in a dingy hotel with another equally un-informed Democratic freshman and found, all in all, that being a member of the legislature of one of the greatest states in the Union was a be-wildering and frustrating experience.

After two years, he almost decided to forget the whole business and take a good job offered him in the City of New York's Buildings Depart-ment. At the urging of Tom Foley, his ward leader, however, Smith decided to stick it out and give the Assembly another try. Foley also gave him two pieces of advice. One was: "Never promise anything that you are not perfectly sure you can deliver. Most people who come to public men are not looking for the truth. They like to be jollied. The safest practice is to tell them the truth, and after they have tried out a dozen other people, they will come to the conclusion that you were right in the beginning." The other was, "Don't speak until you have something to say. Men who talk just for the pleasure of it do not get very far."[9]

Smith had too much pride and common sense to speak in the Assembly or introduce bills until he was clear in his mind what it was all about, and he was safe from possible embarrassment. Not being in the law or insur-ance business, he was not able to carry on two professions at once. Un-like many of his fellow assemblymen, he did not rush back to New York for long weekends and show up at the legislature only from Tuesday to Thursday. He put in a full work week at the capital, diligently reading bills and reports. He educated himself for his job.

Gradually he made headway. In 1906, his third year in the Assembly, he obtained a seat on the Insurance Committee. This was an interesting and informative assignment, since Charles Evans Hughes was conducting that year his famous investigation into the malpractices of the insurance industry. In the following session he served on the committee to consider a new charter for New York City. His efforts won grudging praise from the Citizens Union, a silk-stocking reform organization that usually took a glum view of Tammany's representatives. In 1906 the Union termed him "intelligent and active, somewhat above the average of machine men" and two years later rated him "increasingly active and aggressive; very much above average in intelligence, force and usefulness, though still in-clined to follow machine in support of bad measures."[10]

Smith also began to emerge as a leader in the Democratic caucus. His native wit and charm won him friends. In 1905 he acquired a sturdy com-rade-in-arms in Robert F. Wagner, a young lawyer of German immigrant parentage who resembled Smith in his shrewdness as a politician and his capacity to learn as he went. Smith and Wagner shared rooms together for several years.

In 1911 the Democrats captured the governorship and both houses of the legislature for the first time in many years. Smith was elected majority leader and Wagner, by then a senator, was elected leader in the upper house. Smith also became Chairman of the Ways and Means Committee. This job delighted him. He was able to go over every appropriation bill in minute detail and learn countless facts about the state government which fascinated him.

Smith dropped down to minority leader the next year, but in 1913, when the Democrats resumed control, he was elected speaker. During these years of legislative leadership, Smith was a loyal and undeviating agent for the programs and objectives of Charles Murphy, the taciturn ruler of Tammany Hall. Smith used to say decisions were made in "an unbossed Democratic caucus." This prompted a wag on the New York *World* to define an unbossed caucus as Murphy at one end of a telephone wire and Smith at the other. A bossed caucus would have been Murphy in Albany giving his instructions in person. William Allen White later observed of Smith that "he took orders until he could give them." Smith, of course, would have defined the relationship differently, but White was essentially correct. This was the way of the organization, and Smith was an organization man to the core.

Smith carried out missions such as opposition to strict liquor control and to Governor Hughes's efforts to ban racetracks. In 1911 he and Wagner tried unsuccessfully to push through "Blue-Eyed Billy" Sheehan, Murphy's candidate for the United States Senate. He put across the so-called "Murphy Charter" for New York City over the outraged screams of the good-government groups. In 1913, when Governor Sulzer proved unresponsive to the suggestions of Tammany, which had elected him, Smith and Wagner had the legislature impeach him on the basis of some trivial violations of the campaign-expenditures law. Sulzer was an honorable if erratic executive. Many political organizations have denied renomination to politicians who became too independent, but the impeachment of Sulzer was a peak in the high-handed, ruthless enforcement of obedience to a political organization.

Smith was a tough and efficient leader. He rounded up the votes, led the debates, and carried out his agenda expeditiously. As Speaker, he gaveled bills through with dispatch. As a rough-and-tumble debater on the floor, he was unsurpassed, and his sense of humor rarely deserted him. He once suggested to the author of an amendment that he should have used "and" instead of "or" in expressing his legislative intent. The other assemblyman resented this correction and challenged him to cite the grammatical rule that applied to the case. Smith paused a moment, and then replied, "I will refer the gentleman to the grammatical rule that says 'When a pluperfect adjective precedes a noun, insert a plus.' "

There was another and more important side to Smith's development during these years than that of the smart tactician and manipulator. He was fighting steadily for social welfare and labor reforms that would help the lives of the ordinary people of the state. He fought for a workman's compensation law to protect laborers injured in accidents, for a law preventing child labor, for an eight-hour day for women workers, widows' pensions, stricter public-utility regulation, and health and housing legislation.

In 1911, 145 women lost their lives when the Triangle Shirt factory burned. The building was unsafe and there were not enough exits. Scores of women were trapped inside, and others jumped from windows to their death in a frantic effort to escape. This grim tragedy aroused the public to an awareness of the evil sweatshop conditions that had long prevailed. The legislature created an investigating committee of which Wagner was chairman and Smith vice-chairman.

The Factory Commission, as it was known, had the duty of inquiring into a wide range of problems, including:

"1. Hazard to life because of fire; covering fire prevention, arrangement of machinery, fire drills, inadequate fire escapes and exits, number of persons employed in factories and lofts.

"2. Danger to life and health because of unsanitary conditions; ventilation, lighting and heating arrangement, hours of labor.

"3. Occupational diseases such as industrial consumption, lead poisoning, and bone disease.

"4. Adequate inspection.

"5. Manufacturing in tenement houses.

"6. Laws and ordinances already existing, and the extent to which they were enforced."[11]

The commission sat for sixteen months, or rather it walked, climbed, crawled, and poked through good, bad, and worse factories during that length of time. Frances Perkins, later to be Roosevelt's Secretary of Labor, was a member of the Commission. She recalled some of these inspection trips in her book *The Roosevelt I Knew*: "We used to make it our business to take Al Smith . . . to see the women, thousands of them coming off the ten-hour night-shift on the rope walks in Auburn. We made sure that Robert Wagner personally crawled through the tiny hole in the wall that gave egress to a steep iron ladder covered with ice and ending twelve feet from the ground, which was euphemistically labelled 'Fire Escape' in many factories. We saw to it . . . [they] got up at dawn and drove with us for an unannounced visit to a Cattaraugus County cannery and that they saw with their own eyes the little children, not adolescents, but five-, six-, and seven-year olds, snipping beans and shelling peas. We made sure that they saw the machinery that would scalp a girl or cut off a man's arm. Hours so long that both men and women were depleted and exhausted became realities to them through seeing for themselves the dirty little factories."[12]

Smith visited factories "where he knew that little children, who had been at work there a few minutes before, were huddled into an elevator and held there between floors until the Commission's visit was over. He saw whole families, mothers with their children, little boys and girls, working all the daylight hours and seven days a week in the canneries and the fields."

The Factory Commission issued a three-volume report recommending that night work for women be forbidden, women be banned from foundry work, a fifty-four-hour week and ultimately a forty-eight-hour week be required for women, and workers be given one day's rest in every seven. The report also recommended that factories provide seats for women workers, child labor be curbed, and that the law require every factory to have adequate stairways, fire escapes, and sprinkler systems. The report lashed out at tenement work and recommended stricter sanitation and safety inspection regulations. These and other suggestions became the charter for social reform in New York, and Smith fought for them all. Under his leadership in the legislature and later in the governor's office, they were eventually all written into law.

Smith frequently used his rather formidable talent for sarcasm during this long running battle for the Factory Commission recommendations. During one hearing, the canners opposed the bill giving workers one day's rest a week. They produced several clergymen who argued that the cannery workers were nearly destitute and needed seven days' wages. Smith looked at them sourly.

"If the good Lord were to revise the Decalogue, which He isn't going to do," he said, "I have no doubt that He would pick a committee from these gentlemen to do it and that one commandment at least would be rewritten to read, 'Remember the Sabbath Day to keep it holy, except in canneries.' "

The Consumers League, the Committee on Safety, the New York Child Labor Committee, and many other social-welfare organizations cooperated in the work of the Factory Commission. Samuel Gompers of the AFL and Mary E. Dreier, president of the Women's Trade Union League, were members of the Commission. Prominent social workers and settlement house leaders such as Lillian Wald, Frances Perkins, and Florence Kelly worked with Smith in the investigation.

This was Smith's first intimate relationship with reformers of this type. Previously as a clubhouse politico and young assemblyman, he had stood around with the ward hacks in Albany and New York and passed off sneering jokes about social workers and dumb do-gooders. Now he began to distinguish between the silk-stocking mugwumps who fluttered with horror over machine politics and these earnest, informed, socially conscious people who really wanted to do something for working people. He came to have a more tolerant attitude toward women in politics. Eventually, he came out for equal suffrage and as governor appointed many women to government positions.

More important, these social workers and intellectuals imparted a new coherence to his own impressions and pragmatic intuitions. His thinking took on a new dimension and began to fill out into a self-sufficient philosophy of society and government. As Norman Hapgood and Henry Moskowitz were later to comment in their semiauthorized biography, *Up from the City Streets*, the Factory Commission gave Smith "a permanent set of contacts . . . which any progressive legislator and executive needs. Smith was quick to realize their value.

"For years he had been oppressed by the absence of general ideas and general purposes in both political organizations. Those general ideas and general purposes were now made available to him."[13]

In fighting for the reforms of the Factory Commission, Smith often found himself opposed by those same Republicans who clamored so loudly against racetracks and Tammany and the saloon. Now, as spokesmen for the business community, these so-called reformers stood fast against another kind of reform. Smith and his adversaries spoke from different moral orders and appealed to conflicting hierarchies of values. Each could rightly think himself honest and a sincere champion of good government.

In putting through the Factory Commission proposals, Smith used the same tactics he practiced in achieving Boss Murphy's political ends. He cajoled and pressured, traded votes and favors, appealed to loyalty and made use of friendship. Some of his friends on both sides of the aisle in the Assembly were members of that cynical fraternity known as the Black Horse Cavalry who trafficked with lobbyists, held up businessmen with "strike bills," and operated for cash on behalf of insurance companies and private utilities. Smith steered clear of their lucrative entanglements and later, as governor, his rigidly honest leadership broke much of the effectiveness of these influence rings. But he could not have accomplished anything by "passing on the other side of the street." He had friends alike among the reactionaries of Bill Barnes's Republican machine and the Tammany disciples of narrow and ferociously corrupt Crokerism. He had a first-name acquaintance with good and evil. Smith grew up in the machine and grew out of it, but even as he transcended it, he remained alert to its potentialities for good as well as its limitations. It was of this period in his life that William Allen White remarked, "He keeps his old friends with his heart and makes new ones with his head."

3

Twelve years in the Assembly brought Smith statewide fame, experience, and valuable friendships, but in 1915 he was forty-two, had no money, and was still trying to take care of a wife and five children on thirty dollars a week. If he had been a lawyer, it might have been different but he was not. His envy of the financial opportunities open to the lawyer may have accounted for the cynicism and distrust with which he regarded the legal breed. Observing a law student at his studies, he once remarked, "There's a boy learning to take a bribe and call it a fee."

A functioning machine, however, is mindful of its own. In 1915 Tammany somewhat unexpectedly moved Smith into the job of Sheriff of New York County. The sheriff was at that time legally entitled to half the fees he collected. In two years Smith was able to save $105,000 which provided the backlog of financial security for his later career. He easily defeated the incumbent Republican sheriff. He was even endorsed for the post by the Republican *New York Tribune* and the conservative Citizens' Union. Concerning this endorsement, the New York *World* observed urbanely: "The Citizens' Union endorsement has always been part of the honest graft of Republican candidates for main offices. . . . It is a scandal that Charles F. Murphy should pander to the moral sentiment of the community and permit a respectable candidate to be nominated for Sheriff."

After two quiet years in the sheriff's office, Smith was elected president of the board of aldermen in 1917 on a citywide ticket headed by John F. Hylan of Brooklyn. Hylan's chief claim to recognition was his home residence, for Brooklyn was due for recognition from the party. Hylan was a self-educated man, but unlike Smith there was not much native material to develop. The motorman-turned-lawyer remained a bumbler and a blunderer with a talent for inferior rhetoric and a capacious unconcern for facts. Smith deplored Hylan in private and loyally supported him in public.

The 1918 election ended this strain on Smith's good nature. The Democrats, with enthusiastic upstate legislators leading the way, nominated Smith for governor. He squeezed through by 14,000 votes over Governor Charles Whitman, the Republican incumbent.

Smith was the first man actively identified with Tammany to be elected governor in more than fifty years. He later recalled that Tammany leader Murphy said to him after the election, "Al, it is a great thing for you, Mrs. Smith and the children and your mother. The organization will stand behind you like one man so that you may make good in the office of governor. I am anxious to see you make good so that we can show the people that a young man who has come from the lower east side and has been closely associated with all the phases of party activity, can make good."[14]

Smith himself felt this motive for success keenly. He thought of his mother, his wife and children, and his other relatives and friends in the old ward as well as his new friends among the social workers and the intellectuals. He was determined to succeed and to justify their confidence.

Smith's appointments to state office were conspicuously enlightened. Especially notable was the selection of Colonel Frederick Stuart Greene as superintendent of the Highway Department. This agency gave out roadbuilding contracts and was an important political prize. Greene, however, was an engineer and not a politician, and he sometimes gave the party faithful short shrift. Smith knew that when it came to building roads, good government would be the best politics in the long run. "Of course, he is a so-and-so in May," he reportedly explained to aggrieved politicians, "but think what an angel he is in November."

Smith appointed a Reconstruction Commission to study many of the state's economic and financial problems, including housing, unemployment, and taxation. Frances Perkins remembered that the first meeting called to discuss the Commission was held in the evening at the Governor's mansion. Smith asked his wife and his mother to attend because there would be ladies present. Mrs. Belle I. Moskowitz, secretary of the Commission, was later to become his most important adviser, and more influential with him than any man.

Prohibition came to the fore during Smith's first term. He unsuccessfully urged the rejection of the Eighteenth Amendment. This dreary and unprofitable issue was to dog his steps throughout the rest of his active public career.

The years 1919–1920 were the time of the first big red scare in America and of a lingering mood of wartime conformism and orthodoxy. Five Socialists had been elected to the New York Assembly. In 1920 the Republican-controlled legislature voted to oust them from their seats. Although it was an internal problem of the legislature over which he had no control, Smith spoke out against this arbitrary act. It was "inconceivable," he said, "that a political party duly constituted and legally organized should be deprived of its right to expression so long as it had honestly, by lawful methods of education and propaganda, succeeded in securing representation, unless the chosen representatives are unfit as individuals. . . . Our faith in American democracy is confirmed not only by its results, but by its methods and organs of free expression. They are the safeguards against revolution. To discard the methods of representative government leads to the misdeeds of the very extremists we denounce and serves to increase the number of the enemies of orderly free government."

After ousting them, the legislature conducted lengthy public hearings to prove that the Socialists were hostile to the American form of government and favored its overthrow by force. Charles Evans Hughes and many prominent members of the bar came to their defense, but were unsuccessful. As soon as the seats were declared vacant, Smith immediately ordered a special election so that the voters in those districts would not be denied representation. The five Socialists ran again and all were re-elected.

Hughes and other intelligent conservatives joined Smith in opposition to the legislature's action. For Smith to speak out was an especially courageous and useful action. The Democratic voters from whom he drew his own political strength were not particularly well equipped to understand the significance of this issue. Many of them, like Smith himself, were Catholics, and the philosophy of the Church, with its distrust of secularism and its opposition to revolution in Russia, could easily be misapplied to justify the repression of dissent. Many of Smith's followers were also readers of the Hearst papers which were busily at work inflaming the public mind and screaming for 100 percent Americanism. Under these circumstances it would have been safer and much easier for Smith to wave the flag and go with the crowd. Instead he stood up for common sense. It was a mission of political education that a leader of his background was peculiarly fitted to do, and he did it.

The legislature also set up the Lusk Committee to investigate revolutionary radicalism. Lusk and his colleagues went through all the hijinks which similar committees of Congress have more recently made familiar on a national scale. The Lusk Committee recommended several pieces of legislation, including a curb on free speech, a loyalty oath for school-teachers, the registration of private schools, and state regulation of private school courses of study so as to prevent the young from being indoctrinated with radical ideas. The legislature passed three of these bills. Smith vetoed them.

One bill provided severe penalties for what was termed "criminal anarchy," and established a special agency to ferret it out. In his veto message, Smith declared, "The traditional abhorrence of a free people of all kinds of spies and secret police is valid and justified and calls for the disapproval of this measure."

Rejecting a bill to establish a loyalty test for teachers, he said: "Opposition to any presently established institution, no matter how intelligent, conscientious or disinterested this opposition might be, would be sufficient to disqualify the teacher. Every teacher would be at the mercy of his colleagues, his pupils, and their parents, and any work or act of the teacher might be held by the Commissioner [of Education] to indicate an attitude hostile to some of the institutions of the United States or of the State.

"The bill," he continued, "unjustly discriminates against teachers as a class. It deprives teachers of their right to freedom of thought, it limits the teaching staff of the public schools to those only who lack the courage or the mind to exercise their legal right to just criticism of existing institutions. The bill confers upon the Commissioner of Education a power of interference with freedom of opinion which strikes at the foundations of democratic education."

In a third statement vetoing the bill to register private schools and control their courses of study, Smith observed that "the clash of conflicting opinions, from which progress arises more than from any other source, would be abolished by law, tolerance and intellectual freedom destroyed and an intellectual autocracy imposed upon the people."

He reminded the legislators of Benjamin Franklin's remark that "they that can give up essential liberty to obtain a little temporary safety deserve neither liberty nor safety."

"But I go further," Smith added; "the safety of this government and its institutions rests upon the reasoned and devoted loyalty of its people. It does not need for its defense a system of intellectual tyranny which, in the endeavor to choke error by force, must of necessity crush truth as well."[15]

Smith's vetoes killed the bills, but in the succeeding Republican administration they were repassed and signed by Governor Miller. Smith did not give up the fight. Upon returning to office in 1923, he recommended repeal of these pieces of repressive legislation. Aided by the somewhat calmer state of public opinion at that time, and by his own skill at political pressure, he succeeded.

In 1923 he also pardoned Jim Larkin, a radical agitator who had been imprisoned under the state's criminal-anarchy law. Larkin had advocated a revolution to establish a dictatorship of the proletariat. In freeing him, Smith denounced this Communist theory:

"I pardon Larkin, therefore," he said, "not because of agreement with his views, but despite my disagreement with them. The public assertion of an erroneous doctrine is perhaps the surest way to disclose the error and make it evident to the electorate. And it is a distinct disservice to the State to impose, for the utterance of a misguided opinion, such extreme punishment as may tend to deter, in proper cases, that full and free discussion of political issues which is a fundamental of democracy."[16]

Smith carried his deep convictions about civil liberties into the field of censorship. Although as a good Catholic he opposed birth control, he never used his power to obstruct the dissemination of propaganda by the Birth Control League, and never advocated any coercive legislation against it. "Censorship in any form cannot be tolerated in a democratic government," he once observed.

In 1923 he and Jimmy Walker, then majority leader in the state senate, succeeded in defeating a book-censorship bill sponsored by the Society for the Suppression of Vice. An upstate Republican offered the bill, which also had support from some city Democrats. Passages from D. H. Lawrence and other authors were read aloud in the senate to the accompaniment of much smirking and headshaking. Several senators spoke of the ruinous effects of bad books on a woman's virtue.

"I have heard with great interest the addresses of the gentlemen on the other side," Walker said, "and I have the utmost respect for what they have said. But I submit, gentlemen, that they are either naïve or confused. Why all this talk about womanhood? I have never yet heard of a girl being ruined by a book."

Smith in his statements argued that the existing statutes against lewdness were sufficient protection against obscene books and that any more restrictive legislation would be an invasion of traditional American freedom of expression. Between them, Smith's eloquence and Walker's wit sank the "Clean Books" bill.

Smith struggled repeatedly but unsuccessfully for the repeal of the motion-picture censorship law which gave to a three-man board the power to censor or ban any movie.

"Censorship cannot exist without censors," Smith pointed out in a message in 1924, "and no purely administrative body should have the right to impose its opinion of what should or should not be published or exhibited upon any citizen whose conduct did not transgress the law of the land. The power in one group of men to prevent the publication or exhibition of anything that does not transgress the law is a power which of necessity destroys initiative and shackles freedom of speech."[17]

4

Smith was narrowly defeated for reelection in 1920 by Nathan Miller. Bucking the Harding landslide, he ran one million votes ahead of the national Democratic ticket.

In retirement, he worked at a salary of thirty thousand dollars a year as chairman of the United States Trucking Corporation. Not unexpectedly, he proved an able business executive, reorganizing the firm's operations and putting it in the black. He also served by appointment from the outgoing President Wilson as a member of the National Board of Indian Commissioners and by appointment from Miller as a member of the New York Port Authority.

Two years later, he ran against Miller again and defeated him by 386,000 votes, at that time a record-breaking majority. The campaign between Miller and Smith was a genuine test between two conflicting social philosophies. Miller was a capable, high-minded, and thoroughgoing conservative. Discussing proposed social legislation, he had said: "I assert that it is the function of the state not to make life comfortable, not to remove these cares which the sentimentalists say afflict the hard-working people, not to make it certain that regardless of their industry and thrift they will be taken care of whether they are employed or not. I say that if you are to have the stimulus which is necessary to human progress you must leave to the individual himself the provision for his old age or for his unemployment or for his sickness."

When the votes were counted, he wired Smith, "Evidently the voters prefer your brand of government to mine."

Smith was reelected by safe majorities in 1924 and 1926 over Theodore Roosevelt, Jr., and Ogden Mills, respectively, two attractive conservative scions of the aristocracy. The Republicans were not, after Miller's defeat, to return to power in New York State for twenty years, and then only under the leadership of a leader who accepted without question all the basic social reforms Smith pioneered.

As governor, Smith continued to be as fascinated by the mechanics and organization of the state government as he had been as chairman of the Ways and Means Committee. He became entranced with the analogy between the state government and a business corporation. The legislature, he often said, was his board of directors and the voters his stockholders. It was not really a sound comparison, but it was effective political shorthand in arguing for governmental reforms. Under his leadership, the 189 agencies and commissions were consolidated into twenty departments. The long ballot was scrapped and only four policy-making offices placed before the people for election. In 1927 he introduced the cabinet system in New York State government. He overhauled the chaotic appropriation system and introduced an executive budget. Many useless jobs were abolished, civil service was strengthened, and managerial economies made. He advocated the lengthening of the governor's term to four years and the scheduling of state elections in nonpresidential years, changes not brought about until a decade later.

Most of these structural reforms appear, in retrospect, to have been only common sense. Many of them had earlier been proposed by Elihu Root and Charles Evans Hughes. If the Republicans in the legislature had gone along with them, they would have passed with little attention. By fighting them, they focused attention on Smith and helped build him up as a national figure.

"The fact of the matter is: it is not my program," Smith once sensibly conceded. "The real truth about it is I could not think that all out myself."

Smith was busy at more than reaping the field that Hughes and Root had sown. He put through an extensive body of social legislation. He signed the law giving women teachers equal pay with men. During his time in office, the state contribution to education increased from $9,000,-000 annually to $82,000,000. He obtained a law encouraging private enterprise to undertake slum clearance and housing development, and unsuccessfully championed more ambitious housing plans. He obtained the forty-eight-hour week for women workers and strengthened the workmen's compensation law. He spoke in favor of the Child Labor amendment despite the massed opposition of Catholic bishops, and unsuccessfully urged the legislature to submit it as a referendum to the voters. He saved Niagara and other waterpower sites from exploitation by the private utilities.

Smith was also interested in roads, parks, and grade-crossing elimination. He barnstormed the state in behalf of various bond issues to finance projects in these fields.

His campaign for the $15,000,000 bond issue to build parks and bathing beaches on Long Island for the people of New York City encountered the adamant opposition of wealthy Long Island property owners. He was attending a public hearing on the subject when one suburbanite complained that this plan would bring "the rabble" to Long Island. The presiding officer did not notice this remark, but Smith heard it and let out an anguished scream.

"Hey!" he cried. "Rabble! I am the rabble!"

On another occasion, one of the opponents sadly inquired where a poor millionaire could go nowadays to find peace and quiet. Smith suggested he try a hospital.

The level of Smith's appointments steadily rose the longer he stayed in office. In addition to the notoriously honest Colonel Greene, the Highway Commissioner so well disliked by politicians, he named Frances Perkins chairman of the Industrial Board that administers the workmen's-compensation law and the factory code. He appointed Bernard Shientag as Industrial Commissioner. Both Shientag and Miss Perkins had served with him during the Triangle fire investigation. He appointed Mark Graves, who had been Miller's budget director, to a top position in the Tax Department. He retained several of Miller's other appointees. He filled the post of state architect by the then uncommon method of asking the American Institute of Architects to recommend several qualified men. When it was later discovered that the man he had selected from their list was not a Democrat, Smith is reported to have said, "I didn't ask him what his politics were. After all, I was hiring an architect and not a precinct captain!"

Two of Smith's most controversial selections were Robert Moses, whom he named secretary of state, and Mrs. Belle Moskowitz, who served on the Port Authority and as his principal braintruster. Moses was a wealthy young Republican with a Phi Beta Kappa key from Yale, a Ph.D. from Columbia, and two years of study at Oxford. He had worked for the Bureau of Municipal Research and proved himself an expert at governmental reorganization, city planning, and many other subjects. Moses, brilliant, opinionated, and wonderfully irritating, ingratiated himself with no one except Smith, who respected his mind and came to be fond of him personally.

Mrs. Moskowitz, a graduate of Columbia Teachers College, and a professional social worker, was originally a Republican who had campaigned in 1912 for Theodore Roosevelt's Progressive Party. Her husband was Henry Moskowitz, Director of the Madison Street Settlement House and an independent Democrat who had served as Market Commissioner in the anti-Tammany administration of Mayor Mitchel. She had long been active as a labor arbitrator and a worker for women's suffrage.

It is curious that Charles Murphy and his Tammany associates who had broken and impeached Governor Sulzer a few years earlier over this very issue of patronage should have been so tolerant of Smith's enlightened approach. Undoubtedly their pride in "one of our own" who had made good gave Smith unusual leeway. Murphy, moreover, was growing old. He knew death had one hand on his shoulder, and he had sufficient imagination to want to end his career on a high note. What better way than to give Smith latitude and build him up as a candidate for President?

In the middle 1920's the lesser bosses and some of the rank and file in the organization began to resent Smith's frequent appointment of Republicans and his development of an entourage of nonpartisan experts. They complained that he was surrounding himself with Jews and intellectuals, and grumbled, "Al is going highhat." Smith, however, was too powerful to care about such criticisms and few dared make them to his face.

By then, Smith had gone a long way from the old Fourth Ward and the political ethics of Fourteenth Street. Crucial in this development was his irrevocable destruction of the remnants of the political power of William Randolph Hearst.

The eccentric, power-hungry publisher had had a checkered career in New York and national politics during Smith's lifetime. In 1905 and again in 1909, he had been an independent anti-Tammany candidate for mayor. On the other hand, in 1906 he was Tammany's candidate for governor. By 1917 his intermittent wars with the organization had ended in a negotiated peace. He and Murphy joined hands in electing John F. Hylan as mayor. Hylan took Hearst's advice on policy and to Tammany he gave the patronage. To the practical minds of the organization it seemed an eminently agreeable compromise.

Smith was largely a bystander in most of this feuding and maneuvering. Busy with his work in Albany, he did not often come in contact with Hearst. In 1917, as a candidate for the presidency of the Board of Aldermen, and in 1918, as a candidate for the governorship, he had Hearst's editorial support. During his first year as governor, he politely ignored most of the publisher's suggestions. Hearst never enjoyed being ignored. In the summer of 1919, his newspapers opened up with a vicious attack on Smith for his alleged collusion with the milk trust. The cost of milk in New York City was high at that time and there was profiteering but the governor could do little about it except remonstrate with the legislature for its failure to act. The milk problem was under the control of a commission whose members were selected by the legislature and whom Smith could not remove, no matter what their unfitness. Smith had asked for action but in vain. Hearst's *New York Evening Journal* ignored all this.

"Governor Smith is whimpering and whining, but babies in New York are dying for lack of milk," it cried. The paper charged incorrectly that the governor had the power to fix the price of milk and had refused to do so. It printed horrible pictures of starving children and worried mothers and ran cartoons of Smith as a dog and a viper. Smith took this in silence for a time. Then he spoke out. He characterized the Hearst papers as "foul, dirty, slimy." He termed Hearst "the greatest living enemy of the people whose cause he pretends to espouse." He challenged the publisher to appear with him in a public debate on the issue. When Hearst did not reply and the Hearst papers did not carry any mention of the proposed debate, Smith asked him what kept "his filthy sheets strangely silent." Despite the silence, arrangements for the debate went ahead anyway for the night of October 29th at Carnegie Hall.

Hearst of course did not appear. The hall was filled to overflowing. Smith did not leave the audience in suspense for long.

"I am going to ask," he said, "for your absolute silence and attention. I feel that I am here tonight upon a mission as important not only to myself but to this city, this state, and this country as I could possibly perform. Of course, I am alone.—I know the man to whom I issued the challenge, and I know that he has not got a drop of good, clean, pure, red blood in his whole body. And I know the color of his liver, and it is whiter, if that could be, than the driven snow.

"In his morning edition he has a picture of me with a laboring man cartooned on one side, and a mother and her children on the other. The heading of it is: 'Answer these people, Governor Smith'; I want to say to this audience that I was anxious to bring him on this platform so that he could answer to these people. They need no answer from me. They need it from him. They need it from the man that is exploiting them. They need it from the man that is sowing in their minds and in their hearts the seeds of disorder and discontent to suit his own selfish purpose."

Smith was in superb form. His face red with anger and his voice often thick with emotion, he took up Hearst's charges one by one and refuted them. As always, he was speaking off the cuff with only a few notes and his extraordinary memory to guide him. His voice, with all its native harshness, rose and fell, cracked and roared. He hammered the rostrum and he pointed with scorn. An honest, angry man of God from the East Side was cussing out the Devil and setting his people free. It was melodrama and it was great.

"Early in my remarks," he said, "I said something about misleading the poor. I cannot think of a more contemptible man—my power of imagination fails me to bring into my mind's eye a more despicable man—than the man that exploits the poor. Any man . . . that conjures up for you a fancied grievance against your government or against the man at the head of it, to help himself, is breeding the seeds of anarchy and dissatisfaction more disastrous to the welfare of the community . . . than any other teaching I can think of because, at least, the wildest anarchist, the most extreme Socialist, the wildest radical that you can think of may at least be sincere in his own heart. He may think that it is right when he preaches it. But the man that preaches to the poor of this or of any other community discontent and dissatisfaction to help himself and to destroy, as he said he would, the governor of the state, is a man as low and as mean as I can picture him."

Smith spoke for some two hours. In conclusion, he said: "Nobody that ever went up to the Governor's office went there with a graver sense of the responsibility of that office than I did. What could there possibly be about me that I should be assailed in this reckless manner by this man? I have more reason, probably, than any man I will meet here tonight to have a strong love and a strong devotion for this country, for this state, and for this city.

"Look at what I have received at its hands: I left school and went to work when I was fifteen years of age. I worked hard, night and day; I worked honestly and conscientiously at every job that I was ever put at, until I went to the governor's chair at Albany. What can it be? It has got to be jealousy, it has got to be envy, it has got to be hatred, or it has to be something that nobody understands, that forces me to come down here, into the city of New York before this audience, and urge them to organize in this city to stay the danger that comes from these papers, to the end that the health, the welfare and the comfort of this people, of the people of this state, may be promoted and we may be rid of this pestilence that walks in the dark."

As he ended, the audience rose in a wild ovation, and then proceeded to pass a resolution calling for a "sound public opinion directed against the insidious and disintegrating opinions" of the Hearst newspapers.[18]

Smith's speech destroyed the fake milk scandal. Curiously enough, the Hearst papers the next year supported Smith for reelection, a striking proof of the fact that the publisher's "crusades" were based on nothing more substantial than his own calculated opportunism and the state of his digestion at the moment.

In 1922 Hearst was eager for another try at public office. His money, his newspapers, and his connections with the Hylan administration still gave him considerable political strength. He wanted to be governor and he charitably let it be known that he would have no objection if Smith ran for United States senator on the same ticket. Actually, Hearst was prepared to take either office himself. His agents made overtures to Smith, but he rebuffed them. When the delegates gathered in Syracuse in late September for the nominating convention, the issue was still in doubt. Murphy, still at peace with Hearst, was as always amenable to a deal, but left the decision to Smith. The majority of upstate delegates detested Hearst, but the Tammany men, who had the largest bloc of votes, were eager to placate him because their jobs and contracts depended on Mayor Hylan, and Hylan was a Hearst man. One after another of these sweaty, beefy, cigar-chewing brethren paraded into Smith's suite and urged him to be reasonable. He must, they insisted, come to terms with Hearst. If he did not go along, they argued, then the boys, his friends, would be out in the cold at City Hall. Smith was unmoved.

"The answer is NO! NO! I won't run with Hearst. I won't do it for you, Murphy, McCooey, or all of you together," he told them.

The tension mounted. Opinion among the delegates circulating in little groups in the lobbies swung back and forth. Smith was warned that if he did not give in, he would be defeated on the floor of the convention. Hearst had the votes, he was warned.

"I'm damned if I will," he replied. "I'm damned if I will! I may be licked, but I'll lick Hearst, too, if I never do anything again."

On the day of the voting, opinion began to turn imperceptibly in Smith's favor. With hours to go, Hearst's managers became stricken with panic. They realized they could not beat Smith down. Hearst did not want to be defeated in a straight-out fight on the floor. He wired a request that his name not be presented. The fight was over. Smith was nominated by acclamation. Hearst's political career was ended.

The lead story in the next morning's New York *World* began: "Alfred E. Smith not only is the Democratic nominee for Governor but is undisputed state leader of his party. He made his fight on a principle from which he never swerved. Even his foes who saw his struggle single-handed against Hearst, Hylan, Murphy and McCooey . . . admit his supremacy."[19]

From then on, Smith was bigger than Tammany Hall, bigger than his party. Two years later Murphy died. The next year after that Tom Foley, the boss of the Fourth Ward who had started Smith on his political career, died. The successors to these old powers were not men who could overshadow the governor. George Olvany, the new leader of Tammany, for example, had been one of Smith's aides in the sheriff's office. This represented a subtle and far-reaching change in the Tammany scheme of things. For the first time in its history, the real leader was not an organization boss who stayed out of public office but a man with a great public office and with interests and obligations that far transcended Tammany. The old balance of power in the boss-candidate relationship had been altered and, as it turned out, altered irreparably.

The mayoralty election of 1925 was the conclusive proof of Smith's new dominance. Hylan was seeking a third term. Smith opposed him. Though he disliked the mayor's subjection to Hearst's influence, what was more important, he had no respect for him as a man.

"I supported him the two times he was a candidate," Smith observed, "—and if I say it myself, I made more intelligent speeches for his election than he was able to make himself."

Smith ended Hylan's career as he had that of Hearst three years earlier.

Hylan's defeat was useful because, like Hearst, he was a demagogue whose useless rabble-rousing aroused the ordinary voters but directed their energies away from any useful solutions of practical problems. He thundered against Wall Street, the "plunderbund," and the British, but he was too incompetent to accomplish anything lasting once elected. It took an honest, effective, liberal politician of the stature of Smith to reach the masses of ordinary voters and get them to distinguish the real from the sham. A conservative could not have done it. The misfortune was, however, that in defeating Hylan, Smith did not choose a more reliable man for his purposes than the lighthearted James J. Walker. By dictating to Walker the selection of an honest man as his first police commissioner and by occasional interference behind the scenes, Smith tried to keep the new administration moving along constructive lines. But it was impossible to control the situation in the city from Albany. Walker failed badly to provide in the city the kind of enlightened, honest government Smith gave at the state level.

Although the 1925 victory proved stillborn, it did mark Smith as a responsible party leader of impressive stature. It was after this election that Senator Borah was heard to remark, "The Democratic Party has a candidate for President."

5

It was inevitable that Smith's ambitions should turn toward the Presidency. The Democratic Party seemed bankrupt of talent in the 1920's. Despite the handicaps of his religion and machine background, he was governor of the largest state in the Union and the most colorful and piquant figure on the national scene.

Smith was first placed in nomination at the San Francisco convention of 1920. Bourke Cochrane, an old-time Tammany spellbinder, made the nominating speech. Smith stood amid the crowd at the back of the hall and with simple vanity enjoyed the words and the demonstration that followed. He knew it was only a compliment and one of the delaying maneuvers leading to the nomination of James Cox, the real choice of the party bosses at that convention.

Four years later, the movement was serious. It was a mark of Boss Murphy's essential provincialism that he believed bringing the convention to New York would aid Smith's chances. The convention quickly became deadlocked between Smith and William G. McAdoo, and the party for 103 desperate ballots proceeded to tear itself apart. Prohibition was a major issue, and one which by its very nature was guaranteed to stir more emotionalism than good sense. Behind it stalked the ugly shadow of the Ku Klux Klan. Smith, being a practical politician, was not originally in favor of bringing the Klan to the floor for discussion, but he could not restrain his liberal and Catholic backers who insisted on a resolution denouncing the KKK. It failed by a narrow margin.

Early in the convention Smith saw that he was not going to be nominated. The sensible thing would have been to withdraw, but he could not. There were no strong second-rank candidates. His withdrawal would probably have thrown the nomination to McAdoo who, rightly or wrongly, had become the symbol of racial bigotry and fanaticism on the liquor issue. Such a withdrawal would have seemed an abandonment of the party to the enemy. Smith decided he had to stay in as long as McAdoo had a chance. This decision, like other choices he had to make in connection with his presidential efforts, was bad for him personally, and he knew it, but the situation seemed to him beyond his control. McAdoo, having more votes, was a long time in giving up his dream. The final nomination of the honorable and unexciting John W. Davis brought the jungle warfare to a dispirited end. Smith capped the anticlimax by making a dreary speech to the convention which unintentionally sounded like a paean of self-praise.

Smith's chances in the election of 1928 and in all future presidential elections were probably destroyed in those acrid, smoke-filled, hate-filled days of the 1924 convention. The only successful strategy a Catholic presidential candidate could adopt, as John F. Kennedy later demonstrated, was to appear the embodiment of reasonableness, and to stay that way, forever passing out sweet-smelling sleeping potions to the restless dragons. Rage he could never afford, even the rage to live and to claim what seemed rightfully his. Smith was a man of normal emotions in an abnormal situation.

In the four years that followed, Smith tried the way of a cautious man. He remained cannily silent on the prohibition issue. He began to talk more about waterpower, the tariff, the World Court, and other national issues in an effort to refute William Allen White's wisecrack that he was "a Galahad who has never ventured abroad." Carefully prepared biographies were circulated which set his Tammany background in proper perspective and made earnest appeals to the rural parts of the country to understand this man from the sidewalks.

"He is the first of our national heroes to be born amidst din and squalor," Norman Hapgood and Henry Moskowitz wrote in their best-selling biography, *Up from the City Streets*, in 1927. "His story suggests that in the future our vast cities may do better by humanity than we have feared. It is possible that their evils may be reduced, and that their sons may show not less energy, persistence, and initiative than have come heretofore from the silences and long labor of the ax and the plow."

Looking into his environment, they found "many elements tending to favor activity, independence, quickness of mind, and persistence. It will be decades before we reach any firm conclusion about whether our crowded streets are less promising soil for greatness than the solitary furrow and the village store."

The authors examined the parish and the ward in which Smith grew up. "The 18,000 people who composed the parish were wholesome. The differences were not fundamental between them and the kind of people who would have made up a town of 18,000 in the Middle West. They were unquestioning, like the people in the Middle West. A point of view of life had come to them and they accepted it. The people in the Middle West might be Presbyterians; these were Catholics. The people in the Middle West might have come from England and Sweden and Germany; all of these came from Ireland. But there was no dissent in either case. Virtue was virtue, vice was vice."

Hapgood and Moskowitz went from these early pages to write a penetrating and valuable book about Smith, but it is doubtful if this heavily defensive statement of the case for city life and city people had quite the effect in Iowa and Texas that was hoped. Virtue is indeed virtue everywhere, and vice is vice, but the differences were fundamental between urban and rural America in the 1920's. The differences bred by religion, racial origin, and way of life might be only accidental but they were crucial. Only time and social and economic change would alter them. The words that tried to bridge the gap had the false ring of an inferiority complex. Village America felt itself threatened. It did not want to be told how really similar the alien and the new were, but rather how it could protect itself against their encroachment and their swift, oncoming mastery.

Since the McAdoo candidacy disintegrated and no competing candidate emerged, Smith easily obtained the nomination in 1928. Before accepting, he wired the delegates that he was opposed to the mumbo jumbo in the platform concerning prohibition and would insist on recommending to the voters substantial modification of the Eighteenth Amendment. The convention gave way.

William Allen White, writing in 1928, gave a portrait of Smith as he emerged on the national scene as a presidential candidate: "Now meet and consider Alfred Emanuel Smith, Governor of the State of New York. Observe a stocky man, yet never pudgy, five feet seven, who looks five feet nine or ten sitting down, for he has a long, sturdy body. He is blond, well kept, with clear, fine, healthy skin, pink and white in fact, blue eyes, and fair hair that at one time may have been red—or it may have been tow in childhood. He is smooth-shaven, oval-faced, mean-jawed, with a pugnacious set to his head, which wags with fine self-assertion; a self-assertion that is never quite vanity. And as he talks one begins to realize that he is merely gesticulating with his long neck above sloping shoulders, over a broad chest set upon a scaffolding of nimble legs. He is articulate in every inch of his body. Now let's dress him, for Alfred Emanuel Smith, Governor of New York, is a dresser—which brands him for a city chap, as do the kind of clothes he wears. Behold a pink, hair-striped collar on top of a dark wine-colored bow tie, set above a V of shirt which shows small brownish-crimson figures on a white background with a slight pink thread running through it. Protruding from the top pocket of a dark, well-tailored coat are the scarlet tips of a handkerchief. Tan shoes, with appropriate silk socks, set off his properly creased gray trousers. He is a tailored man, who gives thought to wherewithal he should be clad; again the habit of a city chap. His blue eyes, looking casually at a man or a scene, remain curtained; bright flickering specks under dark lashes. Only when his emotions begin to rise do his eyelids open. Then his eyes glow with some incandescence which reveals a deeply earnest nature. His laughter is casual and incidental, but purpose glows in those wide scathing eyes."

He gives "an impression of balance—this kind of balance: a big heart and a clear brain; a balance that makes a man capable of loyalties based upon qualities of both heart and mind. He can be loyal to a friend; but can go to the stake for an idea over the body of his friend—and keep his friend. Nice persons and well-bred come into his office and, seeing him spitting nervously on the carpet as he smokes a big brown cigar, are shocked at his manners."[20]

Although he had anticipated his nomination, he was ill-prepared to wage a national campaign. "July and August of 1928 were probably the busiest months in my life," he wrote in his autobiography. "Many of the national issues were new to me. I had made no detailed study of them and was without knowledge of the party's attitude." This lack of preparation was inexcusable but characteristic. Smith had buoyant self-confidence, and his mind was such that he could confront issues only when they left the realm of speculation and came before him in the shape of specific, practical problems.

Hoover's great victory was inevitable. It was also inevitable that Smith should attribute his defeat to his religion, the prohibition issue, and the ugly whispering campaign. The undercover stories hurt him deeply in a way that only the victim of such a smear attack can perhaps fully comprehend. Smith was able to indulge in the melancholy pastime of comparing his vote in the rural areas of many border and midwestern states with that of dry Protestant Democrats running on the ticket with him. "I was probably the outstanding victim of the last half century of a whispering campaign," he wrote in his autobiography. Yet the fact remains that he would not have won even if the South had remained solid and he had carried all the doubtful border states. Bigotry and prohibition contributed to his defeat but they were not decisive. He was defeated in the North and he was defeated by prosperity. He failed to carry New York or any of the larger industrial states.

Will Rogers, who concealed a good deal of political shrewdness behind his whimsical manner, advised Smith in a magazine article in October, 1927, not to run the next year. He put his finger on Smith's central difficulty: "You got no Issue.

"You can't lick this Prosperity thing," Rogers wrote, "even the fellow that hasn't got any is all excited over the idea.

"You politicians have got to look further ahead; you always got a putter in your hands when you ought to have a driver."[21]

Smith tried to meet the prosperity issue by the self-defeating tactic of proving he was as safe, sound, and well liked by business as anyone could desire. He named John Raskob, a financial associate of the Du Ponts as Chairman of the Democratic National Committee, and Jouett Shouse, a wealthy corporation lawyer, as its executive director. His campaign featured endorsements by prominent businessmen. On national issues, many of which he did not fully understand, he took positions close to the viewpoint of the business community. He adopted the Republican attitude in favor of immigration restriction as a means of keeping American wages high—a fallacious theory also favored by the leaders of the American Federation of Labor. Smith argued that restriction of immigration had begun under the Democrats although, in fact, the best Democratic tradition on the subject was contained in the messages of Cleveland and Wilson vetoing restrictive bills. On the tariff issue, Smith veered away from his party's historic low-tariff position. He argued for modification of the prohibition amendment but did not quite advocate repeal. Here his hedging did him no good, since in the eyes of both friends and foes of prohibition he stood as a symbol of the "dripping-wet," total-repeal viewpoint. He made gestures toward the farmers, but he did not have any farm plan bold enough to cope with the agricultural depression or stir the imagination of farm audiences. In his autobiography written a year after his defeat, Smith dismissed the farm issue with two sentences: "The farmer is inherently a Republican. I never made any impression on any considerable number of them in New York State."

It is hard to escape the conclusion that Smith's self-education, which had carried him so far, had not yet carried him far enough. Before 1928 he had not traveled widely in the midwestern and far western part of the country. He had not learned enough about the people and their problems in those regions. He had not developed an adequate staff to brief him on the details of national issues and to prepare broad-gauged solutions. He did not have sufficient time in a six-week tour to explain himself and the issues to the people of the whole country. He seemed to have forgotten that outside the industrial East, the Democratic Party was in terms of organization a shambles, and that not since Wilson's campaign in 1912 had a Democratic candidate stumped the country with a positive, constructive program on domestic issues. He had very little newspaper support. The reservoir of ignorance about economic issues was wide and deep. There simply was not time in one short campaign to overcome all these obstacles. Considering the many difficulties, he did a great deal. It was a genuine accomplishment to have polled more than fifteen million votes. His remark about the farmers undervalued his achievement. A later study showed that in Iowa, for example, while he had run poorly in the towns and cities, as was to be expected, he had drawn 43 percent of the vote from the farmers themselves, nearly double the figure polled by Cox eight years earlier. Senator Norris of Nebraska and Senator Blaine of Wisconsin, two progressive Republicans, had also rallied to his cause. These straws in the wind should have given him hope that in a later campaign he would have been able to swing to his side the midwestern liberal wing of the Republican Party, a feat that Roosevelt accomplished four and eight years later.

Smith's losing campaign was actually rich with meaning for the future. He stimulated and focused the political power of the millions of city voters of immigrant background. They voted in heavier numbers than ever before, and they voted Democratic. The revolutionary political pattern of 1928 made clear for the first time what was to be the power structure of the New Deal. In the nation's twelve largest cities (New York, Chicago, Philadelphia, Pittsburgh, Detroit, Cleveland, Baltimore, St. Louis, Boston, Milwaukee, San Francisco, and Los Angeles), the Republicans in 1920 polled an overall majority of 1,638,000 votes. This GOP majority declined slightly in 1924. In 1928 Smith converted it into a majority of 38,000 for the Democrats. He carried New York, Boston, Cleveland, St. Louis, and Milwaukee, and ran neck-and-neck in all the others except Los Angeles.

Democratic predominance in the cities is familiar today, but it was not prior to 1928. Until then, the Democratic Party was not much more of an urban party than were the Republicans. If the Democrats traditionally carried Boston and New York, the Republicans won Philadelphia,

Chicago, and St. Louis. Smith swung whole racial groups, such as the French Canadians in New England and the German Catholics in the midwestern cities, heavily into the Democratic column.

As Samuel Lubell has remarked, "Smith split not only the Solid South but the Republican North as well." Hoover carried 200 southern counties for the Republicans, but Smith carried 122 northern counties away from the GOP.[22]

The sons and daughters of the millions of immigrants who came to this country between 1880 and 1914 were coming of voting age in 1928. Smith was their spokesman. His program of the protective state was responsive to their needs. These voters and these ideas set in motion a profound shift in the nation's balance of political power. The economic misery that began a year later was the catalyst that brought these elements to solution. For Smith the depression came a year too late.

Yet when all analysis was done, it remained a bleak fact that a man qualified ·by integrity, talent, and achievement had been denied the Presidency in a campaign marred by religious hatred, racial bigotry, and snobbery toward a self-made man. Several states in the traditionally most loyal section of his party had rejected him. Thousands, and perhaps millions of voters, who admired his public record still voted for the other candidate. It was not that he had become just another defeated candidate. It seemed rather that the country had rejected Smith as a person, his family and his social origins, his vision of America. His thirty long years of self-education, of personal growth, of honest achievement seemed to have no meaning and no value after all. It is not surprising that in the years that followed Smith did not move on to new ideas and further growth but turned back inward upon himself. The promise of Brooklyn Bridge had not been fulfilled.

CHAPTER ELEVEN

Boston Irish

IN MAY, 1906, the city of Boston gave a banquet in honor of William O'Connell, its new Catholic archbishop. Mayor John F. "Honey Fitz" Fitzgerald told the audience: "The high reputation of the government of this Catholic city, compared with places like Cincinnati and Philadelphia, proves the mass of the Catholic people to be upright and clean in their political relations."[1]

The faintly defensive note within this proud statement reflected the newness of the Irish Catholics as the majority group in Boston. It was only sixty years since the famine-era Irish had come swarming into this Puritan city and only twenty years since they had drawn equal in numbers with the Protestant Yankee element. The first Irishman had been appointed to the Boston police force in 1851; the first Irishman had been elected mayor in 1886; the Irish won a majority of seats on the City Council in 1899; they elected their second mayor, Patrick Collins, in 1901. Fitzgerald had succeeded him. In 1906 it was too early to determine what effect the city's new masters would have on Boston's "high reputation."

1

The Irish in Boston found themselves in a situation that was unique in several ways. In other large American cities immigration was a gradual process continuing for a hundred years, and immigrants were drawn from a wide range of countries. But in Boston the Irish erupted on the scene in the 1840's in large numbers, and for the next forty years they were the only alien, immigrant group in Boston's midst. By the time the Italians, Russian Jews, Lithuanians, and other groups began to arrive in the 1880's, the Irish were already almost a majority of the entire city. In New York and Chicago, the Irish in the nineteenth century enjoyed brief periods of numerical hegemony, but very quickly they had to fall back upon their special advantages of language and early arrival and all their highly developed skills of political leadership to maintain themselves as first among their equals in the immigrant community. In Boston, the Irish could rely upon the sheer strength of numbers alone. The other immigrant groups did not come to the city in sufficient quantity to endanger Irish supremacy. This made for inbreeding and a complacent parochialism. Politics, for example, became an Irish family affair. But more than politics was affected. Social encounters of all kinds were not, as elsewhere, many-sided affairs. In Boston they were essentially two-dimensional, involving only the Irish and the Yankees.* This meant that social antagonisms were not easily diverted, diffused, and blurred. It was all too easy to keep one's hostilities in focus on a single target.

Second, the Irish were in competition with a uniquely accomplished and prestigious native group. Boston was already an old city when the Irish arrived. The Yankee aristocracy, soon to be dubbed the Brahmins, had a coherent sense of identity and a proud past. Their ancestors had started the movement toward the American Revolution with the Boston Tea Party, and evidences of that heroic past were everywhere in Boston and its environs: the Old North Church, Faneuil Hall, Bunker Hill. The stories of the deeds of James Otis, John Hancock, and the Adamses leaped up from the pages of every Irish child's grade-school textbook. Moreover, the Boston Yankee had produced most of the nation's literary genius in Emerson, Thoreau, Hawthorne, Alcott, and the rest. The institution of Harvard College, already more than two centuries old when the Irish arrived, dominated the local educational scene.

The weight of this history, these great names, and these awesome institutions was oppressive to the Boston Irish. It could not help but produce in them a massive inferiority complex. At every turn, society seemed to be looming up and asking: What achievements and leaders do you have to compare with these? The Irish who went to Chicago and St. Louis and the other cities of the Middle and Far West had the advantage of growing up with their city. Those who went to New York and Philadelphia encountered wealthy classes that were fluid and diverse in their makeup, and less directly continuous with the past. The Irish who went to Boston could not have been worse off, psychologically speaking, unless they had gone to Charleston, South Carolina. Ideally, the Boston Irish would have assimilated for themselves as much of their community's past as they could use and tolerantly ignored the rest. But

* The term "Yankee" should be understood as including not only the descendants of the original colonial settlers but also those who emigrated to the city from the farms and small towns of New England throughout the nineteenth century and also the Protestant immigrants from Nova Scotia and other parts of eastern Canada. The term "Brahmins" refers to Yankee aristocrats.

in each generation, the contemporary struggle with the Yankees for power made it difficult to identity with Yankee heroes and achievements of the past. The principal competitive cultural resource the Irish possessed was their religion, but it would be a long time before Catholic culture and Catholic prestige symbols could rival effectively those of the older element in the community. The Irish, understandably but unfortunately, often eased their resentments and inferiority feelings by cries of discrimination. The social and economic discrimination was real enough, but neither exaggeration nor self-pity was useful in combating it.

A third factor that helped bring about the peculiar Boston situation was the deadness of the city's economy. Since Boston has always been a banking, shipping, and distribution center, its economic vitality has been dependent upon the well-being of the New England hinterland it serves. Cheap Irish labor made possible rapid industrialization in the region after the Civil War. Shoes and textiles were the principal products, and they were the basis of many fortunes. But this prosperity was not rooted in any natural economic advantages. It was based on the cheapness of immigrant labor and the fact of being first in the field and thus having the jump on the rest of the country. By the turn of the century, the rest of the nation had overcome the time lag and recruited laborers cheaper than those of New England. The results were that shoe factories shifted their location to St. Louis and that the cotton mills began to slip away to the South. In 1900 there were 14,000,000 active cotton spindles in New England; forty years later, there were only 4,700,000. The textile cities of Lowell and Lawrence, north of Boston, had previously been called "the Lancashire of America," and this analogy proved disagreeably exact. Their hegemony in textiles, like that of Lancashire, was founded on ephemeral conditions. In the twentieth century New England's position as a textile producer declined in the nation as that of old England declined in the world.

Boston and its economic region suffered from the myopia of the ruling class. Despite the prosperity in the decades after 1865, Boston's industrial history was actually a series of lost opportunities. Although Boston was second only to New York as a money market, the city did not reap any substantial benefit. Local capitalists, for example, failed to tie the city in with one of the transcontinental railroad routes to the West despite the fact that they helped finance several of them. This meant that although Boston because of its northerly position is one day closer to Europe than is New York, it declined as a port since it had no direct access to middle-western markets. Boston capitalists even surrendered control of the local Fitchburg & Boston, and Boston & Albany railroads to outside interests.

Early efforts in the locomotive and heavy-engine industry came to nothing. Yet there was no compelling reason for this failure. Philadelphia and Wilmington, which became the centers of this industry, were not much nearer the source of raw materials than Boston. Although Boston had the edge over New York in the manufacture of ready-made clothing in 1870, it soon dropped behind. Later, the automobile industry had its beginning in nearby Springfield, Massachusetts, but this potential was never fulfilled. These missed opportunities cannot be accounted for by the necessities of geography. There were a few aggressive outsiders who came to Boston, utilized technological innovations and new business methods, and licked the handicaps of geography. Samuel Zemurray who created the United Fruit Company and the men who developed the United Shoe Machinery Corporation proved that brains could still outwit nature. Boston's business backwardness was due to the deadness of enterprise and the immobility of capital. The spirit of aggressive adventure was gone. Why was this so?

2

The slow contraction of Boston's rate of economic expansion was both a cause and a symbol of the silent shrinkage of the spirit experienced by a large part of the Yankee community in the late nineteenth and early twentieth centuries. The older families began to sterilize their capital by tying it up in trust funds, which tended to prolong these families in power because their wealth was less easily dissipated. Although this trend, in part, was only conforming to the familiar pattern of finance capitalism everywhere, it was also a response to and an insulating vacuum against the pressures of the ever-growing numbers of Irish who threatened the old values and the old ways. The trustee system was a holding action against the future.

The further this process went, the harder it became to drop old attitudes and develop new ones to fit the city's changing business problems. This rigidity of mind did not help old businesses to survive or new ones to grow. As dividends fell and enough attractive new employment opportunities did not develop, a growing sense of panic seized all sections of the community. The old families found it harder to discover safe, respectable niches for their less bright younger sons. Lacking a sufficient number of sinecures, they sometimes moved these scions into positions of responsibility where their imcompetence endangered the interests of all. At the same time, the ambitious sons of the Irish and other immigrants found the way ahead blocked. The more restless and

energetic moved to New York and other cities. They were the expend-
ables. Boston could do without them—or thought it could. One of those
who left was Mayor Fitzgerald's son-in-law, Joseph Kennedy, who
abandoned Boston after World War I for the more abundant business
opportunities of New York. In his old age "Honey Fitz" made of his
son-in-law's departure a parable of Boston's decline.

The dynamic Yankee businessman of the old era had begun to harden
by the 1850's into the conservative Brahmin. By 1900 this class had
retreated still further. The archtype of a once virile and creative ruling
group became the Back Bay gentleman who reputedly reinvested his
dividends and lived on the income from his income. The drop in quality
from the elder Holmes to the late George Apley was a measure of the
toll the past century had taken of the Boston aristocracy.

While the members of this *rentier* class occupied themselves with
their sailboats and their genealogies, the managers of the economy moved
crabwise. Men whose thinking was molded by their service in the banks
and trust companies of State Street fumbled over the small decisions and
tried to avoid the big ones. Caution, traditionally a watchword of the
Boston financial district, was exalted into an even higher plane in its
hierarchy of values. Much that was only vulgar—inertia, ignorance,
economic nepotism—masqueraded as high-minded New England conservatism. Gone were the men who would take a chance on the future of
their own city or who would make a sacrifice to save the prosperity of
their state and region.

This withdrawal and inertia of Boston's wealthy people and its
business community conditioned the outlook on life of the Irish majority
in the years from 1900 to 1940. Because the city did not enjoy the
economic expansion that invigorated other major cities, the Irish made
very slow progress into the middle and upper classes. By the end of this
period, only four of the thirty directors of the Boston Chamber of
Commerce were of Irish descent. None of the major department stores
and only one small bank were under Irish control. When John Gunther
visited Boston near the end of World War II, he was astonished to
discover that the New England Council, a businessmen's organization
formed in 1925 to spearhead a regional recovery drive, had never had
an Irishman as an officer, a committee chairman, or a member of the
executive committee.[2] In short, ethnic and class lines almost exactly
coincided. The majority who had the political power felt themselves
distinctly separated from the minority who had the economic power, and
the separation was not only along economic lines, as it would be elsewhere, but also along nationality, religious, and cultural lines. Moreover,
the visible failure of the city to progress economically meant that the

working class did not respect or have confidence in the business leadership even on the latter's own terms, that is, on economic terms. State Street could not reasonably assert that its stewardship of the economy had brought prosperity to the city.

Boston's population increased from 560,000 in 1900 to 780,000 in 1940. Since the economy did not expand, there was throughout this period, except briefly during World War I, a chronic labor surplus. The number of persons engaged in manufacturing remained virtually constant: 52,000 in 1900 and 57,000 in 1940. Approximately half those who had jobs were employed in comparatively low-paid and static occupations such as clerical and sales jobs, and domestic and service work. The occasional unemployment of manual laborers that had been familiar before World War I spread and became endemic in the city after the war. Throughout the 1920's when the rest of the nation was enjoying an economic boom, Boston regularly sustained an unemployment rate of 12 to 15 percent. The great depression of 1929 and afterward further narrowed the horizon and darkened the scene.

The Irish reacted to this economic squeeze by struggling to find a protected job in the civil service. The competition for openings as teachers, policemen, firemen, school janitors, and clerks became intense. Jobs in the large private monopolies such as the telephone and electric-light companies were equally desirable. Two of Boston's recent mayors exemplify this occupational pattern. Maurice Tobin, mayor from 1938 to 1945, began as a clerk and rose to divisional traffic manager for the telephone company. John Hynes, mayor from 1950 to 1960, began as a clerk in the city Health Department and spent twenty-nine years in the municipal bureaucracy. He was city clerk when he resigned to run for mayor in 1949.

Security and status became ruling obsessions for the Irish at their economic level as it had for the Back Bay Brahmins at theirs. Instead of sharing the more characteristic American attitude of confidence and optimism where material matters are concerned, the spirit that says there is "more where that came from" and plenty to spare for all, Boston developed the ethos of a civil service city. Too many Bostonians had the less attractive attitudes of the frustrated bureaucrat: "Pass the buck, don't stick your neck out, and keep your nose clean." The lack of necessary economic and social elbow room made everyone hold rigid and tense as twentieth century Boston came gradually to resemble a giant subway car in the five o'clock rush: no space to move and every seat occupied even to the end of the line.

3

Boston's two-dimensional social character, the weight of its history, and the sluggishness of its economic life account for the modern stereotypes about the city and about the Boston Irish. However, the city was, in addition, not favored by fate with leaders on various fronts who could have mediated and transcended the conflicts these unique factors created. One of the ways in which a city explains itself to itself, articulates its problems, and defines its common aspirations is through its newspapers. Boston was unusual throughout this period in having eight newspapers: the *Herald, Globe, Post,* and *Record* in the morning and the *Traveler, Globe, Transcript,* and *American* in the evening.* The Boston press has often been unfairly attacked or, rather, criticized for the wrong reasons. It is doubtful if the Boston papers in this period were more parochial or more sensationalist or less diligent in covering the news of the metropolis than most newspapers elsewhere in the country. Their real failing was that they either represented a fragment of the community and ignored the rest or sought universal acceptance by the evasion of problems and issues. Either way, no paper could affirmatively answer the question: Who speaks for all of Boston?

The distinctive journal of the Brahmins was the *Transcript,* which passed out of existence in 1939. The *Transcript,* as the many satires and anecdotes about it demonstrate, epitomized one element of Boston. There is the limerick:

> "There was a young maid from Back Bay
> Whose manners were very blasé;
> While still in her teens
> She refused pork and beans
> And once threw her *Transcript* away."

The *Transcript* was the guardian of the genteel tradition. In politics in the 1880's and 1890's, it expounded the view of the Mugwump Republicans, although it could never quite bring itself to endorse Democrat Grover Cleveland. Its genealogy articles, its lengthy obituaries of proper Bostonians, its fantastically detailed coverage of minor social and church meetings, and its high-grade coverage of music, literature, and the arts were the paper's strongest features because they dealt with the strongest interests of the *Transcript*'s unique reading public.[3] In the twentieth cen-

* There was a ninth if the *Christian Science Monitor,* a church-financed paper with a national audience, is counted as a Boston newspaper.

tury it continued to voice its low-tariff views and to scold the Republican Party leaders in a proprietary fashion. Well before its demise, T. S. Eliot wrote:

"When evening quickens faintly in the street
Wakening the appetites of life in some
And to others bringing the *Boston Evening Transcript.*"[4]

As the Brahmins yielded active leadership to their bankers, trustees, and corporation managers, this upper middle class found in the Boston *Herald* an organ for a more modern, ready-to-wear brand of conservatism. This shift was personified in the the career of Robert Lincoln O'Brien, longtime Washington correspondent and briefly editor of the *Transcript* who switched to the *Herald* shortly after 1900. The *Herald*'s owners, who included the proprietors of the United Shoe Machinery Company and several wealthy businessmen, had bailed the previous owner out of his financial difficulties but had been unable to make the paper pay until they hired O'Brien. He made the *Herald* a financial success by close attention to the business end of the paper and by stolidly espousing the views of orthodox Republicanism. A characteristic editorial was one that appeared at the climax of the 1932 election entitled, "Our Congressmen." The editor urged the reelection of all Republican congressmen and closed with the exhortation: "[Even] if you haven't had time to examine the qualification of your congressional representative, don't hesitate to mark a cross for the Republican."[5]

Under such a policy, the *Herald*, being published in an overwhelmingly Democratic city, inevitably became the paper of the bedroom suburbs and not of Boston itself. In an effort to establish contact with the Irish masses, at least for advertising purposes, the paper's management acquired an afternoon outlet, the *Traveler*. Through huge headlines and flamboyant news treatment, the *Traveler* acquired a sizable Irish readership but always addressed itself to the least common denominator of its audience's tastes and interests, not to its needs or ideals. A paper that only reflects is a paper that cannot lead.

The *Boston Globe* resolved the problem of a schizoid community in a different fashion. The tradition of the *Globe*, which had both morning and evening editions, was set by its publisher, General Charles Taylor, whose twin maxims were (1) "Every reader of the *Globe* must find his name in the paper at least once a year," and (2) "No story should appear . . . whose writer could not shake hands the next day with the man about whom he had written." General Taylor was a very amiable and popular man, who, as Oswald Garrison Villard put it, was "without a vestige of a social policy." His intense parochialism was illustrated in his reply to an excited employee's announcement of the alarming news that the *Herald* had engaged another London correspondent. Taylor exclaimed, "Then, by God, we'll have to get another in South Boston!"[6]

The *Globe* was admirably fair and impartial in its coverage of the news. Over the years it had some outstanding reporters such as the great Frank Sibley, who distinguished himself by his coverage of the Sacco-Vanzetti case, and Louis Lyons, who did excellent stories on the Boston school system and other local problems and eventually became curator of the Neiman Foundation at Harvard. But the *Globe* was unique in the nation in that it never took a stand in any election, local or national. Its editorial page featured a staff-written column signed "Uncle Dudley" which often offered excellent analyses, but when it came to conclusions, it specialized in a curious kind of benign obfuscation. The *Globe* under General Taylor and his heirs called itself an "independent" newspaper, but it confused neutrality with independence. Seeking to anesthetize all basic issues and offend no one, it served the business community by its indomitable refusal to admit there were any social issues. Boston could not find its voice in the *Globe*.

The morning *Record* and the evening *American* were standard Hearst tabloids. Insofar as the Boston Irish had a spokesman, it was the *Post*. This was a paper famous among newspapermen for its elaborate array of headlines and subheadlines that told the gist of a news story before the reader ever arrived at the "lead" sentence. It also followed the practice of starting thirty or more stories on the front page and then after one or two paragraphs "jumping" to an inside page. E. A. Grozier, the publisher of the *Post*, had an instinct rivaling General Taylor for what was required to produce a successful hometown newspaper. Every local murder, sick child, and brave dog was found worthy of a feature story in the *Post*. The paper, which because of mismanagement by a subsequent publisher went out of existence in 1956, dominated the morning field through most of the first half of this century. But Grozier was a circulation man, first and last, and he had no social philosophy or political viewpoint. The result was that the *Post* was as alien a product to Yankee and suburban Boston as the *Transcript* was to the Irish. Moreover, the paper's relationship with its Irish constituency was equivocal. It did not so much speak to and for them as cater to their tastes and obey their known prejudices. While its rivals were to some extent outsiders, guilty of conscious insincerity, the *Post* was too much a member of the family. Its Irish readers had a genuine affection for it, but the paper except on rare occasions did them the disservice of flattering and agreeing with them when it should have led them.

In New York, Al Smith was helped enormously by the support and the educating influence of the *World* and the *Times*. Both these papers were enlightened on national and international issues, responsive to the needs of the working class on questions of social reform, and spoke for the interests of the whole community. They helped knit together the native elements and the immigrant communities, the rich and the poor, the traditional past and the emergent future. The Groziers, the Taylors, and the men who owned the Herald-Traveler Corporation were not worse than the run-of-the-mill of American publishers; when one criticizes them, one is really only deploring the fact that none of them had the social vision or the capacity for leadership of a Pulitzer or an Ochs. Boston was not notoriously ill-served by its press, but it was a community badly in need of an extraordinarily good press to bridge its divisions. No publisher emerged to meet its special needs.

4

The Roman Catholic Church also failed signally in the years before 1940 to mediate between the Irish and the Yankees. Unlike the ordinary Protestant church which is a voluntary association of worshipers, the Catholic Church is greater than the total of its parts. Under creative leadership, this independent authority of the Church might have been directed toward lessening the drift to group solidarity and intergroup conflict. Such leadership was not forthcoming.

Any religious group has two distinct though interdependent functions: it propagates a body of religious dogma and social philosophy, and it serves as a social institution interacting with other social forces on the public scene. In Massachusetts in the first half of the twentieth century, the Catholic Church as the champion of certain principles was at once querulous and quiescent and as an institution profoundly conservative. This was due largely to the influence of a single man, William Cardinal O'Connell, Archbishop of the Boston diocese 1907–1911, Cardinal, 1911–1944.

O'Connell was born in Lowell in 1859, the youngest of eleven children. His Irish immigrant parents had graduated from the textile mills and risen to comparative affluence within the small Irish community. Moving out of the Irish slums to Chapel Hill, a predominantly Protestant, middle-class district, they were among Lowell's first "lace-curtain Irish." His father died when O'Connell was four years old, but the estate, together with the earnings of the older children, enabled the boy to obtain a good education. After attending the public grade school and high school, he spent five years at St. Charles's College in Maryland and at Boston College from which he graduated in 1881. After four years of study in the American College at Rome, he was ordained a priest and returned to the United States to serve as a curate in Boston.

O'Connell had grown up in a time when Yankee versus Irish, Protestant versus Catholic tensions in Massachusetts were still acute. In his memoirs he denounced those Irish who changed their names and dropped their religion as the price of assimilation, denouncing them as "contemptible toadies [who] went over body and soul to the enemy and sold their glorious inheritance for a mess of pottage. No sooner had they taken their places among the Protestants than they were given places which as Catholics they never would have obtained. And so some of the Murphys became Murfies; some of the O'Briens became Bryants; some of the Delaneys became Delanos. But, be it said to the credit of the Catholics of those times, such betrayal and treason were stamped as ignominious and detestable."[7]

Despite the comfortable economic circumstances of his family, O'Connell was acquainted with the hardships of the working class. While in high school, he obtained a summer job in a textile mill.

"For the first hour or two I had the greatest delight in scattering the fluffy cotton mass on to the table of the carding machine and watching it with fascinated eyes pass through the machinery, come out in great bands of soft white, downy stuff, automatically twist itself around the huge bobbin . . . [but] the thought came to me, "What if I were condemned to do this all my life!" And the poetry of mechanical motion began to turn into a very serious prose. I began to feel faint from the disgusting smell of the oil, whose vapor filled the atmosphere of the room. I looked around me and saw my boyish companions, who at that moment looked to me like shriveled old men.

"The stench of ammonia that rose from the chemical room near-by made my eyes run water and almost stifled my breath. I suddenly felt a weakness as if I were about to faint. I stopped the machine and leaned against it in an endeavor to recover. Somehow I felt I could never start that machine again."

When the noon lunch hour came, the future Cardinal told his companions: " 'Boys, I can never stand this as you do; the noise, the smell, the eternal monotony of the grind would crush me in a week. Good-bye boys, I'm going home.'

"I left the mill then, and I never returned. . . . Now the whole point of this story is this: Here I was a boy nearly twelve years old, perfectly normal, healthy and strong; yet, one half-day in that atmosphere seemed to me like a hundred years. Fortunately for me I was not compelled to work in the mill at such a job as that. But how about the thousands of other boys of my age not even so healthy or well as I was, who were compelled to work by circumstances, the chief of which was the miserable economic conditions of their families, due to overwork and a disgraceful underpay? The maw, the mills demanded victims, and the forced poverty and the unjust recompense and the greed of the industrialists helped to supply them."[8]

Father O'Connell's first parish was in one of Boston's poorest working-class neighborhoods. It was the period when Cardinal Gibbons and Archbishop Ireland were fighting their major battles to prevent the Papal condemnation of the Knights of Labor and to align the Church on the side of social justice. O'Connell was a youthful admirer of their efforts.

But the passage of time and changed circumstances altered his outlook. In 1895, after ten years as a parish priest, O'Connell was recalled to Rome to take over the rectorship of his alma mater, the American College. In Rome he entered into the fashionable international society centered upon the Papal Court and the wealthy expatriates living nearby. "I went," he wrote later, "not frequently, but at least occasionally, to these great houses and kept in touch, and obtained a very considerable knowledge of how the world was run in general from those who, by their power and influence, were really running it. And let it be said, remembering that this was the end of the nineteenth century and the beginning of the twentieth, the machinery of the world was working well, and there was peace and prosperity everywhere, both in Europe and in America."[9]

Two of O'Connell's close friends were "the very rich and very hospitable" Drapers. General Eben Draper's substantial contribution to the McKinley campaign had bought him the ambassadorship to Rome. In private life he was the proprietor in Hopedale, Massachusetts, of mills where non-union labor worked long hours for low wages under conditions similar to those which the youthful O'Connell had experienced in the mill in Lowell.

Another friend O'Connell made in Rome was Cardinal Merry Del Val, a Spaniard, and the extremely conservative "gray eminence" of Pope Pius X. Under Del Val's patronage and because of his own very considerable intellectual powers, O'Connell rose rapidly. In 1901 he became Bishop of Portland, Maine; in 1907, Archbishop of Boston; and four years later, a cardinal. For thirty-eight years, from 1906 until his death in 1944 at age eighty-five, Cardinal O'Connell dominated the Catholic scene in Boston. Since the Catholic Church was a formative influence on the Irish, this meant that he did much, both in a positive and a negative sense, to shape the mind of the Boston Irish.

O'Connell early dropped his youthful liberalism. By the time he became cardinal and thereafter, his influence on all social and economic

questions was uniformly conservative. He associated socially with leading
bankers, businessmen, and members of the Brahmin families. He resided in
a large mansion built along the lines of a Renaissance Italian palace, and
in his later years, he spent so much of his time traveling to Europe and to
his winter estate on the island of Nassau that he was irreverently dubbed
"Gangplank Bill." The public ideals of the Yankee business community
became his ideals.[10] He gave no impetus in his archdiocese to the propa-
gation of the social doctrines embodied in the papal encyclicals *Rerum
Novarum* (1891) and *Quadragesimo Anno* (1931). Nor was there any
recognition of the fact that the overwhelming majority of his fellow
Catholics were in the low-income group and that a sizable number of
them were for long periods unemployed. The social problems of Boston
called urgently for the Church to leave its ivory tower and go into the
marketplace to spread its social teachings. But no such missionary effort
was attempted.

Cardinal O'Connell's chief positive contribution was his dogged assertion of the importance of simple integrity in public office. He reiterated
with relentless regularity the message "Thou shalt not steal," and anyone
familiar with Boston politics would agree the point was worth making.
Over the decades this preaching gradually had a useful influence, but its
effect was much less than it might have been if it had been part of a
broader message that struck home with real impact in the daily lives of
tens of thousands of impoverished, frustrated Boston Catholics in the
1920's and 1930's.

On the negative side, Cardinal O'Connell permitted the Church's moral
teachings to be trivialized and distorted through a politically operated
censorship of books, movies, and legitimate plays. He consistently
sanctioned the misuse of public authority in the moral field, which only
served to produce embarrassing anomalies and to give his Church and his
adopted city a bad name throughout the nation. Thus, the Old Howard, a
famous burlesque theater, flourished while Eugene O'Neill's *Strange Interlude* had to open in a suburban movie house to avoid Boston's theatrical
censorship. Charles Morton, an urbane connoisseur of Boston manners
during years as a writer for the *Boston Transcript* and the *Atlantic
Monthly*, once chronicled the careers of some of those who have held the
post of Clerk of the Licensing Division (that is, Boston's official public
censor). There was, for example, "John M. Casey, who retired on a
pension in 1932 after twenty-eight years of service, during which Boston
censorship, as the magazine *Equity* put it, 'was a unique example of its
kind.' Casey's retirement festivities were also unique—a vast banquet at
the Copley Plaza at which the manager of the Old Howard bestowed on
him a purse containing a thousand gold dollars, a gift from the theatrical

men of Boston. A three-page telegram from Izzy Herk, head of the Empire Burlesque Association, was offered in evidence, but unfortunately not read.

"Casey's successor was Stanton R. White, a twenty-eight-year-old son-in-law of Mayor [James M.] Curley's brother, who had held a civil-service post as county paymaster until 'they said I had to take an examination.' Still feeling his way, but aware of the public interest in his work, White made a try at defining the responsibilities of his office. The standard for the stage would be, he declared, what he considered fit for 'my own boy or girl, if they were fifteen or sixteen years old, to see and hear.' The *Boston Evening Transcript* commented optimistically: 'This would appear to be something of a slackening of the city censorship as practiced during the regime of John M. Casey, when the twelve-year-old mentality was popularly believed to be the deadline.' White was equally obliging in letting it be known how he proposed to pursue the standard he had established: 'I guess I'll just have to sorta use my head.' "

Morton also accurately described the cultural mythology:

"The stereotypes underlying the censorship are picturesque. The Yankee is depicted as rich and therefore dishonest—educated and therefore depraved, and seeking to gratify his unnatural tastes through the sinister but otherwise unintelligible productions intended for the New York stage. No censorship could curb sufficiently the base appetites of the Yankee, so the assumption goes, but the city government must fight the good fight anyhow.

"The official concept of the other inhabitants of Boston limns them as hard-working, pious folk, ready for a fight or a frolic after a day of honest toil, broadminded enough to enjoy a bit of burlesque but profoundly hostile to such nastiness as the Yankee affects in his public entertainment."[11]

Cardinal O'Connell, a patron of music and a man of sophisticated taste, knew better than to believe in these stereotypes, but he allowed the Church's moral teaching to be confined, oversimplified, and debased within them. What was true of the seriocomic censorship of the serious theater was likewise true of books. "Banned in Boston" became an incitement to the prurient and a boon to the vulgarly commercial, not a safeguard to the innocent. Again, there was an anomaly. Books were banned, although fewer than 10 percent of the public buys books (or attends the legitimate theater). Was *Forever Amber* really a threat to the morals of Boston Catholics? Or was the Church by sanctioning government censorship for avowedly moral grounds only making itself a party to politically motivated attacks on the Brahmin scapegoat?

During Cardinal O'Connell's nearly forty years of leadership, Boston Catholics were permitted to erect a double standard. Their adoption of the Puritanical (and, in a true sense, quite un-Catholic) standards of the old Yankee-founded Watch and Ward Society not only failed to elevate the tone of moral life in Boston but also served as an egregious Irish cultural revenge upon the Yankee community which was powerless to fight back at the polls. This double standard should have been of particular concern to Cardinal O'Connell since anyone seriously concerned with ethics recognizes that hypocrisy is the first danger to be guarded against in making moral judgments. Only the cardinal could have provided his people with leadership on these issues as against the cant and doubletalk of the politicians and part of the press. Only he could have placed the Church's teachings in proper perspective. It weighs heavily against his record in history that he failed to do so.

Again, as with Boston's newspaper publishers, it was not that Cardinal O'Connell was markedly more conservative or unenlightened than many other clerics elsewhere, particularly of his generation. It was rather that Boston because of its uniquely severe internal conflicts and difficulties was exceptionally in need of progressive and constructive leadership from its most powerful clergyman. O'Connell was not more reactionary than some others, but Boston could least afford a reactionary.

5

Rejection of a society or a body of ideas may be as secure a form of adjustment as acceptance. So it seemed for the early Irish in Boston. They tended during the first generation to withdraw from their new neighbors and to reject the life and values of the larger Boston community. The Yankees of 1840 were optimistic, individualistic, increasingly secular, and believers in reform. The Irish, bred to disaster in the old country and suffering in the new, were understandably pessimistic, fatalistic and, in a certain sense, conservative. But as time passed, it became difficult for the Irish to remain in ghetto-like seclusion. Inevitably, they began to make gestures toward the larger society around them. One of these gestures took the form of a discreet flirtation with the Yankee element. The first generation, having experienced the worst of the economic deprivation and the brunt of the conflict with the hostile, nativist working class, might have been expected to become radicals. In fact, however, the first political leaders to emerge from the Irish community in the period from 1870 to

1900 were moderate in outlook and conservative in style. As leaders in the Irish nationalist movement, they exemplified and affirmed both for Ireland and for Irish Americans in this country the characteristic American faith in education, in individual self-improvement, in limited government. They cooperated with the more liberal Yankee leaders and they emulated native standards of political behavior. The foremost spokesman of this generation was John Boyle O'Reilly, the newspaper editor, romantic novelist, and poet, who by the time of his death in 1890 had been fully accepted into the Boston literary establishment. There was another side to him than that of the respectable man of letters. Like Patrick Ford, his nationalist and editorial contemporary in New York, O'Reilly had a crusading zeal and a humanitarian sympathy for the underdog that sometimes prompted him to endorse radical economic programs. Here he did not carry the bulk of the Irish community with him. In politics, the more representative figure was Patrick A. Collins.

Born in Ireland in 1844 and brought to the United States as an infant, Collins quit grade school to work in an upholstery shop, as a coal miner, and later as an office clerk. By indomitable spirit and self-discipline, he obtained a college education and graduated from Harvard Law School. Entering politics, he conformed to the prevailing middle-class ideal of a dignified gentleman and a political reformer. He was on good personal terms with Grover Cleveland and with Richard Olney, his strike-breaking Attorney General, whom Collins supported for President in 1904. During the second Cleveland administration, Collins was American Counsul General in London. He strongly opposed William Jennings Bryan's leadership of the Democratic Party.

During his two terms as mayor from 1901 to 1905, Collins enjoyed considerable Republican support and was well regarded by the business community. As Andrew J. Peters, himself a conservative Boston mayor, staidly expressed it in the *Commonwealth History of Massachusetts:* "Collins had the confidence and respect of the citizens of Boston, irrespective of party, and honestly endeavored to check the rapidly growing tendency to extravagance in city government."[12]

The Yankee community, for its part, responded favorably to this emerging Irish leadership. Yankee Democrats such as Josiah Quincy, mayor of Boston in the 1890's; William E. Russell, governor, 1890–1893; William Saltonstall (father of the present-day Republican senator), and Charles F. Adams tried within the limitations of their own outlook and background to assimilate the Irish masses to the traditions of their party. The Yankee community, which had a long tradition of reformist and humanitarian activity, also created numerous charitable and social service agencies to assist the poor. The Irish were at first reluctant to make use of

> "The organized charity scrimped and iced,
> In the name of a cautious, statistical Christ."

But this reluctance could not, of course, be blamed upon the Yankees.

While the well-intentioned ladies of Marlborough Street busied themselves with their charities, and O'Reilly wrote his commemorative poems to heroes of the Abolitionist movement, and Mayor Collins and Mayor Quincy symbolized a putative rapproachement of the Irish and Yankee communities, other men at another level were coming to terms with the social system as they found it. In scattered sections of the city, Irish politicians capitalized on their native shrewdness and their acquaintance with their neighborhood to build islands of political power. Despite the steadily increasing Irish vote, it was the end of the century before the Irish and the Democratic Party took firm control of the city. This meant that city politics was in the inchoate state that New York City politics had been forty years earlier before Tammany consolidated its power under Tweed, "Honest John" Kelly, and their successors. There was no central organization. No clear dichotomy existed between the boss and the candidates. There were various ward bosses who themselves were often candidates; their organizations were personal and local; their discipline feeble. Loose citywide alliances were easily made and easily broken. On the surface, it seemed as if these elements would gradually coalesce into a conventional big-city machine, and the usual accommodations would take place between political power and the economic interests. But Boston was not to have such an easy passage from the past to the future.

For fifty years the relations between the two groups in the community had been exacerbated. There were resentments seeking expression, inferiorities that gnawed and strained, injustices that demanded revenge. The long Irish-Yankee struggle for control of the city now nearing its climax was not to be resolved and then passed over in any smooth and painless fashion. The different forms of *modus vivendi* envisaged by the literary men, the respectable politicians, and the greasy-thumbed ward bosses were alike insufficient. The first were too suave to give passion its catharsis; the last too simpleminded. For what was wrong with the rival ward bosses, and what the Irish sensed was wrong with them, was that after they had captured the scraps of local office they were content to be the agents rather than the principals in the struggle for power. Saloonkeepers, tailors, and contractors by profession, they wanted simply to keep things running as they had been in their ward and take their share of the graft. Whatever the brand of buncombe they served up to voters at election time, everyone knew they were pensioners of the streetcar company, the gas company, the railroads, or some other dominant interest in the established order, still firmly controlled by the old families. It was a low and lethargic arrangement. This kind of easygoing, trickle-down politics was adequate to the needs of expansive, prosperous, heterogeneous cities like New York and Chicago. The Boston Irish demanded something more, but what that something would be they did not know.

It is the first generation that meekly obeys the foreman, defers to the teacher, respects the corner cop. It is the later generations that rebel. Since the older people can remember the quite different society from which they emigrated, they never fully overcome their initial feelings of mingled fear, awe, and gratitude. They rarely learn to speak up as if they really believe they own the world about them by right rather than by sufferance. The second generation who can remember no society other than America look out on the world around them with quite different eyes. In Boston in the late 1890's, the members of the first American Irish generation, those born in the 1860's and 1870's, were coming to maturity.

As the century closed, these younger Irish came roaring out of the slums and tenement houses propelled by a hard, aggressive urge to strike out at the world, to choke down all inner feelings of inadequacy, to master and punish their foes. Since the channels to conspicuous success in business were partly choked, politics was the obvious open road. A score of young politicians came to the fore in these years. Each knew the others, and all at some point in their careers worked together, yet each would someday be the bitter enemy of the others. What they shared was not a common program that could keep them together as allies, but a common protest of no clear content. They were spokesmen of a vague restlessness, a mood, a sentiment. They expressed an insurgency born of pride, resentment, and ambition. These Irish of the new generation were proud of their Irish blood, resentful of Yankee wrongs (real and imagined), and ambitious of great achievement. No longer was there the feeling that they were merely as good as the Yankees, no longer the eager pathetic hope for tangible tokens of acceptance. Those feelings were gone, those battles won. Now the dominant mood was a cocky, chip-on-the-shoulder self-confidence, a belief that they were better than the Yankees and—so the feeling went—if those old Yanks didn't like it, why then, damn them, they could lump it. Either way it did not matter: their day was done.

Revolt was in the air. The young politicians sensed the mood, but they were never able to reduce this nebulous congeries of faith and fear, of ancient hatred and youthful idealism to an intellectually coherent platform. It was like a mysterious tune; all knew the melody but no two could agree on the lyrics. It should not be astonishing, therefore, that these young politicians ended their careers half a century later as cynical, embittered old men, hating one another and seeking in vain for the cause of their own disintegration.

These young men were rebels, not reformers. "Reform," "economy and efficiency," and "civil service" were the monopoly of the Yankee politicians. To the culturally isolated Irish politicians, one Yankee was the same as another, and these genteel slogans were meaningless shibboleths, "blinds" to bolster the rule of the old order.

"Big Tim" O'Flaherty, the hero of Joseph Dinneen's novel *Ward Eight*, summed it up when he said to the Yankee settlement house worker:

"You're not actually suggesting that I become a reformer? . . . He's as bad down here as an informer, and as cordially hated."[13]

What did this mean in practice? It meant that these Irish politicians would usually be found on the side of labor when it was a clearcut capitalist-labor issue. Most were from working-class homes, and the concrete economic problems of the wage earner were something they could understand. But it also meant that they could never wage a battle on a broad liberal front simply because once they left labor's section of the battleline they could not tell their friends from their enemies. The big guns of the Irish community were too often silent or misdirected for lack of a philosophical range finder.

The older men of the Collins-O'Reilly-Quincy school, accustomed to appealing to a middle-class "independent" electorate on issues, were no match for the "Big Tims" come questing for power. Nor were the fat bosses of the beer-and-lollipops tradition adequate to the changed social scene. The impulse to violence was too close to the surface. Something more imaginative would be needed.

As Boston entered the twentieth century, it was already tense with internal conflict and undischarged hostilities. The scene was prepared and the time was right for the emergence of a master demagogue. History was not long in producing one.

CHAPTER TWELVE

The Legend of Jim Curley

1

IN NOVEMBER, 1949, James Michael Curley was defeated for re-election as Mayor of Boston. He had known many ups and downs but this was the final defeat from which there was to be no comeback. One gray morning the week after election, a young writer went to City Hall to interview Mayor Curley for a magazine article. The appointment was for eleven-thirty but, in keeping with the lordly inefficiency of Curley's last administration, the writer was not admitted to the inner office until two-fifteen in the afternoon. Once there, he found several other claimants for the mayor's attention sitting on high-backed chairs ranged along one wall. The room was baronial in size, and these chairs were such as to make a six-footer dangle his feet like a child.

Curley and his male secretary sat at desks facing each other by the windows. Curley, his tall frame humped with age, his leonine head thrust forward, his cheeks sallow and his eyes flecked with yellow, showed the ravages of his seventy-five years. As each interview came to an end, those who remained moved one seat closer to his desk rustling uneasily like patients in a dentist's office. The next-to-the-last claimant was a salesman in his early thirties. Though he had never met the mayor, he leaned forward and whispered to Curley some statement that seemed to justify his claim to a respectful hearing. After the mayor nodded his assent, the young man made his request in low tones. In a moment or two, the mayor cut him off with an upward gesture of his hand.

"Get me Dr. So-and-So at City Hospital," he said.

His secretary put through the call. The mayor and the salesman waited in silence. Everyone else in the room eavesdropped with a heavy show of unconcern.

"Hello, Doctor. Fine, fine. Doctor, I have a young man here in my office who comes very well recommended. He sells a fine product—it's a little something to kill the odors in the morgue."

The mayor mentioned the product's name, and then listened. He turned to the salesman and said, "He says they have a lot of that on hand already."

The young man leaned forward and whispered with some urgency.

"It's a very fine product and I think we should help his company out," the mayor said. "We could buy some and keep it in reserve, couldn't we? Fine, I'll send him right down."

"What's your name?"

The salesman gave his name, and the mayor repeated it into the phone. "Fine. Thanks, Doctor. Goodbye."

The salesman shook hands, and left. The writer moved up to the right hand of power. Curley inclined his head gravely. His voice rumbled up sweetly from the depths of his diaphragm:

"Ah, young man, and what can I do for you?"

2

Exactly fifty years earlier, James Michael Curley had won his first public office. Defeated the year before for the Boston City Council, he decided in the fall of 1899 that he would leave nothing undone to achieve victory. It was an advantage for a candidate to have his name at the top of the ballot, since many uneducated voters put a cross beside the first name they saw. Since position on the ballot was determined by the order of filing nomination papers, Curley decided his name must head the list. Adopting a tactic that older politicians had used, he, his brother John, and a score of brawny friends went with their nominating papers to the registrar's office on the night before the filing day and barricaded the entrance.

"It was some siege," Curley recalled in his memoirs. "Several times that night flying wedges of rowdies tried to crash our lines, but we plugged them as they came in. John suffered a broken jaw, and my cohorts and I took a pounding, but when the clerks and registrars arrived the following morning, we still held the fort, and my name topped the ballot. Years later, the law was changed, and ballot position was determined by lot."[1]

Curley was successful in that campaign, and his career was launched. The reliance on raw, physical power that marked its beginning remained one of its several enduring characteristics. He never broke this early habit nor mastered his quick, impulsive temper.* A career that began in turbulence never completely lost an aura of aggression and violence.

* In 1924, middle-aged and mayor of Boston, Curley met a newspaper publisher who had been attacking him, and knocked him down in the street. Six years later, waiting to make an election-eve broadcast, he heard the chairman of the Democratic State Committee broadcast an attack on him from the adjoining studio. Curley rushed

During the succeeding fifty years, Curley followed a pattern that had no analogy elsewhere in America. Other states had their "grand old man" who won election after election and became a local institution. But no other figure knew such remarkable fluctuations and yet lasted so long. He was four times elected to Congress and four times mayor of Boston and he held several other offices from alderman to governor. Yet he was also defeated once for the House of Representatives, once for the Senate, twice for the governorship, and six times for mayor of Boston. He made as many comebacks as a fading opera singer. The explanation for his unique durability and resilience did not lie in any well-organized party machine. Though he was organizationally entrenched in a few wards in Boston, he had no citywide system of ward leaders, precinct captains, and clubhouses. He was never "boss" of Boston in the sense that Frank Hague ruled Jersey City or Tom Pendergast controlled Kansas City.

Curley was less powerful than a party boss and more significant than a conventionally successful party leader. He was the idol of a cult, arbiter of a social clique, and spokesman of a state of mind.

3

Curley was born in a Boston slum on November 20, 1874. His father and mother had come to Boston as adolescents from their native Galway a few years earlier. When his father, who was a hodcarrier, died, his mother worked as a scrubwoman to support James, ten, and his brother John, twelve.

Curley had no formal education beyond grade school. As a schoolboy, he sold newspapers, worked long hours as a delivery boy in a neighborhood drugstore, then was employed briefly in a piano factory and by a tinsmith. At seventeen, he took a job with a grocer "where I worked for the next eight years, putting up orders and delivering them in a horse-drawn wagon.

"I drove an old gray horse which wouldn't hurry if you lit a fire under him, starting work before 6 A.M. and never getting home three nights a week much before midnight. . . . On the other three days, when I left work earlier, I spent a great deal of time building up my muscles in a local gymnasium. I needed bulging biceps and a strong back, since while delivering groceries I often had to carry a barrel of flour up three or four flights of rickety tenement stairs."[2]

---

him and chased him down the stairs. On the day of his inauguration as governor in 1935, he had a brief scuffle at the State House with the retiring governor, an arch-enemy.

Meanwhile, he had taken a civil service examination in the hope of becoming a fireman. ("I was . . . lured by the prospect of retiring at the end
of twenty years.") But Curley had too much energy and too strong a
"killer instinct" for the yawns-and-checkers routine of fire-station existence. Nagged by ambition and a fierce, unfocused instinct for personal
power, he fumbled his way toward some larger career.

That politics should have become his vocation was almost inevitable
in that social context. Curley had certain conventional political assets. He
was tall, had a strong face, and a powerful if untrained speaking voice.
He was an active Catholic who taught Sunday school and passed the collection plate at Mass. Having always lived in the same neighborhood, he
had a sizable circle of acquaintances. He was a regular worker in the
leading Irish fraternal society, the Ancient Order of Hibernians. Yet he
did not fit the stereotype of the young politician as an affable, hail-fellow-
well-met. Curley was not a backslapper. In those years he did not dance
or drink. He smoked an occasional cigar, but only to make himself appear
older than he was. Though strong and muscular, he was bored by athletics
and never good at them. He was more serious and studious than his fellow
workingmen, attended night classes, read books borrowed from the local
public library, and tried to study law on his own. Although widely
acquainted, he had, then as later, few personal intimates. He was an egotist, a lone wolf, already developing into the manipulator, slightly
estranged from the crowd, and therefore able to manipulate its sentiments
and partly transcend its values. Curley, like the equally sober young Al
Smith, was a success in politics because he liked "to run things," and his
fellows were willing to delegate responsibilities to anyone so eager to take
them over. ("I had no time for girl friends, since I was kept busy serving
as general chairman of committees that organized picnics, outings, min-
strel shows, church suppers and dances. As a member of the Ancient
Order of Hibernians, I raised funds for welfare projects and went around
the neighborhood visiting the sick and needy. In 1896, as in previous years,
I served on the general committee that made arrangements for St. Patrick's
Day, which culminated in the big parade in South Boston on March 17.[3]")

When Curley entered politics, rival leaders regularly used bullies to
break up one another's rallies, brought their cheering claques to meetings,
and employed gangs of repeaters and ballot-box-stuffers on election days.
It was a hard school, and Curley learned all the lessons. At many rallies
in the early years, Curley, sturdily built and just under six feet, used his
fists on opposition bullies and hecklers. But Curley had more than
physical strength going for him. He had a talent for savage invective and
slashing repartee which with years of practice became increasingly sharp
and witty. Uncommonly industrious, he applied his native intelligence to

the many small problems involved in building political support. "Counted out" by the existing machine in his first race, he used brute force, guile, and persistence to win a year later. After his victory, he organized his own political club—named the Tammany Club after its obvious model. Over the next eleven years, he served continuously in public office, first as a member of the old Boston Common Council (seventy-five members with three members elected from each of the twenty-five wards), then as a representative in the state legislature, an alderman, and finally as a member of the reformed, small City Council. Curley, having lost his job as a grocery deliveryman because he spent too much of the boss's time on his own political errands, worked as a salesman for a wholesale bakery supply house, briefly operated a saloon, and finally opened an insurance agency that remained his nominal occupation for a long period during which politics became his real livelihood.

At his political club, Curley conducted naturalization classes for immigrants and practiced his public-speaking techniques by holding debates. He also performed the other services of a ward boss:

"I used to meet groups of unemployed and take them to City Hall and employment agencies to find jobs for them. In the course of two years, I secured jobs for about seven hundred men and women, often finding it necessary to fill out job applications for them. I took others to the police station or court where I intervened in their behalf, spending hundreds of hours over the years in the company of judges, probation officers and attorneys."[4]

It was a short step from this sort of constituent service to the crime that put Curley's name on the city's front pages. He was arrested for taking a civil service examination for letter carrier on behalf of a needy but dull-witted constituent. Before attempting this impersonation, Curley looked up the law; as far as he could discover, the only penalty for taking an examination for another person was to be blacklisted from taking future civil service examinations. But there was another statute Curley did not know about. He soon found himself serving a sixty-day term in the Charles Street Jail as punishment for his bold ruse. While in jail, he was elected to the Board of Aldermen, a popular vindication that became, for both his enemies and his friends, part of the developing Curley legend. To his enemies, he was a man who had clearly committed an illegal act and an offense against public morality; he passed through his subsequent career forever stigmatized, in the newspaper phrase, as "once convicted for fraud." To his supporters, Curley's action was not a crime but an endearing gesture. Many of Boston's poor had been peasants on the farms of Ireland and Italy where the "government" was an alien force. In the United States, the distinctions between the various branches and levels of government bewildered them. Civil service examinations seemed only one more example of red tape, and every bit as confusing or frightening as any other encounter with a bureaucracy. A simple matter of routine for an educated American could often be an adventure of Kafkaesque proportions for an immigrant. (One can imagine the misadventures: "But how do I get to City Hall? Where is this office, please? Not in here, over there and two doors to your right! Sign the third and next-to-bottom lines.") Although the Boston Irish were better acclimated than many of the newer immigrants, they still could identify with these sentiments of uneasiness and fear. Against this background, Curley's feat of impersonation could be interpreted as the natural act of a friend and his action portrayed as a heroic deed.

What the voters conferred, Curley did not propose to yield lightly: "Although my sentence was not scheduled to expire until noon, I was released fifteen minutes before that hour on the first Wednesday in January. . . . I stepped into a waiting carriage and proceeded to City Hall where a friend warned me that Daniel J. Whelton, President of the Board of Aldermen, planned to declare my seat vacant [because of his penal offense].

"It was relatively warm for a January day, and the large window directly behind the presiding officer's chair was open. I took the first seat nearest Whelton in the council chambers, and just before the meeting opened, stepped up to him and said: 'I understand that you propose to move that my seat be declared vacant.'

" 'Yes,' he said, 'I do.'

" 'Well,' I answered, 'I just want to inform you that if you present such a motion, you will go through that window.' The window was on the second floor, and he apparently realized it would be a rather uncomfortable landing on the hard surface below. He glared at me, rapped for order and proceeded with the business of the day without making any reference to me."[5]

In subsequent campaigns, when charges about this incident were revived, Curley supporters silenced them with the cry, "He did it for a friend!"

4

As a city and state legislator, Curley began to stand out from the mob of other aspiring young politicians not only by his assiduity in pushing labor and social-welfare measures (which most of his Irish rivals also supported) but also by his skill in dramatizing such issues.

For example, city laborers were traditionally laid off without pay during inclement weather while supervisors, clerks, and others holding white-collar jobs remained on the job and drew full salary. Any politician with an instinct for an issue could see there was an injustice here. However, it occurred to Curley that the more effective approach was not to champion those who were worse off but rather to attack those who were well off. He introduced an order that would make it mandatory for all employees to be laid off without pay on inclement days. As he had anticipated, there were angry protests from the clerks and foremen. These protests attracted attention to the discrepancy between the supervisors and the laborers and led to a new policy of paying everyone on an equal basis.

Firemen customarily lived at the firehouse and had only one day off in every fifteen. Curley as a state legislator led the fight for the two-platoon system, giving the firemen twelve hours off out of every twenty-four, the bill was vetoed by the Republican governor. Later, in his first term as mayor of Boston, Curley instituted this twelve-hour day for firemen.

But the epitome of Curley's flair in this direction was what he did for the scrubwomen. "My mother was obliged to work . . . as a scrubwoman toiling nights in office buildings downtown. I thought of her one night while leaving City Hall during my first term as Mayor. I told the scrubwomen cleaning the corridors to get up: 'The only time a woman should go down on her knees is when she is praying to Almighty God,' I said. Next morning I ordered long-handled mops and issued an order that scrubwomen were never again to get down on their knees in City Hall."[6]

Told and retold at countless rallies, the story of Curley and the scrubwomen became an immensely effective chapter in the growing Curley legend.

5

In 1910 Curley was elected to Congress, but this was only a preliminary test for higher office. With his executive talent and imperious temper, Curley naturally made the offices of mayor and governor his goals. In 1913, early in his second term in the House, he announced his candidacy as mayor. It was expected that his opponent would be the incumbent, Mayor John Fitzgerald. The latter had been mayor for six of the previous eight years and at fifty was at the peak of his career. He and Curley had parallel careers except that Fitzgerald, being eleven years older, reached each of the rungs in the ladder earlier. Elected mayor in 1905, succeeding Patrick Collins, he was the first American-born son of Irish parentage to reach that office. (He was also Boston's first mayor not to have a moustache or beard.)

"Their talents were comparable, but personally they were direct opposites. Fitzgerald had a pleasant tenor voice, whereas Curley never had been known to sing in public. [Fitzgerald] was affable, genial, friendly, the kind of person upon whom a nickname is easily fastened. He was known throughout the city as Honey, Fitzy, John F. or the Little General. He was short, quick, lively and bouncy, always smiling, dwarfed by the commanding height and personality of Curley. Curley had no nickname. Few persons ever called him 'Jim,' except in print. He was always James Michael Curley or merely Curley. . . . John F. neither smoked nor drank. He loved chocolates and hated liquor. He was born in 1863, not far from the Old North Church where Paul Revere hung out his lanterns, one of nine sons of the neighborhood grocer, and grew up an athlete who could not help being elected captain of the team. He was educated in near-by Eliot School and Boston Latin School, a two-letter man, baseball and football; [he] did not go on to college, but served transient apprenticeships of various kinds. He got into politics because an Irish boy could not get a job in any bank, or a white-collar job with a railroad."[7]

Fitzgerald is a significant figure because he represents the more normal, conventional alternative to Curley. He accepted the political system as he found it; he had become a boss in his own ward, and in seeking citywide power he naturally entered into an alliance with other ward bosses. As mayor, he respected their local prerogatives and allocated patronage and favors in accord with understandings he had reached with them.

It was Fitzgerald who presided over the transition of political power in the city from the Yankees to the Irish and who bore the brunt of the struggle. At the turn of the century, the two segments of the community were equally matched in population, and it was still possible for a Yankee Republican to be elected mayor. Fitzgerald won his first term as mayor in 1905 by a slender margin. When he sought reelection two years later, he was defeated by an equally narrow margin by George Hibbard, a Yankee Republican elected on an economy-and-efficiency platform. The business community, increasingly apprehensive about the prospect of Irish control of the city, tried to curb the power of the ward machines by sponsoring a new municipal charter which replaced the Board of Aldermen and the City Council with a single legislative body, much smaller and with fewer powers, and concentrated authority and responsibility in the hands of the mayor, whose term was lengthened from two to four years. In an effort to take city politics out of the rut of the two-party rivalry, elections were made nonpartisan. This was an attempt to find a shortcut through the Yankee-Irish conflict rather than face its implications squarely. The framers of the charter refused to acknowledge the stubborn fact that in any free system, power sooner or later gravitates to the majority group. The only positive course is to try to educate the majority and have confidence in its intelligence and goodwill. But the business-community reformers were at bottom pessimistic about their Irish fellow citizens and their educability in civic affairs. Their shortcut led immediately to failure. In the first election held under the new charter in 1909, James J. Storrow, an able, public-spirited banker and the candidate of the reform forces, was defeated for mayor by Fitzgerald who squeaked through by 1,402 votes. The reformers charged that he won because he appealed to Irish feelings of racial and religious solidarity rather than debate the real problems confronting the city. The Fitzgerald supporters countered that Storrow had spent enormous sums in an effort to buy the election.

Fitzgerald was not the ominous figure the reform forces depicted. He was actually a rather urbane expression of Irish protest and unrest. As far as his manner was concerned, he was much closer than Curley to the genteel tradition of the preceding generation. Although the Good Government Association and the business community had fought his election, he did not attack or disavow their basic values. On the contrary, he was a booster and salesman of the Chamber of Commerce type. He coined the slogan "A Bigger, Better, and Busier Boston," and was an indefatigable spokesman for the interests of Boston as a port. He was on good terms with Cardinal O'Connell and the clergy. The emerging "lace-curtain" Irish regarded him as colorful but respectable. Those outside the Irish community who deplored Fitzgerald's triumph little realized that he would be succeeded by a man to whom their objections and fears would apply much more than to the amiable "Honey Fitz."[8]

As the Irish saying goes, Fitzgerald delivered the body, but Jim Curley captured the wake. When Curley announced his candidacy, Fitzgerald, after a lengthy period of indecision, chose to withdraw. His decision caught the public and the party bosses by surprise. It appears that he calculated that a fresh face would more easily defeat Curley and that his own career would benefit from a period out of the limelight. Whatever his calculations, he erred. After he voluntarily relinquished the mayoralty, he never held elective office again.*

* Fitzgerald made impressive but narrowly unsuccessful races for U.S. senator in 1916, for U.S. representative in 1918, and for governor in 1922. In 1930 his name was on the Democratic ballot for governor but he withdrew before Primary Day.

The ward leaders chose as their candidate Thomas J. Kenny, a successful lawyer and politician from South Boston, who proved a cautious and dull campaigner. The Good Government Association endorsed him, and Fitzgerald and Storrow, enemies four years earlier, united to back him against Curley.

Curley waged a slam-bang, hell-raising campaign, denouncing all other politicians, assuring the voters he would be independent of the ward machines, and would do away with Fitzgerald's "Sunday kitchen cabinet" (meetings with the ward bosses). He dismissed the Democratic City Committee as "a collection of chowderheads" and "eggshells." He wound up his campaign in his opponent's home territory and told a hostile audience: "You're nothing but a pack of second-story workers, milk-bottle robbers and doormat thieves. I'll be elected mayor of Boston, and you don't like it. Here I am. Does any one of you bums want to step up here and make anything of it?"

Curley paid not even lip service to the traditional political standards. He derided the Good Government Association as "goo goos." He denounced the business leaders as "the State Street wrecking crew." He characterized bankers as "insolent, arrogant sharpies, swindling the city of all they could get away with, while at the same time prating about the high cost of government."[9]

Curley had no newspaper support and, until the very end of the campaign when Martin Lomasney, the boss of the West End, endorsed him, no support from any other prominent political figure. But his exciting speeches and his dramatic exploitation of the deep-seated anger, envy, and resentment in the Irish working classes brought him victory. He won 43,000 to 37,000, carrying sixteen of the twenty-six wards, and running ahead in all the lower-income sections of the city.

Curley's stunning victory over the powerful opposing coalition demonstrated the intensity of the previously inarticulate discontent with the city's existing political arrangements. The majority of voters wanted something more, something more striking and dramatic, something more expressive and emotionally satisfying than the stale and wearisome round of musical chairs which the old-style ward bosses had been playing for thirty years. Curley met that need. He had the ruthlessness, the style, the gift for the memorable phrase, and an utter unscrupulousness about means that enabled him to dominate the scene. He personalized all community problems, centered all conflicts around himself, and had

---

In 1942 he made his last race, being overwhelmingly defeated for the U.S. Senate nomination. Except for this final setback, his defeats were primarily due to errors of timing and luck. He ran for the right office in the wrong year, or vice versa. He was fortunate only in his posterity.

such vast egotism and such a grand sense of himself as the protagonist and prototype of his people that countless Bostonians leading drab workaday lives were able to identify with him and find release and vicarious satisfaction. The more he was attacked, the more they loved him. The more broadly he painted his emotional effects, the more comprehensive became his appeal. The more he exacerbated Irish-Yankee antagonisms, the more he vented repressed resentments and hatreds. For the next forty years he acted out a personal legend that provided a catharsis for the Boston Irish.

Certain adventitious circumstances assisted Curley. If the previous generation of politicians had organized a unified political machine, the experience of other cities suggests that although Curley might have been able to defy it successfully once, it would have eventually tamed or broken him. Rebels, like reformers, rarely win a second term. But the Democratic Party in Boston had little coherence or internal discipline. It was a feudal system, and Curley, like a Renaissance king, was able to pick off the barons one at a time. He was further aided by the changes made in the reform charter of 1909. As long as city elections are fought on a two-party basis, there is some value in controlling the formal apparatus of the party. But since the reformers had made municipal elections nonpartisan, the party machinery was irrelevant and politics became purely personal. This made it easier for Curley, the outsider, to legitimize his position even though his opponents controlled the Democratic City Committee. Moreover, the charter, by centralizing power in the hands of the mayor, gave Curley (or any strong personality) an excellent opportunity and weakened the city's legislative branch, the natural stronghold of the ward bosses.

As Curley gradually starved out, bought off, and beat down the various ward bosses, he did not replace their organizations with a unified machine of his own. Having bucked the system successfully, he was extremely wary of dispersing any power in the hands of local subordinates. "Build up a ward politician and someday he will betray you"[10]—that was his constant fear. Trusting no one, Curley became the lone general in an army of privates. He endeavored to make every appointee and every recipient of a favor feel personally indebted to him. During his administrations, the mayor's office was always thronged with humble people seeking aid who in other big cities would have been siphoned off at the level of the precinct captain or the district leader. Evenings and weekends, constituents kept his phone ringing almost constantly. Favor seekers hung about the entrance to his home as he left for work in the morning and congregated in the approaches to his office in City Hall. This highly centralized system, or lack of system, would have appalled the mayors and party bosses who were Curley's contemporaries in other large cities. (It is impossible to imagine Edward J. Flynn in the Bronx or Frank Hague in Jersey City allowing himself to be badgered and importuned in this way.) But it gave Curley a secure personal hold over the hearts of thousands of Bostonians.

Curley's method of operation enabled ordinary men and women to have or at least feel that they had direct personal access to the source of power. From the conventional politician's viewpoint, this method had the serious defect of centering all frictions and disappointments on the Number One Man himself. If Curley received all the credit, so also did he monopolize the blame and the resentment. But here lay the secret of his amazing resiliency. In any impersonal Tammany-style organization, power adheres to the office rather than to the man, and once deprived of the key position, whether it be Grand Sachem or Cook County Chairman, the old leader is virtually wiped out as a political factor. But in Boston, Curley remained a real political force as long as he lived because there were thousands of voters who recalled past favors or who had once had favorable sentiments toward him which under the right circumstances could be reawakened. No caucus of the executive committee could vote out Robin Hood.

Since Curley did not organize a stratified, functioning machine, he was not able to impose his will on the party when it came to nominations for other local and state offices. He had to cajole and negotiate with the various members of the City Council much as a President deals with members of Congress.* After he eventually captured control of the Democratic City Committee, he kept it a paper organization. Curley was content to be the most powerful single figure in Boston politics and to have an enormous personal following that would vote for him but that he could not deliver to anyone else.

Curley did not achieve this preeminence overnight. When he sought reelection in 1917, he was defeated because the old-line factions opposing him shrewdly entered three Democratic congressmen in the race to split his vote. The winner was Representative Andrew Peters, a conservative Yankee Democrat; but in Curley's mind the villain was Representative James Gallivan of South Boston who finished a strong third and whose support was drawn from voters who otherwise would probably have supported Curley.[11] Impelled by anger and vindictiveness, Curley the following year foolishly challenged Gallivan for his

---

* The *Boston Post*, Nov. 4, 1931, has a full account of Curley's failure to purge three members of the City Council in that year's midterm election. The *Boston Herald*, Dec. 1, 1947, has an article by W. E. Mullins, *Herald* political columnist, pointing out that there was then only "one reliable Curley man" on the City Council.

seat in Congress. Running in his enemy's personal stronghold, Curley was again defeated. But in 1921, in an extremely close election, Curley obtained a second four-year term in City Hall. From that time forward, he consolidated his popularity. The following fifteen years were the period of his maximum power. He was mayor from 1921 to 1925, and again from 1929 to 1933, and governor from 1934 to 1936. He could easily have been reelected mayor in 1925 and again in 1933, but the legislature had meanwhile changed the law to forbid successive terms by the same man. The business community and the reformers who had originated the "strong mayor" charter now realized the scope of their error and made yet another shortcut attempt to mitigate their mistake. But, again, it could be argued that the ban on reelection helped Curley as much as it hampered him. Since for selfish reasons he did not want a successor whose background and personality appealed to his own following, he made behind-the-scenes deals with the Republican minority and dissident Democrats to allow the office to fall into their control. These deals resulted in weak administrations whose ineptitude served, from Curley's standpoint, the useful negative purposes of avoiding the accumulation of anti-Curley resentments among the voters, forestalling the emergence of a strong rival, and highlighting his own accomplishments against the drab background of pseudo reform.

6

Curley's durable political strength had a serious basis. He devoted substantial sums to developing the City Hospital; during each of his four administrations large additions and improvements were made. He developed the mudflats along the South Boston ocean front into a mile-long beach, built several bathhouses, and an excellent solarium. He also constructed numerous playgrounds, stadiums, and recreational facilities. In short, he put into practice a theory of positive government that had tangible benefits for voters, particularly those in the low-income brackets. These gains were visible, while the economies and stabilized tax rate that were the only accomplishments of intervening administrations were invisible. Moreover, when it came to administrative efficiency as distinguished from economy, Curley, despite his whims and vagaries, was undeniably a more energetic and effective executive than any of his Boston contemporaries.

A second source of Curley's strength was that his administrations provided jobs. In a city plagued with chronic unemployment, Curley's expansive spending for medical and recreational facilities, as well as the more conventional public works projects (tunnels, subways, and street widening), was always popular. The question of direct relief versus public works projects that later became a national concern was already an issue in Boston throughout the ostensibly prosperous 1920's.

Curley's talents as a master showman were another of his important political strengths. The Irish, as all their history makes clear, are highly politicized people. To an Irishman, the proper song is not "I Love a Parade" but "I Love an Election Night." Politics, because it is taken seriously, can also serve as a source of entertainment, and an Irishman considers himself a connoisseur of political style. Moreover, Boston is an unusually politically conscious city. Every family has a politician, a hopeful aspirant, or an active party worker in its bosom. Familiarity breeds the attitude that political struggles are sporting affairs, matters of gamesmanship. "James Michael" was the greatest gamester of them all.

A brief study of the 1921 mayoralty election exemplifies Curley as he rounded into the top of his form. His opponent that year was John R. Murphy, then sixty-six, a respectable old-timer whose roots went far back into a past era of Boston politics. From 1876 to 1885, he had been business manager of John Boyle O'Reilly's newspaper, *The Boston Pilot*. (O'Reilly was his brother-in-law.) Murphy made the nominating speech at the Democratic city convention for Hugh O'Brien who became the first Irish Catholic mayor in 1886. He was rewarded with the job of Wire Commissioner. Subsequently he served as state representative, state senator, and Water Commissioner, and was an unsuccessful candidate for mayor as far back as 1899. At the time of his campaign against Curley, he was Fire Commissioner in the administration of Mayor Peters.

Curley's approach, as always, was a frontal attack on his opponent's strongest point, his long experience. He derided Murphy as "an old mustard plaster that has been stuck on the back of the people for fifty years."

At one point in the campaign, Murphy and Curley appeared on the same platform. Murphy reviewed his long career and various qualifications. When Curley's turn came, he rose, struck a Murphy-like pose, squinted toward the audience, and croaked, "I don't see anybody here that I welcomed back from the Civil War."

Curley, without hesitation, slandered his opponent by trumping up a baseless religious issue. Murphy was a practicing Catholic, but he had recently moved near Trinity (Protestant) Church. Curley charged that Murphy had moved so he would not have so far to walk to church.

"He has not only joined a Masonic order but he has also become a communicant of fashionable Trinity Church," Curley cried.

Murphy spent several nights on the stump denying this charge. Then Curley revived it in slightly different form:

"Where was James M. Curley last Friday night? He was conducting a political meeting in Duxbury. And where was John R. Murphy last Friday night? He was eating steak at the Copley Plaza."

Curley sent squads of his followers to the saloons and door-to-door in the tenement districts spreading these rumors: "Murphy intends to divorce his wife and marry a 16-year old girl," or, "The counterman at Thompson's Spa told me Murphy ordered a roast beef sandwich last Friday."[12]

Curley won by fewer than 2,700 votes. It is possible that in Boston in 1921 there were that many credulous voters but it is not likely. This whispering campaign and these low blows were not the central effort of Curley's campaign; their only purpose was tactical, to throw Murphy off stride and keep him busy denying rumors while Curley pressed forward on the offensive. The cynicism of this kind of campaigning could not be kept a secret from the voters, since scores of Curley's camp followers were necessarily "in" on this tactic, talked about it and, perhaps, even improved on Curley's diabolical cleverness in the retelling. The majority of the Boston Irish enjoyed and wanted this kind of eye-gouging, ear-biting, rough-and-tumble political fighting; many of them, having heard Curley on one street corner, would rush a few blocks away to another corner in the hopes of hearing Murphy (or one of his supporters) reply in kind. There was a reciprocal relationship between Curley and his audiences; an audience would have to be conditioned by history and circumstances to have such an avid taste for invective and verbal violence, and Curley, by consistently pandering to that taste, helped confirm it and establish a norm.

Curley made no pretense to sincerity, then or later, in his deliberate use of excessive language. As he remarked in his memoirs: "There are times . . . when, if you want to win an election, you must do unto others as they wish to do unto you, but you must do it first. It is not always sufficient to return blow for blow. 'In a pinch, swing hard' is an excellent proverb for a politician. . . . More than once I have congratulated an opponent just after he blistered me in a speech. It's all part of the great game of politics where the epithets are not to be taken too seriously."[13]

This attitude is obviously close to that of President Harry Truman, who engaged in memorable campaign duels with Republican leaders and enjoyed excellent personal relations with most of them. (It is no accident that the Boston Irish took Truman to their heart in 1948 and gave him an immense plurality. He was their style, "a fighter.")

The wit, scorn, and invective that Curley employed recklessly in the family quarrels of the Boston Irish took on a different aspect when he used them in the Irish-Yankee conflict. Many Irish who disapproved of much of Curley's behavior and would often vote against him in a contest with another Irishman could not help but feel a thrill of pleasure when he gave voice to emotions—hostility, envy, resentment, anger—that are repressed or played down in normal political discourse.

No one could state the case for the Irish more boldly and confidently than Curley did in a letter to a member of the Harvard Board of Overseers: "The Massachusetts of the Puritans is as dead as Caesar, but there is no need to mourn the fact. Their successors—the Irish—had letters and learning, culture and civilization when the ancestors of the Puritans were savages running half-naked through the forests of Britain. It took the Irish to make Massachusetts a fit place to live in."[14]

"The term 'codfish aristocracy,'" Curley once said, "is a reflection on the fish."

He attacked the wealthy Yankees who looked down their noses at him as the descendants of scoundrels who "got rich selling opium to the Chinese, rum to the Indians, or trading in slaves."

He made repeated attacks through the years on the Somerset Club, a Boston men's club, which excludes Catholics.

He made the obvious transposition on the famous description of Boston as the place where the Cabots speak only to Lowells and the Lowells speak only to God. "Boston," he liked to say, "is where the Caseys speak only to Curleys, and the Curleys speak only to whom they damn well please."

When asked by the press to comment on a Republican governor's appointment to public office of Endicott Peabody Saltonstall, Curley wisecracked, "What, all three of them?"

Curley authentically reflected the sentiment of most of the Irish community in his deeply ambivalent attitudes toward Harvard University. To the Irish of Curley's generation, roughly the period 1910 to 1940, Harvard was much more than an educational institution: it was the awesome symbol of Yankee tradition, power, and prestige. Almost from the first arrival of the Irish in the mid-nineteenth century, individual Irishmen had been students at Harvard (as noted earlier, Patrick Collins, the second Irish Catholic mayor, was a Harvard graduate), and by 1900 it was no longer unusual for Boston Irish boys to go to Harvard. But the Irish community as a whole still experienced Harvard and its satellite cluster of private preparatory schools (Groton, Milton, Phillips Andover, and others) as bulwarks of a social and economic system from whose power and privilege most Irish were shut out. (Eton and Harrow, Oxford and Cambridge have been seen by the

British working class in a similar way.) Some Irish complained that Harvard discriminated against them, a complaint that had no basis in fact. Others experienced the choice of Harvard instead of a Catholic college as a surrender or a sellout because in a limited but real sense this choice represented a move away from the values of the Irish Catholic community. If this were not felt by the student himself, it might be felt by his less sophisticated relatives. Curley touched this chord when he boasted that although Harvard had admitted one of his sons, he had destroyed the letter of acceptance and sent his son instead to Holy Cross College, a Jesuit college in nearby Worcester.

The development of Holy Cross and, more particularly, Boston College by the Jesuits introduced a separate factor of rivalry. These colleges did not, in purely secular terms, stand up as rivals to Harvard, but they asserted a religious claim that exercised a considerable hold over the loyalties of the Boston Irish. Moreover, the Irish-Yankee struggle tended at the middle-class level to polarize around the Jesuit colleges and Harvard. The alumni of the Catholic schools competed in Massachusetts with Harvard graduates in business and the professions, specifically law, insurance, real estate, and stock brokerage. The struggles of the Irish to crack the Boston financial district were epochal in the evolution of this emerging Irish middle class, and so were their attempts to win judgeships. Since the governor appointed all judges, and since most governors before 1930 were Yankee Republicans, the judiciary was one of the last strongholds of the old order to yield to Irish penetration. In finance and in the judiciary, the Irish drive to power was in part an effort by Catholic college alumni to break the hegemony of Harvard.

Curley reflected both sides of this Irish attitude toward Harvard, the respect and the resentment. He admired the university and coveted its approbation. Every Curley campaign inevitably featured an endorsement by at least one Harvard professor (it is a large faculty). Words of praise from Harvard professors for Curley's executive skill or his oratorical power were quoted in his campaign literature. Any group of Harvard students who wanted to work for Curley or issue a statement in his behalf were sure of a warm welcome, a fact that periodically exposed him to hoaxes by ingenious editors of the Harvard *Lampoon*. Curley never declined an opportunity to speak at Harvard. But at the same time, he criticized the university and frequently made derisive jokes about Harvard men. His ambivalence on the subject impelled him to extravagant gestures. When Harvard celebrated its tercentenary in 1936, Curley, then governor, showed up with gold-braided military aides, a company of red-coated cavrymen on horseback, and a small military band blaring trumpets and beating drums. Massachusetts governors traditionally attend Harvard Commencement, but this display of military pomp was a revival of a custom that had long since lapsed. Unlike many previous Massachusetts governors, Curley did not receive an honorary degree.

Curley obviously enjoyed these encounters with Harvard, and exploited them politically, but that does not diminish the significance of this conflict for him and for the Irish community.

7

In his oratory, clothes, and manner of living, Curley set the style for a whole generation of Boston politicians, and for many who were not in politics. In his early campaigns, Curley's voice was strong but harsh and unmodulated. Through conscious cultivation, he achieved a smooth, velvety baritone that could caress a hearer with a line of poetry or rise to a thunderous emotional climax. He also acquired an accent that with its broad "a" and dropped "r" was more Harvard Yard than Irish brogue. There was always a gap between what Curley the man was actually like and what Curley the public figure appeared to be in his own conception of himself and in the imagination of his adherents. His beautifully developed speaking voice was his greatest asset in closing that gap and making real the image.

His choice of rhetoric was also an effort in that direction. Not for him the plain, blunt language of Al Smith or the cultivated simplicity of Franklin Roosevelt. He had read widely and eclectically in history and literature and always liked to make a comment worthy of the eighteenth and nineteenth century English and American political masters he admired. When he publicly quarreled with Al Smith in 1932, he made use of the couplet from Scott's *Marmion*:

> "O, what a tangled web we weave,
> When first we practise to deceive!"

When an old supporter turned against him, he naturally rebuked him in Shakespearian language:

> "How sharper than a serpent's tooth it is
> To have a thankless child!"

Curley's adherents, ordinary people of limited education but with a taste for oratory and rhetoric, enjoyed and admired these gorgeous flights.

From the outset of his career, Curley was sensitive to the importance of clothes. He spent part of the $25 he raised for his first campaign in 1898 at Max Keezer's, a famous secondhand clothing store near Harvard where he bought a black dress suit, undoubtedly once the property of a Harvard student, to wear at his rallies in Roxbury. As a young congressman, he admired the white vest worn by Speaker Champ Clark, and for many years thereafter he wore one himself. He frequently wore a black coat and gray-striped trousers to the office. His broadbrimmed gray soft hat and velvet-collared Chesterfield coat were imitated by so many younger politicians they practically constituted a uniform. Curley was more than a political leader; he was a teacher and the exemplar of a social ideal. If he had been simply a politician, attacks on him from outside the Irish community would not have generated the defensiveness they always aroused in his admirers.

During his first administration as mayor in 1915, Curley built a large house in a fashionable section of Boston. The oval-shaped dining room was forty feet long and had a fourteen-foot ceiling, hand-carved mahogany paneling, and a chandelier of Irish Waterford glass. The wide, winding staircase rose two stories without any visible support. The exterior was distinguished by the shamrock carved on each of its shutters. Curley filled the house with expensive furniture, rugs, glassware, and objets d'art.

This house was the object of much gossip, and provoked an inconclusive public investigation of how Curley had acquired the money to build it. But it was also the occasion for much admiration. The ordinary working-class people who were the backbone of Curley's political support appeared not to resent the fact that Curley lived in a rather grand manner. Like movie fans who do not resent their favorite star living in well-publicized luxury in Beverly Hills and baseball fans who do not begrudge a well-paid baseball player receiving thousands of dollars in gifts at a day in his honor, many rank-and-file Bostonians took a vicarious pleasure in their political hero's style of life.

Behind his many masks, Curley remained always a lonely man. His only confidante was his first wife, a tall, plain-faced woman of shrewd if untutored mind who played something approaching a mother role to her tempestuous husband. She had a large fund of common sense, kept a strict rein on her imagination, and served as an informed and incisive private critic. She died of cancer in June, 1930. (Curley remarried several years later.) During his long years of power, his winter and summer homes were usually crowded with politicians and contractors. Curley was engrossed with them because politics was his career, and their flattery pleased his vanity. But he also viewed them with a certain contempt. Like the humbler favor seekers in his home ward in the early days, they were only so much human material to be manipulated. His real inner life, like that of most great egotists, consisted of an endless drama in which he was always the hero and always played to an audience of one—himself. He had no colleagues and no equals. He had only spear-carriers and minor actors in his own romantic drama. He saw himself as variously the greatest mayor Boston ever had, the greatest governor of Massachusetts, the state's most illustrious senator since Daniel Webster, as Secretary of the Navy making ceremonial visits to Japan and other naval powers around the globe, as ambassador to Italy, and even as President.[15]

8

Curley demonstrated his characteristic imagination in the summer of 1931 when he unexpectedly endorsed Franklin Roosevelt for the Democratic presidential nomination the following year. Al Smith was still the overwhelming choice of the state's rank-and-file Democrats, and most Massachusetts politicians were either urging him to seek the nomination again or patiently waiting for him to make up his mind. Curley had nothing to gain from the renomination of Smith, since "the Happy Warrior" had always disliked him and had entrusted his local interests to Curley's enemies, United States Senator David I. Walsh and Governor Joseph B. Ely. Moreover, to anyone not emotionally committed to Smith, the nomination of Roosevelt was the most probable political development. Nevertheless, it took daring for Curley to go against the strong tide of local opinion. Having decided upon his gamble, Curley followed his usual tactic. He did not simply ignore Smith or promote Roosevelt as the better of two good men. In the school of politics in which Curley learned his profession, either of those courses would have been a milk-and-water diet unworthy of a red-blooded man. He waded in and attacked Smith ferociously.

"Smith is a tool of Wall Street," Curley charged. "He is in league with the financial interests of the nation to keep President Hoover in the White House."

Curley persuaded Roosevelt to allow him to enter a slate of pledged delegates in the Massachusetts presidential primary in April, 1932. Although the Smith ticket swept the state, including Boston, by nearly

3-to-1 and captured all the delegates, Curley participated in Roosevelt's final triumph when he arranged to become an alternate delegate from Puerto Rico, styling himself, "Jaime Miguel Curleo." On his return to Boston, he began his first speech with the salutation, "Señors and señoras . . ."

The alliance between Curley and Roosevelt was uneasy from the first. Curley, by instinct and experience, was more sympathetic with the Irish machine politicians in Tammany than with an aristocratic reformer. Roosevelt, on his part, was well aware that Curley took graft and could not be trusted in any office where financial probity mattered. Curley's dreams of the Navy secretaryship had no basis in reality. After much shadowboxing concerning the ambassadorship to Rome, Roosevelt finally offered him the post of Minister to Poland, which Curley declined.

Curley, however, used his early leap aboard the Roosevelt express to get himself elected governor in 1934, his only statewide victory. His two years in office were tumultuous. The session of the legislature during his first year in office was the longest in history up to that time. The official compilation of the governor's papers for those two years is twice as long as that of any of his predecessors.

Curley pushed through a considerable body of social legislation. State employees received the forty-eight-hour week, attachment of wages for debt was banned, the eligibility limit for old-age pensions was reduced from seventy to sixty-five, and a start was made on a low-cost housing program. Numerous laws paralleling those being enacted by Congress at the federal level were adopted. William Green, president of the American Federation of Labor, wrote: "More progressive, constructive, liberal laws were enacted under Curley in two years than under all previous administrations in any ten-year period in the history of the State."[16]

But this record of solid achievement was obscured by the endless uproar created by Curley's aggressive methods and by the fierce determination of the Republican Party and of his enemies within his own party to bring him down. Curley inherited an administration staffed from top to bottom with holdovers from the regime of Governor Ely, his conservative Democratic predecessor, and earlier Republican governors. A governor in Massachusetts serves only a two-year term, but major policy-making officials serve five- or seven-year terms. This is a system deliberately staggered and arranged to make the bureaucracy relatively independent of politics and to limit the scope of the governor's power. Pending the expiration of their terms, top officials can be removed only through impeachment by the Governor's Council. This "relic of royalty," as Curley called it, is a carryover from colonial days. It is made

up of eight men elected from individual council districts with the lieu-
tenant-governor a voting member. The council must approve all appointments, pardons, and contracts. Faced with a 5-to-4 Republican majority,
Curley appointed two of the Republicans to important positions and filled
their places with Democrats. An uproar immediately began that he had
"destroyed the people's barrier."

Having gained control of the Council, Curley impeached several
Republican officeholders. He also refused to reappoint several "nonpolitical" incumbents, notably Payson Smith, Commissioner of Education for the preceding eighteen years, whom he replaced with an Irish
Catholic, James G. Reardon. The press, which was uniformly hostile to
Curley, was easily able to depict this shift as an outrageous example of
political jobbery. But there was another side to the story. Smith's record
was not impressive. Massachusetts in 1935 still had no minimum annual
salary for teachers (some towns paid as little as $600 a year), no state-
wide system for the certification of teachers to guarantee they be of
at least minimum quality, and no statewide system of correlating student
achievement such as the New York Regents' Examination. In short, in
education as in many other areas, Massachusetts was resting on its reputation and had fallen behind.

Curley added zest to the controversy by charging that no Irish
Catholic had ever been appointed to the faculty of any of the state's six
teacher colleges. A survey revealed this was not true, but the Irish had
far fewer positions on these faculties than their numbers would have led
one to expect. Moreover, many Irish teaching applicants, particularly
graduates of Catholic colleges, believed, justifiably or not, that they were
discriminated against by the Yankee-run school boards in the small
towns. The Smith controversy revealed the volcano of passion that
smoldered beneath the surface in many areas of the state's life.

More important to Curley was his rapid falling-out with President
Roosevelt. He had been elected on the slogan "work and wages" and
had assured the electorate that because of his personal friendship with
Roosevelt and his early support of his candidacy, he would be able
to obtain exceptionally large amounts of federal aid for public works
projects. But Roosevelt was not responsive to Curley's requests nor
would he turn control of relief funds over to an administrator recommended by Curley. After a year in office, Curley had accomplished
no more than Ely, his conservative predecessor, who had also been on the
"outs" with Roosevelt. As the *Boston Post* observed editorially:

"Governor Curley didn't actually promise 'work and wages for
all' in his campaign, but a good many persons assumed he did and that
was a fair inference. No doubt he has struggled hard to keep the work

and wages promise, but that is impossible. He may have failed to get the necessary financial cooperation from the Federal Government, but he promised he could."[17]

Curley admitted his failure the same week when he announced his candidacy for United States senator. Curley declared that the pressure of the unemployed, coupled with his own inability to satisfy the demands, had caused him to decide to retire as governor.

"No man could live four years on this job under present conditions," he said in explaining why he would not seek a second term. "I could not have stood it to date, if it were not for the fact that I have regulated my living carefully during the past year. Four or five times a week I have to get a thorough physical rub-down. All this is stimulating but it amounts to working on borrowed time.

"If it were humanly possible to effect any material benefit for these thousands of unemployed, it would, of course, be a source of gratification. But as a matter of fact, the problem is one which is much too large to be accomplished by merely state legislation and state activity."[18]

But the Roosevelt administration and independent liberals had no reason to welcome Curley's decision to shift to the national scene. Considerable differences had developed between Curley and Roosevelt on national issues. In May, 1935, Roosevelt declared the Supreme Court's decision outlawing the N.R.A. was taking the country back to the "horse-and-buggy days." Curley said: "In my opinion, the Supreme Court in its decision in the case of the N.R.A. in disregarding the exigencies of industrial depression and unemployment and in hewing religiously to the tenets of the constitution, acted strictly in accord with the views of even those who would benefit through a different interpretation."[19]

On August 8, 1935, Curley, speaking to the Massachusetts Federation of Labor Convention, urged Roosevelt "to correct the mistakes and evils of the New Deal." On November 2, 1935, he declared that "the Roosevelt policy of trying to stabilize industry overnight is a mistake, and I think the President will realize the necessity of a change in his policy. Instead of demanding reforms immediately, he should approach them gradually."[20] On the issue of American adherence to the World Court which was before the Senate, he rallied to the support of William Randolph Hearst, the leader of the opposition, whom he called "that clarion of the plain people of America."[21]

In January, 1936, speaking to a conference called to stimulate private employment, Curley renewed his criticism of Roosevelt and his advisers, the "brain trusters." "A majority of the so-called super-intellectuals, who are socially inclined, believe that unless we get reform with recovery we will never get reform. My personal opinion is that the main thing is to get recovery and then get reform. These super-intellectuals want reform regardless of recovery. They want to eat their apple and have it too. They can't have both."

He reported he had recently been advised by "representatives of two large industries that they are ready to spend money in developments but they are holding off because of the uncertainty. What is true of these two, is, I believe, true of all other industries. There is no incentive to spend money when we have ten million unemployed and when the relief rolls are so large as to make taxation excessive."[22]

These criticisms were part of the familiar line of attack that the conservatives in the business community had intitiated against the New Deal: the presumed choice between recovery and reform, the complaint of "excessive taxation," the scorn for the impractical intellectuals in the administration, and the promise that business expansion awaited only the return of "sound" policies.

Curley was needling the President because the latter had denied him the patronage and control of relief expenditures he desired. Curley was also mercurial where national issues were concerned. But his drift away from Roosevelt and the New Deal represented something more profound than either political tactics or personal vagaries. No one in 1934 would have predicted that in two years Curley would be echoing the conservatives, just as no one in 1936 would have predicted that in 1940 John L. Lewis would be campaigning against Roosevelt and for a Wall Street utilities lawyer. Yet in both cases the evolution was not only logical but almost inevitable. There were striking external similarities between Lewis and Curley: both had great physical brawn and both frequently used their fists as well as their brains on the way to the top. Both were self-educated and apparently cultured, yet their outlook was really shaped by the struggle for power. Learning was but a tool to be used for a larger end; each could quote "the immortal bard of Avon" but neither was truly educated. Both had acquired a rare personal charm and a flair for grandiloquent oratory. But more important than these personal similarities was the similar environment from which they came. Curley spoke for the Boston Irish masses, a people culturally and economically isolated; Lewis for the coal miners, a body of workers economically depressed and physically isolated. Each in his career had known violent ups-and-downs and each had finally reached the culmination of his career because of political circumstances created by the New Deal. Yet neither was prepared to cooperate effectively in a broad social movement, for they had worshiped naked power and knew not how to use it. For lack of a social philosophy, for lack of a broad-gauged understanding and sympathy with radically diverse elements, the titanic energies of these two men, which should have been harnessed for the common good, were frittered away in meaningless personal strife.

9

Curley suffered an ignominious defeat in 1936. He easily wrested the senatorial nominination away from Marcus Coolidge, the dim Democratic incumbent, but he lost the election to Henry Cabot Lodge, then only thirty-four and with no experience except two terms in the state legislature. Curley suffered a double defection. The Union Party organized by Father Charles E. Couglin entered a candidate in the race who polled over 120,000 votes. This was almost equal to Lodge's plurality of 134,000. If there had not been a Couglinite third candidate, most of this support would have gone to Curley and he would have finished in an approximate "dead heat" with Lodge. But in addition, Curley was badly cut by "lace-curtain" Irish, particularly in the outlying parts of the state, who disliked his flamboyant style, and by independent liberals who objected to his attacks on the New Deal.

More significant than the 1936 election was the mayoralty contest in Boston the following year. Curley returned to the people he had always known, confident that from this secure base he could rebuild his shattered political fortunes. He encountered instead the most decisive defeat he ever suffered in a Boston election, losing the city by 25,250 votes.

The victor was Maurice J. Tobin, subsequently governor of Massachusetts and Secretary of Labor in the Truman Cabinet, who had been a Curley protégé.

Several factors played a part in Tobin's sweeping victory. One was his youth. He was thirty-six, while Curley was sixty-three and suddenly seemed old. Where Curley had previously always seemed to personify youth and action against the forces of reaction and inertia, Tobin now made brief remarks such as: "My opponent first ran for mayor in 1913. I was twelve years old that year." Where past candidates had always focused their attack on Curley, Tobin shrewdly refused to give him that psychological advantage. He rarely mentioned Curley, and his brief, fleeting references seemed more damning than a full-length arraignment: "I will not mention my opponent's record. You all know it too well."[23]

Another factor was active support by the *Boston Post*. This paper was usually neutral in mayoralty campaigns because the presence of several Democratic candidates gave the contest a "family" character.

But in 1937 the *Post* endorsed Tobin and crusaded for him. The *Post* and Cardinal O'Connell, who had long disliked Curley, joined hands to make that dislike politically effective. It was the *Post*'s custom to run a quotation each day in a page-wide box over its masthead. On election day, the box read:

"Voters of Boston: Cardinal O'Connell, in speaking to the Catholic Alumni Association, said, 'The walls are raised against honest men in civic life.' You can break down these walls by voting for an honest, clean, competent young man, *Maurice Tobin*, today. He will redeem the city and take it out of the hands of those who have been responsible for graft and corruption."

To those who read this statement quickly and failed to notice the change in punctuation, it seemed that the cardinal was directly endorsing Tobin. His Eminence became extremely preoccupied and was "unable" to see an emissary from Curley who wanted him to disavow the use of his name in this connection.

Another factor was strong business community and Republican Party support. The old leadership of the minority party in Boston that had often collaborated in deals with Curley behind the scenes had been displaced by a younger, progressive faction headed by Henry Parkman, a scion of the same family as the famous nineteenth century historian.

But the newspapers, the cardinal, and the Republicans had at various times in the past opposed Curley with little effect. The crux of the matter was to be found in changing attitudes within the Irish community itself.

The significance of this pivotal election was pointed up in a speech by Joseph A. Scolponetti, a long-time Curley supporter. It was in a sense the swan song of Curley and those other insurgent politicians who had emerged at the turn of the century:

"Shall we, the Democrats of Boston, permit division in our ranks? We number a 3-1 majority. Can we be divided by an ignominious Press and intolerant Bigots? These pretenders of government are not our friends. They seek to Republicanize our city and state again. For more than one hundred and fifty years these Tories held the reins of Government. In politics we of the newer races were Outcasts. In business our forefathers were cowed with coolie wages. We were without standing and without right, but out of the hardships of the virile O'Briens, Collins, Fitzgeralds and Curleys there came a new day.

"We are not approaching the Dawn of a New Era. It is here. We are in the sunlight of a New Day. Let's enjoy it! The dawn of a New Era came when Jim Curley became Governor. It came when he cleared the barriers in the Department of Education and appointed the youthful

Jim Reardon . . . [other Irish appointments listed]. Shall we Democrats of Boston destroy these advantages? Can you not see enemies knocking at our gates? Shall we surrender?

". . . To you, his people, I make this call to arms. Will he be crucified? If crucified he must be, will the nails be driven by the Bantrys, the Normans and the Parkmans? I know Jim Curley. I know his people. The flower of love is in their hearts. The breath of loyalty is in their souls. The truth of God is in their minds. No, they will not fail this Man of Destiny, James M. Curley."[24]

In the years from 1934 to 1937, the old insurgent crusade begun in the 1890's reached the heights of victory and then died away, its banners dragging in the dust. For over thirty years, Curley and a host of lesser men had painted visions of a golden era that lay at the end of the trail. The only obstacles to attaining the promised land were the prejudiced, reactionary Yankees. Finally, in January, 1935, Curley became governor, which meant the Boston Irish and their allies, the Italians and other "new immigrants," took over Beacon Hill.*

Curley did "clear the barriers." But the promised land proved to be a grand illusion. Within eleven months, Curley confessed the job too big for any one state (and by implication for any one man) to handle. For the first time, the immigrant poor began to realize that perhaps the whole trouble lay not with the Yankees or the bankers or "the pirates of Back Bay"; perhaps it was a regional or a national problem. The great majority of Irish and other immigrant community voters turned toward Washington where alone there was a man with a program that seemed capable of genuine achievement. But strangely enough, Curley, for what seemed to the average man an obscure reason, had broken with Roosevelt and the New Deal and had begun to blame his own failures on the Washington "braintrusters," the "super-intellectuals."

There is nothing more dangerous for a politician than for him to announce his program is completed, that he has no fresh vision of the future. Scolponetti said: "We are in the sunlight of a New Day. Let's enjoy it!" With one-quarter of his listeners unemployed and thousands of others barely struggling to survive on low wages, this exhortation was more ironic than inspiring.

In the mid-1950's, nearly twenty years after the 1937 mayoralty election, when Curley in his old age had been transformed from a politically potent figure to a kind of cultural artifact—an object of detached interest, half scientific and half sentimental—the usual ex-

* There had been a previous Irish Catholic governor—David I. Walsh in 1914-1915 —but Walsh was much too dignified, restrained, and middle class to satisfy the emotions to which Curley appealed.

planation offered for his political downfall was that the welfare state
had outmoded his style of politics. The combination of social security,
unemployment compensation, minimum wages, and trade unions had
undermined Curley as it had his notorious colleagues in the profession
of political boss: Edward Kelly in Chicago, Frank Hague in Jersey City,
and the successive leaders of Tammany Hall in New York. This is the
explanation offered in the novel *The Last Hurrah* by Edwin O'Connor
in which a character attributes the defeat of Skeffington, the fictional
boss modeled on Curley, to "Roosevelt . . . and good old, remote, impersonal Washington."[25] This is sound enough as far as it goes; the
welfare state has undoubtedly lessened the dependence of the average
voter on the local political leader and the local party machine. This
explanation, however, does not account for the durability of the
political machine. The operations of the Democratic Party machine in
Chicago under Mayor Richard Daley or in Philadelphia under Congressman William Green, Jr., in 1962 are not remarkably different from
those of similar machines thirty years ago before the arrival of Roosevelt
and the New Deal. Nor, in the specific case of Boston, would it account
for Curley's defeat in 1937, which occurred after the social security
law had been enacted but before it went into operation. This period
was the nadir of his career: in 1936 he was defeated for the Senate; in
1937, for mayor; in 1938, for governor. Over the next dozen years, as
the welfare state developed and its economic effects became fully felt,
Curley actually grew stronger, rather than weaker. In 1941 he came
back strongly against Tobin, losing by only 9,200 votes. (The vote was
Tobin, 125,000, and Curley, 116,000.) The next year he slid easily into
a safe berth as a congressman where he served one term and part of a
second before running for mayor again in 1945. This time he was
victorious; he polled slightly fewer votes than he had four years previously, but his opposition was divided between two candidates, enabling
him to become a minority mayor. In 1949 he was defeated for reelection;
but, unlike the fictional Skeffington, he did not lose in a landslide; he
was overturned in a close, hard-fought election. John B. Hynes, his
opponent, polled 138,000 to Curley's 126,000. Curley's ninth and tenth
races for mayor, in 1951 and 1955, do not count; they were token races
in which Curley sought publicity and campaign funds and did not
seriously expect to gain office.

   Curley's political significance can be comprehended only in cultural
terms. His main political strength was his ability to define, dramatize, and
play upon the discrimination, resentments, and frustrations suffered by
the Irish community in its long passage from a despised immigrant minor-

ity to a politically irresistible but economically blocked majority. In the middle of the 1930's, three circumstances developed concurrently that were Curley's undoing. First, he became governor and was able to clear the last discriminations obstructing the Irish, at least the last discriminations that were directly curable by political means. He thereby exhausted what had been a durable issue. Second, education, the passage of time, and the slow accumulation of wealth had produced a new majority within the Boston Irish community. This majority, made up in part but by no means entirely of persons of middle-class incomes, had become detached from the values Curley espoused. Quite independent of any economic effects of the developing welfare state, these voters no longer saw the problems of Boston or the world in the simplified terms in which Curley presented them. They were more skeptical of emotional appeals, more sophisticated about the complexity of public problems, and less tolerant of routine graft. The third circumstance was the extraordinary depth and scope of the great depression, which produced a volume of unemployment that overwhelmed Curley's personal, *ad hoc* methods of dealing with economic problems. He characteristically reacted to these changed circumstances with attacks on other leaders and other groups, specifically, on Roosevelt and the New Dealers. Here Curley overreached himself: he ran 210,000 votes behind Roosevelt in the 1936 senatorial election. Retreating to Boston, he lost the mayoralty the next year to Tobin because the new majority was for the first time strong enough to reject him. His defeat was overwhelming because part of the lowest-income group, which had always been the hard core of his strength, was disillusioned with his gubernatorial failure to solve the unemployment problem and had hopes that Tobin would be more effective in getting federal money. When the hope was not fulfilled, Curley recaptured this strength in subsequent elections. The recession of 1937, which persisted in Boston until the outbreak of World War II, convinced the least well-off segment of the Boston Irish of the truth of the old adage Curley and his adherents assiduously promoted for decades: "Curley spends money, and that means jobs. When the other guys are in, business is always lousy."

The election returns of 1941, 1945, and 1949 reflect this attitude. Of the city's twenty-two wards, the first eleven (with the exception of Wards 4 and 5, which are the Republican Back Bay–Beacon Hill area) are the worst parts of the city in terms of income and housing. Here Curley ran well: Charlestown, East Boston, South Boston, the North and West Ends, and Roxbury. The higher numbered wards, from 12 through 22, represent the more affluent parts of the city. Here Curley, except in one or two neighborhoods, did poorly. But "affluence" is only a comparative term. There are many workingmen and their families and many poorly paid schoolteachers, salespeople, and clerks living in these wards. The cleavage was cultural as much as economic. In these areas, the old gang code was losing its force; religion and education were producing an insistence on more rigorous standards of public ethics and public behavior. A growing sophistication made these voters impervious to the old appeals.

During the last dozen years of his active career, from 1937 to 1949, Curley did not change scapegoats in midfield. He might have been expected to substitute as an object of attack some other group for the Yankees who within Boston itself had dwindled to numerical insignificance. There was considerable anti-Semitic feeling in Boston during the war years. One private organization tallied 611 anti-Semitic incidents in 1942-1943, including 60 cases of physical violence.[26] After the war, when a public housing project was built in South Boston, there was an angry undercover dispute as to whether Negroes should be admitted to the project. Curley made no attempt to exploit these and similar tensions. He always followed the course of appealing to all minorities and trying to align them with his faction. For example, as a representative, he printed in the *Congressional Record* a list of the thousands of American Jews who had won the Congressional Medal of Honor and similar awards for bravery or who had been killed in action. He mailed thousands of reprints to Jewish voters in Massachusetts and elsewhere. (The *New York Times* criticized him for wasting the taxpayers' money, while the now defunct radical newspaper, *PM*, praised him.) Curley ran well in the two wards where most of Boston's Negroes lived; he stressed the patronage he had conferred, such as his appointment of the first Negro physician to the staff of the City Hospital, and in his last years he joined the National Association for the Advancement of Colored People. Similarly, he ran as well in the Lithuanian neighborhood in South Boston as in that section's Irish neighborhoods. American urban politicians traditionally try to make an appeal as comprehensive as the membership list of the United Nations. Curley acted within that tradition, and deserves credit for helping to avoid what might otherwise have deteriorated into an ugly situation in wartime and postwar Boston.

Curley was seventy-one when he took office for the last time in January, 1946. Weakened by diabetes, high blood pressure, and other ailments, he was much less the dominating executive and political showman than in the past. His manner, if not his methods, had mellowed. He sallied forth against fewer present enemies and more often recalled past encounters; all passions were spent except the simple will to survive, and the hardy old aggressiveness was veined with sentiment and reminiscence. His conviction and five months in federal prison in the middle of his term for an unimportant mail-fraud offense seemed, even to many of his enemies, a gratuitous and irrelevant humiliation.

10

On November 12, 1958, Curley died. When his will was probated, it showed a net estate of $3,768, insufficient to cover the bequests he had made. Money had always been a marginal concern for Curley. He had been a thriftless grabber who liked dollars in order to enjoy the gesture of giving them away, or to shower expensive baubles on his friends and womenfolk. But these were only trimmings. He was in the game, not for money, but for power and the thrill of its exercise. His sin was in the higher use of that power, and it is not to be found on any court records or on the ledgers of any bookkeeper.

The difference between Al Smith and Curley is instructive, and the difference lies in the moral examples they provided. Smith, in the decade from 1918 to 1928, made his name and the name of New York synonymous with good state government. It is largely because he established such a high standard of competence, integrity, and effectiveness that succeeding governors from both parties have been men of quality. Smith took what was best and strongest in the immigrant community from which he came and merged it in a pragmatic synthesis with the best traditions of the larger society into which he moved.

Curley, on the other hand, never transcended the boundaries. He exploited the sufferings and the inexperience, the warm sentiment, the fears, and the prejudices of his own people to perpetuate his personal power. He solved nothing; he moved toward no larger understanding; he opened no new lines of communication.

For more than thirty years, Curley kept the greater part of the Boston populace half-drunk with fantasies, invective, and showmanship. He was a model to countless younger politicians who needed a more clear-headed guide. His appeal to emotionalism muddled almost every issue. He did all this with wit and panache, but he nevertheless committed two mortal sins against the public good: his bad example debased the moral tone of political life in a great city for a generation, and his words distorted the people's understanding of reality.

But he was, of course, the victim as well as the protagonist of this tragedy. He was as competent an executive as Smith. He had political skills, eloquence, daring, and imagination that should have brought him national recognition and acceptance in terms of the Cabinet post or the major ambassadorship he craved. But the antagonisms and failures in the sad history of the Irish and the Yankees in Boston made it uncommonly difficult for any man to break free. Curley did not, and to the end of his days he remained a self-crippled giant on a provincial stage.

CHAPTER THIRTEEN

The Irish in Literature

1

W HEN F. SCOTT FITZGERALD'S FIRST NOVEL was published in 1920, Mrs. James J. Hill, the wife of the railroad millionaire, told the manager of a St. Paul bookstore, "I've been looking for someone to write the life of Archbishop Ireland and now I think I've found him. They tell me there is a fine young Catholic writer who has just published a religious book, *This Side of Paradise*."[1]

When this anecdote reached him, Fitzgerald must have been greatly amused. He was the first Irish Catholic to become a major novelist in this country, but he was already moving away from Catholicism. After he married Zelda Sayre in the rectory of St. Patrick's Cathedral on April 3, 1920, and attended his daughter's baptism the following year, he rarely, if ever, attended any ceremony in a Catholic Church. Moreover, his conquest of national fame was so swift and complete that he never became identified in the public mind as Irish at all. He differed notably in this respect from Irish literary figures of a generation or two earlier, such as the poet John Boyle O'Reilly and the essayist Finley Peter Dunne, both of whom were readily recognized as symbols and spokesmen of different aspects of the immigrant experience.

Desiring worldly success, and keenly aware of what would later be called his "image," Fitzgerald may well have played down his religion and ancestry in order not to be stereotyped. He wanted to win acceptance as an artist in his own right, unconnected with any distracting associations with Pat-and-Mike jokes, the Irish brogue, and other cultural clichés. Seeing the Church solely as an Irish-American institution, he judged it provincial and unfashionable, a place for immigrant priests and servant girls. This early attitude was detected by Monsignor Sigourney Webster Fay, an erudite, cultivated priest who was an important influence on him during his prep-school and college years. Monsignor Fay, according to a Fitzgerald biographer, "told Shane Leslie, a young Irish author visiting this country [in 1917], that Fitzgerald thought it very clever and literary to leave the Church, but that he was rebelling against his upbringing and they must do their best to keep him in. Leslie had influence with Fitzgerald; he was handsome and well-connected and had been at Cambridge with Rupert Brooke. In Fitzgerald's presence he and Fay would discuss the grandeurs of Catholicism, its saints, statesmen and intellectuals, its Augustines, Richelieus, and Newmans. Fitzgerald drank it all in, later remarking that Fay and Leslie made the Church seem 'a dazzling, golden thing.' "[2]

Monsignor Fay, who reappears as Father Darcy in *This Side of Paradise*, did not win the struggle to hold his protégé for the Church. Fitzgerald became an agnostic, but the intimations of mortality ("ashes to ashes, dust to dust"), the capacity for awe, the sense of life's mystery and man's frailty, and the demanding moral standards that he learned from his experience of Catholicism stayed with him all his life. His biographer, Arthur Mizener, has observed: "He had been brought up a Catholic, with all that means in the way of habitual convictions. If it is too simple to say, as one of his contemporaries did, that 'when Scott ceased to go to Mass he began to drink,' it is true that his unfaltering sense of life—especially his own life—as a dramatic conflict between good and evil was cultivated, if not determined, by his early training. . . . It takes a sense of sin which lies far deeper than any nominal commitment to a doctrine to be as powerfully affected by immoral conduct as Fitzgerald was."[3]

2

Fitzgerald's work is intimately bound up with his Irish background but in a more complex and less obvious way than that of the earlier Irish writers. Malcolm Cowley noted: "Like [Finley Peter] Dunne, he had been accepted into the ruling Protestant group, and unlike Dunne he wrote about that group, so that his Irishness was a little disguised, but it remained an undertone in all his stories; it gave him a sense of standing apart that sharpened his observation of social differences."[4]

Edmund Wilson, a close friend and Princeton contemporary of Fitzgerald, had long before stressed the importance of this factor. "In regard to the man himself," Wilson wrote in the *Bookman* in 1922, "there are perhaps two things worth knowing, for the influence they have had on his work. In the first place, he comes from the Middle West. . . . The second thing one should know about him is that Fitzgerald is partly Irish and that he brings both to life and to fiction certain qualities that are not Anglo-Saxon. For, like the Irish, Fitzgerald is romantic, but also cynical about romance; he is bitter as well as ecstatic; astringent as well as lyrical. He casts himself in the role of playboy, yet at the playboy he incessantly mocks. He is vain, a little malicious, of quick intelligence and wit, and has an Irish gift for turning language into something iridescent and surprising. He often reminds one, in fact, of the description that a great Irishman, Bernard Shaw, has written of the Irish: 'An Irishman's imagination never lets him alone, never convinces him, never satisfies him; but it makes him that he can't face reality nor deal with it nor handle it nor conquer it; he can only sneer at them that do . . . and imagination's such a torture that you can't bear it without whiskey. . . . And all the while there goes on a horrible, senseless, mischievous laughter.' "[5]

Irish references recur throughout Fitzgerald's work. When, in *Tender Is the Night*, Rosemary Hoyt suggests to Dick Diver that he have a screen test, he tries to conceal his embarrassment for her, "his face moving first in an Irish way." In the story "Babylon Revisited," Charles Wales, the main character, was ". . . thirty-five, and good to look at. The Irish mobility of his face was sobered by a deep wrinkle between his eyes." The opening scene of *This Side of Paradise* is a portrait of the hero's extravagantly Celtic mother, née Beatrice O'Hara.*

But Fitzgerald's Irishness was more than a matter of physical descriptions, names of characters, and the undertones of his writing. It is, as Wilson and Cowley have suggested, basic to understanding his view of life as an artist. The main theme of his writing is the relationship of men of no social background, such as Jay Gatsby, or of shabby genteel background, such as Dick Diver, with women of high social status such as Gatsby's dream girl, Daisy Buchanan, or of great wealth such as Nicole Diver. There is a horror of poverty and mean obscurity. There is an endless fascination with the freedom, the secure style, and the virginal selfishness and self-possession of the very rich. Wealth is seen as a lure, a destructive force, an incitement of illusions for which men pay a terrible price. Other American writers have been preoccupied with this theme; Theodore Dreiser's *An American Tragedy*, for example, is a powerful work, but its emotional force comes exclusively from the intensity of Clyde Griffiths's hunger for luxury and success and not from the interplay between the illusions of the hero and the realities of the rich. Fitzgerald developed this

* Leslie Fiedler also argues that the Irishness of Fitzgerald's characters is a clue to understanding his work. "Almost all the main characters, whatever their outsides [in *Tender Is the Night*], turn out to be F. Scott Fitzgerald. Dick Diver, the protagonist, who seems from a distance the assured aristocrat, the obverse of the author, reveals on the first close-up the Irish lilt, the drunkenness, the tortured sensibility that are Fitzgerald's. . . . Even the young moving-picture actress, Rosemary Hoyt, turns out to be a version of the author. She is Irish (always a clue), full of embarrassment and guilty pride at a too-sudden success" (Leslie Fiedler, *An End to Innocence* [Beacon Press, Boston, 1955], pp. 178–179).

theme of the heartbreak and moral failure at the center of America's material success much more subtly than any of his contemporaries because he had the insight and sensitivity to make use of the opportunities for experience and observation that his "lace-curtain" Irish Catholic background gave him.

The well-to-do Irish in American cities in Fitzgerald's formative years, the first two decades of this century, stood near and yet outside the golden circle of the Protestant establishment in this country. They were privy and prey to the small snobberies and shades of difference that set off the very rich, very Protestant, very respectable from those who were near but not quite in. As the Irish were at the edge of two worlds, of the insiders and the great unwashed, it is not surprising that in Fitzgerald they produced a great master of the novel of manners and society. Fitzgerald always had the double vision of the insider and the outsider at Vanity Fair. Nick Carraway, the narrator in *The Great Gatsby*, remarks early in the novel: "High over the city our line of yellow windows must have contributed their share of human secrecy to the casual watcher in the darkening streets, and I was him too, looking up and wondering. I was within and without, simultaneously enchanted and repelled by the inexhaustible variety of life."[6]

3

Fitzgerald's vantage point in life was made possible by his maternal grandfather, an Irish immigrant. Philip Francis McQuillan came to this country with his parents from County Fermanagh, Ireland at age nine in 1843. As a young man, he moved to St. Paul, Minnesota, and built a thriving wholesale grocery business. When he died in 1877, he was one of the city's leading businessmen, and left a fortune of more than a quarter-million dollars.

His oldest daughter was Fitzgerald's mother. Mollie McQuillan Fitzgerald was an intelligent, bookish, imaginative woman but plain-featured and a dowdy dresser. On the edge of spinsterhood, she married a longtime suitor, Edward Fitzgerald. He was also partly of Irish ancestry, but little is known of his father, who died young. On his maternal side, he was related to several distinguished Maryland families. Among his ancestors was Francis Scott Key, for whom he named his son. Edward Fitzgerald was a small, neat, dapper man who wore a Vandyke beard, carried a cane, and had the fine southern manners his son so much admired. But he was a failure in business and drank heavily, though in a quiet, discreet way. After he lost his job as a salesman for a soap company in 1908, when his son was twelve, the family moved in with Grandmother McQuillan. Her fortune supported them in comfort. Fitzgerald's mother could not have enhanced her son's confidence in his father, and indirectly in himself, by asking, as she often did, "If it wasn't for your Grandfather McQuillan, where would we be now?"

Also on the scene were two of Mrs. Fitzgerald's spinster sisters. One soon died of tuberculosis, but the other, Miss Annabel McQuillan, stern and conservative, dressed in black and attending Mass daily, lived on and was remembered by her nephew as "the real matriarch of my family, a dried up old maid, but with character and culture."

At dancing classes and private schools, Scott and his sister met children considerably wealthier than themselves, and were socially accepted, but their parents barely moved in society at all. His mother was ambitious for her children but cared nothing for society herself, and as she grew older became mildly eccentric. Her attitudes intensified Fitzgerald's social insecurities. He became keenly aware of the discrepancy between his mother's strong character and lack of style and his father's ineffectuality and social grace. Although the money and strength came from his mother's side, he could not help but regret, with youthful snobbishness, that her family was, as he once wrote, "straight 1850 potato-famine Irish." Because his parents had reversed the normal masculine and feminine roles of strength and dependency, of authority and grace, Fitzgerald did not see adult social relationships from the angle of vision of the ordinary boy. Nothing seemed simple to one with his imagination, and everything in the social scene was subject to his personal verification. As he later recalled in a letter to John O'Hara, "I spent my youth in alternately crawling in front of the kitchen maids and insulting the great."[7] This experience made for a sometimes painful childhood, but it helped him as a novelist. Among other ways, it enabled him to become one of the few novelists who could create wholly credible feminine characters.

His religion was not a social handicap in St. Paul, which had a prosperous Irish Catholic community and where Mrs. James J. Hill, the wealthiest woman in the city, was a Catholic. But when he went east to attend Newman School, he was faintly defensive that he was not entering one of the better-known and more fashionable prep schools such as Hotchkiss or Groton. When a girl in St. Paul claimed never to have heard of Newman, Fitzgerald answered, "It's a good school—you see, it's a *Catholic* school."

Newman, situated not far from Princeton, had been intended, too optimistically as it turned out, as a kind of Catholic Eton. It had a lay faculty, and its students, drawn mostly from successful Irish families, were preparing for Ivy League rather than for Catholic colleges. "The school flourished in an atmosphere of hilarious chaos and Irish individualism which would have horrified the renowned Cardinal for whom it was named. . . . The Newman of this period has been compared to Clongowes Wood, the famed Jesuit school outside Dublin, where the students showed a like talent for writing, acting, leading and rebelling."[8] But it does not appear that Fitzgerald received as good a classical education at Newman as James Joyce and Oliver St. John Gogarty did at Clongowes Wood.

At Newman and more rapidly at Princeton, Fitzgerald began to pull away from St. Paul and his Irish Catholic background. Princeton was a citadel of the eastern Protestant upper class, a training ground for the American equivalent of the British Establishment. Fitzgerald as a middle westerner, a Catholic, and a boy of middling economic circumstances began as an outsider. But he identified completely with his new surroundings, and by means of his social and literary gifts he quickly won complete acceptance. Once the triumph of his first novel, *This Side of Paradise*, published in 1920 when he was twenty-four, put the seal of financial success on him, it was as if he had always been to the manner born. But it was in his movement from his "lace-curtain" Irish background into the larger society that he developed insight into certain styles of life and his remarkably true feeling for the psychological nuances of the rich and the *arrivistes* that marked his major literary works.

4

His early novels, *This Side of Paradise* and *The Beautiful and Damned*, together with his short stories in the *Saturday Evening Post*, helped create the stereotype that still survives of Fitzgerald as the spokesman of the Jazz Age. He and Zelda became the archetypes of the new generation of the 1920's, the hard-drinking, sexually emancipated young men and their flappers living it up in speakeasies and on weekend house parties. This legend was composed of equal parts publicity and substance. The Fitzgeralds enjoyed being the center of attention, and they had the gaiety and high spirits to originate their legend and the vanity and inventiveness to embellish it.

In important respects, however, Fitzgerald went counter to the stereotype and to the taste of the twenties. Critics who have looked behind the legend at the writing itself have invariably been struck by his conservatism in sexual matters. He alludes to the occasional adulteries of his characters, but these sexual events are never set forth in detail. He portrays women with delicacy and restraint. His language parallels his treatment of sex; his characters never use four-letter words or coarse expressions. Although the twenties were a time of technical innovation in fiction, Fitzgerald

Illustrations

Above: "The smell of the potato rotting in the fields rose and mingled with the odors of death in the cottages and along the hedgerows." (Starving families gather at the gate of the workhouse during the Irish famine.)

Below: "To the question, What did they seek? the answer is the same for them as for all men. They sought a door that would open and give them access to hope." (Emigrants receive the priest's blessing before leaving for America.)

EMIGRANT ARRIVAL AT CONSTITUTION WHARF, BOSTON.

Above: Emigrant arrival at Constitution Wharf, Boston: "Whenever possible, they followed old routes of settlement to the neighborhoods where other Irish had come a few years earlier. . . . Those already arrived held Saturday-night 'kitchen rackets' to welcome the 'greenhorns.' "

Below: "The shanty Irish might have been the individual's own grandmother who did, indeed, smoke a clay pipe and keep a pig or a goat in what became Central Park." (The east side of Fifth Avenue between 116th and 117th streets in 1893, the kind of neighborhood in which many American Irish of this era lived and grew up.)

CORCORAN LEGION

FIFTH REGIMENT.

COL. WILLIAM McEVILY

A FEW GOOD MEN ARE WANTED

TO FILL UP CAPT. WM. L. MONEGAN'S COMPANY.

This is a splendid opportunity for young men to join a Crack Regiment. You will have good officers, who will pay every attention to your welfare.

All Promotions will be made from the Ranks!

Relief Tickets will be immediately issued to Families of Volunteers.

The highest Bounties will be paid, and good Quarters, Rations and Uniforms furnished.

This Regiment is quartered at STATEN ISLAND, in a position highly favorable to the health and good condition of the men.

THOSE WISHING TO JOIN CAN APPLY TO

Lieuts. MICHAEL McDONALD, and DANIEL H. McDONNELL, Recruiting Officers.

No. 52 FIRST AVE., COR. OF THIRD ST.

BAKER & GODWIN, Printers, Printing House Square, opposite City Hall, N. Y.

"Throughout the North, the Irish had volunteered for the army. No fewer than thirty-eight Union regiments had the word 'Irish' in their names."

Yankee Sullivan lost the American heavyweight championship in 1853 after a bareknuckle bout lasting thirty-seven rounds.

THROUGH AGES THOU HAST SLEPT IN CHAINS A NIGHT—ARISE NOW MAN AND VINDICATE THY RIGHT

I remain as usual Mike Walsh

Mike Walsh, at Tammany Hall, in 1843

DRAWN FROM LIFE & ENGRAVED BY S.H. GIMBER.

PUBLISHED BY THOS. M. SPEDON. 25 PINE ST NEW YORK.

"The more orthodox leaders had little enthusiasm for Walsh, but his popular following was great. At Tammany meetings, the crowd often shouted insistently for Walsh until the presiding officer had to let him speak."

"Cardinal Gibbons believed American Catholicism could not secure its faith or fulfill its opportunities by proscription and withdrawal; it could validate its principles only by practicing them on the American scene."

"In 1892 he went to work in the Fulton Fish Market as a clerk at twelve dollars a week and all the fish he could eat. He worked a twelve-hour shift from 4:00 A.M. to 4:00 P.M. and on Friday from 3:00 A.M."

"Bigotry and prohibition contributed to his defeat but they were not decisive. He was defeated in the north and he was defeated by prosperity." (Al Smith campaigning in Milwaukee in 1928.)

Above: Boston Mayor John F. Fitzgerald in 1910 with his daughter Rose who is the mother of President Kennedy. "It was Fitzgerald who presided over the transition of political power from the Yankees to the Irish."

Below: James M. Curley campaigns with Franklin D. Roosevelt in Massachusetts in 1932. "The alliance between Curley and Roosevelt was uneasy from the first."

"The humor and satire of Finley Peter Dunne and his alter ego, 'Mr. Dooley,' were the wisdom of an American Irishman, perpetually fascinated by the ways of politics, a profession in whose larger claims he had no belief." (Caricature by Spy.)

Above: "No other American writer has better depicted his chosen theme than F. Scott Fitzgerald, this exile from the lace-curtain Irish parlors of St. Paul, who became the poet of our mocking affluence."

Below: Mayor Curley (center, with raised hat) returns to Boston on bail after conviction for mail fraud, in 1946. "He was the idol of a cult, arbiter of a social clique, and spokesman of a state of mind."

Above: "Stark Young wrote of Laurette Taylor's performance in *The Glass Menagerie:* 'She is the real and first talent of them all. . . .' She herself once said, 'Give the Irish a miserable thought and they create an Ibsen drama.'"

Opposite: "It was logical, if not predictable, that the first serious, important playwright in the United States should have been Eugene O'Neill."

Below: "When the catastrophe of 1929 shocked and disoriented millions of middle-class and working-class Irish, the first voice calling them to abandon their old heroes and strike out in a new direction belonged not to a politician but to a priest, Father Charles E. Coughlin."

"If there was one figure other than Franklin D. Roosevelt himself who personified the idealism and toughness, the intellectual stylishness and operational verve of the middle years of the New Deal, it was Thomas Gardiner Corcoran."

"It was not Joe McCarthy's destiny to become a domesticated hatchetman. This was not the aim of the man who had dragged down the titans of the Senate, wrecked Dean Acheson's career, made a Secretary of the Army grovel before him, fired bureaucrats at will, and added a new word—an extension of his name—to the English language."

"The new President and his administration bodied forth in full and accurate form the three main themes of the history of the Irish in this country: the poetry, the power, and the liberalism."

wrote in the conventional forms that had been perfected in the nineteenth century. Clean, "natural" prose was the vogue, but he had no fear of the long, complex sentence replete with several modifiers. He was one of the few serious writers of his period who consciously tried to write beautiful and graceful prose, as distinguished from the merely economical and functional.

In an age that sneered, or at least pretended to sneer, at conventional verities, and that prized a skeptical knowingness above other intellectual qualities, Fitzgerald never passed himself off as hard-boiled or cynical. Like Dick Diver, he had "the old interior laughter" that made solemnity or pretense of any kind ultimately impossible. Always true to his own view of life, he mourned any vision of lost innocence, worked hard to express just the right nuance of sentiment, and used expressions such as "a willingness of the heart" that most of his contemporaries could not have written without embarrassment.

His undeceived moral intelligence, the "spoilt priest" within him, was always a spectator at his own revels. He was a romantic about the possibilities of experience and a moralist about the consequence of it. A year before his death he wrote his daughter: "Sometimes I wish I had gone along with (Cole Porter and Rodgers and Hart and that gang), but I guess I am too much a moralist at heart, and really want to preach at people in some acceptable form, rather than to entertain."[9]

5

Fitzgerald's reputation rests securely on his two major works, *The Great Gatsby* and *Tender Is the Night*. The former ranks with Hemingway's *The Sun Also Rises* as a very nearly perfect short novel. It is a timeless story of a talented young man who invents his own identity and sacrifices his integrity for the sake of twin illusions: that mere wealth brings happiness and that he can recover the love of a woman whom he had known in one brief, romantic encounter in the past. It is also a striking portrait of one segment of American life at a certain time. The book captures the febrile gaiety, the ephemeral glamour of the bootlegger, the incoherence of old and new social groupings among the rich and the newly rich, the undercurrents of grossness and lawlessness, and the engaging innocence of a people that still felt young and full of hope as the great boom of the 1920's got underway.

Daisy Buchanan, the object of Gatsby's aspirations and the unwitting agent of his destruction, symbolizes the tyranny of material possessions over men's imaginations:

"He [Gatsby] had intended, probably, to take what he could and go

—but now he found that he had committed himself to the following of a grail. He knew that Daisy was extraordinary, but he didn't realize just how extraordinary a 'nice' girl could be. She vanished into her rich house, into her rich, full life, leaving Gatsby—nothing. He felt married to her, that was all. When they met again, two days later, it was Gatsby who was breathless, who was, somehow, betrayed. . . . [He] was overwhelmingly aware of the youth and mystery that wealth imprisons and preserves, of the freshness of many clothes, and of Daisy, gleaming like silver, safe and proud above the hot struggles of the poor."

At the end of the story, the irresponsibility of Daisy and her husband have led to Gatsby's death: "They were careless people, Tom and Daisy— they smashed up things and creatures and then retreated back into their money or their vast carelessness, or whatever it was that kept them together, and let other people clean up the mess they had made. . . ."[10]

No one can read that passage and still accuse Fitzgerald of romanticizing the rich. He was fascinated by the "youth and mystery" that wealth imprisons and preserves, but his preoccupation heightened, rather than diminished, his extraordinarily acute powers of observation and his capacity for implicit moral judgment.

Tender Is the Night, published in 1934, nine years after *Gatsby*, is a much more ambitious and correspondingly less successful novel. It has brilliant scenes, and passages that are beautifully written. Fitzgerald can introduce a walk-on character and in half a sentence make her both a recognizable person and an effective symbol: "The hostess—she was another tall rich American girl, promenading insouciantly upon the national prosperity. . . ." He can make a mood immediately vivid: "the gray gentle world of a mild hangover of fatigue when the nerves relax in bunches like piano strings, and crackle suddenly like wicker chairs."

Although he had little interest in ideas or generalized conceptions, Fitzgerald in the visit to the battlefield in *Tender Is the Night* expressed better than any historian or philosopher the essential character of the First World War:

"See that little stream—we could walk to it in two minutes. It took the British a month to walk to it—a whole empire walking very slowly, dying in front and pushing forward behind. And another empire walked very slowly backward a few inches a day, leaving the dead like a million bloody rugs. No Europeans will ever do that again in this generation. . . . The young men think they could do it but they couldn't. They could fight the first Marne again but not this. This took religion and years of plenty and tremendous sureties and the exact relation that existed between the classes. . . . This kind of battle was invented by Lewis Carroll and Jules Verne and whoever wrote *Undine*, and country deacons bowling and marraines in Marseilles and girls seduced in the back lanes of Wurttemberg and Westphalia. Why this was a love battle—there was a century of middle-class love spent here. This was the last love battle."[11]

Fitzgerald, however, had struggled with and reworked this novel through so many versions that it does not quite hang together right. As he decided after its publication, the book gains coherence and force if the opening section in which the young actress Rosemary Hoyt appears is shifted to its logical place in the middle of the story. The novel is better read as rearranged and edited by Malcolm Cowley in the 1953 edition. But the central difficulty is with Dick Diver. He is not completely believable as a psychiatrist. Although a good psychiatrist admittedly has to have a touch of the poet to apply his scientific knowledge wisely, Dr. Diver is too much the poet. He clearly has the sensibility, vulnerability, and anguish of an artist, of Fitzgerald himself, and not enough of the detachment and discipline of a scientist and professional man dealing every day with patients.

The failure of the central character invalidates *Tender Is the Night* as an objective work of art, and yet one cannot read it without being deeply moved. When Dick Diver raises his right hand and with a papal cross blesses the beach where he had achieved his social triumphs and then fades out as an obscure figure in a far-off country town, the effect is heartbreaking. To explain this contradictory reaction, one can only fall back upon a romantic and subjective concept of criticism which the drama critic Stark Young once invoked in writing about Eugene O'Neill: "What moved us was the cost to the dramatist of what he handled. . . . Even when we are not at all touched by the feeling itself or the idea presented, we are stabbed to our depths by the importance of this feeling to him, and we are all his, not because of what he says but because saying it meant so much to him."[12]

We mourn Dick Diver because through the veil of fiction we see the handsome, gallant, tortured face of Scott Fitzgerald. We know that Nicole Diver was really his Zelda and that all the while he was writing this book, she was not, like Nicole, winning her way back to mental health, much as Fitzgerald would have liked to emulate Dick and surrender his psychic strength to her if such was possible, but rather she was sinking ever deeper into illness. We know further that he wrote the book under harrowing circumstances of financial indebtedness, deepening addiction to alcohol, and the impossible commands of his conscience to be mother as well as father to his daughter. *Tender Is the Night* was to be his masterpiece, compressing into one powerful work all that he had learned and suffered in living in a particular way with a particular group of people in a particular time. It was to be his epic about America's moneyed class and the waste and splendor of their lives. If he failed quite to achieve what his imagination intended, it is nonetheless a majestic failure. No other American writer has better depicted his chosen theme than this exile from the "lace-curtain" Irish parlors of St. Paul, who became the poet of our mocking affluence.

II

6

It is John O'Hara writing and it is James Malloy, a young newspaperman who very much resembles the author, talking in O'Hara's second novel, *BUtterfield 8:* "I want to tell you something about myself that will help to explain a lot of things about me. You might as well hear it now. First of all, I am a Mick."

Malloy explains to his girl friend that although he buys his clothes at Brooks Brothers and does not eat salad with a spoon, he is indubitably a "Mick." What is worse, years of study have convinced him that there are not two kinds of Irish, but only one. All Irish faces have an ineradicable resemblance whether they are seen at the Dublin Horse Show or at a Knights of Columbus picnic in Pennsylvania. This exposition fails to clarify anything very much, but Malloy persists. Eventually, he makes himself clear. The Irish are, in a word, "non-assimilable." Some of them, like the members of his own family, may have ancestors dating from pre-Revolutionary War days and be eligible to join the Society of the Cincinnati, but in the eyes of most Americans, the Irish are still outsiders. An Irish actor like James Cagney is cast as the perfect gangster type because, Malloy argues, the tough young Irishman fits Protestant America's stereotype of an outlaw. Malloy's girl friend, who had previously thought of her escort as another middle-class boy from the country club set, finally accepts his argument but at the end of the conversation is still somewhat puzzled.[13] Of John O'Hara it might be said that the issue has puzzled him all his life.

The social stigmata of the "lace-curtain" Irish which Scott Fitzgerald transmuted into his own kind of poetry are bleeding wounds in the writing of John O'Hara. Everything that, in Fitzgerald's case, remained implicit or submerged in the relationship between his social background and his writing is explicit and barely reworked in the case of O'Hara. He has picked at his Irishness like a scab. It is one of the furious impulses that agitate his work, but he has never fully confronted his own past and made peace with it. His evasiveness has impoverished his fiction. His inability to identify with his Irish heritage and to feel at ease with himself as an Irishman is the crux of his failure to develop successfully as a major novelist.

O'Hara was born in Pottsville, Pennsylvania, in 1905. His father, Patrick Henry O'Hara, was one of the town's leading doctors, but preceding generations had been, in his son's words, "shanty Irish." His mother, Katherine Delaney O'Hara ("she went to an expensive school and spoke French and played bridge") was a member of a distinguished Irish family that had lived in that part of Pennsylvania for generations.

Pottsville was, as O'Hara later wrote, a "small room," a city of under 25,000. It became the "Gibbsville" of most of his novels and, except physically, he may be said never to have left its confines. Mahantongo Street where the fashionable rich lived became "Lantenengo Street."

"Born the son of a doctor and the eldest of eight, O'Hara was destined to live at Sixth and Mahantongo when those of high fashion lived above 11th, to go to St. Patrick's Parochial School while his contemporaries went to Mrs. Thurlow's. The interior quarrel of O'Hara's childhood was a subtle one, for he was not a boy 'from the wrong side of the tracks.' He rode in the chauffeured cars of the rich, attended their parties, went to dancing school with their children and fell in love with their daughters. But he did not go to Philadelphia's Peter Thompson for his custom-made clothes, and he did go to St. Patrick's Church where he was altar boy at 7 o'clock Mass every morning. ('Years later,' says a friend, also a non-observing Catholic, 'O'Hara attributed the fact that I had stayed in the Church longer than he to my not having been an altar boy. He disliked what he regarded as the peasant status of the Catholic Church.' ")[14]

O'Hara did not attend the prep schools of his dreams and did not attend college at all. After a period at the Keystone State Normal School, he went at fifteen to New York City's Fordham Prep where he was "honorably dismissed" after a year because of failing grades. (His highest mark, 76, was in English.) He finally graduated from Niagara School in 1924, at age nineteen, valedictorian of his class, and winner of honors in English and Spanish. He returned home to a job on the local paper, the *Pottsville Journal.* This must have been in some way an embittering experience, because most of his works include savage satire of small-town newspapers and portrayals of local publishers as greedy and mean-spirited.

His hope of eventually going to Yale ended the following year when his father died, "had a funeral as big as a gangster's or a politician's . . . and left no money to speak of."

O'Hara soon left Pottsville for the wider horizons of New York. During the next several years, he held several newspaper jobs and had odd writing assignments. He briefly handled the Bergdorf Goodman account for public-relations man Benjamin Sonnenberg and did press agentry for Warner Brothers' studio. While working for Warner's, he wrote the advertising campaign for *Public Enemy*, the first of the great gangster films, which starred James Cagney.

O'Hara was in those years the kind of Irishman about whom the old-fashioned term "mucker" used to be applied. Hard-drinking, quick to take offense, carrying a large Irish chip on his shoulder, he was a young country-club buck striving for big-town sophistication in a raccoon coat and a button-down shirt from Brooks Brothers. But, underneath, there was a genuine talent.

7

O'Hara, who had been contributing short stories to the *New Yorker* for several years, broke through to fame with his first novel, *Appointment in Samarra*, in 1934. It remains his best work. He followed the next year with *BUtterfield 8*, less interesting but an immense popular success. There then followed a long period in which O'Hara wrote little of consequence. Busy earning a living, he turned out film scripts, a minor novel about Hollywood (*Hope of Heaven*, 1938), a musical comedy (*Pal Joey*, 1940), and columns of comment for various magazines. He did write numerous short stories, and some of these were outstanding.

Meanwhile, his success was bringing him closer to "the affluent and socially prominent life that he had studied and coveted since childhood, but," as Beverly Gary reported in the *New York Post*, "he was still as much observer as participant."

" 'John used to sit in front of the window of his apartment with a pair of binoculars and watch the yachts go by,' says a friend. 'He had the Social Register on his lap and checked the flags of the boats against it, to see which yacht belonged to whom.'

"Though he could now afford the best table at '21,' Peal shoes, the best liquor (once when he was annoyed with Wolcott Gibbs, he ordered a glass of the finest brandy with the sole purpose of throwing it in his friend's face), was a member of the Players Club, and maintained an East Side apartment and a summer house in fashionable Quogue, Long Island, O'Hara though not disenchanted, still resented the things that were beyond his grasp.

"He yearned to belong to a socially elite club, had even suggested to his amused fellow members at the Players that they adopt colors and hatbands, and was always slightly jealous of his friend John McClain's membership in New York's Racquet Club. The mock Phi Beta Kappa key

O'Hara sometimes carried, engraved with the word "Nope," was his wry comment on the irretrievable years he wished he could have spent at Yale."[15]

It was not until 1949, fifteen years after *Appointment in Samarra*, that O'Hara published his next major work, *A Rage to Live*. This was the first of four long novels that he wrote over the next decade. *Ten North Frederick* was published in 1955, *From the Terrace* in 1958, and *Ourselves to Know* in 1960. These novels received unfavorable notices from most of the critics, but they sold well. The adverse criticism evoked from O'Hara a testy defensiveness. The contradictions between the reactions of himself, his readers, and his critics are at the heart of O'Hara's situation as a writer.

Since he has a superb talent for dialogue, social observation, and some nuances of character, he writes fiction that is consistently readable. Even *From the Terrace*, his longest work, has the unwearying fascination of gossip about people one knows. This accounts for his popularity, but good gossip is not enough to make good fiction. Serious critics keep complaining that O'Hara has betrayed his talent by letting it slip out of his control. They do him the painful honor of comparing him, not to other best-selling popular writers, but to the best serious writers of any time. By this absolute standard, he is not the great novelist of manners that his talent has always seemed to promise. O'Hara's response to this criticism is so excessive as to pose a question. Edmund Wilson, for example, in *The Boys in the Back Room*, wrote a sympathetic and, on balance, favorable account of his early work. But O'Hara responded with a bad-tempered *ad hominem* attack ("Of course a grown man who is still known as Bunny is suspect automatically," he grumbled.)

O'Hara's talent in his longer fiction is out of control and his work out of focus because his writing is in the service of a private obsession. One hears speaking through his work the inarticulate, half-strangled, half-conscious rage and resentment of every Irish man and Irish woman who was ever turned down for a job in an old-line Protestant law firm, ever snubbed for the "sin" of having gone to the wrong college, ever left out of a fashionable party, ever patronized for wearing slightly wrong clothes. The tragedy is that O'Hara does not give these emotions direct and honest expression. He cannot help but hear that raging voice since it is also his own, but he tries to escape it. His elaborately styled personal way of life is a defense against it. Unfortunately, so is his fiction. He writes about the kind of person he is not and the way of life he has not experienced. His main characters, Grace Caldwell Tate in *A Rage to Live*, Joseph Chapin in *Ten North Frederick*, and Alfred Eaton in *From the Terrace* are all members of the upper-class Protestant establishment. They are expertly observed and the surfaces of their lives are described with loving care, but after hundreds of pages they remain dull people. This is because their emotional insides, the only part of them that O'Hara has to imagine, are sawdust. He is not interested in them for themselves; they are the stalking horses of his fantasies. They are projections of himself acting out his dream that in a better world he would have been born rich and Protestant, gone to Yale, been elected to the Racquet Club, and idled away his life with the very few who could possibly be his social equals. His characters' manners and clothes and clubs and horses and houses and silver services are real to him; the rest of them is faked up to serve a need exterior to themselves: the need of their creator's private obsession. His characters have a fitful vitality because O'Hara endows them with strong and usually uncontrolled sexuality. But this fails to bring them fully alive because it periodically forces his fictional people to act out of character. The single, the married, the adolescents, the dowagers not only have remarkably similar sexual encounters in O'Hara's fiction but also talk about them with unnatural candor and uncharacteristic vulgarity. Sex beguiles and distracts, but it does not lend lasting reality to the airless, lifeless inner nature of his principal characters.

O'Hara has rationalized the adverse judgments of the critics on the grounds that they dislike writers about the rich and prefer novels about bums written by beatniks. This is a curious conviction on the part of a writer who has lived through the extraordinary critical revival that Fitzgerald's writings have enjoyed. O'Hara has bracketed himself with earlier writers about the rich such as Henry James and Edith Wharton, but they were both insiders who chose to write about the small upper class in which they were born and moved with ease.

Significantly, O'Hara has never written a novel in which an Irish Catholic is the protagonist. He wrote a brief, memorable portrait of his own father in an early short story, "The Doctor's Son"; he never followed it up, although his father promised to be a much more interesting and attractive hero than the assorted failures, the Eatons and Chapins, he has depicted. Nor has he written the brilliant novel about the wealthy Irish Catholics of New York that would seem clearly within the range of his interest and talent. That he has acquaintance and insight into this group is evident from his brief sketch of Paul and Nancy Farley, minor characters in *BUtterfield 8*.

There are Irish Catholic characters in most of his novels and many of his stories, but they are always of two kinds. The first are the standard types: the machine politician, the newspaper reporter, the shrewd old priest, the kitchen maid, who are sketched in with a few lines of dialogue or a passage of social history. They are serviceable minor characters and readily recognizable, but they never become more than types. The second kind is the distinctly unpleasant social climber, usually a man. In *Appointment in Samarra*, Julian English's disintegration begins when he yields to the drunken impulse to throw a highball in the face of Harry Reilly, the *nouveau riche* businessman who is his creditor.[16]

O'Hara skillfully implies that English had an exaggerated fear of Reilly's vindictiveness, but he makes that fear comprehensible in terms of the town's social pattern. When English has committed suicide, O'Hara adds an excellent ironic touch: "I liked English," Reilly says to his sister, "and he liked me, or otherwise he wouldn't have borrowed money from me. I know that type. He wouldn't borrow a nickel from me if he didn't like me." A moment later, he adds to himself: "He was a real gentleman. I wonder what in God's name would make him do a thing like that?"[17]

Although Reilly is presented unsympathetically, he serves an artistic purpose as a foil to English, the disorganized snob. In Creighton Duffy, a principal character in *From the Terrace*, O'Hara created an improbable New York–and–Washington version of a wealthy Irish Catholic who is so loathsome as to be a caricature. Duffy is portrayed stooping to petty personal blackmail, dining on black-market steaks during the war, and conniving with a Communist labor leader for personal power and profit. This inverted hostility toward the Irish is the other side of O'Hara's preoccupation with the Protestant, Anglo-Saxon rich.

O'Hara once remarked: "I am on a first-name basis with two authentic Vanderbilts, two genuine Whitneys and one former Astor, which is darn good for a boy from Pottsville, Pa. By and large, I think the experience has been good for all of us: the snobbish poor, the democratic rich."[18]

Good for John O'Hara the dreamer, perhaps. But good for John O'Hara the writer?

III

8

No writer is more central to the history of the American Irish than James T. Farrell. He wrote about a world that Fitzgerald never knew and that O'Hara knew peripherally as a youth but quickly departed. This was the world of the workingman and of the lower middle class —shoe salesmen and hotel cashiers, painting contractors and railway-express clerks. These were people for whom "lace-curtain" status was beyond reach and the higher social gradations Fitzgerald and O'Hara described beyond imagining. The line of social demarcation for them was between the cold-water-tenement Irish and the steam-heat, apartment-house Irish. The setting of Farrell's major work is the South Side of Chicago, which in his chosen time, 1905 to 1930, was an Irish Catholic stronghold. (It subsequently became a Negro neighborhood.) It is for him what Yoknapatawpha County was for William Faulkner and the Riviera was for Fitzgerald: a real place that, as the artist peopled it with figures from his past and characters of his invention, took on mythic dimensions.

The motif of Farrell's work has been the search for love, integrity, and self-understanding in a comparatively hostile atmosphere. On the South Side of Chicago and in similar neighborhoods in many other cities, these aspirations are often snuffed out by the harshness and brutality of material circumstances or cheated by the counterfeit satisfactions of yellow journalism, sentimentalized religion, Babbitt-like exhortation, and illusions founded upon ignorance. For the Irish as for other nationality groups, the struggle of individuals to understand themselves and to grow is complicated by their early life in immigrant neighborhoods and by their often ambiguous relationship to the past of their own families. The passage of time has eased this complication for the Irish, but for those of Farrell's generation it was crucial, and it remains of substantial importance.

"For many of us Americans," Farrell has written, "there is a gap between our past and our present, between our childhood and our productive manhood. We are the sons and daughters, the grandsons and granddaughters of the disinherited of the earth. Our forebears partook little of the great culture of mankind. Their lives and destinies were hard; their contributions to our civilization were made with their backs. We have come from their poverty. We have a personal past different from the past suggested in the great and inspiring world of culture and ideas. Our beginnings were naive, and we must still understand the difference between our present and our past."[19]

The difference Farrell writes of is the difference experienced by those who are poor and Irish and Catholic in a middle-class, vaguely Anglo-Saxon, and Protestant society. His people know only city streets and crowded tenements in a culture that glorifies the small town and the farm. Those of them who care about books and music cannot help but be sensitive to the fact that notwithstanding the past achievements of the Irish in the arts, their own immediate forebears had often been completely cut off from learning and literature; some of them, like

Farrell's own grandmother, could not read or write. These fathers and grandfathers, struggling against extreme poverty and deprivation, strove first to sustain themselves and then to help their children to move upward. This struggle was costly in terms of frustration, broken hopes, the battles lost to the bottle, the deadening physical labor, the inescapable vulgarity and harshness of life in slums and tenements. If the life was not easy, neither was it easy to describe that life with honesty and candor, with faithful attention to exact details, with dignity and tenderness and compassion. This is what Farrell accomplished in his two great masterpieces, the *Studs Lonigan* trilogy and the Danny O'Neill tetralogy *A World I Never Made, No Star Is Lost, Father and Son,* and *My Days of Anger.*

First of all had to come honesty, for this is the kind of material that converts readily into melodrama, sentimental romance, or sketches for dialect comedians. If Farrell's name has become almost a synonym for honesty and seriousness, this was inevitable, since only a writer with his uncommon passion for telling the truth could render the lives of these people as serious literature. More than one reader has had the reaction of the man who said: "When I first read Farrell, I saw the faces of my family in a book. He gave a dignity to these people that no other writer ever had before him."

To have avoided the temptation to fake, sensationalize, or patronize his people is an important artistic achievement. But Farrell's honesty is one reason for his not having so large an audience as might be expected. Some readers have the reaction of the woman who said: "I don't want to read any more of his books. He writes about the people I've spent all my life trying to get away from."[20]

9

James Thomas Farrell was born in Chicago on February 27, 1904, the son and grandson of hard-working, poorly paid teamsters.

"My father was typical of the tough, two-fisted Irish workingmen of his day. He was a union slugger in the 1914 strike in Chicago, and I have been told that he once beat up Tim Murphy, the gangster. He was a big strapping man, aggressive, with a strong sense of pride and dignity. He was a union man from way back in the teamsters union. . . ."[21]

Since the father rarely earned more than sixteen dollars a week and had several younger children to support, he was forced to let his wife's family raise his son, James. These relatives, whom Farrell has immortalized in his novels as the O'Flahertys, were economically a cut or two above his own family because his uncle was a shoe salesman and his aunt had a clerical job. Growing up in a family earnestly trying to "make something of themselves," attending St. Anselm's parochial school and later St. Cyril's High School (now renamed Mount Carmel), and playing in the streets, parks and dusty backyards of the South Side, Farrell lived a life like that of countless other Irish Catholic youths in other cities during those first three decades of this century. The boys around 58th Street on Chicago's South Side could just as well have been living on Manhattan's West Side or South Boston or, as John Chamberlain wrote, recalling his own youth, on Grand Avenue in New Haven, Connecticut.[22]

Farrell captured in his writing the quality of life in such a neighborhood as it is seen and experienced by an insider. To him, Chicago was not what it appeared to an outsider like Carl Sandburg or Theodore Dreiser, a "city of big shoulders," a pulsing, animated manifestation of power, wealth, and raw energy. "I never felt the wonder of Chicago until I had left it and returned to it many times," Farrell wrote. He saw Chicago in those decades as a network of ethnically based neighborhoods, a confederation of small towns. When he read Sherwood Anderson's *Winesburg, Ohio*, and *Tar: A Midwest Childhood*, he was struck by similarities between Chicago's South Side and Ohio's countryside that one would not have expected: "I felt [close] to Anderson's intimate world. . . . The neighborhoods of Chicago in which I grew up possessed something of the character of a small town. They were little worlds of their own. Many of the people living in them knew one another. There was a certain amount of gossip of the character that one finds in small towns. One of the largest nationality and religious groups in these neighborhoods was Irish-American and Catholic. I attended a parochial school. Through the school and Sunday Mass, the life of these neighborhoods was rendered somewhat more cohesive. My grandmother was always a neighborhood character, well known. I became known, too, the way a boy would be in a small town."[23]

If what Anderson had written about the emotions and experiences of ordinary people was meaningful and moving, Farrell resolved that his own life and the lives of the Irish he had grown up with were worth writing about. After reading Anderson, "My self-confidence grew in one leap." This was critically important because in the late 1920's when Farrell first began to write, few serious novels had been written about the lives of the Irish or of other people of immigrant ancestry. Works such as Stephen Crane's *Maggie: A Girl of the Streets* (1893) and Abraham Cahan's *The Rise of David Levinsky* (1917) were isolated exceptions.

Despite the novels of Theodore Dreiser and the thunderings of H. L. Mencken, the genteel tradition in American literature was still strong and excluded certain types of character, speech, and experience from the domain of serious writing. Farrell had few models to test his early work against. In the thirty years since the publication of *Studs Lonigan*, he has himself become a model for many younger writers, and a major force in revolutionizing and broadening American fiction. It is hard to imagine books such as James Jones's *From Here to Eternity* and Norman Mailer's *The Naked and the Dead* being published and praised if there had not first been a *Studs*.

There was little in Farrell's family and social background that nourished his aspiration to be a writer. His relatives and boyhood friends thought it a little odd to want to read books, and the idea of actually writing a book seemed downright queer. Farrell has described poignantly being called "Four Eyes" because he wore glasses and how he felt that perhaps he really was "a goof." The poetry of Edgar Guest, the editorials of Albert Brisbane, the hortatory essays of Elbert Hubbard, and perhaps a book on the lives of the saints were typical reading indulged in by the people among whom he grew up. A boy who had intellectual interests was supposed to become a priest; otherwise he was just wasting his time.

10

"Studs Lonigan, on the verge of fifteen, and wearing his first suit of long trousers, stood in the bathroom with a Sweet Caporal pasted in his mug. His hands were jammed in his trouser pockets, and he sneered. He puffed, drew the fag out of his mouth, inhaled and said to himself:

" 'Well, I'm kissin' the old dump goodbye tonight.' "

So begins *Studs Lonigan*, the classic story of an Irish Catholic youth in early twentieth century America who is victimized by his belief in an impoverishing dream—the myth of the "tough guy" as hero—and who slowly disintegrates and dies because he has nothing to live for. It is a brilliantly wrought tragedy which lays bare one section of American Irish life. The theme of the book is cultural, not economic, poverty. Studs is not a slum boy.

"Had I written *Studs Lonigan* as a story of the slums, it would then have been easy for the reader falsely to place the motivation and causation of the story directly in immediate economic roots. Such a placing of motivation would have obscured one of the most important meanings which I wanted to inculcate into my story. Here was a neighborhood several steps removed from the slums and dire economic want, and here was manifested a pervasive spiritual poverty."[24]

Studs' father and mother are normal parents. They send him to parochial school and to Mass; they try to set him a good example of hard work and decent, plain living. But somehow the family, the Church, and the school fail to provide the standards and incentives that would make him a responsible and attractive human being. The streets, the neighborhood gang, and the poolroom take over, and their false values shape Studs. He is a normal boy with the usual number of decent, kindly impulses; if anything sets him off from other American boys, it may be, as John Chamberlain has suggested, an excess of Irish adventurousness and imagination. He wants to be a big shot, to have style, to achieve a romantic personal identity. The streets and the boyhood gang capture this adventurousness and imagination and provide him with his only ideal: "to be strong, and tough, and the real stuff." This ideal represses the parts of his nature that are gentle; it fills his mind with anxiety about aggression, fantasies of aggression, and daydreams of physical conquest. To be manly comes to mean simply to be exploitative in sexual relations with women and always ready for a fight with other men.

The first volume of the trilogy depicts Studs as he assimilates these barren values and develops his personal vision of the future. In the second volume, as he encounters frustration and defeat, his daydreams gradually shift from what he intends to do into nostalgic reveries about what he has done. The story might have stopped there with Studs stagnating as a "slob," vaguely unhappy in a dull marriage and a dead-end job. But Studs is also a victim of his times. Most men drink more or less during their young manhood, but "when Studs and his companions began drinking, the worst liquor of the prohibition era was being sold. Those were the days when the newspapers published daily death lists of the number of persons who had died from bootleg liquor and wood alcohol. That was the time when men and boys would take one or two drinks, pass out into unconsciousness and come to their senses only to learn that they would never again have their eyesight."[25] Studs' drinking gravely impairs his health. The great depression that costs him his job is a second adverse circumstance. Studs goes under.

Studs is one of the major fictional creations of the twentieth century. Few college-educated Irish Catholics reach manhood without making his acquaintance twice, once in life and once in the pages of Farrell's novel. It is a book—Joyce's *Portrait of the Artist as a Young Man* is another—that has become part of a young Irishman's coming of age.

11

Farrell reacted against the cultural poverty of Studs' world with indignation and fierce anger. Part of his emancipation from this environment was his breaking away from the Catholic Church. He blamed the Church for failure to instill higher values than moneymaking and "getting ahead," for its failure to affirm culture and learning more vigorously, and for stifling young people's desires to know and to experience by imposing authoritarian restrictions. The anti-Catholicism evident in his early work made Farrell an extremely unpopular figure in the Catholic community. His writing was deplored as nasty and dirty, as putting too much emphasis on sex and four-letter words, and as not giving a true, balanced account of the American Irish.*

As the years passed, however, a change took place on both sides. Despite the dismay and the offended feelings, thousands of Irish Catholics read Farrell. When any serious author is so widely read, it means that he is communicating to his readers something real and penetrating about their common experience. Unsympathetic Catholic critics eventually conceded that while Farrell had depicted only the worst features of Catholic life in America—sentimentalism, Jansenism, and sectarianism—these were, as Frank O'Malley observed in *America*, "features which have made even the staunchest and most knowing Catholic minds wince."[26]

Farrell, for his part, began to see his indignation in a longer perspective. His early bitterness faded and his outlook broadened. In "My Beginnings as a Writer," a chapter in a book of literary memoirs published in 1954 when he was fifty, he tenderly recalled Sister Magdalen, his eighth-grade teacher, and two priests, Father Walter and Father Dolan, who taught him in high school. To these sympathetic teachers he traced his beginnings as a writer. Each of them aroused his interest in his studies and encouraged him to take the first small steps in the direction of self-expression and self-consciousness.[27]

In private, he began to boast a bit about his many Catholic friends and admirers. He took warm pleasure from the letters he received from nuns and priests who told him, in effect, that they shared his distaste for certain aspects of Catholicism and that his books had had a liberating effect within the Church. Although there seemed little likelihood that Farrell would ever return as a communicant to the Church, the emotional break

* As late as 1948, the police in Philadelphia attempted unsuccessfully to ban the sale of *Studs Lonigan.* The attorney for the police was, not unexpectedly, an Irish Catholic lawyer, James Francis Ryan. The transcript of this trial is reprinted in *Reflections at Fifty*, pp. 188-223.

had been largely repaired. It could scarcely have been otherwise, since Farrell, preoccupied as an artist with re-creating and redefining a particular body of experience, could not remain totally alienated from one of the major chords of that experience or fail to find bonds of sympathy with others who had shared the experience but not made the religious break. Moreover, in Farrell's writing, as in that of James Joyce, the effects of years of Catholic education and indoctrination are plainly evident. As John Chamberlain shrewdly observed as early as 1938, in his introduction to the Modern Library edition of *Studs Lonigan:* "If one will inspect the structure of the trilogy closely, one will perceive that it is far more of a moral homily than it is a coldly amoral snapshot. We have no mere 'slice of life' here; if anything, we have a sermon. 'The wages of sin is death.' But the sermon . . . is implicit in the artistic arrangement of the material."

Farrell expresses his moral purpose with his favorite quotation from the notebooks of Anton Chekhov: "Man will only become better when you make him see what he is like."

12

Farrell's greatest gift as a writer is his genius for depicting character. While Studs was becoming part of our national folklore, Farrell went on to create Danny O'Neill, his Uncle Al, his Aunt Margaret, his slatternly mother Lizz, and perhaps the best of all, his grandmother Mrs. O'Flaherty, the unforgettable epitome of all earthy, shrewd, tough, domineering old Irish mothers. Between 1936 and 1943, Farrell published four long novels that comprise the Danny O'Neill series. Relying almost solely upon short passages of dialogue and interior monologue, he makes these people real and engages our concern in their conflicts and development. As Carl Van Doren observed: "You forget that you are seeing this life through the eyes of a selecting novelist. It seems merely to be there before you."

The theme of the four novels is the emergence of Danny O'Neill from the same kind of environment as that which stifled Studs. They relate a triumph of character, a counterpoint to Studs's tragedy. Danny is clearly an autobiographical character, but Farrell presents him with objectivity. We see him whole with his whining weakness, naïveté, enthusiasm, earnestness, youthful dreams, hopes, anger, defeats, and relentless perseverance. The supporting cast of characters is presented with the same objectivity but also with compassion all the more effective for its understatement; they are brought to life, in Van Doren's phrase, "with that habitual tenderness which is quite as characteristic of Mr. Farrell's novels as their toughness."

Farrell's career during the years he was composing these major works followed an uneven course. The first volume of the *Studs Lonigan* trilogy sold only 533 copies in its hard-cover edition; the second and third volumes did slightly better; but in 1937 Farrell was still eligible for the only literary prize he has won, an award of $2,500 from the Book-of-the-Month Club for a novel of quality that had sold less than 5,000 copies. *Studs* had actually gone a few over this limit, but Heywood Broun, one of the book club's judges, successfully battled through its selection. During these years Farrell had a hand-to-mouth existence, living on occasional journalism and publisher's advances. James Henle, the president of Vanguard Press, was for a long time a devoted supporter of his work.

In contrast to the financial adversity, Farrell enjoyed at first a growing critical repute. Except in Catholic journals, he was widely praised for *Studs Lonigan*. Upon the publication in 1936 of *A World I Never Made*, the first of the Danny O'Neill books, his position in the front-rank of American writers was established. Bernard De Voto, writing in the *Saturday Review of Literature*, was typical when he declared that the story was "presented with what I can only call ecstasy," and went "beyond *Studs Lonigan*."

But, meanwhile, Farrell was plunging into political and literary controversies that earned him many enemies, particularly among Communists and the fellow travelers of Communism in liberal circles. As early as 1935, he was attacking the attempts of the pro-Communist clique to set the standards for American writers. When Stalin began his famous purges of the Old Bolsheviks in 1936, Farrell denounced the trials as a hoax. He worked with John Dewey to organize an informal court of inquiry in Mexico to take the testimony of Leon Trotsky in rebuttal to Stalin's charges. Farrell was uniquely feared by the Communist literary faction because he had, unlike most novelists, actually read all of Marx and Lenin. He also had a Swiftian talent for dialectical debate and slashing rebuttal. Had he chosen to concentrate his efforts as a historian and political journalist, he might well have achieved eminence in those fields. As it was, his political activities caused an envenomed attack upon his fiction. Beginning with *No Star Is Lost* in 1938, his work received increasingly hostile reviews. A whispering campaign promoted a stereotype of him as heavy-handed, dull, untalented.

Farrell withstood the attack. During the war and immediate postwar years, *Studs Lonigan* reigned as one of the top best-sellers in the Modern Library series. In 1946 *Bernard Clare*, the first of a new trilogy, sold 39,000 copies, the best sale any of his books had ever achieved in hard cover. For the first time, Farrell knew a brief period of prosperity.

Almost as suddenly, he was stranded by a change in public taste. The

American people, worn by nearly twenty years of depression, war, and unceasing political controversy, were in the mood in the 1950's for rest and romance. The same public that elected General Eisenhower to the White House rediscovered the legend of Scott Fitzgerald and made the gay, irresponsible 1920's a vogue. Just as Fitzgerald's brilliant story of the very rich in *Tender Is the Night* seemed hopelessly beside the point in depression-ridden 1934, so Farrell's realistic novels about the poor and the socially idealistic struck the wrong note for the affluent and nostalgic 1950's. *Yet Other Waters*, for example, which told the story of a young writer and socialist breaking away from the Communists, was a novel too close in spirit and subject matter to the angry thirties. Almost everyone had lost interest in the passions and quarrels of that decade except the men who ran the investigations and security hearings in Washington.

In the face of this renewed adversity, Farrell returned to the scene and the people of his best writing: to the Irish on the South Side of Chicago in the early years of this century. He wrote the beautiful and moving story of the life and death of Tom O'Flaherty, the old teamster who was his grandfather, and of those he loved.

As Farrell worked on this book, he pondered the changes that time had wrought in him since he began twenty-five years earlier to write the story of a boy named Studs and of an Irish neighborhood that had now disappeared:

"We swim well or badly in the sea of time. . . . [Yet] life is wonderful. To understand it, to love it, to make it a little better, and to accept its buffetings as best we can and swim against them, knowing that we swim on and out toward a horizon we can never reach—this is all we can do. . . . I took a volume of Yeats' poems off my shelf. I came upon *The Lamentations of the Old Pensioner*. . . . Lines of it opened doors to my own world of feeling. And over and over again, I read the two final lines:

> " 'I spit into the face of time,
> That has transfigured me.' "[28]

Farrell called his novel *The Face of Time*. Published in 1953, it earned him more critical acclaim than he had won in many years, but it did not make the impact on the reading public that had been expected. Time has transfigured him, and contemporaries have surrendered him to neglect, but he lives imperishably in his art. His portrayal of a vital part of the Irish experience endures.

CHAPTER FOURTEEN

The Irish in the Theater

1

IN THE ENGLISH-SPEAKING WORLD during the first quarter of the twentieth century, the greatest playwrights were Irish—Sean O'Casey, William Butler Yeats, George Bernard Shaw, John Synge—and the most influential experiment was the Abbey Theatre in Dublin where playwrights and actors broke through the excessively artificial conventions, the stylized gestures, and the noise and movement of the nineteenth century theater to express life in a simpler, more natural, and moving way.

Against this background, it was logical, if not predictable, that the first serious and important playwright in the United States should have been Eugene O'Neill, an American of Irish parentage. There was an intellectual link between O'Neill and the theater renaissance in Ireland, for George Cram Cook, the organizer of the Provincetown Players which gave O'Neill valuable encouragement and backing during the early part of his career, had drawn his inspiration from productions of the Irish Players who toured this country. "What he [Cook] saw done for Irish life he wanted for American life—no stage conventions in the way of projecting with the humility of true feeling."[1]

More directly and personally, O'Neill derived from an old and strong Irish tradition in the American theater. For more than seventy-five years, the Irish had been prominent as actors, playwrights, and managers in both the traditional and the popular stage. James O'Neill, his father, was one of many Irish-born actors who had toured the United States for decades, playing both Shakespearean repertory and historical melodramas. Dion Boucicault's dramas about Irish life (*The Colleen Bawn*, *The Shaughraun*, and many others) had been immensely popular in the United States in the middle of the nineteenth century, while the comedies of Edward Harrigan about American Irish life had been equally successful a generation later. Irish comics had been exceptionally prominent in vaudeville. By 1910 George M. Cohan, an older contemporary of O'Neill, had established himself by his extraordinary versatility as the master of the romantic comedy and the light musical play. Cohan was playwright, songwriter, actor, dancer, and producer. Born in 1878, and active in the theater from childhood, he spanned in his career nearly fifty years from the farces and revues of the 1880's to the realistic plays of the 1930's. For millions of Americans, Cohan epitomized the genial, witty, lighthearted, sentimental kind of Irishman, always ready with a quip or a story or a sympathetic tear in his eye, willing to buy a drink or down one, the kind of Irishman about whom songs like "When Irish Eyes Are Smiling" are written. He was the cocky, self-confident Irishman who sang in "Harrigan":

> Proud of all the Irish blood that's in me,
> Divil a man can say a word agin me.

As a songwriter and public personality, Cohan expressed and ultimately came to symbolize the passionate identification with America, the more than life-size patriotism, of the first- and second-generation Irish immigrants. It was natural, for example, that Cohan should write the most popular patriotic song of World War I, "Over There."[2]

Cohan brought his kind of popular theater to its perfect form in the play that he wrote and acted in, *The Song and Dance Man*. A hit of the 1923-1924 Broadway season, this told the story of "Hap" Farrell, a second-rate variety actor who cherished the illusion that he was the very best in his profession. Cohan, who probably *was* the greatest song-and-dance man America ever produced, made "Hap" the embodiment of the whole tradition of the Irish actor as comic entertainer.

O'Neill was in revolt against that comic tradition; Cohan wrote the kind of plays O'Neill most definitely did not want to write. Their paths crossed only once: Cohan played the lead in *Ah, Wilderness!* O'Neill's only sunny, humorous play. The show was a success, and Cohan scored a personal triumph, but the old song-and-dance man reciprocated O'Neill's intellectual disapprobation; he told intimates that the play's humor was "mostly old vaudeville jokes which had been done over and over."[3] O'Neill likewise rejected the other parts of the American Irish theatrical tradition: the heavy romantic style of actors like his father, the historical romances and melodramas, the pure-hearted colleens and honest lads of Boucicault's plays, the gags and stock situations of the "stage Irishman" of vaudeville. Like the Abbey Theatre playwrights, he was desperately determined to present the Irish as real people. But what is significant is that he had a tradition against which to revolt. The theater was his natural home, and he came to the writing of his plays as an inheritor of a communal past on whose resources he could draw and against which he could measure his aims.

2

The lives of O'Neill and his family comprise several of the basic themes of the story of the Irish in this country. James O'Neill, his father, was born in Kilkenny County, Ireland, in 1846, during the worst of the potato famine, and came to America as a child with his parents and nine sisters and brothers. James during his early years in this country experienced hideous poverty. His father deserted the family to return to Ireland, where he soon died; his mother went to work as a domestic, and James quit school at ten to take a job. The family was often hungry and was twice evicted for failure to pay the rent. These sufferings and deprivations disfigured James O'Neill's later emotional life, making him fearful and obsessive where money matters were concerned. One of the recurring themes in his son's plays was human greed and the destructive effects of the search for and the possession of money.

James made his escape from poverty as a young man when he entered one of the favorite Irish professions: the theater. He trained himself to speak without a brogue, memorized Shakespeare, and by unceasing determination became an accomplished actor. The great Edwin Booth once said of his performance as Othello, "That young man is playing the part better than I ever did." But at thirty-six, James O'Neill became diverted from his successful career as a Shakespearean actor by his enormous popular success in the role of Edmond Dantes in *The Count of Monte Cristo*. He played it some six thousand times on tour and earned as much as $40,000 annually, but by the end of his life he had come to regard the play as his "curse." It had led him to forsake the proper development of his career in favor of easy money. After his performances, since the role was physically and emotionally exhausting, the elder O'Neill increasingly found relief in heavy drinking. If there is a specter haunting the Irish, its name is alcoholism. Heavy drinking almost ruined the health of Eugene O'Neill during his youth, and the escape into alcohol is another recurring theme in his plays.

James O'Neill was a devout Catholic, rarely missing Mass on Sunday even when he was on tour, and he was also an enthusiastic Irish patriot. His son was baptized Eugene Gladstone O'Neill because of James's admiration for "the only British Prime Minister who ever tried to do anything for Ireland."

If, through his father, he reached back to the potato famine and the mythic crossing of the Atlantic in steerage, Eugene O'Neill touched through his mother another theme: the rise of the prosperous, "lace-curtain" Irish. Ella Quinlan O'Neill was the only child of a wealthy wholesale grocer in Cleveland, Ohio.* Ella, a pretty and pious girl, was well educated for a woman of that day, having attended a Catholic school, St. Mary's Academy near South Bend, Indiana, where she studied Latin, French, art, and music. When her future husband was appearing in a play in Cleveland, he met her father at church one day. The romance began when the grocer brought his daughter backstage to meet O'Neill. After a decorous two-year engagement, the couple were married in June, 1877. The bride was twenty, eleven years younger than her husband. They were deeply in love, but it was an odd match between the self-educated actor who had raised himself out of poverty by a sustained, imperious act of will and the shy, convent-educated girl from a sheltered, genteel home. Throughout most of her married life, Ella O'Neill traveled with her husband in his exhausting cross-country tours. Although she had married an actor, she never quite overcame the belief that theatrical people were dissolute and not respectable. She tended to hold herself aloof from the other members of the company. At the same time, as an actor's wife, she was no longer welcome in the homes of girls she had known at St. Mary's. "She was deeply hurt," her son later recalled, "that girls from wealthy families she had known in school dropped her after she married my father."

Ella O'Neill bore three sons, the second dying in infancy. The two who survived were James ("Jamie") and, ten years younger, Eugene, born October 16, 1888. Eugene, virtually an only child because his brother was away in boarding school, spent his childhood on tour with his parents. "A child has a regular, fixed home," he wrote later, "but you might say I started in as a trouper. I knew only actors and the stage. My mother nursed me in the wings and in dressing rooms." He recalled those early years as "a succession of one-night stands, of perpetual waiting in the wings, dirty dressing rooms, stuffy trains and shoddy hotels."[4] When he was old enough to attend school, he received a Catholic education, first at Mount St. Vincent-on-Hudson at Riverdale, New York, where he boarded for three years, and later at De La Salle Institute in New York City. O'Neill as a young man broke away from the Catholic Church and never returned to it, but Catholicism had formed his conscience, and throughout his life he oscillated between the opposing poles of religious commitment and nihilist denial, between belief and revulsion. Certain portions of his Catholic experience were particularly influential: the belief in original sin, the stress on the brevity and transitory quality of human life, the view of God as judge, as omnipotent, as He who knows all one's most secret thoughts and dreams.

* The wholesale grocery business was a favorite of Irish immigrant entrepreneurs because it did not require a large amount of capital. It will be recalled that P. F. McQuillan, the grandfather of F. Scott Fitzgerald, was also a wholesale grocer.

O'Neill entered Princeton but withdrew after a year devoted mostly to drinking and collegiate escapades. He spent the next five years drifting. He worked briefly for a mail-order house, explored for gold in Central America (finding no gold but contracting malaria), worked as an assistant ticket-taker in his father's stage company, shipped to Buenos Aires as seaman on a Norwegian sailing vessel, and acted minor roles in his father's interminable production of *The Count of Monte Cristo*. During this period, he was briefly and unhappily married, his first son, Eugene, Jr., being born to this marriage.

In the summer of 1912, O'Neill was reunited with his parents and older brother at the family summer home in New London, Connecticut. He worked for several months as a newspaper reporter before he discovered he had tuberculosis. While O'Neill was recuperating in a sanatorium, he decided that what he wanted to do most in life was write plays. He never swerved from that decision. He was then twenty-four; seven years later, one of his scripts was produced on Broadway, won a Pulitzer Prize, and his brilliant career was launched.

3

In his revolt against the false sentiment and stultifying limitations of the theater of his father's generation, O'Neill had recourse to the true realistic solution: he tried to write honestly and simply about those aspects of life that he knew firsthand. His first one-act plays, never produced, revolved around the problems of an unhappy marriage—clearly his own. One of his first full-length plays was *The Straw*, based on his experiences in the tuberculosis sanatorium; the central character, a dying girl, was based on an Irish girl named Kitty McKay ("Eileen Carmody" in the play) whom he had known there, and the hero was modeled upon himself. In this play, he presented in the heroine and her father contrasting portraits of Irish characters. The father, "Bill Carmody," who bullies and exploits his sick daughter, has a face "bony and ponderous; his nose, short and squat; his mouth large, thick-lipped and harsh; his complexion mottled—red, purple-streaked, and freckled; his hair, short and stubby with a bald spot on the crown. The expression of his small, blue eyes is one of selfish cunning." He talks in a brogue, "crosses himself with pious unction," and scorns people who read books. The heroine is described as resembling her deceased mother, sensitive and thoughtful, the type who, as her father says, "always was dreamin' their lives out." She is pretty with eyes "large and blue, confident in their compelling candor and sweetness; her lips, full and red, half-open, over strong even teeth, droop at the corner into an expression of wistful sadness." But even in describing

Eileen, O'Neill is determined to be realistic; as if fearful of presenting a stereotype "colleen," he describes her as having "a rather heavy Irish jaw."

This play, a failure on Broadway in 1921, aroused the antagonism of some American Irish who felt that O'Neill's depiction of the Carmodys was a slur upon the Irish. This adverse reaction in some sections of the Irish community recurred throughout his career. Nearly thirty years later, many in the audience walked out during a pre-Broadway tryout of *A Moon for the Misbegotten* in Columbus, Ohio. When the producer asked the doorman why they were leaving, the doorman replied: "I don't know. They just said they were Irish."[5]

O'Neill's difficulties were in the great tradition; audiences in both Dublin and the United States had rioted in protest against the depiction of Irish character presented by John Synge in *The Playboy of the Western World*. In this country, the Ancient Order of Hibernians, the most powerful Irish fraternal society, not only crusaded, understandably enough, against the "Pat 'n' Mike" stereotype of the stage Irishman but also attacked the new, serious Irish drama. In 1912 it passed a resolution assailing Synge, Yeats, and "other so-called Irish dramatists." When the Abbey Theatre sent a company on tour in the United States that year, the AOH organized boycotts in major cities, and the management had to provide police protection during performances. This was all wildly ironic, since nothing did more to raise the prestige of the Irish in this country than the works of Yeats and his contemporaries. But the AOH wanted only plays about lovable mothers, virtuous daughters, and manly young men, all behaving themselves in accord with sentimental tradition. The whole concept that plays and novels should be a criticism of life was alien and disturbing to them.[6]

O'Neill was, in fact, intensely proud that only Irish blood flowed in his veins, and he identified strongly with the American Irish. But like the great playwrights in Dublin, he felt his identification with the Irish so keenly that he took to heart their errors and failings, exposing and attacking them in his plays. Those who thought him anti-Irish did not comprehend that for an artist telling the truth is the highest act of love.

4

O'Neill also turned for subject matter to the sea and to the lives of sailors he had known. He had been fascinated by a stoker named Driscoll with whom he had worked on one of his voyages. O'Neill used the name for a secondary character in *Bound East for Cardiff*, one of his earliest plays and the first to be produced—at Provincetown in 1916—but he did not develop the character fully. In that play, a sailor is dying, and Driscoll, a shipmate, jokingly accuses him of wanting to die so that he will go to heaven. The sailor says No, when he dies he will go to hell. He then reviews the bitter, hard life sailors live; most of the play is his dramatic monologue; at his death, Driscoll kneels in prayer.

Driscoll appears full-length and universalized under the name "Yank" in O'Neill's *The Hairy Ape*. Here he personifies man's desperate attempt to rise from the apes and find meaning and justice in life. Driscoll "was a giant of a man and absurdly strong," O'Neill recalled later. "He thought a whole lot of himself, was a determined individualist. He was very proud of his strength, his capacity for grueling work. It seemed to give him mental poise to be able to dominate the stokehole, do more work than any of his mates.

"The voyage after I quit going to sea, Driscoll shipped on again as usual. I stayed behind at Jimmy the Priest's [a bar and cheap hotel in New York]. When the ship returned to New York, Driscoll was the first to swing the saloon doors open and bellow for a drink. We could usually calculate the time of the ship's docking from the moment of Driscoll's appearance. Then I drifted away and later I heard that Driscoll had jumped overboard in midocean. None of our mutual seamates knew why. I concluded something must have shaken his hard-boiled poise, for he wasn't the type who just give up, and he loved life. Anyway, it was his death that inspired the idea for the Yank of 'The Hairy Ape.' "[7]

The sea, Jimmy the Priest's saloon, and two sailors, one Swedish and the other Irish, provided the setting and the supporting characters for one of O'Neill's best plays, *Anna Christie.*

O'Neill originally intended this play to be tragic and in the manner of the great Scandinavian playwrights Ibsen and Strindberg. But the two characters he invented, Anna Christie and her sailor lover, Matt Burke, develop not only a life of their own—something all successful characters must do—but also a positive attitude toward life's difficulties, an attitude mingling stoicism, insouciance, and stubborn hope, which defies the playwright's tragic intent. What he conceived as a tragedy of fate became a triumph of character.

Anna Christie concerns Chris Chistopherson, a middle-aged sailor who deserted Anna and her mother in Sweden and went to sea. He hates the loneliness and the hardships of the sea, but is haunted and compelled by it. After his wife's death, he places Anna with relatives in Minnesota, far inland, away from the sea's temptations. Misfortunes befall her, she becomes a prostitute, seeks out her father, and eventually finds him—working as a barge captain by the sea. His worst fears are confirmed when she falls in love with Matt, a sailor. Will her life be ruined by the sea as his was?

Anna insists upon telling Matt about her past; he leaves in a rage but, after a two-day drunk, returns and they are reconciled. The play ends leaving Chris's fearful question unresolved. But it is difficult to believe that Anna (brilliantly played on the stage by Pauline Lord and in the motion picture by Greta Garbo) will, with her vitality and self-confidence, fail to survive; the same is true of Matt who, as one critic has observed, "possesses all of the exuberance, the pugnaciousness, and the boastfulness of the Playboy of the Western World."[8]

A wholly different but equally successful play of this same period was *The Emperor Jones*. Based on the story of a Negro adventurer who held power briefly on the island of Haiti before the natives overthrew him, the play benefited greatly from the knowledge of what would make striking and effective theater acquired from O'Neill's childhood touring with his father. *The Emperor Jones* in O'Neill's most economically and skilfully constructed play. In eight scenes he portrays the disintegration of a strong, arrogant human being as he makes a headlong flight through the jungle and into his past. The gradually accelerated beat of a drum paces the rising excitement. The dense tropical jungle populated with "formless fears" and echoing with weird noises becomes a palpable force as the author drew upon his memories of the Honduras jungle in his gold-hunting days. The play, performed all over the world, contributed more than any of his other works to making him internationally famous. (It was in a London production of *The Emperor Jones* that Paul Robeson achieved his first success.) Forty years later, time has only confirmed the judgment Alexander Woollcott wrote in the *New York Times* when the play opened: ". . . An extraordinarily striking and dramatic study of panic fear. It reinforces the impression that for strength and originality he has no rival among the American writers for the stage."[9]

5

O'Neill in 1925 turned his attention to two themes that were to beguile and torment his imagination for the rest of his life: one private and psychological, the other historical and cultural. The former concerned his attitude toward his own father. He had hated James O'Neill, rebelled against him, been partially reconciled with him before his death (in 1920), but never forgiven him. He feared and respected his father, seeing him as the embodiment of sternness, strength, greed, egotism. When his father died, he and his brother went on a prolonged drinking spree. The complementary theme was the story of the Catholic Irish and the Protestant Yankees of rural and small-town New England where O'Neill attended prep school and spent his summers. Sexual Puritanism, concealed shame, mad romantic pride, and greed were the fatal flaws O'Neill saw in the Irish character. He projected some of these qualities, notably greed for land, into the Yankee character. On the sexual side, he had a double vision of the Yankee, sometimes (as in *Desire Under the Elms*) seeing him as possessing a natural, unashamed, healthy sexuality, and sometimes (as in *Strange Interlude*) seeing him as timid and inhibited. In Ireland, the Irish and the English had struggled at close quarters for centuries, and the issue had turned on who was to possess the land. It was easy to see that ancient struggle transposed to America in the conflict in New England between the Irish immigrants and the old Yankee settlers. Their struggle for the mastery of this new country was, on the historical and cultural level, the counterpart of the contest within the family between a father and his sons.

O'Neill first drew these psychological and cultural themes together in an exceptionally powerful play, *Desire Under the Elms*. He omitted the Irish half of the cultural conflict, but otherwise the two themes fuse perfectly and intensify one another with great effect. Ephraim Cabot is, at one and the same time, a portrait of the Yankee character as O'Neill conceived it and the epitome of every tough, durable, sexually potent, land-possessing old father any son ever hated. It is impossible not to admire Ephraim as he tells how he wrung a good farm out of the hard-scrabble New England soil:

"When I came here fifty odd year ago—I was jest twenty an' the strongest an' hardest ye ever seen—ten times as strong an' fifty times as hard as Eben [his youngest son]. Waal—this place was nothin' but fields o' stones. Folks laughed when I tuk it. They couldn't know what I knowed. When ye kin make corn sprout out o' stones, God's livin' in yew! They wa'n't strong enuf fur that! They reckoned God was easy. They laughed. They don't laugh no more. Some died here abouts. Some went West an' died. They're all under ground—fur hollerin' arter an easy God. God hain't easy. (*He shakes his head slowly.*) And I growed hard. Folks kept allus sayin' he's a hard man like 'twas sinful t' be hard, so's at last I said back at 'em: Waal then, by thunder, y'll git me hard an' see how ye like it! . . . God's hard, not easy! God's in the stones! Build my church on a rock—out o' stones! an' I'll be in them! That's what he meant t' Peter! (*He sighs heavily—a pause.*) Stones. I picked 'em up an' piled 'em into walls. Ye kin read the years of my life in them walls, every day a hefted stone, climbin' over the hills up an' down, fencin' in the fields that was mine, whar I'd made thin's grow out o' nothin'—like the will o' God, like the servant o' His hand. It wan't easy."

Eben, his son, a softer, gentler man, makes a commentary on the human cost of his father's achievement: "Stone atop o' stone, makin' walls till yer heart's a stone ye heft up out o' the way. . . ."

Ephraim, at seventy-five, having outlived two wives, marries a third, Abbie Putnam, a woman half his age. The two olders sons leave the farm in disgust, but Eben stays to protect his potential inheritance. He worships the memory of his mother and hates his father, who thinks him a weakling. He falls in love with Abbie and they have a child—the new son that Ephraim had wanted. The old man torments him by planting in his mind the conviction that Abbie does not really love him but bore a son so that she herself could inherit the farm. When Eben accuses her of this, she demonstrates the falsity of the charge by smothering the baby. Eben knows now that his father lied and that Abbie did indeed love him for himself alone; her desire was for him and not for the farm. He insists upon sharing her guilt for the murder of their child. As the play ends, the two are led away by the sheriff's men.

The farm is clearly meant to stand for all America. One of the sheriff's deputies says: "It's a jim-dandy farm—no denying it. I wish I owned it." Greed, the terrible need to possess, has disfigured and frustrated the love that Abbie and the beautiful elms symbolize.

6

The success of *Desire Under the Elms* unfortunately tempted O'Neill to move away from his cultural home grounds and to try increasingly ambitious psychological explorations. The experimental plays (*The Great God Brown, Lazarus Laughed*) and the extremely long plays (*Strange Interlude, Mourning Becomes Electra*) written in the next half-dozen years now seem in retrospect to be cumbersome and pretentious period pieces. Psychiatry has become both more sophisticated and more commonplace that it was in 1927 when O'Neill wrote *Strange Interlude*. This case study of a neurotic woman and four men in her life is now only of historical interest.* *Mourning Becomes Electra* is a restatement in modern terms of a Greek tragedy, but, as Eric Bentley has observed, neither O'Neill's actual story nor the Greek tragedy gains anything from combining the two.[10]

O'Neill at the beginning of the 1920's had written: "The playwright today must dig at the roots of the sickness of today as he feels it—the death of the old God and the failure of science and materialism to give

* In 1963 the Actors Studio successfully revived *Strange Interlude*. The public and most critics received it favorably, but I still think it should have been left with the historians.

any satisfying new One for the surviving primitive religious instinct to find a meaning for life in and to comfort its fears of death with. It seems to me that anyone trying to do big work nowadays must have this big subject behind all the little subjects of his plays or novels, or he is simply scribbling around on the surface of things and has no more real status than a parlor entertainer."[11]

The thrust of O'Neill's concern was surely in the right direction. The radical loss of religious faith on the part of millions of people is a major phenomenon of the modern world; it may well be the "big subject behind all the little subjects," but an artist does not discover the truth about society until he has first discovered it about himself. He has to define his personal vision and follow it through, digging into the authentic material provided by his own experience and background. Only by confronting himself can he get at "the roots of the sickness of today." O'Neill in his "big" plays in the late 1920's was relying too heavily upon his intellectual resources, his reading of Nietzsche, Schopenhauer, and Jung, and not enough upon his true strengths—his sensibility, his reliable feeling for the dramatically effective, his integrity, his own experience. In the early thirties, after the exhausting effort of creating *Mourning Becomes Electra* (which took two years and several drafts), O'Neill began to circle back toward his artistic center. His next two plays, *Days Without End* and *Ah, Wilderness!* are two of his less important works, but they are significant in his development because they mark the beginning of this return to his true material: his own and his family's past. *Days Without End* concerns a man who saves his marriage and resolves a deep inner conflict by reembracing religious faith. The play led to rumors that O'Neill was planning to return to the Catholic Church. According to Richard Dana Skinner, the distinguished drama critic of *The Commonweal*, the lay Catholic weekly, who was close to him during this period, O'Neill seriously considered this possibility. "In 'Days Without End,'" Skinner wrote, "O'Neill sought directly, in surrender to the Christ crucified, a truth that would set him free." But whatever intellectual temptations Catholicism may have had for O'Neill, it was intimately bound up with his feelings about his parents and his childhood; it was part of his personal past against which he was still in revulsion.

Ah, Wilderness! was a journey to that past by another route. In this portrait of a sensitive youth growing up in a town very much like New London, O'Neill tried to imagine what his own youth would have been like if he had had a more normal family life and a father he loved. (As it turned out on Broadway, George M. Cohan as the father stole the show and, ironically enough, overshadowed the role of the son.) The play is a happy, romantic dream of what might have been.

Ah, Wilderness! was a hit and *Days Without End* a failure on Broadway during the winter of 1933-1934. They were the last of his plays to be produced for twelve years. During this long hiatus, he worked on a cycle of plays, numbering first five, then nine, and finally eleven plays. The cycle, "A Tale of the Possessors Self-Dispossessed," was intended to tell the history of America through several generations of two families, one Irish and the other Yankee. As the title indicates, it would present O'Neill's pessimistic view that the American story is a tragedy brought about by human greed. If the playwright had enjoyed the good health and vitality in his later years to bring this vast project to fulfillment, it might well have been what he intended it to be—the masterpiece crowning his career. It would certainly have been a testament to the Irish presence in American life. But ill-health sapped his enthusiasm. He completed first and second drafts of seven of these plays, but in the last year of his life, when he sensed death approaching and knew the plays needed further revision, he destroyed six of them.

"We tore them up bit by bit, together," his wife later recalled. "I helped him because his hands—he had this terrific tremor, he could tear just a few pages at a time. It was like tearing up children."[12]

The only play to survive was *A Touch of the Poet* which was produced on Broadway in 1958. Planned as the third play in the cycle, it takes place in a small New England town in 1828, the same setting and a generation earlier than *Desire Under the Elms*. It is the story of an Irish immigrant, Major Cornelius "Con" Melody who makes his living as a tavernkeeper but is determined to pass himself off as a gentleman and impress his Yankee neighbors. He is in an equivocal position because he looks down upon his fellow Irish immigrants as mere "bogtrotters," but the Yankee will not accept him. Yet his fantasied picture of himself, which is sustained by his military title, his courtly manners, and his possession of a beautiful thoroughbred mare, is more important to him than these drab realities. Then his daughter Sara falls in love with a Yankee youth, Simon Harford. When the Harfords oppose a marriage, Con goes to their home to protest and is thrown out by a Negro servant. Humiliated, his dream broken, he decides to face reality in all its bitterness. As a token of this decision, he shoots his mare, the symbol of his pride. But the play is not to be a tragedy, for Sara lures Simon to seduce her, the two decide to get married despite his family's objections, and Major Melody's self-esteem is restored. The play is not successful because O'Neill does not establish the Major as a character of sufficient intensity and force to make his troubles deeply moving to the audience, but the play is entertaining as a sketch of a certain kind of Irish "character." "More Stately Mansions," one of the scripts O'Neill destroyed, was to have been the successor play in which he took up the story of Simon and Sara's children who would be half-Yankee, half-Irish. But only the story of the blarney-ing Major was left upon O'Neill's death, a fragment of a grand design.

7

When World War II began in 1939, O'Neill was fifty-one and stricken with Parkinson's Disease, which produced an increasingly severe tremor in his hands. His own ill-health and the sense of depression evoked by the catastrophe through which the world was passing drew his thoughts away from his cycle of plays and toward his own beginnings. Over the next two years, in a final burst of creativity, he wrote three plays: *The Iceman Cometh, Long Day's Journey Into Night*, and *A Moon for the Misbegotten*. The first two of these are masterpieces, rank-ing with *Anna Christie, The Emperor Jones*, and *Desire Under the Elms* as the five plays by which he will live in history.

In *The Iceman Cometh*, O'Neill returned to the destitute, hard-drink-ing days of his young manhood when he spent many hours in a Green-wich Village saloon, the Golden Swan, better known as "the Hell Hole." The author's spokesman in the play is "Larry Slade." He has sometimes been identified as Terry Carlin, an old Irish drinking companion of the author's early days, but he might also stand for the author himself, since the description could be that of a seedier, down-on-his-luck O'Neill: "tall, raw-boned, with coarse straight white hair, worn long and raggedly cut. He had a gaunt Irish face with a big nose, high cheekbones, a lantern jaw with a week's stubble of beard, a mystic's meditative pale blue eyes with a gleam of sharp sardonic humor in them. . . . He stares in front of him, an expression of tired tolerance giving his face the quality of a pitying but weary old priest's."

The entire action takes place in the saloon in the summer of 1912. As the play begins, Larry explains sardonically: "It's Bedrock Bar. The End of the Line Café, The Bottom of the Sea Rathskeller! Don't you notice the beautiful calm in the atmosphere? That's because it's the last harbor. No one here has to worry about where they're going next, because there is no farther they can go. It's a great comfort to them. Although even here they keep up the appearances of life with a few harmless pipe dreams about their yesterdays and tomorrows, as you'll see for yourself if you're here long."

The two chief characters are Don Parritt and Theodore ("Hickey") Hickman. Each has a dreadful secret which unfolds in the course of the play. Parritt is a member of a radical political Movement. He has just fled from the West Coast where his mother, a leading figure in the Movement, has been jailed for her part in a bombing in which several persons were killed; Larry Slade had once been in the Movement and in love with Parritt's mother. She emerges as the old-fashioned radical woman, totally committed to politics, a believer in free love, a woman deficient in maternal feeling.

"There's nothing soft or sentimental about Mother." her son says. "When she's finished with anyone, she's finished. She's always been proud of that. And you know how she feels about the Movement. Like a revivalist preacher about religion. Anyone who loses faith in it is more than dead to her; he's a Judas who ought to be boiled in oil. . . . To hear her go on sometimes, you'd think she was the Movement."

Parritt's secret is that he betrayed his mother to the police. He tries to take refuge in various protective pipe dreams, arguing first that he did it for patriotic motives and, later, because he needed money to support a whore. But ultimately he breaks down and faces reality: "I may as well confess, Larry. There's no use lying any more. You know, anyway. I didn't give a damn about the money. It was because I hated her. . . . I laughed to myself and thought, 'You know what you can do with your freedom pipe dream now, don't you, you damned old bitch!' "

Tortured by guilt, Parritt leaves to commit suicide. If he has been the victim of a lack of love, Hickey has suffered from an excess of it. Ordinarily, when Hickey arrives in the saloon to go on a drinking spree, he is a welcome figure to the drunks, derelicts, and prostitutes who frequent the place. He means a round of free drinks, gaiety, a good time. But this time he is acting strangely. He is not drinking, and he presses his companions to abandon their respective pipe dreams, arguing that only by freeing themselves from their illusions can they find true peace. Only Larry Slade recognizes that the peace Hickey has in mind is the peace of the grave. Hickey's influence prevails and, one by one, the other characters strip themselves of their dreams and reveal their sad truths. Hickey periodically makes references to his wife, Evelyn, whom he jokingly says is at home in bed with the iceman. The climax of the play is reached when his secret is revealed; he has murdered his wife and the iceman is Death.

Hickey is one of O'Neill's memorable characters. A smiling, wise-cracking, Hoosier salesman, he has built a career on his talent for "sizing people up quick, spotting what their pet pipe dreams were, and then kidding 'em along that line, pretending you believed what they wanted to believe about themselves." A total cynic, he is incapable of love or belief. All he ever wanted was to enjoy the peace of the saloon, ". . . sitting around with the old gang, getting drunk and forgetting love, joking and laughing and swapping lies." But fate has cursed him with a wife who loved him more than he deserved, who forgave his every transgression, who always took him back.

He pretends he killed her so that she would not have to go on forgiving him. If he had deserted her, she would have died of grief, if he had committed suicide, she would have died of a broken heart. "You see, Evelyn loved me. And I loved her. That was the trouble. It would have been easy to find a way out if she hadn't loved me so much. Or if I hadn't loved her. But as it was, there was only one possible way."

But this is only Hickey's own final illusion. When he killed her there was in his heart not love but hatred. He hated her overpowering love and her romantic conception of him because they loaded him down with guilt and made him hate himself.

The Iceman Cometh, although repetitious and prolix, is a brilliant, moving, and dramatically effective portrayal of life on the near edge of hell. The pessimism and fatalism integral to the playwright's view of the world were, in the play's own terms, adequately accounted for by the realistic squalor of the lives of the lost souls in Harry Hope's saloon. O'Neill had once been one of them and could thirty years later still identify with them.

8

The writing of *The Iceman Cometh* made for O'Neill a clearing in the darkness of his past. Having gone that far, he was able at last to penetrate to the core of his experience. He wrote the story of his own family, and it became his finest play, *Long Day's Journey Into Night*.

The play covers a day in the life of the Tyrones who are modeled directly on the playwright's own family: the father, an aging actor, handsome, vain, hard-drinking, and pathologically stingy; the mother, unhappy, cut off from polite society, periodically addicted to morphine; the older son, burdened by a severe Oedipus complex, a failure, able to find emotional gratification only with whores, and far advanced toward becoming an alcoholic; and the younger son (O'Neill himself), restless, a drifter, sensitive, possessing "a touch of the poet" in his makeup. The scene is the family's summer home in New London, Connecticut; the time is 1912; and the events of the play are those that occurred in the lives of the O'Neills that year: Eugene discovers he has a mild case of tuberculosis, and his mother, after a sanatorium cure, relapses into her morphine addiction.

O'Neill gives the younger brother in the play the name of his dead baby brother, Edmund, whom he had never known. The choice of names underscores two circumstances crucial in O'Neill's understanding of himself: that his parents had considered him a substitute for his dead brother and that during his mother's illness after his birth, she was treated by an incompetent doctor who prescribed heavy doses of morphine and inadvertently made her an addict. This misfortune, which shadowed the rest of her life, instilled in her younger son a lifelong conviction, undeserved but ineradicable, of personal guilt and unworthiness.

Long Day's Journey Into Night is an exposition, profoundly sad and relentlessly complete, of the truth that those who cannot learn from the past are condemned to relive it. In Act Two, Scene Two, Mary Tyrone cries out to her husband: "James! You mustn't remember! You mustn't humiliate me so!" And a moment later, he exclaims: "Mary! For God's sake, forget the past!" But neither they nor their sons can forget and break the tyranny of the past. As the critic Kenneth Tynan wrote: "Every conversation leads inexorably up to the utterance of some sudden, unforgivable, scab-tearing cruelty."

As the play progresses the mother steadily retreats deeper into illusion, while Edmund achieves a better understanding of reality, the only possible basis for forgiveness and life. She symbolizes the past become irremediable, while he symbolizes intelligence and art striving to win the future. The father and the older brother are, like the mother, victims of their past; neither can help himself but, as the long day journeys into night, each tries to help Edmund.

The father reveals to him the tragic turning his own career took. He tells him of his terror of poverty, of his fantasy that he will end his days in a poorhouse, of his uncontrollable desire to make money in order to ward off the terror and the fantasy, and how this obsession for financial security caused him to sacrifice his career in Shakespeare in favor of a popular, moneymaking play.

> TYRONE: . . . My good bad luck made me find the big money-maker. It wasn't that in my eyes at first. It was a great romantic part I knew I could play better than anyone. But it was a great box office success from the start—and then life had me where it wanted

me—at from thirty-five to forty thousand net profit a season! A fortune in those days—or even in these. (*Bitterly*) What the hell was it I wanted to buy, I wonder, that was worth—Well, no matter. It's a late day for regrets. . . .

EDMUND: (*Moved, stares at his father with understanding—slowly*) I'm glad you've told me this, Papa. I know you a lot better now.

A short time later, Jamie, in a burst of drunken candor tells Edmund his painful truths:

JAMIE: Listen, Kid, you'll be going away. May not get another chance to talk. Or might not be drunk enough to tell you truth. So got to tell you now. Something I ought to have told you long ago—for your own good. . . . Want to warn you—against me. Mama and Papa are right. I've been rotten bad influence. And worst of it is, I did it on purpose.

EDMUND (*Uneasily*): Shut up! I don't want to hear—

JAMIE: Nix, Kid! You listen! Did it on purpose to make a bum of you. Or part of me did. A big part. That part that's been dead so long. That hates life. My putting you wise so you'd learn from my mistakes. Believed that myself at times, but it's a fake. Made my mistakes look good. Made getting drunk romantic. Made whores fascinating vampires instead of poor, stupid, diseased slobs they really are. Made fun of work as sucker's game. Never wanted you succeed and make me look even worse by comparison. Wanted you to fail. Always jealous of you. Mama's baby, Papa's pet! (*He stares at Edmund with increasing enmity.*) And it was your being born that started Mama on dope. I know that's not your fault, but all the same, God damn you, I can't help hating your guts—!"

EDMUND (*Almost frightenedly*): Jamie! Cut it out! You're crazy!

JAMIE: But don't get the wrong idea, Kid. I love you more than I hate you. My saying what I'm telling you now proves it. I run the risk you'll hate me—and you're all I've got left. But I didn't mean to tell you that last stuff—go that far back. Don't know what made me. What I wanted to say is, I'd like to see you become the greatest success in the world. But you'd better be on your guard. Because I'll do my damnedest to make you fail. . . .

The possibility that Edmund, able to understand and forgive his father and on guard against the influence of the older brother he loves and admires, may break out of the iron circle of the family's past is the only glimmer of hope in this tragedy.

Kenneth Tynan wrote of *Long Day's Journey Into Night:* "No more honest or unsparing autobiographical play exists in dramatic literature. . . . One goes expecting to hear a playwright, and one meets a man."[13]

Stephen Whicher, another critic, wrote in reviewing the play's world premiere in Stockholm in 1956: "The significant fact, however, is not that the work contains autobiographical elements, but that O'Neill has transcended them so completely. The undeniable impact of its current Swedish production, for example, certainly cannot be explained by the self-revelation which the play contains. Audiences are not sitting on hard seats night after night, absorbed in this play for over four hours, just because it gives them information about O'Neill."[14]

O'Neill had transmuted his family's private griefs and conflicts into objective form, in short, into art. His play can be understood as a searing passage from one man's autobiography, as Tynan described it, and as, in Whicher's phrase, *"the* modern tragedy," setting forth contemporary man's deep anguish.

From another perspective, we can give the play a third reading, one in terms of its historical and cultural setting. An important underlying reason for the solidity of the play's artistic achievement is that here again, as he did in *Desire Under the Elms* and as he tried to do, with what success we shall never know, in his projected cycle of plays, O'Neill accomplished the fusion of his psychological and cultural themes. He has told the story of a family in terms of the deepest human emotions—love, hate, pride, envy, remorse. He has also told the story of the Irish Catholics in America in terms of his personal understanding of their long journey.

Long Day's Journey Into Night is not only a great play about one family; it is also the great play about the American Irish. The Tyrones are embedded in the context of their Irish past. They reflect the strains of their relations with their Yankee neighbors. There is the father's chauvinism about all things Irish:

> EDMUND: Yes, facts don't mean a thing, do they? What you want to believe, that's the only truth! (*Derisively*) Shakespeare was an Irish Catholic, for example.
>
> TYRONE (*Stubbornly*): So he was. The proof is in his plays.
>
> EDMUND: Well, he wasn't, and there's no proof of it in his plays, except to you! (*Jeeringly*) The Duke of Wellington, there was another good Irish Catholic!
>
> TYRONE: I never said he was a good one. He was a renegade but a Catholic just the same.

EDMUND: Well, he wasn't. You just want to believe no one but an Irish Catholic general could beat Napoleon.

One of the few humorous moments the Tyrones enjoy comes when Edmund recounts the triumph of his father's tenant Shaughnessy in a quarrel with Harker, a Yankee millionaire concerning some pigs which have broken through a fence and wandered into Harker's pond. The mother refers to Shaughnessy as "That dreadful man!" The father calls him ". . . a wily Shanty Mick, that one. He could hide behind a corkscrew." But neither can resist sharing vicariously in his victory. Edmund tells what happened when Harker came to complain:

> Shaughnessy got a few drinks under his belt and was waiting at the gate to welcome him. He told me he never gave Harker a chance to open his mouth. He began by shouting that he was no slave Standard Oil could trample on. He was a King of Ireland, if he had his rights, and scum was scum to him, no matter how much money it had stolen from the poor.
> MARY: Oh, Lord! (*But she can't help laughing.*)
> [After a further account of Shaughnessy's verbal offensive, the father says] (*admiringly before he thinks*), The damned old scoundrel! By God, you can't beat him! (*He laughs—then stops abruptly and scowls.*) The dirty blackguard! He'll get me in serious trouble yet. I hope you told him I'd be mad as hell—
> EDMUND: I told him you'd be tickled to death over the great Irish victory, and so you are. Stop faking, Papa.

When Edmund's tuberculosis becomes known, old fears and superstitions color the family's discussions of his condition. During the middle of the nineteenth century, tuberculosis had been known for a time as "the Irish disease," since thousands of Irish, weakened by malnutrition during the potato famines, died of it in the old country and thousands more suffered it after coming to America because they lived in crowded, unsanitary conditions. Since other Americans feared them as carriers of the disease, many Irish thought of TB as a hereditary racial curse. James Tyrone reflects these notions:

> TYRONE: . . . I've warned him for years his body couldn't stand it, but he wouldn't heed me, and now it's too late.
> JAMIE (*Sharply*): What do you mean, too late? You talk as if you thought—
> TYRONE (*Guiltily explosive*): Don't be a damned fool! I meant

nothing but what's plain to anyone! His health has broken down and
he may be an invalid for a long time.

    JAMIE: I know it's an Irish peasant idea consumption is fatal. It
probably is when you live in a hovel on a bog, but over here, with
modern treatment—

    TYRONE: Don't I know that! What are you gabbing about, any-
way? And keep your dirty tongue off Ireland, with your sneers
about peasants and bogs and hovels!

The five characters in the play are distinctive individuals and also
archetypes of American Irish character. The father is the immigrant of
remarkable talents whose gifts have been marred by the ordeal of immigration; he has borne the terrible psychic strains of inventing himself as
a new character in a new society. The mother is the conventional, "lace-
curtain" Irishwoman who yearns for the safety and respectability of an
ordinary, middle-class existence. The elder son has, in O'Neill's words,
"the remnant of a humorous, romantic, irresponsible Irish charm—that
of the beguiling ne'er-do-well, with a strain of the sentimentally poetic,
attractive to women and popular with men." The younger son is the
brooding "dark Irishman." Cathleen, the maid, appears as the ignorant
greenhorn recently arrived from Ireland, while offstage, Bridget, the
cook, grumbles about the work and boasts about her relatives.

9

    "The critics have missed the most important thing about me and my
work," O'Neill once told his older son, "the fact that I am Irish."
Throughout his later years, he treasured a compliment he had received
from Sean O'Casey: "You write like an Irishman, you don't write like
an American."

    O'Neill was distinctly conscious of his Irish heritage. He was proud,
for example, that in Gaelic his family name means "champion." He liked
to think of himself as descended from Shane the Proud, a famous
sixteenth century chief of the O'Neill family. According to Croswell
Bowen: "O'Neill especially enjoyed the story of Shane's swimming across
a lake in competition with another Irish warrior for the hand of a beautiful princess. It was specified that the swimmer whose hand first touched
the far shore would win the fair lady. After Shane had swum three-
quarters of the distance across the lake, he realized his opponent was going
to win. Thereupon, he took a dagger from his belt, cut off one of his

hands at the wrist and flung it to the far shore—winning the race and the princess."

When his second son was born, he corresponded with James Stephens, the Irish poet and novelist, asking him for some good Irish names. From a list Stephens sent him, he chose the name Shane Rudraighe O'Neill. He also turned to the Gaelic in choosing a name for his daughter, Oona.

When *A Moon for the Misbegotten*, the last of his plays produced during his lifetime, was being cast, O'Neill imposed an eccentric condition. He insisted that all members of the cast be of Irish ancestry. This was scarcely a tribute to the acting profession, but his request was complied with. Mary Welch, who played the feminine lead, has told how O'Neill cross-examined her when she tried out for the part: "Are you Irish with that pug nose? What percent? From what part of Ireland are your people? I want as many people as possible connected with my play to be Irish. Although the setting is New England, the dry wit, the mercurial changes of mood and the mystic quality of the three main characters are so definitely Irish."

Miss Welch was allowed to read the part when she replied that her forebears were 100 percent Irish from County Cork.[15]

A Moon for the Misbegotten, the last of the three plays which O'Neill composed in 1939-1941, is a full-length portrayal of his brother, Jamie. The tenant farmer, Shaughnessy, an offstage character in *Long Day's Journey* who, with his mischievous pigs and his quarrel with his Yankee neighbor provided a moment of humor, reappears in this play as a major character. He epitomizes the "shanty Irish," tough, brawling, and earthy, who drink hard and "talk hard." He has a daughter who, according to O'Neill's script, "is so oversize that she is almost a freak—five feet eleven in her stockings and weighs around one hundred and eighty. She is . . . immensely strong. . . . She is all woman. . . . The map of Ireland is stamped on her face." Jamie O'Neill appears in this play much the same as he had in its predecessor, as haunted by his love for his mother, now dead, and as seeking escape through alcohol and prostitutes. The play has almost no plot, for it is essentially a portrait of a foredoomed but touching love affair between these two misbegotten ones—the giantess and the emotionally lost man—as they enjoy their brief season under the moon. The play does not quite succeed because O'Neill apparently found it impossible to achieve sufficient objectivity about the older brother he loved and mourned. Except for the mildly bawdy humor of the opening scenes, the tone of the play is too consistently soft, tender, elegiac; there is insufficient conflict to give the play dramatic force.

O'Neill's "Irishness," however, is deeper and more fundamental than the explicit choice of Irish characters in his plays. It pervaded his life and work. He was in the great Celtic tradition of singers and poets, drunk with words. He was a poet *manqué* who made up for his own inability to write good poetry by quoting frequently in his plays from the romantic poets. He had an ear for dialogue, particularly for the hard-boiled American vernacular and for Irish turns of phrase, a better ear than he is usually credited with, as he demonstrated in the talk of Hickey, Harry Hope, and the other barroom characters in *The Iceman Cometh*. Like many Irish, he was sea-haunted, his early experience as a sailor reinforcing the feeling for the ocean traditional in the sons of an island people. He exemplified the characteristic Irish ambivalence toward alcohol in his drinking habits; as a youth, he drank up a storm; but after forty he was, in his phrase, "in temperance." As his fondness for the legend of Shane the Proud indicates, he had an Irishman's romantic sense of the past and liked to think of himself as descended from a line of kings. Although he was married three times (his first two marriages ended in divorce) and his personal life was occasionally flamboyant, there remained in his outlook a persistent strain of Puritanism, deriving from a misunderstanding of his early Catholic training and from his parents' religiosity. This strain in his thought helps account for his fascination with the authentic Puritans and their descendants in New England. It is also linked with his lifelong preoccupation with the religious question which he defined in antireligious, Nietzschean terms ("God is dead"). His latent Puritanism merged with his markedly Irish predilection for gloom; the Puritanism made him think the world was inherently a joyless place, while the Irish fondness for looking on the dark side enabled him to think of himself as peculiarly fated and cursed.

"It was a great mistake, my being born a man," Edmund says in *Long Day's Journey*. "I would have been much more successful as a sea gull or a fish. As it is, I will always be a stranger who never feels at home, who does not really want and is not really wanted, who can never belong, who must always be a little in love with death!"

This Irish pessimism, fatalism and mysticism were much more profound and controlling in O'Neill's outlook than his reading of Nietzsche or his rational reflection on man's situation. It is not too much to say that he was neither a philosopher nor a psychologist—but he was Irish.

In *The Iceman Cometh* and *A Long Day's Journey Into Night*, O'Neill returned to subjects he knew intimately, and treated them in a straightforward, realistic manner. He abandoned the masks, the soliloquies, and the long asides with which he had experimented in the twenties. He made no use of flashbacks or any other juggling with the time sequence. There was no striving for mythic overtones from Greek tragedy. His only technical device was the use in *Long Day's Journey* of the repeated boom of the foghorn, a device reminiscent of those which he used in two of his early great plays, the steamers' whistles in *Anna Christie* and the jungle drum in *The Emperor Jones*. For all else, he depended solely upon his conception of his characters and their use of language.

He beautifully summed up the style of these final plays in a speech of Edmund in *Long Day's Journey*. Congratulated by his father for having "the makings of a poet," Edmund says: "The *makings* of a poet. No, I'm afraid I'm like the guy who is always panhandling for a smoke. He hasn't even got the makings. He's got only the habit. I couldn't touch what I tried to tell you just now. I just stammered. That's the best I'll ever do. I mean, if I live. Well, it will be faithful realism, at least. Stammering is the native eloquence of us fog people."

By means of this "faithful realism," O'Neill did, at the last, "dig at the roots of the sickness of today." He wrote of himself, his family, his sea mates and drinking companions, his Irish and Yankee neighbors, of his and their past. With his native eloquence, he laid bare their lives and made out of their anguish and broken love a thing of beauty.

10

In the shadow of Eugene O'Neill, there emerged an impressive group of other American playwrights, some of them his contemporaries and others a decade or so younger, whose work taken collectively over the two decades after 1920 raised the theater in this country to a new level. Like him, they essayed serious themes, explored issues realistically, and wrote freshly and with psychological sophistication. Among these playwrights were Elmer Rice, Sidney Howard, Paul Green, Maxwell Anderson, and Thornton Wilder. The outstanding member of this generation from an Irish Catholic background was Philip Barry.

There were many parallels in Barry's career with that of F. Scott Fitzgerald. Also born in 1896 and in a medium-size city (Rochester, New York, rather than St. Paul), Barry, after studying in parochial schools, attended an Ivy League college, arriving at Yale two years after Fitzgerald entered Princeton. He, too, supported himself briefly by writing advertising copy. Barry studied dramatic writing in Professor George Baker's famous course at Harvard where his play *You and I* won a prize. When it was successfully produced on Broadway during the 1922-1923 season, Barry, at twenty-six was a success in his profession, two years after Fitzgerald had made his dazzling debut with *This Side of Paradise*.

Barry was a more conventional and less tragic figure than Fitzgerald. However, since the two of them, who were friendly acquaintances during the twenties, shared not only early success but also the same blond good looks and personal charm, it was easy for contemporaries to think of them as the twin "golden boys" of the age. Barry had Fitzgerald's fascination with the rich, with the glittering surface of their lives, with the enlarged potential their wealth afforded them to lead lives that were more graceful and interesting or more desperately empty than those of ordinary men. Barry, too, was a romantic, a moralist, and an observant outsider.

He was a prolific writer whose fluency, light wit, and talent for plot invention enabled him to turn out a number of highly successful romantic comedies. At the same time, he wrote a number of serious, ambitious plays that sometimes earned the enthusiasm of the critics but were never comparably successful with audiences.

Paris Bound, which opened in New York on December 27, 1927, and played for 197 performances, was typical of Barry's romantic comedies. It dealt with the theme of divorce and infidelity in marriage, questions that had become freshly topical in the twenties because of the emancipation of women and the revolution in attitudes toward sex and marriage brought about partly by the influence of Freud. Barry took a moderate position, contemporary in tone but basically conservative. Divorce was no longer wrong in the Victorian sense, but it was still a mistake.

A young husband is unfaithful as his father was before him. Will his wife repeat his mother's mistake and divorce him rather than forgive him? A character in the play tells the young wife: "I don't mean to belittle sex, my dear. I acknowledge quite cheerfully its power and its delights. Sex holds a high and dishonored place among other forms of intoxication. But love is something else again, and marriage is still another thing."

These words clearly reflect the author's attitude, and they might easily be those of an urbane Catholic priest counseling a distraught wife against rash action. Barry's Catholic upbringing structured his moral preoccupations and provided a serious undertone to the fashionable urbanity and easy charm of his plays.

Less than a year later, in November, 1928, *Holiday*, an even more successful Barry play, opened on Broadway. The role of Linda Seton was written for Hope Williams who had scored a personal triumph in a secondary role in *Paris Bound*. In both plays Miss Williams played a wealthy young woman, gay, witty, attractive, but restless and bored because she is too intelligent to be wholly satisfied by conventional upper-class life. Since Hope Williams was in private life a member of a wealthy *Social Register* family who escaped the world of Park Avenue by becoming an actress, her portrayal naturally gave an extra fillip to the public's interest in Barry's theme.

The play has faintly the quality of a period piece. A minor character is described as "well turned out in a morning-coat, striped trousers and spats." Much of Barry's badinage has, like those spats or prohibition-age champagne, not borne up well with time. Here the leading lady and her sister's suitor parody how her stuffy father will conduct the initial interview with the young man:

> "However do you do, Mr. Case?"
> "And you, Miss—ah—"
> "Seton is the name."
> "Not one of the bank Setons?"
> "The same."
> "Fancy! I hear November cats are up four points."
> "Have you been to the opera lately?"
> "Only in fits and starts, I'm afraid."
> "But, my dear—we must do something for them! They entertained us in Rome."
> "And you really saw Mt. Everest?"
> "Chit."
> "Chat."

But this chic if perishable dialogue served adequately to record Barry's observations of the mood of the young, idle rich.

The plot turned on the differing attitudes of two wealthy sisters toward a penniless but intelligent and imaginative young man. Julia Seton falls in love with him but ultimately wants to mold him to the kind of successful businessman and social leader her father is. Her sister Linda (Hope Williams) sees that this would ruin the freshness and spontaneity that makes Johnny Case an attractive human being. He does not know what he wants, but by the end of the play he does know that he wants to take a holiday and discover himself. "You see, I'm a kind of a queer duck, in a way. I'm afraid I'm not as anxious as I might be for the things most people work toward. I don't *want* too much money.... You see it's always been my plan to make a few thousand early in the game, if I could, and then quit for as long as they last, and try to find out who I am and what I am and what goes on and what about it—now, while I'm young, and feel good all the time."

The solution Barry provided for his hero was banal enough: a "holiday" in Europe where he could think things out. Johnny Case was a Dodsworth in search of himself before, rather than after, he had waged his thirty years' war in American business. This romantic affirmation of experience as against the apparent security and smothering materialism of prosperity struck a chord with audiences during the play's long run in the winter of 1928-1929. The two sisters develop the author's theme in a passage near the play's climax:

> LINDA: Your future! What do you want, Julia—just security? Sit back in your feather boa among the worthies of the world? . . . You can't stand this sort of life forever, not if you're the person I think you are, and when it starts going thin on you, what'll you have to hold on to? Lois Evans shot herself, why? Fanny Grant's up the Hudson in a sanitarium—why?
>
> JULIA: I'm sure I don't know.
>
> LINDA: Nothing left to do or have or want—that's why—and no insides! There's not a poor girl in town who isn't happier than we are —at least they still want what we've got—they think it's good. (*She turns away*)—If they knew!

Fitzgerald made a similar criticism of the prevailing materialism when he wrote at this time: "The restlessness . . . approached hysteria. The parties were bigger. . . . The pace was faster . . . the shows were broader, the buildings were higher, the morals were looser, and the liquor was cheaper; but all these benefits did not really minister to much delight."[16]

Barry, like Fitzgerald, was a double figure: both a fellow reveler and an unenchanted moralist at the Bull Market feast. They chronicled the gaiety and foretold the disillusionment.

The angry, unhappy, economically depressed thirties did not provide a favorable background for the kind of play that had made Barry's reputation. There were seven lean years between his successful comedy *The Animal Kingdom* in 1932 and the opening of the play by which he is best remembered, *The Philadelphia Story*, in March, 1939. Early in the first act of this play about a rich Main Line girl, two characters agree about the change in outlook the decade has wrought:

"It's odd how self-conscious we've all become over the worldly possessions that once made us so confident," one remarks.

"I know; you catch yourself explaining away your dough, the way you would a black eye; you've just run into it in the dark or something," the other agrees.

The play starred Katharine Hepburn with Joseph Cotten as her ex-husband and Van Heflin and Shirley Booth as the writer and photographer, respectively, from a news magazine. It concerns a wealthy girl who, like Linda Seton in *Holiday*, is struggling to find an emotional center in her life. Her marriage has failed because of "your so-called 'strength'— your prejudice against weakness—your blank intolerance . . . for human frailty."

"You have everything it takes to make a lovely woman except the one essential—an understanding heart," her father tells her.

Not unexpectedly in a Barry comedy, she does not marry the successful young businessman or the reporter from the news magazine but, after a series of confrontations that awaken her heart, she returns to her former husband.

11

The other side to Barry's playwrighting career consisted of his serious plays, usually on religious or quasi-religious themes. As John Mason Brown wrote in the *New York Evening Post* in 1939: "That there have always been two Philip Barrys writing for our stage has long since been well known to those who have followed Mr. Barry's double life as a dramatist. One of these has been the cosmic Mr. Barry who has fought an anguishing, often arresting, inner struggle as he has gone searching for his God in such scripts as 'John,' 'Hotel Universe,' 'The Joyous Season,' and this winter's 'Here Come the Clowns.' The other Mr. Barry, the first to be heard from and the one his largest public has always doted upon, is the dramatist who has shown an extraordinary flair for badinage and written . . . charming and perceptive tearful comedies. . . ."

In his serious plays, Barry attempted to make a dramatic statement about modern man's religious dilemma: How do we achieve moral responsibility and a coherent attitude toward ourselves and our place in the universe when churches and other institutions have lost much of their former teaching authority and we are haunted by the anguishing thought that God may be dead? His concern with this fundamental dilemma drew the playwright to the ancient questions about evil, free will, and the nature of man.

Barry's *Here Come the Clowns*, the last of his serious plays, survived for eighty-eight performances and succeeded in being, if neither a box-office hit nor a permanent critical success, at least the most talked-about play of the 1938-1939 season.

Here Come the Clowns, which benefited from an outstanding performance in the leading role by Eddie Dowling and a strong supporting cast, including Madge Evans, Dora Dudley, and Hortense Alden, is a fable about the problem of evil in the world. When the reviewers gave what Barry considered confused and unnecessarily contradictory interpretations of his fable, he provided his own in a review which he wrote himself and published a week after the play's opening. "It seems to me," he began, that 'Here Come the Clowns' is an extremely simple play, as easy to understand and as clear in its meaning as any fable might be. The entire action takes place at James Concannon's Globe Theatre and in the backroom of a speakeasy attached to it. If the word 'Globe' means the world, I am afraid that is just what I mean. If the backroom of Ma Speedy's *Café des Artistes* is a small cross-section of the world, populated by some of its apparently less important citizens, that, too, is what I mean. They are not unimportant to me. . . ."[17]

Among those who gather in the backroom are a midget called "The Major"; a ventriloquist with a dummy named Frank Frenzy and a wife who is a lesbian; a dancer, Lew Cooper, who is in love with his partner but for an unknown reason will not marry her; an embittered, alcoholic press agent; and an unemployed stage hand, Dan Clancy (played by Dowling). Clancy, deeply religious, has suffered a series of misfortunes worthy of a modern Job. He is obsessed by his determination to find God and ask Him for the explanation of evil.

An illusionist named Professor Pabst, billed to appear at the Globe Theatre the following week, arrives early and volunteers to entertain his fellow professionals. "He's going to do his act—" one of them whispers. But the Professor says: "Act? I have no act. It is you who have the acts." He conducts a series of revealing interviews. The ventriloquist confesses that he stays with the wife he hates in order to save her from her lesbian tendencies. The midget tells how he and his wife had a normal child whom they gave away for adoption because the boy, at seven, had grown taller than they were. His wife died of remorse; his son ran away from his foster parents; and the Major never again learned of his whereabouts. The dancer turns out to be the Major's long-lost son; he does not marry his sweetheart because he dreads fathering a midget. Next, it is Clancy's turn for the moment of revelation. His estranged wife, Nora, appears. She confesses that she has never loved him, that she wed him only because she was pregnant, and that the dead daughter he mourns was another man's child. Clancy, who thought he had experienced the utmost in suffering, is thus stripped of his only remaining possession: his happy memories.

Finally, old James Concannon appears. He owned the Globe Theatre but has long since disappeared, and his theater is run by a corporation. Clancy had always held him in great reverence. Clancy is delighted to see him reappear because he believes that Concannon has been sent to answer his questions.

"Maybe you can tell me, sir," he begins, "—maybe you can tell me why, for all its pretty scenery, the whole earth is full of human misery, of death and tyranny and torture?"

MR. CONCANNON: You are afraid of death?

CLANCY: I don't savor the thought of it. Not while I've yet to find the meaning of life.

MR. CONCANNON: What else have you to ask?

CLANCY: Well, sir, to come straight out with it, if it's Good that rules over us, why is it Evil that always seems to have the upper hand?

MR. CONCANNON: There must be the occasions for sin, must there not—that Virtue may hold her lovely head aloft? There must be persecution, must there not—to fortify man's faith in heaven? There must be slavery, must there not—that he may know the priceless boon of freedom?

CLANCY: Maybe there must be, but why must we *stand* 'em? Why can't we fight 'em off the face of the earth?

MR. CONCANNON: Submission: it is the Will of God. All must be left to the Almighty Will.

CLANCY: The same old—

THE MAJOR: Tell me if you will, sir—tell me His reason for—for creating things like—tell me—why are—why are freaks?

MR. CONCANNON: Would you deny Him a sense of humor?

THE MAJOR (*starting back as if struck*): Oh, don't—please don't—.

Clancy, shocked at this cruel answer, thinks Concannon must be not God but the Devil. He steps toward him, whereupon Concannon pulls off his wig, moustache, and glasses and turns out to be Professor Pabst. Dickinson, the embittered press agent ("God's in His Heaven, all right, and he's going to stay there"), draws a gun and fires at Pabst but shoots Clancy, who, a moment too late, has intervened.

Clancy, dying, tells the others the answer his long quest for God has brought him: "I see now it's no will of God things are as they are—no, nor Devil's will neither! It's the will of all them like yourself, the world over—men bad by their *own choice*—and the woods full of 'em! . . . Answer? The proud will of man is me answer! . . . It's a fine instrument— the free will of man is, and can as easily be turned to Good as to Bad.

As Barry remarked in his review of his own play, "Clancy at last finds God in the will of man." But if God has any real meaning, this "answer" is only another paradox, as baffling as any Clancy encountered in his quest. However, as Barry explicates it, this paradox is understood as an assertion of faith in man: "I feel that Clancy is but one man ready and willing to go down in the battle with evil, which continues to be fought throughout the world; that all men should live and die fighting it. That it is infinitely better to die in this struggle than it is to live in fear or in the questionable security which follows any compromise with all these things in government and human society that we know in our hearts to be wrong. This at least was Clancy's answer."

12

In *The Joyous Season*, produced in 1934, and *Without Love*, produced in 1942, Barry dealt explicitly with Irish material. *The Joyous Season* concerns a wealthy Boston Irish family which has achieved social and financial success, symbolized by the mansion it now occupies on Beacon Hill. But spiritually and emotionally, the Farleys have lost their way. They have placed too great an emphasis on material comfort and security; but even worse, in Barry's view, they have lost their best Irish quality—their zest for change and adventure. One of the sons quotes their deceased father: "He knew he wouldn't be here to see how the house worked out for us. He'd let us talk him into it, but he wasn't convinced. He kept saying it looked too set, too final. 'When the Irish arrive, they turn British,' he said."[18]

The central character in the play is Christina, a daughter who many years earlier became a nun and has now returned for a brief visit at Christmas ("the joyous season"). According to her father's will, she can choose either the Beacon Hill house or the old family farm as the building for a boarding school to be started by her Order. The family hopes she will choose the farm in which they have lost interest and which is the symbol of their authentic Irish roots. At the end of the play, Christina leaves the decision to them, but in the interim she has reshaped their lives. As in *Holiday*, Barry attacks security as a goal. Christina says: "There is a look in the eye of those who follow their stars. I think they are the happy ones of this world and the next. . . . When the Good Lord made the Farleys, he had a better life in mind for them than one without adventure, side by side in a safe haven. . . . My good hope for all of you is that each will find his star and follow it."

Barry dedicated the play to his sister, a member of the Religious of the Sacred Heart. Because the leading character is a nun and the title has religious significance, most reviewers treated *The Joyous Season* as a religious play. But Barry's message, quoted above, is not specifically religious. The play is actually a study of one of those close-knit, overpoweringly loyal, and interdependent Irish families, and the point Barry is trying to make is not so much religious as racial. He is trying to tell his fellow Irish to remember the earthiness, sense of humor, independence, and other qualities that made them an attractive people in times of adversity and not to let their newly acquired money make them stuffy, dull, and status-conscious. The play does not quite succeed because Barry's satirical knife does not cut deep enough and because Christina is such an angelic figure that a few words from her dissolve the conflicts. In real life, the chains of the past are not so easily broken.

Without Love starred Katharine Hepburn in an attempt to repeat the success of *The Philadelphia Story*.[19] Once again, we encounter the rich but frozen-hearted young woman who needs the right kind of love to thaw her out. She is a widow still grieving for her late husband, and the hero is on the rebound from an unhappy love affair. They decide on a marriage of convenience, a marriage "without love." Love conquers convenience, but only after much intrigue and high politics.

The hero is an ex-newspaperman working as a confidential agent for President Roosevelt. By means of pressure from the American Irish, he hopes to get Eire's government to make its ports available to the British as bases against Nazi submarines. The plot had considerable topical interest because the Irish ports and Ireland's neutrality were matters of concern throughout the war. Barry argued the viewpoint of the growing number of American Irish for whom the ancient quarrel with Britain had been drained of meaning and who wanted their ancestral homeland to take its place alongside the United States in a time of common danger.

Barry died in 1949. A play on which he was working, *Second Threshold*, was completed by Robert Sherwood and produced in 1951, but his career had culminated a decade before his death in the season that saw the production of his best-remembered comedy, *The Philadelphia Story*, and his most deeply felt drama, *Here Come the Clowns*. Both strands in his work were just short of the highest quality. He was like Fitzgerald in his romantic imagination, and in his insight into the lives of the very rich, but he was not the latter's equal in writing beautiful prose or in the depth of his psychological penetration. However, the difference in the quality of their achievement is not so great as their contrasting posthumous reputations would suggest. People do not ordinarily reread old plays as they do old short stories and novels. The work of a dramatist, like that of a journalist, is much more perishable, and its revival is dependent on many factors having nothing to do with its artistic merit. *Holiday*, *Paris Bound*, *The Animal Kingdom*, and *The Philadelphia Story* remain important works in their genre.

In his religious plays, Barry essayed themes as ambitious as those of O'Neill, but his development of them was more poignant than powerful. He could see the issues and invent characters and situations to present them with dramatic effect, but he was ultimately not willing to explore the most painful and discouraging depths into which these issues lead. Dan Clancy and his fellow clowns never break the heart of the audience as do the ravaged Tyrones of *Long Day's Journey*.

Barry achieved a substantial body of work. He was a writer of integrity, never satisfied with his successes and not stalemated by his honorable failures.

13

Among the thousands of Irish actors and actresses in the history of the American stage, Laurette Taylor attained a high, unique, and secure place. Beginning at the turn of the century, she progressed in a long, colorful career from old-fashioned melodramas through sentimental comedies to the realistic plays of the early 1920's and, then, after a long eclipse, made a brilliant comeback in 1945-1946 as the star of Tennessee Williams's first success, *The Glass Menagerie*. Few others in the twentieth century equaled, and none surpassed, her in the range and complexity of her accomplishment in the acting art.

Stark Young wrote of her performance in *The Glass Menagerie:* "Here is naturalistic acting of the most profound, spontaneous, unbroken continuity and moving life. Technique, which is always composed of skill and instinct working together, is in this case so overlaid with warmth, tenderness, and wit that any analysis is completely baffled. Only a trained theatre eye and ear can see what is happening and then only at times. . . . She is the real and the first talent of them all."[20]

She was born Loretta Cooney on April 1, 1884, in New York City. Her mother, Elizabeth Dorsey, was the tenth of eleven children born to a couple who had emigrated from County Galway in the early 1850's. Her father had come from Ireland as a young man.

Laurette (she Gallicized her name for stage purposes) was stage-struck from early childhood. Her mother, who largely supported the family as a dressmaker, loved the theater and backed her daughter's ambitions over the objections of her pious, Puritanical husband. Laurette got her start on the vaudeville circuit. When sixteen, she married the head of a touring company, Charles Taylor, then a well-known playwright and producer of melodramas. Learning to act, she drudged her way through endless one-night and one-week stands across the country in Taylor's productions and in stock companies in the Far West. Their marriage was unhappy. Soon after their two children were born, they were divorced. For the next several years, Laurette had a difficult struggle playing bit parts and trying to establish herself in the legitimate theater in New York.

In 1912 she married J. Hartley Manners. Born in London of Irish parentage, Manners was then forty-two, and after many years as an actor in England, was becoming known in New York as a writer of comedies and romantic dramas. A man of elegant style and imperturbable dignity, he was regarded as a confirmed bachelor until he unexpectedly married the struggling young actress with two small children. Immediately after their wedding, Manners set himself to write a vehicle for his wife. He succeeded beyond all expectations. *Peg o' My Heart* which opened in New York on December 21, 1912, lifted Laurette to Broadway stardom. The play, phenomenally popular, became one of the all-time long-run hits. Laurette played it for six hundred consecutive performances; five road companies toured successfully for several years; she revived it on Broadway in 1921, and many years later it was made into a popular motion picture.[21]

The plot is simple. The Chichesters, an upper-class English family, consisting of a widowed mother, her son Alaric, and her daughter Ethel, have lost their money because of a sudden bank failure. Their only hope of making ends meet is to accept the quirky conditions of a deceased relative's will. Mrs. Chichester is to receive a comfortable income if she will instruct Peg O'Connell, a niece she has never seen, in the ways of being a lady. Peg's mother had been disowned by the Chichesters when she ran off with an impoverished Irishman. Peg, though uneducated, has a heart of gold and turns out to be the real lady in the family. She talks her cousin Ethel out of running away with a married man and rejects her cousin Alaric's insincere proposal of marriage. The naturalness and warmth of this Irish girl contrast with the starchy manners and false values of the Chichesters. Peg's philosophy is: "If there was more honesty in the world there would be less sin."

An important offstage character is Peg's father, whom she idolizes and whose admonitions and nationalistic speeches on behalf of Ireland she frequently quotes.

The play has a fair amount of Irish moonshine prose, as when Peg, having persuaded Ethel not to leave with her married lover, says to her weeping cousin: "Well, then, cry. And may the salt of yer tears wash away the sins of this night and fall like holy water on yer soul! And with the sunlight the thought of all this will go from ye."

The play ends happily when the Chichesters recover their money and Peg marries her true love.

Laurette subsequently starred in *Out There*, *Happiness*, and several other romantic comedies written by her husband. They were box-office successes. The critics usually acclaimed her performances but panned the plays as vehicles that squandered her talent. In 1921 she played Sarah Kantor in Fannie Hurst's *Humoresque*. Creating the role of the old

Jewish woman was an opportunity for a virtuoso display of her artistry. No one at first thought her suited to the part. Jews thought an Irish actress could not do justice to the character, while her Irish fans wrote, "What makes you want to play a Jew?" But with characteristic attention to detail and tireless work, she mastered the role. Alexander Woollcott wrote: "It seems right and true in every inflection of the voice, in every curl of the lip and in every eloquent shrug of the Ghetto shoulders. It is an old woman, her Mrs. Kantor. . . . In the curve of the back, in the brooding tragedy of the eyes, in the immemorial woe that is in the very color of the voice, a race speaks."

Despite the critics' praise, the play was not supported by the public. Laurette's comment: "The Irish and the Jews both must have stayed mad."

In her private life she was flamboyantly and romantically Irish. She was temperamental, charming, moody, whimsical, and outraged by turns. As Ashton Stevens, an old friend and critic, wrote of her: "She was most traditionally Irish. She loved hard and hated even harder. God loved her loves, and the Devil had conditioned her as one of the world's most amusing haters." She herself once said, "Give the Irish a miserable thought and they create an Ibsen drama."

She and Stanislavsky became good friends, but when the great exponent of the acting method cross-examined her on why she did certain things on stage, she had no answer except that they seemed "right" to her. Finally, in self-defense, she decided she did have a method and began to expound it. She called it "my early Irish method."[22]

Throughout the twenties, Laurette was one of the half-dozen leading American actresses, but as her fame grew, personal conflicts accumulated. She began to drink heavily. After Manners died in 1928, she suffered severely from the lack of his stabilizing influence. Columnist Earl Wilson once asked her about her drinking. She replied, "After Hartley died, I went on the longest wake in history." This was not entirely true. Drinking kept her off the stage for long periods, and her career went into eclipse, but she periodically worked in plays and was usually well received. One of the bright moments of this long dark period came in 1939 when she was invited to give a command performance at Franklin Roosevelt's birthday celebration followed by dinner at the White House.

Laurette, according to her daughter, "worshipped him [Roosevelt]. Here at last was a man in high office of incomparable charm and humor, who used his facial muscles, had a gorgeously flexible voice, and was a raconteur and speaker of rare brilliance. He was her ideal. There was a distinct tremor in her voice at the conclusion of the show as she stepped forward to salute him with 'Happy Birthday to you, happy patriot,'—a tremor which had perceptibly deepened when she realized she was within one word of Al Smithing her hero with 'Happy Birthday to you, Happy Warrior.'

". . . After supper, in pursuit of her hero, she failed to note the other guests mounting a broad staircase, and instead virtually crashed her way into the small private elevator which carried Roosevelt and his wife upstairs to their private study. Mortified by her mistake, she pressed her ample person against the elevator's wall and managed to stammer, 'I'm so sorry, Mr. President. I thought the others were following.' Gravely, the President replied: 'I think it is delightful of you to ride, Miss Taylor, when you can walk.' "[23]

By an act of will, she finally brought her drinking under control. She also became at peace in her own mind about her religion. She had been reared as a Catholic, but because of her divorce from her first husband, her marriage to Hartley Manners was not, in the eyes of the Church, a valid union. This fact alternately outraged and depressed her. She raised her two children as Catholics and, with superb self-confidence, considered it only a matter of time before the Church would admit the error of *its* ways. By 1944, when she was sixty, she had ceased troubling herself with the issue. "She had not returned to the Church, but had finally buried the hatchet over the Church's non-recognition of her marriage to Hartley. Catholicism and herself she now treated as separate powers, being respectful but in no way allegiant. Vaguely she felt that the triumph of her struggle against drink had won a thousand indulgences for her soul and that her passport to Heaven did not require the stamp of any formal religion."[24]

In the spring of 1945, she made her comeback as the mother in *The Glass Menagerie*. The play ran almost a year before her health, which had been slowly failing for years, broke down and forced her to withdraw, a few months before her death. Laurette's performances in her final season on Broadway were incomparable. She never played the role exactly the same way twice, but night after night she made the mother come terribly, pathetically, agonizingly alive: conniving to find a suitor for her emotionally withdrawn daughter, summoning her unhappy son to his dismal job with her morning cry, "Rise and shine!" trying to charm the hapless "gentleman caller," and always trailing, like a tattered silk negligee, the shreds of her largely illusory past as a glamorous young lady down on the old plantation.

The New York critics gave her their Critics Circle Award as best actress; she received the Page One best actress award of the New York Newspaper Guild, and headed the annual poll taken by *Variety*. That year, another Irishman was making a striking comeback and winning awards—Frank Fay in *Harvey*. His success delighted Laurette, who always spoke up for the Irish.

"Just think," she would say, "two Irish Catholics—Frank Fay and me—tops on Broadway."

Peg o' My Heart's father would not have expected anything less.

CHAPTER FIFTEEN

A Tale of Two Priests

1

THE ECONOMIC COLLAPSE of 1929 and the twelve years of depression that followed ended a world for the American Irish. The economic disasters that ravaged the industrial and commercial system broke the rationale they had lived by. Although a few Irish had become millionaires and many were still laborers, the majority moved in the great middle range of society and the economy. They were the skilled workers, the foremen, section bosses, and lesser managers, the civil servants and political captains, the lawyers, doctors, insurance brokers, storekeepers, and salesmen. The Irish had one foot in the lower middle class, but their hands reached many rungs of the middle and upper middle class. They were in many ways the people who made the urban capitalist system function, reconciling economic and political power, mediating between new and old groups in the cities, staffing the business system's middle ranks, and making its compromises and adjustments. Most of all, they were important in shoring up the values of the business community because they were the small capitalists and the expectant capitalists.

The cruel deflation of 1929 to 1941 temporarily shattered this psychology in the Irish community. At every turn, events put in doubt the unquestioned values. Small hoards of savings slowly accumulated through years of toil and self-denial disappeared with lightning speed. Mortgages on homes and on small rental properties—two-, three-, and four-family tenement houses, "the poor man's bank account"—were foreclosed. Insurance, with premiums as low as twelve cents a week on policies of $250, which had been paid for years in weekly installments to wheedling door-to-door collectors, had to be surrendered for its cash value. Higher on the economic scale, once-successful salesmen found no customers for real estate or insurance or automobiles. Small construction-company owners stopped building houses and sold their steam shovels and trucks. Foremen and skilled craftsmen counted themselves fortunate to find jobs as laborers. Grocery-store owners saw old customers go on relief or plead for further and further extensions of credit.

Families in substantial middle-class neighborhoods discovered that the big new house with its lace curtains, grand piano, and polished mahogany furniture was too costly to heat and maintain on shrunken incomes. The two-car garage became an irrelevant luxury as these families sold their Pierce-Arrows and Packards. The hundred-share stock certificate became wastepaper: City Service went off the board altogether, and Radio, which had seemed like a bargain at 260, fell to 8. What further ignominy lay ahead? Would they have to take out the telephone next? Had the long trek from the old neighborhood been all in vain? Were yesterday's dreams only a mocking delusion?

When the catastrophe of 1929 shocked and disoriented millions of middle-class and working-class Irish, the first voice calling them to abandon their old heroes and strike out in a new direction belonged not to a politician but to a priest, Father Charles E. Coughlin. Later events have obscured the pivotal role he played in 1930-1933. He was then a pathbreaker and propagandist for the radicalism of the subsequent New Deal. His weekly radio talks enabled his American Irish audience to make more easily and quickly the necessary intellectual transition from the minimalist view of the state ("that government is best which governs least") to a positive belief in an active, creative government. No one else who could reach this audience was preaching his doctrine. Al Smith, growing more conservative rather than more venturesome as the economic crisis deepened, expounded states' rights, neo-Jeffersonian views; Franklin Roosevelt had not yet emerged as the spokesman for a distinct point of view. In Congress, Irish Democrats, as bewildered as their constituency, followed Speaker John Nance Garner in his demands for a sales tax to balance the budget and an end to the "extravagance" of the Hoover administration, or they devoted themselves to the less complicated issues of prohibition and the veterans' bonus. But each week from Detroit, listeners who only two or three years earlier had been serenely committed to business community values and the gospel of success by self-reliance and individual effort heard ringing attacks on "rugged individualism," excoriations of bankers, and demands for government action to provide social justice.

2

Charles Coughlin, born in Hamilton, Ontario in 1891, was descended on both sides from Irish emigrants from County Cork.* A great-grandfather had been a laborer in the building of the Erie Canal, and for three generations the men of the family had worked on the boats on the canal and the Great Lakes. Coughlin, an only child, attended parochial school in Hamilton, and then, at twelve, went to Toronto, forty miles away, to study with the Basilian Fathers at St. Michael's College. Over the next thirteen years, he attended high school, college, and the seminary with the Basilians, and was ordained a priest in June, 1916.† From early childhood, he had been encouraged in his priestly vocation by his pious, devoted mother. In each of his subsequent assignments, he had his parents move to the parish and live near him. They were by his side during his years of fame and subsequent obscurity until their deaths within a short period of each other, both aged eighty-six.

As an undergraduate, Coughlin was a success, playing on a championship Rugby team and serving as president of the senior class. His strongest intellectual interests were literature and public speaking; classmates and former teachers remembered him for his ability to recite passages of Shakespeare from memory and his flair for acting. If Coughlin had become a Broadway star, his contemporaries in college and seminary would have been less astonished than by his emergence as a political and economic pundit.

For seven years after his ordination, Father Coughlin taught English, Greek, and history at Assumption College in Sandwich, Ontario. "My teaching of Greek was a bluff," he recalled later. "It was a very interesting experience—learning Greek while teaching it."[1]

Each evening, the young teacher was tutored on the next day's Greek lesson by an older priest. Learning with one's students is not necessarily a bad way for a teacher to do his job, but Father Coughlin was more at home in his Shakespeare course, which became very popular, and in the "little theater" group that he organized at the college and took on tour.

In 1923 Father Coughlin transferred to regular parish work. After three years as a curate at churches in and around Detroit, he was chosen

---

* Coughlin, although born and reared in Canada, was an American citizen. His father, a native of Indiana, did not foreswear his citizenship when he moved to Ontario. His mother, a Canadian, acquired U.S. nationality after her marriage.

† The Basilians, named for St. Basil, were originally what was known as a "pious society." When Pope Pius XI abolished these societies in 1923 and raised the Basilians to the status of an independent congregation, Father Coughlin chose to leave and enter parish work in the Detroit diocese.

by Bishop Michael Gallagher to organize a new parish in the then raw, half-developed suburban town of Royal Oak, thirteen miles north of Detroit. Bishop Gallagher named the church the Shrine of the Little Flower in honor of Saint Thérèse, the French nun known as "the little flower," who had been canonized a short time before. Since the new parish had a nucleus of only thirty-two Catholic families, the Diocese advanced $79,000 to finance the construction of a small brown frame church, a sum that had to be repaid. The neighborhood was tense because of bad feeling between Catholics and fundamentalist, Bible Belt Protestants from the South and the border states. Two weeks after the new church was built, the Ku Klux Klan set a cross on fire on the church lawn.

Father Coughlin decided to dramatize his difficulties. Through a mutual friend, he met Leo Fitzpatrick, the manager of WJR, a small independent radio station in Detroit. Fitzpatrick agreed that the story of a young priest struggling to build a suburban parish and combating heavy indebtedness and intolerance might make an effective radio broadcast. He agreed to make free air time available if Father Coughlin could pay the $58 for the cost of the lines between the studio and the church in Royal Oak.

Father Coughlin made his first radio broadcast on Sunday, October 17, 1926. Dressed in his vestments and speaking directly from the altar of the Shrine, he denounced religious bigotry and contrasted the religious message of Saint Thérèse, the gentle "little flower," with the hate-filled doctrine of the Ku Klux Klan. He was an instantaneous success. The years of declaiming Shakespeare in the classroom and delivering fiery sermons to small congregations in suburban churches had a spectacular and unexpected fulfillment. Since his first radio talk drew enthusiastic letters not only from the Detroit area but also from states throughout the Middle West, WJR decided to present him as a regular Sunday feature. A week before his thirty-fifth birthday, he had found his true medium.

The Paulist Fathers had used radio previously to give talks on religious subjects, but Coughlin was the first pastor to go on the air regularly. A few months later, in January, 1927, he conducted the first mission and novena over the radio. The response was enormous with mail coming from twenty-three states. Inviting those who wrote him to join his "radio congregation," he organized them into the Radio League of the Little Flower, the members contributing one dollar a year for the upkeep of the church and the incidental costs of the broadcasts. By 1929, stations in Chicago and Cincinnati were carrying his talks.

With $500,000 contributed by his listeners, Father Coughlin moved the original wooden church down the street and, on its exact site, built a huge new Shrine of the Little Flower with a blunt, sawed-off tower, one hundred and eleven feet high and thirty feet square. (The irreverent called it "the silo.") On the facade of the tower above the entrance was a thirty-five-foot stone carving of Christ on the Cross. Since the main theme of Father Coughlin's discourses in these early years was the beauty of charity, he called this the Charity Crucifixion Tower. From his office in the tower's top floor, he now delivered his Sunday broadcasts. The Shrine was immediately a tourist attraction, bringing thousands of visitors each year to Royal Oak.

The basis of Father Coughlin's success on radio was his beautiful baritone voice and the ease, enthusiastic sincerity, and comforting tone of absolute self-confidence with which he spoke. He had excellent diction combined with certain striking personal mannerisms such as a broad "a" and a rolling "r". A master of alliteration and of vivid imagery, he recharged the formal eloquence of pulpit oratory with slashing colloquialisms. Although their oratorical styles are dissimilar, his popular appeal was like that of Bishop Fulton Sheen on television twenty-five years later; and, like Bishop Sheen, he had in those years many Protestant and Jewish admirers.

Father Coughlin built his following initially by making talks on purely religious themes. An interview he gave the *Detroit Free Press* at the time he preached the first radio novena in 1927 describes the nature of his appeal:

"When one thinks of the hundreds of miles travelled by Saint Paul along the coastal cities of Greece, when one vizualizes historically the hundreds of converts which he drew to Christ through his indefatigable labors, he cannot but know the potential good which can be accomplished by his successors who are making use of God's latest gift to man—the radio," Father Coughlin said.

"Until the church services were sent out over the radio, it was difficult to believe that there were so many shut-ins in the country. The most heartening feature of the work is the letters that pour in from these people, men and women, of no denomination and of all denominations, scattered over the land, many of whom have not been able to get into the sunshine in years—and to all of whom the Novena has brought great comfort and spiritual solace.

"*We avoid prejudicial subjects, all controversies, and especially all bigotry.* We all believe in God, in the three Divine Persons, in the birth of the Saviour in the manger, and in His death on the cross at Calvary. At the Shrine of the Little Flower we are trying to put the universal credo into Christianity. Saint Therese is the modern apostle and the radio is the modern medium of preaching the gospel to all nations." [Italics added.][2]

3

It was not until three years later that Father Coughlin stopped preaching the Gospel and ventured into other fields. From January 12 to March 9, 1930, he made a series of broadcasts in which he argued that materialism and atheism had produced political evils: socialism, communism, and nihilism. The series involved him in a brief controversy with Norman Thomas, who complained against his "serious misrepresentation of the nature of socialism and hopeless confusion of it with communism." It also brought him an invitation to testify the following July before a congressional committee investigating communism. He created a sensation by using the committee hearing as a forum to attack Henry Ford:

"A year ago, on the eve of the Automobile Show in New York, Mr. Ford issued a statement that was printed on the front page of every daily newspaper in the United States, that he required 30,000 more workers at his plant in Detroit. As a result of that statement, more than 30,000 men who were out of work flocked to Detroit from Alabama, Mississippi, Tennessee, Texas, and other southern states, and, while the weather was at zero, stood in front of the Ford plant trying to get those jobs. There were no jobs for them, and the only redress they had was to have a fire hose turned on them to drive them away."

Father Coughlin developed the argument that such incidents embittered labor and drove it into the arms of the Communists.

"Getting all those men here in that manner was not done on purpose, was it?" the committee chairman inquired.

"No, it was done through ignorance," Father Coughlin replied charitably.[3]

Coming from a Catholic priest, the charge that the nation's leading industrialist was an unconscious ally of the communists naturally made the front pages. Father Coughlin had begun to demonstrate on the national stage the timing and dramatic flair instinctive to him.

In the fall of 1930, he began broadcasting nationwide on the Columbia Broadcasting System. Beginning with his first talk, "Charity—the Policy of Christ," he attacked laissez faire economics and argued in vehement, if vague, terms for a positive program to combat unemployment and introduce charity and justice into the industrial system. The number of people out of work was growing every week. Although Father Coughlin had no positive program of his own, he evoked a response because no one else was giving voice, week in and week out, to popular fear and discontent. Soon he needed fifty clerks to open his mail.

At the end of each week's talk, he announced his subject for the following week. As 1930 drew to a close, he announced that his first topic in the new year would be "Prosperity." Conservatives, increasingly angry at his inflammatory attacks on private business, protested. Radio stations in Buffalo and Minneapolis–St. Paul announced they would not carry his next talk. This heavy-handed attempt to make him tone down his language was, of course, a superb opportunity for Father Coughlin. On Sunday, January 4, 1931, he began his broadcast with the announcement that because of pressure from "sources which are altogether unknown," he would postpone his remarks on prosperity, and talk instead on free speech. Picturing himself as the tribune of the working class who wished only to speak out against evil, he deplored the "plutocrats" who hoped to silence him. In a fusillade of rhetorical questions, he asked whether he should be a meek lamb and be silent or should he preach his "unpreachable sermon." Free speech was "on trial," and it was up to his listeners to render the verdict.

There could be only one outcome in this contest between an embattled priest and the "altogether unknown" mysterious forces trying to suppress him. In the following week came the largest volume of mail he had yet received. When he finally delivered his "Prosperity" sermon the following Sunday, he had succeeded in giving it a publicity buildup greater than any previous radio address had ever had.

The talk turned out to be a shrill declaration of economic nationalism. The mood of the entire country was isolationist, and the growing number of European countries defaulting in payments on their World War I borrowings intensified the prolonged disillusionment with the Treaty of Versailles, the League of Nations, and internationalism generally. But Father Coughlin mixed these familiar ingredients into a new and startling arrangement. He placed the blame for the depression on international bankers whose pursuit of profits had produced an artificial prosperity based on private loans to Europe, German reparation payments to Britain and France, and British and French war debt payments to the United States. He condemned the Treaty of Versailles (which he pronounced "Ver-sales") as punitive and unjust to Germany, an opinion widely shared in America at that time. He warned that to save their investments the international bankers would try to drag the United States into fresh European entanglements, beginning with United States adherence to the World Court. The logic, and particularly the economic reasoning, that tied together these various opinions was less than clear, but what Father Coughlin lacked in clarity he made up in emotional intensity: "We are forced to admit," he cried, "that the Treaty of Versailles and its manipulations by international bankers has failed to produce peace in Europe or prosperity in America. . . . Perhaps this fact explains so much anxiety in certain quarters for us to join the World Court, to save some of the billions invested by our international financiers in the blood bonds born of an unjust treaty."

In the weeks that followed, Father Coughlin moved from one fresh sensation to another. He attacked Treasury Secretary Andrew Mellon for his opposition to immediate payment of a bonus to World War I veterans, denounced the international oil companies, and went on record against prohibition. His language grew more and more colorful. Describing Mellon as "the billionaire secretary of the treasury," he asked: "Why should [Mellon] insist upon being the guardian for all the ex-soldiers—he who knows not want?" Rebutting the suggestion that the veterans might squander the money, he said: "They were not asked if they would squander their blood on French soil."

Discussing what he called "the oil plot," he contended that three companies had restricted American oil production to provide a market for cheaper Venezuelan oils. He named one company as foreign-owned Royal Dutch Shell, but he did not identify the other two companies because: "I would be charged with indirectly attacking a plutocrat who is too close to our government and insinuating that he had something to do with keeping foreign oil exempt from tariff taxation."

An occasional "blind item" of this kind naturally heightened the suspense and persuaded listeners that the good priest was, indeed, fighting against titanic forces. Father Coughlin astutely tied this mysterious "oil plot" to each listener's own pocketbook: "Meanwhile the price of your gasoline has not dropped very considerably."

"The Slaughter of the Innocents," his first sermon against the Eighteenth Amendment, connected prohibition with the corrupting of the young: "Children could not go into the saloon, but the Volstead Act takes the saloon to the children."[4]

This language was too strong for the Columbia Broadcasting System. Although Coughlin paid for his air time, and CBS had, as he bitterly pointed out, made use of the popularity of his program in selling surrounding time to advertisers, the network refused to renew its contract with him when his 1930-1931 series ended. When he returned to the air the next autumn, he did so on an independent hookup consisting of local stations that agreed to carry his talks on a regular basis and at the same time each Sunday. During the subsequent decade that he remained on the air, he relied upon this arrangement, which had been worked out by Leo Fitzpatrick, the Detroit radio station manager who had discovered him as a radio personality. It is a remarkable testament to Coughlin's popularity that he was able to raise the money to sustain this venture for so long. In 1926 he had paid $58 a week to one radio station in Detroit; in 1929 he paid $1,650 a week for air time on radio stations in Chicago and Cincinnati; in 1931 his 26-station independent network cost him $14,000 a week. Although the costs fluctuated over the decade as his popularity rose and fell and the exact number of stations carrying him varied, his outlay, according to his own statement, never fell below $10,000 a week. For several years, in the early thirties, his mail averaged 80,000 letters a week, and he employed more than 100 clerks to answer it.

Although a year earlier he had prefaced his talks on contemporary issues with the statement that he did so "not with any erratic idea of degrading this pulpit into a political arena," he abandoned this pretense when he resumed speaking in the fall of 1931. Each of his Sunday talks was a political event. He commanded the attention of an enormous audience. As the presidential election approached, Father Coughlin, much more than Al Smith, Franklin Roosevelt, or any other political leader, was the most widely heard voice in opposition to the Hoover administration and the economics of the old order.

4

Although Father Coughlin had admirers in many sections of the country and among diverse elements in the population, the Irish in the cities were the hard core of his following. The cities in the East and the Middle West that carried his program were those with large Irish populations. Later, when he organized his pressure group, the Union for Social Justice, more than half the members of the Board of Trustees had conspicuously Irish names. At the Union's first major rally, the three members of the House of Representatives who spoke were William Connery, Jr., of Massachusetts; Martin L. Sweeney, of Ohio; and Thomas O'Malley, of Wisconsin.

The Irish listened to Father Coughlin and believed in him because he was a priest. With other institutions crumbling and other symbols tarnished, the Church was a tower of certitude. Coughlin knew his audience. He offered no wishy-washy platitudes, no gray alternatives. He painted a big picture, and he painted it in bold, bright colors. He identified an enemy—the bankers and big businessmen who had put selfish profits ahead of justice for all.

There was a sharp need for a scapegoat in the depression. So many families had lost their homes and small businesses through mortgage foreclosures that attacks on banks, on high interest rates, and on financial manipulations of various kinds gratified deep and burning resentments.

Repetition did not exhaust the attractiveness of the attack, nor did the intellectual confusion in Father Coughlin's presentation undermine its
appeal. If the banker is the Devil, can his machinations be denounced and
exposed too often? It was a touch of genius, moreover, for Father
Coughlin to focus most of his attacks not on the local banker, who might
seem too dull and easily comprehensible a fellow to be the source of so
much misery, but on "the international bankers" whose dealings on a
grand scale and in mysterious ways could plausibly be held accountable
for the catastrophe. He called the great financiers by name, and their
very names seemed a malediction as he intoned them in a rolling baritone:
"Jay Pier-pont Morgan . . . Bernard Manass-es Baruch . . . the House of
Rothschild."

Father Coughlin provided Irish Catholics during the crisis of the
depression with a religious justification for their strongly felt but intellectually undefined impulses toward radicalism and rebellion. The Irish
community was intellectually defenseless to meet the economic crisis.
The weight of Catholic teaching tended to be on the side of stability and
to stress respect for private property, duly constituted authority, and
rational and legal procedure. The experience of the Irish in America as
small capitalists and skilled workingmen with capitalist attitudes reinforced this passive, conservative outlook. When the economic and social
system broke down between 1929 and 1933, Irish Catholics had no body
of political ideas to explain this event and point a way out. They did not,
for example, share the socialist rationale that was a tradition in the Jewish
community. They did not share the regional explanations available to the
farmers with their Populist memories: an Irishman living in Boston or
New York could scarcely blame his troubles upon exploitation by "the
East." The Irish had once shared in a tradition of labor radicalism, but by
1929 the great teamster strikes and the organizing struggles of the craft
unions were a generation or more in the past. Several years passed before
this militancy was reborn in the new industrial unions. As the depression
began and deepened, the Irish vice-presidents who surrounded President
William Green in the American Federation of Labor were upholders of
the existing order and as much bewildered as any banker by the steady
deterioration of the *status quo*. There was, in short, little that the Irish
learned in parochial or public school, heard in Church on Sundays, read
in their newspapers, or learned from their parents that prepared them
intellectually for the depression ordeal.

Father Coughlin entered this void with energy, assurance, and an
unceasing flow of colorful, exciting verbiage. He made religion suddenly
and sharply relevant by drastically emphasizing the socially revolutionary
aspects of Christian teaching. He knew what was needed: ". . . inject

Christianity into the fabric of an economic system woven upon the loom of greed by the cunning fingers of those who manipulate the shuttles of human lives for their own selfish purposes." He linked the irresponsible rich with the atheists and communists of Russia: "The most dangerous Communist is the wolf in sheep's clothing of conservatism who is bent upon preserving the policies of greed." He took an event out of the dimness of biblical history and made it an act and a slogan of contemporary meaning: "Drive the money changers from the temple!" The words, heavily laden with echoes from a thousand readings of the Gospel at Sunday Mass, took on the weight of a command from on high.

The Irish did not need Father Coughlin to teach them to resent Herbert Hoover, who had defeated their Al Smith and then failed as steward of the nation's prosperity; but all doubts and inhibitions about denouncing a President of the United States were relieved when Father Coughlin led the way, excoriating Hoover as "the banker's friend, the Holy Ghost of the rich, the protective angel of Wall Street." This sermon in February, 1932, evoked nearly 1,000,000 letters. He used similar religious imagery in his criticisms of other business and political figures; thus, J. P. Morgan, Andrew Mellon, Ogden Mills, and Eugene Meyer were depicted as "the Four Horsemen of the Apocalypse."

Father Coughlin seemed to be bringing Christianity to sit in judgment on the economic order. If he was stronger in singling out evils and pronouncing anathemas than in rigorous, logical analysis, that did not matter. The basic need he filled was that of providing a catharsis. If his proposals for social justice were often vague and self-contradictory, this probably enhanced rather than detracted from their appeal. It enabled each listener to give them content of his own according to his lights.

5

There was one institution other than the Catholic Church that retained and strengthened its hold on the loyalty of most Irish during the depression. That was the Democratic Party. The further Father Coughlin ventured into politics, the more his relationship with this venerable stronghold of Irish power became potentially important. As long as the Republicans were in office, there was no difficulty. Democrats of all shades of opinion enjoyed his attacks on the Hoover administration. Franklin Roosevelt welcomed his open support in the 1932 campaign; the following January, when a wholly admiring biography of Father Coughlin was published, Alfred E. Smith contributed an enthusiastic preface:

"He has righteousness in his heart and brilliance in his mind."* Nor were most observers disturbed by Father Coughlin's use of the pulpit for political purposes. Since Methodist Bishop James Cannon, Jr., and other Protestant clerics had mixed in politics for years, lobbying in behalf of prohibition and opposing Smith in the 1928 campaign, Father Coughlin's sermons against Hoover seemed only a just retribution.

But the election of Roosevelt to the White House placed his political sermons in a new context. Father Coughlin could have returned to purely religious themes or limited himself to discussing political issues in generalized, philosophic terms. But he was by this time much too fascinated by politics to abandon it, and generalized, impersonal discussions were not congenial to his flamboyant temperament. Instead, he tried pragmatically to evolve a dual role as braintruster and spokesman for the new administration. But for the first he was not able, and for the second he was not willing. Not an original or even systematic thinker on economic and political issues, and without specific factual knowledge, he could not be an expert adviser to Roosevelt. Nor could he be content as an influential spokesman and propagandist for the administration. Roosevelt, an even more artful and gifted performer on the radio, did not need a spokesman; his fireside chats were actually competitive to Father Coughlin in a field that the latter had previously had to himself. In any case, Father Coughlin's vanity made it temperamentally impossible for him to be piper of another man's tune. From 1933 to 1936, the relationship of Coughlin and Roosevelt passed through the classic stages of all uneasy alliances: from cooperation to coexistence to conflict.

In the first stage, Father Coughlin warmly embraced Roosevelt and made the latter's cause his own. "It is Roosevelt or ruin!" he cried out to his radio audiences in the autumn of 1932. "The New Deal is Christ's Deal!" he told them the following spring. Roosevelt reciprocated this enthusiasm, picking up, perhaps unconsciously, the now familiar Coughlin imagery: "Drive the money changers from the temple!" Father Coughlin visited the White House and corresponded with the President.

Some of the New Deal's banking and stock-exchange reforms coincided with proposals Father Coughlin had urged. He had also strongly advocated the devaluation of the dollar in terms of gold that Roosevelt put into effect in 1933. But a crusader needs fresh causes to battle for and new infidels to slay. Father Coughlin soon repudiated the gold revaluation as a mistaken project that had principally enriched his old enemies: the international bankers. He launched a campaign to downgrade gold still further and revive the use of silver as a backing for paper currency.

---

* The book was Ruth Mugglebee's *Father Coughlin.* The preface disappeared from subsequent editions. Smith later called Coughlin "a crackpot." Coughlin called him a patron of the House of Morgan.

"Forward to Christ, all ye people! March! March today! God wills it—this religious crusade against the pagan god of Gold!" he cried.[5]

This was a crusade not without its embarrassments. When the Treasury published the list of all holders of silver, the largest in Michigan was Father Coughlin's own secretary. To his faithful admirers, this seemed merely a proof that he practiced what he preached; to his enemies, it was evidence that he hoped to profit secretly from public policies he was supposedly advocating only for the common good. Cynics called his church "the Shrine of the Silver Dollar." However, since speculating in silver was one of the least promising ways of getting rich, the incident was important not because it showed bad faith but because it demonstrated Father Coughlin's bad judgment as he went further and further beyond his intellectual depth.

Soon after the silver disclosure, the *Detroit Free Press* brought out another small but damaging fact. While denouncing the iniquities of Wall Street, he was using the services of a Wall Street broker to handle five hundred shares of common stock that he owned.

The rise of Nazism in Germany meanwhile aroused concern in this country that the same kind of thing "could happen here," and unfavorable attention focused on him. Raymond Gram Swing included him in a book, *Forerunners of American Facism*, published in 1935, in which he wrote: "After reading and hearing many of his [Coughlin's] speeches, I am struck by their technical similarity to those of Hitler."[6]

If Father Coughlin was troubled by the increasingly hostile climate of general public opinion toward his sermons and activities, he showed no sign of it. On the contrary, he seemed to thrive on controversy. In the fall of 1934, he organized an avowedly political movement, the National Union for Social Justice. He soon claimed more than one million members. Whether it was to be simply a pressure group or the nucleus of a new, third party was a secret he kept to himself for the time being, apparently because he had not yet made up his own mind.

Throughout 1935 he vacillated between friendship and hostility toward the New Deal. On March 3rd he said, "I will not support a New Deal which protects plutocrats and comforts Communists."

On March 11th: "I still proclaim to you that it is either 'Roosevelt or Ruin.' I support him today and will support him tomorrow."

Returning to the air in the autumn, he continued these dizzying shifts. Thus on November 17, 1935, he said: "Generally speaking, the New Deal and the National Union possess principles which are unalterably opposed."

On December 1st: "In this age of transition, I am for the principles of the New Deal."

Father Coughlin could not bear to yield first place to Roosevelt, but if he were to try to take his following in some other direction, he would first have to decide what that direction would be. When he publicly mourned the death of Huey Long, many observers took this as a clue that he had hoped to make an alliance in that quarter. Father Coughlin had also to calculate the risks if he decided to pit his popularity against that of Roosevelt. Many of his Irish Catholic supporters were fervently for both Roosevelt and Coughlin. Dreading the prospect of having to make a choice of loyalties, they seized upon his pro-Roosevelt remarks and ignored his criticisms. The one test of strength which Father Coughlin did risk that year emboldened him to go further. He joined with William Randolph Hearst in leading the fight against Roosevelt's proposal that the United States enter the World Court. His fiercely isolationist sermons, which evoked an enormous outpouring of mail to members of the Senate, were credited in the press with a major role in defeating ratification.

6

The floor and the galleries of the House of Representatives were crowded on the afternoon of February 18, 1936. Word had spread that Representative John O'Connor, Democrat from Manhattan, was going to speak about Father Coughlin. O'Connor, the chairman of the Rules Committee, was feuding with the radio priest, who had been attacking him for keeping the inflationary Frazier-Lemke farm-mortgage bill in committee to prevent its coming to a vote. Two days earlier, O'Connor had telegraphed Father Coughlin: "I can guarantee to kick you all the way from the Capitol to the White House, with clerical garb and all the silver in your pocket which you got by speculating in Wall Street."

O'Connor began his speech by withdrawing this threat. It was, he said, unbecoming to himself to make such a remark. He pleaded anger as an extenuating circumstance. Then, his voice shaking, he made an impassioned defense of his career and reputation. He denied he was a tool of Wall Street or that he had been corruptly motivated, as Father Coughlin had insinuated, in sponsoring a private claim bill which Roosevelt had recently vetoed. He assailed his antagonist for abusing his position as a priest and entering politics. "The man has left his calling whether he has gone down or laterally," he said.

Summarizing Father Coughlin's attacks on him, he asked: "How much of that can you stand? Just because you are a member of Congress, just because you belong to the same Church, do you have to take that?"

The House roared its applause.

Representative Patrick J. Boland, of Scranton, Pennsylvania, the Democratic majority whip, congratulated O'Connor.

"I, too, have a reputation at stake," Boland said, "and I do not propose to allow any gentleman under the garb of religion to attack me without putting up a battle to fight him off."

He challenged Father Coughlin to go to Scranton and speak against him. He pointed with pride to his Catholicism, noting that he had seven children being educated in convent schools, and to his Irish ancestry. Then he interjected: "This isn't a case of the Irish fighting among ourselves. I refuse to submit that we are fighting with an Irishman" (laughter and applause).

Representative Martin Sweeney, Democrat, of Cleveland, Ohio, was greeted with boos and a scattering of applause when he finally was recognized. The foremost Coughlinite in the House, Sweeney argued that the issue was not how many children the members had in the priesthood or in Catholic schools, but whether the House was going to be able to vote on a major bill.[7]

The following summer when the National Union for Social Justice had its convention, a group of delegates dressed in black solemnly paraded across the platform carrying a coffin marked "Representative O'Connor."

7

Father Coughlin at this time seemed not greatly changed from the friendly, likable young priest who had come out of obscurity less than a decade before. In 1935 he was forty-four. He had put on a great deal of weight in recent years, but his face was unlined and his brown hair still dark. A stocky figure of medium height and wearing rimless glasses, he communicated a sense of exceptional energy and drive. He liked to play bridge; he occasionally played the piano; he was fond of expensive, well-tailored clothes; he was a chain-smoker; he kept his Great Dane "Pal" at his side in his tower office; he dictated most of his talks and mail to one of his four secretaries, but occasionally he still composed a sermon on his typewriter. Journalists and celebrities who made the trek to Royal Oak to interview him usually came away charmed, sometimes despite themselves. The appraisal of Raymond Gram Swing, a notably unsympathetic observer, was typical of most of these visitors: "Once a caller reaches him —and he can make himself as inaccessible as a bank president—he finds him quite the human being. He is quick, intelligent, friendly, unpretentious in his dealings, leaps up and paces the floor, talks in a flood of language. He smokes cigarettes endlessly. He dots his conversation with manly sounding 'damns' and 'hells.' Furthermore, he is sincere, if sincerity means the aim of his enterprise is not to line his own pockets. But ambition preys on his soul."[8]

8

In retrospect, ambition alone does not suffice to explain it. No goal was in sight to spur mere rational ambition. Only some temperamental levity, some egotism grown narcissistic and diseased, can account for Father Coughlin's invention of the Union Party in the 1936 presidential campaign. It was a grotesque organism with no visible purpose except to serve as his personal vehicle, a function already well served by his Sunday broadcasts. Given Roosevelt's evident personal popularity, the entrenched position of the Democratic Party in both houses of Congress and in most of the state capitals, and the dismal record of previous third parties, no person reasonably astute about politics believed the Union Party could determine the outcome of the presidential election.

Father Coughlin began organizing the new party in the spring of 1936. It was nominally an alliance of his National Union for Social Justice with Dr. Francis E. Townsend's old-age-pension-plan movement and the Share-the-Wealth movement founded by Huey Long and now directed by the Reverend Gerald L. K. Smith, but Father Coughlin kept all the power in his own hands. He personally chose the party's candidates, Representative William Lemke, a maverick Republican from North Dakota, for President, and Thomas C. O'Brien, a dissident Democrat from Boston, Massachusetts, for Vice-President.

The delegates to the first National Union for Social Justice convention in Cleveland in the second week of August endorsed Lemke and O'Brien by a vote of 8,152 to 1. The lone dissenter, John O'Donnell, an alternate from Pittsburgh, made a three-minute speech explaining that he was all for Father Coughlin and social justice but did not like to see the delegates become the victims of "mob psychology" and "humbly and ignorantly serve the purposes of the Liberty League and William Randolph Hearst." Charles J. Madden, a delegate from the same district, then rose and apologized to the convention for O'Donnell's dissent. The proceedings went forward.

The delegates were not given copies of the constitution of the Union that they were to adopt before they voted it, but were told they would be able to read it in an early issue of Father Coughlin's new magazine, *Social Justice.* The constitution's key provisions established the Union's headquarters in Royal Oak, empowered Father Coughlin to name the members of the Nominating Committee and the Board of Trustees, and required a candidate for president to be a member of the Board of Trustees. The latter provision was rendered superfluous when Helen Martin, a delegate from the Bronx, nominated Father Coughlin for president of the organization. He had no opponent.

Louis E. Ward, the author of a hagiographical biography of Father Coughlin, and an unsuccessful aspirant for the Democratic nomination to the United States Senate from Michigan, drew up the platform. Except in its monetary proprosals, it was a remarkably conservative document, affirming belief in the Constitution, a government of checks and balances, and the preservation of states' rights. It protested the New Deal "usurpation" of legislative power through "must bills," patronage, and "gags" on free debate.

A highlight of the convention was a lecture on Father Coughlin's ideas on banking by Father L. A. Tobin, pastor of St. Catherine's Church in Vernon, New York. By this time Father Coughlin had abandoned his concern with both gold and silver and turned his attention to the Federal Reserve System and its power to create money based on the business loans of its member banks. Characterizing Federal Reserve notes as "fictitious money," he insisted that only money issued by the Treasury at the specific direction of Congress was genuine. This reflected a strangely primitive concept of money, banking, and credit dating from the preindustrial era.

Father Tobin demonstrated the simplicity, if not the usefulness, of this concept by means of a board containing one large electric-light bulb and six small bulbs hooked up in sockets. The biggest bulb, he explained, represented the Federal Reserve System and the six little ones the businesses that feed it. One after another he turned on the little bulbs and the big bulb glowed brighter, sapping the current from the little fellows. Then he demonstrated what Father Coughlin would do about it by turning off the big bulb entirely. All the little ones glowed brighter, and their combined brilliance exceeded that of the big bulb. The delegates roared their approval of this thesis which they had heard Father Coughlin expound so often over the radio.

The assembled press corps found it difficult to take all of this seriously. The delegates regarded the reporters with hostility. During the ceremonies on the opening day of the convention when Father Coughlin's appearance touched off a wild demonstration, one woman, shouting, "Two, four, six, eight, who do we appreciate—Father Coughlin!" beat a reporter over the head with her pocketbook and screamed epithets at the press.

Father Coughlin played up to this conviction of his followers that he and they were victims of press prejudice.

"So much misinformation has been spread about my beliefs in the Tory bank-controlled press," he told the delegates at one session, "that the time is ripe for me to reveal once and for all just what I believe and do not believe about money. I will talk in short sentences and speak slowly so that the representatives of the press will have no trouble in following me."

A great roar of boos rolled toward the press. Father Coughlin quickly assured the reporters he thought they were "honest."[9]

The attacks on the press, the muddled criticisms of the banking system, the conservatism of the platform, and the choice of Lemke, a spokesman for the midwestern grain growers, as standard bearer make it clear that the Union Party was essentially a protest by people who felt confused, dispossessed, and temporarily displaced by events. They did not want to go forward to something; they wanted to go back to the old, safe *status quo,* the world as it had existed before the catastrophe of 1929. They were small grocers who feared the competition of the big chain stores; they were small residential property owners whose rents had vanished or shrunk and who feared higher taxes; they were farmers who felt they could make a success with a fresh start if only their mortgage debts were wiped out as Lemke had proposed; they were policemen, firemen, and civil service clerks whose jobs kept them outside the rising industrial trade-union movement, whose social attitudes were conservative, and whose psychology made them fear and resent the many changes taking place in the society around them. In short, Father Coughlin's following was made up of people who wanted to be conservative if circumstances would permit them. The press, the bankers, the government were, these people felt, conspiring against the small man.

"What we strive for," ran a typical Coughlin sentence, "is not revolution, but restoration of principles shelved by the type of radical who identifies prosperity with plutocracy." Abolition of the Federal Reserve System, he argued, meant "freeing the little corner bank from the Federal octopus."

Father Coughlin's political difficulty was that he was not alone in making this kind of appeal. Since the New Deal reforms had done a great deal to rescue the property and living standards of the middle classes, many voters in these groups voted for Roosevelt in gratitude. Still others who shared the social attitudes expressed by the Union Party preferred to vote for the Republicans, the traditional party of conservatism. Despite Father Coughlin's attempt to broaden his party's appeal by running Lemke and linking it with the Townsend and Huey Long movements, there was, in fact, only one segment of the lower middle class on which he could rely: his own personal following among the Irish and, to a lesser extent, German Catholics of the East and Middle West. Even here, circumstances worked to reduce his effectiveness. If his own name had appeared on the ballot, the party might have polled a somewhat larger vote, but Lemke had no glamour or interest for the urban Irish. Nor were they really much interested in Father Coughlin's monetary and banking proposals. Crankish notions about money and banking are the intellectual tradition of the impoverished farmers dating back to the Greenbackers in the 1870's, the Populists, and William Jennings Bryan. But the Irish have never had any interest in these panaceas. The Irish in the big cities deserted the Democrats when Bryan was the candidate in 1896. Tammany Boss Croker epitomized the typical Irish attitude when, after listening to an argument on the respective merits of gold and silver, he remarked, "I'm in favor of all kinds of money." The heart of Coughlin's appeal to the Irish did not lie in his positive program but in his authority as a priest, his personal magnetism as communicated through his dramatic oratory, and his skill in venting emotion upon scapegoats.

Working against this appeal was the deep-seated loyalty to the Democratic Party. Second, there was loyalty to the new trade unions. Coughlin favored government-controlled unions and government-directed collective bargaining along corporatist lines. These opinions put him in frequent conflict in Detroit with the new Committee for Industrial Organization (CIO) trying to organize the automobile workers. Labor groups supporting Roosevelt publicized the fact that the Shrine of the Little Flower had not been built by union labor. These loyalties to party and to union were stronger among men than among women. Women voters also tended to place greater credence in Father Coughlin's political views simply because he was a priest. As a result, some Irish homes that year witnessed for the first time since the introduction of women's suffrage an uncharacteristic political division between husband and wife; the husband supporting Roosevelt and the wife Lemke.

Thoughout the summer and fall of 1936, Father Coughlin resorted to increasingly frantic and vulgar oratory to rally his following for Lemke. He called the President a "liar" and "communistic" and "Franklin Doublecross Roosevelt." He defined the choice between Republicans and Democrats as one "between carbolic acid and rat poison." But this intemperate language only weakened him. He did not sufficiently realize that much of his strength derived from his unique status as a priest. To Catholics, and especially to the Irish, a priest is a figure of more than ordinary dignity; he is a traditional source of authority and wisdom. Father Coughlin's followers were people inwardly divided; they wanted to be respectable and proper but they also wanted to rebel and protest. A priest who voiced radical, rebellious sentiments in dignified, stentorian tones and by use of religious imagery was uniquely positioned to heal this division. But Father Coughlin literally tore off his Roman collar, harangued audiences in an open-necked, sweat-stained shirt, screamed invective and abuse, threatened to beat up a reporter, and made a public bet which he later canceled that Lemke would outpoll Republican Alf Landon. When he abandoned his dignity and priestly manner, Father Coughlin lowered himself in the eyes of many to just another cheap, shouting politician. The louder he shouted, the less he could perform the reconciling function his followers craved.

"I will discontinue radio broadcasting if I do not swing at least 9,000,000 votes to Lemke," Father Coughlin promised. Since the National Union for Social Justice claimed 6,000,000—it was sufficient to send in a postcard to be counted a member—and since his radio audience was estimated as high as 30,000,000, this must have seemed to Father Coughlin a reasonable forecast.

Lemke polled 882,479 votes. Father Coughlin retired from the radio.

9

When Father Coughlin, to the surprise of no one, returned to broadcasting less than three months later, it was under markedly different circumstances. The death of Bishop Gallagher in January, 1937, took away his original patron and most stubborn defender. The new Archbishop, later Cardinal, Edward Mooney reflected the consensus among both liberals and conservatives in the Church that the time had come to curb his diocese's most famous pastor.

Archbishop Mooney almost immediately clashed in public with Father Coughlin. When the latter characterized President Roosevelt's appointment of Hugo Black to the Supreme Court as an act of "personal stupidity," the archbishop in a public statement declared it unbecoming for a priest to make derogatory personal remarks about the President. In the same statement, he contradicted Father Coughlin, who had said no Catholic could be a member of the CIO on the grounds that the union preached class warfare that was contrary to the principles of Christianity. The archbishop took the sensible position that there were communists in the CIO but that it was the duty of Catholics to combat their influence and not to abandon the union to them.[10]

Archbishop Mooney eventually invoked a section of Canon Law that empowered him to censor a priest's public addresses; he appointed a three-man board to review Father Coughlin's radio talks before delivery, but he softened this blow by appointing to the board three priests known to be friendly to Father Coughlin. When he tried to extend this censorship to *Social Justice*, Father Coughlin sold the magazine to one of his lay followers; his name was removed as editor and publisher, but his picture appeared on the masthead, and no one doubted who was still laying down the editorial line. The archbishop ran into similar obstacles when he tried to bring his rebellious subordinate's various organizations and money-raising activities under his control. It turned out that Father Coughlin had ingeniously created a complex of corporations and wholly owned subsidiaries which enabled him to maintain control yet evade formal responsibility.[11] Outmaneuvered on this front, Archbishop Mooney chose to bide his time.

Father Coughlin continued on the air for another three years, and before he was done he wrote a brief but ugly chapter in the story of the American Irish. It is true, as Richard Hofstadter has observed, "there has been a curiously persistent linkage between anti-Semitism and money and credit obsessions."[12] But in the case of Father Coughlin, anti-Semitism took the place of those declining obsessions. The extremely poor showing of the Union Party in the 1936 election apparently undermined his confidence in his economic panaceas. For a time, he drifted aimlessly, becoming just another anti-administration voice in the chorus against the "court packing" plan of 1937 and the government reorganization bill the following year. These positions placed him in an increasingly ironic and embarrassing alliance with the old-line conservatives he had once pilloried.*

In the fall of 1938, at a time when anti-Semitic virulence was reaching new intensity in Nazi Germany, Father Coughlin began a campaign of open attacks on Jews in this country. Anti-Semitism had been present as a kind of unpleasant undertone in his talks and writings for several years, but it had not at first seemed serious or important. He had put forward, for example, the curious notion that silver is a Gentile currency and gold is a Jewish currency. He had frequently attacked Henry Morgenthau, the Secretary of the Treasury, but he had also occasionally praised him.

In one of his speeches to the convention of the National Union for Social Justice in August, 1936, Father Coughlin had talked of monetary questions at length in terms of an obnoxious racial stereotype but still within bounds that could be considered reasonable:

* In 1938 he endorsed Rep. John O'Connor, by then a target of the Roosevelt purge. Reminded of their earlier feud, he brushed it aside: "He [O'Connor] has learned a lot since then."—*Washington Post*, Aug. 20, 1938.

"The first principle of Christianity is 'love thy neighbor as thyself,' but I regret to say that our ancestors in thousands of cases did not practice what they believed. We find them persecuting the Jews and driving them from every nation in Europe except the Papal states. Why? Because they were bad Christians.

"They forced the Jews to own the only thing a Jew could own when every ten or fifteen years or so Jews were kicked out and driven from pillar to post in a most un-Christian manner. Jews owned only what their ingenuity permitted them to own, really—gold which they could easily carry with them. Under this persecution the natural talents of the Jew were nurtured.

"Oh, you can talk of the persecution of the Irish, the Poles and the Huguenots, there still never was such persecution as we Christians inflicted without reason upon the Jews."

Later in the same speech, he cautioned: "Don't blame the Jews for everything. That's Hitlerism."[13]

Shortly before Bishop Gallagher's death, he and Father Coughlin made a joint repudiation of anti-Semitism. "Father Coughlin," according to the *New York Times*, "standing beside the Bishop's chair, denied he was anti-Semitic or Fascist or that he regarded the Jewish international bankers as more reprehensible than the others.

" 'They [the bankers] are all tarred with the same stick,' interjected the Bishop."[14]

Anti-Semitism, as Father Coughlin preached it from 1936 onward, was a matter of innuendo and association, not direct argument. He pictured the nation as in the midst of a great struggle between the forces of Christ and of anti-Christ. Leading the forces of anti-Christ were the communists, and his favorite tactic was to challenge the Jews of America to "officially condemn" communism. He said:

". . . We believe in the principle of 'love thy neighbor as thyself.' With that principle, I challenge every Jew in this nation to tell me that he does or does not believe in it. I am not asking the Jews of the United States to accept Christianity and all of its beliefs, but since their system of 'a tooth for a tooth and an eye for an eye' has failed, that they accept Christ's principle of brotherhood."[15]

Father Coughlin characterized Bernard Baruch and Eddie Cantor as "the two most dangerous Jews in America." He compared Baruch to a prince called Mannasses who had, he said, dismembered Isaiah. *The Catholic Encyclopedia* lists this story as only a legend, but Father Coughlin not only asserted it as established fact but also insisted that Baruch's middle name was Manasses, notwithstanding the financier's statement that it was Mannes.

It would seem that Archbishop Mooney could have done more to halt Father Coughlin's shocking descent into anti-Semitism, but he could have done so only by a naked display of his ecclesiastical authority. His board of censors did, it is believed, cut out many of the more violent passages in Father Coughin's proposed talks, but their import was still clear. Nothing prevented *Social Justice*, operating outside the archbishop's control, from publishing the Protocols of the Elders of Zion and other pieces of anti-Semitic literature long before exposed as hallowed fakes. Perhaps remembering the many difficulties that ensued when the New York hierarchy attempted to suppress Father McGlynn's preaching in the 1880's, Archbishop Mooney was reluctant to deprive Father Coughlin of his freedom of speech and order him to be silent. Choosing instead to be lenient, the archbishop fell back upon that stately ecclesiastical manner that baffles and exasperates outsiders because it relies so heavily on time and a plenitude of rope.

George Cardinal Mundelein of Chicago deemed that something more explicit was needed. He issued a succinct statement which became the standard but not very satisfying position of anti-Coughlin Catholics: "As an American citizen," Cardinal Mundelein declared, "Father Coughlin has the right to express his personal views on current events, but he is not authorized to speak for the Catholic Church, nor does he represent the doctrine or sentiments of the Church."[16]

Father Coughlin meanwhile was fascinated by the spectacle of the Spanish Civil War. To his impressionable and hyperactive imagination, it began to seem entirely plausible that a similar resort to force would be possible in this country to overthrow the Roosevelt administration, the Jews, and the communists. He began to speak approvingly of "Franco's way" and "the Franco solution." His speeches throbbed with intimations of coming violence: "Christian American forces unite to the last man. . . . Rest assured we will fight and we will win. . . . The Christian Way is the peaceful way until, all argument having failed, all civil authority having failed, there is left no other way by the way of defending ourselves against the invaders of our spiritual and national rights. . . . Call this inflammatory, if you will. It is inflammatory."[17]

He encouraged the formation of rifle clubs and quasi-military squads of young men, similar to "storm troopers," under the name of the Christian Front. "It is gratifying," he wrote in *Social Justice* (June 20, 1938), "to learn that so many persons are interested in making arrangements for the establishment of platoons 'against the day' when they will be needed. The day is not far distant—perhaps a matter of two years."

The national director of the Christian Front was John F. Cassidy of New York, and the organization was strongest in Brooklyn, the Bronx, and Queens. It tried to popularize a boycott of Jewish-owned stores under the slogan "Buy Christian for Christmas." Orators at Front rallies talked menacingly of "blood running in the gutters of New York." The Front had a considerable body of elderly and middle-aged sympathizers, but its active cadre consisted of aimless young rowdies and misfits. They had no competent leaders and caused nothing more than minor incidents.

On January 13, 1940, the Federal Bureau of Investigation raided a Christian Front meeting in New York City, arrested seventeen members on charges of "conspiring to overthrow the government of the United States by force," and seized eighteen rifles plus clubs and homemade bombs. The FBI claimed the rifles had been stolen from the 169th Infantry Armory by a reservist who was a Front member.

Father Coughlin promptly disavowed the arrested men as "fakers" and dismissed the Front as "a Communist organization designed to foment trouble." This denial of responsibility evoked much derisive criticism from his enemies. One suspects it may also have brought protests from his own following. A week later, he reversed himself: "I freely choose to be identified as a friend of the accused. It matters not whether they be innocent or guilty. . . . My place is at their side until they are released or convicted. There I take my stand."[18]

When the defendants were acquitted on June 24th, Father Coughlin predicted: "The Christian Front movement will emerge more vigorous and potent than ever."* But its time and his own were rapidly waning. When he offered as his candidates for President and Vice-President the bizarre combination of Wendell Willkie and Charles A. Lindbergh, Willkie immediately repudiated his support.

His financial support was dwindling. Contributions to the Radio League of the Little Flower, which defrayed the cost of his broadcasts, were as follows:

1937	$404,469.
1938	574,416.
1939	102,254.
1940	82,263.[19]

Because of lack of funds, Father Coughlin went off the air in 1940. *Social Justice* continued to publish until shortly before Pearl Harbor, expressing not only an isolationist viewpoint but also republishing with little change anti-British, anti-Russian, and anti-Semitic materials dis-

* This acquittal led to one of history's small ironies. The inability to convict the Christian Fronters contributed to the passage of the Smith Act in 1940, making it a crime to advocate the overthrow of the government by force and violence. This law is the basis for the conviction of Communist Party leaders after World War II, prosecutions much applauded by surviving Coughlinites.

seminated by the official Nazi propaganda service. When the Justice Department called this similarity to the attention of Archbishop Mooney, he took steps privately.[20] *Social Justice* ceased publication. Father Coughlin passed from squalor to silence.

10

The advent of the New Deal in 1933 represented a triumph for another Irish Catholic priest quite different from Father Coughlin in spirit and outlook. John Augustine Ryan at sixty-three was nearing the end of his long, distinguished career. In the previous twenty years, he had no near equal as an unsparing critic of the "lace-curtain" complex and the success values that animated the Irish community (as they did most other Catholics and other Americans). As early as 1907, in an article provocatively entitled "The Fallacy of Bettering One's Position," he argued that the "indefinite improvement of one's economic condition and the unlimited elevation of one's standard of living" were not the proper goals of a Christian society and, indeed, were detrimental to a "right and reasonable life." When Charles Coughlin was still a student, Ryan in his books *The Living Wage* and *Distributive Justice* argued the cause of social justice, urging an overhaul of the freebooting capitalist system to provide for the welfare and security of unorganized workers and consumers.

A native of Minnesota, Ryan was a protégé of Archbishop Ireland and, later, of Cardinal Gibbons. In his career he carried forward the meaning of the struggles and achievements of the two great figures of the golden age of the American hierarchy. His teaching at Catholic University and his prolific writings were a leavening influence on the younger generation of Catholic priests and lay intellectuals. He was an indirect influence on Al Smith in the shaping of a social reform program for New York. But most of the clergy and the more prosperous Irish who set the pace in the Catholic community in the first decades of this century resented him as a disturber of the peace. They reacted to his steady stream of social criticism and reform proposals with lethargic indifference. The more hostile asked the smug question, "Are you a Roman Catholic or a Ryan Catholic?" Millions of working-class Catholics never heard of him. He wrote for *America, Commonweal, The Catholic World*, but these and similar publications had comparatively small circulations. There was no national Catholic newspaper or weekly magazine that reached a mass audience and that could have provided an outlet for his views.

"For some two or three years before I returned to the Catholic University in 1915," Ryan later recalled, "I had occasionally considered the project of establishing and editing a weekly journal devoted to the discussion of industrial problems and reforms in the light of Catholic social doctrine. Since the best place for such a publication would evidently be New York City, I put the matter before the Cardinal Archbishop, His Eminence, John M. Farley. His reply and attitude were unfavorable. This is not surprising, for I was still regarded as 'too radical' by many Bishops as well as others; moreover, very few members of the hierarchy at that time [1914] were sufficiently interested in the social question to appreciate the need or the utility of such a publication."[21]

Now in the autumn of his life, his ideas had come into season. As the post-1929 debacle worsened, the number of "Ryan Catholics" grew rapidly.

11

John Ryan was born in 1869 on a farm in Dakota County, Minnesota, twenty miles south of St. Paul. He was one of eleven children born to an immigrant couple who had come from County Tipperary, Ireland, ten years earlier. His parents were pious, hard-working, and intelligent but meagerly educated, and very poor. The family lived in a small, two-bedroom house, and struggled to make a living out of their two farms, heavily mortgaged at interest rates of 10 and 12 percent. The neighbors were all Irish Catholic immigrant families. They were convinced Democrats except in 1884 when Ryan's father and many of his neighbors crossed party lines to vote for James G. Blaine.

The home had few books, but these included *The Life of Christ, The Life of the Blessed Virgin*, and a volume entitled *Ireland As She Is, As She Has Been, and As She Ought to Be* which contributed to making him a lifelong, ardent Irish patriot. Each week young Ryan and his parents faithfully read Patrick Ford's *The Irish World and American Industrial Liberator*. "One could not read the *Irish World* week after week," he later wrote, "without acquiring an interest in and a love of economic justice, as well as political justice."

Until he was seventeen, Ryan attended the ungraded public district school, where the level of instruction did not go much above the equivalent of the sixth grade. Then he spent a year at the Christian Brothers' School in St. Paul. When the legislature was in session, he spent as many afternoons as he could listening to his hero, Ignatius Donnelly. Then at the height of his powers, Donnelly advocated the social reforms desired by the farmers and the Knights of Labor. His fellow students nicknamed Ryan "the Senator."

Since his parents could not afford to educate him for the priesthood, his grandfather came to his assistance, contributing $200 a year to defray his tuition. Ryan spent the later years of his preparation for the priesthood in the new St. Paul's Seminary that James J. Hill, the railroad magnate, had built as a gift to Archbishop Ireland.

Ireland selected Ryan in 1898, after his ordination to the priesthood, to study at the newly founded Catholic University in Washington. Ryan's interest was economics. As a schoolboy, he had come across a dog-eared copy of Henry George's *Progress and Poverty*, and the subject never ceased to fascinate him. Economics was not taught either at the seminary or in the School of Theology to which he was assigned at Catholic University, but on his own he read voluminously. After two years at Catholic University, he presented as his dissertation, "Moral Aspects of Speculation on the Exchanges," a critique of the classical defense of the function of the market speculator in the economy. The conclusions he reached foreshadowed by more than thirty years the basic philosophy of the Securities and Exchange Acts.

"According to Archbishop Ireland's intention," Ryan later wrote, "I was to spend only two years as a post-graduate student at the Catholic University [before returning to St. Paul to teach]. However, the Archbishop had not made the appointment . . . before he departed for Europe in the late summer of 1900. . . . Giving myself the benefit of the doubt I went back. In November the Archbishop wrote me . . . that his failure to give me a teaching assignment was due to inadvertence, but that . . . I might remain . . . for the rest of the year. As a matter of fact, he permitted me to remain for two years longer."[22]

Out of these two extra years of graduate study came *A Living Wage*, an epoch-making book published in 1906. The book was the first full-length exposition in the United States of one of the social principles laid down by Leo XIII in his Encyclical *Rerum Novarum*, fifteen years earlier. Ryan argued that every laborer has a moral right to a living wage that will provide him with the material goods required to lead a Christian life. This moral right is founded on his intrinsic worth as a person and is second in importance only to his right to life itself. If a laborer is willing and able to work, "the *obligation* of providing him with the material means of living decently" rests upon society and, more specifically, on his employer. The latter cannot escape this responsibility by hiding behind the terms of the so-called "free" contract. "The fact is that the underpaid laborer does not *willingly* sell his labor for less than the equivalent of a decent livelihood any more than the wayfarer willingly gives up his purse to the highwayman. It is the superior *economic force* (which consists essentially in the ability to wait, while the laborer must go to work today or starve) possessed by the employed that enables him to hire labor for less than a Living Wage."

Ryan observed, "As a determinant of rights, economic force has no more validity or sacredness than physical force."

Although the employing and landowning classes have the responsibility to see that labor is adequately paid, if they fail to meet their obligations, it becomes the duty of the state "to compel employers to pay a living wage whenever and wherever it can . . . put into effect the appropriate legislation."

These views marked a substantial step forward from the opinions of Archbishop Ireland and the other progressive Catholic leaders of the preceding generation. As early as 1900, in his first magazine article, Ryan had taken the position, contrary to that of Ireland, that "the right to contract freely is . . . like every other right, limited."

After reading *A Living Wage*, the archbishop told Ryan, "I assure you I do not examine many books so thoroughly. I disagree with some of the positions that you take but not with many of them."[23]

By the time the book was published, Ryan was teaching at the seminary in St. Paul where he remained until 1915. Throughout that period Ireland, whatever his private reservations may have been concerning Ryan's liberal doctrines, encouraged and sustained him in his work. Ryan's professorship was in the field of moral theology, but he added courses in economics and sociology. They were the first such courses taught in any ecclesiastical seminary in the country.

In July and August, 1909, Ryan wrote a two-part article in the *Catholic World* entitled "Program of Social Reform by Legislation." The first section was devoted to legislation needed on behalf of wage earners. Ryan proposed a minimum-wage law, an eight-hour day, public housing, and government insurance against unemployment, sickness, accidents, and old age. He urged sixteen as the minimum working age for children, creation of a conciliation and arbitration service, and a government-operated employment agency.

The second article concerned protection of consumers against monopoly, argued for government ownership of railroads and other public utilities, federal regulation of the prices charged by industrial monopolies, federal regulation of the stock market and the grain market, progressive income and inheritance taxes, and a tax on the increase in the value of land.

Nearly a quarter-century before there was a New Deal, Ryan had spelled out its legislative program, including some objectives that it did not achieve, such as sickness insurance. In the intervening years he discarded government ownership of public utilities in favor of government competition with monopolies, an idea embodied in the Tennessee Valley Authority. Some of Ryan's proposals had been urged as far back as 1892 in the platform of the Populist Party for which he cast his first vote. Other of his suggestions were made by secular reformers in the Progressive movement. Proposals of this kind, however, had never been formulated and articulated within the Catholic community and in terms of Church teaching. Here Ryan was a pioneer. What was also unusual in his program was the blending of agrarian and urban reforms. The Populists and the Bryan Democrats had been almost exclusively spokesmen of agrarian unrest, combating high railroad rates and high industrial prices. Ryan incorporated into this agrarian antimonopoly tradition a novel plan for public housing and a plea for protection of the industrial workers.

In 1911 Ryan wrote and had introduced in the Minnesota legislature a minimum-wage bill covering women and minors; two years later the bill became law. He also took an active part in various movements for economic and social reform in St. Paul, and served as chairman of the State Child Labor Committee. Conservative Catholics criticized these outside activities. The same elements that had fought Gibbons and Ireland twenty years earlier during the "Americanism" controversy still regarded it as unseemly for a Catholic priest to engage with non-Catholics in secular activities. Rumors spread that Ryan was out of favor with the Church hierarchy or that *A Living Wage* might at any moment be put on the Index of forbidden books.

"In these [reform] activities," Ryan later wrote, "I found only a handful of Catholics who were prominent. Few were leaders. This condition I always deplored although I had some idea of the reasons for it. Intelligent and competent Catholics were willing to work for laudable objectives in a Catholic organization, but seemed timid or fearful about associating with non-Catholics for similar purposes."[24]

Ryan saw no difficulty in working with Protestants and Jews for aims he considered desirable and at the same time disassociating himself from them when they espoused birth control and other causes he opposed. He freely joined organizations such as the Saturday Lunch Club in Minneapolis. "The Club included one socialist, two single taxers, and less than a dozen Catholics. It aided greatly in bringing about the selection of more competent and more socially minded representatives in the state legislature, more effective regulation of public utilities and better social and labor legislation. . . . As for the Catholics outside the organization . . . the Saturday Lunch Club was 'a radical bunch,' but they never took the trouble to find out what radicalism meant or how the objectives of the Saturday Lunch Club compared with Pope Leo's encyclical 'On the Condition of Labor.' "[25]

Ryan in 1913 decided to seek a transfer to Catholic University where he would have fewer of the burdensome duties of seminary teaching and more time to pursue his other work. Catholic University was eager to have him, but Ireland was not willing to let him go. Ryan used friends in the hierarchy to intercede in his behalf until Ireland one day expostulated, "Positively, that man is bombarding me with Bishops!" When Ryan told Ireland that Cardinal Gibbons was interested in having him go to the university, the archbishop replied, "You may tell the Cardinal to mind his own business."

Finally, in 1915, however, Ireland yielded up his brilliant protégé and Ryan took his professorship in Washington. The following year, he produced his second major work, *Distributive Justice—The Right and Wrong of Our Present Distribution of Wealth.* In succeeding years he became director of the Social Action Department of the National Catholic Welfare Conference set up in 1920, an officer of the Catholic Association for International Peace organized in 1927, served on the board of the American Civil Liberties Union, crusaded on behalf of freeing the political prisoners arrested during and after World War I, wrote on behalf of the Child Labor Amendment, and fought prohibition.

Ryan was frequently under attack. The Lusk Committee of the New York legislature in 1920 deplored "a certain group in the Catholic Church with leanings toward Socialism under the leadership of the Rev. Dr. Ryan, professor at the Catholic University of Washington." But, then and later, he enjoyed controversy.

During the 1930's Monsignor Ryan was Father Coughlin's most trenchant and persistent critic within the Catholic community. When Coughlin first began preaching on economic issues, Monsignor Ryan welcomed him to the fight and said he was "on the side of the angels." But as the Roosevelt administration progressed, the two differed. Monsignor Ryan was a hearty defender of the New Deal program, serving as a member of a three-man board of appeals for the National Recovery Administration. For him, the NRA business codes, the Wagner Labor Relations Act, the Social Security Act, and the minimum-wage law represented the fulfillment of ideas he had been advocating for thirty years. He took particular umbrage at Father Coughlin's use of *Rerum Novarum* and other papal encyclicals to support his monetary theories and to discredit the New Deal. Coughlin liked to point out to interviewers that he was born in 1891, the year of *Rerum Novarum*, perhaps intending to suggest to the gullible that the same guardian angel had presided over both events. This irritated Ryan, the first and foremost popularizer and interpreter of these encyclicals in this country, who had a distinctly proprietary feeling about them.

During the 1936 campaign, Monsignor Ryan attacked Coughlin and defended Roosevelt in a radio address paid for by the Democratic National Committee. Ryan said he had accepted the Committee's invitation to talk, ". . . because I love truth and hate lies."

"I take up first the despicable assertion that the President of the United States is a communist," he said. "Men who make and repeat this charge apparently believe that during a political campaign the Eighth Commandment should be suspended, abolished, thrown out of the window.

"For the benefit of my non-Catholic hearers, I observe that, in the Catholic version of the Ten Commandments, the eighth is: 'Thou shalt not bear false witness against thy neighbor.' "

After disposing of these "ugly, cowardly, and flagrant calumnies," he described Roosevelt's programs as only "'mild installments of too long delayed social justice."

He contrasted his own experience as an economic expert with that of Father Coughlin. He recalled that he published his first article on an economic question forty-five years earlier: "That takes us back to the year in which Father Coughlin was born. It is more than thirty years since I published my first book, entitled "A Living Wage." At that time, Father Coughlin had not yet entered college. That book of mine was the first publication in this country which placed the laborer's moral right to a living wage upon a solid basis of principle, fact, and argument."

Saying that he had recently begun his thirty-fifth year as a teacher of economics, Ryan continued: "In the light of this experience, I say deliberately to the laboring men and women of America that Father Coughlin's explanation of our economic maladies is at least 50% wrong and that his monetary remedies are at least 90% wrong. Moreover, Father Coughlin's monetary theories and propositions find no support in the encyclicals of either Pope Leo XIII or Pope Pius XI. I think I know something about these encyclicals myself."

In graceful recognition of this support, Roosevelt asked Monsignor Ryan to pronounce the Benediction at the close of his inauguration the following January. This was the first inaugural ceremony to have a Benediction as well as an Invocation. It also marked the first time that a Catholic priest ever participated in a presidential inaugural.[26]

When Father Coughlin later preached anti-Semitism, Monsignor Ryan again did battle with him. In an article in *Commonweal* of December 30, 1938, entitled "Anti-Semitism in the Air," and in a radio broadcast the following March, he made a vigorous rebuttal to racism in any form.

Monsignor Ryan was not only incomparably better informed and more intelligent on social and economic problems than Father Coughlin but he was also squarely within the Church's orthodox philosophy as expounded by the modern Popes. He had gained the official endorsement of the American hierarchy for his social views in 1919 when a committee of bishops issued through the National Catholic War Council a statement on social reconstruction that he had written. The twelve-point "Bishops' Program," urging extensive labor and social welfare reforms, had little impact during the prosperous and somnolent twenties, but after 1930 these ideas moved into general circulation. When Pope Pius XI in 1931, on the fortieth anniversay of *Rerum Novarum*, issued a new social Encyclical, Bishop Shahan, the rector of Catholic University, remarked, "Well, this is a great vindication for John Ryan."[27]

Seven years later, the New Deal had reached flood tide and begun to ebb. Robert H. Jackson, then solicitor general and later Supreme Court Justice, looked back and said: "Liberal political thinking in America has been profoundly influenced by the 'Bishops' Program of Social Reconstruction.' . . . What suffering might have been spared to men had the voice of the Bishops been heeded by those who came to power in 1920 instead of having to wait for the disaster-born administration of 1933."

An Irish Catholic could only add that much of the moral confusion and evil that Father Coughlin ultimately caused could have been avoided if the Church before 1929 had spread Monsignor Ryan's teachings more energetically in its schools and among the laity. Father Coughlin had great impact because he could trade upon the ignorance of his listeners, invent and improvise theory as he went along, and get away with it for a time because few priests other than Monsignor Ryan had tried to expound Christian social doctrine properly.[28]

CHAPTER SIXTEEN

The New Deal: The Opportunity

Hidden within the unexpected dilemma of the economic depression was an opportunity for the American Irish. If the collapse of the old order meant at every income level a drastic liquidation of savings and of hope, its political effect was to transform the Democratic Party, to which the overwhelming majority of Irish belonged, into the nation's majority party. Moreover, in Franklin D. Roosevelt the party had a leader unusually hospitable to talents from diverse sources. Unlike Grover Cleveland and Woodrow Wilson, his two Democratic predecessors in the period since the Civil War, he was able to tilt with the Irish machines as a reformer, cooperate with—and make use of—them as a party leader, and all the while look beyond them to encourage rebels and outsiders in the Irish community who did not fit the traditional machine stereotypes. Because of the Democratic Party's success and the hospitable atmosphere of the New Deal, the Irish for the first time were able to develop their talent for politics and public service at the national level.

1

In national terms, the Irish in 1932 were no further ahead than they had been at the turn of the century. With the lonely exception of Associate Justice Pierce Butler on the Supreme Court, no Irish Catholics had been appointed during that time to any important places in the executive and judicial branches of the federal government. Early in the century, Finley Peter Dunne had written a long, angry letter to his friend Theodore Roosevelt, pointing out that the Protestant Anglo-Saxon politicians of both parties were eager to make use of Irishmen to do the dirty work of politics but forgot the Irish when it came to filling the important places in government. Roosevelt responded to this letter with a somewhat shamefaced and mollifying reply. Although Dunne may not have known it, the thrust had struck home, since Roosevelt had begun his own career as the protégé of an immigrant Irish wardheeler, Joe Murray.[1]

Occasionally, an Irish figure received a diplomatic appointment or a piece of second-rank patronage. Typical was Maurice Egan, the man of letters whom Theodore Roosevelt named Minister to Denmark in 1907 in reward for his services as an unofficial contact with the Catholic hierarchy on Church-State problems in the Philippines and elsewhere. Egan, who kept his post under Taft and Wilson, accomplished the sale to the United States of the Danish West Indies (the Virgin Islands) in 1917.

The most important Irishman in the federal government prior to the New Deal was Joseph Tumulty, private secretary to Woodrow Wilson. Tumulty performed multitudinous duties that are now taken care of by a half-dozen presidential assistants. He was a brilliant success in handling the press, the patronage-hungry politicians, and Congress, and he rendered to his chief an almost fantastic personal loyalty. But Wilson several times considered firing him, and finally rewarded his devoted service with a cold rejection.[2]

In his relations with the Irish community, Wilson did not look behind the middle-class reformer's stereotypes of the "corrupt political machine." For all his great qualities, his idealism and moral courage, Wilson sadly lacked a saving sense of humor about the human situation and his own place in it. It did not occur to him, for example, to reflect that the Irish machine politicians whom he disdained were, notwithstanding their many sins civic and otherwise, instrumental in putting him first into the governorship of New Jersey and then into the White House. The largely Irish, old-line organization headed by "Jim" Smith imposed him on the party as its candidate for governor in 1910. His nomination for President by the Baltimore convention two years later is usually attributed to William Jennings Bryan, who shifted his support from Champ Clark after the latter accepted the support of Tammany. But Tammany's swing to Clark and Bryan's dramatic denunciation took place on the tenth ballot, and Wilson was not nominated until the forty-sixth. Bryan blocked Clark, but it was a decision of two Irish machine politicians, Roger Sullivan of Illinois and Tom Taggart of Indiana, to switch their delegations to Wilson that made the latter's nomination possible.[3] Is there not something entertaining in the thought that Jehovah in bringing forward his Scotch-Irish Presbyterian servant Woodrow made use of these particular human agents? Unfortunately, Wilson's urbanity did not extend so far.

Wilson was also victimized by the narrow and uncomprehending concept of nationality that was fashionable in his time. He himself had deep attachment for and identification with England and Scotland and with British literature, laws, and traditions. This identification, the more profound because it was mostly unconscious and regarded as "natural," was shared, to a greater or lesser extent, by a majority of Wilson's fellow citizens; it was this sentiment that finally decided the nation to enter the war on the side of the Allies in 1917. Wilson was not self-conscious or self-critical about this Anglophilism because he was, quite rightly, secure in his own mind that it in no way contradicted or conflicted with his loyalty to the United States. But because he was insufficiently self-conscious and self-critical, he did not recognize that multiple loyalties were equally natural and understandable for other Americans. He did not extend to the Irish, the Germans, the Poles, the Italians, and other more recent immigrants the same confidence in their American patriotism that he had in his own. Instead, he viewed them as "hyphenates," and misinterpreted their ties of sentiment with the old country as symptomatic of "divided loyalty." The First World War brought these issues to a head, but even before the war began, Wilson had misconceived the situation. In May, 1914, speaking at the dedication of a monument to Commodore John Barry, the Revolutionary War hero, Wilson praised Barry as an Irishman whose "heart crossed the Atlantic with him." He attacked those Americans who "need hyphens in their names because only part of them has come over."

The Irish were naturally incensed at this gratuitous attack on their patriotism. There were several indignant articles in the Irish press pointing out that thousands of Irishmen had died in the Civil War to save the Union that Wilson's southern ancestors had done their best to break up. More to the point, however, Wilson's position did a disservice to his own otherwise noble concept of America and its mission in the world. If America is an idea, and not just a body of land, if Americans began in 1776 an experiment of significance to all mankind, then it was obviously in the interests of all Americans, not just those of Irish ancestry, that Ireland achieve freedom and democracy. Wilson erred in describing American loyalty in tribalistic, totalitarian, exclusive terms.[4] The corollary of this kind of "100 percent American" patriotism is isolationism, not the internationalism Wilson desired.

Wilson, it should be added, was not completely tone-deaf to the sentiments of the American Irish community and those of other Americans who identified Ireland's cause with the triumph of this country's democratic ideals. Four days after Congress declared war, he instructed the American ambassador in London to take up confidentially with the British government the question of self-government for Ireland.

"The only circumstance which seems now to stand in the way of an absolutely cordial co-operation with Great Britain by practically all Americans," Wilson noted, ". . . is the failure so far to find a satisfactory method of self-government for Ireland. This appeared very strikingly in the recent debates in Congress upon the war resolution and appeared in the speeches of opponents of that resolution who were not themselves Irishmen or representatives of constituencies in which Irish voters were influential, notably several members from the South. If the people of the United States could feel there was an early prospect of the establishment for Ireland of substantial self-government, a very great element of satisfaction and enthusiasm would be added to the co-operation now about to be organized between this country and Great Britain."[5]

As the war progressed, however, and the pressures of the Peace Conference enveloped him, Wilson exhausted his comparatively small store of tolerance for the Irish. He became impatient and bitter toward the noisier and more radical advocates of the Irish cause in the United States. Where sympathy and compassionate words would have assuaged Irish sentiment, his self-righteous strictures about "hyphenated Americans" served only to enflame opinion and estrange a substantial section of Irish support that could have been retained. Irish dissatisfaction with the Wilson administration's record on Ireland contributed importantly to the defeat of the Democratic presidential ticket in the large cities in 1920. Warren Harding, the Republican candidate, made unprecedented inroads, carrying Boston by 40,000 votes and New York City by 434,000.

2

During the dozen years of normalcy that intervened between Wilson and Franklin Roosevelt, the Irish remained out of the national picture as successive Republican administrations failed to make any effort to broaden their party's base. The only two Irish politicians of note in the Grand Old Party during these years were William J. "Wild Bill" Donovan and Patrick J. Hurley. Donovan, a World War I hero, an outstanding federal prosecutor in western New York, and later an Assistant Attorney General, was inexplicably passed over by his good friend Herbert Hoover for the post of Attorney General in 1929. Hurley, an Oklahoma lawyer and oilman, was Secretary of War in the Hoover Cabinet. The successful careers of Donovan and Hurley had no perceptible impact on the political course of the American Irish community. Oddly enough, these two colorful Irishmen were among Franklin Roosevelt's favorite Republicans; both saw important service during World War II, Donovan as the head of the Office of Strategic Services and Hurley on missions to Russia and China.

The emotion of the Irish community was overwhelmingly invested in the futile attempts of 1924 and 1928 to place Al Smith in the White House. More than one Irishman lowered his head and wept when that dream finally died at the Chicago convention in July, 1932. (Defeated, and the deed performed by that ancient enemy, William Gibbs McAdoo!) But the younger men, those born in the decade from 1890 to 1900, and including some who had wept for Smith, were quick to respond to the challenge the new leader and the New Deal offered. They were the contemporaries in political life of the literary men—Eugene O'Neill, F. Scott Fitzgerald, Philip Barry—who had already come to prominence in the 1920's, literary success being more readily achieved by the young than other kinds of success. Over the next twenty years, the Irish of that generation comprised a brilliant company of public servants. They were active in many and various fields, including party management, organizing and staffing the new administrative agencies, running the Congress, and in law, diplomacy, and national defense. There was Thomas G. Corcoran of Rhode Island, born in 1900, the most gifted and versatile of the New Deal "brain trusters," and for several years Roosevelt's indefatigable quarterback. John McCormack, born in 1891, and Joseph E. Casey, born in 1898, both of Massachusetts, became two of Roosevelt's most effective and dependable lieutenants in the House of Representatives. James A. Farley, born in 1888 and the oldest of this group, and Edward J. Flynn, born in 1892, both New Yorkers but with quite different styles, became the ablest national party managers of their day. Joseph P. Kennedy, born in 1888, made real an old American Irish dream by becoming ambassador to Great Britain. (He later presided over the fulfillment of an even more splendid American Irish dream.) Frank Murphy, born in Michigan in 1890, was a successful Governor-General of the Philippines, Governor of Michigan, and Attorney General.

These and others like them, men in their thirties and early forties when Roosevelt came to power in 1933, were the first generation of American Irish to play significant roles on the national stage. For them and for the American Irish community as a whole, the economic breakdown of 1929-1933 afforded the occasion for a major breakthrough from the provincial confines of city and state politics. None of these figures became a real presidential possibility, but as a group they made possible the transition from Al Smith to John F. Kennedy.

3

Franklin Roosevelt's choice for Attorney General was Senator Thomas Walsh of Montana, for twenty years one of the dominating figures of the Senate. Walsh, a man of formidable talent as a lawyer, possessed rigorous integrity and uncompromising liberalism. Almost singlehanded, he had broken the Teapot Dome scandal. He had exposed the dubious practices of lobbyists for various industries seeking higher tariffs. During A. Mitchell Palmer's "red scare" after the First World War, Walsh had championed the rights of radicals and dissenters. Throughout the conservative, isolationist years of Harding and Coolidge, he was one of the few in public life who kept alive the liberalism and internationalism of the Wilsonian period, campaigning for the Child Labor Amendment to the Constitution and for United States adherence to the World Court.[6]

When the offer came from Roosevelt early in 1933 to join the Cabinet, Walsh's only reluctance stemmed from his concern that the new President might not be a convinced liberal.

Confiding his fears to a friendly newspaper correspondent, he said: "Do you think he is tough enough? Will he stick with it when the going is hard?"[7]

He overcame his doubts, and accepted. He was then seventy-three, picturesque with his sweeping white moustache, craggy white eyebrows, and dark, alert eyes, but tired and worn from his years of public work. Two days before the inauguration, he died.

The remaining Irishman in the new administration was its political gatekeeper and general panjandrum, a big, strapping six-footer of wide girth, bald dome, and warm smile. Not yet forty-five, James Aloysius Farley from Grassy Point, New York, was Postmaster General, chairman of the Democratic National Committee, and, though he did not suspect it then, at the peak of his power. Farley, in his physiognomy, his geniality, his genius for organization, and his enormous capacity for work, personified the popular stereotype of a likable Irish politician. He made the national chairmanship for the first time under any administration a command post of power and influence. He thereby inadvertently also created the tradition in the Democratic Party that the office normally go to an Irish Catholic. It had, in fact, not previously been an Irish or a Catholic monopoly.

Farley grew up in Grassy Point, a Hudson River town thirty-five miles outside New York City. After his father died when Farley was eleven, his mother ran a combination grocery store and saloon, but like many other Irish mothers had a low opinion of the uses of whiskey. Her son tended bar after school, but under her influence he became a confirmed teetotaler. After high school he worked as a bookkeeper and then joined the United States Gypsum Company where he became a star salesman of building materials. Inheriting his ardent Democratic faith from his parents, he was electioneering for the party before he could vote. Although Grassy Point was a Republican town, Farley was elected town clerk. Most of the compensation of the office consisted of fees from persons who wanted a license to hunt, fish, get married, or own a dog. Farley needed the money, but he was ambitious, shrewd, and self-controlled. He refunded his share of the license fee to the purchaser and each time, of course, won a friend. "Although . . . the added funds would have been most welcome," Farley later recalled, "I was far more concerned about building a political future than I was about cash on hand."[8]

In 1918, when he was thirty, he was elected chairman of the Rockland County Democratic Committee, which gave him membership in the gatherings of the state party leaders. Five years later, Al Smith appointed him to the State Boxing Commission, where he promptly annexed the chairmanship. The incumbent chairman was George F. Brower, while the third member was William Muldoon, a former wrestler and athletic promoter who had suffered a stroke and at nearly eighty years of age was no longer at his mental best. The commission met formally on Tuesdays and sometimes informally on Friday. A few months after Farley went on the commission, Brower went to the hospital for an operation. That Friday Farley met with Muldoon and emerged from the meeting to inform reporters that the Boxing Commission had a new chairman—Mr. Farley.

"We decided," he explained, "that it would be wise to rotate the chairmanship."

Brower expostulated from his hospital bed that the Friday session was not a regular meeting of the commission.

Farley turned aside all complaints with a bland smile.

"I have only the highest regard for Mr. Brower and the manner in which he discharged the duties of his office," was his only comment.

Brower grumbled, "At least he could have waited until I came out of the ether."

The chairmanship never rotated again. Farley subsequently explained that the rotating system was considered a failure and that it was better to have a permanent chairman.

The Boxing Commission paid no salary, but it was an excellent opportunity to do favors by passing out complimentary tickets to fights. Farley "made the life of the fight-promoter one of constant anguish" in his zeal to get passes for friends. For one championship match, he was said to have passed out $30,000 worth of free tickets, prompting promoter Tex Rickard to remark, "Jim, you give me back the 'Annie Oakleys' and I'll give you back the fight."[9]

When he could not get passes, Farley bought tickets and distributed them to friends. Rickard's published figures for the Dempsey-Sharkey fight in 1927 listed Farley as buying $9,024 in tickets. They were worth much more if sold to speculators, but again Farley was more interested in winning friends than making a financial profit.

The Boxing Commission was often in the news in the late 1920's, not always in a favorable sense. The famous sportswriter W. O. McGeehan dubbed the commissioners "The Three Dumb Dukes." But Farley took it all good-naturedly. His name and picture were in the newspapers, and he was making friends.

By 1928 Farley had organized his own building-supplies company and was secretary of the Democratic State Committee, running Franklin Roosevelt's campaign for governor from headquarters in the Hotel Biltmore. Farley developed a much closer relationship with Roosevelt than he had ever had with Smith, who regarded him as a good-natured country boy, willing but not very bright. Smith had dealt with thousands of Irish political workers, and Farley did not seem notably impressive to him. Smith could also be brusque and arrogant. Farley privately resented the treatment he sometimes received at his hands. Roosevelt was more perceptive. He saw in Farley a capable organization man with a wide personal acquaintance yet one not tied personally to Smith nor identified with Tammany. Farley responded to Roosevelt's confidence. It was only much later that he began to believe that Roosevelt was also condescending to him in another, more subtle sense.

By 1930 Farley was state chairman. When Roosevelt won reelection as governor by a majority nearly twice as big as Smith had ever polled, Farley announced, "I do not see how Mr. Roosevelt can escape becoming the next presidential nominee of his party."

The next spring Farley began crisscrossing the country, talking to party leaders. He was a member of the Elks, and he informed the curious that he was on his way to a convention of that fraternal organization or just looking up an old Elk here and there. No one was misled by this explanation, but then Farley had not expected otherwise. Returning from his travels, he dictated between six thousand and seven thousand letters to people he had met, always careful to add some personal reference to show it was not a form letter. He wrote to every county chairman in the country, whether friendly to Roosevelt or not, asking him to keep Farley informed on opinion in his district. His indefatigable energy, highly developed memory for names, faces, and personal details, and his tireless letter writing enabled him to organize the best political intelligence system in the nation. It was a vital component of Roosevelt's success at the convention and in the election.

After the bitter falling-out between the two men ten years later, their respective partisans argued the merits and importance of Farley's work. Farley's friends insisted, in effect, that he had put Roosevelt in the

White House and contributed greatly to keeping him there. Roosevelt's admirers countered that with a candidate of his quality, any political manager could have accomplished what Farley did. It is a meaningless debate. Farley was "selling" an extraordinary candidate, but his services to Roosevelt in the preconvention period and during the early years of the new administration were indispensable in the sense that it was necessary that someone perform them, and with comparable skill and devotion. The best candidate cannot win without assistance of the kind Farley provided. If Farley had not existed, Roosevelt would have had to invent him.

Farley's record as Postmaster General was on a level with most of those who have occupied that routine office. His notable contribution was to boom the sale of new issues of stamps. This promotion of postal business was not without its pitfalls. The department issued a commemorative stamp of "Whistler's Mother" only to discover that someone had thoughtfully added a basket of flowers to the portrait. Farley had to act swiftly to retrieve the art critic vote.

Farley's real work lay elsewhere. His first task was to mediate between the administration and the local party organizations in the dispensing of thousands of federal jobs. Although hostile critics pictured him ravaging the civil service, and coined the term "Farleyism," he handled patronage astutely and without serious embarrassments and scandals.

It is one task to distribute the patronage, but an undertaking of another dimension to make use of it in behalf of the legislative program of an administration with a far-reaching reform program. The Democratic Party in 1933 was by no means a uniformly liberal organization. Many of its elements had little or no enthusiasm for the social changes the White House proposed. Farley coordinated his patronage maneuvers and organization work in the states with the legislative ends of the administration. He was for several years a tactful and effective emissary on Capitol Hill. He helped make the conventional political system operate in the interests of the New Deal.

Farley's third contribution was to build up and hold together the party in the country. In many states before 1930, the Democrats were only a "post-office party" of negligible importance. In many areas the Democrats entered no candidates for local and county offices and state legislatures. Counterbalancing these states were the big city organizations in the East and North, tied to the administration by party loyalty and tradition but not by intellectual commitment or personal sympathy. Farley kept open a channel of communication to Washington for the city machines while he also did much to stimulate party organizational work in the "virgin" states. It was this latter side of his job, what Roosevelt called "Jim's missionary work," that Farley liked best. A nonsmoker and nondrinker, he did not find the smoking-car conviviality of conventions and hotel room caucuses to his taste; he was easily bored by the endless palaver. But traveling through the country and meeting individuals with his big smile and vigorous handshake, he was the successful salesman. Back in his Washington office, a huge room with ornate walnut panels, seated at his desk cluttered with mementos, including a picture of himself when he was twenty-three, bearing the inscription, "Presented to Jim, himself, in memory of his hair, Franklin D. Roosevelt," signing endless letters in green ink—"Sincerely, Jim," and chewing gum all the while, he was the high priest of a flourishing new order of which Roosevelt was the prophet and loyalty the creed. Letters of encouragement, approbation, congratulations, advice, polite refusal, and firm direction flowed from his office. "It was good to see you with Joe in Kansas City. . . . I remember your two fine sons. . . ." Only the splashing of the fountain in the courtyard below matched the steady flow of green ink.

4

If there was one figure other than Franklin D. Roosevelt himself who personified the idealism and toughness, the intellectual stylishness and operational verve of the middle years of the New Deal, it was Thomas Gardiner Corcoran. "Tommy the Cork" wrote presidential speeches, drafted laws, pressured congressmen, recruited talent for government agencies, deployed task forces on special problems, connived with friendly newsmen to advance administration objectives in the press, and generally inspired, calculated, cajoled, and advised. A President is many men, and Corcoran was several of them. The New Deal years were a period when the purposes of government were freshly defined, when intelligence was applied to the solution of social problems in a more direct, concentrated way than for some generations past; government became an exciting affair, a creative enterprise, an occasion for total commitment. In that time of all-night huddles, numerous speech drafts, long-distance telephone calls, and recurrent crises, Corcoran functioned at the top of his powers. He had a taste for power and the opportunity for its exercise: he asked for nothing more.

Corcoran, Irish Catholic on his father's side and of pre-Revolutionary Yankee stock on his mother's, was born in Pawtucket, Rhode Island, on December 29, 1900. A brilliant student throughout his school days, he won numerous prizes and medals, was valedictorian of his class at Brown

University, barely missed out on a Rhodes Scholarship, graduated first in his class at Harvard Law School, stayed to take a master's degree in jurisprudence, and served a year as law clerk to Justice Oliver Wendell Holmes. False modesty, it was observed, never afflicted him. When he was Note Editor of the *Harvard Law Review*, he once remarked: "I just wrote a Note that will be quoted by the Supreme Court someday."

Since Pawtucket obviously offered insufficient scope for his talents, and Washington under Calvin Coolidge's regime was something less than stimulating, Corcoran turned naturally to Wall Street, the nation's power center in the 1920's. He spent five years there as an employee in Cotton & Franklin, a major corporate law firm. He saw Wall Street, as he liked to recall later, "at its top and its bottom—two years of boom and three years of bust." But Wall Street in either condition was not enough to preoccupy all his mind and energy. Corcoran, with his Irish schoolmaster's passion for explaining things to others, had partially supported himself at Harvard by giving private lectures to less bright students; he now kept himself busy finding jobs for classmates and protégés and pushing the careers of friends. He also read the classics, wrote unpublished poetry, learned to play the guitar, accordion, and piano, mastered the entire repertoire of Gilbert and Sullivan, and his own repertoire as an amateur chef. An outdoorman who skied, climbed mountains, and once served as Trail Master for the Appalachian Mountain Club, Corcoran was an accomplished man whose energy, charm, and social gifts were as impressive as his intellectual power and played an important part in his subsequent success.

Corcoran arrived in Washington ahead of the New Deal. When the Reconstruction Finance Corporation was organized under the Hoover Administration in 1932, the senior partner of Cotton & Franklin was asked to recommend young attorneys for the new agency, and Corcoran was one of those he proposed. During his eight years in government service, from 1932 to 1940, Corcoran never left this agency and never held any higher post than that of assistant general counsel. It was an anomaly of the New Deal that one of its half-dozen key figures held such an inconspicuous post. But the obscurity and comparatively limited duties of Corcoran's job had consequent advantages. Beginning in 1934, when his work came to Roosevelt's attention and he began his spectacular rise in influence, Corcoran was enabled to roam freely from one task to another or, more exactly, superintend several at once, and remain unencumbered by the formal responsibilities of a job higher in the government hierarchy.

Corcoran had a "roving commission" from Roosevelt to deal with diverse problems that could not be confined in any single department or agency. Several of the New Deal programs were not suitable for administration by existing agencies, either because they cut across bureaucratic lines of authority or because the old agencies could not be relied upon to bring to them the requisite enthusiasm and imagination. For those reasons, new agencies had to be invented to execute them. Corcoran, with the help of his law-school professor Felix Frankfurter, recruited talent for these new agencies. Among those hostile to the New Deal, this network of allies came to be known alternately as Frankfurter's "happy hot dogs" or Corcoran's OGPU. It was, in fact, a remarkably flexible *ad hoc* invention for coping with the manpower problems of government in a time of rapid expansion and of problems without precedents. Corcoran, by a few telephone calls to friends, could pull together a group of lawyers and other experts on a few hours' notice to draft a bill, a set of regulations, a speech, or a statement for a congressional hearing. This was particularly necessary prior to 1939 when Congress finally passed an administrative reorganization act giving the President, for the first time, an adequate White House staff.

Corcoran formed with Benjamin V. Cohen an informal partnership, thus bringing to the national scene the combination of an Irishman and a Jew that had earlier become familiar in the ethnic alliances of local politics, law, and the stage. Cohen, the son of a scrap-iron merchant in Muncie, Indiana (made famous as "Middletown, U.S.A."), was six years older than Corcoran, had been a brilliant student at the University of Chicago Law School, had also taken a postgraduate year at Harvard and practiced law on Wall Street during the 1920's. The two first met in the winter of 1933-1934 when they helped James M. Landis draft the Securities and Exchange Act regulating the stock market. They soon were inseparable. On the surface it was a striking example of the proverb that opposites attract: Cohen, tall, thin, somewhat shy and retiring, chain-smoking cigarettes and dribbling ashes down his rumpled clothes, bemused and philosophical in manner; Corcoran, short, tending toward stoutness, a nonsmoker who fueled himself on endless cups of coffee, aggressive, voluble, and extroverted. But underneath, the two were fundamentally the same: first-class minds that could master the intricate details of a law or a contract and that also had a taste for speculation about men and history. Basically, they were idealists, but they tried to gird their ideals and their optimism with a protective edge of cynicism as became two worldly young realists.[10]

5

The access of the Irish to power in Washington was first and most visibly evident in the halls of Congress. The political revolution brought on by the depression converted many traditionally Republican states in New England, the Midwest, and Far West to the Democratic side. In almost every instance, Irish politicians were the chief gainers. The Irish had maintained their stubborn commitment to the Democratic Party through the long decades of its minority life in states where it rarely won an election. When the upheavals of the depression put the party in the majority, the Irish were priority claimants. The elections of 1930, 1932, 1934, and 1936 saw a growing number of Irish senators and con-gressmen coming to Washington, sometimes as the first Democrats from their areas in half a century or more. In 1932 the voters elected to the Senate Augustine Lonergan in Connecticut, Ryan Duffy in Wisconsin, and Pat McCarran in Nevada; two years later, Nebraska sent Edward R. Burke, and Wyoming, Joseph O'Mahoney. Some of the Irish Demo-crats elected in these landslides, particularly in the Midwest, were only one-termers, but in other areas, such as southern New England, Pennsyl-vania, and the Rocky Mountain States, the revolution was consolidated.

Typical of the local revolutions that were sending new young Demo-crats to Congress was the development in the Third District in Mas-sachusetts. Boston had for two generations been an Irish Democratic stronghold, but outside the metropolis Massachusetts was barren country for Democrats. State tickets were heavily weighted with Boston Irish candidates; these local figures from Roxbury or South Boston spoke conventionally of "carrying the campaign from the sandy shores of Cape Cod to the rocky heights of the Berkshires." But these candidates, in fact, were rarely seen in the "Yankee country" beyond Boston. The third District was typical of several in the middle and western portions of the state. The largest community did not exceed twenty thousand people. The Yankee farmers working thin, unproductive soil earned a modest living from the growing of hay and apples and the raising of dairy cattle. The towns were crossroads trading centers where the farmers shopped on Saturdays, attended band concerts on the green on a summer evening, and worshiped in the white clapboard churches with their prim steeples rising above maples and elms planted in Revolutionary days. There were many Irish and lesser numbers of Italians, Poles, and French Canadians working in the textile mill towns, but socially they kept to themselves and politically they were a minority.

Joseph Casey was a native of Clinton, the largest of the Irish mill towns in central Massachusetts. His people were factory workers, one generation removed from the immigrant adventure. He was the first of his family to break away from the mill. In public school he had been a bright student and accomplished athlete. After high school he went to Boston University Law School, passed the bar, and began practice. It was 1921, and he was then twenty-three. He was an ardent Democrat but even more he was a convinced liberal. In 1924, when the Democrats nominated Wall Street lawyer John W. Davis for President, Casey was running for Congress. (It was easy for a young Democrat to obtain the nomination in this overwhelmingly Republican district.) He stumped not for Davis but for Robert La Follette, the Progressive Party candidate. He spoke at factory gates and in lodge halls, exhorting apathetic audiences to vote for La Follette because he would give the workingman and the small farmer a decent break. It was a hopeless cause. Since "Silent Cal" Coolidge, Massachusetts' own Yankee son, was the Republican candidate, the farmers were solidly behind him. The culturally isolated mill-town workers had previously scarcely heard of La Follette. Coolidge won by 500,000 votes. Casey, like most other Democrats that year, went down to a smothering defeat.

For the next decade Casey devoted himself to his increasingly success-ful practice as a trial lawyer. He was active in the campaigns of Senator David I. Walsh, a fellow townsman who in 1914-1915 had been the state's first Catholic governor. Walsh had been elected to the Senate in 1918 with the aid of Republicans and independents favoring Wilson's international program. Once in the Senate, however, Walsh feared to brave the storm of Irish denunciation of Wilson. He turned his back on the League of Nations. He also became an exponent of protectionist dogma—"high tariffs mean high wages." This retreat from internation-alism was the watershed in Walsh's career, but this was to become clear only in retrospect. His pro-labor record and his attacks on prohibition served him well; throughout the twenties, he was the only Democrat to gain success in Massachusetts politics.

In 1934 Casey ran for Congress again in the Third District. Frank Foss, the same stalwart Republican conservative who had defeated him ten years earlier, was unworried. He showed up one day at Casey's headquarters, inspected the office, and congratulated his opponent's workers for their civic spirit, expressing the opinion that working in a campaign was always a profitable experience for a young man. The spirit of the New Deal was pervasive, however, and everywhere it was undermining the hold of the stalwarts. Casey traveled the winding country roads and across the bleak hills that autumn, visiting with farmers in their fields and talking with housewives in their kitchens. When the returns came in on election night, he was victorious by three hundred votes, the first Democrat elected to Congress in the history of the dis-trict.

Casey rapidly made his mark in the House as an articulate and resolute exponent of the New Deal program. He played an active part in support of the minimum wage-and-hour law, social security, public housing, and other social welfare legislation. He proved to be one of the very few New England congressmen willing to attack the private power companies that had long been politically sacrosanct in the region. He championed the rural electrification program and worked to popularize it among farmers in Massachusetts. He regularly voted for Tennessee Valley Authority appropriations, although the TVA was unpopular in New England because its cheap power rates supposedly drew industry away from the North. After the disastrous New England floods of 1937, he and Senator Frederick Brown of New Hampshire introduced the Brown-Casey bill to create a Connecticut River Valley Authority that would construct multiple-purpose dams for flood control, hydroelectric power, and prevention of soil erosion. President Roosevelt endorsed the plan, but the private power companies blocked its passage. Had the bill become a law, the New England States might not have suffered from recurring floods such as that in 1955, which inflicted over $1,000,000,000 damage. When Representative Martin Dies of Texas began to go on the rampage, Casey at the request of the House leadership accepted the disagreeable assignment to the House Un-American Activities Committee. There, for two years, he waged an uphill struggle to protect the rights of witnesses and keep Dies's investigations on the track. Casey broke with the high-tariff and isolationist policies of David I. Walsh, voting for reciprocal trade and the repeal of the neutrality laws. By 1940 Casey had become a valued and trusted friend of Roosevelt and one of the administration's half-dozen principal lieutenants on the House floor and in the Appropriations Committee.

Casey meanwhile steadily strengthened his political position in the Third District. In two successive, hard-fought campaigns, he increased his majorities. By 1940 he was so uniformly popular that he entered both the Democratic and Republican primaries. Massachusetts, like California, permitted cross-filing, but it was an uncommon practice since the party divisions were sharp and well defined. Casey startled the Republicans by almost capturing their nomination. The next year the Republican legislature banned cross-filing. At the same time, the opposition conceded Casey was unbeatable. The legislature in redistricting the state added Democratic towns from neighboring Republican districts and established the Third District as overwhelmingly Democratic. Casey, in a half-dozen years, had converted his area from a Republican to a Democratic stronghold. Now, at forty-two, he had a safe seat and could, if he wished, look forward to a long career in the House.

John W. McCormack (who in 1961 became Speaker of the House) was Casey's close friend. McCormack, several years older, had been elected to the House in 1926 from a safely Democratic district in

Boston. With the Irish politician's usually acute sense of where the power lies, McCormack had recognized that in the House his party was predominantly a southern institution. He chose to live in the Washington Hotel, the residence of John Nance Garner of Texas and other southern congressmen. Unlike most northern big-city representatives who are members of the "in Tuesday–out Thursday Club," McCormack spent his weekends in Washington. He devoted himself assiduously to his committee work, developed friendships, and soon was as much a master of parliamentary tactics and lore as the most professional Southerner.* McCormack was instrumental in rounding up northern votes to elect Representative Sam Rayburn, Garner's protégé, as majority leader in 1937 in a bitter contest against the reactionary John O'Connor of New York. When Rayburn became Speaker three years later, McCormack was the natural choice to succeed him as majority leader.

McCormack gave the New Deal domestic legislative program strong and sustained support. Like Casey, he, too, broke with the isolationism that had been traditional with the Massachusetts Irish after the League of Nations debacle of 1919-1920 and that Walsh, the state's senior senator, symbolized. While Walsh was a leading speaker for the isolationist America First Committee, McCormack introduced the Lend-Lease bill in the House and managed its passage on the floor; he voted for Selective Service and otherwise supported Roosevelt's interventionist foreign policy. Later, in the post–World War II period, he was to lead the fight for the British loan of 1946, the Marshall Plan, and other internationalist measures.

Casey's break with Walsh was more spectacular because he was the latter's fellow townsman and had been his protégé, but McCormack's divergence was not without its quiet drama. Although his district was staunchly Democratic, it included South Boston and adjacent neighborhoods where old-fashioned isolationist sentiment was strongest. He would have been more popular in 1940-1941 if he had adopted an America First position or had avoided commitment. McCormack earned respect by his willingness to give leadership on foreign-policy issues.

---

* The seniority system works in favor of congressmen from the one-party South, but this is only a partial explanation of their disproportionate influence. Southern congressmen, for various reasons, tend to look upon the House as a lifetime career and devote themselves to it in the way that only a few Northerners do. McCormack was one of those exceptions; from the first, he resolved to be "a House man."

6

Of all the personalities who came to the center of the national stage during the New Deal, the most romantically and flamboyantly Irish was Frank Murphy. While others were shaped by the interplay between their Irish heritage and American life, Murphy was someone Ireland could have produced unaided. He stepped, as it were, directly out of the pages of James Joyce or a play of Sean O'Casey; one can visualize him mourning Parnell in the committee room on Ivy Day, or standing with Padhraic Pearse and defying the British during the Easter Week rising, or fasting to death with Terence MacSwiney in his prison cell. Rebel, ascetic, romantic, priest *manqué*, and orator, Frank Murphy brought the spirit of the Irish revolutionary tradition to the stirring adventures of the New Deal. "Crisis," he liked to say of his own career, "has become a banality." His very Irish sense of the histrionic thrived on it.

His grandfather was hanged by the British in Ireland; his father emigrated to America as a youngster, joined the Fenian movement, and at sixteen was briefly jailed in Canada for his part in the picaresque Fenian attempt to liberate Ireland by conquering Canada. His father then settled down as a country lawyer in Harbor Beach, Michigan, where he was known as the town radical, an ardent Bryan Democrat, and dedicated Anglophobe.

Murphy had never been outside his hometown before he journeyed at the age of sixteen to Ann Arbor to attend the University of Michigan in 1909, "his pants ending a good six inches above his shoe tops, his worldly goods in a telescope bag." He was an exceptionally thin, spindly-legged youth with dark red hair who played an intense but mediocre game of football, studied hard, participated in campus politics, made the college honor society, and acquired the nickname "Wild Mustard." After college and law school, he clerked in a law firm in Detroit and taught a night-school class in English for Hungarian immigrants. After a notable record in World War I in which he became a captain at twenty-five, Murphy studied briefly at Lincoln's Inn, London, and at Trinity College in Dublin. Ireland in 1919 was in the midst of the revolutionary upheavals that finally culminated in independence. Murphy became friendly with Sinn Feiners, was shadowed by British police, and was sorely tempted to join the fray, but family obligations drew him back to Michigan. Before leaving, he visited Blarney Castle and kissed the Blarney Stone twice, an action that friends and enemies alike considered wholly unnecessary.

Since he had early formed his private motto—"All clients are bastards," Murphy sought public employment and found it as an assistant federal district attorney. During the next three years he achieved extensive newspaper publicity through his convictions of grafters and bootleggers. Reporters who enjoyed his audacious style and craggy red eyebrows nicknamed him "The Airedale." In 1922 he was elected a Records Court judge. Securely launched on a political career, he was never out of public office until his death. Murphy startled his fellow judges by his enthusiasm for liberal ideas in criminology; he created on his own authority a private sentencing board consisting of himself, a psychiatrist, and a sociologist.

When Murphy ran for mayor in 1930, he said in his initial campaign speech, "What Detroit needs is the dawn of a new day, the dew and sunshine of a new morning." He was promptly labeled in the newspapers, the "Dew and Sunshine candidate." Since Detroit has nonpartisan elections and the two parties were not at that time effectively organized as citywide machines, Murphy was free to run in the style he liked best: as a lone wolf. He won by a substantial majority. As mayor, he conducted an administration that was an unorthodox combination of financial reform, rigid economy, social welfarism, and radical rhetoric. He professed to disdain all professional politicians, insisted righteously that he never made appointments on any basis except merit, and skillfully dramatized his appointments of Republicans, Rhodes Scholars, and nonpolitical experts. But at the same time, he was up-to-date on his Christian social ethics and quoted readily from the Papal Encyclical *Rerum Novarum*, and its sequel, *Quadragesimo Anno*, which came out during his first year in the mayor's office. He asserted that it was the city's duty to feed the unemployed, and he strained the city treasury's resources to do so, but he also busily cut padded payrolls and skimped on normal expenses to hold overall expenditures close to pre-depression levels. He was the only politician of those days who could act like a social worker with one hand and a banker with the other, while all the time maintaining intact the gentle otherworldly air of a modern St. Francis.

In 1933 Roosevelt appointed Murphy as Governor-General of the Philippines. He stayed three years, returned home, and was elected governor of Michigan. The two jobs, one in Manila and the other in Lansing, highlighted the two conflicting sides of his nature. In Manila he earned what was then the very handsome salary of $18,000, lived in a palace, and had the military pomp and panoply that went with his viceregal office. In Lansing, where the governorship paid only $5,000 a year and there was no executive mansion, he lived in one room at a nearby hotel. A bachelor who did not smoke or drink alcohol, tea, or coffee, he kept up a steady routine of cold showers, calisthenics, horseback riding, and fruit-and-vegetable dinners. He frankly delighted in the elegance and power of his post in the Philippines, which appealed to the aesthetic and romantic side of his nature; he enjoyed the spartan life in Lansing which appealed to the monkish, ascetic side of his nature. He never joined clubs because he regarded them as breeding grounds of social discrimination. When he vacationed in Palm Beach, he prided himself for years on never entering Bradley's casino. But why choose Palm Beach at all? Perhaps only a man who loved luxury could appreciate what self-denial and self-restraint really meant. Or maybe Murphy had only an Irish fondness for dramatic contrasts.

Two days before Murphy took office as governor of Michigan, a sitdown strike was called at General Motors. Most of his two years as governor were taken up with strike mediations. He resolutely refused to use troops to clear the factories of strikers; by patience in marathon negotiating sessions, he achieved peaceful settlements in a half-dozen major strikes. In retrospect, his course of action seems only elementary common sense; a show of force that led to bloodshed would have been irresponsible. But those shortsighted conservatives who mistook the sitdown strikes as dress rehearsals for another French Revolution were tireless in their attacks upon Murphy for his refusal to "get tough" and "take a stand for law and order."

Murphy's religiously oriented conception of public issues enabled him to see the industrial strife of 1937–1938 from an angle of vision different from the usual liberal or conservative clichés of class warfare. The sitdown strikes, he said, were a "reassertion of the personality—the dignity of the offended human reasserting itself after the frightening experience of the Depression."[11]

Murphy had expressed his philosophy of government in an article in *The Commonweal* several years earlier: "Forty-two years ago the great Pontiff, Leo XIII, pointed the way in his encyclical, 'On the Condition of the Working Classes.' He said: 'Rulers should . . . anxiously safeguard the community and all its members.' "

Murphy, in his characteristic ringing style, asked: "Does the safety of the commonwealth mean merely things—materials, bonds and dollars, brick and stone, pavements and public buildings, battleships and custom barriers, tariffs and laws? Or does it mean something more—human beings and their souls: their aspirations, culture, health and happiness? Does it mean just things you can see and touch or does it mean the imperishable splendors of man and life? Answer that question and define the answer in such a way that the verdict will be confirmed in the court that is supreme above all, and we have our course charted for us."

A skeptic might consider that these words charted something less than a perfectly clear course. In giving a further definition, Murphy, if he did not precisely chart a course, did reveal something of himself and his personal vision:

"The enlightened administrator must put his very soul into the fight to guard against undernourished children, neglected old folks, and victimized wage workers. He must plan, yes, but mere plans and words are not enough. He must act, and his acts must be written into the statutes in the form of old age pensions, better factory laws and general social legislation; they must be in brick and stone in the shape of hospitals for children; they must be in dollars and cents and bread and butter in the form of relief and succor for employees victims of an unemployment they did not create.

"It is a high ministry, that of government," Murphy concluded. "It is putting Christianity to work, and by that standard its success or failure will be measured."[12]

Murphy took his religion seriously, as he did everything else about himself; this had its good side, but not everyone, and particularly not the press, was able to take him quite as seriously as he took himself. During the tense Chrysler strike negotiations that took place during Easter Week, Murphy told the press outside the meeting room: "The spirit of Good Friday prevails in the conference, the spirit of sacrifice."

A reporter spoke up: "Well, tell us, Governor, just who is being crucified now?"

Murphy was defeated for reelection as governor in 1938, but a week after leaving office, he became Attorney General in the Roosevelt Cabinet. Standing in the President's private study and placing his hand on the Bible his mother had given him long before, Murphy took the oath of office on two verses from Isaiah:

"But he shall judge the poor with justice and shall
reprove with equity for the meek of the earth. . . .

"And justice shall be the girdle of his loins; and
faith the girdle of his reigns."

Murphy, in the weeks that followed, swiftly reorganized the Justice Department, replacing almost every member of its top echelon, vigorously pushed the prosecution on criminal charges of Boss Tom Pendergast of Kansas City and of members of the old Huey Long gang in Louisiana, and flew about the country on tours of exhortation and surprise inspection. As 1940 opened, Murphy, ever more glamorous, shaggy-browed, and dramatic at forty-six, seemed a knight needing only fresh dragons to slay and more glorious victories to win for self, country, and Christian virtue.[13]

7

An administration dedicated to "driving the moneychangers from the temple" was not hospitable to men of talent from the business community. The values of conventional financiers and corporation executives were not those of the New Deal. Roosevelt, moreover, personally distrusted the economic oligarchs whose reckless policies, in his view, had brought on the disaster of 1929 and who were fast becoming his most implacable enemies. It is not surprising, therefore, that the businessman who breached this distrust and achieved the most spectacular career of any business figure in the administration, the more spectacular because it was uncommon, should have been a baroque, unorthodox, and Irish financier named Joseph P. Kennedy.

Kennedy, born in 1888, was the grandson of immigrants and the son of a ward boss in East Boston. Although his family was not poor, he began working at an early age. After school hours, he peddled papers, sold candy on an excursion steamer, and took tickets on a sightseeing boat when Dewey's fleet visited Boston Harbor after the Spanish-American War. He attended parochial school until the seventh grade, when he transferred to Boston Latin, the city's famous old school for talented youngsters. There he had what *Fortune* later termed "a Frank Merriwell adventure." He was president of the senior class, colonel of the school regiment, and won the Mayor's Cup for the highest batting average in high school baseball. In the best tradition, Kennedy accepted the trophy from Mayor John F. "Honey Fitz" Fitzgerald and six years later married the mayor's daughter. In the interim, he had graduated from Harvard, where he made Hasty Pudding but not any of the more exclusive social clubs. Kennedy was a member of the class of 1912 which classmate Robert Benchley described as having produced "only one Bishop of Albania," "only one member who caught a giant panda," and only one "village clerk of Hewlett Harbor, L.I."[14]

Kennedy was ferociously ambitious, and his objective was not a giant panda or a village clerkship. He worked as a bank examiner and moved into the presidency of a small bank (the youngest bank president in the United States at twenty-six), served during World War I as assistant general manager of Bethlehem Steel's shipyards, and then turned to the movie industry. He integrated the Keith-Albee-Orpheum movie-house chain, became president of Film Booking Offices of America, and special troubleshooter for First National Pictures. During the depression he helped reorganize Paramount Pictures and Radio Corporation of America. He also became a well-known plunger and "pool" operator on Wall Street. By

1934 he was a millionaire several times over, and had ulcers to match his brick-red hair, volcanic energy, and marvelous mastery of sulfurous profanity.

At first glance Kennedy was an odd choice to become chairman of the Securities and Exchange Commission, newly created to reform and police stock-market practices. Observers noted that while making his fortune on Wall Street, he had engaged in some of the trading practices that were now under attack. Roosevelt, however, had known Kennedy since his days at Bethlehem Steel. Kennedy had been a money raiser and campaign adviser in 1932. Cognizant of Kennedy's financial activities, Roosevelt made the appointment in the belief that it took a smart speculator to police other speculators.[15]

This calculation proved wise. In his fifteen months in office Kennedy organized an able staff, promulgated a stern code of trading practices, and enforced the law with vigor. After an interlude in private life, he returned in 1937 to become chairman of the Maritime Commission. Kennedy conformed to the image of a high-pressure executive: sitting at his desk in shirtsleeves, the windows thrown wide open, three telephones on his desk in rapid use, barking orders laced with cusswords, working sixteen-hour days, and flying thousands of miles each year. His combative methods failed to untangle the maritime industry's many problems. "I should like to report in relinquishing my post," he wrote the President in February, 1938, "that the ills of American shipping had been cured. . . . Candor compels me to say, however, that the shipping problem is far from being solved."

Roosevelt's confidence in him was unshaken. In a "My dear Joe" letter, he replied, "You have maintained your justly earned reputation of being a two-fisted, hard-hitting executive."

Kennedy departed the Maritime Commission to become American ambassador in London. He was the first Catholic and the first Irishman to be appointed ambassador to the Court of St. James's. His selection was a characteristically imaginative Roosevelt move. In a time when war was approaching and England and the United States were drawing closer together, what could more effectively disarm isolationist criticism than to have an Irish ambassador in London? No one could say of Kennedy what had been said of Walter Hines Page in the Wilson administration that he was more pro-English than the English.

As Boston's Joe Kennedy, the man with "nine children and nine million dollars," sailed for Britain, it seemed a masterstroke.

CHAPTER SEVENTEEN
The New Deal: The Aftermath

F OR MOST OF THE FIGURES drawn from the Irish community, their rendezvous with the New Deal ended in various kinds of defeat and disappointment. None had cause to regret the work he had accomplished during the Roosevelt years; it was rather that none of them achieved the complete fulfillment of his public career that his talents and achievements had forecast. The patterns broke off, scrappy and unfinished, or became sadly distorted.

1

James A. Farley was the first to depart, and his was the most spectacular leave-taking. He was victimized by the delusion that periodically afflicts professional political managers—the belief that having been instrumental in electing other men they can easily become candidates for major office and elect themselves.* This transition is, in fact, about the hardest to make in politics; the public is deeply reluctant to accept a manipulator from the smoke-filled back rooms of politics as a candidate for high office. This may be because the public feels that the hardened professional politician has intimate knowledge of, and shares the guilt for, deals, compromises, and money-raising methods that the voters would like to believe their candidates are not involved in. Although his disability in this area was clear to objective observers, Farley gradually persuaded himself from 1937 onward that he could overcome it. For emotional reasons deep within himself, he very much wanted the formal anointment, the reassuring balm, that only a victory direct from the hands of the voters can confer. Only in this way could he rise above his past as a rural ward-heeler, as one of the "Three Dumb Dukes" on the Boxing Commission, as

* Compare the similarly unhappy experience of Leonard Hall, the "Republican Jim Farley." Hall, an impressively successful GOP National Chairman from 1953 to 1956, failed badly when he tried to obtain his party's nomination for governor of New York in 1958.

the professional spoilsman ("Farleyism"), and as political agent and front man for Roosevelt.

Two other factors helped bring about Farley's break with Roosevelt. He was constantly in need of money. He published his memoirs, *Behind the Ballots*, in 1938 to earn extra income.* Since his wife did not like Washington society and lived most of the time in New York, Farley maintained quarters in both cities, shuttled between the two, and frequently had his attention drawn by friends to the lucrative possibilities in private life if he left Washington and entered business in New York. At some point after 1938, he came to the private decision that if he could not achieve his higher political ambitions, he would quit politics and turn to money-making. Second, Roosevelt's increasingly radical and venturesome course in politics alienated Farley. There was the 1937 "court-packing" plan about which Farley had private reservations but which he loyally supported and lobbied for in public. Then came the "purge" of 1938 in which Roosevelt attempted unsuccessfully to unseat several conservative Democratic senators in the party primaries. As an orthodox politician brought up on the canons of party regularity and unity, Farley was shocked by this application of philosophical criteria within the party. He felt the President and the New Dealers were interfering in a preserve that was properly his own. He naturally did not like those liberals around the President, such as Tommy Corcoran and Harry Hopkins, who regarded Farley's brand of politics as old-fashioned and, in some respects, irrelevant.

Farley's personal ambitions, his desire to make money, and his resentment at Roosevelt's intervention in party management drove him in the direction of the conservatives in the party. He increasingly aligned himself with Vice President John Garner, Senators Carter Glass and Harry Byrd of Virginia, and other anti-New Deal southern Democrats who, for reasons of their own, were happy to encourage his presidential ambitions.

As a presidential figure, Farley had two weaknesses, each of them fatal. First, he was not strong enough to carry his own home state. When New York Governor Herbert Lehman proposed to run for the Senate in 1938, Farley and other party leaders were unanimous in pressing Lehman to run instead for reelection. Lehman was the only Democratic candidate capable of defeating Thomas E. Dewey, the Republican nominee. He finally agreed to run, and did defeat Dewey in an extremely close race. If Farley had been a strong potential vote-getter in his own right, he could have stepped into the breach, and the Lehman "draft" would have been unnecessary.

---

* The book was ghosted by a former newspaperman, Edward M. Roddan, who in later years was on the staff of Senator Brien McMahon of Connecticut. McMahon obtained for him an appointment from President Truman as ambassador to Uruguay, thus carrying forward the old American tradition of political ghostwriters becoming diplomats.

Farley's second weakness was that he had no discernible position on the issues and was not identified in the public mind with a program. During the winter of 1939–1940, when he was conducting a "shadow campaign" for the presidential nomination, his views on economic and social problems never progressed much beyond exhortations to harmony and cooperation. Speaking at a party banquet in New York in April, 1940, for example, Farley said: "The solution of our economic problem seems to be a simple one. Why not bring together in frank discussion the leaders of industry, transportation, finance, agriculture, and labor? Let them submerge their selfishness. Let them acquaint each other with their problems. If they do, and are frank with each other, I am confident that out of such a discussion a workable plan that will fit in with the liberal economy of the present day can be formulated. This solution is possible and sound."[1]

The National Recovery Administration (NRA) and similar ventures in government-industry cooperation in the early years of the New Deal might never have occurred for all the cognizance that Farley took of them in these bland homilies.

Farley's real ambition in 1940 was to run for Vice-President on a ticket headed by Cordell Hull. Although Roosevelt killed this dream when he decided to seek a third term, Farley was nominated for the Presidency in a stirring speech by Carter Glass and fought the issue out to the bitter end. He resigned the chairmanship of the Democratic National Committee, left the Cabinet, and entered private business, but he did not entirely leave politics. He refused to quit as state chairman and did not do so until 1944. This gravely embarrassed Governor Lehman and President Roosevelt, who had to maneuver around his hostility in their necessary political operations and who, as the party's chief officeholders, were entitled by custom to have a state chairman in whom they had confidence.

Farley clung to office for a purpose. He achieved it in 1942 when he transformed the Democratic State Convention into a butchershop where he carried out a public bloodletting. He forced through the nomination of his candidate for governor—John Bennett, Jr.—over the open opposition of his party's President, governor, and two United States senators. He triumphed with the delegates because he collected on every favor he had ever performed in his official roles as Postmaster General, national chairman, and state chairman; he spent that officially earned gratitude for the private end of punishing Roosevelt. The roll calls at the convention tore the party apart and left a heritage of enmity and resentment.

It was an extraordinary display of ruthless and irresponsible personal bossism. And for what? Farley's empty triumph gratified only personal pique and personal vanity. He broke the professional politician's rule that the party's welfare is bigger than the fate of any man, that the party should never be split when a compromise is possible, and that a "pro" does not publicly weaken officeholders whom the party organization has a vested interest in keeping in office.*

When Dewey overwhelmingly defeated Bennett in the fall election, Farley was destroyed as a political figure. For decades afterward, he turned up at national conventions, providing an item of color for sentimental journalists; in 1958, at age seventy, he projected himself as a possible candidate for the United States Senate but was ignored. He was a ghost at these party gatherings. In a critical time, Farley, the apostle of party unity, party spirit, and party discipline had put himself first. He collected a reward of his own choosing at the 1942 convention. Nobody owed him anything after that.[2]

2

Frank Murphy served an exciting year as Attorney General. As an Irish moralist, he most enjoyed the part of his work that involved tracking down wrongdoers. By aggressive enforcement of the criminal laws, he stayed on the front pages of the nation's newspapers almost every day. Among the cases prosecuted during his tenure were those of Tom Pendergast, the Democratic boss of Kansas City; Enoch ("Nucky") Johnson, the Republican boss of Atlantic City; Federal Judge Martin Manton; Governor Richard Leche and other prominent politicians in the corrupt Louisiana political machine, as well as a considerable number of less well-known gamblers and gangsters. Joseph Alsop and Robert Kintner in their syndicated column quoted President Roosevelt as telling a visitor that before Murphy was done, he would make the achievements of Tom Dewey, then Manhattan's Republican district attorney, look like "small potatoes." They speculated on a 1940 Democratic "dream ticket": Roosevelt and Murphy.

In January, 1940, Roosevelt unexpectedly appointed Murphy to the Supreme Court on the death of Justice Pierce Butler, the Court's only Catholic member. Although he protested vehemently that he would prefer to stay in the Cabinet, Murphy finally accepted. Most lawyers would not consider a place on the Supreme Court an unhappy ending to their career. But for Murphy it was. He was simply not suited by temperament or in-

---

* Carmine De Sapio destroyed himself politically in 1958 when he made a remarkably similar error of judgment. He forced through the nomination of a Senate candidate over the public opposition of Governor Averell Harriman and Mayor Robert Wagner. Neither Farley nor De Sapio had learned the lesson of the political revolution which Al Smith effected in 1924-1925. Since Smith's time, the New York electorate expects the governors and the mayors to give orders to the party "bosses," not the other way round.

tellectual interest for the politically detached and impersonal style of life required of a judge. Murphy was a politician to his fingertips. Like Fiorello La Guardia or Al Smith, he was an egotist and an actor who desperately, almost physiologically, needed an audience and a place in the center of the stage. Without the response of an audience and the sense of being part of a great unfolding drama, Murphy functioned, but not well or happily.

Murphy spent nine years on the Court before his death in 1949. He sublimated his frustrations by taking increasingly absolutist and doctrinaire positions on questions of individual liberties and minority rights. His opinions, particularly his concurrences and dissents (for he infrequently found a majority of his colleagues who would endorse both his views and his language all the way), contained much beautiful and impassioned writing. But his opinions were flawed by his frequent need to take a position beyond what the merits of the case required. His instincts for self-dramatization and for a messianic view of himself—his sister, according to *Time*, once said, "He looks more like Jesus Christ every day"[3]— became more rather than less pronounced with the passing years. The sheltered world of the Court with its slow pace and stately routines was no place for an Irish rebel in search of a cause.

3

Joe Kennedy, first Irishman and first Catholic to become American ambassador to Great Britian, began his diplomatic career in London early in 1938 in a blaze of favorable personal publicity and ended it in Boston not quite three years later on a sad and sour note. His large family and his informal manners made him excellent newspaper copy; he gave interviews in his shirtsleeves, put his feet on his desk, and punctuated his remarks with occasional bursts of profanity; shortly after his arrival, he scored a hole-in-one at golf. He breezily told the British Navy League: "We try to understand your need for a great merchant fleet. We hope you will try to understand our need for a small one."

Kennedy had been in London less than nine months when the crisis caused by Germany's demands on Czechoslovakia reached its climax. He responded to the crisis in a manner becoming an efficient, hard-working ambassador; having developed close personal relations with Prime Minister Neville Chamberlain and Foreign Secretary Viscount Halifax, he worked closely with them in the weeks leading up to the Munich settlement. If he privately shared their optimistic assumptions about the scope and nature of Hitler's ambitions, he was well within his rights. Moreover, repre-

senting a nation that at the time was no more than a sympathetic bystander, he was not morally in a strong position to urge the British to
pursue a warlike policy.

Kennedy, however, soon passed beyond private consultation and
advice. In a public speech in London shortly after the Munich agreement
was signed, he said: "It has long been a theory of mine that it is unproductive for both democratic and dictator countries to widen the division now
existing between them by emphasizing their differences which are self-
apparent. Instead of hammering away at what are regarded as irrecon-
cilables, they could advantageously bend their energies toward solving
their common problems by an attempt to re-establish good relations on a
world basis.

"It is true that the democratic and dictator countries have important
and fundamental divergencies of outlook which in certain matters go
deeper than politics. But there is simply no sense, common or otherwise,
in letting these differences grow into unrelenting antagonisms. After all,
we have to live together in the same world whether we like it or not."[4]

There was nothing astonishing in these views in 1938. Twenty years
later, identical language had become part of the conventional wisdom concerning the differences between the democracies and the Communist bloc.
Nuclear weapons have made the prospect of settling those differences by
military means terrible to contemplate. But in 1938, nuclear weapons did
not exist and conventional war was still a possible instrument of foreign
policy. Winston Churchill and his supporters argued that it was better to
risk war than to yield to Hitler and face the certainty of war later and on
worse terms. Kennedy made an error of judgment in committing himself
on this question in public. He forgot what ambassadors are supposed to
bear in mind, which is that today's opposition may be tomorrow's government. When Churchill did come to power eighteen months later, he
naturally was not favorably disposed toward Ambassador Kennedy.

Kennedy meanwhile tried to eliminate some of the "self-apparent differences" between Nazi Germany and the democracies. He floated a
"trial balloon" suggesting that the 600,000 German Jews be resettled in
colonial territories in Africa and Asia. As it turned out, only this plan
offered any hope of saving the Jews from extermination since, for most of
them, liberation came too late. There was some basis of hope for the
proposal. As late as 1940 Hitler seriously considered the resettlement of the
Jews on Madagascar as an alternative to the policy of mass murder. Unfortunately, the Germans ignored Kennedy's proposal, and it came to
nothing.

He was actuated by humanitarian convictions, as well as diplomatic
motives, in putting forward his idea. Two months earlier, speaking at a

memorial service for the first Episcopal bishop in the United States, Samuel Seabury, he made a thinly veiled attack on the Nazi persecutions: "In certain parts of the world, the profession and practice of religion is being called a political offense. Men and women are being deprived of their natural born citizenship, and they are being thrown out of the land of their nativity because they profess a certain religion which political authorities have decided to uproot. . . . We are blessed that our two countries are imbued with certain old-fashioned but still useful qualities—respect for the rights of others and for the sanctity of engagements as well as a genuine love of freedom for the individual!"[5]

When war came, Kennedy rose to the challenge with all the zest and volcanic energy that had made him a successful businessman and New Deal administrator. With nearly ten thousand Americans resident in England for whose protection he was responsible and, in addition, many American business interests vexed with war-created problems, Kennedy worked long days at the embassy. But if his energy was in the job, his heart was not. Kennedy was deeply pessimistic about Britain's chances. He not only doubted whether Britain could stand up militarily to Hitler's attack; he feared also that if Britain did survive it would be as a highly regimented, totally mobilized society in which most of the personal and business freedoms he cared about would have been lost. These two gloomy judgments, inextricably intertwined, led him to the further conviction that the United States would be wasting men and resources trying to save Britain. He could not help but bring to bear on the situation his lifetime of business experience, and that experience plus his shrewd trader's mind told him that Britain was, so to speak, a losing proposition.

It was this fundamental difference in assessing the outlook in 1940 that caused Kennedy's break with Roosevelt. The President, more optimistic by nature, and relying as much upon intuition and sentiment as upon any hardheaded estimate of Britain's military chances, was willing to go the limit in aiding Britain.

When Kennedy left London in October, 1940, it was known that he was going home to resign as ambassador. The British government and press gave him a warm sendoff. The London *Times* wrote: "Whether he comes back to us or not, he has earned the respect due a great *American* Ambassador who never for a moment mistook the country to which he was accredited for the country of his birth." The *Evening News* observed: "It is Mr. Kennedy single-handed who has strengthened Anglo-American friendship in London." A columnist in the *Daily Herald* quoted Kennedy as saying: "I did not know London could take it. I did not think any city could take it. I am bowed in reverence." It is doubtful if

Kennedy expressed it that way, but in any event the columnist added enthusiastically: "Forever, in deeds if not in written words, Britain and America are Allies. Largely, that is Joseph Kennedy's work. Goodby, Joe! Heaven bless you! Your job is done."

A certain amount of calculation probably entered into these cordial assessments of Kennedy's ambassadorial career, since Britain was hard pressed and wanted the goodwill of this influential American. But there was also an element of genuine tribute to a hard-working, charming, unorthodox man who had labored for nearly three years in a most difficult transition period when Britain was arguing itself into making a military stand against Hitler, and the United States was arguing itself out of isolation and into the world community.

Upon his return home, Kennedy made a radio broadcast urging Roosevelt's reelection. The following week, while visiting Boston, he talked in his hotel room with Louis Lyons of the *Boston Globe* and two reporters from the *St. Louis Post-Dispatch*. Kennedy apparently assumed the conversation was "off the record" or, more likely, in accordance with a custom familiar among Washington political correspondents "not for direct attribution to the source." Lyons, however, denied Kennedy had placed any restrictions on their talk. He gave him straight police-reporter treatment, printing his most revealing remarks in direct quotation.

Kennedy had said: "I'm willing to spend all I've got to keep us out of the war. There's no sense in our getting in. We'd only be holding the bag. What would we get out of it? Democracy is finished in England. It isn't that she's fighting for democracy. That's the bunk. She's fighting for self-preservation, just as we will if it comes to us. As long as she can hold out, give her what it takes, whatever we don't have to have, and don't expect anything back."

Concerning Colonel Charles Lindbergh, then a major isolationist spokesman, Kennedy said, "Lindbergh isn't crazy either, you know."

On Mrs. Roosevelt: "She bothered us more on our jobs in Washington to take care of the poor little nobodies than all the rest of the people down there put together. She's always sending me a note to have some little Susie Glotz to tea at the Embassy."[6]

This remark about Mrs. Roosevelt is the most persuasive evidence for Kennedy's contention that there was a misunderstanding between himself and Lyons as to whether their interview was on the record. There was no reason for Kennedy to make a gratuitous public attack on the President's wife, particularly as he was, at least nominally, still a member of her husband's administration.

Kennedy's other remarks about the war, democracy, and Lindbergh seem much less extraordinary a generation later than they did at the time. These were the words of a man who prided himself on being plain-spoken, ruthlessly practical, contemptuous of propaganda, and realistic, even cynical, about human nature. In short, Kennedy was the same blunt, lay-it-on-the-line fellow who had been enchanting Washington and London for years with his candor. Kennedy was in character, but the context had changed. His version of realism was out of season.

The Lyons interview contributed an element of personal discord to what had been a disagreement over policy. It not only brought Kennedy's career as ambassador to a close; it also ruptured permanently his relations with Roosevelt and the administration. Kennedy, still a comparatively young man at fifty-two, was well equipped by experience to have been an exceptionally useful administrator of one of the war-production agencies, but he played no role in the war effort. As long as Roosevelt remained in the White House, Kennedy frittered away his time in unsuccessful conservative cabals to capture control of the Democratic Party. With the end of the war and the beginning of a new political era, Kennedy found a new usefulness and political fulfillment in helping to plan and advance the careers of his sons.

4

While James Farley and Joseph Kennedy broke with the Roosevelt administration and dropped out of national politics, and Frank Murphy found himself immolated on the Supreme Court, the national career of Joseph Casey, the brightest of the young Irish New Dealers in the House of Representatives, failed of its early promise through miscalculation and bad luck. But, as the Duke of Wellington said of Waterloo, it was "a damn close run thing."

Having so entrenched himself in his central Massachusetts district by 1941 that the Republican-controlled state legislature reapportioned it as "safely Democratic" territory, Casey had the alternative of making a career for himself in the House, as his close friend John W. McCormack of Boston had chosen to do, or seeking a quicker route to power by running for the Senate. He chose the latter course. In 1942 he became the Democratic candidate against Henry Cabot Lodge, then seeking reelection to his second term.*

* One of Casey's two opponents in the Democratic primary was John F. "Honey Fitz" Fitzgerald, who had come within 33,000 votes of defeating Lodge's grandfather in a Senate race in 1916. But at seventy-nine "the Little General" was well past his prime and did not make a strong race. Even in Boston, where Fitzgerald was strongest, Casey swept 18 of the 22 wards.

Lodge, young, handsome, and with a propensity for oratorical liberalism, had an aura of progressivism. He had attracted many Democratic votes in his "Jack the Giant Killer" victory over Jim Curley six years earlier and, like his grandfather, had paid assiduous court to what he took to be the prejudices and predispositions of the Irish, the Italians, and other voting blocs in the state. From the outset of his career, this had led him to follow a most tortuous course. "As everyone knows," he had said in his victory statement in 1936, "I am a liberal and . . . a friend of labor. Everyone also knows that I will not permit either predilection to override the dictates of my own conscience."[7] He did not explain why there should be any conflict between one's liberalism and one's conscience.

As a freshman senator, Lodge in 1938 supported the Fair Labor Standards Act which set minimum wages and maximum hours, but in view of the intensity of feeling in New England against "unfair" southern competition, this vote on the liberal side was not risky. Otherwise his first-term record was conservative and evasive. In 1937 he was one of sixteen senators to vote against the slum-clearance bill; in 1938 he twice voted against cloture during an antilynching bill filibuster; in 1939 he was one of four senators to vote against the confirmation of William O. Douglas to the Supreme Court; and that year also he cast the deciding vote against an amendment to increase the appropriation for public works projects to relieve unemployment; and in 1942 he was one of only four senators to vote against an amendment to the Social Security Act increasing appropriations for the care of crippled children.

Foreign-policy issues were at the heart of the 1942 campaign. Casey entered the campaign as the protagonist of internationalism. He had broken with Senator David I. Walsh, his onetime mentor and the grand old man of the Democratic Party in Massachusetts, on the question of support for Roosevelt's foreign policy. Against the still strong isolationist sentiment within the Irish community in Massachusetts, Casey had voted for and spoken throughout the state in support of the draft, repeal of the neutrality laws, passage of the Lend-Lease bill, and all-out aid for Britain. Lodge until Pearl Harbor had stayed at or near the isolationist position. When the war began in 1939, Lodge said: "The fight in Europe is not our fight. It is theirs. If the British and French empires cannot stand without our help, then they deserve to fall."[8] In the next two years, he followed a vacillating course that *Time* summed up this way:

"He voted to limit the use of United States forces to the western hemisphere, to restrict transfer of naval craft, to make a two-billion dollar loan instead of Lend-Lease. Then he voted for Lend-Lease, then to retain the neutrality act, then to declare war, thus taking all sides."[9]

Since many Republicans remembered how Lodge's grandfather had sabotaged entry of the United States into the League of Nations in

1919–1920, and were fearful that Lodge might play a similar role after World War II, Casey attracted considerable Republican support. Courtenay Crocker, who polled 23,000 votes in the Republican primary against Lodge, and J. Ernest Kerr, for ten years the executive secretary of the Republican Club of Massachusetts, headed a long list of distinguished Republicans who endorsed Casey. Not since the Bull Moose revolt thirty years earlier was the state's Yankee community so deeply divided. The Citizens Committee for Casey included no fewer than four Cabots, three Grays, and two Peabodys. Republican newspapers such as the *Springfield Republican* and the Pittsfield *Berkshire Eagle* bolted Lodge, while a sizable academic contingent at Harvard and the Massachusetts Institute of Technology was organized in Casey's behalf by the historian Sidney B. Fay.

These gains, however, were partially offset by defections among the hard-core group of Boston Irish who put their isolationist convictions ahead of their normal Democratic allegiance; Senator Walsh stayed in Washington and sat out the campaign. District Attorney William Foley, a longtime power in Boston politics, encountered Casey late in the campaign, and remarked bitterly: "You are not running for the Senate. You're standing for Parliament!" The size of this old-guard isolationist vote was not great; Casey on election day polled percentagewise the normal Democratic vote in Boston except in South Boston and Dorchester, where he ran about 4 percent behind the rest of his ticket.

A much more important factor than these marginal defections was the apathy toward politics that prevailed in wartime. Lodge won by 80,000 votes, defeating Casey 721,000 to 641,000. The total vote was 400,000 below the previous off-year election of 1938 and 700,000 below the presidential election of 1940. Moreover, the fall-off in voting was much greater among Democrats than among Republicans. The Republican vote dropped only 226,000, whereas the Democratic total fell by 465,000; between those two figures is a differential of 239,000, which is nearly three times the margin by which Casey lost.

In retrospect, it can be seen that the chief importance of the 1942 senatorial campaign was educational. For the first time an Irish Democratic candidate in Massachusetts argued openly and consistently for America's assumption of her world responsibilities. For the first time a candidate eschewed demagogy and sentimental rhetoric and dwelt on the hard facts of international life. Some Irish of the older generation rebelled and voted against him, but the overwhelming majority followed his leadership. Casey's failure, like that of Adlai Stevenson a decade later, was a worthwhile and productive failure because it helped educate the citizenry about the nature of the world they lived in and about the responsibilities that world entailed.

After the election, Roosevelt sounded out Casey as to whether he would be willing to become chairman of the Democratic National Committee and manage the next presidential campaign. Casey agreed. But weeks passed and he heard nothing more. Then the selection of Robert E. Hannegan as National Chairman was announced. When Casey inquired of Roosevelt why his own appointment had fallen through, the President explained that Representative McCormack and other mutual friends had suggested that it was unfair of him to ask Casey to take the National Chairmanship since he had no private means and should be permitted to go into private law practice to earn money for his growing family.

The incident is of historical interest only because it demonstrates how many small factors are involved in a crucial decision. The following year, Roosevelt, after deciding to drop Henry Wallace from the ticket, had in mind as alternative candidates for Vice-President, Senator Harry Truman and Justice William O. Douglas. Hannegan, by some astute maneuvering at the Democratic National Convention, brought about the nomination of Truman, his political patron. Casey, much more of a New Dealer than Hannegan, would in that context have preferred Douglas, a better-known liberal, than Truman. If Casey had become National Chairman in 1943, presidential history might have taken a quite different turn.

As events developed, Casey did resume his law practice, and was highly successful. In 1948 he had his second brush with destiny as a would-be President maker. Having established after the war a personal friendship with General Dwight Eisenhower, Casey became a pivotal figure in the effort in the spring of 1948 to persuade him to become a candidate for the Democratic presidential nomination. Casey used with the General much the same argument that the leaders of the internationalist wing of the Republican Party used successfully four years later: Eisenhower's unique prestige in the United States and abroad was a national asset that he should put to work in the cause of peace. "I knew I had lost my man," Casey recalled later, "when after I had made my fervent argument about how much the world needed him, he said to me: 'But if I accept the Democratic nomination, how will I explain it to my Kansas Republican friends? They wanted to enter me in their convention, and I refused.' "[10]

In 1950 the Caseys took the Eisenhowers as their guests to the Broadway opening of *Call Me Madam*. When "I Like Ike" was sung, it evoked so many encores it stopped the show, and Eisenhower finally had to rise and wave to the other members of the audience. The candidate had been born, but by then he had already passed to the other party and other advisers. Joseph Casey was not to be the architect of an Eisenhower administration.

5

In June, 1938, Representative Bruce Barton, addressing a group of Young Republicans, held up Tommy Corcoran as a model for them to emulate. Barton observed: "It can be said truthfully of him as was said by a contemporary of Sir Walter Raleigh: 'I know that he can toil terribly.' "[11]

As the main protagonist within the administration of more radical, aggressive policies on both the economic and political fronts, Corcoran was at the peak of his influence in 1938. He, Ben Cohen, and economist Leon Henderson had argued against the cut in relief and public-works expenditures that Roosevelt made at the beginning of 1937 in an effort to balance the budget. When the economic recession Henderson had forecast actually occurred in the autumn of 1937, their prestige rose. In 1938–1939, the administration attempted against increasingly stiff opposition in Congress to combat the recession by putting into effect spending and lending policies that they advocated to "prime the pump" of the economy with federal funds. They were active in fights over tax legislation with Treasury Secretary Henry Morgenthau and conservatives in Congress who wanted to appease business sentiment by repealing certain taxes to which businessmen vehemently objected, notably the undistributed profits tax. Here Corcoran and his group were defeated; this tax was repealed in 1939.

In 1937 Corcoran had "toiled terribly" in behalf of the "Court-packing" plan which would have increased the Supreme Court from nine to a maximum of fifteen members by adding a new justice for each member over seventy who failed to retire. Corcoran was popularly but erroneously credited with devising this ingenious solution to the administration's troubles with "the nine old men" on the Court. The assumption of his authorship was easy to make because it fitted so well with his deserved reputation for cleverness, but the plan was actually conceived by Roosevelt and Attorney General Homer Cummings. But if Corcoran had played no part in devising the plan, he did his best to get it adopted. The following year, he was active in Roosevelt's unsuccessful attempt to liberalize the Democratic Party by purging the senators who had voted against the Court plan and other administration proposals.

Corcoran's liberal economic views made him a standard whipping boy for angry businessmen and most of the press. His political activities evoked enmities among conservatives on Capitol Hill and the more orthodox party men headed by Farley. Corcoran was becoming an exposed and vulnerable figure. Meanwhile, another factor weakened his position. This was the growing intimacy between Harry Hopkins and Roosevelt. Although Hopkins and Corcoran usually agreed on matters of policy, there was a keen personal rivalry between them, a rivalry in which Hopkins was eventually triumphant. Corcoran, expansive, dominating, self-confident, was temperamentally less well suited for the role of confidant and agent that the frail, self-effacing Hopkins developed with the President during the war. There was also truth in the observations of Alva Johnston who wrote in the *Saturday Evening Post*: "Tommy gained White House favor when he was connected with victories; he lost it when he was connected with defeats. The bad effects of the court fight and purge became more apparent as time went on.

"Various small things also were reported to have given the falling courtier a timely shove downwards. An alleged remark about the ghost writing of the President's speeches is said to have given offense. The chief ghost during the first Roosevelt term was Dr. Raymond Moley. In his book, *After Seven Years*, Moley quoted Tommy as saying, 'You write the music; he only sings it.' There was always somebody around to show the President a crack like that, laughingly."[12]

The last major service Corcoran performed for Roosevelt was the setting up in 1939 of the Temporary National Economic Committee (TNEC) that conducted the most exhaustive investigation in history into the nature and actual functioning of the nation's economy. Corcoran, an intellectual disciple of Associate Justice Louis Brandeis, shared the latter's view that "bigness is badness," and that rigidly enforced antitrust laws and lively competition are the best prescription for the health of business and democracy. The appointment of Thurman Arnold as Assistant Attorney General in charge of a rejuvenated Anti-Trust Division in the Justice Department coincided with the organization of the TNEC. These moves reversed nearly twenty years of government policy which had begun with the encouragement of industry-wide trade associations by Herbert Hoover in the 1920's and continued with the NRA codes of cooperation. The revival of interest in the late 1930's in trust-busting and government-enforced competition is one of Corcoran's enduring legacies from his half-dozen years of power.

Another legacy is the pervasive influence of his example and his personal legend in establishing a government career as an ideal in the minds of countless younger men. This ideal would have taken hold in any event but, as it was, Corcoran defined it and put the mark of his personal style on it. The New Deal shattered the "genteel tradition" in politics that had largely obtained during the seventy years from the Civil War to 1933. The old tradition had held that "politics is dirty business" unfit for gentlemen, that the "business of America is business" and therefore only second-raters and failures go into government, and that government is best when it is smallest and governs least. The Irish, because of their circumstances in American life, had never shared these genteel beliefs and illusions. They knew that government is power, and power exists to be used. They knew that politics is no dirtier than the human beings who participate in it. They knew, further, that politics in its highest form is the search for justice and that those who decry politics and "big government" are usually men and interests who do not want any public agency to redress the private balances of power. The positive view of politics and government traditional in the Irish community was familiar in City Halls across the country. Al Smith brought it to bear at the state level in New York. In the Washington of the thirties, when the age of positive government began on the national level, Corcoran applied it *con brio* and with high intelligence and imagination.

He and his protégés were the first of successive generations of young men in high office: the general counsels, administrative assistants, and high-level bureaucrats who are not in the front lines of elective office themselves but who fashion the programs, ghost the speeches, and, as was said of Corcoran, "play the government as if it were a piano." The telephone is their indispensable weapon. Wherever he was, Corcoran placed his calls through the White House switchboard so that he could truthfully begin his conversation: "This is Tommy Corcoran calling from the White House." He and his protégés and imitators know that ours is a government of men as well as a government of laws. To know an unlisted telephone number or a senator's personal idiosyncrasy is often more useful in getting things done than any formal procedure. They could be called, to use a faintly pejorative term, "operators." But this is misleading. Corcoran did not operate just for the sake of operating. During his years in government, he used his energy and skill in the service of his convictions and ideas. In authoring stock-exchange reforms, abolishing public utility holding companies, pushing Keynesian spending and tax policies, revitalizing the antitrust program, and trying to liberalize the Democratic Party, Corcoran was active on many fronts in behalf of a single coherent philosophy. He was a brilliant public servant.

Corcoran resigned as assistant counsel of the Reconstruction Finance Corporation in 1940. Because of his increased vulnerability and insecurity, he decided that his position as minister-without-portfolio had become untenable and that if he were to continue in government service he needed the prestige and statutory authority of a definite office. He could no longer rely solely upon Roosevelt's personal favor. That fall, he managed the Independent Citizens' Committee set up under the co-chairmanship of Mayor Fiorello La Guardia of New York and Senator George Norris of

Nebraska to win votes for Roosevelt's reelection. After the election, Corcoran and his friends began maneuvering to get him a suitable post.

On January 20, 1941, the day of his third inaugural, Roosevelt wrote Corcoran words of high praise: "I need intelligent, devoted and selfless men. You have been one of those few and must continue. Few men have been understanding of the forces of history against which we have contended and against which we must now rally more powerfully and more astutely than ever. I have always thought you were one of those few."

Roosevelt went on to express his understanding of Corcoran's equivocal position: "You must know that I understand fully how much your front-line fighting has put you 'on the spot'; and that you can no longer contribute effectively without portfolio. As our plans unfold, National Defense will have positions of rank and responsibilities where your great talents and powers will be desperately needed."

But notwithstanding the cordial words, Roosevelt temporized. He pleaded that he needed time and, for the present, offered only an appointment as Special Assistant to the Attorney General "to await a definite assignment."[13]

Corcoran declined this offer and opened a private law practice. Of the several posts for which he was considered, the one he most desired was Solicitor General. When it became vacant later that year, five Justices of the Supreme Court signed a round-robin letter to Roosevelt proposing Corcoran for the position. When Corcoran asked Justice Felix Frankfurter if he would sign, Frankfurter refused and rebuked him for impropriety. Since Corcoran had lobbied Roosevelt tirelessly to appoint Frankfurter to the Court, he was naturally incensed at this pretentious attitude on the part of his old friend and former professor. A bitter quarrel ensued, and the two never spoke to each other again.[14]

The reason Roosevelt usually gave for his failure to appoint Corcoran to a high position was his fear that it would lead to a costly fight over confirmation in the Senate. This concern had some basis, but Roosevelt risked bruising confirmation struggles on behalf of other friends (as, for example, Edward Flynn, nominated as Minister to Australia in 1943, and Henry Wallace, nominated for Secretary of Commerce in 1945). The confirmation obstacle was not insuperable. It is hard to avoid the conclusion that Roosevelt was guilty of serious ingratitude in his failure to reward one of his ablest and most devoted collaborators.

Corcoran, as had Joseph Tumulty, his accomplished if less dazzling counterpart in the Wilson administration, stayed on in Washington, performing in that jungle of law-*cum*-politics where much money is to be made but where reputations are often damaged. Masking his disappointment in pride, he remained friendly with Roosevelt, but his influence at the White House declined sharply from 1943 onward because he counseled the President to distrust Stalin and to play the Germans and Russians off against each other. Having no faith in cooperation among the Big Three, he wanted postwar foreign policy to be based on a bold program of American imperialism. At the time, this approach was completely uncongenial to Roosevelt.

Over the years, Corcoran maintained his interest in politics, raising campaign funds for liberal Democratic senators such as Wayne Morse of Oregon, Mike Mansfield of Montana, and Claude Pepper of Florida.

Making money and advising political figures behind the scenes were no substitutes for the great public career he had envisaged for himself. During the New Deal years, when he was busy staffing agencies with young Harvard Law School graduates, he had thought of himself as restoring the political style of the early days of the Republic when men of genius held high office while still very young. What has been called "the Corcoranization of the Government" was a conscious back-to-Hamilton-Jefferson-Madison-Adams movement. Later, this idea gave way to the idea of emulating Justice Brandeis, who made a fortune representing corporations and then, at forty, turned to public service and nonprofit cases as "the people's lawyer." A private fortune would provide independence and freedom from money worries. He talked about this theory to a *Time* magazine interviewer in 1938.

"If voluble Partner Corcoran's preachments about successful Americans then are practiced," *Time* wrote, "both Lawyer Corcoran and Lawyer Cohen will be ready again for their country's call to service, about 1960. They will have served their governmental novitiate. They will also have made their pile. They should by that time be senior bastions in the 'bridge of men' between private and public life about which Partner Corcoran likes to talk. . . ."[15]

When 1960 came, Corcoran at fifty-nine was a millionaire several times over. If his close friend Lyndon Johnson had become President, perhaps he would have returned to the government and proved his own theory. As it was, he took pleasure in the grimly Darwinian view of history he learned from Justice Holmes. Corcoran liked to repeat a story Holmes had told him. Holmes used to pass William Lloyd Garrison's statue in Boston, look up at it, and ponder that if he were a conservative of his father's generation and had heard Garrison preaching, he would have said to himself: "This is a very dangerous man, for he is willing to say, 'Let the social order perish if only my ideas triumph.' If he were a liberal friend of his father, he would have laughed and said, 'How foolish to worry, for the social order does not perish. Only the personnel at the top changes.' If he had been a philosopher and overheard these two, he would have said, 'How foolish both these men are because they do not see that the liberal and the conservative are but opposite sides of the shears that cuts the pattern of the future.'" And, Holmes concluded, if he had been "that sardonic man in Heaven," he would have said, "These humans are all foolish, including the philosopher, for they do not realize that it is man's destiny to fight. And the handsomer and fairer and more honest your opponent, the higher the tragedy."[16]

CHAPTER EIGHTEEN

McCarthyism

J OE MCCARTHY was that rare man who made himself a legend in his own lifetime and for all the years beyond.

The fervor of his followers, the fury of his enemies, and his own frenetic energy made it certain that no historian in the future can write about America in the decade after World War II and overlook his name and the movement he personified—McCarthyism.

His career was brief. In little more than seven years, the arc of his career curved upward from obscurity in February, 1950, to astonishing national and international notoriety, crashed to humiliation and defeat in 1954, faded into near obscurity once more, and ended in death on May 2, 1957.

Yet in the crowded hours of his power and fame, his image darkened the sky. His colleagues in the United States Senate, except for a few, cowered before him. He helped destroy a Secretary of State, helped drive one national administration from office, and wrung humiliating concessions from a second. His influence ravaged the diplomatic service and other branches of the government, breaking careers, unmaking reputations, and immobilizing policy. There was no one too humble, be he Army dentist or State Department file clerk, and no one too august, be he veteran senator, syndicated columnist, or the President of the United States, to escape McCarthy's inquisitorial concern. He began public life as a Democrat and became a Republican, but always stood apart from both parties. Having indicted the Roosevelt-Truman era as "twenty years of treason," he very soon after Republican Dwight Eisenhower entered the White House began speaking of "twenty-one years of treason."

The man at the center of this legend was a gambling man who took incredulous delight in the furor, who believed that it was, in a way, all the product of a dream in which the dice always come up seven, and there was nothing to do but ride his streak. Now that the streak is over and the tale is ended, what sort of man was Joe McCarthy? And what was the meaning of McCarthyism?

1

Joseph Raymond McCarthy was born on a lonely farm in a remote, rural area near Appleton, Wisconsin, on November 14, 1908. He was the fifth of seven children in the family of Timothy and Bridget McCarthy. They were pious, hard-working, close mouthed people inured to the rough life and the isolation of back-country farming. The McCarthys lived in what was known as "the Irish settlement," a small enclave of Irish in an area overwhelmingly populated by German, Dutch, and Scandinavian settlers. Joe McCarthy was three-quarters Irish and one-quarter German. His mother, Bridget Tierney, had been born in Ireland, while his father, Timothy McCarthy, was native born, the son of an Irish father and a German mother.*

McCarthy attended grade school in a one-room country school. Except for an occasional Saturday afternoon at the movies in Appleton, it was an all-work-and-no-play childhood. He grew into a barrel-chested, short-armed, burly young man. He quit school at fourteen. He was not much given to playing baseball or any of the other youthful games. An inner restlessness drove him away from the farm to take a job as a storekeeper in a neighboring town when he was nineteen. There the urge to acquire an education suddenly burst upon him. At twenty, he enrolled in the local high school and completed the four-year course in one year.

With some meager financial assistance from his father, he then worked his way through the college and law curriculum at Jesuit-run Marquette University during the next five years. He waited on table, tended furnaces, shoveled snow, and played a terrific game of poker to eke out his finances. Admitted to the bar, McCarthy pursued a desultory practice in small towns, dabbling in Democratic Party politics on the side. Defeated for district attorney in 1936 as a Democrat, he switched to the Republicans and three years later, at thirty-one, he was elected a county judge.

From this first campaign on, McCarthy's political rise was enveloped in a miasma of rumors of borderline illegalities, double-crossing, and fast dealing. His election was challenged, unsuccessfully, on grounds he had exceeded the legal limit on campaign expenditures and had misrepresented his opponent's age (the man was sixty-six but McCarthy regularly referred to "my seventy-three-year old opponent" and sometimes cheerfully raised him to eighty-nine). As a judge, he was severely censured by

* At the peak of McCarthy's influence, an elderly Irish Catholic priest of the author's acquaintance criticized McCarthy for being "too timid" in pursuing communists. He did not disclose what he wanted McCarthy to do, but he was clear about the cause of this defect: "It's the German in him. The Germans are sluggish and cautious. If he were pure Irish, he'd fight more."

the Wisconsin Supreme Court for destroying the records in a vital case before it could come up for appeal. He was also criticized for turning his court into a divorce mill. When McCarthy presided, it was remarked that "justice took off her robes and put on a track suit."

When war came, McCarthy joined the Marine Corps. In the days of his fame, this military service, like all else about him, became a subject of controversy. In his first autobiography for the *Congressional Directory* (February, 1947), he wrote: "In June of 1942 applied for enlistment in Marine Corps as buck private and was later commissioned." Subsequent biographical material contained similar statements, although when reporters consulted Navy Department records, it turned out that McCarthy had never been a private. He was commissioned as a First Lieutenant and sent directly to Officers' Training School. After a year of training in the United States, he was assigned as an intelligence officer with the First Marine Air Wing stationed in the New Hebrides. His job was to take down information from pilots returning from a mission and correlate their reports. It was a routine ground assignment, but his political campaign literature always described him as "Tail Gunner Joe."

Once in 1946, after making a speech at Badger Village, a housing development for married veterans studying at the University of Wisconsin, McCarthy was asked by one of the ex-G.I.'s, "Why do you wear built-up shoes?"

McCarthy hesitated. Then he dramatically reached down, removed one shoe, and held it in the air.

"I'll tell you why I wear this shoe," he thundered. "It's because I carry ten pounds of shrapnel in this leg!"

The audience lapsed into awed silence. The meeting soon broke up. It was some time before any of his listeners realized that no human being, whatever shoe he wore, could walk with ten pounds of shrapnel in his leg. McCarthy had not an ounce of shrapnel in him; he had injured his foot in an initiation ceremony when his troopship crossed the international dateline.

In his political speeches, he was fond of recalling "some of the less pleasant days we spent on the South Pacific islands:

"I was with a Marine dive-bombing squadron . . . and one of my tasks at night after we lost pilots or gunners was to write home to the young wives or mothers. . . . If, as was often the case, I had to explain why [the] body, having been lost at sea, his grave would remain forever unmarked, I might try to tell that unfortunate young woman that the greatest headstone any fighting man could desire would be the vast moon-swept, windtossed Pacific Ocean.

"I recall one evening particularly. It was after the raid on Rabaul, one of our roughest strikes. A great number of letters had to be written that night. As I sat in my dugout going over them, the Chaplain came in. I asked him what I could possibly say to these women to explain for the loss of their loved one. . . . The Chaplain told me to write that we made the solemn promise that when this gory, bloody mess is over, there will arise a world that will be to some extent cleaner and finer and more decent."

It was a very moving story. The only trouble was, McCarthy never lived in a dugout, writing letters was not part of his job, and in any case, he could not have written very many, since in the whole war his unit lost a total of five officers and two enlisted men.

He served a little more than a year in the South Pacific, taking time off in 1944 to run in the Republican primary for the United States Senate. He was defeated, but made a strong showing. Deciding not to return to active duty, he resigned the following winter and returned to the bench, six months before the war ended.

McCarthy made his first lunge toward power in 1946 when he upset Robert M. La Follette, Jr., in the Republican senatorial primary by 5,300 votes; it was a minority victory since two also-rans split 60,000 votes between them. Since the Democratic Party was traditionally weak in Wisconsin, McCarthy's victory in the primary virtually assured him of election. He was then only thirty-eight. He had shoved, elbowed, grimaced, shouted, and clowned his way into every photograph, every political meeting where a vote was to be won, every opportunity that came his way. An undistinguished young judge on a rural circuit, he had fought his way into the Senate by the sheer rush of his energy and his absolute refusal to be rebuffed. A Wisconsin friend said of him: "Joe has ambition the way some men have a nervous tic."

McCarthy's first three years in the Senate were dreary enough. Only in retrospect was it possible to see that, in part, they prefigured his later career. He assailed the handling of sugar rationing; it was later learned that the lobbyist for Pepsi-Cola, which was having sugar difficulties, lent him $20,000. He served on a special committee to investigate the housing shortage; he subsequently signed his name to a promotional pamphlet distributed by the Lustron Corporation, a manufacturer of prefabricated housing, for which he received $10,000. The pamphlet, largely ghosted by a public-relations man employed by Lustron, was appropriately entitled. "A Dollar's Worth of Housing for Every Dollar Spent." He was active in a Senate investigation of the "Malmédy massacre" which concerned the trial of German SS troops convicted of killing American soldiers taken prisoner in the Battle of the Bulge. McCarthy championed the cause of the German soldiers who claimed they had been "framed." He made such a violent attack on Senator Raymond Baldwin, the Republican chairman of the investigating committee, that the latter privately gave this as one of his reasons for resigning from the Senate to take a state judgeship.

None of these activities on behalf of Pepsi-Cola, Lustron, and the Malmédy killers lifted McCarthy out of the ruck of obscurity. He was still a backbencher in February, 1950, when he discovered the issue of communism.[1]

2

McCarthy, on the eve of his ascent to national fame, was a rogue. He was a rascally, blarneying, happy-go-lucky adventurer. He was a hard drinker, he loved to gamble at dice, poker, or the races, and he was fond of parties and conversation. He was not a man to be trusted where money or truth was concerned, but, for all that, he was a man to be enjoyed. And roguery remained the essence of his personality in his years of power. It is important to bear this in mind because his actions from 1950 to 1954 and the bitter controversies they provoked inflated him into a shining knight to his admirers and a figure of satanic, Hitler-like evil to his enemies. But he was no hero and no Hitler. He never believed in any principles or body of political convictions, least of all in the movement that was given his name, "McCarthyism." Even when he appeared most dangerous and aggressive, one always had the lurking sense that he might on a whim drop the whole thing and skip to Mexico.

The dictionary defines a rogue as: "A vagrant, an idle, sturdy beggar; a vagabond; tramp. The term . . . loosely applied . . . to various wandering, disorderly, or dissolute persons. . . .

"A dishonest person; a knave; a cheat. Scamp; rascal; worthless fellow . . . pleasantly mischievous, waggish, or frolicsome."

The word, which is of unknown origin, has also a special meaning that President Eisenhower and a considerable body of Republican politicians came to appreciate: "Rogue elephant—A vicious elephant which separates from the herd and roams alone; hence any large animal with habits like those of a rogue elephant—sometimes used attributively of persons."

The period in which he flourished was one of postwar reaction, a time of torpor and conservatism. But McCarthy was not in quest of respectability; he was markedly different in style and motivation from more typical politicians of the Eisenhower period, such as Richard Nixon. In an age of conformity, McCarthy was, as Richard Rovere observed, "the least conformist of politicians. He followed no leader and stamped with no herd. He was a chronic oppositionist, a dissenter for dissent's sake; he had to depart every majority and to attack every authority. He never thought positively. He denounced the very institutions that are customarily thought of as the fortresses of American conformity: the Army, the Protestant clergy, the press, the two major parties, the civil service. . . . He reached the heights at a time when the rules of politics were being rewritten by public relations and advertising men, opinion samplers, professional elocutionists like Robert Montgomery, and the moguls of television. While his contemporaries were slavishly adapting themselves to the ways urged upon them by these people, McCarthy paid no attention to any of it."

The Senate, if it is not the world's most exclusive club, is nevertheless a club where the old-timers very soon take the measure of a new member. By the beginning of 1950, when McCarthy had been in the Senate for three years, his colleagues had sized him up as a lightweight, an occasional troublemaker but mostly a "good-time Charley." Indeed, it was this very reputation that lured the Truman administration and the Senate Democratic leadership into the trap of providing him with his great opportunity. McCarthy made his first speech on communists in government at Wheeling, West Virginia, on February 9, 1950 which was two weeks after Alger Hiss had been sentenced to prison for perjury concerning the theft of State Department documents. Secretary of State Dean Acheson, a personal friend of Hiss, had committed a grave error of judgment by making the statement, "I will not turn my back on Alger Hiss." (James Reston of the *New York Times* once observed how much trouble Acheson would have spared himself if he had expressed the same sentiment in more colloquial terms: "I won't kick a man when he's down.") The Justice Department had prosecuted the Hiss case successfully in court, but Acheson's silly statement, together with the fact that the case had originally been broken by the Republican-controlled House Un-American Activities Committee, placed Truman and the Democrats momentarily on the defensive. Ordinarily, they would not have become exercised by the speeches of an unimportant opposition senator, particularly when those speeches had been delivered in out-of-the-way places during the Lincoln Birthday speechmaking season. But under the circumstances, the Democrats decided to counterattack. They thought they saw a chance to corner and destroy the issue of "softness toward communism" in the person of McCarthy who seemed likely, on his past performances, to be an ineffectual exponent of that issue. Senate Majority Leader Scott Lucas took the unusual step of sponsoring a resolution directing the Foreign Relations Committee or one of its subcommittees to investigate

McCarthy's charges. The chairman chosen for the subcommittee was Millard Tydings, Maryland Democrat, a wily veteran of twenty-four years in the Senate with an irreproachable conservative record. If they had realized they had a dragon by the tail, Lucas would not have been so eager to press for an investigation or Tydings so amenable to chairing it. They would have followed the usual policy of ignoring McCarthy's charges, deprecating them as routine partisan vaporings, or at most conducting the kind of slow-motion inquiry where charges die from procrastination and polite study. Instead, they pushed for immediate public hearings, hoping to unmask McCarthy.

Once the Tydings Committee hearings began, McCarthy displayed a masterful sense of the uses of publicity and unexpected personal resources as an infighter. The very quality of roguishness that had caused his colleagues to discount him proved to be his source of strength. Where a more cautious man would have taken care not to overextend himself and would have embellished a central lie with edgings of fact, McCarthy, boldly and recklessly, followed one sweeping assertion with another still more breathtaking; when disaster confronted him in the shape of denial or convincing refutation, he responded, lightheartedly, waggishly, almost frolicsomely, with some fresh invention or wild diversion. It was all a game, and the faster the chase, the merrier for all. If men's careers and reputations and the policies of the government had not been at stake, McCarthy's performance before the Tydings Committee could be regarded as an entertaining *divertissement*. Perhaps only a splendid Irish rogue could have carried it off so well.

At the same time, the unusual excitement the Tydings Committee hearings aroused in the spring of 1950 in Washington and throughout the country revealed for the first time the depth of the popular feelings of rage and suspicion about the communist issue. McCarthy had tapped a richer vein of anxiety than either he or his smug antagonists had suspected. That was why this unpromising man in rumpled clothes, an indifferent orator with awkward gestures, a poseur with ill-formed ideas and ignorant of the facts on the very issue he exploited, was able to bewitch masses of people and turn the country topsy-turvy for four years. He had touched upon a raw nerve in the national psyche at the critical moment when that generation of Americans was passing through a profound crisis of confidence.

The terribly wearing strains of the cold war, following upon the emotional ordeal of World War II and soon to be intensified by the sacrifices of Korea, made the country receptive to a search for a scapegoat. The American communists and their fellow travelers were not only real enough to serve the purpose but they could also be identified, risking a strain upon credulity, as the cause of every item on the calendar of disillusionment from high taxes to continued draft service. Someone must be responsible for all this, someone must be made to pay dearly, and McCarthy with simpleminded persistence pointed at the most obvious suspect. He tied in the fear, hatred, and weary resentment of communists with distrust of the State Department. Every frustrated isolationist, every spiritually dispossessed American dreading the foreign entanglements of the cold war in an atomic age responded to his cry.

McCarthy had said at Wheeling: "I have here in my hand a list of 205 . . . a list of names that were made known to the Secretary of State as being members of the Communist Party and who nevertheless are still working and shaping policy in the State Department."

The 205 "communists" subsequently became 205 "bad security risks," then 57 "card-carrying communists," and then 81 "cases." It was easy to trace the origins of these figures, their spurious nature, their inherent contradictions and implausibilities. All this the Tydings Committee did. But issues of political loyalty are inherently slippery, and standards of government security are not susceptible of quick definition or description. The Tydings Committee killed the minnows, but the shark of suspicion remained below the waters.

In the background, working all the time to predispose public opinion in McCarthy's favor, was the still-fresh memory of the Hiss case. If McCarthy seemed an improbable figure, everyone remembered it was that shaggy assemblage, the House Un-American Activities Committee, which had uncovered Hiss. If it seemed dubious that Professor Owen Lattimore of Johns Hopkins University could really be, as McCarthy charged, the "number one Soviet spy in this country," everyone remembered that two years earlier no one had suspected that suave, respectable Alger Hiss, president of the Carnegie Foundation, was a Soviet agent. If McCarthy never seemed to produce any substantial evidence in the mass of documents and photostats he was constantly shuffling ("I hold in my hand . . ."), everyone recalled that Whittaker Chambers had seemed equally unpersuasive at first but had finally produced incriminating documents. Might not McCarthy in 1950 draw forth from his bulging briefcase something as decisive as Chambers had taken in 1948 from a pumpkin? The Hiss case had deeply jarred the nation's complacency about communism. McCarthy could not have made the impact he did if the Hiss case had not prepared the way.

The Korean War, which began in June, 1950, four months after McCarthy's Wheeling speech, was a second factor working in his favor. The shock of the war, which broke with no warning and in a part of the world most Americans knew nothing about, dramatically underscored the seriousness of the tension with Russia. The casualty lists, the draft calls, and later the reimposition of price controls stunned a people who only five years earlier had won a great war and thought they had achieved peace, if not forever, at least for their time. When the Chinese communists entered the war in the autumn and, by so doing, made a clearcut victory within the confines of Korea impossible, the resulting stalemate added a sense of frustration to the sense of shock. If the Hiss case gave McCarthy his opening, the Korean War accounted for the durability of his appeal.

A third factor that worked to McCarthy's advantage was the bad luck that befell his political opponents. In the congressional elections of November, 1950, Senator Lucas, the Democratic majority leader; Senator Francis Myers of Pennsylvania, the Democratic majority whip; and Senator Tydings were defeated for reelection. It is possible in retrospect to see that McCarthy was not actually instrumental in their defeat, with the partial exception of Tydings. Lucas and Myers held seats that were by any standard marginal; Illinois and Pennsylvania had in the recent past been Republican strongholds and, despite the many changes effected by the New Deal, they were states in which a Democratic candidate still needed in 1950 a confluence of many favorable forces to achieve success. Maryland, a traditional Democratic state, began in 1950 a sharp swing to the Republicans that brought about that year not only the defeat of Tydings but also a victory for the Republicans in the governorship contest and, two years later, gained them the other Senate seat and a majority of the state's delegation to the House of Representatives. Negroes, trade unionists, and liberals had their own reasons for not supporting the very conservative Tydings for reelection. McCarthy's effort against him played a part in his defeat, but by itself would probably not have been decisive. Nevertheless, in politics what counts, particularly in the short run, is not the deep-seated cause of an event but the quick interpretation people place upon it. In 1950 the defeat of the three Democratic leaders tended to be ascribed to McCarthy.

This was significant in the inner life of the Senate. The Democratic losses in the North and West placed the party in the Senate firmly in the control of its southern bloc. Tydings, a border-state man, had been one of the hierarchs in that bloc. His defeat was as ominous and upsetting in its own way to conservative southern senators as the revelations of the Hiss case had been to the public at large. It meant—no man is safe from McCarthy. The Southerners who had previously ignored or dismissed him were now mindful of Tydings's fate and their own political skins. They shrank back from him in fear. Over the next three and one-half years, scattered individual senators—Herbert Lehman of New York, William Benton of Connecticut, William Fulbright of Arkansas—did lonely battle with him, but none of them was a real Senate insider. It was not until the spring of 1954, when the southern bloc, working through Senator John McClellan of Arkansas, decided to throw its weight actively against him, that McCarthy had anything to worry about. His reputation as the conqueror of Millard Tydings made the Senate for him a privileged sanctuary.

McCarthy used the Senate chamber principally to launch attacks safe from libel suits. He tried deliberately to overpower and silence his critics. Of columnist Drew Pearson, for example, he said: "It appears that Pearson never actually signed up as a member of the Communist Party and has never paid dues [but] if the loyal newspaper editors and publishers and radio-station owners refuse to buy this disguised, sugar-coated voice of Russia, the mockingbirds who have followed the Pearson line will disappear from the scene like chaff before the wind.

"The American people can do much to accomplish this result. . . . It should be remembered that anyone who buys an Adam hat, any store that stocks an Adam hat, is unknowingly and innocently contributing at least something to the cause of international communism by keeping this Communist spokesman on the air."

Adam Hats withdrew its sponsorship of Pearson's broadcasts. Pearson survived, but McCarthy had scored a triumph.

He soon followed with attacks on *Time* magazine, the Milwaukee *Journal*, the Madison *Capital Times*, and other newspapers. He often spoke to an empty chamber. His colleagues, by their withdrawal, expressed their silent disapproval, but also their fear.

3

In 1951–1952 McCarthy spent most of his time out of Washington carrying his fight to the country. The scene varied but the rhetoric was always the same. His favorite audiences were veterans' groups. Preceded by a color guard and wearing an overseas cap, McCarthy paraded to the rostrum amid cheers. Then came a mass recitation of the pledge of allegiance to the flag.

His opening was a sally of heavy humor:

"Well, it's good to get away from Washington and be back here in the U.S.A."

McCarthy was no formal orator. He rambled on for an hour or more, without a text, mixing broadside attacks with sentimental reminiscences of wartime service, indignation with humor, and all expressed in earthy colloquial language.

"Take my word for it, I don't enjoy this task," he would say. "It is a dirty, disagreeable job, but a job which must be done. When I was a boy on the farm, my mother used to raise chickens. The greatest enemy the chickens had were skunks. In order to protect mother's chickens, my three brothers and I had to dig out and destroy those skunks. It was a dirty, foul, unpleasant, smelly job. And sometimes after it was done, people did not like to have us sit next to them in church."

His natural tenor voice rose shrilly or fell to a half-strangled guttural cry. "Hyenas," "traitors," "left-wing, bleeding-heart, phony liberals!" he shouted at various times.

He held up miscellaneous, vaguely identified documents in his left hand and waved them: "I hold in my hand . . ."

Midway through his talk, he would take off his coat. Moments later, he would roll up his shirtsleeves. He sweated. He loosened his tie.

He challenged Dean Acheson to sue him for libel. He promised that he would not run out on his fight against the State Department: "My mother used to say, 'Joe is too dumb to quit anything he starts.'"

After discussing two or three of his "cases," sometimes naming individuals and sometimes describing them only with a term such as "a State Department official," he would move toward his peroration: "As I fight day after day in Washington against the Reds and their friends, my mind goes back to the nights in the islands. I was in a Marine dive-bombing squadron. One night, the Chaplain stopped in my dugout and . . ."

After long verbatim "quotes" from the chaplain, he asked his audience for their help and their prayers.[2]

There was a rough artistry in these performances. His triumphs came through the solid identification his listeners often made with him. He was, they felt, a regular, two-fisted, ordinary guy, trying to do a tough job and refusing to be taken in by the hifalutin words and fancy explanations of the "doubledomes" and the "smart alecks." He knew the score.

The Republican victory of 1952 brought him a crucial measure of power in the form of the Senate Investigating Subcommittee chairmanship. He obtained official status as an investigator, he could name a staff, and he had the power to subpoena witnesses. Since the planning and administrative work required for any systematic inquiry bored him, he delegated the substance of his authority to Roy Cohn, whom he appointed subcommittee counsel.

For one heady year, while McCarthy turned the Voice of America organization upside down, bypassed the State Department in negotiations with Greek shipowners over trade with communist China, and held secret hearings at the Fort Monmouth Army radar center, the agents of the Eisenhower administration talked hopefully of "teamwork." Mc-

Carthy, some seemed to think, was a roughneck boy who, if handled with sympathy and patience, could be persuaded to slick down his hair, straighten his tie, and take his proper place in the choir.

McCarthy had no taste for this kind of reform. His was a Napoleonic egotism. Had he played it safe, had he made a businesslike deal with Vice-President Richard Nixon, had he abided by any one of a dozen truces with the administration, he could have become an esteemed party figure with a safe Senate seat for life and an endless vista of well-paying Lincoln Day audiences listening to his stock oration, "Twenty Years of Treason."

It was not McCarthy's destiny to become a domesticated hatchet man. He had only contempt for the petty brokers of small personal causes. Let others have their cushiony jobs, their official limousines, their tawdry respectability. These were not the aims of Joe McCarthy, the man who had dragged down the titans of the Senate, wrecked Dean Acheson's career, made a Secretary of the Army grovel before him, fired bureaucrats at will, driven Pearson from the networks, raged at newspapers with impunity, shaken whole departments of the government to their foundations, and added a new word—an extension of his own name—to the English language.

Granting the difference in historic size, what Albert Guérard has written of Napoleon is applicable here to McCarthy's imperial vision:

"Honors and wealth: these he grabbed as he went, roughly, abundantly, contemptuously, for his aim was beyond them. It was even beyond power: power was but his instrument, 'his violin,' as he put it. His sole aim was glory. . . .

"The very nature of such a thirst for glory is to be unquenchable. The morrow of every victory is an anti-climax: there must ever be new prodigies, each more dazzling than the last. He was the eternal Don Juan of politics and war. He put it himself with daring and forcible humor: 'God the Father's job? Not for me; no future to it; a blind alley.'

"Hence also his wild gambling with fate. It was not in his nature to cash his chips and retire. To rest satisfied, to calculate on safe and modest profits would seem to him craven and commonplace: the true hero stakes his all—world empire or downfall."[3]

McCarthy was no world historical figure, but the disease of the little Corsican had eaten deep into his bones. Just as Napoleon's victories required Waterloo and St. Helena for their logical working out, so also McCarthy's roaring triumphs inevitably led to the mad folly of the Army hearings and the nadir of censure.

The road led inexorably back to where it had all begun: the marble magnificence of the Senate Caucus Room. There, in the springtime of 1954, where but four years before he had had his melodramatic and inconclusive confrontation with the Tydings Committee, McCarthy and his corporal's guard—Roy Cohn, young, sleek, overconfident; David Schine, blondly handsome and arrogant in his fatuity; Francis P. Carr, sleepy-eyed and inert; James Juliana, dark eyes flashing and manner faintly contemptuous; Don Surine, sullen and remote—there in those April days, they slowly bled to death as surely as the Grand Army on the retreat from Moscow.

McCarthy could have avoided the hearings before they began if he had compromised. The problem of the Army's cooperation with his investigation was not so acute that it could not have been resolved to his satisfaction, particularly given the supine character of Army Secretary Robert Stevens.

McCarthy, however, could not accept anything less than total surrender. During the early stages of the hearing, a face-saving arrangement could still have been worked out. But McCarthy pressed recklessly forward.

In Joseph Welch, the Boston attorney who represented the Army Department in the hearings, he met a courtly, witty, and deadly antagonist. The "cropped photograph," the recorded telephone conversations, the jumbled documents, the unfolding of Cohn's arrogance at Fort Monmouth, and finally Welch's tearful, dramatic reprise to McCarthy's attack on the loyalty of one of Welch's young associates were climactic defeats along the road.

Senator Karl Mundt's flabby manner as presiding officer provided McCarthy with his fatal opportunity. If Mundt, the ranking Republican on the subcommittee who chaired the hearings since McCarthy stepped down to the rank of a witness, had run the inquiry with a firm, judicial hand, the television audience might soon have found the proceedings tedious and technical. But Mundt, in a misguided attempt to be helpful to McCarthy, permitted him to interrupt at will; McCarthy, who rarely restrained himself, was therefore without any exterior check on his recklessness. McCarthy, for all the leeway he had, was never quite able either to outcircle Welch or to overpower him and, in the end, it was the memory that the television audience carried away from the scene that undid him, the memory of McCarthy first bellowing and finally croaking:

"Point of order, Mr. Chairman . . . point of order . . . point of order."

The expression became the butt of a thousand jokes. Fear cannot live with laughter. The rich vein of anxiety McCarthy had struck was temporarily, at least, played out and laughter trickled in its place.

The following December the Senate finally passed a resolution "condemning" McCarthy, but this was important mostly for its psychological effect within the Senate itself where the condemnation broke the spell of fear he had cast for four years. The more decisive judgment had been rendered against him a month earlier when the voters shifted control of Congress from the Republicans to the Democrats. He could be held partly responsible for the Republican defeat because the antics of the Army-McCarthy hearings impaired the Eisenhower administration's prestige. The number of seats that shifted was actually slight, but in the context, the press interpreted it as a defeat for McCarthy just as it had interpreted the GOP victories four years earlier as his triumph. The change in party control meant that McCarthy was deprived of his committee chairmanship. This was a more important factor in his subsequent rapid decline than is usually understood. Although it is true that he had risen to national influence in 1950 to 1952 without the benefit of any committee power, he was then imputing communism and subversion to an administration controlled by the opposition party and one that was, on all fronts, losing the confidence of the country. But after 1954 he was attacking a Republican administration that still retained the confidence of the majority of the people. Moreover, since most Republican politicians and newspapers were naturally eager that their party's first administration in twenty years should succeed, they now withheld from McCarthy the tolerance they had given him a few years earlier when he was attacking Truman. If he had remained a committee chairman, he would at least have had the naked authority to run hearings, subpoena witnesses, and keep himself alive in the press. Deprived of his chairmanship, he had nothing to fall back upon except his own capacity to create tumult by fresh accusations and sensations. In the comparatively hostile political climate that set in by the autumn of 1954, his inner resources were not adequate to this challenge.

"I'm happy to have this circus ended so I can get back to the real work of digging out communism, crime and corruption," McCarthy declared on Thursday evening, December 2, 1954, after the Senate voted 67 to 22 to condemn his behavior. "That job will start officially Monday morning after ten months of inaction," he said, adding that the censure hearings had been "a farce" and "a foul job."[4]

This was the authentic McCarthy cry, but there was no tomorrow. The projected investigation of "communists in defense plants" petered out. Two and one-half years later, McCarthy was dead.

4

McCarthyism was a major crisis in the coming of age of the Irish Catholic community in the United States. It derived strength from the worst, the weakest, and the most outdated parts of the Irish experience in this country. But it also evoked and tested the best in that experience. It was fed by old parochialisms, old prejudices, old misunderstandings. But it was also combated by growing sophistication and deeping moral and political maturity. McCarthy, it must be noted, had several sources of support in addition to the Irish Catholic community. His closest allies were Protestant Republican senators from the Middle West and Far West—William Jenner of Indiana, Karl Mundt of South Dakota, and Herman Welker of Idaho—and the Republican Party in these areas provided him with his political base. McCarthy is examined in the present context only insofar as he, to a degree, was an Irish Catholic phenomenon.

A Gallup poll taken in January, 1954, when McCarthy was at the peak of his influence, reported that 58 percent of American Catholics responded favorably to the question: "In general, would you say you have a favorable or unfavorable opinion of Senator Joseph R. McCarthy?"

The figures for the three religious groups were:[5]

	FAVORABLE	UNFAVORABLE	NO OPINION
Catholics	58%	23%	19%
Protestants	49	28	23
Jews	15	71	14

The discrepancy among religious groups would probably have been wider if the poll had asked the question only of Irish Catholics, instead of all Catholics.

Many Irish Catholics who fell for McCarthy's appeal had at the bottom of their minds a conviction they would not articulate in intellectual terms but which they deeply felt. This was the belief that very few Americans outside the Catholic faith have any real religion or understand what it means to take religion seriously. Only the Catholics, so this feeling goes, believe that God is literally present in their churches; only Catholics make a great point of going to church every Sunday in foul weather or fair, in summer vacations or in winter snow. Since one sees everyone but fellow Catholics as in various stages of backsliding toward agnosticism and atheism, it naturally follows that if religious freedom is to be kept alive in this country it is up to the Catholics. ("Religious freedom" is thought of as the right to exercise religious belief and live in a religiously oriented milieu—a right menaced on all sides by secularism and irreligion. The contrary idea that Catholics are themselves a threat to the religious liberty of others is a notion not much examined by the people under discussion.) It follows, furthermore, that only Catholics can fully grasp the sinister nature of communism, an avowedly antireligious movement. Communism is the work of Satan; one should not compromise with Satan in politics anymore than one should compromise with sin in one's private life. And how do Catholics know that they alone possess religion and must go to any lengths to save it? Because in past generations other Americans have persecuted Catholics and tried to prevent them from having full religious freedom. The memory of the Maria Monk fraud, the Know-Nothing riots, the bigotry of the A.P.A., the Ku Klux Klan, and the defeat of Al Smith seemed to demonstrate that other Americans hated true religion. This religious bigotry in the past had in some ways isolated and set apart the Irish, who were the leaders of the Catholic community. The cultural isolation and the residual resentment against past discrimination convinced many Irish that they had a special mission to save America for religion in the struggle against communism. They felt that only they knew what the struggle was all about and that the liberals and the atheists and the Jews and the half-agnostic Protestants did not know.

This parochial view of America and of the religion of other Americans was shared by a considerable number of American Irish. It was a view more common among the older generations than the young, and among the poor and the uneducated than among the affluent and better schooled. But attitudes based on this view could be observed in various individuals at all age, income, and educational levels. These attitudes provided the general background for McCarthy's success with the Irish.

Several specific sources in the American Irish experience nourished McCarthyism. They include an insufficient understanding of the range and complexity of the Irish people's own history in this country; a comparable failure to understand the splendor and full significance of Catholicism as an intellectual heritage; a faulty and inadequate political tradition; anxieties about social status, and an undercurrent of tension with Jews.

In trying to understand and evaluate these various influences, one has to distinguish between what McCarthyism was and what it drew strength from. The two were not identical. McCarthy, for example, was not an anti-Semite and did not make use of anti-Semitism in his activities. He was as devoid of prejudice as he was of principle. He was an adventurer, not a hater. But there is a minority strain of anti-Semitism within the Irish community, and most Irish anti-Semites rallied to McCarthy's standard. The hard-core Coughlinites of the late 1930's were among the McCarthyites of the early 1950's. These people were distressed when McCarthy confided so much authority in a pair of Jewish youths, Roy Cohn and David Schine, but they rationalized their disappointment on the usual grounds that Cohn and Schine were the "exceptions," the "good Jews." Anti-Semitism was a secondary and submerged but real factor in the McCarthyite complex.

Anxieties about their own social status made some Irish particularly predisposed to respond favorably to McCarthy's appeals for 100 percent Americanism, but those anxieties did not produce McCarthyism nor were they more than a secondary influence in sustaining it. In *The New American Right*, edited by Daniel Bell, several contributors stress the sociological origins of McCarthyism and other movements of the "radical right." Bell lists among the "mélange" of groups supporting McCarthy, "the rising middle-class strata of the ethnic groups, the Irish and the Germans." Richard Hofstadter speculates that McCarthyism ". . . is in good part a product of the rootlessness and heterogeneity of American life, and above all, of its peculiar scramble for status and its peculiar search for secure identity." He sees these status concerns as being most intense among those old-family, Anglo-Saxon Protestants who are losing caste and among those families in immigrant groups that are rapidly gaining it.[6]

My own view is that McCarthyism was primarily a political, not a social, phenomenon. It depended upon McCarthy's personal ingenuity and upon a specific set of historical circumstances, including the Hiss case, the cold war, and the Korean War. Undoubtedly the tensions and conflicts of middle-class life made some Irish peculiarly responsive to the appeals of McCarthy, but the Irish have been advancing socially and economically in the open competition of American life for many decades before McCarthy appeared in 1950 and have continued in the years afterward. Their "touchiness," their resentment at social snubs, their desire to assert their American patriotism, and their desire to "make good" socially were much more intense thirty or forty years earlier. By 1950 many of these status concerns had faded out, and most Irish were mellowed by the feeling that they had comfortably arrived. Moreover, McCarthy did not have his strongest support in the Irish community among the more successful and those actively rising on the social scale. The blatancy and crudeness of his appeal were vaguely disturbing and offensive to these wall-to-wall, two cars-in-the-garage Irish. Like suburban voters of other nationality backgrounds, these Irish more typically preferred the blandness of Dwight Eisenhower or, later, the well-mannered, Ivy League liberalism of John Kennedy. McCarthy was strongest in the poorer, old-line Irish neighborhoods in South Boston, Brooklyn, and Chicago where working-class and lower-middle-class families still lived. These were the people who had been left behind in the scramble; they did not suffer status anxieties due to social and occupational mobility for the simple reason that they were not mobile. They had not advanced beyond where they were a generation or two generations earlier. Their suspicions, prejudices, and resentments were of a simpler, more old-fashioned, more primitive kind.

More important than vague status anxieties in motivating a favorable Irish response toward McCarthy was their unique intellectual and political orientation. Too much Irish Catholic intellectual energy had for too long been devoted to valid but entirely negative attacks on communism. In the second year of the Korean War when McCarthyite emotions were rising, the *Commonweal* observed editorially: ". . . for many people, sterile anti-Communism has become the hallmark of Catholicism; it is the one characteristic note of our periodicals, sermons, academic addresses, speeches at Communion breakfasts. In many minds anti-Communism is actually a synonym for Catholic Action. It should give us pause that as men in their desperate need have stretched out their hands for life-giving bread, we Christians have been offering them the dead stone of anti-Communism."

What the United States and the world badly needed were "the good tidings of Christianity and their implications for the family, in politics and throughout human society."[7]

If there had been sufficient understanding on the part of Irish Catholics as to the positive implications of their religion in the political and social sphere, they would not have been vulnerable to the appeals of a political adventurer whose approach was so singularly lacking in charity, who irresponsibly disregarded complexities, reduced every question to labels and slogans, and made open appeals to unreason and nonintelligence.

Only the conviction that anticommunism was, in itself, the supreme good could adequately explain why Christians, including many priests supposedly well trained in Scholastic thought, could not only condone but approve of a man who said, as McCarthy did, "If you will get me a slippery-elm club and put me aboard Adlai Stevenson's campaign train, I will use it on some of his advisers, and perhaps I can make a good American of him." Or his subsequent statement that a friend named Indian Charlie had advised him that, when in trouble, he should hit his opponent in the groin.

Father Robert Hartnett, editor of *America*, the Jesuit weekly, and the editors of the *Commonweal* steadily tried to combat McCarthyite attitudes in their editorials throughout the early fifties. This wrong, misdirected kind of anticommunism was also the target of a famous speech by Bishop Bernard J. Sheil in April, 1954.

"It is not enough to say that someone is anti-Communist to win my support. It has been said that patriotism is the scoundrel's last refuge. In this day and age anti-Communism is sometimes the scoundrel's first defense," Sheil said.

Bishop Sheil defined affirmative anticommunism in several ways, including the defense of democratic procedures, the clarification of the difference between treason and nonconformity, support of military measures to resist communist intimidation, and, most of all, "seeing to it that conditions here and abroad are such that they don't provide a fertile breeding ground for Communism.

"If a man is truly anti-Communist, . . . he is interested in such matters as seeing to it that people get enough to eat, have decent homes, are able to raise their children in dignity. His scope is broad. He is interested in measures to share the wealth of 'have' nations with the 'have nots.' He is interested in breaking down the barriers that separate people—national barriers, religious barriers, class barriers. He is interested in making a better place of his own little corner of the world and of doing all he can to see that others are not in want.

"I judge an anti-Communist—the real thing, not the cops-and-robbers version—by how well he does these things. . . . By this standard, a number of famous anti-Communists, I'm sorry to say, simply don't measure up."

Bishop Sheil stressed that in giving his opinion on McCarthyism he was expressing only his own opinion and not that of the Church and that on political matters, a Catholic's statement—even a bishop's—has only his own personal weight behind it: "I know that there are many in my Church who do not agree with me on this. So be it. Time will tell which of us is right."

In conclusion, however, Sheil stressed the inescapable moral point: "Although the Church takes no position, and will not, on such a matter of public controversy, the Church does take a position on lies, calumny, the absence of charity, and calculated deceit. These things are wrong—even if they are mistakenly thought of as means to a good end. They are morally evil and to call them good or to act as if they were permissible under certain circumstances is itself a monstrous perversion of morality. They are not justified by any cause—least of all by the cause of anti-Communism which should unite rather than divide all of us in these difficult times."[8]

Bishop Sheil's speech had an impact, among other reasons, because it was delivered in the same week in which Joe McCarthy was the featured speaker at a Communion Breakfast attended by six thousand Catholic members of the New York City police force. Monsignor Joseph McCaffrey, retiring after thirty years as Catholic chaplain of the police force, introduced McCarthy as "one who has devoted time and talent and his life to the exposure and uprooting of Communists." Monsignor McCaffrey noted that despite McCarthy's mistakes, "which have been few," he obviously had the appreciation of the audience, and "certainly he has mine." Cardinal Spellman of New York attended the breakfast, shook hands with McCarthy, and applauded his remarks.[9]

Three weeks earlier, James A. Farley said on St. Patrick's Day that McCarthy had done "a pretty good job in efforts to drive the Communist elements out of government." On that same day, McCarthy addressed a large dinner in Chicago of the Irish Fellowship (boycotted by Democratic National Chairman Stephen Mitchell, an Irish Catholic) and heard himself eulogized by the chairman as typifying the spirit of the American Irish.

5

McCarthy, the only Irish Catholic Republican ever elected to the Senate in the Middle West, had an ambiguous relationship to the dominant Irish Democratic political tradition in this country. He derived moral sanction from the permissive and ethnocentric code of ethics that the Irish political machines had developed in the cities, but he was not subject to the social disciplines and restraints that the machines normally impose on their members. He grew up on a farm in an isolated rural section where the Irish families were a tiny minority and in a state, Wisconsin, which had never known an Irish-dominated political machine. Having switched from the Democrats to the Republicans, he was also outside even the normal party loyalties and disciplines. "It is an advantage to be a Republican with a Democratic name," he once remarked.

It is a point of historic irony for the present study that McCarthy could probably not have created "McCarthyism" and become a national figure if he had come from a state where the Irish were numerous and if he had remained a Democrat. In the states where the Irish are politically strong, their political machines tolerate certain kinds of political corruption but they also impose a code of party loyalty, regularity, and obedience to the leadership. As social institutions, these machines are conservative; they have large and permanent interests to protect and therefore, like most social institutions, are hostile to the adventurer and the demagogue. No man can be allowed to become bigger than the party or to sacrifice the party's interests to his own fantasies and fanaticisms. Too many jobs and contracts are at stake. There have been numerous Irish Democratic politicians in the big cities who held exactly McCarthy's views on communism and subversion in government. Typical in New York in the 1930's was State Senator John McNaboe of Manhattan who sponsored an investigation of communism in the New York City school system.

McNaboe was denied renomination in 1940, and that was the usual fate of the McNaboes in the Democratic Party. They were cut down before they became more than local nuisances. This was not because their views were unpopular; the very political leaders who sabotaged their careers might sympathize with their opinions, but a party organization has too many interests and is subject to too many diverse pressures to tie itself to any single issue. The complex makeup of the Democratic Party and the middle-man role of the Irish within it are important in this connection. Since victory depends upon keeping together a coalition of Irish, Jews, Italians, Negroes, trade unions, and liberal independents, the Irish Democratic politicians do not bring to the fore erratic personalities like Joe McCarthy. They prefer duller but safer types. It was no accident that Wisconsin with its more fluid politics and antimachine traditions produced Joe McCarthy.[10]

Although the Irish machines would not have brought forth McCarthy, their adherents were vulnerable to his appeal. Their political traditions and habits of mind emphasized the sheer fact of power and put little stress on civil liberties or the proprieties of campaigning. Accustomed to political campaigns that were hard fought, savagely argued family fights, many Irish did not really understand the criticism of McCarthy as an "alley fighter" or a traducer of men's reputations. "I approve of his objectives but I don't like his methods," was a mealymouthed evasion not coined by an Irishman. The "fighting Irish" rather liked McCarthy's "tough guy" style. They did not sympathize with State Department employees or defeated politicians who were victims of McCarthy's techniques. Who ever said public life was a vocation for gentlemen? Or, as the old question went, "What was a man with a paper skull doing in Garrity's saloon in the first place?"

Although vulnerable to McCarthy's appeals, the Irish as Democrats were unable to do very much to translate their approval into practical terms. The Democratic Party organizations in the big cities were frequently criticized for failure to speak out against McCarthy and for truckling to McCarthyite sentiment. But it is equally noteworthy that the Irish political machines never broke over to give McCarthy any active, positive support. The fact that he was a Republican made McCarthy's career possible, but in the end it handicapped him because it cut him off, as a practical matter, from one of his fervent sources of support.

McCarthy's attacks on the Democratic Party did not weaken him with the hard core of his following, but they offended and cut him off from many Irish Democrats who resented passages in his famous "twenty years of treason" speech: "The hard fact is that those who wear the label—Democrat—wear with it the stain of a historic betrayal. . . . It is a political label stitched with the idiocy of a Truman; rotted by the deceit of an Acheson; corrupted by the red slime of a [Harry Dexter] White.

"This is an indictment of the Democratic Party—not of each and every member of that party, for there are those who hold their heads high alongside the very best Americans and who refused to yield. But they . . . were far too few to hold the lever that controlled the political destiny of a nation for two decades."[11]

Hearing or reading this speech, most Irish could not help but remember that at every level of government from the city hall to the President's Cabinet they had played important roles in governing the nation during those "twenty years of treason" and that in many places the Democratic Party was virtually an Irish creation. McCarthy attracted the enthusiasm of some Irish Democrats, and engendered conflicting impulses in the minds of many more, but all the time he was working against a powerful tide of old associations, loyalties, and community history.

Irish Democratic political figures who chose to fight McCarthy did not suffer any grievous consequences in their own constituencies. Senator Brien McMahon of Connecticut was active in the work of the Tydings Committee and signed its report. He was a close adviser to Senator William Benton, his Connecticut colleague, in the latter's running battle with McCarthy. Joseph O'Mahoney of Wyoming, defeated for reelection to the Senate in 1952, entered private law practice and successfully defended Owen Lattimore against a federal indictment. O'Mahoney regained a Senate seat in 1954 in a campaign featured by strong McCarthyite attacks on him. When the Senate voted to condemn McCarthy in December, 1954, six of the eight Catholic senators who were present voted in favor of the resolution.

McCarthyism fed upon parochialism and ignorance. This was an ignorance not only about the intricacies of the communist movement—a subject on which some of the most erudite and sophisticated Americans lost their way—but about the history of the Irish in this country, the relationship of the Irish to other groups in American society, and the nature of the religious and intellectual heritage the McCarthyites thought they were protecting by their kind of anticommunism.

Consider the matter of American Irish history. One did not have to be guilty of Joe McCarthy's barbaric excesses to exhibit an overly simple view of what is really a complicated story. Thomas Murphy, for example, turned in a masterly performance as prosecutor in the two Hiss trials, served ably as Police Commissioner of New York City, and in 1951 became a federal judge. But in a St. Patrick's Day address during the height of the McCarthy era, Murphy said: "I can't even recall one Irish name among the many thousands called before the House Committee on Un-American Activities. If there was, he probably changed his name."

Discussing the "galaxy of Irishmen in the vanguard of our country's fight against Communism," he stated that only one witness who testified in behalf of Alger Hiss was Irish. "He was one of the psychiatrists and besides he came from Harvard. In fact we could pair him . . . with . . . the colored maid [a government witness]," Murphy said.[12]

Murphy was speaking in a light vein, making an after-dinner speech not a sociological survey. His remarks, however, typify a durable attitude in the Irish community. In 1962 *Time* magazine did an article on Catholic intellectuals that discussed the question "Where are the Catholic Salks, Oppenheimers, Einsteins?" Soon afterward *Time* ran in its letters column a one-line letter signed "Joseph Kerrigan" that stated: "No Einsteins, but also no Rosenbergs."[13]

This expressed concisely the connection that seems to exist in some minds between intellectual distinction (Einstein) and treason (Julius and Ethel Rosenberg, executed as spies). Like Murphy's speech, the letter also reflected the stereotyped view that persons of Irish Catholic background do not become communists. But the historical record tells a different story.

"The American communist movement owes a great deal to the Irish and the Irish-American radicals. The Irish escaped the handicaps of the other foreign-born elements in the movement. Accepted as Americans, they considered themselves natives and acted accordingly. The Irish communist contingent consisted of a small number of individuals. In leadership, however, they commanded a position relatively out of proportion to their numbers. From the Irish contingent the communists got organizers, writers, editors, speakers, trade union leaders and valuable contacts with important elements in other trade unions. The Irish constituted a virile, aggressive element which boasted of revolutionary traditions and was proud of the achievements of the Irish revolutionists."[14]

These words are from the memoirs of Benjamin Gitlow who helped organize the American Communist Party, eventually became its leader, and then was expelled from the Party because he defied Stalin.

William Z. Foster, the longtime boss of the American Communist Party, and Elizabeth Gurley Flynn, the best-known of the Communist women leaders, are both of Irish ancestry. Foster was born in Taunton, Massachusetts in 1881. "His father, an English-hating Irish immigrant, washed carriages for a living. His mother [was] a devout Catholic of English-Irish stock."[15]

Elizabeth Gurley Flynn's father was a Catholic; she was baptized and briefly attended a convent school, but not raised as a Catholic. She begins her memoirs: "My ancestors were 'immigrants and revolutionists'—from the Emerald Isle. . . . There was an uprising in each generation in Ireland, and forefathers of mine were in every one of them. The awareness of being Irish came to us as small children, through plaintive song and heroic story. . . . As children, we drew in a burning hatred of British rule with our mother's milk. Until my father died, at over eighty, he never said *England* without adding, 'God damn her!' Before I was ten I knew of the great heroes—Robert Emmet, Wolfe Tone, Michael Davitt, Parnell, and O'Donovan Rossa."[16]

Foster, Gurley Flynn, and other, less well-known Irish communists are not representative figures, but they are, nevertheless, part of the history of the American Irish. Only someone ignorant of that history could contend that there have been no Irish radicals, including communists.

The misunderstanding of history is linked to a larger failure of American Catholics led by the Irish to bring to fruition the intellectual heritage of their Church. Cardinal Gibbons, Archbishop Ireland, and Bishop John Lancaster Spalding in the last quarter of the nineteenth century attacked this problem. Father John Tracy Ellis, professor of church history at Catholic University, has summed up what those leaders had to contend with: "The absence of a viable intellectual tradition at once Catholic and American, the lack of any serious cultivation and patronage of the intellectual vocation, the absorption of the overwhelming majority of Catholics of the middle and lower classes in making a living, and the well-nigh universal unfriendliness to Catholic ideas among the general population—all these combined to make it uncommonly difficult for the few who sought to lift the level of Catholic thought."[17]

Despite great progress, these obstacles had been only partially overcome by the middle of the twentieth century. Some sectors of the Irish community remained prejudiced, philistine, and provincial. As a result, they had inadequate defenses against McCarthy's appeal. What was needed was an intellectual and political tradition that would make a future demagogue's offenses against integrity and fair play appear immediately alien and suspect. The Irish had the historical sources for such a tradition in the achievements of clerics like Cardinal Gibbons and Archbishop Ireland, the writing of liberal editors like Patrick Ford and John Boyle O'Reilly, the satire of Finley Peter Dunne, and the staunch integrity of political leaders like Alfred E. Smith and Frank Murphy. Moreover, the Irish had shared in and been influenced by the more general political movements—the progressivism of Theodore Roosevelt, the "new freedom" of Woodrow Wilson, and the "new deal" of Franklin Roosevelt. When the crisis of McCarthyism occurred, there were Irish Catholics who spoke up for the best in their own past, as witness the fact that McCarthy was steadfastly combated by *America* and *Commonweal*, the two most influential Catholic weeklies; by Senator McMahon, the most constructive Irish political figure on the national scene in the early postwar years;

by political leaders like Stephen Mitchell and Paul Butler, successive chairmen of the Democratic National Committee; and by many professors, journalists, lawyers, and countless decent private citizens. The difficulty was that those who fought McCarthyism were not sustained by a "viable intellectual tradition" and by a well-understood political tradition of liberalism and fair dealing. In the absence of such a tradition, a "mucker" was able to present himself as typifying the best of the Irish.

The national crisis that McCarthyism provoked, however, pointed up the distance between certain Irish attitudes and the best ideals of the nation. The crisis was, in this sense, a painful educational experience that brought half-conscious stereotypes out into the open, tested limits, and clarified standards. If there are any grounds for hope in the McCarthyite experience, it is that this crisis may have speeded the development and articulation of a sounder intellectual and political tradition.

CHAPTER NINETEEN

President John F. Kennedy

PEG: Ye know, that [dog] could never be President of the United
   States. But if ye had a child he might grow up to be President.
ETHEL: That's very Irish.
PEG: It's very human, too.

—J. HARTLEY MANNERS
Peg o' My Heart, 1912

"... It makes the prophet in us all presage
The glory of a next Augustan age
Of a power leading from its strength and pride,
Of young ambition eager to be tried,

"... A golden age of poetry and power
Of which this noonday's the beginning hour."

—ROBERT FROST
January 20, 1961

1

THE ELECTION of John Fitzgerald Kennedy as the thirty-sixth
President of the United States was a liberating and enlarging political act that strengthened our whole society. Since the United States is
organized around the ideals of radical popular democracy, making no
compromises with monarchy, state-supported churches, military castes,
racial elites, or hereditary establishments of any kind, the large, tacit prohibition against Catholic citizens that had existed in the political order was
a significant national weakness. In 1960 the people broke this ancient, un-
healthy taboo against a Catholic in the White House and brought our
practices another step closer to our ideals.

John Kennedy's election was charged with a special significance for
the American Irish. The winning of the Presidency culminated and

consolidated more than a century of Irish political activity. It wiped away the bitterness and disappointment of Al Smith's defeat in 1928; it removed any lingering sense of social inferiority and insecurity. To a people for whom politics had long been one of their chosen professions, the election of Kennedy was a deeply satisfying accomplishment in which every Irishman could take vicarious pleasure.

The shift in values implicit in the change from Dwight Eisenhower, conservative and relying upon the business community, to John Kennedy, liberal and dependent on the political and intellectual professions, signified another kind of Irish success. The new President and his administration bodied forth in full and accurate form the three main themes of the history of the Irish in this country: the poetry, the power, and the liberalism. Kennedy was a man of words, an inveterate reader, an orator of considerable power, a companion and admirer of men of the highest intellectual attainments, a man of good taste, sensibility, and imagination. There are banal Irishmen, silent Irishmen, Irishmen whose minds, despite other sterling virtues, are underdeveloped areas. Conceivably, one of these might have become the first American Irish President, but it would have been a pity and a paradox. A people who have produced so many bards, singers, orators, actors, dramatists, poets, and good talkers deserved to have as their greatest political leader a man who loved the language and could use it. And what they deserved they, in this instance, happily obtained.

The search for power has been the main motif of Irish history in the country. Kennedy was a man of power, who openly pursued the authority of the Presidency, and relished its exercise. Beginning with the first of those who came out of the immigrant ships, the Irish have had an instinct for power and an understanding that political power exists to be used. They made the vocation of politician an honorable one, and used their political machines as one means to lift themselves out of exploitation and poverty. In 1928 the electorate rejected a man direct from the machine. Since there have been Irish in the cities who fought the machines, others who entered politics from the ranks of business and campaigned on economy-and-efficiency platforms, and still others who grew up in non-machine states, it is conceivable the first American Irish President might have come from outside the big-city Irish political system. In 1928 Senator Thomas J. Walsh of Montana had been a viable alternative to Smith. In 1960 Senator Eugene McCarthy of Minnesota, who stirred the convention with his memorable nominating speech on behalf of Adlai Stevenson, admirably represented this nonmachine tradition. A former sociology professor at St. Thomas College in St. Paul, McCarthy is a spokesman in politics for the progressive Catholicism and middle-western reformism which Monsignor John Ryan and Archbishop John Ireland exemplified in previous generations.

But the logic of history was against the possibility that the first Irish Catholic President would come from outside the machine-dominated politics of the big cities of the East and industrial Midwest. Irish voting strength is principally in these cities and their suburbs. Because of the special handicaps a Catholic candidate would have to overcome in winning the nomination and election, success logically required a massive, united effort by the Irish political community behind a single figure. Such an effort was not likely to develop around a candidate who did not have ties with and was not acceptable to the big-city Irish political system. This factor had worked against Tom Walsh in 1928 and would, hypothetically, have worked against Eugene McCarthy had he been seeking the nomination in 1960. A candidate had to be not only Irish and Catholic but also "safe" in the sense that he would cooperate with the big-city machines and not try to reform or disturb the patterns of power they had developed. John Kennedy was this kind of candidate.

Both his grandfathers were ward bosses in Boston. Although reared in fashionable neighborhoods and exclusive schools, he began his career in 1946 by returning to the tenements of East Boston and the political haunts of his grandfathers. In his two campaigns for the United States Senate, he built a personal organization in the rest of the state drawn mostly from younger men and business and professional people not previously active in politics, but in Boston he entrusted his interests to State Senator John Powers, the boss of South Boston. Kennedy reaffirmed this expedient alliance in 1959 when he endorsed Powers in his campaign for mayor against a reform candidate.* When he began to seek the Presidency, his advance agent was John Bailey, the Irish Catholic boss of the Democratic Party in Connecticut, whom he later made chairman of the Democratic National Committee. Kennedy's own education and cultivation and his father's wealth placed him at some distance from the stereotypes of Irish political activity that had so harmed Al Smith. This distance was all to his advantage as a national candidate, but he had never lost contact with the realities that lie behind those stereotypes. At the Democratic National Convention in 1960, the backing of the old-line organizations and their Irish bosses—Mayor Richard Daley of Chicago, Congressman William Green of Philadelphia, and Congressman Charles Buckley of the Bronx—was crucial to his success. Kennedy, his brother and manager Robert, and his personal staff, the "Irish Mafia," were hardheaded, unillusioned, unashamedly power-seeking men. They made use of old Irish

* Notwithstanding this endorsement, Powers was defeated in a major upset.

insights into political behavior and old machine organizing techniques suitably updated and transposed for an age of television and rapid communication. For better or for worse, the first Irish Catholic President was in the mainstream of his people's political experience.

Kennedy was a liberal, an Irish Catholic liberal. He could easily have been a conservative, but again history and circumstances made it more likely and more fitting that he go to the White House as the protagonist of those who most need a champion: the old in need of medical care, the unskilled in need of a minimum wage, the Negro in search of justice, the slum child in need of a better home, and, beyond America's shores, all those who hunger and wait. It was more likely that he become a liberal because choosing to enter politics as a Democrat, Kennedy chose thereby to make his career in the party that nationally is a coalition of minorities and has a strong liberal tradition. It was more fitting because the Irish began as have-nots. All but a few started with only their hands and their hope. By 1960 all but a few had worked their way up out of the worst poverty, but it would ill become them to forget the others who came later or had higher walls to climb—the Negro, the Puerto Rican, the Mexican—and who still sweated, struggled, and shivered in the old rookeries, still received from life the back of the hand. It was right that at least the first Irish Catholic President should speak up for the "east side of America" even if most Irish no longer dwell there.

2

John Kennedy was an aristocrat and the representative of an American dynasty with all the advantages in life that such an inheritance confers. Although four years younger than Richard Nixon, his Republican opponent for the Presidency, he was, in a sense, twenty years ahead of Nixon from the day he was born because he entered the race of life with that serenity, security from abrasive money worries, and self-confident style that inherited wealth and family prestige can provide.

By the time he was born in May, 1917, his grandfather had been twice mayor of Boston, and his father, a rising young businessman, was already well on the way toward his first million. Young John was brought up to believe that, as a matter of course, all men of his family were successful and that any barrier would come tumbling down if enough energy, brains, and determination were applied to the assault. If an East Boston politician's son could become Ambassador to the Court of St. James's, might not the ambassador's son become President of the United States?

Joseph Kennedy was a classic dynasty-founder, empire-builder type.

He had ravenous ambition, cupidity, energy, audacity, and charm. The astonishing thing was that such a man did not break or cow the spirit of his sons. Instead, they inherited his energy and brains, and he successfully instilled in them his exceptional competitive drive. John was the second of four sons. His older brother, Joseph, Jr., who was killed in World War II, and his younger brothers, Robert and Edward, more nearly resembled their father in their outgoing temperament. John, by contrast, was a loner, a self-contained person. It may be that in the intensely competitive family situation he withdrew somewhat into himself, learned to keep his own counsel, and put a layer of insulation between himself and other people. Members of his family cannot remember any instance when he cried or had a tantrum as a child. Likewise, as an adult, he was even-tempered and coolly self-disciplined. He was not cold, and he could be a most charming and companionable man, but there was a part of himself always reserved, kept aloof, not completely dissolved in the chemistry of the situation. That is why long before he became President he was always a dignified figure, though his hair was rumpled and everybody called him "Jack." That is why people sometimes described him as cold, though he had extraordinary emotional intensity and verve.

Kennedy had an excellent mind, and received a quality education at Choate and Harvard. Like many boys from a privileged background, he was not strongly motivated toward winning academic honors. His academic record, therefore, was spotty. In his first years at Harvard, he was probably more concerned with making the swimming team than the dean's list, but he finished strong and graduated in the top half of his class. More important, somewhere along the way he acquired the habit of reading. He was one of the top politicians of his time who regularly read serious books as a form of relaxation. Kennedy had an exceptionally absorptive mind: he soaked up information and remembered it. He was quick and keen at understanding complicated problems, respected learning and expertise, and was at ease with scholars.

It was a happy circumstance for the Irish that Kennedy was a mediocre athlete and became a bookish man. The Irish have contributed more than their share to the national cult of football and to the impoverishing ideal of man as simply a sweaty, locker-room figure. Since too many Irish boys have grown up with the idea that the most important goal in four years of college is not in attaining intellectual excellence but in making the team, it is just as well that Kennedy was a skinny, often sickly 150-pounder, not heavy enough or fast enough to make any varsity team, despite his earnest ambitions. The sports that became popularly associated with Kennedy in the White House—swimming, sailing, and "touch" football—are those in which even women can participate. Physical stamina and physical courage were basic elements in Kennedy's makeup, as his gallant wartime heroism demonstrated, but important as they were, they did not comprise the whole man. Instead of just reading Westerns or detective stories, Kennedy wrote two books and was a regular reader of history, biography, political analysis, and serious novels. Americans are so fact-conscious and so technique-oriented that Kennedy's course in rapid reading and ability to read 1,200 words a minute received more attention than the excellent quality of what it was he read. Nevertheless, his intellectual interests became well-known and provided a useful example. Although the Irish have produced men of letters and learning since the Dark Ages, and innumerable good teachers, neither the American Irish in their picture of themselves nor the popular folklore about the Irish gives much place to them as people who are important for what they do with their minds. Kennedy's intellectual distinction helped change that picture.

Fate intervened three times in Kennedy's early life. His older brother had political ambitions and, if he had not been killed, he would have sought the congressional seat that Kennedy won. Second, Kennedy had a miraculous escape from death as a PT boat skipper in the Pacific. Fate intervened a third time in 1954-1955 when he was critically ill from a war-time back injury. If a delicate operation involving the fusion of two spinal discs had failed, he might have died or been crippled. Instead, he made a complete recovery. Any man can look back at his life and see critical turning points, but Kennedy, as the second son of a family with the highest ambitions and an almost royal sense of destiny and as a man twice near death, had a more than ordinary awareness of fortune's role. This awareness did not instill in him any strain of pessimism or melancholy, both fairly common characteristics of the Irish temper, but strengthened his nerves in times of crisis and imbued him with fatalism. More than most men, he was emotionally prepared for the tragic fate that was his.[1]

3

Kennedy grew into his liberal convictions by rational reflection and enlightened self-interest. This set him apart from most other liberals in his party who, more typically, came from low-income families, whose fathers were workingmen or small farmers, who had some firsthand knowledge of being out of work, going on strike, or making ends meet during hard times. Those few who came, as Kennedy did, from wealthy families were usually motivated by convictions or sentiments that drew them to champion the underdog. Kennedy, however, began in 1946 with

little more than the Democratic Party allegiance he inherited. Having
lived in fashionable suburbs, first in Brookline, Massachusetts, and then
in Bronxville, New York, and attended private schools, he had no firsthand acquaintance with economic misery, racial injustice, or the deprivation of civil liberties. There was very little in his background to make
him a liberal. Indeed, the pressures from his father and friends would tend
more to make him an economic tory and a McCarthyite. Only Kennedy's
aloofness and cherished sense of personal independence saved him from
this reactionary fate. Although he had studied briefly under Professor
Harold Laski and had studied under some liberal professors at Harvard,
he did not enter politics with any youthful radical convictions. He entered politics in a typical Irish way: it was a profession in which a man
could build a career.

Entering the national scene comparatively young, being a member of
the House of Representatives at twenty-nine, he had not yet defined
himself as a public man or formed his body of political convictions. Since
he had to vote on every issue as it came along, the hesitancies, incon-
sistencies, and odd lapses that naturally occur over a period of years if a
man is trying to make up his mind on fundamentals and think (and feel)
his way to a coherent philosophy were, in his case, spread on the public
record by his votes in Congress and by his chance remarks.

In 1952 when Kennedy ran successfully for the Senate against Henry
Cabot Lodge, an article in *The New Republic* by John P. Mallan, then a
Harvard teaching fellow, caused a minor sensation:

"On November 10, 1950," Mallan wrote, "a young Massachusetts
Congressman told an informal gathering of Harvard University students
and professors—of which this writer was a member—that (*a*) he could
see no reason why we were fighting in Korea: (*b*) he thought that sooner
or later we would have to get all these foreigners off our backs in Europe;
(*c*) he supported the McCarran [Internal Security] Act and felt that not
enough had been done about Communists in government; (*d*) that he
rather respected Joe McCarthy and thought he "knew Joe pretty well
and he might have something"; (*e*) that he had no great respect for Dean
Acheson or indeed almost any member of the Fair Deal Administration;
(*f*) that he personally was very happy that Helen Gahagan Douglas had
just been defeated in California by Richard Nixon . . . ('because she was
not the sort of person I like working with on Committees')."[2]

Kennedy disputed the accuracy of these quotes, but he did not deny
most of the substance of the article. There was a certain impropriety in
printing remarks that had not been made on an indisputably public occasion; any man in political life has opinions on men and issues which
for perfectly good reasons he may choose to keep confidential. But what
was essentially wrong with the Mallan article was neither its accuracy

nor its propriety but its misjudgment of Kennedy. It interpreted his random criticisms and dissents as proof that he was a conservative who occasionally voted liberal for opportunistic reasons. This imputation of hypocrisy wounded Kennedy, whose most engaging personal traits were candor and openness to argument. He was at the time neither conservative nor liberal, but independent, skeptical, and sometimes undecided.

"I'd be very happy to tell them I'm not a liberal at all. I never joined the Americans for Democratic Action or the American Veterans Committee. I'm not comfortable with those people," Kennedy remarked soon afterward.[3] Yet less than a decade later, he was quite at ease with leaders of both organizations and, as President, appointed a dozen prominent members of Americans for Democratic Action to high posts in his administration. By 1960 he regarded himself as fully and authentically liberal as any of his critics on the left.

What was uncongenial and "not comfortable" for him about liberals, however, probably always remained so. The difference is that liberals have a definite picture of what society should be like. In politics, they judge men and measures according to this Platonic ideal conception. The great depression and the extraordinary force of Franklin Roosevelt's personal leadership confirmed and deepened this intellectual tendency. The New Deal reforms, some of them achieved only after bitter class warfare, polarized national politics. The rise of the industrial trade unions with their vested interest in certain government programs and their year-in, year-out propaganda on political and economic issues tended to keep them polarized. Politics in this country acquired much more ideological content than it had ever had before. There developed on most issues a clearcut division of forces, a set of liberal positions, and a fairly rigid definition of the liberal "line." Although independence of thought and political dissent were admired in the abstract, deviations were not, in practice, welcomed or even readily tolerated. In the postwar years, this became true in the foreign as well as in the domestic field. Once the confusions engendered in 1947-1948 by Henry Wallace were resolved, and once Harry Truman by his personal victory in 1948 established himself in liberal eyes as Roosevelt's legitimate (rather than accidental) successor, the liberal position on foreign policy became firm. For the next several years, it was expected that if a politician were a liberal, he would necessarily support not only the Marshall Plan but also the NATO Treaty, the Berlin airlift, and the war in Korea; he would protect Roosevelt's reputation by rejecting attacks on the wisdom of the Yalta agreement and uphold Truman by defending the rightness of his China policy; and since the reactionaries unfairly attacked Dean Acheson, he would stoutly praise Acheson's conduct of foreign affairs.

There was nothing in the experience or political background of John

F. Kennedy to prepare him to accept a dutiful role in this liberal scheme of things. What he resented was not so much the positions liberals arrived at as the fact that he was expected to accept them uncritically. He was not comfortable with many liberals because they had an orthodoxy and he did not. They knew the answers and he was still trying to ask questions. Since he had escaped the economic trauma of the depression and had a nonideological political background, he had—if he was to be a liberal at all—to think his way through to liberal positions. He had no "gut reactions" he could trust.

Sometimes the results of his independent thinking delighted liberals. When the American Legion opposed public housing, he told the House, "The leadership of the American Legion has not had a constructive thought for the benefit of this country since 1918." At other times, liberals were distressed. In 1949 he placed a large share of the blame for the fall of China on the Democratic-controlled State Department.[4] In private, as Mallan subsequently put in print, he expressed doubts about Dean Acheson's judgment and the wisdom of the United States getting tied up militarily in Korea. He worked conscientiously on labor legislation and voted against the Taft-Hartley Act in 1947, but he expressed open reservations about the all-or-nothing mentality of the union leaders that prompted them to picture that law as "a slave-labor bill." He worked hard for public housing, but he also expressed a recurring interest in the subject of economy in government expenditures, a question that in the postwar folklore of politics had become almost exclusively an issue for conservatives. Perhaps most suspicious in liberal eyes was Kennedy's tendency to find his personal political friends not among fellow liberals in the House, but among young men of no strong convictions, such as George Smathers of Florida, who defeated Claude Pepper, an old liberal hero, for the Senate in 1950. One suspects Kennedy was at times consciously and deliberately having fun by shopping around for wisdom from his father and *The New Republic*, from Herbert Hoover and the CIO. Ideologically speaking, he liked to live dangerously by espousing conservative doubts as well as liberal sentiments. His latent strain of iconoclasm, which was the source of his dry wit, and his desire to be widely popular, a desire which may have been all the deeper in an emotionally reserved man, made it hard for him to become totally committed.

By 1960 Kennedy had resolved his inner contradictions and worked himself around to a coherent liberal position on major issues. The environment of his party had been partly responsible; he was, after all, building a career in a party that is predominantly liberal; "all the pressures," as he once remarked, "worked toward that end." By experience, he found that he agreed with the liberals much more often than with the conservatives.

And by reading and reflection, he came to accept most of the liberal positions on public policy—if not the liberal view of human nature.

In all this development, Kennedy was not simply acting out a political version of the romantic novel about the young man in search of himself, a latter-day *Bildungsroman*. Rather, he personified political traditions that were specifically Irish and Catholic. The Irish political machines were built upon essentially conservative, pragmatic insights and intuitions about human nature. They operate on the theory that most men act in politics on the basis of immediate interests of which food, clothing, shelter, a job, and elementary self-respect are primary. It is much more important to obtain these goals for individuals and to push forward the interests of the group as a whole than it is to forward any social grand design. Inevitably, this means working with the society and the economy as one finds it, and using such leverage as one has to exact such immediate rewards as one can. The whole idea that one would lose an election for the sake of an abstract principle is alien to this Irish tradition. Equally alien is the notion that the interests of the present generation should be sacrificed for the sake of some future benefit. Since their politics was founded in the first instance on old country and neighborhood ties, the Irish put much emphasis on loyalty and on personal leadership. One gives one's allegiance to a party organization or to a man, and ideally to both welded together, but not to issues as such. It is in this tradition that Kennedy grew up. From boyhood, he was nurtured in it by the reminiscences of his grandfather, his father's dinner-table observations, and his own experiences in his first campaign for the Democratic Party nomination for Congress. This tradition acted as a barrier for him, as it still does for many in the Irish community, against the ideological, issue-oriented politics that began to emerge in the 1930's. These political attitudes are a more important source of the tension and division between the Irish and other Democrats than the reasons usually ascribed, such as Al Smith's treatment at the hands of Roosevelt or Jim Farley's defection on the third-term issue.

Kennedy also personified a Catholic attitude toward politics. One suspects he was slightly uneasy about the nature of his relationship to his Catholic heritage. He attended a Catholic school for only one year of his education (Canterbury School in Connecticut, an excellent prep school run by Catholic laymen), and he had differed with the Catholic hierarchy on federal assistance for parochial schools. In 1960 he prepared himself for what turned out to be a crucial confrontation with Protestant ministers in Houston, Texas, by receiving an extensive briefing on Church-State problems from John Cogley, a former editor of *The Commonweal*. Suffering from voice strain, he put his questions and comments to Cogley in writing. After a long discussion of a complicated issue,

Kennedy wrote: "It is hard for a Harvard man to give pointers on theology. What will they think at Fordham and B.C.?"[5]

More than he may have realized, however, Kennedy had an approach to the fundamentals of politics identical with Catholic teaching. Politics, the Church holds, is the search for justice. But since the Kingdom of God is not of this world, heavenly perfection is not to be expected in politics. Only rarely does one face a black-and-white moral choice in politics; most political problems fall into the area of prudence where men have to choose between various alternatives each of which has something to commend it. Sophisticated moral judgment in politics involves the ability to weigh these alternatives, make relevant distinctions, and take into account time and circumstances. The political order, although part of an overarching moral system, has an autonomy of its own. When Christ said, "Render unto Caesar the things that are Caesar's and to God the things that are God's," He intended that the first half of the statement should have equal weight with the second.

The Reverend John Courtney Murray, S.J., the foremost American Catholic theologian, has offered a striking description of what the political order, the City of Man, should be like: "The climate of the City is . . . distinctive. It is not feral or familial but forensic. It is not hot and humid, like the climate of the animal kingdom. It lacks the cordial warmth of love and unreasoning loyalty that pervades the family. It is cool and dry, with the coolness and dryness that characterize good argument among informed and responsible men. Civic amity gives to this climate its vital quality. This form of friendship is a special kind of moral virtue, a thing of reason and intelligence, laboriously cultivated by the discipline of passion, prejudice and narrow self-interest. It is the sentiment proper to the City. . . . It is in direct contrast with the passionate fanaticism of the Jacobin: 'Be my brother or I'll kill you!' Ideally, I suppose, there should be only one passion in the city—the passion for justice. But the will to justice, though it engages the heart, finds its measure as it finds its origin in intelligence."[6]

Cool, dry, reasonable, intelligent—the words, although written in an entirely different context, could easily form a description of John Kennedy. One can almost hear echoing through Murray's passage the flat Boston tones of the President saying: "When all the facts are available, we will make a judgement. . . ." One is also reminded of one of the President's favorite political maxims: "In politics, you don't have friends —you have allies."

From family history, from the folklore of the old hands in Boston who were his first political tutors, and from his own experience in months of campaigning in 1946 when he climbed countless flights of stairs to attend house parties, canvassed neighborhood tradesmen, and shook hands with thousands of voters, Kennedy arrived at some of the basic Catholic understanding of man's political nature as set forth in the philosophy of St. Thomas Aquinas.

The force of this Catholic position becomes clearer when it is contrasted with rival views. Perfection in politics, it has been said, is a Protestant vision. In the past thirty years, a neo-realist school of Protestant theologians has arisen under the leadership of Reinhold Niebuhr to attack this millennial view and to reassert the importance of the contingent and the prudential. But the rhetoric of perfectionist politics is durable. General Eisenhower demonstrated this in 1952 when he characterized what was, after all, just another partisan campaign as a "moral crusade." No Catholic politician who understood his own religious philosophy could make such a claim. This Catholic view is also antithetical to the unformulated tenets of the new secular liberal orthodoxy which tends to hold that the opposite of "liberal" is not "conservative" but "bad." Liberalism, too, though secular, has its millennial, perfectionist undertones, equating liberalism with progress and both with virtue. In the theology of liberalism, the children of light still contend with the children of darkness, but under different names.

The discrepancy between the Irish-and-Catholic traditions of politics and the liberal traditions did not become fully apparent in this country until the late 1930's. Liberals in the nineteenth and early twentieth centuries had worked in municipal reform movements and fought the Irish political machines, but when state and national legislation on social issues was at stake, middle-class liberals cooperated with machine congressmen from working-class districts. Social reformers often found unlikely allies as Frances Perkins did in "Big Tim" Sullivan. Their common interests as city dwellers drew together the Protestant middle-class liberals, the Jews and the Irish in opposition to conservative rural interests. Liberals sympathized with the cause of Irish independence as they did with all nationalist democratic movements. During the 1920's these good relations entered a honeymoon stage. Al Smith in New York brought into his administration former Bull Moose Progressives, Jewish socialists, and other reformers and liberals. In the legislature, Jimmy Walker could have qualified as a founding member of the American Civil Liberties Union with his famous witticism on book censorship: "I have never yet heard of a girl being ruined by a book." The Irish Catholics, the liberals, and the intellectuals were as one in their disgust with prohibition, Wilsonian internationalism, the Ku Klux Klan, and the small-town "boobs" who knifed Smith in 1928. H. L. Mencken and the lowliest Tammany precinct captain could agree that the people wanted beer. Anne Nichols's *Abie's Irish Rose*, which was fantastically popular as a stage play through most of the decade, expressed in homely, sentimental terms the good relations between Irish and Jews, and this amity was part of the basis of the "era of good feelings" that prevailed in urban America in the period.

This mood persisted through the early thirties as liberals of almost all shades of opinion and social backgrounds rallied to Roosevelt. But the Spanish Civil War of 1936-1939 proved a turning point. This was the first major issue on which most Irish Catholics divided from other groups in the liberal coalition. For Catholics, Franco's war was the opening round in the great struggle against world communism; for liberals, the Spanish Loyalists were defending freedom and democracy in the opening round of the war against fascism. There was some truth in both points of view, as well as some exaggeration and distortion, but without arguing the merits of the Spanish Civil War, one can see that strains between Catholics and secular liberals go back to this quarrel. Each side is still trying to prove it was right about Spain.

A series of diverse, unrelated issues over the next twenty-five years served to sharpen and exaggerate the distinction between the Irish-and-Catholic political traditions and the liberal tradition. The disaffection of some well-to-do Irish over Roosevelt's handling of the sitdown strikes, the lingering isolationism of a part of the Irish community in 1940-1941, and on a lower level, the ugly anti-Semitism of Father Coughlin and the Christian Fronters, made liberals increasingly suspicious of Irish Catholics. After World War II, quarrels over the place of religion in the public schools, aid for parochial schools, and certain local laws, backed by Catholics, requiring the closing of businesses on Sunday worsened relations.

The dissension carried over into practical politics. The nomination of Harry Truman as Roosevelt's vice-presidential candidate at the 1944 Democratic Convention was a triumph of the Irish machines (in alliance with the Southerners) over Henry Wallace who had the almost solid backing of the liberal community. In 1952 the Irish machines were instrumental in choosing Adlai Stevenson as the presidential candidate in preference to Senator Estes Kefauver. Eight years later, they discarded Stevenson, by this time the liberal idol, in favor of Kennedy.

The divergence in approach and emphasis between the Irish Catholic and liberal traditions presented Kennedy with perhaps his most complicated and diffuse set of problems in his long quest for his party's presidential nomination. These problems became entangled with the mere fact of his religious affiliation and with what that affiliation was supposed to imply. Kennedy destroyed all the specific religious issues by the stands he took on federal assistance to parochial schools, an ambassador to the Vatican, and Church-State relations. To have an issue, there have to be two sides but Kennedy took the same side as his secular liberal opponents. Nevertheless, the lack of communication and of confidence continued to prevail. Questions repeatedly arose about the authenticity and whole-heartedness of Kennedy's political convictions. He found these queries baffling, and mistrustful liberals found his responses not wholly persuasive. The difficulty was that he was really being asked, not to commit himself on this or that specific issue, but to commit himself to a more crusading spirit, a more abstractly intellectual and idealistic view of politics, and a more dogmatic temper of mind. An outlook and habits of mind that were real and natural for most liberals were unreal and unnatural for Kennedy. Only after he won the Presidency and organized a strikingly liberal administration did it become wholly clear how unfounded the more serious of these liberal doubts had been. He, like Al Smith, demonstrated that one did not have to follow a prescribed route to arrive at progressive and enlightened public policies. But the underlying differences persisted: most liberals felt they had found in John Kennedy a strong ally and a prudent field marshal, but not a hero.

His attitude toward Joe McCarthy became a part of the controversy over the character of Kennedy's liberalism, but it was actually a separate problem. Although the political customs of the Irish community did not stress civil liberties or provide immediate support for an anti-McCarthy stand, Kennedy was not so tone deaf on the McCarthyism issue in the 1950-1954 period as his defensive explanations in later years suggested. He never publicly praised McCarthy or expressed McCarthyite sentiments on the issues raised by communism, loyalty and security investigations, and civil liberties generally. He went on record against loyalty oaths and unrestricted wiretapping. He voted against the confirmation of Robert Lee, a McCarthy protégé, as a member of the Federal Communications Commission, and of Scott McLeod, the McCarthyite security chief of the State Department, as ambassador to Ireland. In 1953, when McCarthy fought the nomination of Charles Bohlen as ambassador to Russia, Kennedy voted to confirm him. His own position on civil liberties was, from the outset, trustworthy.

Nor was his difficulty a lack of political courage. If the McCarthy issue had arisen for him in uncomplicated form as a naked question of courage, he would have met it straightforwardly. In 1947, as a freshman congressman, he refused to sign a petition asking clemency for James M. Curley, then in prison on a conspiracy conviction. Curley had been Kennedy's immediate predecessor representing the district in Congress, and he was a much greater political force among the voters of Boston than Joe McCarthy ever was. McCarthy's political strength in Boston was potential and debatable; Curley's was real and demonstrable. But Kennedy bravely refused Majority Leader John McCormack's request to sign the petition, being the only Democratic holdout in the Massachusetts delegation. Similarly, Kennedy was the first Massachusetts senator of either party to support the St. Lawrence Seaway, a project opposed for decades by those, among them Kennedy's own grandfather "Honey Fitz" Fitzgerald, who feared its economic effect on the port of Boston.

Kennedy's difficulty in confronting the McCarthy problem squarely had a personal origin. His father and several members of his family admired McCarthy. His brother Robert worked for the McCarthy Committee as minority staff counsel for a year and remained on friendly personal terms with McCarthy up to the latter's death. It was largely out of deference to his brother's sensibilities that Kennedy kept confidential for a year and a half the fact that he had decided in 1954 to vote to censure McCarthy, and would have done so if he had not been gravely ill when the vote came. When John Madigan, a Chicago newsman then on the staff of *Newsweek,* prodded him on a television panel show into making his position public, Kennedy did not resent the questioning, but his brother Robert stayed angry at Madigan for many months afterward.[7]

Kennedy had such a strong family feeling and so much reticence in disclosing his emotions that one suspects that for a long time he preferred to suffer the painful gibes ("Why doesn't Jack show more courage and less profile?") than disclose his private reasons. However, in 1959, he did remark to two political writers preparing a book about him: "How could I get up there and denounce Joe McCarthy when my own brother was working for him? It wasn't so much a thing of political liability as it was a personal problem."[8]

4

Electing the first Catholic President was like running the four-minute mile or orbiting the earth in space. After it had been done once, many others would in the future do it again. After a time the memory of how formidable the old barrier had been would grow dim.

The man most responsible for the election of the first Catholic President was John Kennedy himself. He began his assault with as much care and intensive preparation as any athlete or astronaut. He knew, partly from sound instinct and partly by cool, farsighted judgment, what was required of him. First, leaving aside the problem of his religion, he would have to be on all other grounds an especially strong candidate.

This Kennedy was: a better-than-average speaker, a tireless campaigner, an excellent organizer of his own time and the time of his staff, a shrewd negotiator with his political peers, and a figure who in appearance and personal style made a broad-gauged appeal. He was discernibly Irish and Catholic, and this was an asset in the big industrial states, but gone were all traces of the cultural stereotype that Al Smith had embodied, such as the brown derby, the big cigar, and the East Side accent.

Second, with respect to his religion, Kennedy knew that he would have to maintain his sense of humor under the most severe provocation. He could never court martyrdom, never seem defensive or embittered. He was confident that a majority of Americans would accept him for President but only after he had justified the proposed experiment of a Catholic in the White House by answering every fair question and some that were unfair. Whenever possible, Kennedy struck a light note in speaking of the religious issue. Appearing at the Alfred E. Smith Memorial Dinner in New York in 1959, on the same program with Governor Nelson Rockefeller, Kennedy said: "I think it well that we recall at this annual dinner what happened to a great governor when he became a presidential nominee. Despite his successful record as a governor, despite his plainspoken voice, the campaign was a debacle. His views were distorted, he carried fewer states than any candidate in his party's history. He lost states which had been solid for his party for half a century or more. To top it off, he lost his own state which he had served so well as a governor. You all know his name and his religion—Alfred M. Landon, Protestant."

Kennedy added, "While the memory of this election still burns deeply in our minds, I for one am not prepared to say to Governor Rockefeller that the Republicans should not nominate a Protestant in 1960."[9]

Kennedy also understood that if it became necessary to confront the religious issue seriously, he should cast it in some simple and manageable form. In the West Virginia primary he put it in terms of patriotism, reminding his listeners that no one had asked his brothers or himself their religion when they volunteered to serve their country in time of war. In September 1960, making his climactic speech on this issue before the meeting of Protestant ministers in Houston, Texas, he stressed his support of the Constitution and its clear separation of Church and State. He made these basic arguments with passion and earnestness, but above all, he kept himself unfailingly courteous, patient, and good-tempered.

Kennedy made his first major move in national politics in 1956, when he tried to obtain the nomination for Vice-President on the ticket headed by Adlai Stevenson. This was conceived as a dry run for the Presidency, giving him and his small staff valuable experience in conducting a campaign. In the unlikely event that Stevenson defeated Eisenhower, Kennedy as Vice-President could build himself up as his logical successor. If Stevenson were defeated, Kennedy would not be held responsible. His father opposed this vice-presidential venture, reasoning that much of the blame for Stevenson's prospective defeat would be shifted to Kennedy's religion, but his son overruled this objection.

Despite his narrow defeat for the nomination, the 1956 Democratic Convention was a personal triumph for Kennedy. Stevenson chose him to make the nominating speech in his behalf and to narrate the film depicting the party's history. His thrilling race with Kefauver was more like a sports event than an ordinary political struggle in its psychology and the character of its excitement. Kennedy emerged from defeat a glamorous figure. The contest made real, in a vivid way that months of speculation and analysis could not, how close a Catholic could come to a place on the national ticket. One needed only a minimum of imagination to see that this young politician was within striking distance of the final breakthrough and that given four years of effort he could make up the small margin between defeat and victory.

It was inevitable that the Irish, being so strongly situated within the Democratic Party would, when the candidate was right and the time appropriate, make another attempt to win the Presidency. During the Roosevelt years the Irish had moved into the national political scene and obtained the broad range and variety of experience that had been lacking to the Al Smith generation. Irish figures held important posts at every level of the federal government including the Cabinet, the administrative commissions, Congress, and the Supreme Court. The great distance between the municipal and national levels had been closed, and only the Presidency remained beyond their reach. None of the men around Roosevelt—Corcoran, Farley, Joseph Kennedy, and the others—had enjoyed careers that properly positioned them to try for the Presidency; moreover, the memory of Smith's traumatic defeat was still too recent. The seven years of the Truman administration were in many respects a shadow Irish regime. Truman was the product of an Irish political machine, the Pendergast organization in Kansas City. Robert Hannegan, an Irish politician from St. Louis, had engineered Truman's nomination for Vice-President in 1944, and became his first Postmaster General. Irish politicians of straight organization backgrounds gained high place, although most of them, such as Maurice Tobin, the Secretary of Labor; J. Howard McGrath and James McGranery, successive Attorneys General; and Mathew Connelly, Truman's Appointment Secretary, were men of only routine ability, and inferior to their predecessors under Roosevelt. With Truman, the big-city political organizations enjoyed the most cordial relations they had ever had with the White House under any Democratic administration.

Senator Brien McMahon, the author of the law establishing civilian control of atomic energy, and the ablest Irish political figure in the immediate postwar period, had decided in 1951 that he was the man to break the Catholic taboo. Like Kennedy five years later, McMahon decided to try first for the Vice-Presidency. When he fell fatally ill in the spring of 1952, the possibility of an Irish Catholic on the ticket that year disappeared. The development of Kennedy as a presidential possibility, therefore, had behind it a logical political history.

Kennedy, with characteristic boldness, tried to turn the political handicap of his religion into an advantage. When he was seeking the vice-presidential nomination in 1956, he had Theodore Sorensen, his principal assistant, prepare a memorandum arguing that the key to a Democratic victory was to nominate as Stevenson's running mate a Catholic who could win back the states which have a high percentage of Catholic voters. These are also the populous, industrial states with weight in the Electoral College. The memorandum listed fourteen states which had 261 electoral votes, just five short of the majority needed to elect a President. They were: Rhode Island (60 percent Catholic in population), Massachusetts (50 percent), Connecticut (49 percent), New Jersey (39 percent), New York (32 percent), Wisconsin (32 percent), Illinois (30 percent), Pennsylvania (29 percent), Michigan (24 percent), Minnesota (24 percent), California (22 percent), Montana (22 percent), Maryland (21 percent), and Ohio (20 percent).

The memorandum pointed out that the Democrats had carried 13 of these 14 states in 1940, 12 in 1944, and 8 in 1948, adding each time the refrain, ". . . Without which the Democrats would have lost the election.

"In 1952, none of these states went Democratic, all 261 of their electoral votes went to Eisenhower—and the Democrats lost their first presidential election in 24 years."

The memorandum concluded: "Has the Democratic era ended? Has the party permanently lost its political base among the Catholics and immigrants of the large Northern cities that made a Democratic victory possible in 1940, 1944, and 1948? . . . A Catholic Vice-Presidential nominee could refashion this base as Al Smith did and begin a new era of Democratic victories, without costing even the few electoral votes Smith did."

After showing the memorandum privately to a number of Washington correspondents, and generating a number of favorable stories based on it, Kennedy released it publicly—and patriotically—on July 4, 1956, under the name of John Bailey, the Connecticut national committeeman and Kennedy's unofficial campaign manager. Bailey at that time did not stress Kennedy specifically; he pushed only the view: "We need a Catholic on the ticket."[10]

As far as the 1956 election was concerned, the Bailey memorandum was unsound. Most voters simply do not cast their ballots in a national election on the basis of the identity of the vice-presidential candidate. If Kennedy had been on the ticket instead of Kefauver, it is extremely doubtful that Stevenson would have run substantially stronger against Eisenhower in Catholic neighborhoods. Kennedy was fortunate that his political drawing power was not put to this inherently unfair test. This is particularly true when we bear in mind that voters of Irish ancestry— the group within the Catholic community for whom a candidate named Kennedy would have an especially strong appeal—had been comparatively loyal to Stevenson and the Democrats. In 1952 in the first Stevenson-Eisenhower campaign, there had been a shift of perhaps 10 to 15 percent of Irish Catholic Democratic voters into the Eisenhower column compared to the Truman-Dewey election four years earlier. Nevertheless, according to an exhaustive study by political scientists at the University of Michigan, the Irish Catholics were exceeded only by Jews and Negroes in their loyalty to the Democratic ticket in 1952. It is estimated that 55 percent of the Irish Catholics voted for Stevenson and 38 percent for Eisenhower (5 percent did not vote and the vote of 2 percent could not be ascertained). This is a markedly higher percentage than Stevenson obtained from other ethnic groups, such as the Germans, Scandinavians, Poles, and Italians.[11] Even if the Irish Catholics had voted as heavily for Stevenson as they had for Truman, he would not have been elected. In the second Stevenson-Eisenhower campaign in 1956, the shift of Irish voters to the Republican ticket continued. If Kennedy had been Stevenson's running mate, he might have cut these losses, but in view of Eisenhower's large majority the net effect would have been unimportant.

In 1960 Kennedy all but disavowed the Bailey memorandum. The memorandum's contention that a Catholic vice-presidential candidate would be sufficient to attract Catholic voters for the Democrats was obviously harmful to a man who was, by then, interested only in the top place on the ticket. To discourage suggestions that he take the vice-presidential nomination, Kennedy was forced in 1960 to contend that religion should not be taken into account in the choice of any nominee and that the whole idea of putting a Catholic on the ticket for vote-catching purposes was repugnant to him. Nevertheless, his nomination clearly drew the issue of his ability to regain Catholic votes for the Democratic Party. Broadly speaking, he made good on the vote-getting potential that had so beguiled professional politicians for more than four years. He carried ten of the fourteen most Catholic states in the Union, losing only Ohio, Wisconsin, Montana, and California. His gains in heavily Catholic areas were well above the national average; in the nation as a whole there was a drop of approximately eight percentage points from Eisenhower's 1956 popular vote of 57 percent to Nixon's 49 percent, but in many Catholic neighborhoods the drop was twenty to twenty-five percentage points. Dr. George Gallup estimated that more than three out of every five Catholics who voted for Eisenhower in 1956 switched to Kennedy four years later. An analysis has been made of the vote in the 96 counties which are more than 50 percent Catholic and the 75 counties which are 40 to 50 percent Catholic. Fifty-four of these 171 counties showed a Republican loss of 20 percent or more, which is two and one-half times as great as the national average. Ninety-seven counties had Republican losses ranging between 8 percent and 20 percent; the remaining seventeen counties showed losses less than the national average, while only three showed a Republican gain.[12]

But there are many imponderables in these statistical analyses. Kennedy's gains among Catholic voters were nearly offset by his losses among Protestant voters in rural Ohio, rural Pennsylvania, some sections of California, southern Missouri, and Oklahoma and the Dakotas. As one Democratic analyst remarked, "Kennedy's religion elected him and it also very nearly defeated him."[13] On balance, his religion aided him because New York and Pennsylvania, where it definitely helped, carry heavy weight in the Electoral College. But the balance was close.

The role of the Irish in the election is less easily isolated than that of Catholics as a group. By 1960 the Irish had become so well integrated into the society and, at the higher income levels, so diffused into heterogeneous neighborhoods that voting statistics become difficult to interpret reliably. A voter's Irish Catholic background was still an important shaping influence on his political behavior but the measurement of that influence was elusive. However, one can draw many inferences from personal observation and from the pragmatic judgments of politicians. Clearly, Kennedy was both a cultural and a regional hero on his native ground of southern New England, where the enthusiasm and solidarity of the Irish made possible his huge majorities in Massachusetts, Rhode Island, and Connecticut. Irish strength was important in New York where Kennedy carried middle-class Irish neighborhoods in Queens and Brooklyn by old-fashioned majorities, incidentally sweeping to defeat the only Republican congressman in Brooklyn. The Irish contributed to his huge Philadelphia majority, which was indispensable to his carrying Pennsylvania. But his appeal to Irish Catholics was not uniformly compelling. In New Jersey his failure to make any headway among well-to-do Irish voters in the suburbs accounted for his relatively meager 22,000 vote majority. Nor in Illinois did he win back those wealthier Irish who live in Chicago's bedroom suburbs. His victory in that state by a scant 8,000 votes is primarily to be credited to his overwhelming vote in the Negro wards.

Private polls taken by Kennedy during the campaign indicated that some Irish voters actually resolved their doubts in Nixon's favor simply to prove that there is not an "Irish Catholic bloc vote." Kennedy, as a Catholic symbol and a putative victim of discrimination, made his greatest appeal to Italian voters. This is probably because among Americans of Italian ancestry, it is the present generation that is making the great transition from the old immigrant neighborhoods into the larger society and from the working class into the many levels of the middle class. This transitional generation is understandably sensitive to social slights, religious prejudices, and various forms of discrimination. The middle-class Irish Catholics, most of whom made this same transition one and two generations earlier, tended less readily than the Italian voters to identify with Kennedy. In any event, Kennedy did not make quite as spectacular gains among conservative Irish Catholic voters as he and most politicians in his party had hoped.

From a longer perspective, there was clearly an element of nostalgia on the part of those politicians who had hoped that Kennedy could counteract the effects of economic affluence and turn the clock back to the 1920's and early 1930's when Irish and Democrat were virtually synonymous. For three decades there had been a small but steady drift of Irish into the Republican party, and Irish figures had increasingly gained recognition in Republican ranks. In 1936 William F. Bleakley, an Irish Catholic from Westchester County, was the Republican candidate for governor of New York. Four years later, Thomas J. Curran became Republican chairman in New York County (Manhattan). In Connecticut in 1938, John Danaher became the first Irish Catholic ever elected as a Republican to the United States Senate. Of Danaher's father, who switched the family's allegiance to the GOP, the story used to be told of the old Irish Catholic lady who said to her friend, "Have you heard the news? John Danaher has become a Republican!" The other replied: "It can't be true. I saw him at Mass just last Sunday."

Between 1940 and 1946, New York, Pennsylvania, Michigan, Wisconson, Minnesota and California sent Irish Catholic Republicans to Congress.[14]

After his election in 1952, Eisenhower made a definite gesture to Irish Catholics, as well as trade unionists, in choosing Martin Durkin, the head of the Plumbers' Union, as his Secretary of Labor. When Durkin resigned after several months, Eisenhower replaced him with James Mitchell, another Irish Catholic. Mitchell, who had been a personnel executive for retail stores, was more typical than Durkin of those middle-class Irish who were joining the GOP. In 1960 Richard Nixon seriously considered Mitchell as his vice-presidential candidate, which suggests that it is probably only a matter of time before the Republicans place an Irish Catholic on their national ticket.

As the Irish as a group become more affluent, it is natural that a growing number of them should join the more conservative party. Kennedy could not reasonably be expected to reverse this trend. His personal appeal retarded this development but, in all likelihood, only for the short term.

Although experts might long dispute about the combination of voters and the strokes of fortune that brought about his narrow victory, John Kennedy in November, 1960, was concerned only with the future. He was determined to be President of all the people. Whether in the exercise of his best abilities he would prove, in Robert Frost's formulation, more Irish or more Harvard was for the future to determine. Yet he was conscious also that he had a special responsibility over and above that of any of his predecessors. The day after his election when a reporter congratulated him on breaking the historic barrier against a Catholic in the White House, Kennedy replied: "No, I have not broken it. I have only been given the opportunity to break it. If I am not a successful President, the barrier will be back higher than ever."[15]

The most significant chapter in the American Irish story was about to begin.

CHAPTER TWENTY

Kennedy and After

IN THE GLARING SUN of a Dallas afternoon, the nightmare returned. History, which the Irish people on two continents had thought to have mastered for once, asserted its old power with an act of sudden, cruel caprice. John F. Kennedy, their chosen hero, the first Irish Catholic President of the United States, the leader of the free world, a man of intelligence, physical beauty, personal grace, and rare vitality, was dead. Not his sturdy courage nor his coolness in crisis, not his prudent preparations nor his gift for diplomacy had availed him against his enemy. He joined the company of lost leaders—Michael Collins, Terence MacSwiney, Charles Stewart Parnell, Wolfe Tone, Patrick Sarsfield, and all the others reaching back in an unbroken line through the mists of defeat and old pain. He became one with those who "always went forth to battle and . . . always fell." He who wanted so much to cope with real problems and master practical issues became a romantic hero and a tragic martyr; he who had been a leader became a legend. What should have been the Age of Kennedy, "a golden age of poetry and power," became only a brief, shining interlude, measured in days instead of years. The promised land of what was to be now became the forbidden country of what might have been. John Kennedy became one of history's tantalizing if's. He had time only to give a hint of his native power, a glimpse of his developing stature, a preliminary measure of his intended achievement, and then he was gone. Time foreshortened and opportunity foreclosed—this was the essence of John Kennedy's tragedy.

1

When he entered the White House, John Kennedy was a superb political technician. The story of his thousand days in the Presidency was of his uneven but measurable growth into a political strategist and a moral force.

Kennedy's original objective was to make the United States into a leaner, more effective competitor of the Communist powers for world leadership. He judged the 1960's to be a crucial decade. It was not that he believed that the cold war would explode into a nuclear hot war or be ended by negotiations; rather, he regarded the coming decade as the time when the free world would either move decisively ahead or fall irretrievably behind in the competition with the Communist world. He saw his task as organizing the nation's manpower and resources for a long struggle in which freedom would contain, penetrate, and eventually outlast the forces of totalitarian tyranny. He wanted to put the nation's economic house in order, eliminate the waste of both inflation and recession, reduce needless poverty and unemployment, improve the education and physical fitness of the nation's youth, place foreign aid on a dependable long-term basis, and build a balanced military defense. He hoped to finance and assist Latin America through a peaceful social revolution by the Alliance for Progress. Britain was to be encouraged to join the Common Market, and then Western Europe, thus strengthened, was to collaborate with the United States in the evolution of a new trade and political partnership. This was his "grand design" for an invincible Atlantic community.

This framework of policy rested on the assumption that the United States was not merely ricocheting from one temporary crisis to another; it was in a deep, permanent crisis and had to organize itself and its allies to confront that crisis. Kennedy was convinced that if only he could awaken the moral energy and mobilize the full resources of this country and its allies, the drab tyrannies of Russia and China could not prevail against us. Seen in this broad perspective, many disparate people, events, and situations were integrally related. From the restless youth in the congested slums of Harlem to the unemployed ex-coal miners in the tumbledown villages of West Virginia, from dusty, sun-baked India to the cold, dark, trackless reaches of outer space, from the first Peace Corpsmen in Tanganyika to the Strategic Air Command bomber pilots over the North Pole, from the villages of Vietnam to the streets of West Berlin, a whole civilization struggled to put its affairs in order and to defend its ramparts, to save itself and thereby to save man's last, best hope for freedom.

Kennedy, both as chief executive of his own country and as *de facto* leader of the free world, had an immense educational task to get the people and the press of the United States, Canada, Britain, Western Europe, India, and Latin America to recognize the magnitude, the seriousness, and, above all, the interrelatedness of this epic struggle. The allies, inevitably and quite humanly resentful of America's new dominance and its new place as a superpower, were also plagued by special difficulties: Canada, flexing the muscles of a new nationalism; Britain, shorn of empire, exhausted by the sacrifices of two wars, and in search of a viable national role; Western Europe, materially revived but still emotionally depleted by the orgy of fascism, by the wounds it inflicted and the guilts it engendered; India, pursuing a profitless quarrel with Pakistan while the Chinese enemy rumbled in the Himalayas; and Latin America, beset in most of its member states by ruling classes too selfish and shortsighted to improve the social welfare of their people while there was still time to avoid destructive, blood-drenched revolutions.

The core of Kennedy's problem was at home. Only if he could alter the tone of American public opinion, only if he could call the American people to a new vision of service and idealism would he enable the country to meet the severe demands that he thought it would have to meet not only in the sixties but throughout the rest of the century. Kennedy had proved his skill as a political negotiator and a dextrous manipulator during his long conquest of the Presidency, but what was needed now was not better process but better content.

For the eight years of the Eisenhower Administration, the loudest sound in America had been the oink-and-grunt of private hoggishness. The Eisenhower years had been years of flabbiness, materialism, and self-satisfaction. It had been the age of the slob. There is always a bit of slobbism in all of us—the lazy voice that suggests that we take it easy, cut a corner, put security first, and measure everything by how much money there is in it for us.

For eight years President Eisenhower had told his fellow citizens, in effect, that putting the pursuit of private gain ahead of everything else was perfectly all right. During the 1960 campaign, Richard Nixon picked up the theme. Over and over again, he had said: "I don't say America is perfect—we're just the best country in the world! My opponent says we've been standing still—look around you at the shopping centers and the highways and the factories and the homes and the schools. Do you think America could have made all this progress if we had been standing still?"[1]

That comfortable argument ignored the brutal fact that America was not going to contain the Communist powers with shopping centers. We were not going to confound Castroism in Latin America by opening another snug subdivision on Long Island or prevent India from falling to communism by putting another television set in the rumpus room.

People never need a President to tell them to put their own selfish interests first; most of us are quite efficient in that department already. What America needed in 1960 was a President who would speak up for the public interest, who would remind Americans of their neighbor down the street or halfway across the world, who would prod his fellow citizens to do that day what needed to be done if theirs was to be a better country and a better world in the days to come. The real enemy Kennedy had to combat was the mood of slobbism in the country. The measure of his success would not be the number of bills he persuaded Congress to pass but the extent to which he elevated and redirected public opinion.

History showed it could be done. Theodore Roosevelt had awakened the sleeping public conscience to the evils of "the malefactors of great wealth" after the torpor of the McKinley years. Woodrow Wilson had educated part of his generation and posed a reverberating challenge to all of posterity by his crusade for internationalism. Franklin Roosevelt had made positive government an accepted fact of life and had firmly committed his party to a progressive position.

Kennedy felt keenly the responsibility to give a new lead to public opinion. The suppressed Gaither Report of 1957, the Rockefeller report on national defense, and similar studies had convinced him that U.S. defenses were in an alarming condition. Although improved intelligence data proved that the "missile gap" argument of the 1960 campaign was based on a misconception of relative U.S. and Soviet strength, he had been sincere in raising it. He conceived his role as not unlike that of Winston Churchill, who, in the late 1930's, tried to awaken a complacent Britain. He set out to create a new mood of national unity and patriotic resolution.

"Ask not what your country can do for you but what you can do for your country," he cried out in his Inaugural message.

"The tide of events has been running out and time has not been our friend," he warned in his first State of the Union message ten days later.

"There will be further setbacks before the tide is turned. But turn it must. The hopes of all mankind rest upon us," he said.

When the Bay of Pigs invasion failed, Kennedy resorted to an even more strident and compelling clarion call. Speaking to the American Society of Newspaper Editors on April 20, 1961, he said: "The complacent, the self-indulgent, the soft societies are about to be swept away with the debris of history. Only the strong, and the industrious, can possibly survive."

When his militant rhetoric failed to impress Nikita Khrushchev and the latter took a menacingly belligerent line concerning the Berlin question, Kennedy took the nation—verbally—to the brink of war. Speaking on July 25, 1961, he declared: "We do not want to fight—but we have fought before." Berlin, he told his countrymen, is "the great testing place of our courage and will."

To back up those words, he mobilized Army reserves, increased the military budget, and announced a new start on a program of civil defense shelters.

All this was more rhetorical bluff than resolute action, more posture than policy. Kennedy did not send the Marines into Cuba; he avoided giving the Cuban exile brigade any sustained air cover or overt assistance during the Bay of Pigs invasion. When the East Germans, only nineteen days after his July 25 speech, erected the Berlin Wall, the United States did—nothing. In Southeast Asia, Kennedy dramatically linked the fate of Laos with the security of the United States, but he settled for a soft, unstable compromise.

These discrepancies between words and deeds do not mean the deeds were wrong. On the contrary, they were probably the right deeds on all three occasions. But these discrepancies pointed up the fact that during his first year in office, Kennedy had not yet developed a means of describing to the American people the true nature of their role and responsibility. Will and nerve and courage were all demanded, but these were less important perhaps than sheer staying power. In a conventional war, Roosevelt or Churchill could speak for a nation totally committed to struggle and triumph. The people faced a black-and-white situation; it was we or the enemy. But Kennedy had a more complex and elusive task. The cold war is a dirty gray business, diffuse and shapeless. Churchill could call for "blood, sweat, and tears." It is hard to make eloquence out of just sweat.

Beyond sheer staying power, the greatest cold-war demand on the American people was for more political inventiveness and flexibility. The times called for innovation as well as durability. The three accomplishments in foreign affairs during his first year in office for which Kennedy will be remembered favorably in history are the founding of the Peace Corps, the decision to place a man on the moon by 1970, and the formation of the Alliance for Progress. All three appeal to men's sense of adventure, raise the challenge of doing a difficult thing well, and summon men to seek beyond self. In short, they are triumphs of moral and political imagination. Of the three, the Alliance for Progress was the most important and uniquely Kennedy's own. The idea for the Peace Corps had originated two years earlier with Hubert Humphrey. The man-in-space program had a natural appeal to a nation not accustomed to coming in second in any major competition, and it is likely that any Democrat elected in 1960 would have proposed it. But the Alliance for Progress was a program on a vast scale, unlike the Peace Corps, and it had no domestic lobby to support it, unlike the man-on-the-moon project, which had the political and propaganda backing of the aerospace industry. The Alliance was unorthodox. Although the United States had financed the

Marshall Plan and other aid programs, it had never tied financial assistance to a program of political and social reforms sure to be unpopular with the ruling classes in the recipient countries. If the Alliance failed, the hope for a liberal solution to Latin America's problems was doomed. If it succeeded, democracy would have scored a tremendous victory: the free societies would have proved that they could lift the underdeveloped countries out of stagnation and misery without resort to totalitarian political coercion and economic regimentation. In retrospect, nothing is more tragic about Kennedy's unfulfilled promise than the fact that he did not live to provide his inspiration and personal leadership to the Alliance throughout the balance of the decade.

2

In domestic policy, Kennedy often acted as if an invisible leash restrained the leap of his imagination. He was inhibited by his belief that he did not have the support of a majority of the American people for his program. He had polled less than 50 per cent of the popular vote and had barely defeated Nixon. If his opponent had been Eisenhower, he would not have won. Instead of gaining seats in Congress as the winning party in a Presidential election normally does, the Democrats had actually lost 20 seats in the House. As a practical matter, these losses deprived Kennedy of a working majority in the House. As a psychological fact, they convinced him, as did the narrowness of his own winning margin, that he lacked a mandate. He was not only the youngest elected President but also the first Catholic in the White House. These special circumstances confirmed in him the belief that he had to proceed with care. By reassuring millions of Eisenhower-Nixon voters that he was, indeed, trustworthy, he seemed determined to win in the public opinion polls that massive majority which had been denied him in November, 1960.

To win this broader support, Kennedy organized an essentially bipartisan Administration. To all the major policy-making positions in foreign and fiscal affairs, he appointed Democrats who had been politically inactive and Republicans. His Secretary of State—Dean Rusk—was such a Democrat; he had been a career official in the State Department before becoming president of the Rockefeller Foundation. Republicans received the other top posts: Douglas Dillon in Treasury, Robert McNamara in Defense, and John McCone in Central Intelligence. For the job as head of the White House foreign-affairs staff, Kennedy chose McGeorge Bundy, a lifelong Republican and the biographer of Henry L. Stimson, who had been Hoover's Secretary of State. Kennedy encouraged the highly conservative William McChesney Martin, Jr., to stay as head of the Federal Reserve Board. He placed Christian Herter, who had been Eisenhower's last Secretary of State, in charge of tariff negotiations with the European Common Market. For disarmament negotiations in the spring of 1961, he turned to Republicans Arthur Dean, who had been John Foster Dulles's law partner, and John McCloy, the former head of the Chase Manhattan Bank. To head a commission to review the foreign aid program, Kennedy selected General Lucius Clay, long-time colleague and intimate adviser of Eisenhower who had helped organize the latter's administration in 1952–53. Kennedy's choices for major ambassadorships were equally orthodox: to London, a man who had served as ambassador under both Truman and Eisenhower; to Paris, a general; and to Rome, a career diplomat.

These appointments reassured those Republican voters who had presumably feared that Kennedy might be radical or irresponsible. They also underlined the Kennedy Administration's continuity with the past and its solid identification with the eastern Establishment. Kennedy had promised to "get America moving again"; he had not said anything about getting it moving in a significantly different direction.

Caution was the dominant theme in the formulation of Kennedy's domestic program. Throughout the 1960 campaign, he had berated Eisenhower for failing to sign an executive order forbidding racial discrimination in housing. Kennedy repeatedly declared that the problem could be resolved "with a stroke of the pen." But he himself was in office almost two years before he signed such an order. Moreover, the order he signed was significantly less comprehensive than had been expected. On the broader issues of civil rights, Kennedy during his first two years in office sounded no call to advance. After his nomination in the summer of 1960, he asked Representative Emanuel Celler, head of the House Judiciary Committee, and Senator Joseph Clark to draft the next Administration's civil rights legislative program. But this was only political window dressing. After the election, Kennedy submitted no legislative recommendations on civil rights. He stayed neutral when the Senate liberals attempted in January, 1961, to revise Senate Rule 22, the pro-filibuster rule. He said privately that it would "tear the country apart" if he advanced the Celler-Clark proposals. Instead, the Administration chose to "litigate rather than legislate." Over the next two years, vigorous enforcement of the laws and the initiation of numerous suits against voting discrimination brought some results, but litigation proved no substitute for additional laws.

Aside from his silence on civil rights, Kennedy asked Congress for a broad range of economic and social welfare legislation. He was successful, in part, as Congress during his first year enacted a major housing bill, an increase in the minimum wage, and a program to assist economically depressed areas. He was unsuccessful on the more ambitious and controversial issues such as medical care for the elderly under Social Security and federal aid for elementary and secondary schools.

The central drama on the domestic front, however, was in Kennedy's ambiguous and often awkward relations with the nation's business community. As the son of a wealthy speculator, he was in no real sense hostile to business. He had no intention of denouncing the "economic royalists," as had Franklin Roosevelt, or excoriating Wall Street, as had Harry Truman. Such fervor and outsized rhetoric were alien to Kennedy; he regarded the antagonisms they bred as wasteful. As a chief executive whose overriding interest was foreign affairs and whose highest aim was to mobilize the nation's energies to wage the cold war more effectively, he wanted to enlist business's cooperation. But notwithstanding any personal predilections of his own, he was inevitably heir to the suspicion and hostility which most businessmen felt toward the Democratic Party and which had built up during the twenty years of Roosevelt and Truman. He unintentionally confirmed those suspicions and hostilities by his appointments to the major regulatory commissions: Frank McCulloch as chairman of the National Labor Relations Board, Paul Dixon as chairman of the Federal Trade Commission, and Joseph Swidler as chairman of the Federal Power Commission. These appointments, which from a liberal standpoint were outstanding, represented Kennedy's effort to consolidate his relations with leading liberal Democratic senators with whom he had not been especially close in former years and with major interest groups which had backed his election. Thus McCulloch was a former administrative assistant to Senator Paul H. Douglas of Illinois. Dixon had been staff director of the Senate Anti-Monopoly Subcommittee under Senator Estes Kefauver of Tennessee. The choice of Swidler, a former official of the Tennessee Valley Authority, was popular with consumer and public power organizations, while that of McCulloch was well received by the trade unions. These appointments and others like them raised the hackles of many businessmen; the choice of Douglas Dillon as Secretary of the Treasury and of textile businessman Luther Hodges as Secretary of Commerce failed to offset their adverse reaction. Unlike Eisenhower, who had hobnobbed with big businessmen, Kennedy had few of them in his circle of friends; and he was more likely to turn for advice on economic issues to academic economists ("theorists" as they were usually stigmatized in the business press).

Kennedy's attitude toward businessmen was most nearly like that of Theodore Roosevelt. He was for the business system, but he wanted to curb and discipline its excesses. He judged business by its self-proclaimed values: honesty, competition, productivity, stable money. But he discovered that for many in the business world, honesty did not extend to paying their fair share of income taxes; they were quite content to have other taxpayers pay the bill for yachts, hunting lodges, theater tickets, nightclub jaunts, and other so-called business expenses. He discovered that competition did not entail any desire for vigorous enforcement of the anti-trust laws. He discovered that although stable money (more often known as "a sound dollar") was nominally a high priority for businessmen, they were, in fact, as reluctant as trade unions to observe any impartial wage-price guidelines based on productivity.

Kennedy tried conscientiously to woo the business community without surrendering complaisantly to it. By administrative order, the Treasury Department provided business with revised tax depreciation schedules that saved business $1.5 billion annually. Subsequently, the pro-business majorities in the House and Senate committees voted far more generous tax relief for depreciating plant and equipment than the President had asked for and effectively ignored his plea to reform expense-account abuses. Senator Albert Gore of Tennessee described the language of the 1962 law on expense accounts as "legislative endorsement of widespread abuse and scandalous avoidance of taxes." Bernard Nossiter, the economics writer for the *Washington Post*, described the bill as "more like a business lobbyist's delight than the answer to the problems with which Kennedy first proposed to grapple."[2]

In signing the tax law, however, Kennedy adopted the passive tactic of proclaiming a defeat a victory. He said blandly: "This is an important bill—one possessing many desirable features which will stimulate the economy and provide a greater measure of fairness in our tax system."

When an investigation disclosed disgraceful profiteering by private drug companies and reckless practices in the inadequate testing and premature use of dangerous drugs, Senator Kefauver drafted an ambitious bill to remedy these evils. But he received no support from the Kennedy Administration. On the contrary, officials of the Health, Education, and Welfare Department collaborated with Senator Everett Dirksen of Illinois and other enemies of the bill within the Senate Judiciary Committee in an effort to write a relatively innocuous, noncontroversial substitute. Only the scandal of thalidomide, a harmful drug which caused babies to be born deformed, prompted the Administration to change sides and support Kefauver.[3]

Taxes and drug regulation were but two of several moves by the Administration to prove its benevolence toward private industry, but these tactics failed. They could not counter the effect in businessmen's minds of the steel crisis of April, 1962. After Kennedy and Secretary of Labor Arthur Goldberg had persuaded the steel union to settle for a noninflationary wage increase that stayed within the Administration's wage-price guidelines, U.S. Steel and the other companies unexpectedly informed the White House they were raising steel prices well above the level required by the wage settlement or permitted by the guidelines.

Kennedy regarded the steel companies' move as a direct challenge to the office of the Presidency. The companies were saying, in effect, that they were going to set their own prices and would not brook any presidential interference. Kennedy launched an aggressive public-relations campaign against the steel industry. He denounced its action as a broken pledge and contrary to the economic interests of the nation. The White House spurred the Kefauver subcommittee to conduct an investigation of steel industry costs and profits. The Treasury Department let it be known that the expense accounts of steel executives were about to receive a tax audit. The Justice Department hinted that anti-trust action against U.S. Steel might be in the offing. These aggressive threats worked. The industry rolled back the price increase.

A few weeks later, the stock market broke sharply. Like most market breaks, it was a normal corrective after a prolonged speculative price rise. But many brokers and speculators tagged it "the Kennedy slump," characterizing his attack on steel prices as a blow to business confidence. Kennedy observed that those who were blaming him for the fall in the stock-market prices had not given him any of the credit when those same prices had been rising, but this sensible observation did not stem the hostile gossip.

The Kefauver subcommittee meanwhile attempted to persist in its steel inquiry. If successful, such an inquiry would have laid the basis for an informed public judgment on whether the steel industry's costs justified a price increase. Over the long term, only such public understanding could sustain the Administration's anti-inflationary wage-price guidelines. Kefauver and his staff sought the answers to these still largely unanswered questions: "What are the steel industry's labor costs and how do they compare with foreign costs of producing a ton of steel? Are the profits on each ton high, low, just right? Does the industry have enough funds for new investment? Could it get more by higher prices or lower prices?"[4] When Kefauver's staff prepared a questionnaire designed to elicit information on these and similar questions, U.S. Steel and seven smaller firms agreed to supply the information, but Bethlehem Steel and three others refused. The Kefauver subcommittee voted to cite the recalcitrant firms for contempt of the Senate, but the full Judiciary Committee defeated the resolution. The steel inquiry eventually collapsed.

President Kennedy made no effort, publicly or privately, to compel the steel companies to provide the necessary information. The Administration had disengaged itself from this investigation. The Justice Department dropped the prospective anti-trust suit; the Treasury Department shelved the audit of steel executives' expense accounts. Thus the steel confrontation of April, 1962, petered out. It was valuable as a fresh defense of the prerogatives of the Presidency (and it was in this light that Kennedy preferred to view it), but it was an isolated incident, not the opening stage of a concerted effort to make government wage-and-price restraints based on productivity into a viable, permanent policy. It was a commando raid, not a campaign.

A postscript to the steel crisis was the President's famous speech at the Yale University commencement in June, 1962. Here he argued that many of the economic problems confronting the nation were technical rather than political in nature. There was, he suggested, a failure of communication between leaders in business and government which caused them to work at cross purposes although they shared many common objectives. He attributed this communications failure to the persistence of conservative myths such as the sanctity of a balanced budget.

The Yale speech was sensible, incisive, modern-minded. It told the members of the graduating class little that their professors of economics had not been telling them for the previous four years. But to their conservative parents and to many in the business community, Kennedy's words were incendiary radicalism. Among those well-disposed toward the President's arguments, the speech had seemingly little impact because it was not tied to action. In one sense, he was right that many public issues are problems in semantics and technique. But in a deeper sense, these issues are truly political. That is, no progress is made in resolving them until men's interests and emotions as well as their powers of reason are involved. Kennedy's actual policies were helping to enrich conservatives where the practice of their own mythology would have impoverished them, but as long as they could, they naturally preferred to have their profits and their myths, too. Kennedy could not defeat and dispel the myths by dry rational argument but only by showing the rest of the people how the perpetuation of these myths hurt *their* interests and by arousing them to fight against them. This, Kennedy was deeply reluctant to do.

But the cool tactician's most glittering triumph was still to come. Beside it, the steel crisis paled and the Bay of Pigs was an event of little consequence. In October, 1962, United States intelligence obtained photographic proof that the Soviet Union, contrary to its firm official denials, was establishing missile bases in Cuba. Once completed, these bases would have seriously altered the balance of American and Russian power upon which world peace depended.

To counter this threat, Kennedy laid down a naval blockade around Cuba and warned the Soviet Union that war might ensue. After the most anxiety-laden week since World War II, Khrushchev drew back. The missiles were withdrawn. Kennedy had triumphed. It was the kind of test of will and nerve which Kennedy had been forecasting since the beginning of his presidency and for which he had been preparing himself all his life. It was his proudest moment.

Several days afterward, the congressional elections of November, 1962, confirmed the bright readings of the pollsters. For the first time since 1934, an incumbent Administration held its own in the House and Senate in a mid-term election. The Democratic showing demonstrated the young President's high standing in the country.

Yet as the the second year of his presidency drew to an end, the old questions recurred. What was the larger context within which he operated? Toward what vision did this gifted pragmatist strive? Walter Lippman formulated the problem as well as it could be and offered a provocative answer.

"The Administration has, of course, had some legislative successes...," Lippman wrote in *Newsweek* (January 21, 1963). "But it has not yet been able to win for itself a general understanding of its purposes. We must wait to see if it can do this. We have yet to find out whether the country can be converted by persuasion at a time when business is fairly good and there are only scattered pockets of unemployment. Although President Kennedy is very popular, he has not yet been able to carry the country with him. He has not yet won over the minds of the people. This may be because he has not yet conquered their hearts by opening his own."

3

Only ten months elapsed between the appearance of that article and John Kennedy's assassination. During that time, he made the decisions and entered into the commitments that make much clearer the nature of his purposes. The year opened with a severe disappointment. General de Gaulle vetoed Britain's entry into the Common Market. Kennedy's "grand design" for the Atlantic community had been predicated upon the admission of Britain and its trading partners, the "outer seven," into the economic and political institutions of a federal Europe. The Trade Expansion Act of 1962, which had been Kennedy's highest priority legislative objective the previous year, was intended to facilitate lower tariffs and much closer American economic relations with this new, enlarged European bloc. De Gaulle's veto defeated Kennedy's imaginative design; it not only divided the Atlantic community economically but proved to be the prelude to a series of moves that undercut American military and political strength in Europe.

Out of that defeat and the greater triumph of the Cuban missile confrontation, Kennedy bred a new program in foreign affairs. He originally had seen the United States chiefly as the leader of a grand coalition of the free and himself as the spokesman and organizer of a more arduous, concerted effort on every front where communism threatened. He had declared in his Inaugural message: "Civility is not a sign of weakness, and sincerity is always subject to proof. Let us never negotiate out of fear. But let us never fear to negotiate." Although honestly intended, this seeking for peace through negotiation was, he had judged, a matter of second priority. The restoration of American military preponderance, the invigoration of its political nerve, and the strengthening of its alliances came first.

After two years in office, Kennedy was gradually coming to reverse those priorities. The Cuban missile crisis had amply proved that the Soviet Union respected America's military power and political nerve. At the same time, France's veering away from its former close cooperation with Britain and the United States postponed into the indefinite future any prospect of gaining substantial advantage from the Russians by dealing with them from a position of tight allied unity. At the very moment when the free countries were growing in wealth relative to the Soviet Union and should have been in a position of strength, France dissipated that strength in an anachronistic, delusive search for national "grandeur." Under these circumstances, Kennedy chose to concentrate his efforts on narrowing the areas of disagreement between the United States and the Soviet Union. Where formerly he had exhorted his fellow Americans to a keener effort and warned darkly of coming perils, Kennedy now struck a new note. He spoke with pride of the many contributions his country had made toward blocking the spread of communism and maintaining peace.[5]

The clearest expression of Kennedy's new mood in foreign policy was his address at the American University commencement on June 10, 1963, the most important speech of his presidency.

"History teaches us," he said, "that enmities between nations, as between individuals, do not last forever. However fixed our likes and dislikes may seem, the tide of time and events will often bring surprising changes in the relations between nations and neighbors. . . .

"So let us not be blind to our differences—but let us also direct attention to our common interest and to the means by which those differences can be resolved. And if we cannot end now our differences, at least we can direct attention to our common interests and to the means by which those differences can be resolved. And if we cannot end now our differences, at least we can help make the world safe for diversity. For, in the final analysis, our most basic common link is that we all inhabit this small planet. We all breathe the same air. We all cherish our children's future. And we are all mortal."[6]

Within weeks, agreement on the nuclear test ban treaty followed. Such a treaty had been in the diplomatic mill for several years, and at least twice before, agreement had seemed very near. Kennedy's conciliatory speech, it would appear, was important in bringing the long search to a successful conclusion. Three months later, Kennedy took his second step in defusing the explosive hostilities between the United States and the Soviet Union. He agreed to the sale of American wheat to relieve impending food shortages in Russia.

Kennedy was too canny a realist to expect that peace and genuine friendship with the Russian rulers were imminent. "They do not wish us well," he once remarked matter-of-factly to a television interviewer. But he understood that with imagination, persistence, and the willingness to run certain political risks at home, he could work with the Russian leadership in ways that would enhance the possibilities of peace. He had found the main line on which he could exercise his talents for statesmanship.

On the domestic economic front, Kennedy at the beginning of 1963 asked for a major income-tax reduction although the budget was unbalanced. This was an effort to put Keynesian economic theory into practice. If a drop in the rate of taxation stimulated business activity and resulted in little, if any, actual drop in tax revenue, the theory would be proved. One of the myths Kennedy had deplored in his Yale speech would be demolished.

While the tax bill was still under consideration in Congress, the pace of events in the South forced Kennedy to make an unqualified commitment, politically and legislatively, to the cause of Negro equality. Over the objections of some of his cautious advisers who worried about the political repercussions in Congress and the South, he forthrightly endorsed a comprehensive package of civil-rights bills in June, 1963. For the first time, a President of the United States defined the civil-rights issue in its true, fundamental terms as a moral question challenging the conscience and good faith of all Americans. Two days later the Southern Democrats voted overwhelmingly to defeat the Administration's request for a fresh authorization of funds for the depressed areas program. In appropriations committees, the Southern chairmen began a deliberate slowdown of the routine money bills. The cautious advisers had not been wrong; the legislative and political price of defying the Southern bloc in behalf of civil rights was going to be high. But Kennedy had made his irrevocable commitment. The long siege was on.

Neither the tax bill nor the civil rights bill had been enacted when President Kennedy left for Texas on November 21. He moved in those last weeks and months under a cloud of criticism. Karl E. Meyer, an American writing in the British weekly *New Statesmen* (October 18, 1963), reported what was then a common liberal opinion: "The criticism one hears of Mr. Kennedy is not that his intentions are bad, but that his leadership is feeble. There is no context for political debate, no felt sense of direction or priorities, no shape or purpose in public opinion. The President seems reluctant to take the country into his confidence, to share his heart and hopes; he rations himself like a wasting resource."

Tom Wicker, reviewing *J.F.K.: The Man and the Myth*, a savage attack on Kennedy by Victor Lasky, wrote in the *New York Times* (September 8, 1963): "There is enough substance in Mr. Lasky's diatribe to make it clear that . . . dispassionate analysis is needed to help us understand and weigh a President who promised so much more—in words and in person—than has been delivered."

James Reston, in his Washington column in the *Times*, wrote on October 25, 1963: "The difference between what public men here say in public and what they say in private is greater today than at any time since the war."

Contrasting the public optimism of officials with their private pessimism, Reston wrote of the President: "What he thinks is desirable or essential is politically impossible.

"Consequently, while he and his associates go on talking publicly about the progress they have made, privately they are beginning to fear that, given the existing form of American society and the existing balance of political power, the evils they complain about simply cannot be remedied. They admit privately they are confronted with radical economic, social and political problems, but they are afraid of adopting in a Presidential election year radical policies to meet these problems.

"The result is that they talk moderately and optimistically in public and radically and pessimistically in private. This poisons the atmosphere in Washington and debases the whole political process."

What was being complained about in these various critiques was Kennedy's refusal to engage in open political combat with the enemies—

in Congress and in the country—of his domestic program. As Lippmann observed, Kennedy believed "that measures have to be worked through by arrangements with Congress. He does not ever want to force measures as leaders do—as the two Roosevelts did, as Wilson did. He is a man who works it out politically. He's one of them. He's one of the boys. That's his method."[7]

That method was bringing results. By November, 1963, the tax and civil rights bills were certain of passage. At one of his last press conferences, Kennedy urbanely observed that these bills were having an eighteenth-month, rather than a nine-month, delivery period. He talked calmly of the rhythms and cycles of change, plainly implying that he was patiently waiting for the tide to cease ebbing and begin flowing.

But that method, the patient practice of inside politics, was not bringing another, less tangible kind of result. It was not changing the tone of public opinion; it was not altering the context in which public issues were being debated. That tone and that context appeared substantially the same as in Eisenhower's time. If the presidency was a place of moral leadership, "a bully pulpit" in Theodore Roosevelt's phrase, Kennedy was making insufficient use of it.

His reluctance had several sources. If he spoke out sharply and often on social issues, he would antagonize some of the Eisenhower-Nixon voters he wanted to win to his personal following. He would undercut his own tactics of conciliating and reassuring them. Kennedy thought it shrewder to play personal rather than programmatic politics; he judged that it was easier to change the minds of hostile voters about a man—a friendly, reasonable, dignified man with a lovely wife and family—than to convert them through the abstractions of a program. If he stirred up controversy on domestic issues, he would diminish that atmosphere of national unity which, at least during his first two years in office, he had deemed essential to promoting his foreign policy objectives. This was an arguable proposition, since Harry Truman and the Republican-controlled 80th Congress of 1947–48 had feuded bitterly over domestic legislation but had cooperated to pass the Marshall Plan and aid for Greece and Turkey.

Nevertheless, Kennedy worried about "dividing" the country. As a practical man, he instinctively focussed on the hard immediacies of bargaining on Capitol Hill rather than on broader, more diffuse undertakings directed toward public opinion.

The deepest source of his reluctance, however, was personal. He was a reserved man who had disciplined himself so tautly that he could not publicly articulate or dramatize his deepest feelings. Possessing so many of the intellectual virtues—skepticism, tolerance, openmindedness, prudence—he found it impossible to comprehend to what extent most other people live in and off their emotions. He reasoned that one ought to be able to disarm anger with a display of calmness and to convert prejudice with a statement of facts. But his Irish political sense made him skeptical of the effectiveness of rational appeals to the public, and by temperament, he was reluctant to stir darker depths of feelings than he was familiar or comfortable with. By the same token, he underestimated the breadth and intensity of the positive feelings he aroused. He steered away from controversy because he did not feel confident of his hold on the emotions and imagination of the majority of the people. He was loved more than he knew. He could not comprehend that what he sought in public support and approbation and affection he already had in as large a measure as any leader could expect.

"I didn't think I'd get such a fine reception," he remarked after leaving Houston and Fort Worth for Dallas.[8] It was an old weakness for him. It had complicated his approach to the problem of McCarthyism when he was a young senator. He had not understood then that nothing he could say against McCarthy would have seriously impaired his own standing with his Massachusetts constituency. To the Irish and their immigrant allies, he was a golden hero acting out a legend of success and unselfish public service which accorded with their highest aspirations. Far above the grubby realities of machine politics which they knew all too well, Kennedy was going to be a leader fit to stand by John Adams and Daniel Webster and the other heroes of an older Boston. Too many of their unfulfilled aspirations, too many of their dreams, too much of their love already had become invested in him for them to abandon him over McCarthyism or any other single issue. But Kennedy did not realize this. Again, as President, he did not realize the extent to which he had become a vehicle for the nation's social idealism. He did not realize that his programs had more popular backing than was visible on Capitol Hill, that his championship of the Negro and the unemployed and of the old in need of medical care, his realism on economic issues, and his manifest eagerness to work for peace had touched a popular nerve and created a vast reservoir of latent support. His style of governing, his acts of boldness, and his infrequent speeches of explanation had already endowed him with enemies and admirers, with hatred—though he sought none—and with love—though he did not know it.

Kennedy was the finest heir of the power-seeking Irish political tradition, and his death the ultimate ironic comment on that tradition. He would not have scorned the description of pragmatist, but it is not as a pragmatist that he is remembered. The pragmatist, according to William James, "turns away from abstraction and insufficiency, from verbal solutions, from bad *a priori* reasons, from fixed principles, closed systems, pretended absolutes and origins. He turns towards concreteness and adequacy, towards facts, towards action and towards power."[9]

Power is ephemeral, and facts lose their force. What is remembered of John Kennedy is not that he conquered power but the grace and verve and civility with which he wielded it. What is remembered are not his political skills but his intellectual virtues. He is remembered not for his deeds but for his qualities, and of these the foremost were intelligence and courage. In short, he is remembered for the force of his moral example.

His Irish inheritance provided him with political skills, and his own emotional makeup provided him with caution. The political skills and the caution crippled him almost as much as they served him. But not quite. For despite them, he had made the hard journey from tactician to strategist; despite them, he had entered the hearts of his people.

4

The Kennedy years in the White House brought to a rounded fulfillment the long story of Irish adjustment in America. On balance, it has been a success story. There have been individual and collective defeats but, over-all, the Irish progress in this country testifies to the validity of the open society and the continuing success of the American democratic experiment.

The Irish have succeeded in the fields in which they chose to concentrate their efforts—politics, religion, theater, literature, the law and law enforcement, medicine, and sports. The pages of the metropolitan newspapers are rich in evidence on the activities of the American Irish. The *New York Times* for Thursday, December 10, 1964, for example, printed no fewer than seven stories about men of Irish ancestry who had achieved conspicuous success in their chosen occupations.

On page 30, there was a news account of the reelection of W. A. Boyle as President of the United Mine Workers. He had succeeded to the presidency of the union a year earlier on the death of the late Thomas Kennedy.

On page 45, there was a review of a book about the possibility of life in outer space entitled *We Are Not Alone*, written by Walter Sullivan, the *Times'* science correspondent.

On page 47, appeared the obituary of a financier, Peter P. McDermott. The obituary read in part: "Peter McDermott, who entered Wall Street as a runner and office boy in 1902 and rose to become a wealthy broker, died Tuesday. . . . Mr. McDermott was senior partner in the firm of Peter P. McDermott & Co., which he founded in 1925 with one associate. The firm now has eight partners, two memberships on the New York Stock Exchange and four on the American Stock Exchange. . . . Mr. McDermott was a director for several years in the late 1920's of the Hibernia Trust Company. The banking house later became the Colonial Trust Company and then was absorbed by the Meadowbrook National Bank."

On page 61, the amusement page, was an advertisement for a new motion picture, *Cheyenne Autumn*, directed by John Ford and starring, among others, the actor Arthur Kennedy.

On page 72, in the sports section, a news story reported that John F. Kennedy of the New York Racing Association had been elected executive secretary of the Jockey Club, one of the most influential posts in the field of horse racing.

On page 82, in the business section, there was a photograph of Edmond Hanrahan. The accompanying story reported that Hanrahan, a former chairman of the Securities and Exchange Commission and a partner in the New York law firm of Sullivan, Donovan, Hanrahan, McGovern and Lane, had been elected a director of the American Truck Leasing Corporation.

Reading the *Times* with an eye for the doings of the American Irish is, in one sense, a tour de force. But December 10, 1964, was not an exceptional day. On other days, the reader of the *Times* could learn about the activities of Francis Cardinal Spellman at the Vatican Council, the political conferences of Senator Robert F. Kennedy, the law enforcement work of District Attorney Frank Hogan and Police Commissioner Vincent Broderick, and the memoirs of movie actor Pat O'Brien. In short, it is incontestable that the Irish have entered a fairly wide spectrum of occupations in the United States and have fared well.

Among the Irish themselves, there is a tendency to feel that their old political hegemony is disappearing as the Negroes take over the slums of the big cities and the Italian middle classes push their way forward. This conviction is most widely shared and most valid in New York City, where the old Irish monopoly power has disappeared. Elsewhere, a judgment of Irish political decline would be premature. In the late 1940's, as an older generation of political leaders passed from the scene—Frank Hague in Jersey City, Ed Kelly and Pat Nash in Chicago, and James M. Curley in Boston—there were many articles by journalists and political scientists about "the passing of the old-time bosses" and "the end of an era." But in 1965, Boston, Philadelphia, Detroit, Chicago, and San Francisco still had mayors of Irish extraction. These mayors were more sophisticated than their predecessors and their cities better governed, but the pattern of political organization had not changed radically over the previous twenty years and the political skills and interest traditional among the Irish were still evident. Outside New York, both the Irish and the political machines that were their creation have proved more durable than the writers of the 1940's had foreseen.[10]

Although the drift of the Irish to the suburbs has visibly destroyed Irish political control in New York City and undermined it in other big cities, this change has had offsetting compensations. Because it weakened the old stereotype of the Irish political boss, it gave the Irish new political respectability, making it easier for them to win state and national offices. Much of the energy that was once invested in City Hall, and stalemated at that level, is now prominently at work in the Federal Government. As the old-style Irish machines declined somewhat in the cities, many more Irish names appeared in the Cabinet, the Supreme Court, and places of leadership in Congress.

At the national level, the Irish have played their familiar path-breaking role for other immigrants. President Kennedy appointed the first person of Italian ancestry to serve in the Cabinet—Anthony Celebrezze—as Secretary of Health, Education, and Welfare, and the first of Polish ancestry—John Gronouski—as Postmaster General. Only the refusal of Congress to upgrade the housing agency to Cabinet status prevented him from appointing the first Negro—Robert Weaver. As it was, Weaver was the first Negro to head a major independent agency. In a broader sense, the election of Kennedy made all things potentially possible for politicians from other minority backgrounds. He broke the barrier against a Catholic in the White House not only for Irish Catholics but also for Italians, Poles, and others. Similarly, the election of a Jew as President or Vice-President, which had formerly seemed outside the realm of practical possibility, now became plausible. Kennedy's scrupulous conduct in office on all religious issues had proved to the Protestants and the nonbelievers of the nation that they had nothing to fear from a chief executive whose religious faith differed from their own.

The papacy of John XXIII, which paralleled in time the rise to power of John Kennedy and was also tragically brief, substantially affected the reputation and the cultural environment of the American Irish. They still retained in the church hierarchy an approximation of their old preponderance. In 1886 when James Gibbons became a Cardinal, the Irish comprised 35 of the 69 bishops in the American Church; eighty years later three of the five Cardinals and nineteen of the thirty-three Archbishops were Irish. Of the bishops, more than 40 per cent—108 out of 259—were identifiably Irish. Outsiders had tended to lump them together as one indistinguishable bloc, the notoriously conservative American Irish hierarchy. But the deliberations at the Vatican Council in Rome brought out a much different picture. Except for an occasional ultraconservative such as James Cardinal McIntyre of Los Angeles, most American bishops voted with the progressive side on most issues. They intervened energetically when it appeared that the Papal Curia was undercutting the liberal schema on religious liberty and on relations with the Jews. They supported the reform of the liturgy and the much wider use of the English language in place of Latin. Fugitive ideas which only five or ten years earlier had found no home except in the pages of *Commonweal* now received the approbation of most American bishops. The reformist impulse in the Church was clearly stronger and more widely shared than anyone had foreseen before the Council provided the historic opportunity for action.

While the voting of the American bishops belied their stereotype, the rapidly developing ecumenical movement transformed the cultural atmosphere in which the Church moved in this country. Old religious antagonisms suddenly seemed un-Christian; the complex of defensive "ghetto" attitudes uncritically accepted by many Catholics now appeared unnecessary. A new spirit of confidence animated the American Catholic community as constructive dialogue with Protestants on theological issues replaced the suspicious reserve and fusty apologetics of an earlier generation. The Irish, who had once been foremost among Catholics in erecting defensive positions, now provided many leaders in the movement to breach them. Even the most entrenched institutions, such as the parochial school, came under critical re-examination. "Never in the history of a large country like the United States has the image of the Church been changed so profoundly and so rapidly," Father H. A. Reinhold, the leading Catholic liturgist, wrote.[11] The brief era of the two Johns—John XXIII and John Kennedy—had ended forever what remained of the political, religious, and cultural isolation of the American Irish. They are now moving in the broad mainstream of American life.

In sports, the Irish are no longer prominent. There are no Irish boxers worthy of comparison with yesterday's heroes, John L. Sullivan and Gentleman Jim Corbett. The last heavyweight champion of Irish ancestry was James J. Braddock, who lost the title to Joe Louis in 1937. It has remained largely a Negro monopoly ever since. There are far fewer Irish baseball players than in the days of Connie Mack and "Big Ed" Walsh. But this development is in the normal evolution of immigrant groups rising on the ladder of American life. Since professional sports are often physically dangerous and their financial rewards precarious, they appeal most to the sons of the newest, most impoverished ethnic groups. In the 1960's, these are the Negroes and Puerto Ricans.

The more significant areas of life in which the Irish have been notably underrepresented—both in numbers of people engaged and of persons in leadership positions—are science and industry. These are important deficiencies. Science is, in the modern world, the most prestigious intellectual activity. Business, in all its various forms, is naturally the field in which the majority of people make their living.

The low turnout in science and in business has obvious historical origins. The industrial revolution passed Ireland by because England used its power to thwart Ireland's economic development and because Ireland has no coal, iron, petroleum, or other natural resources. Italy and Poland are two other countries that have produced large numbers of immigrants to the United States and that have shared the same difficulties: serious misrule and a lack of industrial resources. Poles and Italians likewise have not been prominent in the middle and top ranks of American business and industry. (They had additional handicaps which the Irish did not have, such as unfamiliarity with the English language and later arrival in the United States.) A second influence deflecting the Irish from careers in science and in industry in the past has been the character of Catholic education. Catholic schools have traditionally emphasized Greek, Latin, religion, philosophy, and the liberal arts curriculum. They have held up to their students not the inquiring, skeptical scientific investigator as a model, but the well-rounded, classically educated gentleman and scholar. It is also probably true that a person whose life is religiously centered tends to think that he already knows the answers and that, in subtle ways, this leads him or her away from a career in science.

Catholic education has undergone far-reaching changes in the past twenty-five years and will experience still further change in the years ahead. Notre Dame University under the presidency of Father Theodore Hesburgh in 1965, for example, was far different from the school where Knute Rockne coached and the "Four Horsemen" played forty years earlier. Great strides have been made in Catholic schools since World War II in the teaching of science. Irish Catholics, both lay and clergy, have played an active part in pushing for these changes. Nevertheless, the underrepresentation of the Irish in science, with the exception of medicine, continues to be a marked feature of their situation in American life.

In business, the Irish in the 1960's were not much differently situated than they had been at the turn of the century. Notwithstanding individual Irish millionaires in mining, railroading, meat packing, and other specialized fields, the typical Irish businessman was still a merchant, contractor, or real-estate broker. These are all occupations in which little capital was needed to begin and in which in years past it was often an advantage to be Irish and to have political connections with City Hall or personal ties to the Irish community. As great, impersonal organizations have developed in industry in the twentieth century, such as General Motors and International Business Machines, the Irish, like other Americans, have entered the ever-growing ranks of white-collar employees and technicians. Since the turn of the century, a considerable number of Irish have followed up the initial exploits of Thomas Fortune Ryan in the Wall Street financial district. They have triumphed both on its wildly speculative side and, to a lesser extent, on its more orthodox side. There have been market speculators such as Joseph P. Kennedy and Bernard "Sell 'em Ben" Smith; there have been investment bankers such as James V. Forrestal, president of Dillon, Read before he entered government service, and stockbrokers such as the above-mentioned Peter P. McDermott and John Coleman, a former chairman of the Board of Governors of the New York Stock Exchange. There are no Irish investment banking firms comparable to the great Jewish (Kuhn, Loeb; Lehman Brothers) or Yankee (Morgan) banking houses. This is because the Irish entered the financial district relatively late; they came as outsiders and lone wolves. They had behind them neither family capital nor any communal banking or business tradition.

There lingers a waning yet persistent sentiment in the Irish communities in most big cities in the East and Middle West that the Irish are discriminated against in the higher levels of business, industry, and finance. This attitude has long been endemic in Boston. In 1960, the same year in which John Kennedy was elected, an American Irish writer in Philadelphia observed: "The city's banks . . . are grouped according to Proper Philadelphia and 'other.' All of the prestige institutions but one have old line gentlemen for presidents. Of the thirty-five business firms employing 1,000 or more, only two have presidents with recognizably Irish names."[12]

Although prejudice undoubtedly existed in the past, particularly in such conservative cities as Boston and Philadelphia, it can be overplayed as an obstacle to Irish advancement. The Irish cannot have it both ways. They cannot be strongly represented in the Church, in politics, and the law, and also be prominent to the same degree in all other fields. Each ethnic group has only so many persons of talent in each generation. If the Irish had wanted to devote to finance and business the same energy and talent they have devoted to politics, there might be today several Irish figures on Wall Street to rank with Lehman and Loeb and Schiff. Certainly the financial district did not place any higher barrier to the Irish Catholics than it did to the Jews.

The range of occupations in which the Irish have achieved their successes in the United States is suggestive about the group as a whole. The Irish have evinced an unusual interest in gaining positions of authority in the most conservative institutions in our society—not only in the Catholic Church, which is readily understandable, but also in government and political parties, banking, the judiciary, the police, and the public schools. If there is a single concept that distinguishes the Irish in America, it is their dual preoccupation with security and power. The fact that the Irish in many large cities control City Hall, the police, the courts, and sometimes the public school system gives them a distinctive attitude toward issues affecting public order, the security of the streets, and civil liberties. They are for law and order in part because it is they who enforce and administer the laws and maintain order.

Fundamentally, the Irish have been a people outside of the business system and never fully have been reconciled to its values. At the lower levels, they have been obsessed with the security of civil-service jobs because they have been more impressed by the failures and vicissitudes of capitalism than by its opportunities and rewards. At the higher levels, this same alienation reappears as an aristocratic disdain for mere money-making. Repeatedly, there recurs an aspiration for the honors of high public office and a belief that government service is really the highest calling. The Kennedys are archetypes. Joseph Kennedy accumulated a huge fortune, but what he really coveted was the Ambassadorship to Great Britain, and his ambition was to found a family dynasty to rival the Adamses or the Roosevelts. His son John epitomized this attitude when he remarked of politics: "It beats chasing a dollar." In the same spirit, Thomas E. Murray, successful inventor and industrialist, devoted the last two decades of his life to public affairs, including a term on the Atomic Energy Commission and an unsuccessful bid for a U. S. Senate nomination in New York in 1958. James Forrestal left Wall Street for service in the Navy and Defense Department. A protégé of his, John Connor, resigned the presidency of Merck & Co., the drug manufacturing firm, to become Secretary of Commerce in the Johnson Cabinet in 1965. The Irish are not unique in their esteem for public life, but it remains their most distinctive common concern and tradition.

Political power cannot be a morally worthy end in itself. Those who exercise it are ultimately judged by the means they used to obtain it, the manner of its exercise, and the ideals it served. Only if these moral criteria are controlling can men advance toward the highest political civilization. John Kennedy's legacy as a public man points in this direction. He rose to the presidency on the backs of the Irish political machines and on his father's money—although his own talents and leadership qualities were even more decisive in his success—and for the use of those means he was often criticized. He weakened the force of that criticism by the grace with which he exercised the authority of the presidency once it was his and by the nobility of the ideals for which he was striving at the time of his death. What F. Scott Fitzgerald wrote of his hero in *The Great Gatsby* might well have been written of Kennedy that sunny morning as he entered Dallas in triumph:

"He had come a long way to this blue lawn, and his dream must have seemed so close that he could hardly fail to grasp it. He did not know that it was already behind him, somewhere back in the vast obscurity beyond the city, where the dark fields of the republic rolled on under the night.

"Gatsby believed in the green light, the orgiastic future that year by year recedes before us. It eluded us then, but that's no matter—tomorrow we will run faster, stretch out our arms farther . . . And one fine morning—

"So we beat on, boats against the current, borne back ceaselessly into the past."

It was not the fact that Kennedy obtained the power of the presidency that was important, for there have been many presidents whom no one but the historians can remember. What mattered was that he exercised that power in a manner and for ideals that were morally worthy. He thus contributed toward further civilizing the conduct of politics and heightened the quality of public life. The means he used in the everyday conduct of life gave meaning to the tragedy of his death. For Americans, and particularly for his fellow Irish, he provided inspiration and standards to meet the tragic realities that lie beyond power and success.

Notes

[1] Quoted in *New York Times*, Jan. 28, 1957, p. 26.

[2] William Manchester, *Portrait of a President* (Little, Brown, Boston, 1962), p. 71.

[3] Thomas Beer, *Hanna, Crane, and the Mauve Decade* (Knopf, New York, 1941), p. 115.

[4] See, for example, Michael J. O'Brien, *A Hidden Phase of American History: Ireland's Part in America's Struggle for Liberty* (Dodd, Mead, New York, 1920). Mr. O'Brien was the historiographer of the American Irish Historical Society.

[5] UPI dispatch in *Santa Barbara News-Press*, March 19, 1962.

CHAPTER ONE

Notes

[1] Sean O'Faolain, *King of the Beggars: A Life of Daniel O'Connell* (Viking Press, New York, 1938), p. 328.

[2] Sean O'Faolain, *The Irish, A Character Study* (Devin-Adair, New York, 1949), pp. 43–45.

[3] *Ibid.*, p. 82.

[4] *The Variorum Edition of the Poems of W. B. Yeats*, ed. by Peter Allt and Russell K. Alspach (Macmillan, New York, 1957), pp. 146-147.

[5] O'Faolain, *King of the Beggars*, pp. 98-99.

[6] *Ibid.*, p. 41.

[7] *The Works of William Carleton*, (P. F. Collier, New York, 1882), 3 vols.

[8] My account of O'Connell is based upon O'Faolain's excellent biography, *King of the Beggars;* the quotation making the analogy with Tammany Hall is p. 308.

[9] O'Faolain, *King of the Beggars*, p. 227.

[10] I have read many works of history and fiction that have contributed to my understanding of the Irish background but that are not specifically cited in this chapter. Among them, I would particularly note George W. Potter, *To the Golden Door* (Little, Brown, Boston, 1960); Arnold Schrier, *Ireland and the American Emigration, 1850–1900* (University of Minnesota Press, Minneapolis, 1958); *A Treasury of Irish Folklore*, edited and with an Introduction by Padraic Colum (Crown Publishers, Inc., New York, 1954); and *1,000 Years of Irish Prose*, edited by Vivian Mercier and David H. Greene (Devin-Adair, New York, 1952).

CHAPTER TWO

Notes

[1] Quoted in W. F. Adams, *Ireland and Irish Emigration to the New World from 1815 to the Famine* (Yale University Press, New Haven, 1932), p. 342.

[2] Quoted in George W. Potter, *To the Golden Door* (Little, Brown and Co., Boston, 1960), p. 165.

[3] Carl Wittke, *The Irish in America* (Louisiana State University Press, Baton Rouge, 1956), p. 45.

[4] Joseph Gurn, *Charles Carroll of Carrollton* (P. J. Kenedy, New York, 1932), p. 4.

[5] Michael J. O'Brien, *A Hidden Phase of American History: Ireland's Part in America's Struggle for Liberty* (Dodd, Mead and Co., New York, 1920), pp. 37b-37c. On Barry, see William Bell Clark, *Gallant John Barry* (Macmillan, New York, 1938).

[6] Charles P. Whittemore, *A General of the Revolution: John Sullivan of New Hampshire* (Columbia University Press, New York, 1961), pp. 2-3.

[7] Dixon Wecter, *The Saga of American Society* (Scribner, New York, 1937), p. 207.

[8] *The Diary of Philip Hone*, edited with an Introduction by Allan Nevins (Dodd, Mead and Co., New York, 1927). For derogatory references to Irish, see entries for Sept. 12 and Dec. 17, 1835; on the death of Lynch, Sept. 7, 1837.

[9] *The Diary of George Templeton Strong*, edited by Allan Nevins and Milton H. Thomas (Macmillan, New York, 1952), 4 vols. This entry was for July 7, 1857 in the volume for 1850–1859, p. 348.

[10] Oscar Handlin, *The Uprooted* (Little, Brown, Boston, 1951), Chapter One; also, p. 80.

[11] Robert Ernst, *Immigrant Life in New York City, 1825–1863* (King's Crown Press, New York, 1949), p. 133.

[12] John Higham, *Strangers in the Land: Patterns of American Nativism 1860–1925* (Rutgers University Press, New Brunswick, N.J., 1955), Chapter One.

[13] Oscar Handlin, *Boston's Immigrants, 1790–1880* (Harvard University Press, Rev. Ed., Cambridge, Mass., 1959), pp. 14-15.

[14] Ray A. Billington, *The Protestant Crusade, 1800–1860* (Macmillan, New York, 1938; reissued, Rinehart, New York 1952), pp. 72-76.

[15] Billington, *op. cit.*, pp. 220–231.

[16] Strong, *Diary*. These entries are in the volume for 1835–1849, pp. 228, 232-233, 240.

[17] Billington, *op. cit.*, pp. 412–416.

CHAPTER THREE
Notes

[1] M. R. Werner, *Tammany Hall* (Doubleday, Doran & Co., New York, 1928), pp. 26-27.

[2] Florence E. Gibson, *The Attitudes of the New York Irish Toward State and National Affairs, 1848–1892* (Columbia University Press, New York, 1951), Chapter Two.

[3] *Irish American*, Sept. 25, 1852.

[4] Charles W. Elliott, *Winfield Scott—the Soldier and the Man* (Macmillan, New York, 1937), p. 638.

[5] *Irish American*, Oct. 23, 1852.

[6] Arthur M. Schlesinger, Jr., *The Age of Jackson* (Little, Brown, Boston, 1945), p. 408.

[7] *Ibid.*, pp. 408-409.

[8] *Ibid.*, p. 490.

[9] *Irish American*, March 20, 1858.

[10] *The Poetical Works of Charles G. Halpine (Miles O'Reilly)*, ed. by Robert B. Roosevelt (Harper, New York, 1869), p. 289.

[11] F. Phisterer, *New York in the War of the Rebellion* (J. B. Lyon Co., Albany, N.Y., 1912), p. 70.

[12] *New York Tribune*, July 18, 1863, quoted in Gibson, *New York Irish*, pp. 155-156.

[13] *Harper's Weekly*, Aug. 1, 1863.

[14] José Ortega y Gasset, *Invertebrate Spain* (W. W. Norton, New York, 1937), p. 26.

CHAPTER FOUR

Notes

[1] Arthur Mann, *Yankee Reformers in the Urban Age* (Belknap Press, Cambridge, Mass., 1954), pp. 14-15.

[2] Edwin L. Godkin, *Problems of Modern Democracy* (Scribner, New York, 1896), pp. 200-201.

[3] Richard Hofstadter, *The Age of Reform* (Knopf, New York, 1955; Vintage Edition, 1960), pp. 174-186, discusses these two political traditions from a different perspective.

[4] Conrad Arensberg, *The Irish Countryman: An Anthropological Study* (Macmillan, New York, 1937), p. 84.

CHAPTER FIVE
Notes

[1] Florence Gibson, *The Attitudes of the New York Irish Toward State and National Affairs, 1848–1892*, pp. 211-212.

[2] M. R. Werner, *Tammany Hall*, pp. 120-121.

[3] *Ibid.*, p. 108.

[4] Gibson, *op. cit.*, p. 224.

[5] *New York Tribune*, Nov. 2, 1868.

[6] There are numerous accounts of the Tweed Ring. I have principally used Denis Tilden Lynch, *"Boss" Tweed* (Boni and Liveright, New York, 1927); Denis Tilden Lynch, *The Wild Seventies* (Appleton-Century, New York, 1941); and Werner, *Tammany*, pp. 104-275.

[7] *Harper's Weekly*, Sept. 21, 1872.

[8] *The Nation*, April 18, 1878.

[9] Allan Nevins, *Abram S. Hewitt, with Some Account of Peter Cooper* (Harper, New York, 1935), pp. 465-467.

[10] *Ibid.*, pp. 513-514.

[11] T. Lothrop Stoddard, *Master of Manhattan* (Longmans, Green, New York, 1931), p. 23.

[12] William Allen White, *Masks in a Pageant* (Macmillan, New York, 1928), p. 13.

[13] H. W. Walker, "The Trail of the Tammany Tiger," series in *The Saturday Evening Post*, March–April, 1914.

[14] Stoddard, *op. cit.*, p. 128.

[15] Werner, *op. cit.*, pp. 349-354.

[16] Finley Peter Dunne, "Lexow," *Mr. Dooley in the Hearts of His Countrymen* (Boston, 1899).

[17] Alfred Henry Lewis, *The Boss and How He Came to Rule New York* (New York, 1903).

[18] W. A. Swanberg, *Citizen Hearst* (Scribner's, New York, 1961), pp. 242-252.

[19] Mortimer Smith, *William Jay Gaynor* (Regnery, Chicago, 1951), p. 117; the quotations from Gaynor are also from this admirable short biography, pp. x-xi.

CHAPTER SIX

Notes

[1] Julia Cooley Altrocchi, *The Spectacular San Franciscans* (E. P. Dutton, New York, 1949), p. 21.

[2] *Ibid.*, pp. 98-99.

[3] William Martin Camp, *San Francisco: Port of Gold* (Doubleday, Garden City, N.Y., 1947), p. 117.

[4] Altrocchi, *op. cit.*, pp. 176-177.

[5] Hubert Howe Bancroft, *Retrospection, Political and Personal* (The Bancroft Co., New York, 1913), pp. 198-200.

[6] Altrocchi, *op. cit.*, pp. 67, 102, 157-158.

[7] Wells Drury, *An Editor on the Comstock Lode* (Farrar and Rinehart, New York, 1936), p. 31.

[8] Mark Twain, *Roughing It* (American Publishing Co., Hartford, Conn., 1872; 1886 edition), p. 185.

[9] Drury, *op. cit.*, p. 32.

[10] *Ibid.*, pp. 63-66.

[11] See *New York Times*, April 20, 1912, for her adventure on the *Titanic;* also, Wecter, *Saga of American Society*, p. 248.

CHAPTER SEVEN
Notes

[1] There are three biographies of John L. Sullivan which differ only in details: Roy F. Dibble, *John L. Sullivan: An Intimate Narrative* (Little, Brown, Boston, 1925); Donald Barr Chidsey, *John the Great* (Doubleday, Doran, Garden City, New York, 1942); and Nat Fleischer, *John L. Sullivan* (Putnam's, New York, 1951). I have mostly relied on Dibble's book.

[2] My account of McNelly's career is based on the standard work, Walter Prescott Webb, *The Texas Rangers* (Houghton, Mifflin, Boston, 1935). I have also consulted Tom Lea, *The King Ranch* (Little, Brown, Boston, 1957). This quotation is from Webb, p. 460.

[3] Webb, *op. cit.,* pp. 235, 237.

[4] Tom Lea, "Cattle Raids on the King Ranch," *The Atlantic,* May, 1957, pp. 47-52.

[5] Quoted in Webb, *op. cit.,* pp. 238-239.

[6] Adjutant General's Military Papers, June, 1875. Quoted in Webb, *op. cit.,* pp. 239-241.

[7] Webb, *op. cit.,* p. 255.

[8] Walter Prescott Webb corresponded with Callicot in the latter's old age and persuaded him to write this eyewitness account. Since his account is so much more vivid than words of mine could be, it seemed best simply to quote it. This manuscript appears in Webb, *op. cit.,* pp. 261-262 and 263-264.

[9] Quoted in Webb, *op. cit.,* p. 287.

[10] *Ibid.,* p. ix.

CHAPTER EIGHT

Notes

[1] Monsignor John Tracy Ellis, *The Life of James Cardinal Gibbons*, 2 vols. (Bruce Publishing Co., Milwaukee, 1952), II, p. 6.

[2] *Ibid.*, I, p. 317-319.

[3] Stephen Bell, *Rebel, Priest, and Prophet: A Biography of Edward Mc-Glynn* (Devin-Adair, New York, 1937); Sylvester L. Malone, ed., *Dr. Edward McGlynn* (New York, 1918).

[4] Ellis, *op. cit.*, I, p. 447.

[5] *Ibid.*, I, p. 327.

[6] *Ibid.*, II, p. 223, 253.

[7] *Ibid.*, II, pp. 636, 618n., 619.

[8] Rev. James H. Moynihan, *The Life of Archbishop John Ireland* (Harper, New York, 1953), p. 142.

[9] Philip H. DesMarais, "John Ireland in American Politics, 1886–1906," Georgetown University M.A. thesis, typescript, 1951.

[10] Archbishop John Ireland, *The Church and Modern Society* (McBride, Chicago, 1897), I, pp. 46-47.

[11] Gertrude Himmelfarb, *Lord Acton: A Study in Conscience and Politics* (University of Chicago Press, Chicago, 1952), p. 41.

[12] Ellis, *op. cit.*, I, pp. 398-399; II, p. 40n.

[13] It is another of history's ironies that the Jesuits and Catholic University have, so to speak, exchanged sides on these issues in our own time. Although Catholic University has a number of distinguished scholars who exert a progressive influence, among them Monsignor John Tracy Ellis, Gibbons's biographer, it has become on theological issues a stronghold of the extreme conservatives. The leader of this group is Monsignor Joseph Fenton, Dean of Theology at Catholic University and editor of the *American Ecclesiastical Review*. The foremost progressive figures in contemporary American Catholic theology, meanwhile, are two Jesuits, the Reverend John Courtney Murray and the Reverend Gustave Weigel.

[14] H. J. Browne, *The Catholic Church and the Knights of Labor* (Catholic University of America Press, Washington, 1949); Ellis, *Gibbons*, I, pp. 491, 494-495, 503, 511-521.

[15] An excellent survey of this period in Church history is Robert D. Cross, *The Emergence of Liberal Catholicism in America* (Harvard University Press,

Cambridge, Mass., 1958), especially, Chapter VI, "Perspectives on Social Change," pp. 106-129. J. T. Smith, *The Catholic Church in New York*, 2 vols. (New York, 1905), has many useful insights on the conservative New York hierarchy.

CHAPTER NINE

Notes

[1] The only Irish Catholic appointed to the Cabinet in the period was Joseph McKenna who served as Attorney General at the beginning of the McKinley Administration. McKenna, a Californian, escaped the subtle social discrimination which retarded the careers of comparable lawyers and politicians in the East and Midwest. But even in McKenna's case, his religion nearly debarred him: "For Secretary of the Interior, McKinley's thoughts turned to Judge Joseph McKenna of California, a bland Irishman with whom he had been associated on the Ways and Means Committee. He had forgotten, if he had ever known, that McKenna was a Roman Catholic. The Judge mentioned the fact during an interview at Canton, and added that his control of the Indian missions would be particularly objectionable to Protestants. Visions of the A.P.A. must have rushed with the speed of light through McKinley's mind, but he did not blink, as he composedly remarked that the position of which he was thinking had nothing to do with the Indian missions. It was the Attorney Generalship. McKenna thought that he would prefer it to any other Cabinet seat, and shortly after he was formally invited to accept it" (Margaret Leech, *In The Days of McKinley*, Harper, New York, 1959, pp. 106-107). Several months later, McKinley elevated McKenna to the Supreme Court.

[2] *Irish World*, Sept. 19, 1874. Quoted in Florence E. Gibson, *The Attitudes of the New York Irish Toward State and National Affairs, 1848-1892*, p. 329.

[3] For a summary of this Irish nationalist activity in the United States in the 1880's, see Gibson, *New York Irish*, pp. 327-369. There are sketches of Ford in *The National Cyclopaedia of American Biography*, and the *Dictionary of American Biography*.

[4] A valuable monograph is Thomas N. Brown, "The Origin and Character of Irish-American Nationalism," *Review of Politics*, XVIII (1956), pp. 346 ff. See also, Brown, "Social Discrimination Against the Irish in the United States," mimeographed pamphlet in the Library of Jewish Information, issued by the American Jewish Committee, November, 1958.

[5] Rev. Robert H. Lord, Rev. John E. Sexton, and Rev. Edward T. Harrington, *History of the Archdiocese of Boston* (Sheed & Ward, New York, 1944), III, p. 394.

[6] Monsignor John Tracy Ellis, *The Life of James Cardinal Gibbons*, I, p. 334.

[7] M. R. Werner, *Tammany Hall*, p. 438.

[8] William L. Riordon, *Plunkitt of Tammany Hall* (Dutton, New York, paperback ed., 1963), p. 48.

[9] Frances Perkins, *The Roosevelt I Knew*, (Viking, New York, 1946), p. 14.

[10] Henry Pelling, *American Labor* (University of Chicago Press, Chicago, 1960), p. 117.

[11] Quoted in *ibid.*, p. 76.

[12] Thomas Beer's chapter "Dear Harp" in *The Mauve Decade* reprinted in *Hanna, Crane, and the Mauve Decade* (Knopf, New York, 1941), p. 123n.

[13] E. J. Kahn, *The Merry Partners: The Age and Stage of Harrigan and Hart* (New York, 1955), and Carl Wittke, *The Irish in America* (Louisiana State University Press, Baton Rouge, 1956), p. 259.

[14] Elmer Ellis, *Mr. Dooley's America* (Knopf, New York, 1941).

[15] Quoted in Wittke, *op. cit.*, p. 154.

[16] Finley Peter Dunne, *Observations by Mr. Dooley* (New York, 1902), pp. 83-84.

[17] Ellis, *Dooley*, p. 90.

[18] *Ibid.*, pp. 90-91, 93.

[19] *Ibid.*, p. 118.

[20] *Ibid.*, p. 95.

CHAPTER TEN

Notes

[1] Norman Hapgood and Henry Moskowitz, *Up from the City Streets: Alfred E. Smith. A Biographical Study in Contemporary Politics* (Harcourt, Brace, New York, 1927), p. 349.

[2] Alfred E. Smith, *Up to Now—An Autobiography* (Garden City Publishing Co., Garden City, N.Y., 1929), p. 20.

[3] Hapgood and Moskowitz, *op. cit.*, pp. 10-11.

[4] Henry F. Pringle, *Alfred E. Smith: A Critical Study* (Macy-Masius, New York, 1927), pp. 94-95.

[5] Smith, *op. cit.*, p. 296.

[6] Pringle, *op. cit.*, pp. 99-102.

[7] Constance Rourke, *American Humor* (Doubleday Anchor Books ed., 1953; orig. ed., Harcourt, Brace, 1931), p. 93.

[8] Pringle, *op. cit.*, p. 108.

[9] Smith, *op. cit.*, pp. 76-77.

[10] Pringle, *op. cit.*, pp. 151-152.

[11] Hapgood and Moskowitz, *op. cit.*, pp. 63-64.

[12] Frances Perkins, *The Roosevelt I Knew*, p. 22.

[13] Hapgood and Moskowitz, *op. cit.*, p. 65.

[14] Smith, *op. cit.*, pp. 281-282.

[15] Hapgood and Moskowitz, *op. cit.*, pp. 193-194.

[16] *Ibid.*, p. 195.

[17] Statements on censorship are in Pringle, *op. cit.*, pp. 339-341.

[18] *Ibid.*, pp. 27-32.

[19] New York *World*, Sept. 30, 1922.

[20] William Allen White, *Masks in a Pageant* (Macmillan, New York, 1928), pp. 463-464; other quotations from White have been from this same essay.

[21] Will Rogers, *How We Elect Our Presidents* (selected and edited by Donald Day, Little, Brown, Boston, 1952), pp. 52-53.

[22] Samuel Lubell, *The Future of American Politics* (Harper, New York, 1952), pp. 34-35.

CHAPTER ELEVEN

Notes

[1] *The Independent*, May 31, 1906.

[2] John Gunther, *Inside U.S.A.* (Harper, New York, 1946), p. 512.

[3] For an excellent, entertaining account of *The Transcript* in its final days, see the articles of Charles Morton in *The Atlantic*, February–March, 1961.

[4] T. S. Eliot, "The *Boston Evening Transcript*," in *The Complete Poems and Plays* (Harcourt, Brace, New York, 1952), p. 16.

[5] *Boston Herald*, Nov. 7, 1932.

[6] Oswald Garrison Villard, *The Disappearing Daily* (Knopf, New York, 1943), p. 178.

[7] William Cardinal O'Connell, *Recollections of Seventy Years* (Houghton, Mifflin, Boston, 1934), p. 9. For his childhood and family background, see pp. 3-4.

[8] *Ibid.*, p. 5.

[9] *Ibid.*, p. 191.

[10] William Cardinal O'Connell, *Sermons and Addresses* (Boston, 1925 ff.); see especially, Vol. 9, pp. 59-70, 266-267. In his memoirs, he wrote: "There was plenty of wealth in New England, especially among the rich merchants of Boston, but it never succeeded in turning their heads. They were then and they have still remained true to the best ideals of commercial and social life." —O'Connell, *Recollections*, p. 374.

[11] Charles Morton, "The Censor's Double Standard," *The Reporter*, March 14, 1950.

[12] Albert Bushnell Hart, ed., *Commonwealth History of Massachusetts*, IV, 77.

[13] Joseph Dinneen, *Ward Eight* (Harper, New York, 1936), p. 206.

CHAPTER TWELVE

Notes

[1] James Michael Curley, *I'd Do It Again: A Record of All My Uproarious Years* (Prentice-Hall, Englewood Cliffs, N.J., 1957), p. 49. Despite its inaccurate details and its rather helter-skelter arrangement, this is the best book on Curley because it gives an authentic and lively sense of him as a human being.

[2] *Ibid.*, pp. 41-42.

[3] *Ibid.*, pp. 45-46.

[4] *Ibid.*, pp. 62-63.

[5] *Ibid.*, p. 71.

[6] *Ibid.*, p. 36.

[7] Joseph F. Dinneen, *The Purple Shamrock* (W. W. Norton, New York, 1949), pp. 93-94.

[8] John Henry Cutler, *"Honey Fitz": The Colorful Life and Times of John F. ("Honey Fitz") Fitzgerald* (Bobbs-Merrill, Indianapolis, 1962) is an informal, anecdotal biography.

[9] Dinneen, *op. cit.*, p. 119. For accounts of 1913 campaign, see also, Curley, *op. cit.*, pp. 110-122.

[10] Interview with James M. Curley, December, 1949.

[11] The vote was Peters, 37,000; Curley, 28,000; Gallivan, 19,000; and Rep. Peter Tague, 2,000.

[12] Curley, *op. cit.*, pp. 157-159.

[13] *Ibid.*, pp. 6, 348.

[14] Quoted in Van Wyck Brooks, *New England Indian Summer* (Dutton, New York, 1940), p. 412.

[15] Personal interview with Curley. He frequently avowed his ambitions to be Secretary of the Navy and ambassador to Italy. See Curley, *op. cit.*, pp. 247-250, and Dinneen, *op. cit.*, pp. 199-200 and 205-212. When Curley attended the Democratic National Convention in 1936, he paraded to his hotel followed by wardheelers carrying signs, "James M. Curley, Man of Destiny, Watch 1940" and "Curley in '40."

[16] James M. Curley, *Addresses and Messages to the General Court . . . for the Years 1935-36* (Boston, 1936), Foreword.

[17] *Boston Post*, Dec. 14, 1935.

[18] *Ibid.*, Dec. 6, 1935.

[19] Curley, *Addresses and Messages*, p. 160.

[20] *Boston Herald*, Aug. 9, 1935; Nov. 3, 1935.

[21] Curley, *Addresses and Messages*, p. 609.

[22] *Boston Herald*, Jan. 27, 1936.

[23] This account of the 1937 campaign is based upon the *Boston Herald* and *Boston Post*, Oct. 15 through Nov. 5, 1937.

[24] This excerpt from the speech was published as a paid advertisement in most Boston newspapers, Nov. 1, 1937.

[25] Edwin O'Connor, *The Last Hurrah* (Little, Brown, Boston, 1956), pp. 373-375. I offered a similar analysis in my article on Curley's defeat ("Ex-Mayor of the Poor," *The Reporter*, Jan. 17, 1950), but for reasons detailed in the text I no longer consider it an adequate explanation.

[26] Mary K. Fitzgerald, "The Real Bostonians," *The New Leader*, April 3, 1948, p. 9.

CHAPTER THIRTEEN

Notes

[1] Andrew Turnbull, *Scott Fitzgerald* (Scribner, New York, 1962), p. 339.

[2] *Ibid.*, p. 78.

[3] Arthur Mizener, *The Far Side of Paradise* (Houghton, Mifflin, Boston, 1951), p. 85.

[4] Malcolm Cowley, *The Literary Situation* (Viking Press, Compass Books Edition, New York, 1958), p. 153.

[5] Edmund Wilson, "F. Scott Fitzgerald," *Bookman*, March, 1922, reprinted in Wilson, *The Shores of Light* (Farrar, Straus and Young, New York, 1952), pp. 27-35.

[6] F. Scott Fitzgerald, *The Great Gatsby* (in *Three Novels of F. Scott Fitzgerald*, Scribner, New York, 1953), p. 28.

[7] Quoted in Mizener, *op. cit.*, p. 15.

[8] Turnbull, *op. cit.*, pp. 33-34.

[9] Edmund Wilson, ed., *The Crack-Up* (New Directions, New York, 1945), p. 305.

[10] Fitzgerald, *The Great Gatsby*, pp. 113-114 and 136.

[11] Fitzgerald, *Tender Is the Night*, pp. 117-118.

[12] Stark Young, *Immortal Shadows* (Scribner, New York, 1948), p. 91. This is a review of O'Neill's "Dynamo," Feb. 11, 1928.

[13] John O'Hara, *BUtterfield 8* (Random House, New York, 1935. Modern Library Paperback ed.), pp. 66-68.

[14] Beverly Gary, "A Post Portrait: John O'Hara," second of six articles, *New York Post*, May 18-24, 1959. I am indebted to Miss Gary's excellent series for most of the biographical data on O'Hara.

[15] Gary series, *New York Post*, May 21, 1959.

[16] O'Hara, *Appointment in Samarra* (Modern Library edition), see pp. 12-13 for a vivid portrait of Reilly.

[17] *Ibid.*, pp. 297-298.

[18] *New York Post*, May 18, 1959. See also a painfully embarrassing letter from O'Hara to the *New York Herald Tribune*, published as, "Don't Say It Never Happened," April 8, 1962, in which he argues his father was not a parvenu and did own five automobiles at once.

[19] James T. Farrell, *Reflections at Fifty* (Vanguard Press, 1954), Foreword, p. 10.

[20] Personal sources.

[21] Personal interview, 1953.

[22] John Chamberlain, Introduction to the Modern Library edition of *Studs Lonigan* (New York, 1938), p. viii.

[23] Farrell, *Reflections at Fifty*, pp. 164-65.

[24] Farrell, Introduction to *Studs Lonigan* (Modern Library ed.), p. xii.

[25] *Ibid.*, p. xiii.

[26] Frank O'Malley, "James T. Farrell," *America*, June 23, 1951, pp. 311-313.

[27] Farrell, *Reflections at Fifty*, pp. 156-163.

[28] *Ibid.*, pp. 64-65, 40-41.

CHAPTER FOURTEEN

Notes

[1] Edwin A. Engel, *The Haunted Heroes of Eugene O'Neill* (Harvard University Press, Cambridge, Mass., 1953), pp. 4-5.

[2] Gilbert Seldes, "Song and Dance Man," *The New Yorker*, March 17 and 24, 1934, reprinted in *Profiles from the New Yorker* (Knopf, New York, 1938).

[3] Croswell Bowen and Shane O'Neill, *The Curse of the Misbegotten: A Tale of the House of O'Neill* (McGraw-Hill, New York, 1959), p. 237. Apparently, O'Neill and Cohan got on well together at first until Cohan began adding bits of personal "business" and making the play run late. See Arthur and Barbara Gelb, *O'Neill* (Harper, New York, 1962), pp. 769-770, 775-776.

[4] For biographical background on O'Neill, I have consulted Bowen, *op. cit.*, and Gelb, *op. cit.*

[5] Bowen, *op. cit.*, pp. 135, 325-326.

[6] John O'Dea, *History of the Ancient Order of Hibernians and Ladies' Auxiliary*, 3 vols. (Philadelphia, 1923), III, 1470-1471.

[7] Bowen, *op. cit.*, p. 32.

[8] Engel, *op. cit.*, p. 42.

[9] *New York Times*, Nov. 4, 1920.

[10] Eric Bentley, "Trying to Like O'Neill," reprinted in *In Seach of Theater* (Vintage Books, New York, 1955), pp. 220-234, particularly pp. 231-232. Although I share Bentley's dislike for the plays of O'Neill's middle period, I do not agree with his overall low estimate of his work.

[11] Quoted in Engel, *op. cit.*, p. 95.

[12] Quoted in Bowen, *op. cit.*, p. 358.

[13] Kenneth Tynan in *The* (London) *Observer*, Sept. 28, 1958.

[14] Stephen Whicher in *The Commonweal*, March 16, 1956.

[15] Bowen, *op. cit.*, pp. ix; 314; x-xi; 112; 323. See also John Henry Raleigh, "O'Neill's Long Day's Journey Into Night and New England Irish-Catholicism," *Partisan Review* (Fall, 1959), Vol. XXVI, No. 4, pp. 575-592.

[16] Andrew Turnbull, *Scott Fitzgerald*, p. 183.

[17] Quoted in Burns Mantle, ed., *Best Plays of 1938-39* (New York, 1939).

[18] Philip Barry, *The Joyous Season* (Samuel French, New York, 1934), p. 143.

[19] Philip Barry, *Without Love* (Coward-McCann, New York, 1943).

[20] Stark Young, "The Glass Menagerie," *The New Republic*, April 16, 1945.

[21] *S.R.O., The Most Successful Plays of the American Stage*, compiled by

Bennett Cerf and Van H. Cartmell (Doubleday, Garden City, N.Y., 1944), pp. 331-406.

[22] Marguerite Courtney, *Laurette* (Rinehart and Co., New York, 1955), p. 422; Ashton Stevens, in *Chicago Herald-American,* Dec. 10, 1946.

[23] Courtney, *op. cit.,* pp. 384-385.

[24] *Ibid.,* p. 418.

CHAPTER FIFTEEN

Notes

[1] My account of Father Coughlin's family background and early career is based on Ruth Mugglebee, *Father Coughlin of the Shrine of the Little Flower* (L.C. Page, Boston, 1933). The quotation on teaching Greek, p. 104.

[2] *Detroit Free Press*, Jan. 17, 1927.

[3] Mugglebee, *op. cit.*, pp. 195-196.

[4] *Ibid.*, pp. 213-229.

[5] Radio broadcast, Nov. 19, 1933.

[6] Raymond Gram Swing, *Forerunners of American Fascism* (Messner, New York, 1935), p. 49.

[7] *New York Times*, Feb. 17, Feb. 19, 1936; *Congressional Record*, Vol. 80, part 2, pp. 2313-2320.

[8] Swing, *Forerunners of Fascism*, p. 51.

[9] My account of the National Union for Social Justice convention is based on the *New York Times*, Aug. 8-19, 1936.

[10] Statement in *Michigan Catholic*, official diocesan newspaper; *Washington Post*, Oct. 10, 1937.

[11] *Look*, March 26 and April 4, 1940.

[12] Richard Hofstadter, *The Age of Reform* (Alfred A. Knopf, Inc, New York, 1955), Vintage edition, p. 81.

[13] *New York Times*, Aug. 15, 1936.

[14] *Ibid.*, Sept. 4, 1936; see also Bishop Gallagher's obituary, Jan. 21, 1937.

[15] *Ibid.*, Aug. 19, 1936.

[16] For Baruch episode, see John McCarten, "Father Coughlin: Holy Medicine Man," *The American Mercury*, June, 1939; for Cardinal Mundelein's statement, see *New York Times*, December 12, 1938.

[17] Quoted in *Commonweal* (editorial), Jan. 26, 1940.

[18] *New York Times*, Jan. 14 and Jan. 22, 1940.

[19] These figures became known in 1942 when the books of the League, which had long been kept confidential, were made available during an investigation by the Michigan state unemployment compensation commission.—*Washington Times-Herald*, March 11, 1942.

[20] Private source. The National Union for Social Justice passed out of existence in 1944 when Father Coughlin and two of his secretaries signed dissolution papers and filed them with the Michigan Secretary of State.—*Washington Post*, Aug. 18, 1944.

[21] Monsignor John A. Ryan, *Social Doctrine in Action* (Harper, New York, 1941), p. 96. His early article, "The Fallacy of Bettering One's Position," appeared in *The Catholic World*, November, 1907.

[22] Ryan, *Social Doctrine*, p. 70.

[23] *Ibid.*, p. 27.

[24] *Ibid.*, p. 124.

[25] *Ibid.*, p. 126.

[26] *New York Times*, Oct. 9, 1936; Jan. 21, 1937.

[27] Ryan, *Social Doctrine*, p. 242.

[28] Quotation from Attorney General Jackson, in Ryan, *Social Doctrine*, p. 151.

CHAPTER SIXTEEN

Notes

[1] For Dunne's letter, see Ellis, *Mr. Dooley's America*, p. 208; for Murray's role in electing Roosevelt to the Assembly, see Henry F. Pringle, *Theodore Roosevelt* (New York, 1931), pp. 59-60.

[2] John M. Blum, *Joe Tumulty and the Wilson Era* (Houghton, Mifflin, Boston, 1951).

[3] Arthur Link, *Wilson: The Road to the White House* (Princeton University Press, 1947). Link observes that Wilson's nomination was "not the result of the work or influence of any single man or group of men," and lists a half-dozen factors that were important. He concludes ". . . and, finally, the support of machine politicians brought over the votes without which Wilson could never have been nominated" (p. 465).

[4] There is an interesting discussion of this question, using the contemporary example of American Jews and Israel in Oscar Handlin, *Race and Nationality in American Life* (Doubleday, New York, 1957), pp. 245-254.

[5] Wilson to Secretary of State Robert Lansing, April 10, 1917, National Archives. Quoted in Charles Callan Tansill, *America and the Fight for Irish Freedom: 1866-1922* (Devin-Adair, New York, 1957), p. 230.

[6] Josephine O'Keane, *Thomas J. Walsh: A Senator from Montana* (M. Jones Co., Francestown, N.H., 1955).

[7] Interview with Ruth Finney, long-time Scripps-Howard correspondent in Washington, 1950.

[8] James A. Farley, *Behind the Ballots* (Harcourt, Brace, New York, 1938).

[9] Drew Pearson and Robert S. Allen, "The President's Trigger Man," *Harper's*, March, 1935; Alva Johnston, "Big Jim Farley; He Gets the Blame," *Saturday.Evening Post*, June 27, 1936.

[10] Alva Johnston, "White House Tommy," *Saturday Evening Post*, July 31, 1937; *Time*, Sept. 12, 1938; Alva Johnston, "The Saga of Tommy the Cork," *Saturday Evening Post*, Oct. 13, Oct. 20, Oct. 27, 1945; *Fortune*, September, 1937.

[11] "The Labor Governors," *Fortune*, June, 1937.

[12] Frank Murphy, "The Moral Law in Government," *The Commonweal*, May 19, 1933.

[13] *Time*, Jan. 9, 1939; Jan. 23, 1939; Aug. 28, 1939.

[14] "Commissioner Kennedy," *Fortune*, September, 1937.

[15] *New Republic*, July 11, 1934; *Literary Digest*, July 7, 1934; "Big Business, What Now?" *Saturday Evening Post*, Jan. 16, 1937.

CHAPTER SEVENTEEN
Notes

[1] *New York Times,* April 19, 1940.

[2] James A. Farley, *Jim Farley's Story—The Roosevelt Years* (Whittlesey House, McGraw-Hill, New York, 1948). See pp. 347-358 for his defense of his conduct in 1942.

[3] *Time,* January 23, 1939.

[4] Speech to the Trafalgar Day Dinner of Britain's Navy League, *Time,* October 31, 1938; *New York Times,* October 20, 1938.

[5] *Time,* Sept. 12, 1938.

[6] *Boston Globe,* Nov. 8, 1940.

[7] *Boston Herald,* Nov. 5, 1936.

[8] *Boston Globe,* Sept. 14, 1939.

[9] *Time,* July 7, 1942.

[10] Interview with Joseph Casey, 1952.

[11] *Time,* Sept. 12, 1938.

[12] Alva Johnston, "The Saga of Tommy the Cork," *Saturday Evening Post,* Oct. 27, 1945.

[13] Elliott Roosevelt and Joseph P. Lash, *F.D.R.: His Personal Letters* (Duell, Sloan and Pearce, New York, 1950), II, p. 1150.

[14] There was no impropriety involved in Corcoran's attempts to obtain this appointment. Solicitors-General, like Justices of the Supreme Court, are not delivered by the stork. For a blow-by-blow account of work on behalf of Frankfurter's own appointment, see *The Secret Diary of Harold L. Ickes* (Simon and Schuster, New York, 1954), II, 539-540, 545-552.

[15] *Time,* Sept. 12, 1938.

[16] Personal Interview with Thomas G. Corcoran, 1958.

CHAPTER EIGHTEEN

Notes

[1] My account of McCarthy is based principally on my own work as a reporter for the *New York Post*; see particularly, Oliver Pilat and William V. Shannon, "Smear, Inc.—The One Man Mob of Joe McCarthy," a series of twelve articles in the *New York Post*, Sept. 4–Sept. 23, 1951. I have also used "McCarthy: A Documented Record," *The Progressive* (special issue), April, 1954; "McCarthy Record," *Congressional Quarterly*, April 30, 1954; Jack Anderson and Ronald W. May, *McCarthy* (Beacon Press, Boston, 1952); and Richard Rovere, *Senator Joe McCarthy* (Harcourt, Brace, New York, 1959). The case for McCarthy is stated in, William F. Buckley, Jr., and L. Brent Bozell, *McCarthy and His Enemies* (Henry Regnery, Chicago, 1954).

[2] This description of a typical McCarthy performance is based on numerous speeches by him that I covered as a reporter for the *New York Post*. The language was always much the same, but these specific quotes are from his address to the Veterans of Foreign Wars' convention in New York City, Aug. 30, 1951.

[3] Albert Guérard, *Napoleon I* (Knopf, New York, 1956), pp. 67-68.

[4] *New York Times*, Dec. 3, 1954.

[5] *Time*, Jan. 25, 1954.

[6] Daniel Bell, ed., *The New American Right* (Criterion Books, New York, 1955), pp. 14-15, 41-42. Talcott Parsons makes the same diagnosis, p. 136.

[7] *The Commonweal*, Oct. 12, 1951.

[8] Bishop Sheil gave his address in Chicago before the International Education Conference of the United Automobile Workers Union on April 9, 1954. The full text of his speech was carried in the *New York Post*, April 18, 1954.

[9] *New York Times*, April 5, 1954; *New York Post*, April 5-6, 1954.

[10] On McNaboe, see his obituary in the *New York Times*, June 22, 1954.

[11] Associated Press dispatch printed in the *Washington Post* and other newspapers, Feb. 5, 1954, containing extracts from a speech McCarthy gave the previous evening in Charleston, West Virginia.

[12] *New York Times*, March 18, 1951, p. 70; see also letters in "Dear Editor" column, *New York Post*, March 21, 1951.

[13] *Time*, Feb. 9 and March 2 (letters column), 1962.

[14] Benjamin Gitlow, *The Whole of Their Lives* (Scribner, New York, 1948), p. 37.

[15] Theodore Draper, *American Communism and Soviet Russia* (New York,

1960), p. 61; William Z. Foster, *Pages From a Worker's Life* (International Press, New York, 1939).

[16] Elizabeth Gurley Flynn, *I Speak My Own Piece* (Masses & Midstream, New York, 1955), pp. 13-33.

[17] Monsignor John Tracy Ellis, *American Catholicism* (University of Chicago Press, Chicago, 1955), pp. 114, 117.

CHAPTER NINETEEN

Notes

[1] My interpretation is based primarily on interviews and personal knowledge. In addition, James M. Burns, *John F. Kennedy: A Political Profile* (Harcourt, Brace, New York, 1960) is an excellent account of Kennedy's personal and political development.

[2] John P. Mallan, "Massachusetts: Liberal and Corrupt," *The New Republic* (Oct. 13, 1952), pp. 10-12.

[3] Paul F. Healy, "The Senate's Gay Young Bachelor," *The Saturday Evening Post* (June 13, 1953), p. 27.

[4] Quoted in Burns, *op. cit.*, pp. 75, 80.

[5] Interview with John Cogley, September, 1961.

[6] John Courtney Murray, "America's Four Conspiracies," in *Religion in America*, ed. by John Cogley (Meridian Books, New York, 1958), p. 16.

[7] Private source.

[8] Ralph G. Martin and Edward Plaut, *Front Runner, Dark Horse*, (Doubleday and Co., Garden City, 1960), p. 202.

[9] Quoted from the text of Kennedy's speech.

[10] "Can Catholic Vote Swing Election?" *U.S. News & World Report*, Aug. 10, 1956; the text of the Bailey Memorandum is reprinted in *U.S. News & World Report*, Aug. 1, 1960.

[11] Angus Campbell, Gerald Gurin, and Warren E. Miller, *The Voter Decides* (Row, Peterson, Evanston, Ill., 1954), p. 77.

[12] "The 1960 Elections: A Summary Report with Supporting Tables," paperbound, April, 1961. Prepared by the Research Staff, Republican National Committee, pp. 11-12.

[13] George Belknap, formerly consultant on polling to the Democratic National Committee, interview, February, 1963.

[14] Moses Rischin, "Our Own Kind," A Report to the Center for the Study of Democratic Institutions, Santa Barbara, Calif., 1960, p. 11.

[15] Private source.

CHAPTER TWENTY

Notes

[1] *The Speeches, Remarks, Press Conferences, and Study Papers of Vice President Richard M. Nixon,* August 1 through November 7, 1960, Part II (U.S. Government Printing Office, Washington, 1961). Nixon made essentially this same argument throughout the last two weeks of the campaign, extemporizing his language. See, for example, p. 869, final two paragraphs.

[2] Bernard Nossiter, "Shadow and Substance on the New Frontier," *The Progressive,* January, 1963, pp. 19-21.

[3] Richard Harris, *The Real Voice* (Macmillan, New York, 1964), see especially, p. 170.

[4] Nossiter, *op. cit.,* p. 20.

[5] *Public Papers of the Presidents of the United States, John F. Kennedy,* January 1 to December 31, 1962 (U.S. Government Printing Office, Washington, 1963), television and radio interview, December 17, 1962, pp. 902-903. Kennedy concluded a lengthy exposition of American services to the world: "My goodness, we have done a tremendous job in this country!"

[6] *Public Papers, John F. Kennedy,* January 1 to November 22, 1963 (U.S. Government Printing Office, Washington, 1964), pp. 461-462.

[7] Lippmann interview, *Washington Post,* May 3, 1963, p. A12.

[8] Evelyn Lincoln, "My Twelve Years With Kennedy," *Saturday Evening Post,* Aug. 28, 1965, p. 46.

[9] William James, *Pragmatism* (Longmans, Green and Co., New York, 1910), p. 51.

[10] Detroit and San Francisco, although they have elected Irish mayors, were not cities which have had typical Irish political machines such as New York and Chicago have developed.

[11] H. A. Reinhold, "No Time to Stop," *Commonweal,* August 20, 1965, p. 585.

[12] Dennis Clark, "Philadelphia's Irish: Hamstrung Hibernians," *Greater Philadelphia Magazine,* March, 1960.

Index

The author would like to thank the following authors and publishers for permission to reprint various selections in this book:

The Bruce Publishing Company for permission to quote from *The Life of James Cardinal Gibbons*, Vols. I & II, Monsignor John Tracy Ellis, The Bruce Publishing Company, Milwaukee, Wisconsin, pp. I-707, II-735, $17.50. Copyright 1952.

Harcourt, Brace & World, Inc. for permission to quote from *Up From the City Streets: Alfred E. Smith: A Biographical Study of Contemporary Politics* by Hapgood and Moskowitz, and from "The Boston Evening Transcript" by T. S. Eliot.

Harper & Row for permission to quote from *Social Doctrine in Action* by Monsignor John A. Ryan, Copyright 1941 by Harper & Row, Publishers, Incorporated.

Houghton Mifflin Company for permission to quote from *The Texas Rangers* by Walter Prescott Webb, and from *The Recollections of Seventy Years* by William Cardinal O'Connell.

Alfred A. Knopf, Inc. for permission to quote from *Mr. Dooley's America* by Elmer Ellis.

Little, Brown & Company for permission to quote from *The Age of Jackson* by Arthur M. Schlesinger, Jr., Copyright 1945 by Arthur M. Schlesinger, Jr.

The Macmillian Company for permission to quote from *The Variorum Edition of the Poems of W. B. Yeats*, edited by Peter Alt and Russell K. Alspach, 1957, and from "John L. Sullivan" by Vachel Lindsay.

Joseph F. Dinneen, Sr. for permission to quote from his book, *The Purple Shamrock*, published by W. W. Norton & Company, Inc.

Prentice-Hall, Inc. for permission to quote from *I'd Do It Again: A Record of All My Uproarious Years* by James Michael Curley © 1957 by Samuel Nesson, published by Prentice-Hall, Inc., Englewood Cliffs, New Jersey.

Vanguard Press, Inc. for permission to quote from *Reflections at Fifty* by James T. Farrell, Copyright, 1954, by James T. Farrell.

The Reporter for permission to quote from Charles W. Morton's "The Censor's Double Standard," published in *The Reporter* on March 14, 1950.

Random House, Inc., for permission to quote from *The Straw, The Iceman Cometh,* and *Desire Under the Elms* by Eugene O'Neill. *The Straw:* Copyright 1921 and renewed 1948 by Eugene O'Neill. Reprinted from *The Plays of Eugene O'Neill* by permission of Random House, Inc. *The Iceman Cometh:* Copyright 1946 by Eugene O'Neill. Reprinted from *The Plays of Eugene O'Neill* by permission of Random House, Inc. *Desire Under the Elms:* Copyright 1924 and renewed 1952 by Eugene O'Neill. Reprinted from *The Plays of Eugene O'Neill* by permission of Random House, Inc.

Samuel French, Inc. for permission to quote from *The Joyous Season, Paris Bound,* and *Holiday* by Philip Barry. *The Joyous Season:* Copyright, 1934, by Philip Barry; Copyright, 1961 (in renewal), by Ellen S. Barry. All rights reserved. Reprinted by permission of the copyright owner and Samuel French, Inc. *Paris Bound:* Copyright, 1927, 1929, by Philip Barry; Copyright, 1955, 1956 (in renewal), by Ellen S. Barry. All rights reserved. Reprinted by permission of the copyright owner and Samuel French, Inc. *Holiday:* Copyright 1928, 1929, by Philip Barry; Copyright, 1955, 1956 (in renewal), by Ellen S. Barry. All rights reserved. Reprinted by permission of the copyright owner and Samuel French, Inc.